Practical Law Office Management

The West Legal Studies Series

Your options keep growing with West Legal Studies
Each year our list continues to offer you more options for every area of the law to meet your course or on-the-job reference requirements. We now have over 140 titles from which to choose in the following areas:

Administrative Law	Family Law
Alternative Dispute Resolution	Federal Taxation
Bankruptcy	Intellectual Property
Business Organizations/Corporations	Introduction to Law
Civil Litigation and Procedure	Introduction to Paralegalism
CLA Exam Preparation	Law Office Management
Client Accounting	Law Office Procedures
Computer in the Law Office	Legal Research, Writing, and Analysis
Constitutional Law	Legal Terminology
Contract Law	Paralegal Employment
Criminal Law and Procedure	Real Estate Law
Document Preparation	Reference Materials
Environmental Law	Torts and Personal Injury Law
Ethics	Will, Trusts, and Estate Administration

You will find unparalleled, practical support
Each book is augmented by instructor and student supplements to ensure the best learning experience possible. We also offer custom publishing and other benefits such as West's Student Achievement Award. In addition, our sales representatives are ready to provide you with dependable service.

We want to hear from you
Our best contributions for improving the quality of our books and instructional materials is feedback from the people who use them. If you have a question, concern, or observation about any of our materials, or you have a product proposal or manuscript, we want to hear from you. Please contact your local representative or write us at the following address:

West Legal Studies, 3 Columbia Circle, P.O. Box 15015, Albany, NY 12212-5015

For additional information point your browser at
www.westlegalstudies.com

Practical Law Office Management 2E

Brent Roper, J.D., MBA

WEST
THOMSON LEARNING

Australia Canada Mexico Singapore Spain United Kingdom United States

WEST LEGAL STUDIES

Practical Law Office Management, 2E
by Brent D. Roper

Business Unit Director:
Susan L. Simpfenderfer

Executive Editor:
Marlene McHugh Pratt

Senior Acquisitions Editor:
Joan M. Gill

Developmental Editor:
Rhonda Dearborn

Editorial Assistant:
Lisa Flatley

Executive Production Manager:
Wendy A. Troeger

Technology Project Manager:
James Considine

Production Manager:
Carolyn Miller

Production Coordinator:
Matthew J. Williams

Executive Marketing Manager:
Donna J. Lewis

Channel Manager:
Nigar Hale

Cover Design:
TDB Publishing Services

COPYRIGHT © 2002 Delmar West Legal Studies is an imprint of Delmar, a division of Thomson Learning, Inc. Thomson Learning™ is a trademark used herein under license.

Printed in the United States
1 2 3 4 5 XXX 05 04 03 02 01

For more information contact Delmar,
3 Columbia Circle, PO Box 15015,
Albany, NY 12212-5015.

Or find us on the World Wide Web at
www.thomsonlearning.com or
www.westlegalstudies.com

ALL RIGHTS RESERVED. No part of this work covered by the copyright hereon may be reproduced or used in any form or by any means—graphic, electronic, or mechanical, including photocopying, recording, taping, Web distribution or information storage and retrieval systems—without written permission of the publisher.

For permission to use material from this text or product, contact us by
Tel   (800) 730-2214
Fax (800) 730-2215
www.thomsonrights.com

Library of Congress Cataloging-in-Publication Data

Roper, Brent D.
  Practical law office management / Brent Roper.--2nd ed.
    p. cm
  "West Legal Studies Series."
  Includes bibliographical references and index.
  ISBN 0-7668-2854-9
    1. Law offices--United States. I. Title

KF318 .R66 2001
340'.068--dc21   2001026285

NOTICE TO THE READER

Publisher does not warrant or guarantee any of the products described herein or perform any independent analysis in connection with any of the product information contained herein. Publisher does not assume, and expressly disclaims, any obligation to obtain and include information other than that provided to it by the manufacturer.

The reader is notified that this text is an educational tool, not a practice book. Since the law is in constant change, no rule or statement of law in this book should be relied upon for any service to any client. The reader should always refer to standard legal sources for the current rule or law. If legal advice or other expert assistance is required, the services of the appropriate professional should be sought.

The Publisher makes no representation or warranties of any kind, including but not limited to, the warranties of fitness for particular purpose or merchantability, nor are any such representations implied with respect to the material set forth herein, and the publisher takes no responsibility with respect to such material. The publisher shall not be liable for any special, consequential, or exemplary damages resulting, in whole or part, from the readers' use of, or reliance upon, this material.

To the wife of my youth,
Shirley Phelps-Roper

Brief Contents

PREFACE x

1 INTRODUCTION TO LAW OFFICE MANAGEMENT 1

2 ETHICS AND MALPRACTICE 45

3 STAFF MANUALS, QUALITY MARKETING, AND PLANNING 109

4 CLIENTS AND COMMUNICATION SKILLS 159

5 TIMEKEEPING AND BILLING 195
   Hands-on Exercises: Abacus Law Docket Control 251
   Hands-on Exercises: Timeslips for Windows 258

6 CLIENT TRUST FUNDS AND LAW OFFICE ACCOUNTING 273

7 CALENDARING, DOCKET CONTROL, AND CASE MANAGEMENT 307

8 HUMAN RESOURCE MANAGEMENT 343

9 FILE AND LAW LIBRARY MANAGEMENT 389

10 LAW OFFICE EQUIPMENT, TECHNOLOGY, SPACE MANAGEMENT, SECURITY, AND LEASES 419

APPENDICES
Appendix A   Succeeding as a Legal Assistant   451
Appendix B   National Law Office Management, Legal Assistant, and Related Associations   463

Glossary 465

Index 473

Contents

Preface x

1 Introduction to Law Office Management 1

The Legal Team 2
Types of Law Practices 16
Law Practice Organization Structures 23
Law Office Management Principles 27

2 Ethics and Malpractice 45

Why Are Ethics and Malpractice Important? 47
Legal Ethics and Professional Responsibility 47
The Unauthorized Practice of Law 54
Competence and Diligence 61
Conflict of Interest 71
Malpractice and Prevention 85

3 Staff Manuals, Quality, Marketing, and Planning 109

Law Practice Policies and Procedures—The Staff Manual 111
Total Quality Management 121
Marketing 126
Planning 142

4 Clients and Communication Skills 159

Why Do Legal Assistants Need to Foster Good Client Relationships and Communicate Effectively? 161
Client Relationships 165
Ethical Duty to Communicate with Clients 162
Communication Skills 175

5 TIMEKEEPING AND BILLING   195

The Difference Between Timekeeping and Billing   196
Why Do Legal Assistants Need to Know Timekeeping and
Billing   197
Kinds of Legal Fee Agreements   197
Value Billing   209
The Ethics of Timekeeping and Billing   209
Legal Expenses   220
Timekeeping   221
Billing   229
Billing From the Corporate and Government Perspective   239

6 CLIENT TRUST FUNDS AND LAW OFFICE ACCOUNTING   273

Why Legal Assistants Need a Basic Understanding of Law Office
Accounting   274
Client Funds—Trust/Escrow Accounts   275
Budgeting   282
Internal Controls   286
Lawyers and NonLawyers Cannot Share Fees   291

7 CALENDARING, DOCKET CONTROL, AND CASE MANAGEMENT   307

Calendaring, Docket Control, and Case Management
Definitions   308
Appointments   309
Deadlines and Reminders   310
Hearings and Court Dates   311
Receiving Documents, Following Court Rules, and Calculating
Deadlines   313
Ethical and Malpractice Considerations   316
Manual Docket Control Systems   321
Types of Computerized Docket Control Systems   323
Overview of Computerized Legal Docket Control Features   325
The Docket Cycle   332
Using a Word Processor for Docket Control   333

8 HUMAN RESOURCE MANAGEMENT   343

Introduction to Human Resource Management   344
The Hiring Process   345
Performance Evaluations   357
Termination   366
Personnel Policies   368
Current Personnel Law Issues   368
Managing Stress   376

9 FILE AND LAW LIBRARY MANAGEMENT   389

Why Legal Assistants Need an Understanding of File and Law Library Management   390
Introduction to File Management   391
Filing Methods and Techniques   392
File Management and Ethics   401
Form Files   402
Introduction to Law Library Management   403
Technology and the Law Library   408

10 LAW OFFICE EQUIPMENT, TECHNOLOGY, SPACE MANAGEMENT, SECURITY, AND LEASES   419

Law Office Equipment and Technology   420
Purchasing Equipment and Supplies   427
Law Office Layout, Space Management, Security, and Leases   431

APPENDICES:

Appendix A   Succeeding as a Legal Assistant   451
Appendix B   National Law Office Management, Legal Assistant, and Related Associations   463

Glossary   465

Index   473

PREFACE

Another class, another boring textbook. Right? Wrong! Law office management is a dynamic subject and a great class. It will make you a better legal assistant. You will learn about real life problems you will encounter on the job and how to deal with them successfully. You will understand how important performing quality work for clients is. You will learn methods for improving your communication skills and your ability to work with clients successfully. You will be shown how to track and bill your time correctly, and how to use your time effectively. Throughout the book, there are explanations about how to avoid ethical problems that will come up. Law office management is anything but boring.

The goal of *Practical Law Office Management* is to educate legal assistant students regarding law office management procedures and systems. Law firms, as well as legal assistants themselves, must have good management skills to survive in today's competitive marketplace. This text is written for the student who wants to understand effective law practice management techniques and systems whether or not he or she will go on to become a law office administrator.

This text is not intended to be an "armchair" text on the theories and principles of management, nor is it a text on how to set up a law office. Rather, this text presents a practical discussion of law office management from a legal assistant's view.

The information presented is national in scope and assumes no prior knowledge of management or the legal field. Sociology, theories, and jargon are kept to an absolute minimum. To present a flavor of how a real law office operates, step-by-step explanations, "how-to" tips, practical charts, recent trends in law office management, and software, and many practical ideas on law office management from the legal assistant's perspective are provided. Information is presented in a manner to encourage students to think independently and to learn by participating.

This book, among other things, will explain what management generally expects of legal assistants and will present good law office systems and practical information about law office management.

Legal assistants must learn to manage themselves in addition to performing their normal duties. This book will help the student manage himself or herself in addition to teaching basic law office systems, such as timekeeping and billing, docket control, financial management, file and library management, computer systems and more. If the student takes the time to learn the management systems in this book, he or she will perform tasks more efficiently, with greater accuracy, and with less work. Sound too good to be true? That is what good management is all about.

A book on law office management has inherent limitations because there are many different management styles, techniques, and philosophies depending on the size and type of firm (i.e., small, medium, and large firms, corporate legal departments), location of the firm (urban, rural, east, west), and so forth. In addition, law office management is such a diverse topic that most people cannot agree on all the topics that should be covered. In light of these inherent problems, a vast and varied amount of information from many different angles is presented.

ETHICS

The importance of ethics is stressed throughout the text. Assuring a high ethical standard in the law office is a major function of law office management. It is very important to your career to be educated regarding ethical issues and to adopt a high ethical standard as a way of life. Every chapter in the text has an in-depth section on ethics. In "Chapter 2—Ethics and Malpractice," the codes of ethics for both the National Association of Legal Assistants (NALA) and the National Federation of Paralegal Associations (NAFPA) are included. At the end of most chapters, there are also ethical related cases. The cases discuss major ethical points in the chapter in real life, actual settings.

ORGANIZATION OF THE TEXT

The text is organized into ten chapters. Chapter 1 is an introduction to the legal environment and to law office management. It is suggested that all students who are new to the legal field read this chapter first. However, from Chapter 2 on, each chapter stands on its own and does not depend on the chapter(s) before it. Thus, instructors can assign the chapters in whatever order they believe is appropriate.

CHANGES TO THE SECOND EDITION

The second edition of *Practical Law Office Management* offers major enhancements over the first version. The text has been completely updated to reflect current management practices and technological advances. However, "old" material that is still relevant has been retained. Topics like ethics, quality, customer services, and communication are featured throughout the text. Some of the quotes in the book, while more than ten years old, are as relevant and important as when they were first spoken or written. Some of the more significant changes include the following.

- Each chapter has a new section entitled "Internet Sites" that lists Web sites where additional information can be found.
- Each chapter has a new section entitled "Suggested Reading" that lists books where additional information can be found. For the most part, the books are published by the American Bar Association, which typically has some of the best law office management-related books on the market.

- Attention to the ethics of law office management has been increased throughout the text. Because ethics discussions are often theoretical, I have also added a section at the end of each chapter entitled "Case Review." The cases are always ethics-related and show how ethical rules are applied in real life. They show what happens when poor management practices are used and point to the devastating consequences to clients and to the legal professional.
- The American Bar Association's Ethics 2000 Commission is currently working on a major revision to the *Model Rules of Professional Conduct*, last revised in 1983. Although the revisions to the *Model Rules* were not complete as this book went to press, I did include references to draft revisions that the Commission was considering.
- The text has many charts, graphs, illustrations, and quotes. All of these have been updated when possible to make the book current.
- Chapter 4—Clients and Communication has been expanded. The chapter contains many suggestions on how to provide outstanding service to clients and how to better communicate and interact with them.
- Chapter 8—Human Resources Management has been updated to include a new section on how to manage stress. Additionally, it includes current ideas on how to manage people and human resource issues.
- Chapter 9—File and Law Library Management has been updated to include in-depth discussions of CD-ROM libraries and performing legal research on the Internet.
- Chapter 10 now includes an in-depth discussion of e-mail from an ethical perspective. It also presents ideas on how to effectively use e-mail while limiting risks inherent in its use.
- New Hands-On Exercises have also been expanded to include "Timeslips for Windows," a timekeeping and billing program, and "Abacus Law," a docket control and case management program.

SPECIAL FEATURES

- Strong, practical coverage of ethics throughout the text
- Ethics cases regarding law office management topics in most chapters
- Citations to the recommended changes to the *Model Rules* by the ABA Ethics 2000 Commission
- Quotes from practicing legal assistants throughout the text
- Hands-on-exercises and software for "Timeslips for Windows" and "Abacus Law" docket control
- Introductions to each chapter that "set the stage" for the chapter
- Up-to-date charts, figures, and graphs to illustrate concepts
- Key terms/concepts defined in the margin
- Listing of Internet sites by topic for each chapter
- List of suggested reading for each chapter
- Expanded discussion questions and exercises at the end of each chapter
- Chapter objectives listed for each chapter
- Practical suggestions on how to succeed as a legal assistant and avoid problems

NEW TO THE EDITION

- More information in Chapter 2 on the subject of confidentiality
- A streamlined Chapter 6 based on user feedback
- Additional technology-oriented material in Chapter 10
- Revised Chapter 6 so that it can be addressed in a more condensed format

SUPPLEMENTS

Several supplements are available for use with the text, including an instructor's manual, and software.

- **Instructor's Manual with Test Bank**   West Legal Studies has provided a downloadable Instructor's Manual online at *www.westlegalstudies.com* in the Instructor's Lounge under Resource. The Instructor's Manual is designed to save the instructor time in organizing and preparing for class. Written by the author of the text, it includes outlines, teaching objectives, discussion ideas, transparency masters, and a test bank.
- **Computerized Test Bank**   The Test Bank found in the Instructor's Manual is also available in a computerized format on CD-ROM. The platforms supported include Windows™ 3.1 and 95, Windows™ NT, and Macintosh. Features include:
  - Multiple methods of question selection
  - Multiple outputs—that is, print, ASCII, and RTF
  - Graphic support (black and white)
  - Random questioning output
  - Special character support
- **Web page**   Come visit our Web site at *www.westlegalstudies.com* where you will find valuable information specific to this book such as hot links and sample materials to download, as well as other West Legal Studies products.
- **Survival Manual for Paralegal Students**   Written by Bradene Moore and Kathleen Reed of the University of Toledo, covers practical and basic information to help students make the most of their paralegal courses. Topics covered include choosing courses of study and note-taking skills. ISBN 0-314-22111-5
- **Strategies and Tips for Paralegal Educators**   Written by Anita Tebbe of Johnson County Community College, provides teaching strategies specifically designed for paralegal educators. A copy of this pamphlet is available to each adopter. Quantities for distribution to adjunct instructors are available for purchase at a minimal price. A coupon in the pamphlet provides ordering information. ISBN 0-314-04971-1
- **WESTLAW®**   West's on-line computerized legal research system offers students "hands-on" experience with a system commonly used in law offices. Qualified adopters can receive ten free house of WESTLAW®. WESTLAW® can be accessed with Macintosh and IBM PC and compatibles. A modem is required.

- **Court TV Videos**   West Legal Studies is pleased to offer the following videos from Court TV. Available for a minimal fee:
  - New York v. Ferguson—Murder on the 5:33:The Trial of Colin Ferguson
    ISBN 0–7668–1098–4
  - Ohio v. Alfieri—Road Rage
    ISBN 0–7668–1099–2
  - Flynn v. Goldman Sachs—Fired on Wall Street: A Case of Sex Discrimination?
    ISBN 0–7668–1096–8
  - Dodd v. Dodd: Religion and Child Custody in Conflict
    ISBN 0–7668–1094–1
  - Fentress v. Eli Lilly & Co., et al—Prozac on Trial
    ISBN 0–7668–1095–X
  - In RE Custody of Baby Girl Clausen—Child of Mine: The Fight for Baby Jessica
    ISBN 0–7668–1097–6
- **West's Paralegal Video Library** includes:
  - *The Drama of the Law II: Paralegal Issues Video*
    ISBN 0–314–07088–5
  - *I Never Said I Was a Lawyer Paralegal Ethics Video*
    ISBN 0–314–08049–X

These videos are available at no charge to qualified adopters.

SOFTWARE TUTORIALS AND HANDS-ON EXERCISES

The text accommodates legal assistant programs that have access to computers by including software tutorials at the end of some chapters. However, these are simply an added feature and computer use is completely optional. This text can be used fully by legal assistant programs that choose not to use computers.

The software tutorials included in the text are completely interactive and allow the student hands-on experience with the software programs. In addition, all of the tutorials are specifically related to law offices and legal applications so the student not only learns how to operate the software, but also learns how to use it in a law office. Educational versions of the software programs used for the tutorials are provided free of charge for schools adopting the text. The programs include Abacus Law Docket Control and Timeslips for Windows Timekeeping and Billing Program.

TO THE STUDENT

Law office management is exciting and ever changing. It is my hope that you will find this book useful as a reference tool in your professional career and that you will use some ideas in it to climb the ladder of success. Remember that just because you graduate from a paralegal program, you do not get to start at the top. Everyone has to start at the bottom and work his or her way up. I started as a runner/clerk and worked up from there. Do not be surprised or disappointed if you start in an entry level job. The experience you will gain is priceless, and through hard work and determination, you will move up more quickly than you think, and you will be better for it because you will have earned it. Also, help your co-workers. You will not be able to succeed without their help. Treat them like you would like to be treated, put the interests of your law office ahead of your own, and you will go far.

If you have an interesting idea, have solved some problem in law office management, or just have a story to tell and you would not mind me using it as an example in a subsequent edition of this book, please do not hesitate to contact me. I am always interested in learning from you. I wish you the best of luck in your endeavors. Brent Roper, 3640 Churchill Road, Topeka, KS 66604.

ACKNOWLEDGMENTS

One of my favorite parts of writing a book is to thank the people who helped me put it together. To all the people who have worked on this project: Thank you for all of your help.

REVIEWERS   Thank you to the reviewers of this second edition for their time and suggestions for improving the text.

> Deborah Meier Carr
> University of Maryland, University College
>
> Valerie Chaffin, CLA
> Meredith College, NC
>
> Susan W. Harrell
> University of West Florida
>
> Sherri Hoffman, PLS, CLA
> Law Office Manager, Hugh W. Farrell and Associates
>
> Kathryn L. Myers
> Saint Mary of the Woods College, IN

PRACTICING LEGAL ASSISTANTS   A special "thank you" goes to the following practicing legal assistants who provided information and quotations for this text. It was a pleasure to include their real life experiences herein.

> Lenette R. Pinchback, CLA
> Andrea L. Blanscet, CLA
> Vanessa Beam, CLAS
> Linda Rushton, CLA

WEST   A special thanks goes to the wonderful people at West, including Joan Gill, Acquisitions Editor, Rhonda Dearborn, Developmental Editor, and Matt Williams Production Coordinator. Without their long hours and help, this book would not have been possible.

OTHER

- My daughter Megan Phelps-Roper and son Joshua Phelps-Roper, who spent many hours helping with the development of this text in various capacities.
- James Publishing, publishers of Legal Assistant Today, 3520 Cadillac Ave, Suite H, Costa Mesa, CA 92626. (800) 394-2626.
- Alan Olson and James Cotterman of Altman Weil, Inc. (www.altmanweil.com) for information from their Survey of Law Firm Economics.
- The American Bar Association (ABA) who as always, was extremely helpful and provided superb information and source material.
- Bill Statsky, who has unselfishly helped me develop my ideas and thoughts as a writer. Bill also provided me with a library of source material.
- Dr. John L. Espy of Washburn University, for his ideas on management techniques and strategic planning.
- A special thanks goes to my wife, Shirley Phelps-Roper, and children, Samuel, Joshua, Megan, Rebekah, Isaiah, Zacharias, Grace Elizabeth, Gabriel, Jonah and Noah who put up with my long hours, and hectic schedule, and who also desperately wanted to see their names in print again. Finally, a special thanks goes to my mom Nanci Toews (and stepfather Jim), my dad Ed Fundis (and step-mother Gloria), and my father-in-law and mother-in-law, Fred and Margie Phelps. Without the love and cooperation of my family, I never could have seen this project through.

Brent D. Roper
3640 Churchill Road
Topeka, KS 66604

> Please note the Internet resources are of a time sensitive nature and URL addresses may often change or be deleted.

Contact us at westlegalstudies@delmar.com

Introduction to Law Office Management

CHAPTER OBJECTIVES

After you read this chapter, you will be able to:
- Discuss the titles and duties of each member of the legal team.
- Explain the trends in legal assistant salaries.
- Identify alternative law office organization structures.
- Identify the functions of law office management.
- Explain the "systems view" of management.

> The firm was more than forty years old and was well established in the legal community. Recently, however, the firm had moved to a particularly high-rent area and had substantial debt, employee turnover was growing, and productivity and client billings were down. The firm was feeling the effects of increased competition in the legal business. New clients were not coming to the firm and it had grown dependent on two large clients for most of its business. Unexpectedly, one of the clients moved its business to a competing law firm. Word had it that the client was less than pleased with the work it had received.
>
> Management decided that a bold move was necessary to save the firm. Clients were interviewed to see how the firm's services could be improved. Analysis was done to discover niche markets the firm could expand into and strong marketing efforts began on the Internet and with existing clients. The idea of merging with another law firm that was stronger while still being a good "fit" was explored. Budgets were developed to help project income and expenses better, a long-term business plan for the firm was drafted, and staff discussions were held to explore ways to increase retention while trimming costs and increasing productivity. Consultants were hired to help the firm's management increase its effectiveness. While the firm had a long way to go, it was on its way to recovery.

Law offices are organizations that provide legal services to their clients, but they are fundamentally a business, and like any business, their function is to make money, operate at a profit, and earn money for their owners. This chapter introduces you to the legal team members who provide services to clients and management to a law office. In addition, it discusses the different structures law offices internally and externally operate in, and gives an overview of the specific functions of law office management.

THE LEGAL TEAM

In a law office, there are many people who make up the legal team. The **legal team** consists of attorneys, administrators, law clerks, librarians, legal assistants, secretaries, clerks, and other third parties (see Figure 1-1). Each person provides a distinct

legal team
A group made up of attorneys, administrators, law clerks, librarians, legal assistants, secretaries, clerks, and other third parties. Each provides a distinct range of services to clients and each has a place on the legal team.

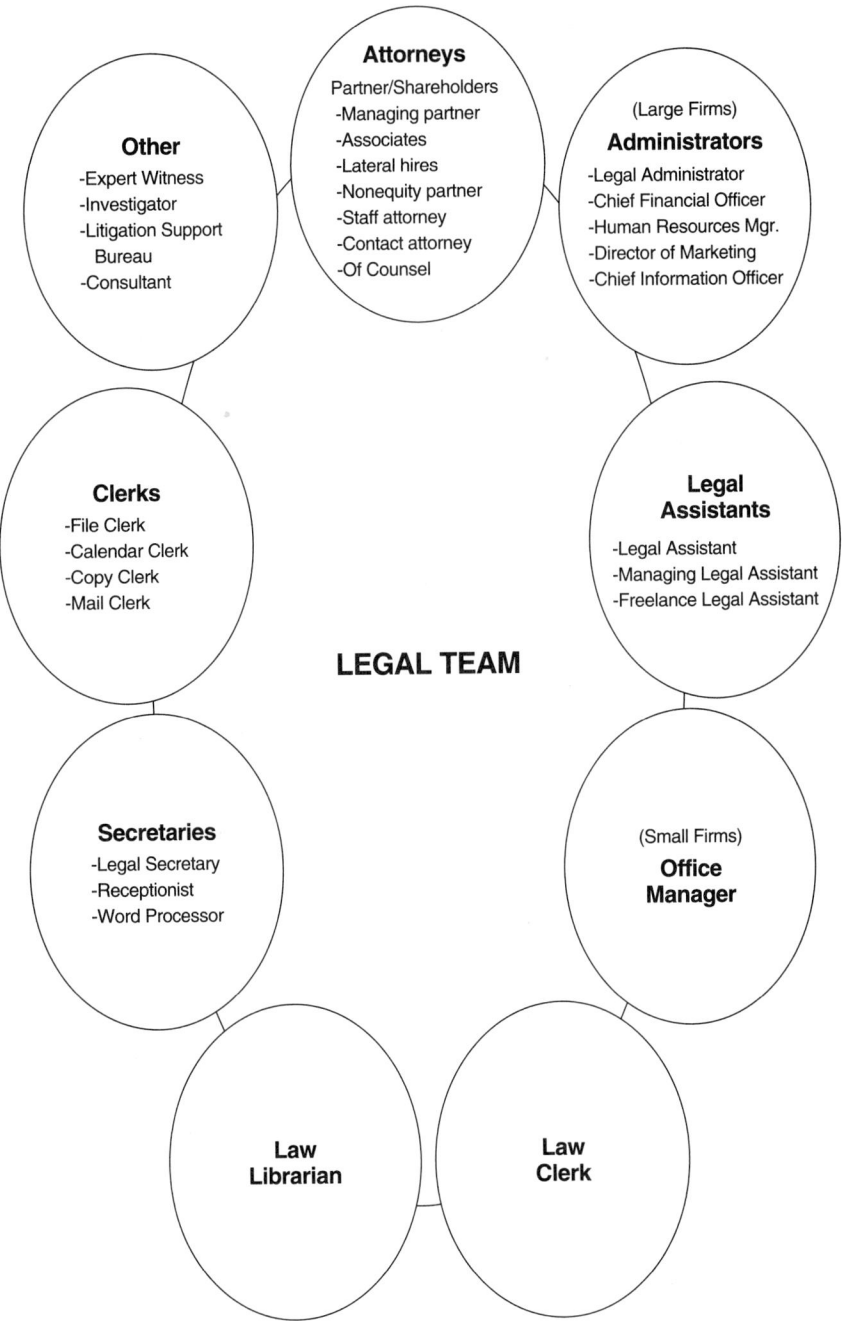

**Figure 1-1
The Legal Team**

range of services to clients, and each has his or her place on the legal team. The positions and job duties in any law office depend on the type and size of the office. A list of job titles and a general description of common duties and responsibilities are provided in this section. It should be noted that job titles are just that, they are "titles" only. Attorneys and law office administrators are far more impressed with a person's actual performance than with a person's job title.

> *Treat everyone, from the senior partner to the mail delivery person, with the same degree of respect and courtesy due any member of the legal team.*[1]

ATTORNEY

attorneys
Licensed professionals who counsel clients regarding their legal rights, represent clients in litigation, and negotiate agreements between clients and others.

Attorneys counsel clients regarding their legal rights, represent clients in litigation, and negotiate agreements between clients and others. Depending on the size of the law office, attorneys may also have administrative duties. There are several kinds of attorneys.

partner or **shareholder**
An owner in a private law practice who shares in its profits and losses.

PARTNER/SHAREHOLDER A **partner** or **shareholder** is an attorney-owner in a private law practice and shares in its profits and losses. In the partnership form of business, an owner of the business is called a partner. In the corporate form of business, an owner is called a shareholder. Partners and shareholders serve primarily the same purpose; it is only the legal structure that is different. For simplicity, "partner" will be used to refer collectively to partners and shareholders, but "shareholder" could also have been used.

Partners attend partnership meetings and vote in the management decisions of the firm. Partners must also make monetary contributions to the firm if the need arises. Partners are sometimes called "equity partners," since they share in the profits or losses of the firm. To become a partner, an attorney must either be an attorney who founded the firm or be voted into the position by the existing partners. Typically, partners do not receive a "salary" but may receive a periodic draw, which is an advance against future profits.

managing partner
An attorney in a law firm chosen by the partnership to run the firm, make administrative decisions, and set policies.

In some firms, a **managing partner** is chosen by the partnership to run the firm and make administrative decisions and set policies. The managing partner reports to the partnership on the progress of the firm. Managing partners are typically elected to serve a set time such as one or two years.

associate attorney
Attorney who is a salaried employee of the law firm, does not have an ownership interest in the firm, does not share in the profits, and has no vote regarding management decisions.

ASSOCIATE ATTORNEYS An **associate attorney** does not have an ownership interest in the law firm and does not share in the profits. The associate is only an employee of the firm who receives a salary and has no vote regarding management decisions. Associates can be hired directly out of law school or come from other firms. Associates who are hired from other firms are known as lateral hires or lateral hire associates. Associates who are candidates for a future partnership are said to be on a partnership track. An associate is usually with the firm between three and ten years before he or she is a candidate for a partnership position, depending on the size of the firm. In large metropolitan firms, the time may be longer. An associate passed over for partnership may or may not leave the firm to practice elsewhere. Sometimes, to keep good associate attorneys who have nevertheless been passed over for partnership, the firm creates a position known as a nonequity partner. A **nonequity partner** does not share in the profits or losses of the business but may be included in some aspects of the management of the firm and may be entitled to other benefits not given to associates. A **staff attorney** is another type of associate. A staff attorney is an attorney hired by a firm with the knowledge and understanding that he or she will never be considered for partnership. Finally, a **contract attorney** is an associate attorney who is temporarily hired by the law office for a specific job or period. When the job or period is finished, the relationship with the firm is over.

OF COUNSEL The **"of counsel"** position is a flexible concept but generally means that the attorney is affiliated with the firm in some way, such as a retired or semiretired partner. "Of counsel" attorneys lend their names to a firm for goodwill and prestige purposes to attract additional clients and business to the firm. An "of counsel" attorney may be paid on a "per job" basis or may be an employee of the firm. He or she does not usually share in the profits of the firm. The "of counsel" arrangement is also used when an attorney is considering joining a firm as a partner and wants to work on a trial basis first.

> *Not only are more firms beginning to see the essential role of administrators, and are delegating to them more and more administrative functions, but there is an accelerating trend toward actually giving them power in addition to their authority.*[2]

ADMINISTRATORS

Administrators are usually found in medium and large firms, although they are beginning to be used in small firms as well. Law office administrators are responsible for some type of law office administrative system such as general management, finance and accounting, human resources, marketing, or computer systems. Administrators are typically nonattorneys who have degrees in business or related fields or who have been promoted through the ranks. Administrators have a broad range of power to make management decisions with the approval of the partnership. Most report directly to a committee or a partner.

Administrators draft annual budgets, prepare and interpret management reports, supervise the fiscal operations of the business, hire and fire support staff, and are responsible for implementing effective systems. In short, administrators are managers hired to relieve management burdens from partners or managing committees. Experienced legal assistants are sometimes promoted to administrative positions. Administration can be a positive career move for legal assistants with good management skills. An excellent source of information regarding law office administration is available from the Association of Legal Administrators (ALA); see appendix B.

---

nonequity partner
One who does not share in the profits or losses of the firm but may be included in some aspects of management and may be entitled to certain benefits.

staff attorney
An attorney hired by a firm with the knowledge and understanding that he or she will never be considered for partnership.

contract attorney
An attorney temporarily hired by the law office for a specific job or period. When the job or period is finished, the relationship with the firm is over.

of counsel
An attorney affiliated with the firm in some way such as a retired or semiretired partner.

administrator
Person responsible for some type of law office administrative system such as general management, finance and accounting, human resources, marketing, or computer systems.

LEGAL ASSISTANTS

legal assistants
A distinguishable group of persons who assist attorneys in the delivery of legal services. They have knowledge and expertise regarding the legal system and substantive and procedural law that qualifies them to do work of a legal nature under the supervision of an attorney.

Legal assistants, also known as paralegals, are a distinguishable group of persons who assist attorneys in the delivery of legal services. Through formal education, training, and experience, legal assistants have knowledge and expertise regarding the legal system and substantive and procedural law that qualify them to do work of a legal nature under the supervision of an attorney.[3] This definition is used by the National Association of Legal Assistants (NALA), but it is not the only one. Figure 1-2 shows four separate definitions for a legal assistant or paralegal as defined by the American Bar Association (ABA), National Federation of Paralegal Associations (NFPA), National Association of Legal Assistants (NALA), and American Association for Paralegal Education (AAfPe). The terms *legal assistant* and *paralegal* often are used interchangeably, with no difference in meaning. This text, as well as the ABA, NFPA, and NALA, all use these terms interchangeably (see Figure 1-2). However, in some parts of the country and in some legal organizations there are various distinctions between the two terms.

> *Legal assistants play a vital role in the delivery of legal services to the public.*[4]

The ABA Standing Committee on Legal Assistants recently stated:

> As we approach [and enter] the twenty-first century, one of the highest priority goals of the American Bar Association is to increase access to legal services... One of the most effective ways to improve access to legal services is through the expanded utilization of well-qualified legal assistants who, with proper training and supervision, can be delegated work that would otherwise have to be done by a lawyer.[5]

The ABA has also recognized the contribution of legal assistants to the legal profession by creating an associate membership category for legal assistants, which allows them to participate in ABA activities and join sections and divisions of the ABA. Many state and county bar associations also allow legal assistants to participate as associate members in their organizations. Legal assistants also have two of their own national professional associations, NFPA and NALA, among others that they may join (see Appendix B).

Although legal assistants may perform many tasks, they are strictly prohibited from giving legal advice to clients, from representing clients in court proceedings, from accepting a client case, and from setting a fee in a matter. This is covered in more detail in the next chapter.

A "traditional" legal assistant works under the direct supervision of an attorney and is accountable to that attorney. There are also other "non-traditional" legal assistants, including freelance or contract legal assistants and independent legal assistants, also called *legal technicians*. A **freelance** or **contract legal assistant** works as an independent contractor with supervision by and/or accountability to an attorney.

freelance/contract legal assistant
Works as an independent contractor with supervision by and/or accountability to an attorney; is hired for a specific job or period.

Organization	Definition of "Legal Assistant or Paralegal"
American Bar Association	"A legal assistant or paralegal is a person, qualified by education, training or work experience who is employed or retained by a lawyer, law office, corporation, governmental agency, or other entity and who performs specifically delegated substantive legal work for which a lawyer is responsible." *ABA Standing Committee on Legal Assistants.*
National Federation of Paralegal Associations (NFPA)	"A paralegal/legal assistant is a person qualified through education, training or work experience to perform substantive legal work that requires knowledge of legal concepts and is customarily, but not exclusively, performed by a lawyer. This person may be retained or employed by a lawyer, law office, governmental agency or other entity or may be authorized by administrative, statutory or court authority to perform this work."
National Association Legal Assistants (NALA)	"Legal assistants, also known as paralegals, are of a distinguishable group of persons who assist attorneys in the delivery of legal services. Through formal education, training and experience, legal assistants have knowledge and expertise regarding the legal system and substantive and procedural law which qualify them to do work of a legal nature under the supervision of an attorney."
American Association for Paralegal Education (AAfPE)	"Paralegals perform substantive and procedural legal work as authorized by law, which work, in the absence of the paralegal, would be performed by an attorney. Paralegals have knowledge of the law gained through education, or education and work experience, which qualifies them to perform legal work. Paralegals adhere to recognized ethical standards and rules of professional responsibility."

**Figure 1-2
Definitions of a Legal Assistant/Paralegal**

These legal assistants are self-employed and market and sell their services to legal organizations on a per-job basis. While they work under the supervision of an attorney, they may do so off-site and for a number of attorneys or legal organizations at the same time.

> *I like the freedom of movement and being able to be my own boss and set my own hours [as a freelance legal assistant]. I'm not restricted to a set schedule, though of course I set appointments with the attorneys or their clients. I can come and go as I please. The client's [i.e. the law firm's] only concern is that I get the work done. I charge an hourly rate, which the law firms bill to their clients. It's a win/win situation. — A freelance legal assistant.[6]*

independent legal assistant
Provides services to clients in which the law is involved, but is not accountable to a lawyer.

Independent legal assistants, or **legal technicians,** provide services to clients in regard to a process in which the law is involved and for whose work no lawyer is accountable.[7] Legal technicians assist in providing "self-help services to the public." Because they do not work under the auspices of an attorney, they are often accused of ethical misconduct and subject to statutes against the unauthorized practice of law. (This is discussed in detail in the next chapter.)

legal assistant manager
Oversees a legal assistant program in a legal organization; hires, supervises, trains, and evaluates legal assistants.

Some larger legal organizations have **legal assistant managers** that oversee the legal assistant program. This may include a full range of duties and responsibilities, including hiring, supervising, training, and evaluating legal assistants.

A recent survey by the National Association of Legal Assistants found that more than 70 percent of the legal assistants responding had some kind of college degree (see Figure 1-3). Both NFPA and NALA have voluntary certification exams. Some states offer certifications as well.

LEGAL ASSISTANT ROLES, RESPONSIBILITIES, AND EMPLOYMENT

People unfamiliar with the legal profession might assume that legal assistants spend a great deal of time in trials and in court. This tends to be a misconception. No mat-

Figure 1-3
General Education Degree Attained

Source: National Association of Legal Assistants, 2000 National Utilization and Compensation Survey

Response	Percent
High School Diploma	28%
Associate Degree	28%
Bachelor's Degree	40%
Master's Degree	4%

ter what kind of law a law office practices, a considerable amount of a legal assistant's time is spent researching background information, plowing through reams of files, summarizing depositions, drafting pleadings and correspondence, and organizing information and files. It is not always exciting, but it is always essential work in every case. In many cases, the facts gathered, researched, and presented determine the outcome of the case. Many duties a legal assistant may perform will never involve a courtroom, such as preparation of wills, real estate closing transactions, drafting discovery, and preparation of business corporation papers.

Defining the work legal assistants do is not always an easy task given the wide variety and versatility of the profession. Figure 1-4 shows some of the more frequent daily duties legal assistants perform. Notice that assisting at trial is the lowest on the chart. Although there is diversity among legal assistant job duties, nearly all legal assistants spend a considerable portion of their time drafting documents and communicating either in writing or orally. A majority of the legal assistants responding to the survey in Figure 1-4 daily draft letters and case correspondence, work with and manage files and cases, calendar and keep track of case deadlines, work with computer systems, draft pleadings and formal court documents, work on miscellaneous office matters, and work with clients.

Most legal assistants practice in a particular area of the law. Figure 1-5 shows the areas in which legal assistants most frequently practice. Notice in Figure 1-5 that 51 percent of the legal assistants surveyed indicated that they specialized in civil litigation. Litigation provides many employment opportunities for legal assistants.

In addition to practicing in many different areas of the law, legal assistants are employed in different kinds of legal organizations (see Figure 1-6). About three-fourths of all legal assistants work in private law offices. Figure 1-6 also shows that about 59 percent of the legal assistants surveyed worked in relatively small firms with ten or fewer attorneys. The size of the law office has an effect on the job duties

Duty	Percentage of Survey Respondents That Daily Perform This Duty
Draft correspondence	80%
Case management	69%
Calendaring deadlines	63%
Automation systems/computers	54%
Draft pleadings	50%
Office matters	45%
Assist with client contact	42%
Court filings	31%
Document analysis/summary	31%
General, factual research	26%
Investigation	17%
Client/witness interviews	15%
Legal research	8%
Deposition summaries	4%
Assist at trial	2%

**Figure 1-4
Daily Functions and Duties of Legal Assistants**

Source: National Association of Legal Assistants, 2000 National Utilization and Compensation Survey

**Figure 1-5
Legal Assistant Specialty Areas of Practice**

Source: National Association of Legal Assistants, 2000 National Utilization and Compensation Survey

Specialty Areas	Percent of Respondents Selecting the Speciality
Civil litigation	51%
Personal injury	34%
Corporate	33%
Real estate	30%
Probate/estates	26%
Contracts	26%
Administrative/Government/Public	25%
Trusts & estates	23%
Insurance	21%
Family Law	21%
Office Management	21%
Medical Malpractice	21%
Employment/Labor Law	20%
Bankruptcy	19%
Worker's Compensation	17%
Criminal	17%

**Figure 1-6
Legal Assistant Employment**

Source: National Association of Legal Assistants, 2000 National Utilization and Compensation Survey

Employer	Percent
Private law firm	74%
Corporation	10%
Public Sector/Government	8%
Insurance Company	2%
Self Employed	2%
Health/Medical	1%
Bank	1%
Other	2%

Number of Attorneys	Percent
1 (sole practitioner)	12%
2–5	30%
6–10	17%
11–20	14%
21–50	14%
Over 50	13%

Figure 1-7
Legal Assistant Compensation Survey

Source: National Association of Legal Assistants, 2000 National Utilization and Compensation Survey

By Years of Legal Experience	Average Total Compensation
1–5 years	$30,342
6–10 years	$37,034
11–15 years	$42,296
16–20 years	$45,402
21–25 years	$46,422

By Region	Average Total Compensation
Far West	$54,335
New England/East	$41,537
Southwest	$39,983
Southeast	$38,821
Great Lakes	$38,807
Plains States	$38,175
Rocky Mountains	$33,238

By Practice Area	Average Total Compensation
Intellectual Property	$46,349
Securities/Antitrust	$43,916
Corporate	$42,088
Employment/Labor Law	$41,453
Environmental Law	$41,876
Contract	$40,604
Insurance	$40,062
Civil Litigation	$39,677
Real Estate	$39,370
Bankruptcy	$37,825
Personal Injury	$37,091
Probate	$36,930
Criminal	$35,456

and salaries of legal assistants. In small law offices, legal assistants usually compose and draft their own documents on a computer and do their own secretarial tasks. In larger firms, legal assistants may supervise secretarial personnel who transcribe documents and perform secretarial duties for the legal assistants.

LEGAL ASSISTANT COMPENSATION

Figure 1-7 contains a national survey of legal assistant compensation. This survey found that the average compensation for all legal assistants was $40,471. The survey found that legal assistants in intellectual property, securities/antitrust, and corporate law departments receive higher compensation on average than do legal

**Figure 1–8
Billing and Overtime**

Source: National Association of Legal Assistants, 2000 National Utilization and Compensation Survey

Billable Hours Expected Per Week	
Number of Hours	**Percent**
25 hours or less	14%
26–30 hours	30%
31–35 hours	32%
36–40 hours	20%
41 hours or more	4%

assistants in other areas of practice. Another national survey showed that only about half of all legal assistants are required to bill clients for their time. When they did bill for their time, the average billing rate was $74 an hour. The most common requirement for hours to be billed by a legal assistant per week is between twenty-six and thirty-five hours (1,352 and 1,820 annually).

Fair Labor Standard Act
Federal law that sets minimum wage and overtime pay requirements for employees.

FLSA exempt
The employee is not required to be paid overtime wages over 40 hours per week.

FLSA non-exempt
The employee is required to be paid overtime wages (time and a half) over 40 hours per week.

EXEMPT v. NON-EXEMPT The **Fair Labor Standard Act (FLSA)** is a federal law that sets minimum wage and overtime pay requirements for employees. It requires that overtime pay (one-and-one-half times their normal rate) be paid to employees who work in excess of forty hours per week. Employees do not need to be paid overtime if they fall into one of the four "white-collar" exemptions: executive, administrative, professional, or outside sales. If an employee is **exempt**, he or she is not required to be paid overtime wages. If an employee is **non-exempt**, he or she is required to be paid overtime wages. According to a recent survey of legal assistants 52.2 percent responding indicated that they were classified as "exempt" by their employer and were not paid overtime wages.

The issue of whether legal assistants should be exempt or non-exempt is hotly debated. The United States Department of Labor, which administers the FLSA, has long taken the position that legal assistants are non-exempt and are entitled to overtime pay for hours worked in excess of forty per week because their "duties do not involve the exercise of discretion and independent judgment required by the regulations" (see Wage & Hour Opinion Letters dated March 20, 1998; February 19, 1998; April 13, 1995; February 10, 1978). The advantage of this long-held position by the Department of Labor is that if a legal assistant is deemed non-exempt, then he or she is entitled to overtime pay, which can be an attractive benefit. Unfortunately, the ruling arguably diminishes the profession by holding that it is not of a prestigious enough nature to warrant exempt status. The Department of Labor's ruling has been widely criticized because it fails to take into account recent practice and utilization of, legal assistants, recognized status of the profession, legal assistants' advanced education and their continuing legal education, the substantive duties they perform, and the degree to which legal assistants exercise discretion and independent judgment in the performance of the job.[8] In 1994, a jury in the case of *Riech v. Page & Addison, P.C.*, (Case No. 3:91-CV-2655-P in the United States District Court, Northern District of Texas, Dallas Division) found that the legal assistants at the Page &

Addison law firm were exempt from overtime requirements. Nevertheless, the Department of Labor did not change its general position on the matter.

> *Paralegals being classified as exempt or non-exempt is a double-edged sword. Being non-exempt protects the paralegal from working "associates on partner track" hours (i.e., large numbers of hours), especially in a cost-minded firm (and what firm is not cost-minded nowadays?) However, paralegals are striving to be recognized as "professionals" and most professionals are exempt employees.*
>
> —Linda L. Rushton, CLA

THE JUDICIAL SYSTEM'S RECOGNITION OF THE LEGAL ASSISTANT PROFESSION

The United States Supreme Court case of *Missouri v. Jenkins*, 491 U.S. 274, 109 S.Ct. 2463, 105 L.Ed. 2d 229 (1989), established that the legal assistant profession has come of age. In that case, the plaintiff was successful on several counts under a federal statute in a civil rights lawsuit and was attempting to recover attorney's fees from the defendant. The federal statutory language allowed the prevailing party to recover "reasonable attorney's fees" from the adverse party. The plaintiff argued for the right to recover the time that both attorneys and legal assistants had spent working on the case. The defendant argued that legal assistant time was not "attorney's fees." Alternatively, the defendant argued that if required to pay for legal assistant time, the amount should be about fifteen dollars an hour, a representation of the overhead costs to the firm of a legal assistant.

The Court found that legal assistants carry out many useful tasks and "reasonable attorney's fees" refers to a reasonable fee for work produced, whether it be by attorneys or by legal assistants and could be compensable as long as the work was not of a clerical nature. The Court also found that under the federal statute, legal assistant time should be compensable at the prevailing market rates in the area for legal assistant's services. The Court noted that the prevailing rate for legal assistants in that part of the United States at that time was about forty dollars an hour and held that the plaintiff was entitled to receive that amount for legal assistant hours expended on the case. This important case defines a legal assistant position not as a secretarial or clerical position but as a professional, fee-generating profession.

Former Chief Justice Warren Burger stated that:

> The "expanded use of well-trained assistants, sometimes called 'paralegals,' has been an important development. The advent of the paralegal enables law offices to perform high quality legal services at a lower cost. Possibly we have only scratched the surface of this development."

While *Missouri v. Jenkins* was a landmark decision for legal assistants, the case involved a federal court interpreting a specific federal statute, the Civil Rights Act. Because fee questions occur under many different situations, it is possible for a court under a different statute to reach a different conclusion. Since *Missouri v. Jenkins,* many federal and state courts have allowed for recovery of legal assistant billable hours [see *Baldwin v. Burton,* 850 P.2d 1188, 1200-01 (Utah 1993), *Cooper v. Secretary of Dept. of Health and Human Services,* No. 90-608V, 1992 WL 63271 at 3(Cl. Ct. March 11, 1992), *Consolo v. George,* 58 F.3d 791 (1st Cir. 1995), *Department of Transp., State of Fla. v. Robbins & Robbins, Inc.* 700 So. 2d 782, Fla.App. 5 Dist. (1997), *Guinn v. Dotson* (1994) 23 Cal. App. 4th 262, *In re Mullins,* 84 F.3d 459 (D.C. Cir. 1996), *Taylor v. Chubb Group of Insurance Companies,* 874 P.2d 806 (Ok. 1994).

> *The recognition by the courts that legal assistants are income-producing members of the professional legal service delivery team, that they perform substantive legal tasks under the supervision of the attorney, and that their fees are properly included as a component in an award of attorney fees has done much to increase the status of the legal assistant profession.*[9]

LEGAL ASSISTANT PROFITABILITY FOR LAW OFFICES

The use of legal assistants is a financially profitable proposition and represents a win-win situation for both the law office and client. Law offices charge clients for legal assistant time. Legal assistant billing rates are substantially more than the salaries law offices pay them, so law offices make a profit by billing legal assistant time. In addition, clients are typically very willing to pay for legal assistant time because the billable rate is substantially less than what an attorney would charge to do the same work.

> *To remain competitive, lawyers need to acknowledge that they are overqualified for much of what they do . . . It is through the expanded use of legal assistants that lawyers can remain profitable while meeting current client demands.*[10]

OFFICE MANAGER

office manager
Manager who handles day-to-day operations of the law office, such as accounting, supervision of the clerical support staff, and assisting the managing partner.

Office managers are typically found in smaller firms. They handle day-to-day operations of the law office, including such activities as timekeeping and billing, supervision of the clerical support staff, assisting the managing partner in preparing a budget, and making recommendations with regard to changes in systems and purchases. Office managers typically do not have degrees in business. Office managers are usually not given as much decision-making power as administrators, and unlike administrators, usually assist a managing partner in managing the law office. Nonetheless, good office managers are important to the survival of smaller firms. Experienced legal assistants are sometimes promoted into office manager positions.

LAW CLERK

A **law clerk** is usually a student who works for a law firm on a part-time basis while he or she is finishing a law degree. Law clerk duties revolve around legal research and writing almost exclusively. Law clerks perform legal research, write legal briefs and motions, and prepare memorandums of law.

LAW LIBRARIAN

A **law librarian** is responsible for maintaining a law library. Maintenance includes purchasing new books and periodicals, classifying, storing, and indexing books, updating the holdings, and coordinating computer-assisted legal research (i.e., WESTLAW, LEXIS, and other services).

SECRETARIES

Secretaries provide assistance and support to other law office staff by taking dictation, performing typing and filing functions, and aiding in scheduling of appointments. Secretaries include legal secretaries, receptionists, and word processing secretaries. Competent legal secretaries have highly specialized skills and perform many services for law firms. Legal secretaries, like legal assistants, have their own local, regional, state, and national associations. It is not uncommon for a person to start employment with a law office as a legal secretary and work his or her way up to legal assistant, office manager, or other position. Receptionists are common in all law offices. Receptionist duties include answering the phone, greeting clients, opening the mail, and making photocopies. Word processing secretaries are common in larger law offices. They type, format, and produce documents using word processing software.

It is not uncommon for there to be friction between legal assistants and secretaries. Problems may occur in law offices where there are no clear descriptions of job duties, where legal assistants are required to do some clerical or administrative work, and where secretaries perform higher level research or case management from time to time. This blurring of the lines sometimes causes confusion about who is supposed to do what. When this happens, it adds pressure to the relationship. Some secretaries also resent legal assistants performing work of a higher level than they are allowed to perform. In addition, some secretaries refuse or resist performing clerical work for legal assistants because they view legal assistants as peers. In any case, legal assistants and secretaries must work together as members of the same team. They must put the needs of the team first and support their coworkers because eventually they will need their help.

> *Get along with the secretaries. You work together. They do not work for you. They are a great ally, but an even greater road block if you get in their way. Give them respect.*[11]

law clerk
A law student working for a law firm on a part-time basis while he or she is finishing a law degree. Law clerk duties revolve almost exclusively around legal research and writing.

law librarian
A librarian is responsible for maintaining a law library. Maintenance includes purchasing new books and periodicals, classifying, storing, indexing, and updating the holdings, and coordinating computer-assisted legal research (i.e. WESTLAW, LEXIS, and other services).

secretaries
Employees who provide assistance and support to other law office staff by taking dictation, performing typing and filing functions, and aiding in scheduling of appointments.

CLERKS

Clerks provide support to other staff positions in a variety of functions. Law offices may have a wide variety of clerks, including mail clerks, copy clerks, file clerks, calendar clerks, and billing clerks. Much of their work involves data entry and physically handling files and documents.

clerks
Employees who provide support to other staff positions in a variety of miscellaneous functions.

OTHER LEGAL TEAM MEMBERS

A variety of other people and organizations make up the legal team. Other team members may include expert witnesses, investigators, litigation support bureaus, and consultants. An **expert witness** is a person who has technical or scientific expertise in a specific field and agrees to give testimony for a client at trial. Professional investigators are hired in cases to gather facts and evidence regarding a case. Litigation support service bureaus are sometimes used in cases that have hundreds or thousands of documents to organize and records to computerize for trial. Law offices use business consultants, marketing consultants, and other types of consultants to give them advice on how to run their business efficiently. Law offices may also use temporary or permanent staffing firms and may outsource jobs, projects, or services as needed, including copying, mail services, and records management.

expert witness
A person who has technical expertise in a specific field and agrees to give testimony for a client at trial.

TYPES OF LAW PRACTICES

To a certain extent, how law office management operates depends on the type of law office. Therefore, it is necessary to review the different types of law practices and their functional effect on management. Usually, people think only of the private law firm as a type of law practice, but there are others as well, including corporate law practices, government practices, and legal aid practices.

CORPORATE LAW PRACTICE

Some businesses have their own in-house law department, including large corporations, banks, retailers, manufacturers, transportation companies, publishers, insurance companies, and hospitals. In a corporate legal department, attorneys have just one client: the business. However, some corporate legal departments see each division or department in the corporation as a "client" for whom they must provide quality legal services.

Corporations that have their own legal department are generally large, with millions of dollars in assets. Unlike private law firms, a corporate legal department is not involved in many administrative functions, such as accounting, since the corporation itself provides these services. Corporate legal departments do not record billable hours, since all costs are covered by the corporation. However, corporate legal departments must still budget, track, and plan activities, and they are responsible for the overall efficiency of their department. Corporate law departments handle a variety of legal concerns in such areas as labor relations, employee benefits, federal tax law, intellectual property environmental law issues, SEC (Security Exchange Commission) filings, general litigation, real estate law, and workers' compensation claims.

> *The benefits of working for a corporation are really great. There is a lot of responsibility. . . . There is more opportunity for upward mobility within the company, since you can contribute your legal skills in other areas, such as sales and marketing. . . . The stress level is lower—it is not as frantic as at a law firm.*[12]
>
> —A corporate legal assistant

Most corporate legal departments are too small to handle all the legal needs of the corporation, so the law departments hire private law firms that specialize in the additional areas they need. This is sometimes referred to as having "outside counsel." The chief attorney for a corporate legal department is called the **general counsel.** The general counsel, in addition to having legal duties, may also be the corporate secretary.

Staffing in corporate legal departments includes secretaries, legal assistants, law clerks, administrators, and attorneys. Most corporate legal departments employ one or more legal assistants. The job duties a legal assistant performs in a corporate legal department are *similar to those performed in* other types of practices. Job duties might include preparing deposition summaries, performing legal research, and drafting documents. Like legal assistants in private law firms, legal assistants in corporate legal departments might also specialize in specific areas such as litigation, real estate, or business law.

general counsel
The chief for a corporate legal department.

GOVERNMENT PRACTICE

Government attorneys, like corporate attorneys, have just one client. In most local, state, and federal agencies, there is a legal department that represents the interests of *each* particular agency. Government attorneys representing agencies or governmental bodies may be involved in contract law, bankruptcy law, tax law, employment law, property law, and environmental law to name a few. Each state also has an attorney general's office. The attorney general operates as the state's chief law enforcement officer and chief attorney. In many instances, when a state or state agency is sued, the state's attorney general's office represents the state. There are many other types of government attorneys, including prosecutors such as local district and city attorneys, state attorneys general, and United States attorneys.

In many ways, practicing for the government is similar to practicing for a large corporation. Government attorneys, like corporate attorneys, do not record billable hours and are not responsible for as many management duties as are their counterparts in private law firms. Government practices are different from the corporate legal department in that politics plays a role in governmental practices. Attorneys and legal assistants are paid according to their civil service classification. Staffing for government legal departments consists of secretaries, investigators, legal assistants, law clerks, and attorneys. The job duties of legal assistants in government practices vary depending on the area of practice, and these duties may be tested for in various civil service exams that are a prerequisite to hiring.

> *Recently I started working for a government contractor after spending my entire career at private law firms. The biggest advantage of being in the government/corporate environment is that the pressure of achieving a certain amount of billable hours every month is no longer there. Also, the attorneys in the corporate and government environment seem to be more laid back than attorneys in private practice.*
> —Linda L. Rushton, CLA

LEGAL AID OFFICES

legal aid office
A not-for-profit law office that receives grants from the government and private donations to pay for representation of disadvantaged persons who otherwise could not afford legal services.

A **legal aid office,** sometimes called a legal clinic or public law office, is a not-for-profit law office that receives grants from the government and private donations to pay for representation of disadvantaged persons who otherwise could not afford legal services. In some cases, legal aid offices or clinics are operated by law schools, bar associations, or other nonprofit entities as a public service to the community. Clients pay little or no fees for legal services. Legal aid offices typically represent the disadvantaged in areas relating to child support, child custody, disability claims, bankruptcies, landlord-tenant disputes, and mental health problems. Staffing for legal aid offices includes secretaries, legal assistants, law clerks, and attorneys. In legal aid practices, legal assistants may be used fairly extensively and are usually given a wide variety of tasks because their use is cost effective. Legal aid offices typically handle civil matters while government public defender's offices handle criminal matters for low-income clients.

> *After ten years of work at the Vermont Legal Aid, I seem to have accumulated cases that never close, clients that never stop calling.... "Can I run this by you?" So why does this work still seem fresh and new to me? Perhaps because no day is like any other....*
> *(A recent case of) helping [a] client through her housing crisis was a team effort, and that is a real benefit of working in this office.*[13]

PRIVATE LAW PRACTICES

The most common way that attorneys practice law is in a private law firm. A private law practice is a firm that generates its own income from representing clients. Private law firms, like any business, are operated to make a profit for their owners.

Practice Setting	Size	Percent	Approximate Number
Private Practice	Solo Practitioner		297,724
Private Practice	Firms of 2–5 Attorneys		95,263
Private Practice	Firms of 6–20 Attorneys		90,218
Private Practice	Firms of 21–50 Attorneys		45,954
Private Practice	Firms of 51–100 Attorneys		28,823
Private Practice	Firms of 101 or more Attorneys		76,493
Private Industry/ Private Association			76,842
Judiciary/Government/ Public Service/Military			95,754
Retired/Inactive			42,673
Education			8,186
TOTAL			857,930*

*Because of rounding the column of figures does not add up to the total shown. *The Lawyer Statistical Report*, "The U.S. Legal Profession in 1995, Clara N. Carson, American Bar Foundation, 1999

Figure 1-9
Number of Attorneys by Practice Setting

Source: 1994 Supplement to the American Bar Association *Lawyer Statistical Report* (see also, www.abanet.org/solo/stats.html).

Private law firms represent a variety of clients and come in all shapes and sizes, from the solo practitioner to international megafirms.

The terminology is somewhat arbitrary, and may depend on the relative size of your community, but, for this text, a small firm is a law office that has fewer than twenty attorneys; a medium-size firm usually has from twenty to seventy-five attorneys; and a large firm can employ from seventy-five to hundreds of attorneys. There are also "megafirms" that employ between five hundred and one thousand attorneys or more. Private practices, no matter the size, have their own unique styles, methods, clients, cultures, and ways of doing things. Thirty-three percent of all attorneys are sole practitioners (see Figure 1-9).

> *For over two years, I have worked for a sole legal practitioner. I am the only paralegal in the office and am directly involved in almost everything that transpires in our office. . . . My input is not only heard, but utilized. I have no billing quotas. While we do keep close track of billable hours, I don't have to justify every minute of my workday. . . .*[14]
> —A sole practitioner's legal assistant

SOLE PRACTITIONER

A sole practitioner is an attorney who individually owns and manages the practice. Anyone who works for the attorney is considered an employee. Sole practitioners sometimes hire another attorney as an employee. The employee attorney would not be entitled to any share in the profits of the practice. Although the sole practitioner has the advantage of freedom and independence, he or she is also ultimately responsible for all or nearly all the legal work performed by the law office and is also responsible for all the management duties. For the sole practitioner to succeed, it is important that overhead costs be as small as possible. Overhead costs are expenses incurred month after month and include such things as rent (thus the term "overhead"), utilities, the lease of equipment such as copiers and computers, and support staff salaries. These are costs incurred whether the attorney is serving one client or one hundred clients. Sole practitioners typically have small offices with a very small law library.

Sole practitioners are typically generalists, meaning they handle a wide variety of cases such as probate, family law, criminal law, and personal injury. The sole practitioner typically refers a case outside of his or her area of expertise to another attorney who is skilled in that matter. Sole practitioners need good management skills for their practice to survive. This may pose a problem because management duties take the sole practitioner away from the actual practice of law, which is the activity that brings in the money.

Staffing can include a secretary, legal assistant, law clerk, and possibly an associate attorney. These positions may even be part time. Legal assistants working in a sole practitioner's office enjoy a great deal of responsibility and diversity in their jobs. Duties include legal research, drafting pleadings and discovery materials, word processing, and interviewing witnesses. Because sole practitioners are generalists, their legal assistants work in many areas of law. In a solo practice, the legal assistant has the opportunity to learn firsthand about law office management and to perform management functions.

LAW FIRMS

Law firms have two or more attorneys in practice together. While there is not as much freedom as in sole practice, law firms do not have as much risk as a sole practitioner has. If a sole practitioner becomes ill, loses a large client, or faces other such catastrophes, the sole practitioner's income may be endangered. In law firms, these problems may be alleviated because more than one attorney is available. Law firms are usually categorized as either small, medium, or large.

> *The (small) size of the law office contributes to the fact that we, as paralegals, are appreciated for more than just our clerical or organizational skills. At times we do research or writing that an associate might do at a larger law office.*[15]
> —Small law firm legal assistant

THE SMALL LAW FIRM The small firm usually has fewer than twenty attorneys. Most small firms have a staff member such as an office manager or an administrator who helps with the day-to-day operations of the business. However, a partner or managing partner is usually responsible for major management decisions such as hiring, firing, distributing profits, and setting salaries. Small firms usually concentrate in a few areas of the law but may also have attorneys who are general practitioners.

A small law office that specializes in only one or two areas of the law is sometimes called a **boutique firm**. The boutique firm normally has several attorneys who practice in the same specialty. Legal assistants who work for boutique firms also usually become specialists in that particular area of law.

boutique firm
A small law office that specializes in only one or two areas of the law.

Disadvantages that hinder small firms include cash-flow problems, the lack of time to recruit, hire, and train new staff, little time for management, and long hours. Staffing positions include clerks, secretaries, legal assistants, office managers, law clerks, and attorneys. Small firms offer legal assistants a relatively large variety of tasks to perform.

THE MEDIUM-SIZE FIRM The medium-size firm usually has from twenty to seventy-five attorneys. Typically, medium-size firms are organized into subject-area departments. Medium-size firms differ from small firms in that most medium-size firms have professional administrators who manage many aspects of the business. Administrators usually report to a managing partner or a committee that has overall management responsibilities. Medium-size firms typically have multiple offices, and it is not uncommon for them to have sophisticated computer systems. Staffing often consists of administrators, law librarians, receptionists, secretaries, legal assistants, law clerks, and attorneys. Legal assistants in medium-size firms have a more structured existence than in smaller firms. The diversity of duties and areas of practice are not as broad as in smaller firms. However, the legal assistant may learn a particular area of law in depth. In addition, the internal structure and lines of communication are more intense and more important than in small firms where colleagues tend to be more familiar with one another.

> *A [mega lawfirm] is an incredible place to work. I'm allowed to do whatever I want to take on . . . The longer I'm here, the more opportunity there is to take on a bigger piece of the process.*
> —Legal assistant in a 1000+ attorney firm.[16]

> *The resources at a large firm are greater than smaller firms. There will be a number of experienced legal assistants to whom an entry-level legal assistant can turn to for a mentor. In addition, there will be more variety of law practiced by the attorneys; therefore, when an issue arises which is not your practice group's specialty, another attorney or practice group in the firm can handle the situation instead of referring it out of the firm.*
> —Linda L. Rushton, CLA

THE LARGE FIRM The large firm has from seventy-five to several hundred attorneys. A few large firms, sometimes called "megafirms" have five hundred to one thousand or more attorneys. Most large firms have practice groups or departments. A large firm might have fifteen or more different practice groups including antitrust, bankruptcy, environmental, estate planning, intellectual property, international, labor/employment law, litigation, patents, trademarks, copyright, property, and tax. The internal structure of these firms is more similar to the structure of business corporations than to other types of law firms. Staffing in large firms typically includes various classes of legal assistants, law clerks, and attorneys in addition to the positions shown in Figure 1-10. Large firms often have as clients large corporations. Many have offices throughout the United States, and some have international offices. Large firms also have resources such as large law libraries, a word processing department, and extensive, technologically advanced computer systems connecting all their offices for information exchange.

Disadvantages encountered by large firms include recruiting and retaining good employees in the vital areas of the practice, getting departments to communicate and work together, and controlling the bureaucracy itself. Large law firms usually employ a large number of legal assistants and treat them formally and professionally, requiring them to attend department meetings, assist attorneys in depositions, and travel as needed. Computers are used extensively by legal assistants. The physical space occupied by a large firm is more lavish than in small and medium-size firms, usually including occupying several floors in a large office building.

**Figure 1-10
Large Law Firm
Administrative Staff
Positions**

Accounts payable clerk	Legal assistant supervisor
Accounts receivable clerk	Library aides
Analysts	Mail clerks
Bookkeepers	Messengers/pages
Chief financial officer/comptroller	Payroll specialists
Computer specialists	Proofreaders
Copy room clerks	Purchasing clerks
Credit/collections manager	Receptionists
Data processing operators	Records/file manager
Director of marketing	Recruiter
Docket clerks	Reservation clerks
Employee benefits manager	Risk manager
Equipment manager	Secretaries
Facilities manager	Telephone operators
File room clerks	Time and billing assistants
Human resource manager	Word processors
Legal administrator	Word processing supervisor

PLAINTIFF/DEFENSE FIRMS

Private law practices may categorize themselves as either more or less plaintiff or defense oriented no matter what the size of the law office. Plaintiff-oriented firms, as the name implies, represent clients who bring claims against others. Plaintiff-oriented firms tend to be smaller than defense-oriented firms, are generally not as well funded as defense-oriented firms, and have fewer employees. Cash flow in plaintiff firms may not be as stable as in defense-oriented firms because in many cases they take clients on a contingency fee basis. That is, the law office recovers fees for the case only if it wins.

Defense-oriented firms, on the other hand, have the luxury of billing defendants, who are typically businesses, according to the time spent on the case. This gives defense-oriented firms a more stable cash flow, enabling them to hire more personnel, purchase advanced equipment, and spend more on litigation services such as hiring expert witnesses and taking as many depositions as needed. Nonetheless, effective management is needed in both plaintiff- and defense-oriented firms.

No matter what type of legal organization, good management, including sound financial management, cost-efficient hiring and training of personnel, efficient use of equipment, and overall leadership, is important.

LAW PRACTICE ORGANIZATION STRUCTURES

Law practices have different organization or management structures. Private law practices are managed by a powerful managing partner, by all partners, or by committees. Corporate and government law practices have either a centralized or decentralized management structure.

LEGAL FORMS OF PRIVATE LAW FIRMS

Management structures of law firms are affected by the firm's legal status. A law firm can be formed as a sole proprietorship, partnership, corporation, or, in some states, a limited liability company. Before the management structure of law offices can be considered, the legal status of law offices must be explained.

SOLE PROPRIETORSHIP In a sole proprietorship, the proprietor, in this case an attorney, runs the business and personally receives all profits and is personally responsible for all losses and liabilities of the law office. However, keep in mind that a sole proprietorship is a distinct type of legal structure. A sole practitioner does not have to use the sole proprietorship form of legal structure. Many sole practitioners are incorporated.

PARTNERSHIP The partnership's legal structure allows two or more attorneys to associate themselves together and to share in the profits or losses of the business. Many group practices use this structure. When a law office is established as a partnership, the founding attorneys are usually named as partners. As growth takes place, the partnership may hire additional associate attorneys.

All the partners are jointly and severally liable for the actions of the firm. This means if one partner commits malpractice and injures a client, each partner may be held individually or jointly responsible. Partners are also personally liable for the debts of the partnership. Partnerships typically use committees to make policy decisions, and partners meet regularly to discuss partnership business.

PROFESSIONAL CORPORATION The professional corporation allows a single shareholder or a group of shareholders from the same profession, such as attorneys, to join to share in the outcomes of a business. When a law office is established as a professional corporation, the founding attorney or attorneys receive shares in the business. As in a partnership, associates are not owners and are only paid a salary. Shareholders can vote to offer additional shares of the business to associates and expand the ownership of the law firm. All attorneys are employees of the corporation and are paid a salary. Besides a salary, shareholders are paid a dividend. The amount of the dividend depends on the profitability of the corporation and on the number of shares owned. Shareholders are not personally responsible for the debts of the professional corporation. The corporate form requires the election of officers and a board of directors.

LIMITED LIABILITY COMPANY The limited liability company (LLC) is a hybrid form of legal structure. It is a combination of the corporate and partnership form. The LLC form of structure is valid in many states. The main advantage of an LLC is that it allows for limited personal liability of company debts for its owners (like a corporation), but is treated like a partnership for income tax purposes.

PRIVATE LAW FIRM MANAGEMENT STRUCTURES

The type of management or governing structure used to manage the business aspect of the firm is the choice of the firm, but the legal structure of the business may dictate some of that management structure. For example, a corporation by law must have a board of directors. Many law practices struggle with the problem of who runs the firm and who has the final say on firm decisions. Possible management structures include the powerful managing partner, rule by all partners/shareholders, and rule by management committee or board (see Figure 1-11).

powerful managing partner
A management structure in which a single partner is responsible for managing the firm.

THE POWERFUL MANAGING PARTNER In a **powerful managing partner** management structure a single partner manages the firm. The managing partner is responsible for day-to-day operations of the partnership while partners vote on major firm decisions. The managing partner may have a specific term of office. In some

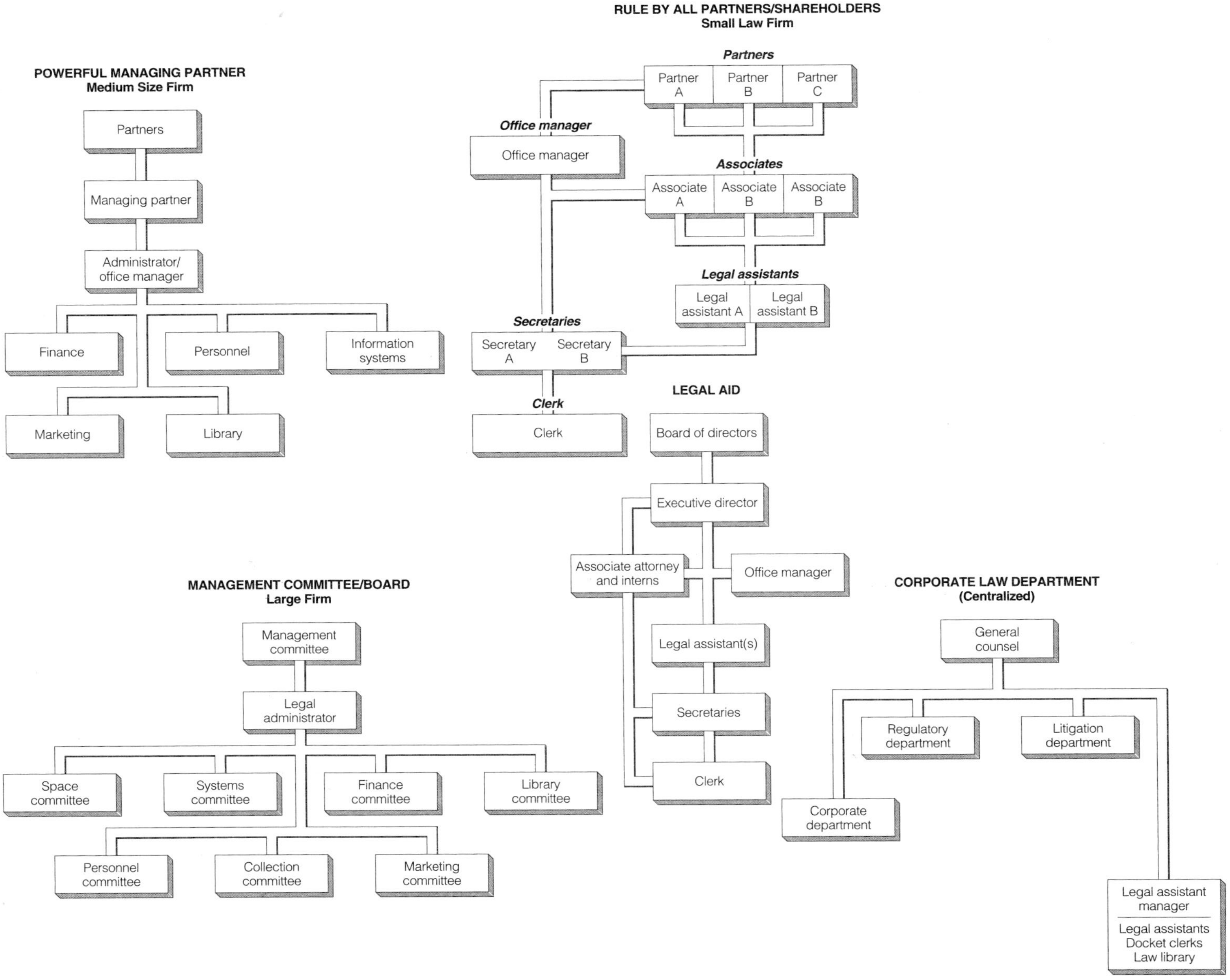

Figure 1-11 Organizational Charts

Source: Legal Assistant Management Association

firms, the position is rotated among the practicing partners. In many firms, the managing partner spends anywhere from 60 percent to 100 percent of his or her time on management responsibilities. This form allows other partners to spend more time practicing law, but places the managerial duties on one partner and reduces the managing partner's time to practice law. The powerful managing partner structure is autocratic, meaning that power rests with one person. In some cases, the other partners may feel they are without a voice in the management of the firm.

> *Smaller firms tend to favor a democratic form of governance. Typically, every partner votes on every management decision. As firm size increases, it soon becomes obvious that this system is too cumbersome to be practical once a firm reaches . . . 12 to 15 partners.*[17]

rule by all partners/shareholders
A management structure in which all partners/shareholders are included in decisions that affect the firm.

RULE BY ALL PARTNERS/SHAREHOLDERS **Rule by all partners/shareholders** is a management structure in which all partners/shareholders make decisions that affect the firm. All the partners or shareholders meet whenever management policies or decisions need to be made. This is a democratic structure, since all the partners have a say in firm decisions and policies. Although this structure allows partners/shareholders involvement in all the decisions of the firm, as the number of partners/shareholders increases, the effectiveness of the group may decrease with more people added to the body. This may foster indecision and a lack of direction.

> *The most common arrangement for mid-size firms is governance by a committee, variously called the executive committee, the management committee, the policy committee, or some equivalent. The committee members serve, in effect, as delegates for the rest of the partners.*[18]

rule by management committee/board
Management structure that uses a committee structure to make management decisions for the firm.

RULE BY MANAGEMENT COMMITTEE/BOARD The **rule by management committee/board** management structure uses a committee structure to make management decisions for the firm. Committees are made up of five to ten members depending on the size of the firm. Committees are typically made up of partners or shareholders. Common committees include the library committee, automation or systems committee, finance committee, and personnel committee. These committees usually report to a management or executive committee. If the committee gets too large, the actions of the committee slow down greatly and can hamper the effectiveness of the firm.

CORPORATE, GOVERNMENT, AND LEGAL AID ORGANIZATION STRUCTURES

Corporate and government law practices have different organizational and management structures than do private law firms. Corporate law departments can be centralized or decentralized. In the past, many, but not all, were centralized, meaning they were usually located in the firm's corporate headquarters but provided legal services for the whole company. Many government practices take a decentralized approach. Most state and federal agencies have their own legal departments that provide legal services only to that particular agency. Like most private law firms, corporate and government practices can have different divisions within the practice such as litigation or labor law. Although many corporate departments are centralized and many government practices decentralized, the choice depends on the type, size, and dynamics of the organization.

The management structure of corporate and government practices is dependent upon the corporation's or agency's own organizational structure as well. Many corporate and government departments have a general counsel responsible for the overall management of the department. The power of the general counsel is similar to that of the powerful managing partner in private law firms. However, the power is diluted, since the general counsel must still act under the auspices of the overall corporate structure or of the legislative or other public body in the government practice.

Legal aid practices, because they are usually nonprofit corporations, are overseen by a board of directors. The board of directors might be made up of law professors, attorneys in private practice, judges, and other interested persons. The board usually hires an executive director who is responsible for the day-to-day operations of the practice. The executive director has attorneys, legal assistants, clerical staff, and administrators who report to him or her.

LAW OFFICE MANAGEMENT PRINCIPLES

There was a time when law office management was viewed as unimportant. Attorneys viewed management responsibilities as something that got in the way of providing legal services to their clients. In truth, some of this view still prevails. This is why a competent legal assistant, able to take over many responsibilities in office management, is a valuable member of the legal team. Today, the highly competitive nature of the legal field and the need to control costs make law office management an important topic. While many might think that management is more important in very large firms than in small law firms or corporate law departments, the opposite is true. Good management skills are equally important in every type of legal practice if the practice is going to be successful in serving clients, providing quality jobs for its employees, and producing profits for its partners or shareholders.

During the past twenty years, there has been an automation revolution that has changed law office management. Until recently, law offices were generally unconcerned with computers, word processing, computerized accounting and billing, state-of-the-art telephone systems, the Internet, copiers, and facsimile machines. However, during the past decade, law offices have spent millions of dollars purchasing this type of equipment. Law offices, like most other businesses, have discovered that purchasing state-of-the-art equipment gives them an edge over their competition, greatly increases staff productivity, and improves the quality of the services they can provide.

DISPELLING A MYTH

A myth about attorneys needs to be dispelled. Many people assume that attorneys automatically make good managers. In truth, it is generally agreed that many lawyers are not very good managers.[19] Although lawyers have gone to school to learn about practicing law, most have no management skills or training. Practicing law and practicing management take very different skills. In fact, there is an adage that says: "The best system for law office management is the system that involves the lawyers least."[20] Although attorneys may realize that management is important, that does not necessarily mean they are proficient at it. As you read this chapter, keep in mind that many attorneys practicing today have never taken a course like this one. Although national and local bar associations are beginning to put emphasis on training attorneys in management skills, they still have a long way to go. Because of the general lack of management training for attorneys, legal assistants with good management skills can be very useful to law firms.

In today's medium- and larger-size firms, the situation is alleviated somewhat with the use of professional administrators. Unfortunately, most smaller firms do not have the resources to hire administrators and must rely on attorneys, legal assistants, and other staff members to deal with problems as well as their other duties. Given the increasing competitiveness of the legal market, effective law office management will be a prime concern for law firms for years to come.

WHY LEGAL ASSISTANTS NEED TO KNOW LAW OFFICE MANAGEMENT

If you think that good law office management does not affect legal assistants, reread the example at the beginning of the chapter about the law office. It is not an uncommon event to have a law practice close or merge. The cost of operating a law office is extremely high, and legal assistants depend on the viability of the law office for their economic survival. Management affects everyone in the practice. Other reasons why good management is important to legal assistants are that well-managed practices run with fewer problems and crises, work flows smoothly, billings and client payments are received in a timely manner, appointments and deadlines are met, ethical problems are taken seriously, staff members are adequately compensated, staff are adequately trained to perform their jobs, and there is less stress.

Practicing good management is hard; it takes time and teamwork, but is well worth the effort. Some signs of poor management include frustrated and unhappy staff members and clients, daily "crises," reduced attorney effectiveness, higher costs, low employee job satisfaction, high employee turnover, increased use of employee sick leave, and low staff morale. From the legal secretary to the law clerk to the legal assistant to the attorney, everyone has a stake in the action. In short, effective management is good for all and should be practiced by all.

PRACTICE MANAGEMENT V. ADMINISTRATIVE MANAGEMENT

practice management
Management decisions about how a law office will practice law and handle its cases.

There are two major aspects of managing a law office: practice management and administrative management. **Practice management (i.e. substantive or case management)** refers to management decisions about how a law office will practice law

> **Figure 1-12**
> **Practice Management v. Administrative Management**
>
> **Practice, Case, or Substantive Management:**
> - What type of <u>cases</u> should we specialize in?
> - Which <u>cases</u> should we accept?
> - How will <u>case</u> files be organized?
> - How will documents for each <u>case</u> be indexed for retrieval later?
> - What form files will need to be created for each type of <u>case</u>?
>
> **Administrative, Office, or "Plant" Management:**
> - Purchasing equipment and supplies for the <u>law office</u>.
> - Hiring and evaluating law <u>office staff</u>.
> - Sending out invoices for the <u>law office</u>.
> - Managing the finances and profitability of the <u>law office</u>.
> - What administrative structure is the most efficient for the <u>law office</u>?

and handle its cases (see Figure 1-12). Practice management decisions include determining the general types of cases the law office will specialize in, how many cases the law office should accept in a given area, and which clients should be accepted or rejected. Practice management is sometimes called "case management" or "file management" because this type of management centers on managing and controlling client files and client cases.

The cases and clients a law office takes on directly affect the profitability of the firm. If a law office undertakes to represent a number of client cases that do not generate any profits because the client did not pay, or the contingency case is lost, or the fees received are unexpectedly low, the economic effects on the law office are quite harmful. Also, if law office staff do not manage and organize cases effectively, then there may be poor quality legal services, reduced profitability, unhappy clients, and ethical complaints.

Administrative management (i.e. office management or "plant" management) refers to management decisions relating to operating or managing a law office, including financial and personnel matters. Administrative management is the focus of this text.

administrative management
Management decisions relating to operating or managing a law office, including financial and personnel matters.

FUNCTIONS OF LAW OFFICE MANAGEMENT

> *In private law practices the primary objective of management is to ensure that the firm provides efficient, high-quality legal services that please clients while earning a reasonable profit.*

Management is the administration of people and other resources to accomplish objectives. In private law practices (i.e. private businesses that provide legal services for a fee), the primary objective of management is to provide efficient, high-quality, legal services that please clients while earning a reasonable profit for the firm. In a corporate or government legal department, where generating a profit is not applicable, the

management
The administration of people and other resources to accomplish objectives.

objective of management is to provide efficient, high-quality legal services to its client at a reasonable cost. Law office management functions include providing financial management, practice management, and human resource (personnel) management; planning for the future; providing organization; setting policies; creating effective systems; providing marketing management; controlling the law office; and providing the law office with leadership. Figure 1-13 contains a detailed list of the duties of each function of management.

financial management
The oversight of a firm's financial assets and profitability to ensure overall financial health.

1. **Financial management** is the oversight of a firm's financial assets and profitability to ensure overall financial health. Financial management is important in any business. A business that does not earn a profit soon goes out of existence. There are many aspects of the financial management of a law firm. Timekeeping and billing, which includes tracking attorney and legal assistant time spent on client matters and billing clients for the time, is a particularly crucial area, as is trust accounting, which entails ethical responsibilities of keeping track of clients monies paid but not yet earned by the firm. Budgeting and tracking firm expenses, revenue, and profitability as well as making payments (accounts payable) and tracking firm receipts (accounts receivable) are also important to the overall success of the firm. Other areas of financial management include purchasing high quality goods and services at the least expensive cost, tracking the assets of the firm (including equipment and furniture), properly investing firm monies that are not currently being used, having a good relationship with a bank to secure loans as necessary, tracking tax liabilities, and having proper insurance to protect the firm's assets.

2. **Practice management**—Management must ensure that the firm's clients receive prompt, quality legal services at a fair cost. Law firms are service providers, and if clients do not receive quality legal services, they *will* go somewhere else to get the service they expect. A firm's lifeblood is dependent upon the ability of management to prudently choose the type of clients it serves, to keep existing clients, and to gain new clients.

> *To "hardwire" clients to your firm, they cannot be taken for granted. That means learning everything possible about clients—their expectations of the firm, their business and their plans for growth.[21]*
>
> *A conviction that the client's needs must be placed above everything else is apparent in successful firms.[22]*

Firms must also develop comprehensive systems to support client services in order to provide only high quality legal services to clients. This includes using knowledge systems such as software, the Internet, the law library, and the collective knowledge of the staff to serve clients. This may also include conducting client surveys to ensure that client needs are being met and to continually develop new ways to serve clients better. Another important practice management component is effective and timely handling of ethical problems and dilemmas. Ethical considerations take a priority in most well-managed law firms. Systems and procedures are developed to address potential ethical problems proactively, and when ethical dilemmas do occur, the firm deals with them in a timely and careful manner.

3. **Human resource management** refers to recruiting, hiring, training, evaluating, maintaining, and directing the personnel who will provide quality legal services to clients. While law firms use technology to serve clients more efficiently, for the most part, client services are delivered to clients by and through a firm's staff. Therefore, the management of that staff is of great concern to most law offices. Firms must recruit and select only staff that are well-trained and competent in their areas of expertise. They must also provide compensation and benefits that will appropriately reward and motivate staff so that they are able to retain the good employees they have. Staff must be constantly trained regarding changes in the law, technology, and client needs. Staff must be managed and evaluated regularly to ensure they are providing competent services to clients. They must be rewarded for services rendered or counseled about problems that occur. The firm must also periodically review its organizational structure, the design of its jobs, and how services are provided to clients in order to make adjustments that ensure its effectiveness.

4. **Planning** is the process of setting objectives, assessing future needs, and developing a course of action to achieve the objectives.[23] Planning is the road map for meeting the firm's goals. Law firms should have short-range and long-range plans or goals. A short-term plan might include raising staff salaries or increasing profitability by 10 percent. A long-term plan for a law office might include opening additional offices in other cities or expanding the practice into new legal areas. Without a plan, the law office goes about its business with no real direction. Successful law practices only happen by careful planning and the execution of good management decisions.

5. **Organization, policies, and creating effective systems**—Organizing is the process of arranging people and physical resources to carry out plans and accomplish objectives.[24] Management must make effective policy decisions to achieve its goals and carry out its plan. Part of this function is the process of creating systems that will bring this about. A **system** is a consistent or organized way of doing something. Establishing good systems is very important to effective law office management. Effective systems save time and money and ensure that all clients receive quality services. A staff manual or staff procedural manual sets out firm policies on how client matters and related items are carried out. A staff manual is a way for firm management to ensure that matters are handled competently, appropriately, with quality and uniformity. There are also many other types of systems in law offices. One of the more important is the firm's information system, including computer hardware and software. Law firms, like most businesses, have grown dependent on technology for delivering high quality, efficient services to its clients. As the need for technology has increased, so has the number of software programs that law offices must use just to stay competitive. These include word processing databases, timekeeping and billing, the Internet, e-mail and many others (see Figure 1-13). Law

human resource management
Recruiting, hiring, training, evaluating, maintaining, and directing the personnel that will provide quality legal services to the clients.

planning
The process of setting objectives, assessing the future, and developing courses of action to achieve these objectives.

organizing
The process of arranging people and physical resources to carry out plans and accomplish objectives.

system
A consistent or organized way of doing something.

Figure 1-13
Law Firm Management Responsibilities

Financial Management		• Timekeeping and Billing • Trust Accounting • Budgeting/Forecasting/Profitability • Financial Reporting/General Ledger Accounting • Accounts Receivable/Cash Flow Analysis • Accounts Payable/Cash Disbursements • Payroll and Employee Benefit Plans • Purchasing and Asset Management • Investments • Banking Relationships • Tax Planning and Reporting • Insurance and Risk Management
Practice Management		• Legal Practice Systems • Legal Practice Quality Control • Planning Client Development • Case Management and Record Keeping Systems • Practice Management Planning • Case Development • Conflict of Interest System • Client Satisfaction • Intranet/Internal Firm Knowledge Systems • Management of Ethics and Professional Conduct
Human Resources Management		• Compensation and Benefit Administration • Recruitment, Selection and Placement • Orientation, Training and Development • Performance Evaluation and Coaching • Employee Relations and Morale • Discipline and Termination • Worker's Compensation • Organization Analysis • Job Design and Development of Job Descriptions
Planning		• Short-term Planning • Long-term Strategic and Tactical Planning • Budgeting/Forecasting • Planning Client Development • Client Satisfaction
Organization, Policies and Creating Effective Internal Systems		• Policy Making/Procedures Manual • Operations and Systems Analysis • Computer Hardware Systems/Networks • Computer Software o Word Processing, Spreadsheet, Database, Timekeeping & Billing, Docket Control, Litigation Support, Computerized Legal Research, Presentation Graphics, Operating System, E-mail, Web Browser/Internet, Specialized Left Software, Groupware • Other internal systems • Facilities Management • Equipment and Automation (Copiers, Telecommunications, etc.)

system of procedures. A staff manual establishes administrative procedures and documents how things will be accomplished administratively. Systems and staff manuals are covered in more detail in a subsequent chapter. However, it is important that you realize from the beginning how important good systems are to effective law office management.

From a financial point of view, proper use of "systems" allows attorneys to delegate more complicated work to legal assistants and in turn allows legal assistants to delegate clerical work to clerical employees. This is a financial benefit to the law office on the substantive side because it allows the firm to do the same amount of work with reduced cost to the firm and the clients. On the administrative side, a legal assistant can perform administrative tasks and relieve the attorney to do substantive legal work for clients. Efficient firms delegate work to the lowest competent level. For example, if an attorney, law clerk, legal assistant, and secretary all have the ability to perform a certain task competently, efficiency says that the work should be performed by the secretary, since the secretary's cost to the law office is the least. Although there is a "cost" to setting up a system, including the time and expertise to develop it, once it is in place the savings are substantial over time.

The legal assistant is in a perfect position to be an innovator of both administrative and substantive systems. Much of what a legal assistant does is amendable to systemization. Any member of a law office who creates or innovates usable and timesaving systems will gain a reputation for his or her ability to solve problems and will be a valued member of the law office team.

INTERNET SITES

ORGANIZATION	DESCRIPTION	INTERNET ADDRESS
American Bar Association (ABA)	Association for attorneys. The site has a large amount of information relevant to individuals working in the legal profession	www.abanet.org
ABA Law Practice Today	ABA site devoted to law practice management	www.abanet.org/lpm
ABA Standing Committee on Legal Assistants	ABA site devoted to the use of legal assistants in legal organizations	www.abanet.org/legalassts
Association of Legal Administrators	National association for legal administrators	www.alanet.org
Law Office Hornbook	A resource for legal professionals seeking information and guidance on issues relating to law firm management and malpractice avoidance	www.hornbook.com
Legal Assistant Management Association	National association for legal assistant managers	www.lamanet.org

Legal Assistant Today	National magazine for legal assistants	www.legalassistanttoday.com
National Association of Legal Assistants	National association for legal assistants	www.nala.org
National Federation of Paralegal Associations	National association for legal assistants	www.paralegals.org

Summary

Law offices depend on a legal team of effective players that includes attorneys, administrators, legal assistants, secretaries, clerks, and others to be successful. There are several types of law practices, including corporate, government, legal aid, and private, and each has its own management structures. Good management is necessary for the effective practice of law in all types of firms and for the overall survival of any type of law practice. Management is the use of people and other resources to accomplish objectives. Specific law office management functions include providing financial, marketing, and human resource management; providing leadership; controlling; organizing; ensuring quality legal services; creating effective systems; making policies; and planning for the future. Good systems are important to law practices since they save time, allow more work to be delegated, increase the quality of the legal services provided, and reduce costs.

Suggested Reading

Law Practice Management, published by the American Bar Association Law Practice Management Section.

Legal Assistant Today, published by James Publishing.

Leveraging with Legal Assistants—How to Maximize Team Performance, Improve Quality, and Boost Your Bottom Line, Arthur G. Greene, American Bar Association, 1993.

Model Guidelines for the Utilization of Legal Assistant Services, American Bar Association, 1991.

National Association of Legal Assistants' [Annual] Utilization and Compensation Survey, National Association of Legal Assistants.

Key Terms

Legal team
Attorneys
Partner or shareholder
Managing partner
Associate attorney
Nonequity partner
Staff attorney
Contract attorney
"Of counsel"
Law office administrators

Legal assistants
Legal assistant manager
Freelance/Contract legal assistants
Independent Legal
Office managers
Fair Labor Standards Assistants Act (FLSA)
Law clerk
FLSA Exempt
Law librarian
FLSA Non-Exempt

Secretaries
System
Marketing
Controlling
Clerks
Expert witness
General counsel
Legal aid office
Office sharing
Boutique firm
Powerful managing partner
Rule by all partners/shareholders
Rule by management committee/board

Practice management (i.e. substantive or case management)
Administrative management (i.e. office management or "plant" management)
Management
Financial management
Human resource management
Planning
Organizing
Leadership
Substantive task
Administrative task

Questions and Exercises

1. Using Figure 1-13, determine what management responsibilities were neglected by the firm in the opening scenario of this chapter. What other measures could the firm take to get back on track? Who is "at fault" for letting the firm deteriorate to this stage?

2. In a private law practice, what is more important: providing quality legal services to clients, making money, operating at a profit, or earning money for its partners/shareholders?

3. As a legal assistant in a large, 100-plus attorney firm, you work for an attorney who is particularly abrasive. This attorney sometimes challenges the quality of your work, even though most of the problem is his or her inadequate or vague assignments. List several methods of dealing with this matter.

4. Review the different definitions of *legal assistant* in Figure 1-2. Consider the various groups the organizations represent and why each might have a different perspective. Compare and contrast the definitions.

5. Using the Internet, WESTLAW, or LEXIS, research the "white-collar" exemptions to the Fair Labor Standards Act. Present your opinion regarding the exempt or non-exempt status of legal assistants under the FLSA. Of the white-collar exemptions, which is the best "fit" if you decide that legal assistants should be exempt?

6. You are a legal assistant with fifteen years' experience. Recently, you began working for a new associate right out of law school. Unfortunately, the new associate thinks she knows more than she really does, is woefully under-experienced, gets defensive when you offer suggestions, and does not listen very well. How would you handle the matter?

7. Compare and contrast *Missouri v. Jenkins*, 491 U.S. 274, 109 S.Ct. 2463, 105 L.Ed. 2d 229 (1989) which allowed recovery of legal assistant fees, with *Joerger v. Gordon Food Service, Inc.*, 224 Mich.App. 167, 568 N.W.2d 365 (Mich.App., Jun 13, 1977), which did not allow recovery for legal assistant fees.

8. You are a legal assistant in an eight-attorney law firm. Your supervising attorney has instructed you to give clerical work to a legal secretary named Pat. Pat has been with the firm for many years and considers herself to have as much legal experience as any legal assistant. She has made it perfectly clear that she will not peaceably make copies for you or help you in any way with any clerical tasks. Pat does not bill clients for her time, but you must. You are

required to bill 1,750 hours annually. You know that you are not allowed to record billable hours for time you spend doing clerical work. You are responding to a Request for Production of Documents in a case in litigation, and you estimate that it will take five hours to copy the documents. How would you handle the matter?

9. As a legal assistant/office manager in a three-attorney firm, you have become quite frustrated. The managing partner who has the final say on major management decisions is seldom in the office. You are having an increasingly difficult time making management decisions because you cannot obtain her input. In addition, you do not know if you have the responsibility to make major management decisions or not. Work is beginning to back up. Discuss recommendations you might suggest for changing the structure of the law office.

10. For each of the questions below, determine whether the situation involves a practice management or administrative management problem.

a) You go to the shelf to get a legal pad and the shelf is empty. None have been ordered.
b) You need a new litigation support program to computerize, organize, and track documents in a particularly large case.
c) Your supervising attorney asks you to find a particular kind of expert witness for a medical malpractice case your firm is handling, and you have not found one yet.
d) You think the firm is concentrating too much in bankruptcy cases. You are concerned that these cases will not produce enough revenue for the firm.
e) You are preparing for trial with your supervising attorney and you notice that the file is not organized well.
f) A client calls and says that his account was not credited for a payment he made last month.

11. You are in your last semester of school and about to graduate with a legal assistant degree. You plan to begin looking for a job. Government practice would give you job security. A corporate law department would be interesting and provide opportunities for advancement. A legal aid office would give you the feeling that you were helping others. A private law office would be exciting and fast paced. Being a freelance legal assistant would let you be your own boss. What type of job would you select and why?

NOTES

1. Terrie I. Murray, "The Unwritten Rules: Survival in a Law Firm," *Legal Assistant Today,* May/June 1998, p. 12. Copyright 1998. James Publishing, Inc. Reprinted courtesy of *Legal Assistant Today* magazine. For subscription information call (800) 394-2626, or visit www.legalassistanttoday.com.
2. Quoted from "How Firms Manage" by Dr. Larry Richard, Altman Weil, Inc., Newtown Square, PA, © 1996.
3. National Association of Legal Assistants (NALA). Reprinted with the permission of the National Association of Legal Assistants, 1516 S. Boston, #200, Tulsa. www.nala.org.
4. Vicki Kelly Brittain, Evidence Required to Prove the Validity of Legal Assistant Fees as a Compensable Component of Attorney Fee Awards, *Texas Bar Journal,* Vol. 63, No. 3, March 2000, p. 260.
5. American Bar Association Standing Committee on Legal Assistants, Guidelines for the Approval of Legal Assistant Education Programs (1997). Reprinted by permission.
6. Carol Milano, "Salary Survey Results," *Legal Assistant Today,* May/June 1993, p. 68. Copyright 1993. James Publishing, Inc., Reprinted with permission from *Legal Assistant Today* magazine. For subscription information call (800) 394-2626, or visit www.legalassistanttoday.com.
7. National Federation of Paralegal Associations (NFPA). Courtesy of National Federation of Paralegal Associations.

8. Xavier Rodriguez, "Paralegal Overtime: Yes, No, or Maybe? An Update," *Texas Bar Journal,* March 2000, p. 267.
9. Vicki Kelly Brittain, Evidence Required to Prove the Validity of Legal Assistant Fees as a Compensable Component of Attorney Fee Awards, *Texas Bar Journal,* Vol. 63, No. 3, March 2000, p. 262.
10. Arthur Greene, *Leveraging With Legal Assistants,* American Bar Association, 1993, p. vii. Reprinted by permission.
11. Terrie I. Murray, "The Unwritten Rules: Survival in a Law Firm," *Legal Assistant Today,* May/June 1998, p. 12. Copyright 1998. James Publishing, Inc. Reprinted courtesy of *Legal Assistant Today* magazine. For subscription information call (800) 394-2626, or visit www.legalassistanttoday.com.
12. Carol Milano, "Salary Survey Results," *Legal Assistant Today,* May/June 1999, p. 71. Copyright 1993. James Publishing, Inc. Reprinted courtesy of *Legal Assistant Today* magazine. For subscription information call (800) 394-2626, or visit www.legalassistanttoday.com.
13. Printed with permission of Vermont Bar Association. This article appeared in the *Vermont Bar Journal and Law Digest,* vol. 19, no. 2 (April 1993) p. 20, by Joan C. Bauer, a legal aid attorney.
14. A sole practitioner's legal assistant. "Am I the Only Small-Firm Paralegal?" *Legal Assistant Today,* March/April 1993, p. 15.
15. Small law firm legal assistant in Peggy N. Kerley, "High-Profile Criminal Defense Cases Attract Top Paralegals," *Legal Assistant Today,* July/August 1992, p. 33.
16. Debra Levy, "Paralegal with a Twist," *Legal Assistant Today,* September/October, 1999, p. 64. Copyright 2001. James Publishing, Inc. Reprinted courtesy of *Legal Assistant Today* magazine. For subscription information call (800) 394-2626, or visit www.legalassistanttoday.com.
17. Quoted from "How Firms Manage" by Dr. Larry Richard, Altman Weil, Inc., Newtown Square, PA, © 1996.
18. Quoted from "How Firms Manage" by Dr. Larry Richard, Altman Weil, Inc., Newtown Square, PA, © 1996.
19. Richard C. Reed, *Managing a Law Practice: The Human Side,* American Bar Association, 1988, 3. *Citing Law Office Economics & Management* (Summer 1977).
20. Ibid.
21. A law firm consultant, Thomas Clay and Charles Maddock, "The 12 Deadly Management Sins," *Pennsylvania Lawyer,* January/February 1999. Reprinted by permission.
22. Thomas Clay, "Profile of a Successful Law Firm," *The Law Firm Management Guide,* 1988, A-15. Reprinted by permission.
23. Ibid., 7.

CASE REVIEW

William Dowsing Davis III v. Alabama State Bar, 676 So.2d 306 (1996).

676 So.2d 306
(Cite as: 676 So.2d 306)

Supreme Court of Alabama.
William Dowsing DAVIS III
v.
ALABAMA STATE BAR.
Dan Arthur GOLDBERG
v.
ALABAMA STATE BAR.
1940686, 1940687.
Jan. 19, 1996.
Rehearing Denied March 15, 1996.

MADDOX, Justice.

Two attorneys appeal from Alabama State Bar disciplinary proceedings. They challenge the sufficiency of the evidence presented at their disciplinary hearing, claiming that the disciplinary proceeding was nothing more than a "witch-hunt" that they say the Bar conducted because it did not approve of the attorneys' advertising practices. They further challenge the penalties imposed as being too severe.

The Alabama State Bar Disciplinary Board found William Dowsing Davis III and Dan Arthur Goldberg to be violating Rule 1.1, Alabama Rules of Professional

Conduct (failure to provide competent representation); Rule 1.4(a) and (b) (failure to keep clients reasonably informed and failure to reasonably explain a matter so as to permit a client to make an informed decision); Rule 5.1 (failure to make reasonable efforts to ensure that the lawyers in their firm conformed to the Rules of Professional Conduct); Rule 5.3(b) (failure to ensure that the activities of a nonlawyer under an attorney's supervision are compatible with professional standards); Rule 5.5 (b) (providing assistance to a person engaging in the unauthorized practice of law); Rule 8.4(a) (violation of the Rules of Professional Conduct through the acts of another); Rule 8.4(d) (engaging in conduct prejudicial to the administration of justice); and Rule 8.4(g) (engaging in conduct that adversely reflects on a lawyer's fitness to practice law). Both of the attorneys were suspended from the practice of law for 60 days.

The record before this Court is voluminous. Several former and present attorneys and secretaries of these attorneys' firm testified at the disciplinary hearing. Several clients of the firm also testified.

These two attorneys were the sole partners in the law firm of David & Goldberg. The firm spent approximately $500,000 annually on advertising, primarily television advertising, and the advertising attracted a large number of clients. As a result of this large expenditure and the volume of clients produced by the advertising, the attorneys implemented several policies, described below, designed to minimize expenses and maximize profits.

The Bar presented evidence, for example, that David and Goldberg allowed nonlawyer secretaries to provide legal services. It was also shown to be common practice at the firm for secretaries to interview clients and prepare legal filings, especially bankruptcy petitions. Evidence also indicated the nonlawyer staff members gave clients legal advice, such as "informing" clients of the differences between Chapter 7 and Chapter 13 bankruptcy. One former associate attorney testified that it was the firm's practice that attorneys would not interview or have any contact with the client before the first scheduled court appearance.

There was further testimony that these two attorneys imposed unmanageable caseloads on associate attorneys, many of whom were inexperienced. Some associate attorneys, for example, maintained caseloads of nearly 600 active cases. Former associates testified that because for the sheer volume of cases, the amount of time that could be spent on each case was so limited as to make it *308 impossible for them to adequately represent their clients. At the hearing before the Disciplinary Board, the attorneys' own expert witness on Social Security law, Charles Tyler Clark, testified that the Social Security caseload, as described by a former associate of the firm, could not have been adequately handled by the one attorney assigned to it.

There was testimony that the firm had an inadequate supply of filing cabinets for case files and that files were simply stacked in various parts of the office, including the employees' break room and the hallway near the bathrooms. The evidence further tended to show that associate attorneys were given the barest of support staffs and that this fact, coupled with the huge volume of cases imposed upon the associates, created a situation in which files were mishandled, resulting in harm to the interests of clients.

The harm resulting from what could be described as a practice of the firm is best illustrated in the testimony of a former client, Brenda Marie Wood. Her husband, Douglas Wayne Wood, suffers from acute peripheral neuropathy and is dying. He was awarded Social Security disability benefits, but did not begin receiving his payments until eight months after he was supposed to. Mr. and Mrs. Wood saw a David & Goldberg television commercial that promised that the firm would "cut through the Social Security red tape" and get its clients' Social Security benefits fast. Because of the statement made in the advertisement, Mr. Wood hired the firm of David & Goldberg in October 1991 to represent him is his claim for past-due benefits. The firm lost Wood's file three times, and each time Wood was required to fill out a new set of forms. Wood was continuously assured by the firm's staff that his claim had been filed, when in fact it had not been. In February 1992, Wood received a letter from the firm informing him that the deadline for filing the claim had passed, and that it was too late to file his appeal.

The associates employed by Davis & Goldberg were also subjected to policies that interfered with their adequate and professional representation of their clients. These policies included the imposition of time limits or restrictions on the amount of time that they could spend with clients and on cases; the imposition of a quota system that required associates to open a specified number of files in a certain time period; and the imposition of a policy requiring associates not to return the phone calls of existing clients, so that the attorneys could free more time to sign new clients.

[1][2] The appellants contend that the Bar did not meet its burden of proof as to the allegations against them. The standard of review applicable to an appeal from an order of the Disciplinary Board is "that the order will be affirmed unless it is not supported by clear and convincing evidence or misapplies the law to the facts." Noojin v. Alabama State Bar, 577 So.2d 420, 423 (Ala. 1990), citing Hunt v. Disciplinary Board of the Alabama State Bar, 381 So.2d 52 (Ala.1980). We disagree with the attorneys' claims that the evidence was insufficient. In fact, the evidence presented amply showed that the two attorneys, in an effort to turn over a huge volume of cases, neglected their clients and imposed policies on associate attorneys that prevented the attorneys from providing quality and competent legal services. The evidence more than met the clear and convincing standard, and the Board's findings that these lawyers had violated the Rules of Professional Conduct are due to be affirmed.

[3] Even though we affirm the findings that these lawyers had violated the Rules of Professional Conduct, we elect to address their argument that the disciplinary proceeding amounted to a "witch-hunt" conducted because the Bar does not approve of the firm's advertising practices. We reject this contention. Instead, we find that the Disciplinary Board properly fulfilled its role of being a guardian of the image of the legal profession, and, thus, acted as a guardian of the profession itself. [FNI] We cannot find, as the *309 attorneys ask us to find, that the Bar was conducting a "witch-hunt." In fact, there was evidence that the Bar examined the attorneys' advertising practices; it could have found that their advertisements were misleading, specifically in that the attorneys did not provide the quality legal service advertised. The Disciplinary Board heard evidence that one specific advertisement was misleading as it related to a United States Supreme Court ruling on the availability of Social Security benefits. Even the appellants' expert witness testified that the advertisement could have been misleading under certain circumstances.[FN2]

> FNI. Justice O'Connor described the need for such protection in her dissent in Shapero v. Kentucky Bar Ass'n, 486 U.S. 466, 488–89, 108 S.Ct. 1916, 1929–30, 100 L.Ed.2d 475 (1988):
>
> "One distinguishing feature of any profession, unlike other occupations that may be equally respectable, is that membership entails an ethical obligation to temper one's selfish pursuit of economic success by adhering to standards of conduct that could not be enforced either by legal fiat or through the discipline of the market. There are sound reasons to continue pursuing the goal that is implicit in the traditional view of professional life. Both the special privileges incident to membership in the profession and the advantages those privileges give in the necessary task of earning a living are means to a goal that transcends the accumulation of wealth. That goal is public service, which in the legal profession can take a variety of familiar forms. This view of the legal profession need not be rooted in romanticism or self-serving sanctimony, though of course it can be. Rather, special ethical standards for lawyers are properly understood as an appropriate means of restraining lawyers in the exercise of the unique power that they inevitably wield in a political system like ours."
>
> FN2. During the cross-examination of Charles Tyler Clark at the Bar disciplinary hearing, the following testimony was presented:
>
> "MR. KENDRICK: This tape that we just listened to on the commercial, the last part of it, if I wrote it down correctly, says, 'Remember, no fee unless we collect. If you received a notice from Social Security or think you were wrongfully denied benefits, call David & Goldberg.'

Now, if somebody just listened to the last half of that tape, they wouldn't have [an] idea that they were talking about children's denial of Social Security benefits, would they?

"MR. NORTH: Mr. Chairman, I object to the last half of the tape. The tape as a whole."

"THE CHAIRMAN: I understand. But I'll let him answer the question. I understand the tape.

"MR. KENDRICK: If somebody walked in the room and turned the TV on and only caught the last half of it, they wouldn't understand that those cases were limited to children—denial of children's benefits, would they?

"MR. TYLER: That would be correct."

[4] This Court recognized that attorneys have a First Amendment right to engage in various forms of commercial speech. [FN3] We uphold the discipline imposed upon these attorneys, but we are not upholding it because they advertised; rather, we uphold it because the advertising was misleading in that the attorneys did not provide what they said they would provide. False and misleading advertising by attorneys can, and probably has, greatly harmed the public's perception of the legal profession, at a time when the public's confidence in attorneys has diminished. Indeed, the vast majority of those in the legal profession think advertising is harmful to the image of attorneys. [FN4]

FN3. This Court recognizes—and has ruled consistently with the United States Supreme Court regarding—the constitutionality of attorney advertising that is not "false, deceptive, or misleading." Zauderer v. Office of Disciplinary Counsel, 471 U.S. 626, 638, 105 S.Ct. 2265, 2275, 85 L.Ed.2d 652 (1985); also see Bates v. State Bar of Arizona, 434 U.S. 881, 98 S.Ct. 242, 54 L.Ed.2d 164 (1977), and Alabama State Bar Ass'n v. R.W. Lynch Co., 655 So.2d 982 (Ala. 1995).

FN4. In a Gallup poll conducted in November 1993 for the ABA Journal, 87% of the attorneys polled stated that they think legal advertising has harmed the public image of attorneys.

James Podgers, ABA Journal, Feb. 1994, 66–72.

Justice O'Connor warned in her dissent in Shapero v. Kentucky Bar Ass'n, 486 U.S. 466, 108 S.Ct. 1916, 100 L.Ed.2d 475 (1988), that the advertising practices of some attorneys, similar to those practices followed by these two attorneys, will "undermine professional standards" by giving an attorney "incentives to ignore (or avoid discovering) the complexities that would lead a conscientious attorney to treat some clients' cases as anything but routine." [FN5] 486 U.S. at 486, 108 S.Ct. at 1928. (For further discussion of *310 Justice O'Connor's dissent, see notes 1 and 5.)

FN5. Justice O'Connor went on to state:

"[B]ecause lawyers must be provided with expertise that is both esoteric and extremely powerful, it would be unrealistic to demand that clients bargain for their services in the same arm's-length manner that may be appropriate when buying an automobile or choosing a dry cleaner."

486 U.S. at 489–90, 108 S.Ct. at 1930.

Evidence was presented that these two attorneys placed advertisements that were false and misleading. There can be no constitutional right to advertise in a false and misleading way. The evidence tends to show that these two attorneys' ethical violations were caused by their advertising practices and desire to turn over a huge volume of cases. The harm caused by this practice seems apparent.

Additionally, this Court finds no error or abuse in regard to the sanction the Board imposed, a 60-day suspension of the licenses of Davis and Goldberg. The violations were serious, and we cannot hold that the Board acted improperly in imposing the punishment. Consequently, the orders of the Disciplinary Board are affirmed.

In their application for rehearing, the attorneys argue that in its opinion of December 15, 1995, the Court erred in upholding the disciplinary sanctions based solely on allegations of misleading of false advertising. They are apparently referring to the Board's acquittal as to the charge of violating Rule 7.1, Alabama Rules of Professional Conduct. The Court affirmed the Disciplinary Board's numerous findings of violations of ethical rules, but did not address the Board's acquittal of the alleged violation of Rule 7.1. Instead, the Court addressed the attorneys' contention that the Disciplinary Board had conducted a "witch-hunt" against them because the Board did not approve of their advertising policies.

However, the Disciplinary Board found the attorneys in violation of Rule 8.4(g), which states:

> "It is professional misconduct for a lawyer to:
>
> ". . .
>
> "(g)Engage in any other conduct that adversely reflects on his fitness to practice law."

As we have stated earlier, much evidence was presented at the disciplinary hearing that proved that the attorneys' advertising practices and the procedures and policies adopted by Davis & Goldberg adversely affected the attorneys' ability to practice law in the manner required by the Rules of Professional Conduct. Further, Rule 8.4(g) is broad enough to require that attorney advertisements be honest and accurate and that an attorney's practice of law centered around such heavy advertisement be professional and competent as generally required by the Rules of Profession Conduct.

The evidence presented to the Disciplinary Board showed that Davis & Goldberg advertised that the firm provided legal services of a very high standard, but that the firm's representation of its clients failed to meet the high standard presented in its advertising. This evidence of a failure on the part of Davis & Goldberg to do what was promised in its advertisements, taken with the evidence regarding harmful policies and practices adopted by the firm in response to the fact that a large number of clients were attracted to the firm by its advertising practices, is more than sufficient to support the Board's finding that the attorneys violated Rule 8.4(g).

1940686 and 1940687—OPINION OF DECEMBER 15, 1995, WITHDRAWN; OPINION SUBSTITUTED; APPLICATION OVERRULED; AFFIRMED.

HOOPER, C.J., and HOUSTON, KENNEDY, INGRAM, and BUTTS, JJ., concur.

EXERCISES

1. Why was the court overly concerned with the two attorneys' business plan "designed to minimize expenses and maximize profits"?

2. Referring to Figure 1-13, analyze what the attorneys did correctly and incorrectly in terms of the responsibilities of law firm management.

3. How could the attorneys have corrected their management strategy?

4. Why was the court not convinced of the attorneys' "witch-hunt" theory but instead focused on the attorneys' clients?

5. Can an associate attorney or legal assistant reasonably maintain quotas of nearly 600 active cases each?

6. The two attorneys asserted that their nonlawyer staff were simply "informing" clients about differences in the law. Why did the court not agree with their conclusion? Do you agree or disagree with the court? Explain your response.

Ethics and Malpractice

CHAPTER OBJECTIVES

After you read this chapter, you will be able to:

- Define what the unauthorized practice of law is and list factors that are used to determine whether a legal assistant is "practicing law."
- Discuss the voluntary ethical codes established by national legal assistant associations.
- Explain the attorney-client privilege and to whom it applies.
- List guidelines that will prevent legal assistants from accidentally revealing confidential client information.
- Explain what a conflict of interest is and what a law office can do to limit conflict of interest problems.
- Discuss what the "Chinese Wall" is and when it applies.

The Johnson & Smith law firm primarily handled bankruptcy cases. The firm employed two attorneys, several legal assistants, and clerical staff. The Bankruptcy Trustee considered the firm to be a "high-volume filer," filing an average of seventy-seven cases per month (nearly 1,000 per year). The firm's standard practice in handling cases was for a legal assistant to:

- hold an initial consultation meeting with the client, without an attorney present
- discuss with the client the bankruptcy chapters available
- assist the client in deciding which, if any, chapter proceedings should be filed
- consult an attorney if a client had a question they could not answer and relay the attorney's response back to the client
- ask the client to complete a questionnaire
- review the questionnaire
- prepare the bankruptcy papers to be filed
- meet with the client again (without an attorney present) for the purpose of having the client sign the papers

In most instances, unless the client specifically requested to meet with an attorney, the client's first contact with the attorney was at the meeting of creditors. The court found that the legal assistants performed many services that constituted the unauthorized practice of law. Adapted from *In re Pinkins*, 213 B.R. 818 (Bankr.E.D. Mich.1997), (included at the end of this chapter).

WHY ARE ETHICS AND MALPRACTICE IMPORTANT?

The importance of high ethical standards and of following your state's ethical rules cannot be overemphasized. Clients and attorneys must have total confidence that a legal assistant understands the many ethical problems that might arise in the practice of law and that the legal assistant's ethical judgment is clear. Ethical problems routinely encountered by legal assistants include unauthorized practice of law questions, conflict of interest problems, and confidentiality problems. Unethical behavior of a legal assistant can cause an attorney to lose a case, destroy client confidence in the entire law office, or lead a client to dismiss the attorney. Unethical behavior on the part of a legal assistant could lead to sanctions, fines, and disciplinary action against the attorney and can cost a legal assistant his job. It also could result in damaging publicity for the law office and could even result in criminal charges being filed against the attorney. Consequently, legal assistants must know how to work through and solve tough ethical problems.

A legal assistant must perform careful, high-quality work in everything he or she does. An error can be very costly and can subject an attorney or law office to a malpractice claim. Malpractice occurs when an attorney's or law office's conduct does not meet the professional standard for the area and injures a client. Malpractice claims can result in a law office being liable for thousands of dollars of damages to injured clients. It is important that legal assistants understand how malpractice occurs and how it can be prevented.

> *Every day, paralegals run into minor or major roadblocks and are faced with situations requiring professional or ethical judgment. The consequences of ignoring or walking away from the sometimes subtle, fine, gray line can have serious ramifications and aftermath.[1]*

LEGAL ETHICS AND PROFESSIONAL RESPONSIBILITY

Legal ethics is an increasingly important and difficult topic for legal assistants in every type of law practice. There are many treatises that cover this topic in depth. This section will cover ethics only from a legal assistant's perspective and will give insight on common ethical problems likely to arise.

Ethics is an important topic not only because a law office or attorney can be disciplined for violating ethical rules but also because legal ethics bears on whether quality legal services are being provided to clients. If a law office or its employee engages in unethical conduct, the reputation of the office will be affected and clients will lose confidence in it. The unethical behavior does not necessarily have to be directly detrimental to the client or the client's case. If a client senses that the attorney or legal assistant is acting unethically toward an adversary, the client may suspect that the attorney or legal assistant could be guilty of the same type of practice toward her. The issues of trust and ethics are closely related and bear directly upon the attorney and client relationship.

When clients lose confidence, they may move their business to another law office, cease referring new clients to the law office, or even sue. Nearly 70 percent of all the new business a law office receives comes from referrals. When a client takes business elsewhere, it has an immediate as well as a long-term effect on the firm, since that source of revenue is also gone for future years. In short, legal ethics has a direct bearing on the "law office's bottom line" and on the long-term success of the firm. Thus, legal assistants and attorneys have both an incentive and a duty to act ethically and to develop systems that stress the importance of legal ethics on a daily basis.

> *Legal ethics is becoming increasingly complex for lawyer and legal assistants alike. With greater accountability to clients, increased mobility for all law firm personnel, and a growing demand to improve the image of the legal profession, it is essential to keep abreast of current developments in ethics and to adhere to professional standards.*[2]

ETHICAL STANDARDS FOR ATTORNEYS

ethical rule
A minimal standard of conduct.

An **ethical rule** is a minimal standard of conduct. An attorney may not fall below the standard without losing his or her good standing with the state bar. Attorneys who violate ethical rules may be disciplined. Such discipline for unethical conduct may include a permanent disbarment from practicing law, a temporary suspension from practicing, a public censure, a private censure, or an informal reprimand. Figure 2-1 shows a procedural example of ethical rules at work.

Ethics has had a long-standing place in the American legal system. In 1908, the American Bar Association (ABA), a voluntary association of attorneys, adopted the Canons of Professional Ethics. In 1969, the ABA updated and expanded the canons into the ***Model Code of Professional Responsibility.*** The *Model Code* was updated in 1983 and is now called ***Model Rules of Professional Conduct.***

Model Code of Professional Responsibility Model Rules of Professional Conduct
Self-imposed ethical standards for ABA members, but they also serve as a prototype of legal ethic standards for state court systems.

The ABA has convened a commission called the Ethics 2000—Commission on the Evaluation of the Rules of Professional Conduct (hereinafter Ethics 2000 Commission) to review the *Model Rules* and make recommended changes to them. A new revision to the *Model Rules* is expected shortly.

Today, nearly all states base their ethical rules on the ABA *Model Rules.* Attorneys in each state are regulated by their individual state bar association and state court system. Although state courts are free to create their own rules of conduct for attorneys, most simply modify either the ABA *Model Code* or ABA *Model Rules* to reflect the specific ethical conditions in their own states. For this text, the

The facts:	An attorney represented a client who was selling a piece of real estate. It was agreed that the attorney's fees would be $6,500. After completing the sale, the proceeds of the sale were placed into the attorney's trust account (i.e. a holding account for client funds). The attorney paid some proceeds to the client, withdrew $14,000 for himself, would not provide an accounting of the funds to the client, and would not respond to many messages left by the client.
The client:	The client, becoming increasingly frustrated with the attorney, calls the local courthouse and asks how to complain about the conduct of the attorney. The client is told to send a letter of complaint to the state's disciplinary administrator in the state's judicial branch. The client is told that the letter should clearly set out who the attorney was and exactly what happened. The client then sends the letter.
The disciplinary administrator:	The state's disciplinary administrator receives the client's letter. The administrator determines that if everything the client says is true, the attorney may have violated Supreme Court Rule 4-1.5 for his state that states "an attorney shall not charge an illegal or clearly excessive fee." The administrator sends a letter to the attorney asking for his side of the story but never receives a reply.
Investigation:	The disciplinary administrator then refers the matter to the State Bar's Investigation Committee, which investigates the matter including interviewing both the client and the attorney. The committee, after a full investigation, recommends that formal charges be filed before the state's bar court to discipline the attorney.
State bar court/ state supreme court:	The disciplinary administrator files formal charges and prosecutes the attorney for the ethical violations before the state's bar court, an arm of the state's supreme court. A hearing or trial is held where both sides present their evidence. The bar court determines that the attorney violated Rule 4-1.5 and disciplines the attorney by suspending him from the practice of law for two years and orders him to pay restitution to the client.

Figure 2-1 Example of Ethical Violation and Subsequent Ethical Proceedings Against an Attorney

ABA *Model Rules* are most often cited, even though some states still model their ethical/disciplinary rules on the older ABA *Model Code.* Although ethical rules are established by state bars or state courts, most states also have a disciplinary administrator who enforces the rules.

ATTORNEY ETHICAL RULES NOT DIRECTLY APPLICABLE TO THE LEGAL ASSISTANT

State canons of ethics, the *Model Code of Professional Responsibility,* or the *Model Rules of Professional Conduct* do not apply directly to legal assistants, but to attorneys only. However, attorneys can be disciplined for the acts of their staff members including legal assistants because attorneys have the duty to adequately supervise their staffs. Rule 5.3 of the ABA *Model Rules of Professional Conduct* states:

> Rule 5.3. Responsibilities Regarding Nonlawyer Assistants
>
> With respect to a nonlawyer employed or retained by or associated with a lawyer:
>
> (a) a partner in a law office shall make reasonable efforts to ensure that the firm has in effect measures giving reasonable assurance that the person's conduct is compatible with the professional obligations of the lawyer:
>
> (b) *a lawyer having direct supervisory authority over the nonlawyer shall make reasonable efforts to ensure that the person's conduct is compatible with the professional obligations of the lawyer;* and
>
> (c) a lawyer shall be responsible for conduct of such a person that would be a violation of the Rules of Professional Conduct if engaged in by a lawyer if:
>
> > (1) the lawyer orders or, with the knowledge of the specific conduct, ratifies the conduct involved; or
> >
> > (2) the lawyer is a partner in the law office in which the person is employed, or has direct supervisory authority over the person, and knows of the conduct at a time when its consequences can be avoided or mitigated but fails to take reasonable remedial action.[3]

This section of the *Model Rules* is important to legal assistants because it requires attorneys to ensure that their staff members operate within the bounds of these rules. The ABA Ethics 2000 Commission is not recommending any changes to this rule. Figure 2-2 is a summary of case where a law office was sued for malpractice and the attorney was suspended from practice because of the unethical acts of a paralegal. If a legal assistant is found to be acting unethically, especially when there is a pattern and practice of doing this, the attorney has an affirmative duty to remedy the situation, even if that means terminating the legal assistant's employment. Thus, there are many incentives for legal assistants to act ethically and to comply with the same rules as attorneys. In addition, this rule ensures that an attorney cannot avoid the ethical rules and accomplish an unethical act by delegating or allowing a staff member to do it.

So, although a legal assistant cannot be disciplined by state regulatory bodies for violating state ethical rules, he would be held accountable by the attorney who hired or supervised him. Legal assistants must understand and abide by any ethical rules governing the conduct of attorneys.

> *In addition to the possible effect upon a legal assistant's continued employment, a breach of ethics may require payment of monetary damages to an opposing party. The legal assistant's failure to conform to ethical standards also may result in specific, demonstrable harm to the client, when, for example, the ethical breach consists of disclosure of confidential information, taking a position in conflict with that of the client, practicing law, or performing professional work in a negligent manner.*[4]

> In April, Asphalt Engineers met with Robert Walston, a legal assistant with Lee and Peggy Galusha, doing business as Galusha Ltd., a private law firm. Asphalt Engineers advised Walston they wanted to file liens against real property involved in three construction jobs that they had not been paid on. They also requested that lawsuits foreclosing those liens be filed, if necessary. At trial, owners of Asphalt Engineers testified that they believed Walston was an attorney. Walston requested and received a retainer payment from Asphalt Engineers. A lien was filed on one of the projects, but not on the other two. The project where the lien was filed was settled.
>
> In June of the same year, Walston requested and received an additional retainer fee. Although Walston indicated that liens had been filed on the remaining two projects, no liens were in fact filed. The time for filing both liens expired. Before Asphalt Engineers discovered that the two liens had not been filed, they brought a fourth another project to Walston to file a lien on. Again, no lien was filed on the project.
>
> The court found that neither of the Galushas had ever met with Asphalt Engineers and that the Galushas allowed Walston, a nonlawyer, to provide legal advice to Asphalt Engineers, failed to file and foreclose liens, failed to adequately supervise Walston, and failed to prevent Walston from actually practicing law, among other things. Subsequently, a jury awarded Asphalt Engineers more than $75,000 in actual damages, attorneys fees, and punitive damages against the Galusha law firm. In addition, Lee Galusha faced ethical proceedings for failing to adequately supervise the legal assistant and for failing to adequately perform legal work for a client. Lee Galusha was subsequently suspended from the practice of law and eventually was disbarred.

**Figure 2-2
Attorneys Liable for Unethical Acts of Legal Assistant**
Source: See *Asphalt Engineers, Inc. v. Galusha*, 770 P.2d 1180 (160 Ariz. 134, 1989).

VOLUNTARY ETHICAL CODES ESTABLISHED BY LEGAL ASSISTANT ASSOCIATIONS

Legal assistants remain largely unregulated. There are, however, self-imposed, *voluntary* ethical standards set out by national or local legal assistant associations. Both the National Association of Legal Assistants (NALA) and the National Federation of Paralegal Associations (NFPA) have adopted ethical canons for their members. Figures 2-3 and 2-4 show the codes of ethics for both associations. Legal assistants cannot be disciplined for not following such voluntary codes. However, following such a code will help the legal assistant avoid ethical problems.

NALA Code of Ethics and Professional Responsibility

A legal assistant must adhere strictly to the accepted standards of legal ethics and to the general principles of proper conduct. The performance of the duties of the legal assistant shall be governed by specific canons as defined herein so that justice will be served and goals of the profession attained. (See Model Standards and Guidelines for Utilization of Legal Assistants, Section II.)

The canons of ethics set forth hereafter are adopted by the National Association of Legal Assistants, Inc., as a general guide intended to aid legal assistants and attorneys. The enumeration of these rules does not mean there are not others of equal importance although not specifically mentioned. Court rules, agency rules and statutes must be taken into consideration when interpreting the canons.

Definition: Legal assistants, also known as paralegals, are a distinguishable group of persons who assist attorneys in the delivery of legal services. Through formal education, training and experience, legal assistants have knowledge and expertise regarding the legal system and substantive and procedural law which qualify them to do work of a legal nature under the supervision of an attorney.

Canon 1. A legal assistant must not perform any of the duties that attorneys only may perform nor take any actions that attorneys may not take.

Canon 2. A legal assistant may perform any task which is properly delegated and supervised by an attorney, as long as the attorney is ultimately responsible to the client, maintains a direct relationship with the client, and assumes professional responsibility for the work product.

Canon 3. A legal assistant must not: (a) engage in, encourage, or contribute to any act which could constitute the unauthorized practice of law; and (b) establish attorney-client relationships, set fees, give legal opinions or advice or represent a client before a court or agency unless so authorized by that court or agency; and (c) engage in conduct or take any action which would assist or involve the attorney in a violation of professional ethics or give the appearance of professional impropriety.

Canon 4. A legal assistant must use discretion and professional judgment commensurate with knowledge and experience but must not render independent legal judgment in place of an attorney. The services of an attorney are essential in the public interest whenever such legal judgment is required.

Canon 5. A legal assistant must disclose his or her status as a legal assistant at the outset of any professional relationship with a client, attorney, a court or administrative agency or personnel thereof, or a member of the general public. A legal assistant must act prudently in determining the extent to which a client may be assisted without the presence of an attorney.

Canon 6. A legal assistant must strive to maintain integrity and a high degree of competency through education and training with respect to professional responsibility, local rules and practice, and through continuing education in substantive areas of law to better assist the legal profession in fulfilling its duty to provide legal service.

Canon 7. A legal assistant must protect the confidences of a client and must not violate any rule or statute now in effect or hereafter enacted controlling the doctrine of privileged communications between a client and an attorney.

Canon 8. A legal assistant must do all other things incidental, necessary, or expedient for the attainment of the ethics and responsibilities as defined by statute or rule of court.

Canon 9. A legal assistant's conduct is guided by bar associations' codes of professional responsibility and rules of professional conduct.

Figure 2-3 National Association of Legal Assistants, Inc. Code of Ethics and Professional Responsibility

Reprinted with the permission of the National Association of Legal Assistants, 1516 S. Boston, #200, Tulsa. *www.nala.org*. Copyright 1975; revised 1979, 1988, 1995.

NATIONAL FEDERATION OF PARALEGAL ASSOCIATIONS, INC.
MODEL CODE OF ETHICS AND PROFESSIONAL RESPONSIBILITY AND GUIDELINES FOR ENFORCEMENT

PREAMBLE

The National Federation of Paralegal Associations, Inc. ("NFPA") is a professional organization comprised of paralegal associations and individual paralegals throughout the United States and Canada. Members of NFPA have varying backgrounds, experiences, education and job responsibilities that reflect the diversity of the paralegal profession. NFPA promotes the growth, development and recognition of the paralegal profession as an integral partner in the delivery of legal services.

In May 1993 NFPA adopted its Model Code of Ethics and Professional Responsibility ("Model Code") to delineate the principles for ethics and conduct to which every paralegal should aspire.

Many paralegal associations throughout the United States have endorsed the concept and content of NFPA's Model Code through the adoption of their own ethical codes. In doing so, paralegals have confirmed the profession's commitment to increase the quality and efficiency of legal services, as well as recognized its responsibilities to the public, the legal community, and colleagues.

Paralegals have recognized, and will continue to recognize, that the profession must continue to evolve to enhance their roles in the delivery of legal services. With increased levels of responsibility comes the need to define and enforce mandatory rules of professional conduct. Enforcement of codes of paralegal conduct is a logical and necessary step to enhance and ensure the confidence of the legal community and the public in the integrity and professional responsibility of paralegals.

In April 1997 NFPA adopted the Model Disciplinary Rules ("Model Rules") to make possible the enforcement of the Canons and Ethical Considerations contained in the NFPA Model Code. A concurrent determination was made that the Model Code of Ethics and Professional Responsibility, formerly aspirational in nature, should be recognized as setting forth the enforceable obligations of all paralegals.

The Model Code and Model Rules offer a framework for professional discipline, either voluntarily or through formal regulatory programs.

§ 1. NFPA MODEL DISCIPLINARY RULES AND ETHICAL CONSIDERATIONS

1.1 A PARALEGAL SHALL ACHIEVE AND MAINTAIN A HIGH LEVEL OF COMPETENCE.
1.2 A PARALEGAL SHALL MAINTAIN A HIGH LEVEL OF PERSONAL AND PROFESSIONAL INTEGRITY.
1.3 A PARALEGAL SHALL MAINTAIN A HIGH STANDARD OF PROFESSIONAL CONDUCT.
1.4 A PARALEGAL SHALL SERVE THE PUBLIC INTEREST BY CONTRIBUTING TO THE IMPROVEMENT OF THE LEGAL SYSTEM AND DELIVERY OF QUALITY LEGAL SERVICES, INCLUDING PRO BONO PUBLICO SERVICES.
1.5 A PARALEGAL SHALL PRESERVE ALL CONFIDENTIAL INFORMATION PROVIDED BY THE CLIENT OR ACQUIRED FROM OTHER SOURCES BEFORE, DURING, AND AFTER THE COURSE OF THE PROFESSIONAL RELATIONSHIP.
1.6 A PARALEGAL SHALL AVOID CONFLICTS OF INTEREST AND SHALL DISCLOSE ANY POSSIBLE CONFLICT TO THE EMPLOYER OR CLIENT, AS WELL AS TO THE PROSPECTIVE EMPLOYERS OR CLIENTS.
1.7 A PARALEGAL'S TITLE SHALL BE FULLY DISCLOSED.
1.8 A PARALEGAL SHALL NOT ENGAGE IN THE UNAUTHORIZED PRACTICE OF LAW.

Figure 2-4 NFPA Model Code of Ethics and Professional Responsibility
Courtesy of National Federation of Paralegal Associations.

CRIMINAL STATUTES REGARDING THE UNAUTHORIZED PRACTICE OF LAW

There are criminal statutes in nearly every state that provide sanctions for nonlawyers who engage in "practicing law." "Practicing law" usually includes providing legal advice to the public or representation of a client in a court of law.

There is no direct regulation of legal assistants, but they are indirectly regulated through state ethical standards for attorneys, nonbinding legal assistant association ethical standards, and criminal statutes barring nonattorneys from practicing law.

THE UNAUTHORIZED PRACTICE OF LAW

Most states have a criminal statute that prohibits a layperson from practicing law. The reason behind such a statute is to protect the general public from individuals who are not qualified to give legal advice because they do not have the proper educational training, have not passed the bar exam, or are not fit to practice law.

Besides criminal prohibitions, there are ethical prohibitions as well. Rule 5.5 of the ABA *Model Rules of Professional Conduct* prohibits attorneys from assisting nonlawyers in practicing law:

Rule 5.5. Unauthorized Practice of Law

A lawyer shall not:

(b) assist a person who is not a member of the bar in the performance of an activity that constitutes the unauthorized practice of law.

The Ethics 2000 Commission is considering the following revision to this rule:

(c) A lawyer shall not assist another person in the unauthorized practice of law.

This rule draws a line that legal assistants cannot cross. Legal assistants are permitted to *assist* a licensed attorney in practicing law. The real question is at what point does one actually "practice law." The ABA, as well as most states, has been unwilling to give a specific definition of exactly what the "practice of law" is, preferring to consider the matter on a case-by-case basis.

> *Simply put, legal assistants may conduct any law-related services at which they are competent, provided they do not engage in the "unauthorized practice of law." The unauthorized practice of law (UPL) is the practice of law by someone who does not hold a current law license.*[5]

Figure 2-5
The "Practice of Law" Versus "Other Work" in a Law Office

Adapted from Arthur G. Green, *Leveraging With Legal Assistants,* American Bar Association, 1993. Reprinted by permission.

"Practice of Law"	"Other Work" in a Law Office
Giving legal advice	Obtaining facts from a client
Representing clients in court proceedings	Communicating information to the client
	Interviewing witnesses
Performing legal analysis and preparing legal documents	Performing limited legal research to assist an attorney with legal analysis
Evaluating a case and selecting an appropriate course of action	Obtaining documents
	Preparing drafts of requests for production of a document
Accepting or rejecting a case	Preparing drafts of interrogatories
Setting a fee	Preparing drafts of responses to requests for production of documents
Sharing a fee with an attorney	Preparing drafts of responses to interrogatories
	Preparing drafts of pleadings
	Preparing correspondence
	Organizing documents and evidence
	Preparing case chronologies
	Preparing deposition summaries
	Preparing exhibit lists
	Organizing and tracking deadlines
	Conducting factual research

While what constitutes the "practice of law" is established by each jurisdiction, Figure 2-5 sets out items that are typically referred to in court decisions as the "practice of law." Figure 2-5 also sets out other work in a law office. Notice in Figure 2-5 that there are many other professional duties that a legal assistant can perform that do not constitute the practice of law.

GIVING LEGAL ADVICE
Legal assistants may not directly advise a client regarding a legal matter. Courts usually apply three tests to determine whether, in fact, legal advice has been given.

- **Did the advice given require legal skill or knowledge?**[7] Generally, the question is whether or not the advice entails specific legal knowledge or legal skill.

> *The temptation to give legal advice is a challenge that almost every legal assistant encounters daily. During the span of a career, legal assistants become quite familiar with certain practice areas. They learn the answers to many common client questions. It can be very tempting to respond to a client's inquiry when one believes that he or she knows the answer . . . the legal assistant should refer the question to the lawyer with a statement such as "That's a question you should discuss with the lawyer."[6]*

- **Was the person advised of his or her legal rights?**[8] This question centers around whether or not a client was specifically advised of his or her legal rights of what the law is or is not regarding a specific issue. While it is true that a legal assistant cannot advise a client of his or her rights without a UPL violation, most courts allow a legal assistant to consult with an attorney regarding a legal question and then convey the attorney's answer to the client. In this instance, the legal assistant is simply a conduit between the client and the attorney. As long as the legal assistant does not advise the client or convey separate thoughts or legal analysis of his or her own, he or she is not giving legal advice.[9] However, when legal assistants do convey legal advice to a client on the behalf of an attorney, it should be clearly stated that the attorney is the source of the information.

> *Avoiding the unauthorized practice of law (UPL) is probably the "finest line" any paralegal is asked to walk. Even experienced paralegals are not always sure how to handle situations involving insistent clients demanding an answer right now, or that acquaintance or family member who just needs some "friendly advice." If you are not sure if the activity you are about to undertake or the answer you are about to give constitutes UPL, the best rule of thumb is not to do it. It is much easier to say to someone, "I'll have to get back to you," or "Let me check with [supervising attorney/employer]," or "I really can't answer that question because I am not an attorney, but I will be happy to find out for you," than it is to find yourself facing charges for UPL and the very real possibility that you will never again be able to work in the legal field in any capacity.*
>
> —Lenette Pinchback, CLA

- **Is the advice not normally given by a non-lawyer as part of another business or transaction?**[10] Many professionals, such as tax accountants and real estate brokers, work in legal areas where they may regularly give law-related advice in the ordinary course of their job. This type of general advice usually does not amount to the practice of law.

For example, in *In re Houston,* 127 N.M. 582, 985, P.2d 752 (N.M. 1999), clients came to an attorney's office when a van they had recently purchased had serious mechanical problems that the dealer refused to repair. The firm filed a lawsuit against the dealer. Approximately eighteen months later, the car dealer filed for bankruptcy. The law firm received the bankruptcy notice, but never told the clients. The clients discovered the bankruptcy from someone else and called the law firm. The attorney's legal assistant handled the call and told the clients that the bankruptcy would not affect the case. The clients were never told that their claim could be lost if a discharge was entered in bankruptcy without an objection to discharge being granted for their claim. After the bankruptcy was closed, the district court dismissed the clients' claim as barred by the discharge in bankruptcy. At no time, from when the clients initially came to the law firm until just before the case was dismissed, did the clients meet with an attorney. The legal assistant gave legal advice specifically related to the effect of bankruptcy on the clients' case. The advice required legal skill and knowledge, arguably included advising the clients of their rights (the conclusion that the clients did not need to do anything because the bankruptcy would have no effect), and was not normally given by a non-lawyer as part of another business or transaction. In addition, the court found that having a legal assistant conduct all meetings with the clients, during which the clients' objectives and the means for pursuing them were discussed and decided, raised serious questions regarding the unauthorized practice of law. The attorney was suspended for eighteen months.

MISREPRESENTATION OF STATUS

Another factor sometimes at issue regarding the giving of legal advice is whether or not the person giving the information to the client or third party clearly identified himself or herself as a legal assistant. Unless otherwise told, a client may rightly assume that he or she is talking to an attorney when, in fact, he or she is not. In such instances, the client may rely on the information from the legal assistant as legal advice. If a client is misled to believe that a legal assistant is an attorney, the client will expect the legal assistant to be able to take certain actions to advance his or her case that the legal assistant may either be insufficiently knowledgeable to undertake or expressly prohibited from taking.[11] To avoid misunderstandings, legal assistants should always disclose their status as a legal assistant and non-lawyer. Notice in Figure 2-3 that the NALA Code of Ethics and Professional Responsibility, Canon 5 states: "A legal assistant must disclose his or her status as a legal assistant at the outset of any professional relationship with a client, attorney, a court or administrative agency or personnel thereof, or a member of the general public."[12]

REPRESENTING CLIENTS IN COURT PROCEEDINGS Legal assistants generally cannot appear in federal or state courts or legal proceedings such as a deposition on behalf of a client. The rights and interests of the parties are more fully safeguarded with attorneys who have extended training and are licensed. However, some administrative agencies do allow a legal assistant to appear on behalf of a client. Some federal and state agencies require non-lawyers to satisfy certain requirements before appearing before them while others do not. Some jurisdictions allow legal assistants to make limited appearances, such as in uncontested matters and small claims court. A legal assistant should carefully check the rules of the jurisdiction before making an appearance in a proceeding.

PERFORMING LEGAL ANALYSIS AND PREPARING LEGAL DOCUMENTS
Legal assistants cannot draft legal documents such as wills, briefs, motions, pleadings, or contracts *without* the supervision of an attorney. Legal assistants routinely draft these types of documents; the distinction is that they do so properly under the direction and supervision of a member of the bar. The attorney is ultimately responsible for the legal documents. The reason for this rule is that legal documents affect the legal rights of clients and parties and therefore require the oversight of an attorney. As long as a legal assistant is actively working under the supervision of an attorney and the attorney maintains a relationship with the client, the legal assistant may interview witnesses or prospective clients, perform legal research, draft pleadings and briefs, and investigate the facts of cases without being accused of the unauthorized practice of law.

> *A legal assistant working for a lawyer in compliance with this rule can prepare documents without fear of UPL violations. It is the obligation of the legal assistant and lawyer to make sure the work product is reviewed by the lawyer before it is filed with a court or agency or shown to a client or third party.*[13]

EVALUATING A CASE, SELECTING OR REJECTING A CASE, AND SELECTING AN APPROPRIATE COURSE OF ACTION The act of evaluating a fact pattern, applying it to the law, considering possible courses of action based on that factual and legal analysis, and working with the client to strategize the best outcome for the client is reserved exclusively for an attorney. It is a fundamental duty of practicing law for an attorney to perform these functions. Legal assistants may, of course, participate in this process, but they must do so under the auspices of an attorney. Also, the act of accepting or rejecting the representation of a client is usually reserved by an attorney because the process includes the evaluation of the case and the potential giving of legal advice to the client. In *Cincinnati Bar Association v. Bertsche*, 84 Ohio St.3d 170, 702 N.E.2d 859 (Ohio 1998), an attorney allowed a legal assistant to operate a satellite office without adequate supervision. The legal assistant interviewed clients, obtained information, prepared documents, operated bank accounts, secured signings of bankruptcy petitions and other documents, and presumably (though not specifically stated) accepted cases (given that it was a satellite office). From time to time, the attorney would visit the office, interview clients, and oversee the signing of documents. The court concluded that the attorney's delegation of such matters to the legal assistant and his lack of supervision over that assistant violated a disciplinary rule regarding a lawyer not neglecting an entrusted legal matter.

SETTING A FEE AND SHARING A FEE Legal assistants are not allowed to set legal fees or directly share in the fees.[14] A legal assistant can provide information regarding fees to a client at the attorney's direction, but the legal assistant should be careful to explain that the setting of the fee was done by the attorney. The ABA *Model Rules of Professional Conduct* specifically state that lawyers may not share fees with nonlawyers:

Rule 5.4 (a)

A lawyer or law firm shall not share legal fees with a nonlawyer . . .
The Ethics 2000 Commission is not considering any revision of this rule.

In *In re Soulisak,* 227 B.R. 77 (E.D.Va. 1998), a lawyer and a nonlawyer worked together to provide legal services in bankruptcy cases. In addition, they agreed to split the legal fees. The agreement was to charge bankruptcy clients $650: $400 was paid to the attorney, and $250 was paid to the nonlawyer to cover paralegal, clerical, and operating expenses. The court found that the nonlawyer provided many of the services to the clients, thereby committing a UPL violation. The court also found the fee agreement to be improper fee sharing.

LEGAL TECHNICIANS, FREELANCE LEGAL ASSISTANTS, AND THE UNAUTHORIZED PRACTICE OF LAW

Recently, a new class of legal assistants, sometimes called "legal technicians," has emerged. What separates **"legal technicians"** from legal assistants is that they market their services directly to the public and do not work under the supervision of an attorney. Bar associations across the country have argued that since legal technicians do not work under the supervision of a licensed attorney but represent clients directly, they clearly violate criminal statutes regarding the unauthorized practice of law. Legal technicians argue that they simply provide forms that have been written by attorneys and help the clients fill in the forms. Cases are being decided on this issue on a case-by-case matter, but many courts have limited or greatly restricted what services legal technicians can provide.

Freelance legal assistants were defined in chapter 1 as self-employed legal assistants who market and sell their services to law offices on a per job basis. Freelance legal assistants are less likely to be accused of the unauthorized practice of law, since they are supposed to be acting under the supervision of an attorney. However, in instances where the freelance legal assistant is removed from the attorney, and where supervision is limited or nonexistent, unauthorized practice of law problems can occur.

legal technicians
People who market their legal services directly to the public.

HOW TO AVOID THE UNAUTHORIZED PRACTICE OF LAW

- **Always have your work approved by a supervising attorney.** No matter how routine the legal document is, always have an attorney review it. Remember, a legal assistant can do many types of activities as long as it is done under the supervision of an attorney, so take advantage of this and get everything approved. Never let an attorney approve your work without reading it. If the attorney says, "I do not have time to review it, I'll sign it and you just send it out, I trust you," bring the document back at another time or find a tactful way to suggest to her that the document needs to be approved the right way.
- **Never let clients talk you into giving them legal advice.** Most legal assistants never intend to give a client legal advice. However, it is easy to give in when a client presses you. This is usually because the attorney is unavailable and the client "needs an answer now." Legal advice might be telling the client what he should or should not do, answering a legal or statutory question, or telling the client what defense or legal argument he should make. The way to handle this problem is to tell the client that you are a legal assistant and cannot give legal advice but that you will either have the attorney call him directly or you will talk to the attorney and call him with the attorney's advice. A frequent problem that can occur when a legal assistant does give legal advice is that if things go wrong, for any reason, many clients will not hesitate to turn on you and say that they relied on your advice. This is why this issue is such a critical one.
- **Do not start sentences with "You should" or "I think."** When you hear yourself say "You should" or "I think," stop and realize that you probably are about to give legal advice. Again, it's not worth the risk.

> *They (clients) sometimes think they can call you and get the same advice they get from the attorney, and unless you have cleared things with your attorney, you are really getting yourself in hot water if you tell them, "Yeah, you don't have to do this, just do that. . . ." Well, that's legal advice. . . .*[15]

- **Always clearly identify yourself as a legal assistant.** When you talk to clients or send letters out on a law office or company letterhead, *always* identify yourself as a legal assistant. It is very easy for a client to say "Well I thought he was an attorney" to a disciplinary administrator or in a malpractice case.

   Never represent to others either directly or indirectly that you are an attorney. In many states, legal assistants are allowed to have business cards and sign letters on the law practice letterhead as long as the title of "legal assistant" or "paralegal" is included.

- **Management should develop ethical guidelines and rules.** From a management perspective, law office managers should publish rules regarding the unauthorized practice of law, tell staff members what they can and cannot do, and provide a policy on the responsibilities of supervising attorneys.
- **Management should make periodic checks of ethical standards.** It is not enough to simply establish rules and then never monitor them to see if they are being followed. Occasionally, management must monitor its staff regarding compliance with law practice rules and state guidelines to ensure compliance. Management should keep staff members up-to-date on changes or clarifications in ethical standards by circulating recent ethical opinions. Publications of legal assistant associations also report on recent ethical opinions. When appropriate, these should be called to the attention of management for general circulation. Another option is for law office management to hold workshops or seminars on ethics. Attorneys, legal assistants, and staff members should be constantly reminded about ethics.

COMPETENCE AND DILIGENCE

> *The drafters of the ABA Model Rules chose to give competence the most prominent place in the body of legal ethics rules. It is the very first rule, Model Rule 1.1. This positioning makes sense because competence is necessary in every matter a lawyer or legal assistant handles and in each step in the delivery of legal services.*[16]

Legal assistants and attorneys must perform legal services in a competent and diligent manner. The *Model Rules* hold that an attorney must be competent to represent the client. That is, he or she must reasonably know the area of law that the client needs representation in and, assuming the attorney does know the area of law, that he or she takes the preparation time to become familiar with the case to represent the client adequately. Model Rule 1.1 states:

Rule 1.1 COMPETENCE

A lawyer shall provide competent representation to a client. Competent representation requires the legal knowledge, skill, thoroughness, and preparation reasonably necessary for the representation.

The Ethics 2000 Commission is considering no revisions to this rule. The purpose of this rule is to insure that an attorney does not undertake a matter that he or she is not competent in and to insure that the attorney has had adequate preparation. The amount of "adequate preparation" depends on what type of legal matter the client has. That is, major litigation will require far more preparation time than, say, the amount of time it takes to prepare a will. The point is that a legal professional should not undertake to represent a client if he or she does not have the skill or preparation time necessary to do so. Legal assistants must have a basic understanding of the law of each area in which they are working. Additionally, they must be able to analyze, organize, and prepare the factual and legal data obtained to perform their job competently.

> *The legal assistant should be able to write clearly and effectively. The legal assistant must understand the goals, manner of, and organization of documents needed in the lawyer's practice, as well as the style and tone necessary for correspondence to clients and others. Although the lawyer ultimately will review all documents, the [legal] assistant should strive for perfection in the initial preparation. In this way, there will be less chance of an error.[17]*

Model Rule 1.3 requires that an attorney act with a reasonable degree of diligence in pursuing the client's case:

Rule 1.3 DILIGENCE

A lawyer shall act with reasonable diligence and promptness in representing a client.[18]

The Ethics 2000 Commission is considering no revision to this rule. Rule 1.3 specifically requires committed, dedicated, and timely representation of a client. Further insight into the rule is contained in the comment to the rule:

> A client's interests can be adversely affected by the passage of time or the change of conditions; in extreme instances, as when a lawyer overlooks a statute of limitations, the client's legal position may be destroyed. Even when the client's interests are not affected in substance, however, unreasonable delay can cause a client needless anxiety and undermine confidence in the lawyer's trustworthiness.

The comment to this rule also notes that attorneys should carry through to conclusion all legal matters undertaken for a client unless the relationship is properly and clearly terminated. The purpose of this rule is to insure that attorneys put forth reasonable effort and diligence in representing a client. Attorneys and legal assistants cannot adequately represent the interests of clients if they ignore the case, if they are lazy and do not work the case, or if they negligently handle the case.

> *As in any business or profession, accuracy, attention to detail, efficiency, timeliness, and economy of effort are all important.[19]*

Attention to detail is an extremely important skill for a legal assistant to possess. Figure 2-6 shows examples of how legal assistants failed to perform competently, not by failing to know the law, but rather by being disorganized or failing to pay attention to details.

Legal Assistant Fails to File Document, Leads to Dismissal of Case

See *Ortiz v. Gavenda,* 590 N.W.2d 119 (Minn.1999).

Israel Ortiz was severely injured on September 24, 1993 when the motorcycle he was driving collided with a truck driven by Bryan Gavenda and owned by Gavenda's employer, Frito Lay, Inc. Israel Ortiz died from those injuries on December 11, 1993. On June 6, 1995 his widow, Frances Ortiz (Ortiz), served a complaint on Gavenda and Frito Lay (collectively Gavenda) asserting a wrongful death claim and seeking damages as the "Trustee for the heirs of Israel Ortiz." Gavenda's answer to the complaint denied liability and alleged that Ortiz's claim "failed to comply with the provisions of Chapter 573 of Minnesota Statutes"— the chapter governing wrongful death actions.

On November 15, 1995 Ortiz signed a petition to have herself appointed trustee for the next of kin of her deceased husband as required by Minn.Stat. § 573.02, subd. 3 (1998). Although the petition and an accompanying Consent and Oath form were properly signed and duly notarized, *a legal assistant for Ortiz's attorney inadvertently failed to submit the documents to the court and, as a consequence, Ortiz was not appointed trustee. The mistake went unnoticed when Ortiz's complaint was filed with the Anoka County District Court on December 6, 1995. The oversight came to light and Ortiz filed her petition to be appointed trustee on January 8, 1997, but by then more than three years had elapsed since her husband's death.* The Minnesota Supreme Court dismissed the action due to the document not being timely filed by the legal assistant.

Legal Assistant Loses Complaint on Desk and Costs Employer Half Million Dollars

See *Legal Assistant Today,* January/February 1999, p. 24.

A legal assistant working for a corporation received a Complaint on her desk regarding a wrongful termination lawsuit. Apparently, the legal assistant was gone the day the Complaint arrived and it was laid on her desk. The legal assistant did not find the Complaint until approximately 38 days later. Under state law there is a 20-day deadline for responding and the Judge granted the plaintiff a default judgment in the amount of $562,489. The defendant corporation appealed the Judge's decision, but higher courts refused to reverse and the judgment against the company stood.

Legal Assistant's $92 Million Dollar Error

William Statsky, *Introduction to Paralegalism,* West Publishing, 1992.

A legal assistant at Prudential mistakenly left off the last three zeros on a mortgage used to secure a $92,885,000 loan made by Prudential to a company that took bankruptcy. Because of the mistake, Prudential had a lien for only $92,885. The error left Prudential's lien $92,792,115 short.

Figure 2-6 Legal Assistants Failing to Act Competently and Diligently

CONFIDENTIALITY AND THE ATTORNEY-CLIENT PRIVILEGE

client confidentiality
Keeping information exchanged between a client and law office staff confidential.

Another basic ethical concept is that of client confidentiality. **Client confidentiality** refers to the need to keep information exchanged between a client and law office staff, including attorneys and legal assistants, confidential. In addition to the ethical rules of maintaining client confidences, there is a rule of evidence, generally called the attorney-client privilege, that an attorney or legal assistant may invoke to avoid revealing the secrets of a client. The purpose of both the privilege and the ethical rules is to ensure that clients can consult with their attorneys without the fear that such statements would be passed to others or used against them later. If clients knew that what they told their attorney could be repeated to others, clients would be reluctant to tell their attorneys the truth. The attorney-client privilege and the ethical rules on confidentiality complement one another to achieve the same end.

THE ATTORNEY-CLIENT PRIVILEGE RULE OF EVIDENCE

attorney-client privilege
A standard that precludes the disclosure of confidential communications between a lawyer and a client by the lawyer.

Generally, the **attorney-client privilege** precludes the disclosure of confidential communications between a lawyer and a client by the lawyer. Thus, if a criminal defendant confessed a crime to his attorney, the attorney-client privilege would prevent the prosecutor from calling the attorney to the stand to testify about the confession. In addition, courts have applied the attorney-client privilege to legal assistants.

> It has long been held that the [attorney-client] privilege applies . . . to members of the bar, of a court, or their subordinates. . . . Examples of such protected subordinates would include any law student, paralegal, investigator, or other person acting as the agent of a duly qualified attorney under circumstances that would otherwise be sufficient to invoke the privilege. 8 Wigmore, Evidence Section 2301 (McNaughton Rev. 1961).
>
> *Dabney v. Investment Corp. of America*, 82 F.R.D. 464, 465 (E.D. Pa. 1979).

For the privilege to be invoked, the communication must have been made in confidence between the client and the attorney for the purpose of obtaining legal advice.

> *A fundamental principle of the lawyer-client relationship is that a lawyer will not disclose a client's confidential information. This cornerstone of legal representation enables a client to speak freely without fear that embarrassing or legally damaging information will be revealed. . .*
>
> *Lawyers or legal assistants may inadvertently waive the privilege if they share the information with a third person to whom the privilege does not extend, remove incriminating evidence from its original position, or divulge secrets to a court under a mistaken belief that disclosure is required. Waiver of the privilege means that the information can be admitted into evidence against the client at trial.*[20]

> **CONFIDENTIALITY OF INFORMATION**
>
> (a) A lawyer shall not reveal information relating to the representation of a client <u>or a former client</u> unless the client <u>gives informed consent, the disclosure is</u> impliedly authorized in order to carry out the representation, <u>or the disclosure is permitted by</u> paragraph (b) <u>or required by paragraph (c)</u>.
>
> (b) A lawyer may reveal information <u>relating to the representation of a client or a former client</u> to the extent the lawyer reasonably believes necessary:
>
> (1) to prevent <u>reasonably certain</u> death or substantial bodily harm;
>
> <u>(2) to prevent the client from committing a crime or fraud that is likely to result in substantial injury to the financial interests or property of another and in furtherance of which the client has used or is using the lawyer's services;</u>
>
> <u>(3) to rectify or mitigate substantial injury to the financial interests or property of another resulting from the client's commission of a crime or fraud in furtherance of which the client has used the lawyer's services;</u>
>
> <u>(4) to secure legal advice about the lawyer's compliance with these Rules;</u> or
>
> (5) to establish a claim or defense on behalf of the lawyer in a controversy between the lawyer and the client, to establish a defense to a criminal charge or civil claim against the lawyer based upon conduct in which the client was involved, or to respond to allegations in any proceeding concerning the lawyer's representation of the client.
>
> <u>(c) A lawyer shall reveal information relating to the representation of a client or a former client to the extent required by law or court order or when necessary to comply with these Rules.</u>

**Figure 2-7
Ethics 2000 Commission Draft Revision of Rule 1.6—Confidentiality of Information**

Reprinted by permission. Copies of the ABA Model Code of Professional Responsibility, 1999 edition, are available from Service Center, American Bar Association, 750 North Lake Shore Drive, Chicago, IL 60611-4497, 1-800-285-2221.

ETHICAL PROHIBITIONS ON REVEALING CLIENT COMMUNICATIONS

There are several ethical rules regarding attorneys preserving client communications, including Rule 1.6 of the ABA *Model Rules of Professional Conduct,* which states:

1.6. Confidentiality of Information

(a) A lawyer *shall* not reveal information relating to representation of a client unless the client consents after consultation. . . . (emphasis added)

Figure 2-7 shows the ABA Ethics 2000 Commission's draft revision to *Model Rule 1.6.*

Canon 7 of the NALA *Code of Ethics and Professional Responsibility* (see Figure 2-3) and section 1.6 of NFPA's *Model Code of Ethics and Professional Responsibility* (see Figure 2-4), although not enforceable, prohibit legal assistants from revealing client confidences.

> *I used to work in a very small town where everyone knew everyone else's business. My mother-in-law would ask me every day how my day went and did I work on any interesting cases. After a few too many short answers indicating my day was fine without offering any "juicy details," she and I got into a very large fight about why I would never talk to her. Once I explained that I was not allowed to discuss the "juicy details," we got along just fine and she never asked again.*
>
> —Andrea Blanscet, CLA

Again, the purpose of these ethical rules is to encourage clients to be completely honest with their attorneys. You also should note that there are many nuances regarding the attorney-client privilege and the ethical rules, including some exceptions to the rules.

Legal assistants have an absolute duty to preserve the confidences and communications of clients. All information must be kept confidential and should not under any circumstances be revealed in casual conversations with anyone outside the workplace. In addition to the moral and ethical reasons for not disclosing client communications, there also is the issue of quality service to the client. If a client learns that her communications have been revealed to outside sources, by whatever means, even if it is by accident, she can lose confidence in the entire firm. If a client cannot trust her attorney, the client will quickly move on to another firm. Remember, if confidential information gets out, it also could actually compromise your client's case.

HOW TO AVOID CONFIDENTIALITY PROBLEMS

- **Resist the temptation to talk about what goes on in the office whether or not it is client related.** There is always a temptation to talk about office politics and other office matters with people outside the firm. Resist this temptation. If you do this, it will only make it easier to talk about client-related matters. Consider that you are a professional and that both your firm and your clients demand anonymity.
- **Only talk about client matters to office personnel on a need-to-know basis.** Never go around your office talking about a client's case to employees who do not have a reason to know about it. You must get in the habit of keeping information to yourself. Why tell someone about client-related matters, even if it is a fellow employee, unless he needs to know for some legitimate reason? Also, even if you are talking to someone who has a need to know, avoid doing so in public places, such as waiting rooms, elevators, and restaurants, where your conversation can be overheard.

> *Discussing a client's case with a friend or relative may be tempting . . . Discussing cases may seem harmless if the names of the parties are changed or shielded. However, talking about cases, even innocently, is a breach of client confidentiality. Client information must never be discussed outside of the firm . . . One never knows who may be acquainted with a client or with someone connected with a case. Concealing names will not be enough to protect confidential information if the listener (or someone else) can put all the pieces together. Revealing the information could result in a lost case, a malpractice suit, and a disciplinary action against the lawyer.*[21]

- **Never discuss the specific facts or circumstances of a client's case to anyone, not even friends or relatives.** There is a specific temptation to talk about interesting cases you have worked on with friends and relatives because you trust them. However, many client secrets have been unwittingly revealed by friends and relatives who have repeated information they never should have been told. The statement "I promise I won't tell anyone" does not work. People do tell. Former girlfriends or boyfriends may reveal knowledge you told them to spite you. Mothers, fathers, brothers/sisters, or friends may inadvertently reveal a confidence you told them that gets back to the client, adverse party, or a member of your law office. When this happens, you will hear about it one way or another, and the repercussions can be severe. Do not take the chance: it is simply not worth losing a client or a job over. You should not even reveal the fact that an individual is or may be a client of your law office.
- **Always clear your desk of other case files when meeting with clients.** If case files are left in the open, other clients can read the files and access confidential information. Be very careful with any case files taken away from the law office.

> *If you get a call from someone outside the office asking for information about the case you're working on, always check with an attorney before divulging information. Don't even admit that your firm represents a particular client unless you're absolutely sure that is public information. Never, ever give out the names of your witnesses, or even divulge that you have witnesses, if opposing counsel calls. (In the case there is a rule requiring you do that, check with the attorney first.)*[22]

**Figure 2-8
Law Office
Confidentiality Policy**

Law Office Policy and Procedures Manual, 4th ed., 2000, American Bar Association. Reprinted by permission.

5.9.2 Confidential Nature of Client Matters

All matters relating to any clients or office matters are completely confidential. Nothing that occurs in the office should be discussed with family, friends, other clients, or anyone else. Particular care should be taken with papers that are transmitted in the office. Papers should not be examined and matters should not be discussed in public places such as restaurants, lobbies, or elevators, where other persons can peruse such papers or overhear conversations. Particular care should be exercised in commuter trains, buses, or any public area where much "law office" talk still continues to be overheard on a daily basis. Even after a case has become a matter of public notice by virtue of its having been filed in court or reported in the press, assume that it is still conficential and do not discuss it publicly.

Staff members should be careful, even in the office, not to leave confidential papers in open or public areas, nor should they leave computer monitors on in places where they can be easily seen by passers-by. It is the policy of the Firm not to use a client's name for the purpose of surveys or in materials that are prepared to describe the Firm without the permission of the billing lawyer(s).

The paper shredder located in _____ should be used for confidential material that must be destroyed; however, such material should not be destroyed without the prior approval of the billing lawyer(s). The use of a confidentiality notice on facsimile (telecopier) transmissions should also be considered as appropriate. Likewise, care must be exercised in dealing with all computer disks, tapes, and other media that contain privileged material. Computers with modems that are accessible through outside telephone lines must be appropriately secured to prevent improper access. Care should be taken when dealing with vendors as well. A confidentiality agreement may exist between the Firm and a vendor or potential vendors making proposals to the Firm.

- **Do not take phone calls from other clients when meeting with a client.** Taking phone calls from other clients while a client is in your office also can expose confidential information. Be aware of who is in your office when talking about confidential information on the phone, and, when possible, keep your door closed when meeting or talking with clients.
- **Management must create policies and systems to ensure confidentiality.** Law office managers also have a duty to create systems that ensure confidentiality. Some of these systems may include locking file cabinets that contain client files, limiting access to client files on a need-to-know basis, requiring files to be checked out, having law office policies on client confidentiality, and developing procedures to ensure that the confidential information of clients is maintained (see Figure 2-8). Most law offices limit

staff members even from revealing to persons outside the office that a particular individual is being represented. Even revealing the names of clients can give the appearance that the law office does not take confidentiality seriously. Although there is an affirmative ethical duty to maintain client confidentiality, there also is the potential for malpractice liability for firms that violate confidentiality. Under a legal malpractice theory, if a law office through its employees reveals client confidences, accidentally or intentionally, it could be legally liable to the client for damages that result.

- **Be careful when responding to discovery requests.** Many times, legal assistants are involved in responding to discovery document requests. It is important that confidential files are labeled appropriately, that each piece of paper that is to be submitted to the opposing party be carefully reviewed to ensure that confidential client information is not given out, and that such information is discussed with the supervising attorney.
- **Be particularly careful when using fax machines, e-mail, mobile telephones, and related services.** There have been many instances where confidential information conveyed over these media has been inadvertently revealed to others. It is particularly easy to accidentally reveal confidential information via fax machine and e-mail.

> *In a pending asbestos case being heard in the Circuit Court for Baltimore, Maryland, a temporary secretary for one of the defense firms pushed the wrong pre-coded telephone number button on the fax machine's automatic dialer and mistakenly sent a top secret report on the psychological profiles of prospective jurors to the opposing side. The plaintiff's counsel, in return, shared the report with the other plaintiffs' firms. As a result, Judge Marshall Levin felt compelled to dismiss all 51 jurors selected for the nation's largest consolidation of asbestos personal injury cases (9,032 plaintiffs and 10 defendants). In his oral opinion, Judge Levin said that, because the defense firm did not take reasonable precautions to prevent the mistake, the plaintiffs' attorneys know the inner most thinking of the defense counsel.[23]*

Faxes should be sent very carefully. An improper or misdirected fax transmission can lead to breach of client confidentiality. All fax cover pages for law offices should have some kind of confidentiality disclaimer on them. The confidentiality of e-mail is also a concern. From the client's perspective, there are many advantages to using e-mail to communicate with legal professionals. The problem with e-mail is the level of confidentiality and security that it affords. Because Internet e-mail passes through many network servers and could be intercepted or read by others at the server level or otherwise, many legal professionals are worried about violating ethical rules regarding client confidentiality and whether the attorney-client privilege has been waived if third parties have access to such information.

The ABA recently issued a formal opinion on this issue. The committee stated:

> A lawyer may transmit information relating to the representation of a client by unencrypted e-mail sent over the Internet without violating the Model Rules of Professional Conduct because the mode of transmission affords a reasonable expectation of privacy from a technological and legal standpoint. The same privacy accorded U.S. and commercial mail, land-line telephonic transmissions, and facsimiles applies to Internet e-mail. A lawyer should consult with the client and follow her instructions, however, as to the mode of transmitting highly sensitive information relating to the client's representation.[24]

The ABA found that e-mail affords users a reasonable standard of expectation of privacy and therefore concluded that unencrypted e-mail could be used to communicate with a client. However, the ABA also found that an attorney had the duty to consider the sensitivity of the issue being communicated, what it would mean to the client's representation if the communication were disclosed, and the relative security of the contemplated means of communication. Arguably, the ABA wants legal professionals to practice a common-sense standard when using e-mail or other form of communication with clients. If communication with a client is highly sensitive, then the legal assistant or attorney should consult with the client as to whether a more secure form of communication is warranted.

Practical considerations for using e-mail ethically include the following:

- Have a policy for the legal organization regarding the use of e-mail and how it will be used to communicate with clients.
- Consult clients about what type of information they want to communicate via e-mail, how often the client receives or responds to e-mail, and other information about the particulars of the client's specific e-mail system or habits.
- Make sure e-mail addresses are accurately entered so that client communication is not sent to others by mistake.
- Send a test e-mail to a client to insure the right e-mail address is being used.
- Add a confidentiality statement to all client e-mails. This is similar to statements that accompany many fax cover pages that state that the information is intended solely for the recipient and any third party that receives it should immediately send it back or destroy it.
- Do not use e-mail at all for particularly sensitive information.

CONFLICT OF INTEREST

> *The exponential growth of law firms, particularly during the last decade, has spawned an increasing number of conflict of interest issues. As firms expand and their client rosters increase, so does the potential that new engagement will create conflicts with the interest of present or former clients.*[25]

Conflict of interest problems also are an important ethical concept. A **conflict of interest** occurs when an attorney or legal assistant has competing personal or professional interests with a client's case that would preclude him or her from acting impartially toward the client.

Conflict of interest problems typically occur when:

- an attorney or legal assistant has a personal, financial, or other interest in a case;
- the attorney or legal assistant is a substantial witness in the case;

conflict of interest
A competing personal or professional interest that would preclude an attorney or legal assistant from acting impartially toward the client.

> *When a staff person who is coming from another law firm accepts a position . . . we conduct a conflict screening with the former firm and, if appropriate, we set up an information barrier within the firm.*[26]

- a law office, attorney, or legal assistant sometime in the past represented a client who is now an adverse party in a current case;
- an attorney and a client enter into business together;
- when an attorney is asked to advocate a position on behalf of a client that is contrary to the position of another of the firm's clients (an issue conflict).

If, for instance, an attorney represented a husband and wife in a legal action and then several years later the husband approaches the attorney to sue the wife for divorce, the attorney has a conflict of interest problem because he had at one time represented both parties. Not only would he have a question as to which client he should be loyal to, but the attorney may have during the first representation been privy to confidences and secrets of the wife that could be used in the divorce case against her.

Rule 1.7 of the ABA *Model Rules of Professional Conduct* speaks to the conflict of interest issue:

(a) A lawyer shall not represent a client if the representation of that client will be directly adverse to another client, unless:

(1) the lawyer reasonably believes the representation will not adversely affect the relationship with the other client; and

(2) each client consents after consultation . . .

Figure 2-9 shows the Draft Revisions of the ABA Ethics 2000 Commission. Most case law in this area presumes that if a firm has represented both parties in the past, there is an actual conflict of interest. It is not necessary to prove that confidences and secrets were exchanged during the first representation. Usually when an actual conflict of interest occurs, the whole firm, not just the attorney involved, is prohibited from entering the case.

Figure 2-9 Ethics 2000 Commission Draft Revision of Rule 1.7—Conflict of Interest

Reprinted by permission. Copies of the ABA Model Code of Professional Responsibility, 1999 edition, are available from Service Center, American Bar Association, 750 North Lake Shore Drive, Chicago, IL 60611-4497, 1-800-285-2221.

Proposed Rule 1.7—Public Discussion Draft
Ethics 2000 Commission
March 23, 1999

Material added to the current Model Rule has been underlined; deletion from the current Model Rule have been struck through.

CONCURRENT CONFLICT OF INTEREST: GENERAL RULE

(a) A lawyer shall not represent a client if the representation of that client will be directly adverse to another client unless:

   (1) the lawyer reasonably believes the representation will not adversely affect the relationship with the other client; and

   (2) each client consents after consultation.

(b) A lawyer shall not represent a client if the representation of that client may be materially limited by the lawyer's responsibilities to another client or to a third, person or by the lawyer's own interests, unless:

   (1) the lawyer reasonably believes the representation will not be adversely affected; and

   (2) the client consents after consultation. When representation of multiple clients in a single matter is undertaken, the consultation shall include explanation of the implications of the common representation and the advantages and risks involved.

(a) Except as provided in paragraph (b), a lawyer shall not represent a client if the representation involves a conflict of interest. A conflict of interest exists if

   (1) the representation of one client will be directly adverse to another client; or

   (2) there is a significant risk that the representation of one or more clients will be materially limited by the lawyer's duties to another client or to a former client or by the lawyer's own interests or duties to a third person.

(b) Notwithstanding the existence of a conflict of interest under paragraph (a), a lawyer may represent a client if each affected client gives informed consent in writing and

   (1) the lawyer reasonably believes that the lawyer will be able to provide competent and diligent representation to each affected client;

   (2) the representation is not prohibited by law; and

   (3) the representation does not involve the assertion of a claim by one client against another client represented by the lawyer in the same litigation.

Rule 1.8 of the ABA *Model Rules of Professional Conduct* also speaks to the conflict of interest issue:

(a) A lawyer shall not enter into a business transaction with a client or knowingly acquire an ownership, possessor, security or other pecuniary interest adverse to a client unless . . .

(b) A lawyer shall not use information relating to representation of a client to the disadvantage of the client unless the client consents after consultation. . . .

Figure 2-10 shows the Draft Revisions of the ABA Ethics 2000 Commission.

Figure 2-10 Ethics 2000 Commission Draft Revision of Rule 1.8—Conflict of Interest-Specific Rules

Reprinted by permission. Copies of ABA Model Code of Professional Responsibility, 1999 edition, are available from Service Center, American Bar Association, 750 North Lake Shore Drive, Chicago, IL 60611-4497, 1-800-285-2221.

Proposed Rule 1.8 - Public Discussion Draft
Ethics 2000 Commission
March 23, 1999

Material added to the current Model Rule has been underlined; deletions from the current Model Rule have been struck through.

CONCURRENT CONFLICT OF INTEREST:
PROHIBITED TRANSACTIONS SPECIFIC RULES

(a) A lawyer shall not enter into a business transaction with a client or knowingly acquire an ownership, possessory, security, or other pecuniary interest adverse to a client unless:

(1) the transaction and terms on which the lawyer acquires the interest are fair and reasonable to the client and are fully disclosed and transmitted in writing to the client in a manner which that can be reasonably understood by the client;

(2) the client is advised in writing of the desirability of seeking and is given a reasonable opportunity to seek the advice of independent legal counsel in on the transaction; and

(3) the client consents gives informed consent in writing thereto to the essential terms of the transaction and the lawyer's role in the transaction.

(b) A lawyer shall not use information relating to representation of a client to the disadvantage of the client unless the client consents after consultation gives informed consent, except as permitted or required by Rule 1.6 [or Rule 3.3].

(c) A lawyer shall not solicit any substantial gift from a client or prepare on behalf of a client an instrument giving the lawyer or a person related to the lawyer as parent, child, sibling, or spouse any substantial gift from a client, including a testamentary gift, except where the client unless the lawyer or other recipient of the gift is related to the donee client.

(d) Prior to the conclusion of representation of a client, a lawyer shall not make or negotiate an agreement giving the lawyer literary or media rights to a portrayal or account based in substantial part on information relating to the representation.

(continued)

(e) A lawyer shall not provide financial assistance to a client in connection with pending or contemplated litigation, except that:

(1) a lawyer may advance court costs and expenses of litigation, the repayment of which may be contingent on the outcome of the matter; and

(2) a lawyer representing an indigent client may pay court costs and expenses of litigation on behalf of the client.

(f) A lawyer shall not accept compensation <u>or direction</u> for representing a client from one other than the client unless:

(1) the client ~~consents after consultation~~ <u>gives informed consent in writing under the conditions stated in Rule 1.7</u>;

(2) there is no interference with the lawyer's independence of professional judgment or with the lawyer-client relationship; and

(3) information relating to representation of a client is protected as required by Rule 1.6.

(g) A lawyer who represents two or more clients shall not participate in making an aggregate settlement of the claims of or against the clients, or in a criminal case an aggregated agreement as to guilty or nolo contendere pleas, unless each client ~~consents after consultation, including~~ <u>gives informed consent in writing that includes</u> disclosure of the existence and nature of all the claims or pleas involved and of the participation of each person in the settlement.

(h) A lawyer shall not<u>:</u>

<u>(1)</u> make an agreement prospectively limiting the lawyer's liability to a client for malpractice ~~unless permitted by law and the client is independently represented in making the agreement,~~<u>;</u> or

<u>(2)</u> settle a claim <u>or potential claim</u> for such liability with an unrepresented client or former client ~~without first advising~~ <u>unless</u> that person <u>is advised</u> in writing ~~that~~ <u>of the desirability of seeking and is given a reasonable opportunity to seek the advice of</u> independent ~~representation is appropriate~~ <u>legal counsel</u> in connection therewith.

(i) A lawyer related to another lawyer as parent, child, sibling, or spouse <u>or by a cohabitating relationship closely approximating marriage</u> shall not represent a client in a representation directly adverse to a person whom the lawyer knows is represented <u>in the same or in a substantially related matter</u> by the other lawyer ~~except upon~~ <u>unless each affected client gives informed</u> consent ~~by the client after consultation regarding the relationship~~ <u>in writing under the conditions stated in Rule 1.7</u>.

(j) A lawyer shall not acquire a proprietary interest in the cause of action or subject matter of litigation the lawyer is conducting for a client, except that the lawyer may:

(1) acquire a lien ~~granted~~ <u>authorized</u> by law to secure the lawyer's fee or expenses; and

(2) contract with a client for a reasonable contingent fee in a civil case.

<u>(k) A lawyer shall not have sexual relations with a client unless a consensual sexual relationship existed between them when the lawyer-client relationship commenced.</u>

**Figure 2-11
Conflict of Interest Examples**

- **Using Client Information to Harm the Client:**
An ambitious associate attorney regularly defends the X insurance company. Client comes into attorney's office and wants to sue X insurance company for a major personal injury claim, not knowing that the attorney has represented the company before. Attorney, in an effort to help X insurance company intentionally lets the statute of limitations run then pays the client $2,500 from his own pocket telling him that the insurance company settled. Attorney had a clear duty to tell the client regarding his conflict of interest. Attorney was disbarred and the law firm was sued for malpractice.

- **Financial Interest:**
Attorney is an employee of county government water district. Attorney uses his position as authority to influence the water board's decision to purchase a piece of land that he owns through a partnership. Attorney also delays $300,000 of sewer connection fees to another of his piece's of land until after the sale of land is completed to a third-party. Attorney had a clear conflict of interest in both cases. Attorney was suspended for two years for the practice of law and pled guilty to using his official office to influence a governmental decision.

It is important that attorneys and legal assistants are loyal to their clients and have no alternative motives that might influence their independent professional judgment to represent their clients. Figure 2-11 provides a few more examples of conflict of interest problems.

As noted before, there are different types of conflicts, including an issue conflict. In an issue conflict, an attorney or firm is taking different positions on the same issues for different clients. The *Model Rules* generally prohibit this. If each client gives an informed consent, then the firm can most likely continue representing the clients. Also, if the legal matters are in different jurisdictions and the firm reasonably believes neither party will be adversely affected, then most likely the firm can continue representing the clients.

CONFLICT CHECKING

Because law offices and attorneys typically represent a large number of clients, it is often difficult for them to remember every client. As a result, it is possible for an attorney to have a conflict of interest but simply not remember the former client. Thus, it becomes the responsibility of management to ensure that before new cases are taken, a conflict check takes place. It is prudent to have a written policy regarding conflict checking (see Figure 2-12).

Many law offices maintain a list of all their former clients and adverse parties so that when a new case is being considered as to whether it should be accepted, the firm will routinely check this list to ensure that there are no conflict of interest problems.

**Figure 2-12
Sample Conflict of Interest Policy**

Law Office Policy and Procedures Manual, 4th ed., 2000, American Bar Association. Reprinted by permission.

> Before any new file can be opened, a conflicts check must be accomplished. Such conflicts check will be completed before requesting an internal file number from the Accounting Department.
> <u>No new file may be opened if such search discloses any potential conflict with any past or present client or adverse party. Any such conflict should be immediately reported to the responsible attorney.</u> A log of each conflicts check will be maintained. Anyone opening a new file for a new client or new litigation matter without conducting the conflicts check will be subject to disciplinary action.

Last Name	First Name	Social Security	Adverse Party	Type of Case	Date
Allen	Alice	515722404	Hays, Jonathan	Personal injury	1/15/91
Allen	Mariam	093342872	Cox Construction	Contract	12/01/92
Barney	Larry	023234912	Barney, Cindy	Divorce	1/08/88
Johnson	Donald	505235682	Beckwith, Eric	Real estate	8/02/90
Kitchen	Jennifer	093239832	State	Admin.\ law	10/06/91
Hall	Electric	235648905	Den, Robert	Collection	3/16/92
Winslow	Harriet	452239423	—	Adoption	6/7/91

Figure 2-13 A Conflict of Interest Data Base

Most law firms now use a computer program to search for conflicts. Some firms use a computerized data base program to do a conflict checking (see Figure 2-13). A data base program is application software that stores, searches, sorts, and organizes data. When using a data base program, it is advantageous to include the client's date of birth or social security number, otherwise a misspelled name may not be picked up by the program. Some accounting, billing, docket control, and case-management programs also can be used to perform conflict checking.

Some insurance companies that issue malpractice insurance to attorneys also require that, before the policy is written, the firm have and consistently use a conflict-checking device.

THE ETHICAL OR CHINESE WALL

Ethical Wall/Chinese Wall
Term for a technique used to isolate the legal assistant or attorney with a conflict of interest from having anything to do with a case.

Although it is the general rule that courts tend to disqualify a whole firm when a conflict of interest problem arises, some courts have carved out an alternative to disqualification. The alternative is called the Ethical Wall/Chinese Wall theory. The **Chinese Wall** alternative occurs when a firm effectively isolates the legal assistant or attorney with a conflict of interest from having anything whatsoever to do with the case, creating a "Chinese Wall" around her (see excerpts of the *Rivera v. Chicago Pneumatic* opinion in Figure 2-14). This is typically done by instructing staff members

Figure 2-14
A Case Upholding the Ethical/Chinese Wall Theory

Rivera v. Chicago Pneumatic, 1991 WL 151892 (Conn. Super.).
The issue presented in this case is whether defendant's motion to disqualify plaintiffs' counsel should be granted where a paralegal formerly employed by defendant's attorneys, and who had been extensively involved in litigation concerning defendant, is now employed by plaintiffs' counsel, and where plaintiffs' counsel has set up screening procedures to ensure that confidences are not divulged.

Defendant Chicago Pneumatic Tool Company (hereafter Chicago Pneumatic) moves to disqualify plaintiffs' counsel, The Reardon Law Firm, on the grounds that plaintiffs' counsel has employed a paralegal formerly employed by defendant's attorneys, which employee had been involved extensively in the defense of similar product liability lawsuits brought against defendant. Chicago Pneumatic states that the employee, Patricia Lannon, "was privy to all stages of the development of (the prior) litigation" and that "her duties included typing and/or filing of all correspondence, including materials which should be privileged as attorney-client communication; typing and/or filing of all internal office memoranda, including those which would be classified as attorney-work product, as they include discussions of strategy, tactics and the evaluation of legal theories and factual witnesses."

It also asserts that Ms. Lannon had access to documents of the client, and was exposed to interoffice conferences concerning the litigation. Ms. Lannon also was privy to discussions concerning trial strategy, the strengths and weaknesses of plaintiffs' case, and defenses to the action. Ms. Lannon in her affidavits annexed to Plaintiffs' Brief does not dispute that she acquired confidential information of the defendant while employed by defendant's attorneys. The matter at issue here is whether the "Chinese Wall" proposed by the plaintiffs is sufficient under the facts of this case to prevent disclosure of the confidential and privileged information . . .

To ensure that continued representation by plaintiffs' counsel does not threaten the integrity of the proceedings, plaintiffs' counsel has erected a Chinese Wall which incorporates the following:

(1) Ms. Lannon will not be permitted to disclose or discuss any information she acquired while employed by defendant's counsel concerning the cases in question;
(2) The files in question will be kept locked and will not be accessible to Ms. Lannon;
(3) Ms. Lannon will not be permitted in the vicinity of the files when others are working on them;
(4) Ms. Lannon's supervisors, Attorneys Horgan and Provatas, will not work on the cases in question, nor will they maintain any files involving defendant;

(continued)

> 5) Ms. Lannon will sign an affidavit and agreement that she will have no contact with the files, nor will she discuss the files with anyone in plaintiffs' firm or disclose any information she acquired in her former position; and
>
> (6) The attorney who will be handling the files, Attorney Nazzaro, will have no direct contact with Ms. Lannon.
>
> See Letter from Attorney Reardon to Attorney Boyce dated March 15, 1991, appended as Exhibit "B" to Defendant's Brief. See also affidavits signed by Ms. Lannon and affidavits of Attorneys Horgan and Nazzaro. Exhibits B and E; and C and D to Plaintiffs' Brief . . .
>
> In this case, the defendant has not met its burden to show that Ms. Lannon has disclosed confidential information to her new employer. Nor has it sustained its burden of proving that the plaintiffs' law firm was tainted or "infected" by the hiring of Ms. Lannon, or that plaintiffs have obtained an unfair advantage over the defendant which can only be remedied by the removal of plaintiffs' attorneys. "The disqualification of a party's chosen counsel is a harsh sanction, and an extraordinary remedy which should be resorted to sparingly." The court in the state of this record is not persuaded to invoke such a remedy. Moreover, the "Chinese Wall" erected to ensure that confidences will not be revealed in the future appears sufficient and reasonable to accomplish that end. The court must presume that plaintiffs' counsel will scrupulously comply with the Rules of Professional Conduct. See, for example, the Preamble, sections 5.1, 5.2 and 5.3.
>
> Accordingly, defendant Chicago Pneumatic Tool Company's motion to disqualify plaintiffs' counsel is denied, so long as the "Chinese Wall" set forth in Plaintiffs' Brief and affidavits remains in effect.

not to talk to the attorney in question about the case, not to disclose any information acquired at the previous firm, and limiting any access the attorney might have to the files of the case by locking file cabinets and placing passwords on computer files.

If the Ethical or Chinese Wall is erected and the court agrees, it will limit the disqualification to the legal assistant or attorney. Not all courts accept the Chinese Wall theory. Again, it would be the duty of management to ensure that the office could lock up the files and to segregate the attorney or legal assistant with the conflict from the rest of the staff. Law offices must also effectively limit access to computers and client data files to build an effective Chinese Wall.

LEGAL ASSISTANT CONFLICT OF INTERESTS

Many courts have extended the conflict of interest issue to legal assistants as well as attorneys. Conflict-of-interest problems usually occur when a legal assistant changes employment. For instance, in *In re Complex Asbestos Litigation*, a legal assistant worked for a law firm defending major asbestos litigation claims. He worked with discovery documents, was a part of the defense team for three years, and attended defense strategy meetings. Subsequently, he was hired by a firm representing asbestos plaintiffs. The defendants moved to disqualify the plaintiff's attorney because of the legal assistant's conflict of interest. (He had knowledge of confidential information gained over several years.) The motion was granted by the court.

Legal assistants should be ready to answer questions about their previous employers when interviewing for jobs to avoid conflict-of-interest problems. The ABA Committee on Ethics and Professional Responsibility recently issued an opinion regarding this matter:

> A law office that hires a nonlawyer employee, such as a paralegal, away from an opposing law office may save itself from disqualification by effectively screening the new employee from any participation in the case the two firms have in common.

The legal assistant should be alert to situations that might present a potential conflict of interest as a result of information gained in past employment and should disclose any questionable situation to the employer.

> *I accepted a [legal assistant job] offer from another law firm, unaware that the attorneys on both sides knew about a potential conflict of interest. When I switched law firms, the former firm's client expressed major concern over the fact that I was now employed by the law firm representing his opponent. I was put behind an ethical wall and could hardly walk anywhere within the firm without having to shut my eyes and ears or look the other direction. Then one morning . . . a senior partner announced that I would be sent home for two weeks until the firm could get a conflict waiver from the other party. My new law firm would continue to pay my salary and benefits, but no one had any idea what was to follow. Finally, after sixteen weeks, the conflict waiver was granted. Do not take any chances with potential conflict of interest matters. Be sure to find out before you accept a job offer what the firm's policy is if a conflict of interest arises.*[27]

HOW LEGAL ASSISTANTS CAN AVOID CONFLICTS OF INTEREST

- **When changing jobs, bring up the issue of potential conflicts in the interview.** Tell the firm whom you have worked for and what types of cases you have worked on. It is better to deal with potential conflict problems up front than for an employer to hire you and then find out there are problems.
- **Be absolutely honest about your past.** Do not hide or deceive employers about potential conflict-of-interest problems. Honesty is always the best policy.

- **If you later find out you may have a conflict, immediately inform your supervising attorney or legal assistant manager and do not have anything to do with the case.** If you later find out after you have been hired by a new firm that you may have a conflict problem, immediately raise the issue with your supervising attorney. Do not volunteer information to the new firm regarding the matter. If you can, approach your former employer and ask for an informed and express written waiver giving consent for you to work for the other firm. Verbal consents are hard to prove, so get it in writing.
- **Management must ensure that conflict of interest problems are checked.** It is also the duty of management to ensure that employees are not hired who have substantial conflict of interest problems, or if they do have such a problem, that the firm knows it up front. For instance, management might want to add a question to its employment form that asks potential employees to state any conflict problems in addition to establishing the conflict checking system mentioned earlier.

RESOLVING ETHICAL PROBLEMS

There is nothing easy about resolving an ethical problem. Typically, ethical issues are complex and messy; they are rarely "black and white." However, the following ideas can help you deal with ethical problems.

> *I took a job in a ten-lawyer firm in a big city. . . . I soon sensed an undercurrent of shady activities by some of the lawyers. My way of dealing with it at the time was to terminate my employment. I got another job and left. I never discussed it with anyone. When you make your own decision in an ethical dilemma, you have to live with its aftermath. . . . At the time, I was not mature enough to handle such a sensitive situation. . . . I would [now] try to work through the problem with my employer because you don't leave problems behind. Your next employment situation will bring other problems. We need to learn how to deal with them to become better practitioners and better people.*[28]

- **Talk to your legal assistant manager or supervising attorney regarding ethical problems.** When you encounter an ethical problem, the first thing you should do is to talk to someone else about it to get a different perspective. Typically, this will be your legal assistant manager or supervising attorney. However, this is sometimes hard to do when the supervising attorney is the one asking you to do something you think is unethical or if the attorney is herself doing something unethical. One way to approach the issue is to discreetly ask the attorney if she thinks this might be a problem. It is important not to be accusatory, but to simply inquire into the issue and to present your point as objectively as possible. You always have the option, no matter how hard it is, to say "no" to the attorney if she asks you to do something that you know is unethical. Also, be sure to check your firm's personnel policy manual. Ethical problems and procedures for handling them are sometimes covered in this type of manual.

> *If there is something that does not feel right, then do not do it. There is nothing wrong with going up the chain of command to obtain clarification of whether something is ethical or not. If it involves an attorney, go to the managing partner or office administrator. If it involves another staff member, go to human resources. It is better to "check" on the situation rather than let it go. If the dilemma is too great and nothing is done to resolve the issue, there is nothing wrong with seeking other employment and working with another group who are more ethically compatible with you.*
> —Linda Rushton, CLA

- **Talk to another attorney or legal assistant in the firm regarding ethical problems.** If you have a hard time talking to your supervising attorney about an ethical problem, talk to another attorney, legal assistant, or the Ethics Committee, if the firm has one. It is important in dealing with ethical problems to take counsel with others, to bounce ideas off others, and to talk about it. It could be that the other people have more experience than you and have had to deal with a similar situation. When talking to another attorney in the firm, use the same nonaccusatory approach. Also, be sure that you are talking to a person you can trust for sincere advice on how to handle the situation. You do not want to be perceived as spreading rumors or stirring up trouble. In larger firms, you also have the option of asking to be transferred.
- **Join a professional legal assistant association.** Professional associations offer a good way to share information and experiences with others, including information about ethical problems. Most professional legal assistant organizations provide guidance on ethical concerns. Use these resources to help you solve your ethical problem.
- **Be familiar with the ethical rules of your state.** It is always a good idea to have a copy of the ethical rules used in your jurisdiction and to review them from time to time.
- **Subscribe to legal assistant periodicals that cover ethical issues.** Many national legal assistant publications routinely carry articles on ethical concerns. Some even have a regular column on the issues of ethics. This kind of timely information can be helpful when dealing with ethical problems.

> *Unfortunately, we are all faced with decisions regarding ethical matters on a daily basis, both in our professional and personal lives. In the professional realm, not all ethical dilemmas are created by clients. Many unethical situations are created by the very person we should be able to count on for support and advice regarding ethics: our supervising attorney. Whether it be "padding" of time entries, attorneys "stealing" time entries from you or other staff members for work the attorney did not perform in order to bill a higher fee, being asked by your supervising attorney to make a statement or undertake some action that you feel is morally or ethically incorrect, or any number of other unethical situations, quite often your conscience must be your guide. If/when you feel uncomfortable about a situation, your first recourse should always be to speak privately with your supervising attorney. Sometimes it is enough to simply state, "I do not feel comfortable doing that." In most instances, you will find that your supervising attorney will have much more respect for you for having the courage to stand up for your personal and professional ethical beliefs. If this is not the case and more drastic steps are needed, again, your conscience must be your guide. I have communicated with other paralegals who have gone so far as to resign a position over ethical dilemmas. However, this is quite rare. Discussion usually solves the problem.*
>
> —Lenette Pinchback, CLA

- **Report ethical violations to the state bar association as a last resort.** If you have tried to work out an ethical problem to no avail, you always have the option of reporting the violation to the state bar association. This is a very difficult decision to make because you may lose your job as a result. Ethical problems are not easy to deal with, and you must be able to live with whatever decision you make.
- **When considering ethical questions, think conservatively.** When you are faced with a hard ethical question, be conservative and do what you know is right, no matter how much it may hurt. Figure 2-15 contains a list of ethical "commandments" that may guide you in this direction.
- **Do not ignore the ethical problem.** A common way to handle ethical problems is to simply ignore them and hope they will go away. Unfortunately, this approach rarely works. In many instances, it simply makes the situation worse. For example, if you see a staff person charging time to a client's case when he is not working on it, it is better to bring the issue to a head then rather than wait for him to do it to twenty clients. Ethical problems are better handled when they first occur as opposed to letting them fester and become far more complicated.

1. Know the ethical rules governing attorneys. If you understand when attorneys are vulnerable to charges of unprofessional conduct, you will be better able to help them avoid such charges.
2. Know the ethical rules governing paralegals. At the start of your paralegal career, promise yourself that you will adhere to rigorous standards of professional ethics, even if these standards are higher than those followed by people around you.
3. Never tell anyone who is not working on a case anything about that case. This includes your best friend, your spouse, and your relatives.
4. Assume that people outside your office do not have a clear understanding of what a paralegal or legal assistant is. Make sure that everyone with whom you come in contact (clients, attorneys, court officials, agency officials, the public) understands that you are not an attorney.
5. Know what legal advice is and refuse to be coaxed into giving it, no matter how innocent the question asked of you appears to be.
6. Never make contact with an opposing party in a legal dispute, or with anyone closely associated with that party, unless you have the permission of your supervising attorney and of the attorney for the opposing party, if the latter has one.
7. Don't sign your name to anything if you are not certain that what you are signing is 100% accurate and that the law allows a paralegal to sign it.
8. Never pad your time sheets. Insist that what you submit is 100% accurate.
9. Know the common rationalizations for misrepresentation and other unethical conduct:
   - it's always done,
   - the other side does it,
   - the cause of our client is just,
   - if I don't do it, I will jeopardize my job.

   Promise yourself that you will not allow any of these rationalizations to entice you to participate in misrepresentation or other unethical conduct.
10. If what you are asked to do doesn't feel right, don't proceed until it does.

**Figure 2-15
Legal Assistant Ethics: The Ten Commandments of a Conservative**

Source: William Statsky, *Introduction to Paralegalism* (Saint Paul, Minnesota: West Publishing Co., 1992), 264.

Suppose a paralegal, in the interest of job preservation, decides to engage in unethical or illegal activity that has been ordered by an attorney. At what point does that paralegal become liable criminally or civilly for such acts? . . .

Nothing at all would insulate the paralegal [from criminal prosecution if the acts are illegal]. Whether the individual is an attorney or a paralegal, the criminal liability is the same. We indict judges and we indict lawyers. There is no reason to believe we will not indict paralegals.—Robert P. Cummins, member of the ABA's Standing Committee on Lawyer's Professional Responsibility.[29]

ANSWERS TO COMMON LEGAL ASSISTANT ETHICAL QUESTIONS

The following are answers to some other common legal assistant ethical questions. The answers are based on general statements of law, but an answer may be different depending on your particular jurisdiction.

- **May legal assistants have business cards and may their names appear on law firm stationery?** In many states, the answer is yes. For business cards, care must be taken to ensure that the nonlawyer status of the cardholder is displayed prominently on the card. Regarding firm stationery, the name of the legal assistant(s) must be set apart from the lawyers' names, and the legal assistant's title must be shown clearly. Some firms print lawyers' names on one side of the stationery and print legal assistants' names on the other.
- **May a legal assistant sign letters prepared on firm stationery?** Yes, provided (1) the letter contains no direct legal advice or opinions, and (2) the legal assistant's status is shown clearly. The best practice is to include the title "Legal Assistant" or "Legal Assistant to X" directly below the typed name in the signature block of the letter.
- **May a legal assistant discuss fee ranges with a client on a preliminary basis, leaving the final discussion and decision to the supervising attorney?** All discussions related to fees must be deferred to the attorney. Even when a firm uses an internal fee schedule, it generally serves as a guideline only. It is solely the attorney's responsibility to measure the situation presented by each case and to set the fee.
- **How often and in what way must a legal assistant identify his or her nonlawyer status?** There is no single, correct way to identify the legal assistant's status. It seems prudent to do so at the beginning of all telephone conversations and at the beginning of every initial conference with a client or witness. For example, regarding a telephone call, one might say, "Hello. This is Jack Samson, Jane Mitchell's legal assistant." If it appears that the other party thinks the legal assistant is a lawyer, that impression should be corrected right away. The issue is not how often identity must be clarified to comply with the rules, it is how often should identity be clarified to protect the legal assistant from charges related to the unauthorized practice of law.
- **May a legal assistant counsel a close friend or a relative about a legal matter when the friend or relative knows that the legal assistant is not a lawyer and when the legal assistant is not paid for the advice?** Other than suggesting that the friend or relative see a lawyer, the legal assistant cannot give advice or comment in any way that may be taken as a legal opinion. The problem arises most frequently at family dinners, parties, and other social events. Friends and relatives can create an extremely uncomfortable situation. Whether the legal assistant is paid or not is irrelevant; legal advice cannot be given by the legal assistant under any circumstances.

Malpractice and Malpractice Prevention

Legal malpractice occurs when an attorney's or law office's conduct in representing a client falls below the standard skill, prudence, and diligence that an ordinary lawyer would possess or that is commonly available in the legal community.

Figure 2-16 shows areas of law that are more prone to malpractice than others. Plaintiff personal injury and real estate matters are among the highest. Practitioners in these areas should take particular precautions to prevent malpractice. Figure 2-17 shows the most common types of errors that resulted in a malpractice claim being filed. Notice in Figure 2-17 that substantive errors accounted for 46 percent of malpractice claims and that failure to know/properly apply the law represented the most common reason for all malpractice claims.

legal malpractice
Possible consequence when an attorney's or law office's conduct falls below the standard skill, prudence, and diligence that an ordinary lawyer would possess or that is commonly available in the legal community.

> If a mistake is found, never offer excuses such as "My secretary must have misplaced it," "The photocopy clerk didn't duplex the pages as I had asked," or "The attorney shouldn't have waited so long to make the assignment." Just fix it. Identify the problem, figure out what went wrong, figure out how to avoid the problem in the future, and solve it. It doesn't matter whose "fault" it is. In an equal team, everyone has an equal responsibility for getting the job done right.[30]

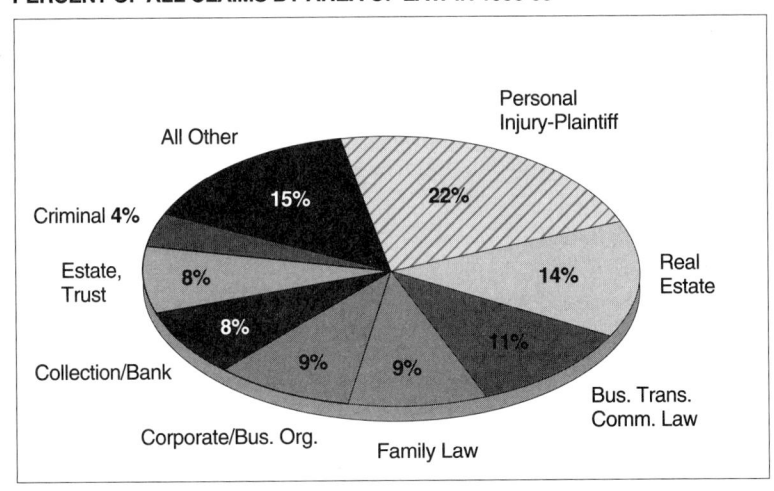

Figure 2-16
Malpractice Claims by Area of Law, 1990–1995

Source: *The Lawyer's Desk Guide to Preventing Malpractice,* American Bar Association, 1999, p. 30. Reprinted by permission.

**Figure 2-17
Malpractice Claims by Type of Alleged Error, 1990–1995**

Source: *The Lawyer's Desk Guide to Preventing Malpractice,* American Bar Association, 1999, p. 30. Reprinted by permission.

Type of Alleged Error

ERROR GROUPING	ALLEGED ERROR	1990–95 Total Number	1990–95 Percent
ADMINISTRATIVE			
	Procrastination in Performance, Follow-Up	981	8.68
	Failure to Calendar Properly	763	6.75
	Failure to React to Calendar	717	6.35
	Failure to File Document-No Deadline	304	2.69
	Clerical Error	242	2.14
	Lost File-Document Evidence	64	0.57
	Subtotal	3071	27.18
SUBSTANTIVE			
	Failure to Know/Properly Apply Law	1248	11.05
	Planning Error-Procedure Choice	1228	10.87
	Inadequate Discovery/Investigation	1157	10.24
	Failure to Know/Ascertain Deadline	788	6.97
	Conflict of Interest	428	3.79
	Failure Understand/Anticipate Tax	221	1.96
	Error in Public Record Search	140	1.24
	Error Mathematical Calculation	50	0.44
	Subtotal	5260	46.56
CLIENT RELATIONS			
	Failure to Obtain Consent/Inform Client	1104	9.77
	Failure to Follow Client's Instruction	572	5.06
	Improper Withdrawal of Representation	242	2.14
	Subtotal	1918	16.97
INTENTIONAL WRONG			
	Malicious Prosecution, Abuse of Process	418	3.70
	Fraud	361	3.19
	Violation of Civil Rights	146	1.29
	Libel or Slander	125	1.11
	Subtotal	1050	9.29
TOTAL		**11299**	**100.00**

DESK GUIDE LEGAL MALPRACTICE

Figure 2-18 also provides some excellent suggestions for helping to avoid costly malpractice claims.

Another way to avoid malpractice claims is by using engagement and disengagement letters. Clients sometimes think attorneys are representing them when, in

Figure 2-18
Ten Ways to Prevent Legal Malpractice

1. Gather factual information from the client to determine the basis of any legal claim and immediately determine and track when the statute of limitations takes effect.
2. Give the client a copy of the written fee agreement specifying the terms of employment and the basis of the attorney's fees in the case.
3. Conduct a thorough conflict of interest check before the client's case is accepted and immediately notify the client in writing if a conflict or a potential conflict is discovered.
4. Investigate the facts of the client's case and the law regarding the case diligently and promptly.
5. Keep the client informed regarding the status of his or her case by providing routine status reports and always inform the client of all developments that might affect the client's rights and ask for his or her participation throughout the case.
6. Charge a reasonable and fair fee for services performed and provide the client with a clear and detailed accounting of the basis for the fees charged.
7. Carefully and thoroughly proofread all documents and e-mails before they go out for mistakes and whenever possible send a copy of the document to the client for his or her approval and review.
8. Immediately tell the client of problems or mistakes as they happen and offer solutions.
9. Do not overestimate the firm's capacity to take on cases outside its expertise and always determine whether there is sufficient time to handle the matter properly.
10. Provide the client with written notice upon the attorney's withdrawal from representation (obtain court approval in matters involving litigation) and promptly provide the client with his or her file and other property he or she is entitled to.

fact, they are not. Law offices should always send an engagement letter or contract that clearly sets out when a case is taken, what the firm is going to do, and on what the fees will be based.

In addition, law offices should routinely send out disengagement letters for any type of case or legal matter, even if the only thing the law office did was to meet with the client in an initial interview (see Figure 2-19). The purpose of the disengagement letter is to clearly set out in writing that the attorney-client relationship was not formed or has ended. A client may not understand that the firm is not pursuing the matter, then come back months or even years later claiming that the attorney committed malpractice against him by not following up on the case.

**Figure 2-19
Disengagement
Letters**

Example 1: Disengagement Letter — New Client where Case Was Not Accepted

Subject: Potential Claim of *Client v. Johnson*

Dear Client:

Thank you for coming in to our office on Tuesday, November XX, 19XX, regarding your legal matter. We are interested in your concerns and appreciated the opportunity to meet with you. However, after further consideration we have decided to decline representation of your interests in the captioned matter.

We have not made a legal opinion as to the validity or merits of your case. You should be aware that any action in this matter must be filed within the applicable statute of limitations. We suggest that you consult with another attorney concerning your rights in this matter.

Again, we will not be representing you in the captioned matter and are closing our file.

Thank you again, and we wish you the best.

Kindest Regards,

Example 2: Disengagement Letter Following Representation

Subject: *Client v. Johnson*

Dear Client:

Thank you for allowing us the opportunity to serve you regarding the captioned matter. The case is now closed. We are closing our files and taking the case out of our active file drawers, in that our work in the matter is finished. We will be sending our file to storage shortly. If you would like evidence or other material that you have provided to us returned, please give me a call so I can get it to you.

We are interested in knowing how you feel about the quality of legal services you received from our firm. We would appreciate it if you would complete the enclosed client survey questionnaire. We are always interested in knowing how we can serve you better in the future.

Again, the captioned case is now closed, and we greatly enjoyed representing your interests.

If you have any questions, please feel free to give me a call.

Kindest Regards,

INTERNET SITES

ORGANIZATION	DESCRIPTION	INTERNET ADDRESS
ABA Center for Professional Responsibility	ABA site devoted to legal ethics	www.abanet.org/cpr
ABA Ethics 2000	ABA site devoted to review and updating the ABA Model Rules of Professional Conduct	www.abanet.org/cpr/ethics2k.html
ABA Standing Committee on Legal Assistants	ABA site devoted to the use of legal assistants in legal organizations, including ethical information related to legal assistants	www.abanet.org/legalassts
American Legal Ethics Library	Comprehensive ethics site	www.law.cornell.edu/ethics
Legalethics.com	Web site devoted to legal ethics, including articles and links to other ethics sites on the Internet	www.legalethics.com
National Association of Legal Assistants	Professional Standards including *NALA Code of Ethics and Professional Responsibility* and *NALA Model Standards and Guidelines for Utilization of Legal Assistants*	www.nala.org/stand.htm
National Federation of Paralegal Associations	*Model Code of Ethics and Professional Responsibility, Paralegals* and related ethics material for legal assistants	www.paralegals.org/Development/home.html
Legal Assistant Management Association	Ethics information related to legal assistants	http://www.lamanet.org/Resources/ethics.html

SUGGESTED READING

ABA Legal Assistant's Practical Guide to Professional Responsibility, American Bar Association, 1998.

ABA Model Guidelines for the Utilization of Legal Assistant Services, American Bar Association (see www.abanet.org/legalassts).

Annotated Model Rules of Professional Conduct, American Bar Association (current edition).

Attorney-Client and Attorney Work Product Privileges: Their Application to Paralegals, National Federation of Paralegal Associations see (see www.paralegals.org/Development/home.html).

Model Code of Ethics and Professional Responsibility, National Federation of Paralegal Associations (see www.paralegals.org/Development/home.html).

NALA Code of Ethics and Professional Responsibility, published by the National Association of Legal Assistants (see www.nala.org/stand.htm).

NALA Model Standards and Guidelines for Utilization of Legal Assistants, published by the National Association of Legal Assistants (see www.nala.org/stand.htm).

Paralegals and Conflicts of Interest, National Federation of Paralegal Associations (see www.paralegals.org/Development/home.html).

Summary

Legal ethics is an increasingly important topic that comes up often for all types of legal assistants. Ethical problems routinely encountered by legal assistants include the unauthorized practice of law, conflict of interest problems, and client confidentiality problems. Although a legal assistant cannot be disciplined by state regulatory bodies for violating attorney ethical rules, he or she can be held accountable by the attorney who hired or supervised him or her. Voluntary ethical codes by national legal assistant associations can help resolve ethical problems.

Legal assistants must be careful to avoid unauthorized practice of law questions. They cannot give legal advice, represent a client in court, accept or reject cases, or set a fee in a matter. Legal assistants must maintain client confidentiality at all times and should not talk about client cases away from the office because this can undermine client confidence and compromise the client's case. Legal assistants must avoid conflict-of-interest problems, especially when changing employment, and also should be careful to make sure that legal malpractice is avoided and that they act prudently and cautiously in handling all kinds of cases.

Key Terms

Ethical rule
ABA *Model Code of Professional Responsibility*
ABA *Model Rules of Professional Conduct*
"Legal technicians"
Client confidentiality

Attorney-client privilege
Conflict of interest
Chinese/Ethical Wall
Legal malpractice

Questions and Exercises

1. You are a legal assistant in the real estate section of a corporate law department. Your company is a large retailer that owns thousands of small retail outlets across the country. You process the leases, review the contracts, and coordinate lease payments with the accounts payable department to make sure the proper lease payments will be made. By the time the lease gets to you, the contract has been reviewed by the attorneys. Typically you assume that the description of the property is accurate, even though you could pull the full file to confirm the description. This is the way that it has always been done. What are your thoughts regarding the adequacy of the description of the property? Is this a good policy? What is the risk if the property description is not accurate? Does it change your answer if your supervising attorney thinks that you are in fact reviewing the contract for accuracy and completeness?

2. You are a legal assistant at a law firm that is representing a company in the process of negotiating a deal to merge with a competitor. You inadvertently mention the possibility of the merger to your father. Without your knowledge, your father purchases a large sum of stock in the company you represent, knowing that when the merger becomes public, the price of the stock will substantially rise. Several months after the transaction, your father gives you a check for five thousand dollars and explains how he made the money. He tells you that he only did it for

your benefit. Disregarding the criminal statutes that have been violated, how would you handle the situation and how could the problem have been avoided?

3. You work for a government agency and are responding to a plaintiff's request for production of documents. One of the requests specifically asks for any notes or memoranda arising out of the facts of the case. In one of the boxes of material the agency has collected on the matter, you find a particularly incriminating memorandum that will virtually win the case for the plaintiffs if it is produced. What do you do?

Assume you go to your supervising attorney about the matter. The attorney responds that she will take care of the matter and thanks you for your diligent work. Several months go by and you are now working on preparing the case for trial. You quickly realize that the document was never produced to the plaintiffs. How would you resolve this situation?

4. You are working on a client's case when the client's accountant calls and asks you for information about the client. You have worked with this particular accountant before and know the accountant is trustworthy. Is there any problem with revealing the information to the accountant? How would you handle it?

5. Your law office just signed an agreement to represent a famous athlete in contract negotiations with his team. A reporter from *Sports Illustrated* calls and asks if your firm is representing the athlete. You read *Sports Illustrated* all the time and are impressed that one of its reporters called your firm. In fact, you are taken off guard by the question. Being typically honest and forthright, you begin to answer. What is your answer?

6. You are a new legal assistant right out of school. You take the first job offered to you. It is at a small firm that is poorly run and not very well respected in the legal community. You work at the firm for only a month and quit. You apply for another position at a different firm and decide not to mention the employment at the small firm, as it was for only a month. You sign the employment application form knowing that it says if you are found to have lied on the application form, you could be terminated. You are subsequently hired by the new firm. Later, you find out the two firms have a highly publicized case they are litigating against each other. What do you do?

7. As a legal assistant in a medium-size law office, you have access to all the resources of the firm, including copy machines, telephones, e-mail and the postage meter. While the firm's staff manual states that the firm's equipment will only be used for firm business, you notice that the other legal assistants frequently use the copier, envelopes, and postage machine for personal use. When you asked one of the other legal assistants in the firm about it, the legal assistant said, "Don't worry about it. Everyone does it." How would you handle the situation?

8. Your law office represents a nonprofit corporation. The executive director of the nonprofit corporation calls you when your supervising attorney is out of the office. The executive director states that an employee is demanding overtime pay, since she worked more than forty hours last week, and saying that, if she is not paid overtime, she will immediately file a wage-and-hour complaint with the appropriate state agency. The attorney will not be in the office the whole week but may call in. You recollect from previous experience that the Fair Labor Standards Act generally states that employees should receive overtime pay for hours worked in excess of forty hours a week, though you are not sure about exceptions to the rule. The executive director presses you and says that he absolutely has to have an answer immediately and that if your firm cannot respond to emergencies, then maybe he will take his business elsewhere. How would you resolve the situation? Give options.

9. As a legal assistant for a legal aid office, one of your jobs is to screen clients. You routinely see new clients and report the facts of each client's case to one of the attorneys. The attorneys then decide which cases they have time to take on. On Monday, a client comes into your office. The client has no money but appears to need an attorney. The client advises you that she has been sued and needs legal counsel to represent her for a hearing in state district court on Friday at 10:00 A.M. before Judge Smith. From your experience, you are sure the attorneys do not have the time to accept this case. After listening to the

client, you respectfully tell her that you do not think the office will be able to represent her. The client then leaves and you prepare a memo to the attorneys. The attorneys subsequently decide not to handle the matter and file is closed.

On Friday at 10:15 A.M., the office receives a phone call from Judge Smith. Judge Smith tells your receptionist that an attorney from your office has five minutes to get over to her courtroom to represent the client or she (Judge Smith) will hold the office/attorneys in contempt of court and levy a fine against the office. Apparently, the client told Judge Smith that she had met with a representative from the legal aid office and had told the representative about the hearing. It was the client's understanding that an attorney from the legal aid office would represent her. Explain how this matter could have been avoided.

10. You notice one of your fellow legal assistants at the legal aid office where you work routinely using fake names and misrepresenting herself when tracking down witnesses or trying to serve subpoenas. Is this unethical or just uncouth? Analyze the situation using either the NALA or NFPA code of ethics.

11. You are a legal assistant for a sole practitioner. You have been working on a motion that has to be filed by 4:30 P.M. At 4:10 P.M., you hand the completed motion to the attorney. The attorney signs the motion and hands it back to you and asks you to copy it and file it. How would you handle this situation? List your options.

12. Analyze from an ethics perspective Figure 2-2, the case of *Asphalt Engineers, Inc. v. Galusha*. Identify the ethical problems you detect.

13. Using the Internet (either a general search engine such as *www.yahoo.com* or visiting NALA's or NFPA's Website), WESTLAW, or LEXIS, research the current status of legal assistant regulation in your state and/or nationally and prepare a brief report about your findings.

14. Read several of the online articles listed in the Suggested Reading section of this text. Prepare a brief summary of at least one.

15. Access the ABA's Website regarding the Ethics 2000 Commission (see *www.abanet.org/cpr/ethics2k.html*). Review several of the Model Rules that were covered in the text. Prepare a brief report on at least one. Determine if additional changes were made to the rule.

16. Using the most current issue of *Legal Assistant Today* magazine, prepare a summary of two articles from an ethical perspective.

Notes

1. Nancy B. Heller, "Dealing with Ethical Dilemmas—Can You Sleep at Night?" October 1992, *On Point* (Newsletter of the National Capital Area Paralegal Association) p. 1. Printed with the permission of Nancy B. Heller, paralegal.
2. *The Legal Assistant's Practical Guide to Professional Responsibility*, American Bar Association, 1998, p. xii. Reprinted by permission.
3. Reprinted with permission. Copies of ABA Model Code of Professional Responsibility, 1999 are available from Service Center, American Bar Association, 750 North Lake Shore Drive, Chicago, IL 60611-4497, 1-800-285-2221.
4. *The Legal Assistant's Practical Guide to Professional Responsibility*, American Bar Association, 1998, p. 5. Reprinted by permission.
5. *The Legal Assistant's Practical Guide to Professional Responsibility*, American Bar Association, 1998, p. 25. Reprinted by permission.
6. *The Legal Assistant's Practical Guide to Professional Responsibility*, American Bar Association, 1998, p. 27. Reprinted by permission.
7. *The Legal Assistant's Practical Guide to Professional Responsibility*, American Bar Association, 1998, p. 27. Reprinted by permission.

8. *The Legal Assistant's Practical Guide to Professional Responsibility,* American Bar Association, 1998, p. 27. Reprinted by permission.
9. *The Legal Assistant's Practical Guide to Professional Responsibility,* American Bar Association, 1998, p. 27. Reprinted by permission.
10. *The Legal Assistant's Practical Guide to Professional Responsibility,* American Bar Association, 1998, p. 27. Reprinted by permission.
11. *The Legal Assistant's Practical Guide to Professional Responsibility,* American Bar Association, 1998, p. 31. Reprinted by permission.
12. *NALA Code of Ethics and Professional Responsibility,* National Association of Legal Assistants. Reprinted with the permission of the National Association of Legal Assistants, 1516 S. Boston, #200, Tulsa. *www.nala.org.* Copyright 1975; revised 1979, 1988, 1995.
13. *The Legal Assistant's Practical Guide to Professional Responsibility,* American Bar Association, 1998, p. 30. Reprinted by permission.
14. *The Legal Assistant's Practical Guide to Professional Responsibility,* American Bar Association, 1998, p. 17.
15. Cynthia Tokumitsu, "How to Avoid the Top 10 Mistakes Paralegals Make on the Job," *Legal Assistant Today,* November/December 1991, p. 34. Copyright 1991. James Publishing, Inc. Reprinted courtesy of *Legal Assistant Today* magazine. For subscription information call (800) 394-2626 or visit *www.legalassistanttoday.com.*
16. *The Legal Assistant's Practical Guide to Professional Responsibility,* American Bar Association, 1998, p. 49. Reprinted by permission.
17. *The Legal Assistant's Practical Guide to Professional Responsibility,* American Bar Association, 1998, p. 51. Reprinted by permission.
18. Reprinted by permission. Copies of ABA Model Code of Professional Responsibility, 1999 edition are available from Service Center, American Bar Association, 750 North Lake Shore Drive, Chicago, IL 60611-4497, 1-800-285-2221.
19. *The Legal Assistant's Practical Guide to Professional Responsibility,* American Bar Association, 1998, p. 53. Reprinted by permission.
20. *The Legal Assistant's Practical Guide to Professional Responsibility,* American Bar Association, 1998, p. 61, 63. Reprinted by permission.
21. *The Legal Assistant's Practical Guide to Professional Responsibility,* American Bar Association, 1998, p. 71. Reprinted by permission.
22. Terrie I. Murray, "The Unwritten Rules: Survival in a Law Firm," *Legal Assistant Today,* May/June 1998, p. 13. Copyright 2001 James Publishing, Inc. Reprinted courtesy of *Legal Assistant Today* magazine. For subscription information call (800) 394-2626, or visit *www.legalassistanttoday.com.*
23. Michael P. Bentzen and Elizabeth A. Brandon-Brown, "Are You Sure Your Fax Transmissions Are Confidential?" *ABA Law Practice Management Publication Network 1,*(3) Winter 1993. Reprinted with permission.
24. ABA Standing Committee on Ethics and Professional Responsibility, Formal Opinion No. 99-413, March 10, 1999—Protecting the Confidentiality of Unencrypted E-mail. Reprinted by permission.
25. Joseph H. Flom and Jonathan J. Lerner, "Lawyer's Conflicts," *Law Practice Management,* March 1991, p. 28. Printed with the permission of Nancy B. Heller, Paralegal.
26. Ann Massie Nelson, "Work with Support Staff to Promote Quality," *Wisconsin Lawyer,* October 1999. Reprinted with permission of the October 1999 *Wisconsin Lawyer,* the official publication of the State Bar of Wisconsin.
27. Susan L. Oder. Reprinted in part from the *Los Angeles Paralegal Association Reporter,* May 1992.
28. Carol Milano, "Hard Choices: Dealing with Ethical Dilemmas on the Job," *Legal Assistant Today,* March/April 1992, p. 72, 78, 79. Copyright 1992. James Publishing, Inc. Reprinted courtesy of *Legal Assistant Today* magazine. For subscription information, call (800) 394-2626, or visit www.legalassistanttoday.com.
29. Phillip M. Perry, "Should You Rat on Your Boss?" *Legal Assistant Today,* March/April 1993, p. 66.
30. Terrie I. Murray, "The Unwritten Rules: Survival in a Law Firm," *Legal Assistant Today,* May/June 1998, p. 12. Copyright 1998 James Publishing, Inc. Reprinted courtesy of *Legal Assistant Today* magazine. For subscription information call (800) 394-2626, or visit *www.legalassistanttoday.com.*

CASE REVIEW

In re Pinkins, 213 B.R. 818 (Bankr.E.D. Mich.1997),

213 B.R. 818
(Cite as: 213 B.R. 818)

United States Bankruptcy Court,

E.D. Michigan,

Southern Division.

In re Darain PINKINS, Walterine Jones, Charles & Shirley Daberkoe, Angela Hall, Pamela Fields, Maretta Roberson, Glenn Peeples, Rahman & Chantay

Harmon, Sabrina Sanders, Phyllis Dunson, Tammy Trombley, Barbara Ellis, Darris

Finney, D'Anyai Asaki, Luis & Denise Sierra, Lashawn & Angela Taylor, Theresa

Singletary, Sandra Asberry, Ralph Knox, Leon Smith, Junotia Robertson, Debtors.

Bankruptcy Nos. 97–40722, 97–40965, 97–42032, 97–42576, 97–42719, 97–42790,

97–42791, 97–42885, 97–43062, 97–43162, 97–43353, 97–43356, 97–43414, 97–43419,

97-43494, 97-43661, 97-43664, 97-44060, 97–44160, 97–44241, 97–44564.

Oct. 14, 1997.

*819 Julie Lesser, Royal Oak, MI, for Debtors.

David Wm. Ruskin, Southfield, MI, Trustee

MEMORANDUM OPINION

STEVEN W. RHODES, Chief Judge.

This matter is before the Court on the Chapter 13 Trustee's objections to fee applications submitted by the Castle Law Office of Detroit, P.C. in 21 cases. The Court conducted a hearing on the objections on August 21, 1997. Because most of the objections relate to all of the fee applications, the Court will address them in one consolidated opinion.

I. Introduction

The Castle Law office ("Castle") handles primarily chapter 13 bankruptcy cases. The firm employs attorneys Julie Lesser and Terri Weik, and several legal assistants and clerical staff members. The Trustee's office considers Castle a "high volume filer," filing an average of 77 cases per month since January 1997. (Transcript of August 21, 1997 hearing (Tr.) at 36.) Castle's standard practice [FN1] in handling initial consultations with clients was that the client met with a legal assistant, who discussed with the client the available chapters and assisted the client in deciding which, if any, chapter proceedings the client should file. If the client had a question and requested an answer from an attorney, the legal assistant would personally ask the attorney and relate the answer back to the client. The client would not meet with *820 an attorney. The assistant gave a questionnaire to the client to fill out and return. The assistant then reviewed the questionnaire and prepared the papers to be filed. The client then returned to sign the papers, again meeting with a legal assistant, rather than an attorney. In most instances, unless the client had specifically requested to meet with an attorney, the client's first contact with the attorney was at the meeting of creditors.

> FN1. The Court is aware that the law firm has since modified some of its procedures. However, this opinion addresses the procedures in effect at the time the fees in question were generated.

The Trustee's primary fee objection is that the firm's clients did not meet with an attorney prior to the meeting of creditors. The Trustee's concern in this respect is that the legal assistant is giving legal advice and acting without direct supervision of an attorney. The Trustee also objects to the similarity of time entries on the fee applications and the lack of detail. The Trustee raises further objections in specific cases in which the fees charged exceed the agreed upon fees, and in cases which were dismissed at or before confirmation and Castle submitted an application for the full amount of the fees.

II. Unauthorized Practice of Law

A.

[1] Michigan law governs whether Castle legal assistants engage in the unauthorized practice of law. In re Bright, 171 B.R. 799, 802 (Bankr.E.D.Mich.1994) (no federal law regulating the extent to which nonlawyers may appear before the bankruptcy court; Michigan law applies). Mich. Comp. Laws Anno. § 600.916 provides in pertinent part:

> It is unlawful for any person to practice law, or to engage in the law business, or in any manner whatsoever to lead others to believe that he is authorized to practice law or to engage in the law business, or in any manner whatsoever to represent or designate himself as an attorney and counselor, attorney at law, or lawyer, unless the person so doing is regularly licensed and authorized to practice law in this state.

M.C.L.A § 600.916; M.S.A. 271A.916.

[2][3] The statute does not identify the activities that constitute the practice of law. Accordingly, "[t]he formidable task of constructing a definition of the practice of law has largely been left to the judiciary." State Bar v. Cramer, 399 Mich. 116, 132, 249 N.W.2d 1 (1976) (citing Comment, Lay Divorce Firms and the Unauthorized Practice of Law, 6 J.L. Reform 423, 426 (1973)). The courts should construe the term with the purpose of the statute in mind, which is to protect the public. Cramer, 399 Mich. at 134, 249N.W.2d 1.

In Cramer, the issue before the court was whether a nonlawyer selling "Do-It-Yourself Divorce Kits" was engaged in the unauthorized practice of law. The court held that it does not constitute the unauthorized practice of law for a nonlawyer to provide or sell standard forms and general instructions for completing the forms, or to provide typing services. Cramer, 399 Mich. at 136, 249 N.W.2d 1. However, the court stated, "[t]o the extent that defendant provides personal advice peculiar to [the client's particular legal situation], she is engaged in the 'unauthorized practice of law.'" Id. at 138, 249 N.W.2d 1.

In Bright, the bankruptcy court addressed whether the services provided by a paralegal constituted the unauthorized practice of law. The paralegal specialized in preparing divorce kits, but also assisted debtors in preparing chapter 7 bankruptcy forms. The practice of the paralegal in that respect was to collect data from the debtor, decide where information should be placed on the forms, and add language to the standard forms not dictated by the debtor. The paralegal also stated that she responded to questions from debtors regarding the interpretation and definition of terms, referred debtors to specific pages of reference books in response to questions and provided information about local procedures and requirements. She also consulted an attorney when a legal question arose and related the response back to the debtor. Bright, 171 B.R. at 800-01. The court noted that there had been no cases in Michigan specifically dealing with the unauthorized practice of law in the bankruptcy setting and looked to bankruptcy cases in other jurisdictions that have attempted to define what constitutes the unauthorized practice of law in the bankruptcy context. Id. at 802. Courts have held that the following activities constitute the practice of law in other jurisdictions:

> ***821** (I) Determining when to file bankruptcy cases. In re Herren, 138 B.R. 989,995 (Bankr.D.Wyo.1992).
>
> (2) Deciding whether to file a Chapter 7 or a Chapter 13. Arthur, 15 B.R. at 54[6] [In re Arthur, 15 B.R. 541 (Bankr.E.D.Pa.1981)].
>
> (3) Filling out or assisting debtors in completing forms or scheduled. In re Glad, 98 B.R. 976, 978 (9th Cir. BAP 1989); In re McCarthy, 149 B.R. 162, 166 (Bankr.S.D.Cal.1992); Herren, 138 B.R. at 993-4; In re Webster, 120 B.R. 111, 113 (Bankr.E.D.Wis.1990); In re Bachmann, 113 B.R. 769, 773-4 (Bankr.S.D.Fla.1990); In re Calzadilla, 151 B.R. 622, 625 (Bankr.S.D.Fla.1993).
>
> (4) Solicitation of financial information and preparation of schedules. Herren, 138 B.R. at 994; In re Grimes, 115 B.R. 639, 643 (Bankr.D.S.D.1990).

(5) Providing clients with definitions of legal terms of art. Herren, 138 B.R. at 995.

(6) Advising debtors which exemptions they should claim. McCarthy, 149 B.R. at 166-7; Herren, 138 B.R. at 995; Webster, 120 B.R. at 113.

(7) Preparing motions and answers to motions. McCarthy, 149 B.R. at 166; Webster, 120 B.R. at 113.

(8) Advising debtors on dischargeability issues. Arthur, 15 B.R. at 54 [6].

(9) Advising debtors concerning the automatic stay. Arthur, 15 B.R. at 54 [6].

(10) Habitual drafting of legal instruments for hire. Arthur, 15 B.R. at 54[6].

(11) Correcting "errors" or omissions on bankruptcy forms. In re Calzadilla, 151 B.R. at 625.

(12) Advising clients as to various remedies and procedures available in the bankruptcy system. In re Calzadilla, 151 B.R. at 625.

Bright, 171 B.R. at 802-03.

[4] This Court finds that the legal assistants of Castle perform many services that constitute the unauthorized practice of law. First, legal assistants explain to prospective clients the difference between chapter 7 and chapter 13. (Tr. at 15.) They are thus defining and explaining concepts and legal terms of art.

Second, Lesser stated that approximately 33% of prospective clients who come to their office for an initial consultation are given other suggestions as to how to resolve their problems without filing bankruptcy. (Tr. at 15.) Because these prospective clients meet only with a legal assistant at the initial consultation, the Court infers that the legal assistant makes the determination that bankruptcy is not the best choice for this particular individual and advises the client of other options. The rendering of advice peculiar to a client's particular situation is specifically prohibited by Cramer, 399 Mich. at 138, 249 N.W.2d I.

Third, it appears that the assistant helps the client determine whether to file chapter 7 or chapter 13. Although Lesser testified that the client makes the choice (Tr. at 15), Lesser also later stated that the decision "by the client and the initial consultant" (Tr. at 16) is immediately reviewed by an attorney. Regardless of that review, the assistant's participation in this important decision constitutes the prohibited practice of law.

Fourth, if the legal assistant is not comfortable answering a specific question, or if the client is not comfortable with the advice given by the legal assistant, the legal assistant asks the attorney what the advice should be and relates that information back to the client. (Tr. at 17.) The primary concern with this practice is that the legal assistant uses his or her own judgment to decide which questions to refer to an attorney and which questions to attempt to answer themselves. There is also a chance that the assistant will not properly phrase the question to the attorney or will not communicate the advice properly to the client. Moreover, and most importantly, the client is entitled to the professional judgment of the attorney.

Lesser stressed that the legal assistants employed by the Castle law firm are very well trained, and that the legal services, although not provided by an attorney, are of the highest quality. (Tr. at 20.) This argument misses the point. Legal assistants are not authorized to practice law.

*822 B.

A number of the Michigan Rules of Professional Conduct provide further guidance on this issue. Michigan Rules of Professional Conduct 5.5 states in part:

> A lawyer shall not:
>
> ****
>
> (b) assist a person who is not a member of the bar in the performance of activity that constitutes the unauthorized practice of law.

The Comment to Rule 5.5 states, "[l]imiting the practice of law to members of the bar protects the public against rendition of legal services by unqualified persons."

Michigan Rules of Professional Conduct 5.3—Responsibilities Regarding Nonlawyer Assistants—states in part:

> With respect to a nonlawyer employed by, retained by, or associated with a lawyer:
>
> (a) a partner in a law firm shall make reasonable efforts to ensure that the firm has in effect measures giving reasonable assurance that the person's conduct is compatible with the professional obligations of the lawyer;
>
> (b) a lawyer having direct supervisory authority over the nonlawyer shall make reasonable efforts to ensure that the person's conduct is compatible with the professional obligations of the lawyer;....

The Comment to Rule 5.3 stresses that the "measures employed in supervising nonlawyers should take account of the fact that they do not have legal training and are not subject to professional discipline."

Michigan Rules of Professional Conduct 1.1 states:

> A lawyer shall provide competent representation to a client. A lawyer shall not:
>
> (a) handle a legal matter which the lawyer knows or should know that the lawyer is not competent to handle, without associating with a lawyer who is competent to handle it;
>
> (b) handle a legal matter without preparation adequate in the circumstances; or
>
> (c) neglect a legal matter entrusted to the lawyer.

Michigan Rules of Professional Conduct 2.1 states:

> In representing a client, a lawyer shall exercise independent professional judgment and shall render candid advice. In rendering advice, a lawyer may refer not only to the law, but to other considerations such as moral, economic, social and political factors that may be relevant to the client's situation.
>
> The Comment to Rule 2.1 indicates that the "client is entitled to straightforward advice expressing the lawyer's honest assessment."

[5] An issue similar to the one before the Court was addressed in State Bar of Michigan Ethics Opinion RI-128, April 21, 1992. [FN2] There, an attorney inquired as to whether his legal assistant could meet with a prospective client, collect information from the client, and forward the information to the attorney, at which point the attorney would prepare the required documents for signing without ever meeting with the client. The Standing Committee on Professional and Judicial Ethics examined the rules cited above and stated,

> FN2. Although ethics opinions are not binding on state or federal courts, they do provide guidance in resolving issues of professional responsibility. Upjohn Co. v. Aetna Cas. & Sur. Co., 768 F.Supp. 1186, 1214 (W.D.Mich.1990).

Taken as a whole, the recurrent theme found in these [ ] rules and comments is that a lawyer's expertise and judgment are an integral part of the service provided to a client. While legal assistants may behave in a very professional manner while interacting with clients and carrying out the multitude of other duties they perform on a regular basis, the fact of the matter is that a legal assistant has not received the extensive, in depth legal training which is required of a lawyer. Without such training, it is possible, perhaps even likely, that a legal assistant, having the only interaction with the client, may not spot an issue or issues that could make a difference in the drafting or representation provided.

RI-128. The Committee further stated that "it is impossible to see how the legal assistant, being the only contact with the law office, could refrain from giving legal advice. ***823** Certainly, any client will have questions regarding legal advice, and if the lawyer is not directly interacting with the client, any advice must be delivered through the legal assistant." RI-128.

[6] Michigan Rules of Professional Conduct 1.4(b), which provides that a "lawyer shall explain a matter to the extent reasonably necessary to permit the client to make informed decisions regarding representation," also infers that it is the lawyer who is communicating with the client. In most instances, clients of the Castle law firm did not meet with an attorney until the meeting of creditors. An attorney cannot adequately represent a client consistent with the

Michigan Rules of Professional Conduct without meeting with the client before filing the case.

C.

In Bright, the court stated that under the Michigan Rules of Professional Conduct, a lawyer is not adequately supervising a non-lawyer if:

(1) the lawyer does not know of the existence or content of meetings between the non-lawyer and the client;

(2) the lawyer relies solely on the non-lawyer as intermediary, neglecting to meet directly with the client; or

(3) the lawyer fails to use his independent professional judgment to determine which documents prepared by the non-lawyer should be communicated outside the law office.

Bright, 171 B.R. at 805.

[7] Lesser stressed that an attorney reviews the file at every step. Specifically, after the initial consultation, an attorney reviews the initial consultation paperwork and determines if the appropriate chapter has been selected. (Tr. at 16.) The attorney reviews the petition and plan. The attorney selects the exemptions. (Tr. at 19.) After the client signs the petition, the attorney makes a final review of the papers and signs them. However, even if the attorney is as personally involved with the file as Lesser suggests, this does not obviate the need for direct client contact. Although it is not improper for attorneys to delegate certain matters to nonlawyer members of their staff, lack of contact or a direct relationship with the client precludes proper delegation. In re Stegemann, 206 B.R. 176, 179 (Bankr.C.D.111.1997).

[8] A further problem arises from Castle's practice of having the legal assistant sign client retention letters. The agreement is purportedly entered into by the client and the attorney. However, the attorney does not sign the client retention letter. (See Ex. I.) This issue was addressed by the Standing Committee on Professional and Judicial Ethics in Op 113. There, the lawyer was prohibited from allowing a nonlawyer employee to sign a client retention letter. The Committee reasoned that since court rules (MCR 2.114) require a lawyer to sign all pleadings, and retention letters are equally important, a nonlawyer may not handle retention letters. See Ethics and Legal Assistants, 71 Mich. B.J. 826 (August 1992).

D.

[9[Various sanctions are available in situations, such as this, involving the unauthorized practice of law. Courts have enjoined the unauthorized practice of law, disgorged fees, denied fees, fined the service provider, and ordered the service provider to pay the bankruptcy trustee's reasonable attorney fees. See Bright, 171 B.R. at 807 (citations omitted). The Court finds under the circumstances of these bankruptcy cases that it is appropriate to deny all fees for the work of legal assistants. The Court cannot award fees for unauthorized and unlawful services.

III. Fees Charged in Excess of Fee Agreement

[10] The Trustee raised objections in the following cases where the amount of the fee application was: greater than the agreed upon fees: Darain Pinkins, 97-40722; Tammy Trombley, 97-43353; Charles & Shirley Daberkoe, 97- 42032; and Barbara Ellis, 97-43356. Lesser explained that the initial fee agreement covered only limited services and, in certain circumstances, additional services were required. The retainer agreement states that the $1,200 fee covers: 1) prefiling consultations, 2) creditor calls, 3) preparation and filing of original petition, 4) attorney representation at meeting of creditors, and 5) attorney representation at one confirmation ***824** hearing. The retainer does not include attorney representation in any court action filed in conjunction with the petition, including adversary proceedings and motions. (See Ex. 1.) Following a review of the fee applications, the Court is satisfied that Castle has charged additional fees only in situations where services were provided that were not included in the initial fee agreement. Accordingly, this objection is overruled.

IV. Fees for Dismissed Cases

[11] The Trustee objects to Castle charging the full fee in the following cases that were dismissed at or before confirmation: Walterine Jones, 97-40965; Angela Hall, 97-42576; D'Anyai Asaki, 97-43419; and Darain Pinkins, 97-40722. The Trustee ques-

tioned whether there was a benefit to the estate in light of the fact that the cases were dismissed. Lesser argued that the dismissals in question were the fault of the debtor and in such instances the law firm should be compensated for the services they provided.

Section 330(a)(3) provides that in determining the amount of reasonable compensation, all relevant factors are to be considered, including:

> (C) whether the services were necessary to the administration of, or beneficial at the time at which the service was rendered toward the completion of, a case under this title.

11 U.S.C. § 330(a)(3)(C).

The Trustee has focused on the subsequent dismissal of the case in his objection to these fees, without identifying any specific charges which he considers objectionable. Because the standard for determining reasonableness considers the fees "at the time at which the service was rendered," it is not appropriate to merely object to the total amount because the case was subsequently dismissed. Lesser argues that in each case in question, the dismissal was the result of actions of the debtor. If any actions by the attorney had contributed to the dismissal, then a reduction in fees would be warranted. However, the Court finds no indication of that in these cases and accordingly this objection is overruled.

V. Services of Clerical Personnel

[12] Castle included in its fee applications expenses for the services of clerical personnel, including the following: Opening of file (file preparation/organization of paperwork, entering client into system); Court preparation for filing; Filing of petition; and Copying of plan/POS to creditors and Trustee. These charges should not be billed separately to clients, but should be included in office overhead. As noted by this Court in In re Woodward East Project, Inc., 195 B.R. 372 (Bankr.E.D.Mich.1996), "it is the normal practice of attorneys in this district that the expenses of . . . clerical services are part of an attorney's office overhead, and are not billed separately to clients." Id. at 377; see also In re Westwood Asphalt, 45 B.R. 111 (Bankr.E.D.Mich.1984); In re Bank of New England Corp., 134 B.R. 450 (Bankr.D.Mass.1991), aff'd, 142 B.R. 584 (D.Mass.1992). Accordingly, expenses for clerical services are not permitted and are disallowed.

VI. Similarity of Time Entries and Insufficiency of Detail

The Trustee objected that each of the 21 fee applications stated the same amount of time for the same type of service. Lesser stated that the firm did not keep contemporaneous time records, and that the fee applications were reconstructed from memory and from reviewing the files. (Tr. at 22-23.)

The Trustee also objected to the lack of specificity of the time records. This lack of specificity necessarily resulted from Castle's initial failure to keep contemporaneous time records and the reconstruction of time records after the fact.

[13] The failure to maintain contemporaneous time records affects the reliability of the records, In re Dawson, 180 B.R. 478, 480 (Bankr.E.D.Tex. 1994), and, although it does not automatically result in the denial of all fees, it does justify a reduction in the fees requested. In re Evangeline Refining Co., 890 F.2d 1312, 1326-27 (5th Cir.1989). Without an opportunity to review actual time records, it is impossible for the Court to determine whether any particular time entry is reasonable.

[14][15][16] Additionally, the description of services provided in the reconstructed fee applications is lacking in detail, making it difficult for the Court to determine if the fees requested are reasonable. Local Bankruptcy *825 Rule 3.03(a)(12)(C) requires the time statement to "describe with particularity the services rendered." Entries such as "Signing Appointment 45 min." or "Phone call to client re: insurance 15 min." fail to adequately describe the services rendered. A fee application which sets forth with specificity the exact nature of the services rendered, the time expended, and the expenses incurred is a prerequisite to making a determination that the services were necessary and reasonable. In re Meyer, 185 B.R. 571, 574 (Bankr.W.D.Mo.1995). The Court "will not indulge in extensive labor and guesswork to justify a fee for an

attorney who has not done so himself." In re Taylor, 66 B.R. 390,393 (Bankr.W.D.Pa.1986); see also J. F. Wagner's Sons Co., 135 B.R. 264, 267 (Bankr.W.D.Ky.1991). The Court finds that a twenty percent reduction in remaining fees is warranted due to Castle's failure to keep contemporaneous time records and resultant lack of detail in their reconstructed time records.

VII. Conclusion

In summary, the Court denies all fees requested for the services of legal assistants and clerical personnel. The Court further reduces the remaining fees for the services of the attorneys by twenty percent. After those deductions, the allowable fees in each case are as follows:

Case Name	Case Number	Amount Requested	Amount Allowed
Pinkins	97-40722	$1,500.00	$863.32
Jones	97-40965	$1,200.00	$730.00
Daberkoe	97-42032	$1,500.00	$706.66
Hall	97-42576	$1,200.00	$550.00
Fields	97-42719	$1,200.00	$573.34
Roberson	97-42790	$1,200.00	$436.67
Peeples	97-42791	$1,200.00	$610.00
Harmon	97-42885	$1,200.00	$526.66
Sanders	97-43062	$1,200.00	$570.00
Dunson	97-43162	$1,200.00	$573.34
Trombley	97-43353	$1,400.00	$740.00
Ellis	97-43356	$1,600.00	$806.67
Finney	97-43414	$1,200.00	$516.00
Asaki	97-43419	$1,200.00	$580.00
Sierra	97-43494	$1,200.00	$563.34
Taylor	97-43661	$1,200.00	$566.67
Singletary	97-43664	$1,200.00	$490.00
Asberry	97-44060	$1,200.00	$493.33
Knox	97-44160	$1,000.00	$506.66
Smith	97-44241	$1,200.00	$616.66
Robertson	97-44564	$1,200.00	$466.66

An order regarding the allowed fees will be entered in each case.

END OF DOCUMENT

EXERCISES

1. What were the main factors listed by the court that persuaded them that the services performed by the legal assistants violated the unauthorized practice of law statutes?

2. Regarding the decision of a client to either file under Chapter 7 or Chapter 13 bankruptcy, suppose the legal assistants argued that they were simply giving information to the client that the client could have gotten from the Internet, in a book, or at the bankruptcy clerk's office, and therefore their conduct did not violate UPL statutes. Evaluate their argument.

3. The attorney for the Castle Law Office argued that the legal assistants were very well trained, and that, while they were not attorneys, their legal services were of the highest quality. Is this a strong argument? How much legal analysis did the court spend on this argument?

4. The attorney for the Castle Law Office argued that, even though an attorney did not meet with clients directly, an attorney did, in fact, review every legal document that each legal assistant prepared and therefore there could be no UPL violation. How did the court handle this argument? Whose argument did you find more persuasive: the court's or the Castle Law Office's? Why?

5. The court concluded that the legal assistants should not have been allowed to sign the client retention letter (i.e., the letter agreeing to represent the client) for the Castle Law Office. What issues are raised by this fact? How did the court handle the matter?

6. For each issue raised by the court regarding the unauthorized practice of law by the legal assistants, what new procedural system would you put in place in the Castle Law Office to allow for correction?

CASE REVIEW

Maloney v. Schwab, 249 B.R 71 (M.D. Pa. 2000).

249 B.R. 71
(Cite as: 249 B.R. 71)

United States District Court,

M.D. Pennsylvania.

In re John C. MALONEY and Christine Maloney, Debtors.

Patricia A. Staiano, United States Trustee, Appellant,

v.

William G. Schwab, Trustee in Bankruptcy For John C. Maloney and Christine Maloney, Appellee.

In re John C. Maloney and Christine Maloney, Debtors.

Sears, Roebuck & Co., Appellant,

v.

William G. Schwab, Trustee in Bankruptcy for John C. Maloney and Christine Maloney, Appellee.

No. 4:97-CV-1940, 4:97-CV-1922.

March 31, 2000.

*72 James G. Watt, Allentown, PA, for John C. Maloney, Christine Maloney, debtors.

Mary Duncan France, Office of the U.S. Trustee, Harrisburg, PA, for Patricia A. Staiano, appellants.

Charles J. Phillips, Baskin, Leisawitz, Heller & Abramowitch, P.C., Berkshire Commons, Wyomissing, PA, for Sears, Roebuck and Company, movants.

Joseph J. Murray, Wilkes Barre, PA, for William G. Schwab, Trustee in Bankruptcy for John Maloney and Christine Maloney, trustee.

MEMORANDUM

KANE, District Judge.

Before the Court is a consolidated appeal docketed in this Court on December 18, 1997. Appellants are Patricia A. Staiano, United States Trustee ("U.S. Trustee"), and Sears, Roebuck & Co. ("Sears"). Pursuant to a briefing schedule set by the Court, Appellant U.S. Trustee filed a supporting brief on August 14, 1998, and an amended supporting brief on August 20, 1998. Appellant Sears filed its supporting brief on August 14, 1998. Appellee William G. Schwab, Trustee in Bankruptcy For John C. Maloney and Christine Maloney, filed no brief in opposition. On October 28, 1998, Judge McClure transferred the above-captioned matter to the undersigned.

This appeal seeks reversal of the Bankruptcy Court's May 12, 1997 Opinion and Order denying the motion of Sears to compel the Chapter 7 Trustee to reconvene the Section 341(a) meeting of creditors to permit the examination of the debtors by Sears' non-attorney representative. Because this Court finds that the court below erred in its legal conclusion that the examination of a debtor at a Section 341(a) meeting of creditors by a non-attorney representative of a creditor constitutes the unauthorized practice of law in Pennsylvania, the decision below will be reversed.

I. Background

On March 5, 1996, John C. and Christine Maloney ("Debtors") filed a voluntary petition under Chapter 7 of the Bankruptcy Code. The U.S. Trustee appointed William G. Schwab (the "Trustee") as the case trustee on March 17, 1996. The meeting ***73** of creditors required to be held pursuant to Section 341(a) of the U.S. Bankruptcy Code, 11 U.S.C. § 341(a) ("Section 341(a) meeting" or "creditors' meeting"), was convened by the Trustee on April 17, 1996.

A paralegal employed by the law firm retained by Sears attended the creditors' meeting on Sears' behalf and requested permission to question the Debtors. The Trustee refused, stating that it was his belief that if he allowed an individual who was not an attorney or an employee of a creditor to question the Debtors, he would be aiding in the unauthorized practice of law. Sears filed a motion on May 8, 1996, requesting that the Bankruptcy Court compel the Trustee to reconvene the creditors' meeting to allow participation by Sears' non-attorney representative. The motion was opposed by the Trustee and by the Debtors. A hearing was held before the Bankruptcy Court on July 16, 1996.

On January 31, 1997, pursuant to her authority under 11 U.S.C. § 341 and 28 U.S.C. § 586(a)(3), the U.S. Trustee directed the Trustee to reconvene the meeting for the purpose of permitting Sears' agent to examine the Debtors. The Trustee withdrew his objection to Sears' motion on February 12, 1997 and notified the parties that he would reconvene the creditors' meeting. On May 12, 1997, the Bankruptcy Court entered an Opinion and Order denying Sears' requested relief and holding that "the examination of a debtor at a first meeting of creditors constitutes the practice of law as that term is interpreted in Pennsylvania" and that "the Bankruptcy Code does not permit a party, unidentified in § 343, to conduct an examination of the debtors at their § 341 meeting, except as permitted by Rule 9010(a)(2)." Opinion and Order at 10, 13.

It is against this factual and procedural backdrop that Appellants appeal the following issues. The U.S. Trustee frames the issues on appeal as follows:

    1. Whether the Bankruptcy Court erred as a matter of law in holding that the examination of a debtor at a meeting of creditors under Section 341(a) of the Bankruptcy Code constitutes the practice of law in Pennsylvania.

    2. Whether the Bankruptcy Court erred as a matter of law in holding that only persons listed in Section 343 of the Bankruptcy Code and their attorneys may examine a debtor at a meeting of creditors under Section 341(a) of the Bankruptcy Code.

Sears frames the issue on appeal as follows:

    1. Whether a non-lawyer representative of a creditor may question a debtor during the meeting of creditors pursuant to Section 341 of the Bankruptcy Code.

II. Legal Standards

[I] This Court has jurisdiction pursuant to 28 U.S.C. §§ 158, 1334. The standard of review for findings of fact with respect to appeals from a bankruptcy court order is the "clearly erroneous" standard. See Fed. R. Bankr.P. 8013; In re Siciliano, 13 F.3d 748, 750 (3d Cir.1994). A bankruptcy court's conclusions of law are reviewed de novo. See Insurance Co. of N. Am. v. Cohn (In re Cohn), 54 F.3d 1108, 1113 (3d Cir.1995).

III. Discussion

Section 341(a) of the U.S. Bankruptcy Code provides that "... the United States Trustee shall convene and preside at a meeting of creditors." 11 U.S.C. § 341(a). The Code further explicitly provides that "[t]he court may not preside at, and may not attend, any meeting under this section including any final meeting of creditors." 11 U.S.C. § 341(c).

Section 343 of the Code provides that the debtor is required to appear for examination under oath at the meeting of creditors. See 11 U.S.C. § 343. The section further provides that "[c]reditors, any indenture trustee, any trustee or examiner *74 in the case, or the United States trustee may examine the debtor." 11 U.S.C. § 343. The examination of a debtor at the creditors' meeting is subject to the parameters set forth in Federal Rule of Bankruptcy Procedure 2004(b) and "may relate only to the acts, conduct or property or to the liabilities and financial condition of the debtor, or to any matter which may affect the administration of the debtor's estate or the debtor's right to discharge." Fed. R. Bankr.P.2004(b).

Federal Rule of Bankruptcy Procedure 2003 specifies that the United States Trustee presides at the creditors' meeting and that the business of the meeting includes the examination of the debtor under oath and may include the election of a trustee or a creditor committee in Chapter 7 cases. See Fed. R. Bankr.P.2003(b)(1). Under the United States Trustee Program, interim trustees appointed by the United States Trustee preside at the creditors' meetings. Trustees, who generally conduct the primary examination at the creditors' meetings and who are responsible for investigating the debtor's financial affairs, are not required to be attorneys. See 11 U.S.C. § 321 (describing eligibility requirements for trustee position, which do not include that person be an attorney).

One additional provision of the Federal Rules of Bankruptcy Procedure is relevant to the issue presented to this Court. Rule 9010(a) provides that:

> A debtor, creditor, equity security holder, indenture trustee, committee or other party may (1) appear in a case under the Code and act either in the entity's own behalf or by an attorney authorized to practice in the court, and (2) perform any act not constituting the practice of law, by an authorized agent, attorney in fact, or proxy.
> Fed. R. Bankr.P.9010(a).

There are a handful of reported cases addressing whether a non-attorney representative of a creditor may question a debtor at a creditors' meeting. Except for the Bankruptcy Court's decision in this case, none hold that the examination of a debtor by a non-attorney at a Section 341(a) meeting constitutes the unauthorized practice of law. See In re Clemmons, 151 B.R. 860 (Bankr.M.D.Tenn.1993); In re Kincaid, 146 B.R. 387 (Bankr.W.D.Tenn.1992); In re Messier, 144 B.R. 617 (Bankr.D.R.I.1992). Two additional courts have addressed the issue of whether non-attorney agents may question debtors at Section 341(a) meetings, but have decided that the issue is a matter of federal rather than state law. [FN1]

> FN1. In In re Gravitt, 1991 WL 497770 (Bankr.E.D.Ky. July 12, 1991), the bankruptcy court relied on an opinion of the Kentucky Bar Association which provided that whether a non-attorney should be permitted to examine a debtor at a Section 341(a) meeting was a question of federal law and that uniformity in these proceedings was desirable. The Gravitt court determined that non-attorneys were permitted to represent creditors and question debtors at Section 341(a) meetings. In State Unauthorized Practice of Law Committee v. Mason, 46 F.3d 469 (5th Cir.1995), the Fifth Circuit determined that Federal Rule of Bankruptcy Procedure 9010(a) explicitly authorized the representation of creditors by non-attorney agents in the bankruptcy process.

[2] This Court is persuaded by the approach of the courts that have considered the issue a matter of state law. Rule 9010(a) of the Federal Rules of Bankruptcy Procedure, set forth above, authorizes

creditors and other specified parties to appear on behalf of themselves, employ an attorney to represent their interests, or use agents as their representatives in any manner that does not constitute the unauthorized practice of law. The qualification on the use of agents and representatives to "perform any act not constituting the practice of law" evidences an intent to permit state law to determine the definition of the practice of law. Accordingly, the relevant question before the Court is whether, under Pennsylvania law, the examination of a debtor at a Section 341(a) meeting constitutes the practice of law.

*75 [3] In In re Clemmons, 151 B.R. 860 (Bankr.M.D.Tenn.1993), the bankruptcy court emphasized the informality of the creditors' meeting in its determination that creditors should be permitted to use non-attorney agents to examine debtors at creditors' meetings under Tennessee law. "The § 341 examination is a simple and inexpensive administrative examination for the benefit of creditors and trustees. It is not an adversary process, but simply a fact finding process." In re Clemmons, 151 B.R. at 862. Section 23-3-203 of the Tennessee Code Annotated describes the practice of law as:

> the appearance as an advocate in a representative capacity or the drawing of papers, pleadings or documents or the performance of any act in such capacity in connection with proceedings pending or prospective before any court, commissioner, referee or any body, board, committee or commission constituted by law or having authority to settle controversies.

T.C.A. § 23-3-101(a). The Clemmons court determined that by applying this definition to the activities engaged in a by a creditor's representative at a Section 341 meeting, it was clear that participation in a creditors' meeting did not constitute the unauthorized practice of law because it did not involve an appearance as an advocate in a representative capacity.

In In re Kincaid, 146 B.R. 387 (Bankr.W.D.Tenn.1992), the bankruptcy court similarly found that the examination of debtors at creditors' meetings did not run afoul of the state statute prohibiting the unauthorized practice of law. The Kincaid court concluded that a creditors' meeting is not a judicial proceeding and does not determine the rights and obligations of parties participating in the process. The court noted that "[t]estimony of debtors at a bankruptcy meeting of creditors is not admissible as direct evidence in a latter adversary proceeding or contested matter." In re Kincaid, 146 B.R. at 389. The bankruptcy court further observed that debtors are required to attend the meetings, but creditors do not lose any substantive rights by failing to attend. See id. at 390. The court also noted that neither the Bankruptcy Code nor the Federal Rules of Bankruptcy Procedure require debtors to be examined by an attorney representing any creditor. See id. Finally, the court decided that Section 341(a) meetings do not involve the concept of advocacy as contemplated in the use of the word "advocate" in the statute prohibiting the unauthorized practice of law. See id.

In re Messier, 144 B.R. 617 (Bankr.D.R.I.1992) involved a slightly different issue. In that case, the bankruptcy court determined that the negotiation of reaffirmation agreements did not constitute the practice of law under Rhode Island law. The bankruptcy court also sua sponte held that when "an agent or employee of a corporate creditor appears at a § 341 meeting, without counsel, to inquire of a debtor within the examination scope permitted under § 343 and the Fed. R. Bankr.P.2004, this does not constitute the unauthorized practice of law within the meaning of R.I. Gen. Laws. § 11-27-1 et seq., and such activity (properly conducted) is permitted in this jurisdiction." In re Messier, 144 B.R. at 619 (footnote omitted).

In Pennsylvania, the unauthorized practice of law is regulated by statute, which provides in relevant part as follows:

> i. General Rule.—Except as provided in subsection (b), any person, including, but not limited to, a paralegal or legal assistant, who within this Commonwealth shall practice law, or who shall hold himself out to the public as being entitled to practice law, or use or advertise the title of lawyer, attorney at law, attorney and counselor at law, counselor, or the equivalent in any language, in such a manner as to convey the impression that he is a practitioner of the law of any jurisdiction, without being an attorney at law or a corporation

complying *76 with 15 Pa.C.S. Ch. 29 (relating to professional corporation), commits a misdemeanor of the third degree upon a first violation. A second or subsequent violation of this subsection constitutes a misdemeanor of the first degree.

42 Pa.C.S. § 2524(a).

The statute prohibits two actions by a non-lawyer—holding himself out as an attorney to the public, and practicing law. There is no allegation in this case that Sears' representative held himself out to the public as being entitled to practice law. Therefore, to run afoul of the statute, the activities conducted by Sears' representative would have to constitute the practice of law.

In the leading case on the unauthorized practice of law, the Pennsylvania Supreme Court stated that it is difficult to precisely define what activities constitute the "practice of law." Shortz v. Farrell, 327 Pa. 81, 193 A. 20 (1937). However, the court found that an attorney applies legal knowledge in three ways:

i. He instructs and advises clients in regard to the law, so that they may properly pursue their affairs and be informed as to their rights and obligations.

ii. He prepares for clients documents requiring familiarity with legal principles beyond the ken of the ordinary layman—for example, wills, and such contracts as are not of a routine nature.

iii. He appears for clients before public tribunals to whom is committed the function of determining the rights of life, liberty, and property according to the law of the land, in order that he may assist the deciding official in the proper interpretation and enforcement of the law.

Id. at 21.

The first two categories described by the court do not apply to the facts of this case. The Sears' representative whose conduct is at issue in this case does not instruct a client on the law. See R. at 15. Further, the record does not disclose that he prepares any document, even routine ones. See R. at 13-19. Accordingly, under Shortz, the only matter at issue in this case is whether the Sears' representative's examination of a debtor at a Section 341(a) meeting constitutes an appearance before a public tribunal.

In Shortz, the Pennsylvania Supreme Court held that an insurance claims adjuster was engaging in the unauthorized practice of law when he appeared before the Workmen's Compensation Review Board ("Board") to examine and cross-examine witnesses. The activities of the adjuster were deemed to fall within the third category of activity—the appearance before public tribunals. See Shortz, 193 A. at 21. First, the court found that the adjuster's representation required him to have a knowledge of relevancy and materiality in order to examine and cross-examine witnesses. Second, the court noted that the record developed before the Board would result in findings of fact that are binding on the courts if there is competent evidence to support the findings. Finally, the court determined that the proceedings, although conducted by an administrative agency, were essentially judicial in nature. Although the members of the Board and its referees are not required to be attorneys, the court noted that the function of persons appearing on behalf of the parties "is to make sure that only proper evidence is admitted, and logically to marshal it for the consideration of the fact-finding tribunal." Id. at 22.

After Shortz v. Farrell, the Pennsylvania Supreme Court further defined the parameters of the practice of law in Dauphin County Bar Ass'n v. Mazzacaro, 465 Pa. 545, 351 A.2d 229 (1975). In that case, the court held that a casualty adjuster who was not an attorney could not represent tort claimants in pursuing damages. The activities pursued by the adjuster included investigating the accident, estimating damages, making a demand on the party from whom recovery was sought, and attempting to negotiate a settlement. See id. at *77 230. The Court noted that to properly value damages and negotiate a settlement required "an understanding of the applicable tort principles (including the elements of negligence and contributory negligence), a grasp of the rules of evidence, and an ability to evaluate the strengths and weaknesses of the client's case vis a vis that of the adversary." Id. at 234. The Supreme Court also recognized that there are instances "when it is clearly within the ken of lay persons to appreciate the legal problems and consequences involved in a given situation and the factors which should influence necessary decisions." Id. at 233. It is when "a judgment requires the abstract understanding of legal principles and a refined skill for their concrete application, the exercise of legal judgment is called for." Id. (quoting Shortz, 193 A. at 21). [FN2]

> FN2. The Bankruptcy Court appeared to place some emphasis on the fact that under Pennsylvania law (as described in Mazzacaro), negotiation of a reaffirmation agreement with a debtor may well constitute the practice of law. However, whether or not negotiation of a reaffirmation agreement constitutes the practice of law in Pennsylvania was not the issue before the Bankruptcy Court. The record in this case does not indicate that the Sears' representative intended to negotiate a reaffirmation agreement with the debtors here. If he had intended to negotiate a reaffirmation agreement, a different issue would have been presented to the Bankruptcy Court, and a different result might permissibly have been reached. See, e.g., In re Carlos, 227 B.R. 535 (Bankr.C.D.Cal.1998) (non-attorney negotiation of reaffirmation agreement with debtor constitutes unauthorized practice of law in California).

Applying these principles to the facts of the instant case, the Court finds that a creditors' meeting held pursuant to Section 341(a) of the Bankruptcy Code does not possess any of the indicia of a fact-finding "public tribunal to whom is committed the function of determining rights of life, liberty, and property" described by the Pennsylvania Supreme Court in Shortz. A trustee makes no findings of fact based on the information elicited at the Section 341(a) meeting. No rights are adjudicated. The tribunal in the bankruptcy process is the court, not the Section 341(a) meeting. Congress specifically intended that the creditors' meeting not function as a tribunal by separating the administrative functions performed at the creditors' meeting from the judicial aspects of the case. See 11 U.S.C. § 341(c) ("[t]he court may not preside at, and may not attend, any meeting under this Section, including any final meeting of creditors").

Not only is a creditors' meeting not a tribunal under Pennsylvania law, but the Court finds that the intended activities of the Sears' representative at the meeting as described in the record did not require an abstract understanding of legal principles or a refined skill for their concrete application. The record in this case indicates that the Sears' representative customarily reviews the debtors' customer file, attends the meeting to ask questions about the merchandise purchased from Sears, describes to the debtors what incentives Sears will offer if debtors reaffirm the debt, and asks questions concerning the debtors' employment. See R. at 14. The testimony of Sears' representative demonstrates that the creditors' meeting is an informal, fact-finding proceeding. [FN3]

> FN3. In its Opinion, the Bankruptcy Court stated that the Unauthorized Practice of Law Committee of the Pennsylvania Bar Association has "considered this very issue and concluded that nonlawyers, whose questioning of a debtor is focused on legal matters in the Bankruptcy Code, 'are engaged in the unauthorized practice of law,' " citing PBA Unauthorized Practice of Law Committee Opinion 96-108. Opinion and Order at 2. The Opinion referenced states that "[i]t is the Opinion of the Pennsylvania Bar Association Unauthorized Practice of Law Committee that non-attorneys participating in Bankruptcy 341 meetings and whose questioning goes beyond mere information gathering to questions focused on legal matters in the Bankruptcy Code are engaged in the unauthorized practice of law as set forth in 42 Pa.C.S.A. § 2524." PBA Unauthorized Practice of Law Committee Opinion 96-108 (emphasis added). That Opinion does not state the proposition that a non-attorney creditor representative engaged in information gathering, of the type described by the Sears' representative here, is engaged in the unauthorized practice of law.

*78 Despite the testimony of Sears' representative regarding the limited scope of his inquiry, the Bankruptcy Court found that the purpose of the creditors' meeting no longer was to assist in the administration of the debtor's estate, but had moved beyond fact-finding to inquisition. The court based its finding on the addition of subsection (d) to Section 341 by the 1994 amendments to the Bankruptcy Code. Section 341(d) requires the trustee to inquire as to whether the debtor is aware of the consequences of seeking a discharge, the ability to file under another chapter, the effect of receiving a discharge, and the effect of reaffirming a debt. See 11 U.S.C. § 341(d). The Bankruptcy Court concluded that this modification opened the door to interrogation on the issues of dischargeability and reaffirmation.

[4] However, in finding that Section 341(d) changed the nature of the proceedings, the Bankruptcy Court misunderstood the intent behind the amendment to Section 341. As noted in the House Report of the Bankruptcy Reform Act of 1994, the amendment to Section 341 "requires the trustee to orally examine the debtor to ensure that he or she is informed about the effects of bankruptcy, both positive and negative. Its purpose is solely informational; it is not intended to be an interrogation to which the debtor must give any specific answers or which could be used against the debtor in some later proceeding." 140 Cong. Rec. H10,766 (Oct. 4, 1994) (emphasis added). Section 341(d) was added to the Code because other protections for the debtor were deleted.

> Since Section 103 of the Reform Act eliminated for most debtors the warnings and explanations concerning reaffirmation previously given by the court at the discharge hearing, it is important that trustees explain not only the procedures for reaffirmation, but also the potential risks of reaffirmation and the fact that the debtor may voluntarily choose to repay any debt to a creditor without reaffirming the debt, as provided in Bankruptcy Code Section 524(f).

Id. As pointed out by the United States Trustee, rather than being a sword for the creditor, Section 341(d) is a shield for the debtor.

IV. Conclusion

Accordingly, for all the reasons discussed above, the Court finds that the Bankruptcy Court erred in its legal conclusion that the examination of a debtor at a Section 341(a) meeting of creditors by a non-attorney representative of a creditor constitutes the unauthorized practice of law in Pennsylvania. This Court holds that, under the facts of record in this case, the proposed examination described by the Sears' non-attorney representative does not constitute the unauthorized practice of law in Pennsylvania. Accordingly, the Court need not address the additional issue raised by the U.S. Trustee on appeal. The Order of the Bankruptcy Court will be reversed in accordance with the foregoing discussion.

END OF DOCUMENT

EXERCISES

1. The court did not find that the legal assistant engaged in the unauthorized practice of law. What were the factors that led the court to this conclusion?

2. What are the differences between the conduct of the legal assistants in *In re Pinkins* and the conduct of the legal assistant in *Maloney?*

Staff Manuals, Quality, Marketing, and Planning

CHAPTER OBJECTIVES

After you read this chapter, you will be able to:
- Discuss what a staff manual is and why it is important.
- Differentiate between a policy and a procedure.
- Discuss why providing quality services is important.
- Explain marketing and various marketing options that are available.
- Identify ethical problems that may arise in carrying out a marketing plan.
- Define "mission statement."
- Explain the planning process.

The law firm of Harris, Martinez, & Baker was a ten-attorney firm that was experiencing growing pains. In response to the problems, the firm hired a consulting firm to offer solutions. The law firm suffered from the following problems.

Law firm staff members received changing and contradictory instructions from partners on policy matters and were frustrated with the lack of effective guidance on how legal services were to be provided. The consulting firm recommended the development of a staff manual to clearly set out what the policies of the firm were regarding a broad range of subjects. The manual would prevent partners from having to decide policy on a fragmented and daily basis and would be a resource for staff members to turn to when partners were unavailable. The consultants recommended that the firm host an Intranet were the staff manual could be accessed electronically by staff and that other internal tools be placed on the Intranet to assist staff in performing their jobs.

There was a general lack of communication among the partners and among staff members. No one knew where the firm was headed. The consulting firm recommended that the firm draft a mission statement, a short-range plan, and a long-range strategic plan to help focus the firm on where it was headed and how it was going to get there. All partners and staff members were to help develop the plan to increase communication. The plan could be placed on the firm's Intranet site so that staff could refer to it at anytime and the plan could be easily changed and modified.

The firm was having a problem bringing in new clients. The consulting firm recommended developing an emphasis on providing quality services to clients. By making quality the number one priority, the firm could receive increased referrals from existing clients and have a product it could market better to the community. The

> consulting firm also recommended that the firm develop a detailed marketing plan that would help it cultivate new clients and expand into new areas.

LAW PRACTICE POLICIES AND PROCEDURES—THE STAFF MANUAL

> Read and digest any staff manual provided. . . . You should know what it says and keep it updated as new policies are published. Despite the comments you will hear describing the manual as out-of-date, it will give you a good overview of office policies. And if the firm bothered to publish the manual, it obviously was important to someone involved in the firm's future and yours. So until you are advised otherwise by someone in authority, presume that the manual states the rules.[1]

In Chapter 1, you were introduced to the "systems" view of management. A system was described as a consistent or organized way of doing something. A system allows managers to create procedures for doing something. By using a system, time is saved, efficiency is increased, and jobs are done uniformly.

One of the ultimate types of systems is a law office staff manual, also called a policy and procedures manual. The purpose of a staff manual is to set out in writing the standing policies and procedures of a law office. The types of policies covered by the staff manual depend on the office, but they can range from personnel policies and how files will be maintained to how letters and pleadings will be formatted (see Figure 3-1). Staff manuals establish and document an efficient and cost-effective way of handling the day-to-day operations of the firm. The manual allows everyone to operate under the same procedures and to quickly find consistent answers to common questions. Without a staff manual, each person develops her own particular method for accomplishing tasks. Law offices need uniformity so that elements are not missed or forgotten. Staff manuals can be used to guarantee each client the same high-quality legal services, every time.

> *In order for . . . staff to provide the quality service that clients require, you need to communicate to them your office and personnel policies and procedures in a clear, effective manner. A staff manual is a necessity to convey . . . policies efficiently and accurately.*[2]

**Figure 3-1
Sample Law Office Staff Manual—Table of Contents**

Law Office Policy and Procedures Manual, 4th ed., Robert Wert and Howard Hatoff, American Bar Association, 2000, p. ix. Reprinted by permission.

Section 1: Introduction
1.1 Purpose and Use of the Manual
1.2 Organization of the Manual

Section 2: Departments and Committees
2.1 Departments According to Principal Areas of Law
2.2 Committees

Section 3: Organization, Management, and Administration
3.1 Firm Resume
3.2 Partners
3.3 Firm Meetings

Section 4: Office Policies
4.1 Diversity
4.2 Policy on Sexual Harassment
4.3 Family and Medical Leave Act
4.4 Code of Personal and Professional Conduct
4.5 Office Hours
4.6 Overtime
4.7 Quality Management/Client Relations
4.8 Weekly Time Report
4.9 Professional Attitude
4.10 Personal Appearance
4.11 Housekeeping

Section 5: Personnel Policies and Benefits
5.1 Employee Classifications
5.2 Compensation
5.3 Leaves of Absence
5.4 Scheduling Vacations
5.5 Holidays
5.6 Personnel Records
5.7 Termination of Employment
5.8 Continuing Legal Education
5.9 Substance Abuse
5.10 Child Care

Section 6: Preparation of Correspondence, Memoranda, and Legal Documents
6.1 Letter Construction
6.2 Memoranda
6.3 Drafts
6.4 Legal Opinion Letters
6.5 Legal Documents

(continued)

Section 7: Office Security and Emergency Procedures
7.1 Emergency Procedures
7.2 Medical Emergencies, Work Injuries, or Accidents
7.3 Data Protection
7.4 Disaster Recovery

Section 8: Financial Management
8.1 Timekeeping Records
8.2 Receipts
8.3 Disbursements
8.4 Petty Cash
8.5 Billing Procedures
8.6 Trust Account

Section 9: File System
9.1 Removal of Files from the Record Room
9.2 The File Opening Form and Worksheet
9.3 Opening a New File
9.4 Returning Files to the Record Room
9.5 Closing Files
9.6 Form Files

Section 10: Technology
10.1 Training
10.2 Word Processing
10.3 Networking
10.4 Docket/Calendar Software
10.5 Time/Billing Software
10.6 WESTLAW/LEXIS
10.7 Security

Section 11: Communication Systems
11.1 Telephones
11.2 Faxes
11.3 Electronic Mail
11.4 Mail Services
11.5 Messenger Services

Section 12: Duplication Services
12.1 Copying Procedures
12.2 Charges for and Recording of Copies Made
12.3 Copyright
12.4 Binding

(continued)

> **Section 13: Equipment, Maintenance, and Supplies**
> 13.1 Supplies
> 13.2 Furniture
> 13.3 Photographic Equipment
> 13.4 Computers
> 13.5 General Maintenance
>
> **Section 14: Library**
> 14.1 Function and Use
> 14.2 Library Organization
> 14.3 Use by Non-Firm Personnel
> 14.4 Client Charges
> 14.5 Department from the Firm
>
> **Section 15: Travel**
> 15.1 Automobiles
> 15.2 Airlines
> 15.3 Hotels
> 15.4 Reimbursement
>
> **Section 16: Miscellaneous**
> 16.1 Marketing
> 16.2 Pro Bono Work
> 16.3 Community and Professional Activities
> 16.4 Malpractice

Staff manuals are particularly helpful when training new employees. New employees can immediately get a feel for how the firm operates and what procedures are to be followed just by reading the manual. This makes the orientation process quicker and less difficult. It is a misconception that staff manuals are only needed in large firms. Small law offices, legal aid offices, and government and corporate law departments need written procedures as well.

> *A small law office I know recently suffered a real crisis. The office had a law office manager that virtually ran all of the systems and procedures for the whole office. She handled all accounting and money transactions, staff payroll, billing, computer use and computer passwords, the firm's form files, everything. Unfortunately, she suffered an unexpected heart attack. She was the only one in the office that knew how all the systems worked. It took the rest of the staff months to piece everything together and the office itself really suffered.*[3]

If a law office does not have a staff manual, consider developing one. Most employers appreciate employees who go beyond their normal job description and take on additional projects that benefit the office. Figure 3-2 shows the steps to put together a staff manual. These types of assignments can sometimes lead to career advancement.

> *You will find that the actual writing of the [staff] manual will bring to light many of the current inefficiencies in your law practice. "It's the way we've always done it" philosophy will slowly give way to "We ought to do it this way, because it is obviously the most cost efficient in terms of time expended."*[4]

WHAT SYSTEMS OR SUBJECTS ARE INCLUDED IN THE STAFF MANUAL?

Figure 3-1 contains a list of systems that are often found in staff manuals. Staff manuals usually cover such items as how the office is organized, ethical and confidentiality policies, personnel-related policies, the use of office equipment, and office procedures for opening new files. Staff manuals can be adapted to the needs of the specific law practice. In general, if management has to reiterate a policy more than once or twice on a matter of importance, the policy should be put in writing.

DRAFTING POLICIES AND PROCEDURES

Staff manuals can contain both policies and procedures. Although the concepts are similar, they also are very different from each other. A **policy** is a specific statement that sets out what is or is not acceptable. A **procedure** is a series of steps that must be followed to accomplish a task. Some firms have separate manuals for policies and procedures. All policies and/or procedures should be detailed, accurate, and succinct (see Figure 3-3). Notice that the procedure in Figure 3-3 is clearly stated, is easy to read, and assigns specific responsibilities, stating *who* is responsible for the tasks. In addition, whenever possible, a due date also is included so that staff members know exactly *when* items are due. When writing policies and procedures, try to strike a balance between having too many details (i.e. overregulating) and having too few. The aim is not to make a bureaucratic, detail-ridden manual, but to have a usable, practical guide.

policy
A specific statement that sets out what is or is not acceptable.

procedure
A series of steps that must be followed to accomplish a task.

ADDITIONAL IDEAS ON ASSEMBLING OR REVISING A STAFF MANUAL

Below are some ideas on putting together or revising a staff manual.

- **Provide electronic access.** Because staff manuals change often, it is best to not have the document in print at all. Instead, give all staff access to the document electronically. This can be done by storing the document on Public or Shared Folders if the firm has an internal computer network (LAN), or on the firm's Intranet. (Intranets are discussed later in this section.)

Figure 3-2
How to Put Together a Staff Manual

1. Approval Stage—Ask approval from your supervisor to begin to put together a list of office procedures. Tell her the benefits of having such policies in writing: to give new employees, to establish minimum acceptable standards in the law office, and to establish a consistent way to handle all client cases the same. You might want to tell your supervisor that you will work on this in your spare time and that it will not affect your regular work (if this is true—always be honest).
2. Information Gathering—Once you have approval to begin working on it, you must gather information. Below are ways to get information regarding your manual.
   a. Call Other Legal Assistants Outside Your Office—Begin by calling your legal assistant friends and acquaintances in other firms. Tell them that you are putting together a staff manual for your office and ask if you could copy or see their firm's staff manual. Many firms will be happy to do this. Some may not want to, but it never hurts to ask.
   b. Contact Any Associations You Belong To—Many legal assistant associations also have resources libraries that have this type of information or have had members that have had similar assignments, so contact them.
   c. Check out from a Law Library or Purchase the ABA *Law Practice Staff Manual* or *Cadence Policy and Procedure Manual*—The American Bar Association publishes the *Law Practice Staff Manual*, 4th ed., 2000. The manual comes on disk. The ABA's manual can be checked out from most law libraries or can be purchased from the ABA for less than one hundred dollars (www.ABANET.org).
   d. Make Observations and Talk to Office Staff—Another way to gather information is to simply observe how the law office operates, how things are being done correctly, and how they could be improved. In addition, talk to all members of the staff (if possible) to get their ideas about how things are being done and how they could be done better. Good insight can be obtained from *all* staff members, including copy clerks, runners, etc.—no one is too low on the "totem pole" to talk to or to get ideas and input from.
3. Drafting Stage—After you have gathered information from many different sources, you are ready to begin drafting the staff manual. As you begin drafting, continue to get the input of other individuals and ask their advice.

(continued)

4. Editing of the Rough Draft—Once you have a working rough draft completed, submit it initially to your supervisor or whoever is supervising the project. Once you have his changes, make the changes and then submit the manual to all staff members for their comments and changes. Coordinate requested changes with your supervisor and make whatever changes are necessary. By including others in the idea and drafting stages, you will make implementing the manual much easier, since other staff members will have an ownership interest in the staff manual.
5. Final Approval by Partners/Executive Committee and Implementation—Before the manual can be finalized, it should be approved by the partners, shareholders or executive committee. Once this is accomplished, the manual should be copied, distributed to all staff, and implemented. During the implementation stage, you will typically find that many changes will need to be made. This is expected.

Docketing Forms
1. **Incoming pleadings.** All incoming pleadings, whether served personally or received in the mail, are entered by the firm's docket clerk in the permanent docket book or computerized record the same day they are received. It is the responsibility of the attorney to see that every incoming pleading reflects a docket date initialed by the docket clerk.
2. **Outgoing pleadings.** It is the responsibility of the secretary to see that a copy of every outgoing pleading is sent to the docket clerk for docketing. No office copy of a pleading is to be placed in the office file until the pleading has been docketed and reflects a docket date initialed by the docket clerk. The entry shall be no later than one day after the pleading is mailed out.
3. **Docket request slips.** All deposition dates, motion dates, hearing dates, etc. should be docketed as soon as they are scheduled. It is the responsibility of the secretary to complete a docket request slip and send it to the docket clerk. The slip will then be returned to the secretary with a docket date initialed by the docket clerk.
4. **Daily and Weekly Docket Reports.** It is the duty of the docket clerk to see that each attorney receives daily and weekly docket reports. Weekly docket reports will be generated and distributed by the docket clerk to attorneys on Fridays for the coming week. Alternatively, attorneys or their secretaries may access the docket system electronically.

**Figure 3-3
Example of a Well-Written Procedure**
Source: Printed with the permission of the NALS.

- **Loose-leaf or three-ring notebooks work well.** If the staff manual cannot be accessed electronically, then put it in loose-leaf form so that pages can be easily updated without having to reprint the whole document.
- **The manual should be accurate, complete, and clear.** The staff manual should be accurate and complete and should be a "how-to" document for the people using it. The manual must be readable and clear so that it can be used as a quick reference guide. Remember, everyone from senior partner to copy clerk will be using the manual; it must be able to be understood by all.
- **List steps to be followed and time frames.** Whenever possible, list a sequence of steps to be accomplished and time frames for each step. This organizes the task and lets the reader know exactly what the individual steps are and when they should be completed.
- **Follow a prototype staff manual.** The ABA publishes the *Law Practice Staff Manual*, 4th edition, which is available at most law libraries or from the ABA www.ABANET.org. The manual is a good place to start if you are drafting one from scratch or redrafting an outdated one. It also comes on disk so that it can be edited quickly and easily.
- **The manual should have a table of contents and an index.** The manual needs to be "user friendly." Also, use a simple numbering system so people can easily cite specific policies.
- **Clarify current questions of staff.** Try to address areas where current staff members have repeated questions.
- **Send it out for review.** Get everyone in the office involved in drafting or revising the manual. It never hurts to get the comments of others and to include them in the process. Consider their suggestions and be open about new ideas and new ways of doing things. The ultimate purpose of the manual is to make the firm as efficient as possible.
- **When writing policies, use titles.** When drafting the manual, never use a person's name to specify who is responsible for a duty; always use a job title.
- **Distribute the staff manual to all employees.** All employees should have a copy of the manual. Typically, staff manuals are handed out to new employees when they are hired.
- **Keep the manual up-to-date.** For the staff manual to be truly useful, it must be kept current. Encourage staff members to submit their ideas for new policies and for revisions in old policies. This is the only way they will truly use the document as it is intended. Law practices are constantly changing, and the staff manual must keep pace. This takes time, but it is time well spent.

STAFF MANUALS FROM AN ETHICS PERSPECTIVE

Staff manuals also are important from an ethical point of view. The manual allows management to draft policies that will deter ethical violations. For instance, a common ethical problem is neglect of client matters. A manual can address this by stating which person is responsible for keeping the calendar, how items will be put on the calendar, and what steps will be taken to avoid missing the deadline. In addition, the staff manual can be used to set out policies on ethical situations, such as the need for strict confidentiality of client information.

STAFF MANUALS ON THE LAW OFFICE INTRANET

An **intranet** is an internal information distribution system based on Internet technology. In short, it is a private "internet" that is used only by law firm staff. A law firm intranet is an internal resource for office staff. When the staff manual is on an Intranet, it is immediately accessible to all staff that have access to a computer, can be updated electronically in one place, and can save thousands of dollars in reduced paper and copying costs. Figure 3-4 shows an example of a law firm intranet. Notice that a law firm intranet can be used to store and disseminate a wide variety of other material.

Intranet
An internal information distribution system used only by a law firm staff.

> *The intranet is a good resource, especially in a large firm. It helps to get information to a large group of people who may be scattered across the nation in different office locations. I have always found the firm directory to be very helpful. Other helpful postings include computer information, such as when the computer system will be shut down for maintenance, or maps for the clients to find the office.*
>
> Linda Rushton, CLA

- Accounting and billing—Access to client time/billing records, firm accounting policies, and accounting forms
- Law library resources—Access to form files, brief banks, CD-ROM products, WESTLAW, LEXIS, and links to many legal sites on the Internet
- Human resources and benefits—Human resource information, including job openings, compensation plans, legal postings, benefit plans, and links to benefit-provider sites
- Continuing legal education—Information related to up-coming CLE seminars, and links to national and local bar association Internet sites related to upcoming CLE seminars
- Client tracking—Client directories, matter lists, contact information, matter numbers, and other client-related information
- Practice areas—Separate pages can be created for each of a firm's departments and specialties. Each specialty can have information specifically related to that area of the law, including links to government regulations and statutes in that area on the Internet, links to case law on the Internet in that area, links to Internet discussion groups on the Internet for that area of law, and resources developed by the firm itself to assist practitioners in that area.

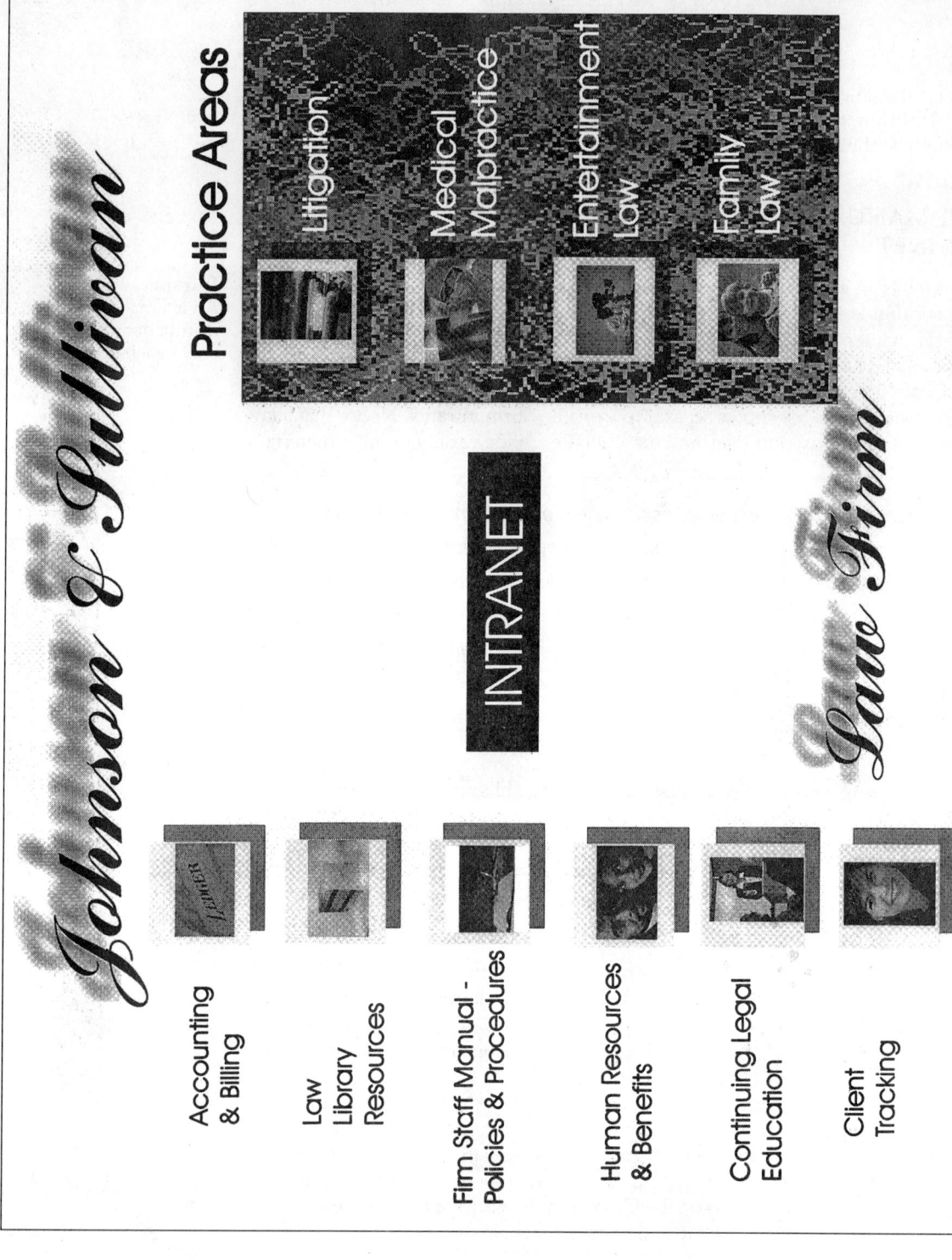

Figure 3-4　Law Firm Internal Intranet

TOTAL QUALITY MANAGEMENT

> *We know exactly what we want in a product or a service, whether it is legal services, a car, or a hamburger and fries: it's quality. Quality is not an accident of nature, nor a gift to the lucky; rather, it is the product of a well-managed organization.* **We** *decide whether ourselves or our organization will have quality as its standard.*[5]

WHAT IS TQM?

> *Clients will most often identify a "quality product" as the [single] most important expectation of their law firm.*[6]

Some might say that total quality management is outdated and has little to do with a legal organization or a practicing legal assistant. Others would say that quality never goes out of style. Because legal organizations must provide quality legal services to stay in business and to please clients—no matter if it is a megacorporation in litigation, an ordinary person needing a will, or serving a corporation in a corporate legal department—that quality must always be the object of focus for a law firm. Legal organizations provide quality legal services through their staff, including their legal assistants. There will always be a market for legal assistants who look out for the client and provide quality legal services. Quality is what distinguishes poor or average legal assistants from exceptional ones. There is also a strong connection between quality and loyalty when it comes to clients. When a client is receiving quality legal services, he or she is usually willing to pay a higher price for those services and has no reason to look elsewhere for a different service provider.

> *Why would a client risk moving his or her business to another firm (and have to pay to educate that firm on his or her business) when his or her current firm, current attorneys, and current legal assistants provide outstanding quality legal services that always meet or exceed his or her expectations?*

Total quality management *(TQM)* is a management philosophy that is based upon knowing the needs of each client and allowing those needs to drive the legal organization at all levels of activity, from the receptionist to the senior partner. From the outset of this book, you have been introduced to the importance of meeting

total quality management
Management philosophy of knowing the needs of each client and allowing those needs to drive the legal organization.

**Figure 3-5
Product-Centered v. Client-Centered Philosophies in a Law Office**

Product-Centered Philosophy	Client-Centered Philosophy
1. Inner forces control the law office.	Client forces control law office decision making.
2. Emphasis is on short-run productivity.	Emphasis on long-range planning for quality and client satisfaction.
3. Law office decisions are forced upon clients.	Law office decisions are made based on client input and meeting clients' needs.
4. Law office provides services they have.	Law office develops new services and modifies existing services based on clients' needs.
5. Law office provides services but does not survey clients to discover whether clients were satisfied with the office's services.	Law office surveys clients before, during, and after services are rendered to ensure clients are satisfied with services and makes appropriate changes based on clients' needs.
6. Law office focuses on short-term profitability and financial success.	Law office focuses on long-range profitability by putting the priority on meeting client needs and providing quality legal services.

client needs and providing quality legal services to clients. TQM is just an expansion on this basic idea. The TQM philosophy of allowing clients' needs to drive an organization, instead of the other way around, was taught to major Japanese corporations in the 1950s by W. Edwards Deming.

The focus of the TQM philosophy is for businesses to compete on *quality*, that is, to compete against other firms on the basis of quality of the service that is provided, as opposed to price or other factors. Figure 3-5 shows the difference between making management decisions based on client needs and based on what is easiest for the law practice to provide.

WHAT ARE SPECIFIC TQM PHILOSOPHIES?

TQM has many nuances and subtleties, but there are several main points to the TQM philosophy.

1. **Management has an overriding duty to ensure that the firm provides quality legal service.** Management must make decisions based on how the decision will affect the quality of the legal services being provided. The distribution of firm assets, including purchases, contracts, and staff employees, must be viewed from the client's perspective and be based on how these decisions will affect the *quality* of the services the firm provides. Likewise, when a legal assistant makes a decision or participates in making a decision about a case, he or she must view that decision in terms of how the decision will affect the quality of legal services, such as deciding what copy service to use, or what litigation support bureau or software to use.
2. **Quality service involves every person in the firm, and everyone must be involved and committed.** Providing quality services begins and ends with

everyone. It is the idea of providing dedication and commitment in everything that is done. It is integrating quality methods into the daily working routine of every member of the staff. It begins with every person taking pride in his or her work.

> *I am a firm believer that the quality of work personally reflects on the paralegal, and I take my work very personally. I know that my name will be attached to everything I do, so I strive to be as perfect as possible, not to say that I do not make mistakes because I am human. Attorneys are perfectionists and any work performed by the legal assistant should be as thorough and complete as possible. Attorneys also count on the legal assistant to be detail-orientated; therefore, the work needs to reflect that as well. Of course, the quality of work rises as the legal assistant gains experience. For an entry-level legal assistant, my advice would be to ask questions and do not stop asking questions, even when you gain experience.*
>
> Linda Rushton, CLA

3. **Quality service is based not on management's or our own perception of quality, but on the perceptions of the client.** In the end, the only person who is going to bring business back to the firm, or refer your services to other businesses, is the client. Therefore, only the client's perception of quality is what counts. Because it is the client's opinion that counts, firms must regularly poll or survey their clients to find out what the firms are doing right, what they are doing wrong, and how they can provide better services to the client. This can be done by interviewing current clients and mailing out client surveys when matters have been resolved, but it is the client's opinions that motivate the firm to change. For a TQM policy to be effective, the firm must be willing to *listen* to the client and to institute *change* to meet the needs of the client. Keep in mind that client needs are constantly changing, so to keep up, the firm must also be willing to change.

> *I used to work for an attorney who was absolutely maniacal about proofreading work products and I used to think she was just being "Type A." As I have progressed in my career, I have learned that there is nothing more irritating than picking up a document that has just been sent out in the mail to find that it is pathetically inadequate in grammar and spelling. Remember, whatever you do it reflects on you, your boss, your firm, and your client.*
>
> Andrea Blanscet, CLA

As a practicing legal assistant, you do not have to wait until the end of a case or matter to ask a client whether or not he or she is pleased with the services you are providing or if there is anything else you can do to be of assistance. Many times, clients will not volunteer that kind of information; you may have to ask.

4. **Quality service depends on individual, team, and ultimately the organization's performance.** In the end, the client will judge the quality of a firm's job based on the client's experience. Thus, everyone involved must be committed to the idea of quality and must be able to share in the financial or other types of benefits the firm receives. TQM eliminates the "we v. they" mentality and rewards all members of the team who contribute. TQM uses project teams to identify and solve problems and increase efficiency.

As a legal assistant, it is crucial that you work as a team member with the other legal professionals that work a client's case. If you see another team member struggling, about to make a mistake, or unable to complete a task in a timely fashion, you have to be willing to help.

> *One of the most important qualities a staff member can have is the self confidence to raise an issue when he or she believes an error has been made without feeling threatened about retaliation.*[7]

5. **Constantly improving systems.** Along with assuring high-quality services, there is also a focus on increasing performance and productivity by constantly improving the systems and the way in which services are provided. This may include purchasing technology, rethinking the ways in which work is performed or routed, deleting repetitive tasks, or doing other things that will increase productivity and efficiency. This is a vigorous process that never ends.

The practicing legal assistant must always be willing to rethink the way something is done. How can I make this better? How can I accomplish this task with higher quality and greater efficiency?

WHAT ARE THE BENEFITS OF THE TQM PHILOSOPHY?

The TQM philosophy offers many benefits.

- **Increased client satisfaction**—The ultimate benefit is that clients are satisfied beyond their expectations, and that based on this satisfaction, they will entrust all their legal services and will refer new clients to the firm.
- **Unity among the management, attorneys and staff**—TQM breaks down the barriers among competing groups in a law practice by focusing everyone on the same goal (unit of purpose) and by allowing all involved to share in the

profits of the business. This can be done by awarding bonuses, giving awards, or recognizing outstanding performance. The "we v. they" mentality is a thing of the past.

> *What is the legal assistant's role in delivering and assuring quality legal services? The legal assistant must accept responsibility for taking the initiative to do what needs to be done to resolve problems and extend first-rate service to the customer (the attorney and the . . . client).*[8]

- **Continuously seeking to improve performance and productivity**—TQM seeks to improve the quality of legal services to clients by increasing staff efficiency and productivity, not just once or twice a year, but constantly to improve the system. This includes all members of the staff checking the quality of their own work, learning advanced technologies, and doing whatever is necessary to provide the client with the best service.

HOW IS TQM IMPLEMENTED?

TQM can be implemented by hiring professional consultants to develop systems for obtaining client feedback and for educating staff members on total quality management techniques. To a lesser degree, TQM also can be implemented by reading about the subject, by simply accepting the principles of TQM, by being responsive to client needs, and by recognizing the effect management decisions have on the quality of legal services being provided. In effect, never forget that quality services are what everything else in the firm depends on.

HOW TQM APPLIES TO LEGAL ASSISTANTS

> *Our organization's philosophy is that quality is not an option, but rather an expected and required performance criteria for all employees of the organization. As a legal assistant manager, satisfactory performance is dependent upon our ability to maximize lawyer and client satisfaction providing the highest level of service possible through the use of legal assistants and, through greater efficiency, to provide this level of quality to our clients at a reasonable and acceptable cost.*[9]

From a TQM standpoint, a legal assistant serves two clients: the attorney (i.e. the internal client) and the end client (i.e. the external client). For a legal assistant to succeed, it is necessary that he or she provide high-quality legal service that satisfies *both* of these clients. Quality should be a way of life whether or not it is officially endorsed by the law office. This philosophy of satisfying clients both internally and externally may lead to advanced career opportunities, increased pay, and better job evaluations. The TQM philosophy also leads to a better work environment because all persons have a say in how things are done.

MARKETING

marketing
Educating consumers on quality legal services.

In Chapter 1, **marketing** was defined as the process of educating consumers on quality legal services that a law office can provide. Thirty years ago, law office marketing was virtually nonexistent. It was not until the landmark Supreme Court case of *Bates v. State Bar of Arizona*, 433 U.S. 350 (1977) that this began to change. In *Bates*, two young attorneys placed an ad in the *Arizona Republic* that stated: "Do you need a lawyer? Legal services at very reasonable fees." In response, the Arizona State Bar Association took disciplinary action against the attorneys. The U.S. Supreme Court held that a ban on attorney advertising was a violation of the First Amendment right to commercial free speech and that it was a restraint of trade. Today, attorney advertising is a given. With nearly one million attorneys practicing law, the "Why should we market our practice?" question has long been forgotten. The increased competitiveness of the legal field has forced law practices to promote themselves or face the reality of getting left behind by losing business to more aggressive firms. In addition, law offices not only compete against other law offices, they also compete against accounting firms when it comes to handling some types of tax matters, real estate companies regarding real estate transactions, and other types of organizations as well. The only question truly left for a law office is *how* to market itself.

> *Many lawyers strongly believe that advertising undermines the dignity of the legal profession. Others argue that it not only allows law firms to operate as businesses, but also provides an important consumer benefit.*[10]

WHY IS MARKETING IMPORTANT TO LEGAL ASSISTANTS?

Marketing is the job of everyone in a private law office. Your job depends on the firm's ability to find and serve additional clients. Therefore, the legal assistant has a vested interest in the marketing function. Your friends, family members, acquaintances, social groups, and fellow legal assistants are worthy of your marketing effort. Make sure people know the name of the organization you work for, network with other professionals, and be prepared to talk to others about what your law office does. By marketing your firm, you will establish that you have an interest in and loyalty to the firm, and you also will be building in some degree of job security. Law offices cannot do business without new clientele.

> *Although my position is in no way a "marketing" position, I find that I inadvertently do a lot of marketing for my firm by virtue of my involvement with my local legal assistant organization. Also, I was recently interviewed by a statewide legal publication regarding an upcoming article about legal assistants. My name, position, and employer were included in the article. These types of things always reflect positively on the firm or organization for which you are employed.*
>
> Lenette Pinchback, CLA

MARKETING GOALS

There is a misconception that advertising and marketing are the same thing. They are not. Advertising is simply getting your name out to the public. Marketing, on the other hand, includes advertising, but is much more. Marketing encompasses providing quality services to clients, gaining insight and feedback into client needs, having a good reputation in the community, and having good public relations. Law office marketing has focused objectives and goals.

- Educate clients and potential clients regarding the firm's array of services
- Educate clients and potential clients as to the particular expertise of the firm in certain areas
- Create goodwill and interest in the firm
- Create positive name recognition for the firm
- Create an image of honesty, ethics, and sincere interest in clients
- Publicize the firm's accomplishments to the profession and community
- Educate clients on changes in the law, thus creating client confidence in the firm
- Improve the firm's competitive position in the marketplace
- Obtain referrals from other attorneys
- Maintain communication with existing clients
- Increase client loyalty and client retention
- Increase staff morale and reinforce the firm's self-image

BASIC RESTRICTIONS ON MARKETING

There are several restrictions on law office marketing. These restrictions involve ethical obligations and are discussed in depth at the end of this chapter, but the most fundamental restriction is that, no matter what the marketing is, it must not be false or misleading.

> *If a legal assistant is asked to input, proofread, or review marketing materials, he or she should take extra care that there is nothing false or misleading contained therein.*[11]

TYPICAL LAW PRACTICE MARKETING OPTIONS

Many larger firms have a marketing department or a marketing director who coordinates the firm's marketing efforts. The importance of having a well-prepared marketing plan is essential to effective marketing. However, you need to have an understanding of what kind of marketing is done in law practice before we get to the plan itself.

- **Quality legal services**—There's that word again: *quality*. Before a firm can market its services, it is essential that it have something of quality to market! Keep in mind that it is always easier to sell a quality product that people want to buy than to sell a product you want to sell. Earlier in this book, it was explained how important existing clients are for bringing repeat business back to the firm and for making referrals to others. This is why quality is so important. Everything a firm does affects quality and therefore affects its marketing effort.

An employee who treats clients rudely, a docket control system that does not work, or billing practices that make clients upset in the end are quality problems. It is for this reason that law office management must ensure quality. Marketing and quality are parts of the same equation.

> *There is no substitute for the quality of the work of the lawyers [and paralegals]. No marketing ploy, no firm brochure, no slick public relations program will cover for the poor work of an attorney [or paralegal].*[12]

Assuming the firm has a commitment to quality, what marketing techniques can the firm employ to get the word out about its great services to clients (see Figure 3-6)?

- **Firm Internet site**—Operating a firm Internet site is a standard marketing practice for many law firms (see Figure 3-7). A definite advantage of a firm Website is that unlike the office itself, it stays open twenty-four hours a day, seven days a week, to local, national, and international customers and clients. A Website is a particularly good idea for a legal organization with a specialized practice. A firm with a unique niche or specialized practice can reach potential clients anywhere in the world. Many organizations have found the marketing potential of a Website to be enormous. In addition, because it operates all the time, it is cost effective when compared to other types of marketing alternatives.

  Depending on the information on the Website, the organization can also provide timely information to clients and potential clients. Many legal organizations offer information in their specialty area that would be useful to their clients. Thus, a Website can provide a service to an organization's clients that hopefully will create goodwill for the firm. A Website can also be used for recruiting employees, such as legal assistants, and other staff. Notice that the law firm in Figure 3-7 uses a Website to inform potential clients about who they are and what their practice areas are, to offer visitors a "resource library" of free information they might find helpful, to provide information about their community activities to create goodwill, to provide

**Figure 3-6
Marketing Options**

Internet site
Firm brochures and resume
Firm newsletter
Information brochures
Public relations:
- Belonging to boards, associations, and community groups
- Speaking at public functions
- Issuing press releases
- Handling publicized pro bono cases
- Volunteering in "law day" activities
- Volunteering staff time to help with fundraisers for community groups

Promotional materials (folders, pencils, with law office logo)
Firm open house
Business cards/letterhead/announcement cards
Public advertising:
- Yellow Page ads
- Newspaper ads
- Television ads
- Radio ads

Client seminars
Marketing to existing clients
Belonging and serving in legal associations
Direct mail (not allowable in some states)

a recruiting site listing open positions and selling the firm to potential applicants, to explain information about their attorneys and their particular areas of expertise, and much more.

We want to be THE online source for information on U.S. immigration law. We have worked for five years to develop a Website that includes nearly 2,000 original articles on immigration law, 100-plus government forms . . . a high-traffic discussion board on immigration law, an advocacy center with information and links to dozens of immigration-related bills pending in Congress . . . and a good deal more. We also distribute an e-mail newsletter that is typically 50-plus pages of the latest news and analysis in our field. By developing strong content, we have been able to develop a regular and substantial readership. The site has had more than 13 million hits to date and the newsletter is e-mailed to 21,000 subscribers every month. . . . It is the engine that has helped our firm grow from a solo practice to one of the nation's largest immigration law firms in just five years.[13]

Johnson & Sullivan

Chicago - Los Angeles - New York - Washington, D.C., London - Tokyo

Law Firm

- Employment
- Attorney Profiles
- Guest Book
- About J&S
- Resource Library
- Practice Areas

Figure 3-7 Internet Site

While firm Internet sites are allowed, there is at least one case where an attorney violated a state's ethical rules by misusing e-mail. In *In re Canter,* Tenn. Sup. Ct., Nos. 95-831-O-H, etc. (6/5/97), the Tennessee Supreme Court found that an attorney who sent an e-mail advertisement message to thousands of Internet groups and lists (called "spamming") had violated the state's ethical rules. The message did not comply with state rules regarding noting that the message was an advertisement and a copy was not filed with the Board of Professional Responsibility as required.

- **Firm brochure/resume**—A firm brochure is typically a pamphlet that informs the general public about the nature of the firm (see Figure 3-8). In many ways, it is like a resume, and some even call it a firm resume. Firm brochures often contain the following types of information.

    (a) History of the firm
    (b) Ideology or philosophy of the firm
    (c) Services offered by the firm (typically the types of law it practices or departments)
    (d) The firm's fee or billing policies
    (e) Description of the firm's attorneys (background, items of interest, awards, degrees, etc.)
    (f) Description of the firm's support staff
    (g) Address and phone number
    (h) Whether the firm has a newsletter or other types of client services
    (i) Notable firm accomplishments
    (j) Important clients the firm has represented (must have client's permission)

Figure 3-8 is a firm brochure for a smaller law office. In some cases, this may be the only brochure the law office has. Larger firms typically take a different marketing approach. Instead of having one brochure that markets the whole firm, they may have separate brochures for each department or brochures that target specific industries. Figure 3-9 is an example of a large law firm's brochure that markets its legal health care department to the health care industry.

- **Firm newsletter**—Firm newsletters are a popular way of maintaining contact with clients and generating goodwill. Firm newsletters can be on a single topic, such as real estate, or on a potpourri of topics. Some firms focus on a different legal issue in each issue: family law, real estate, tax, and so on. It is important that the firm know and understand who its clients are and what type of information would be beneficial to the clients. Another popular topic for newsletters is to inform clients of legislative changes, whether local, state, or national. Newsletters can be produced by using an in-house desktop publishing program, by hiring an advertising consulting firm to produce and help write the newsletter, or by purchasing ready-made legal newsletters. With a ready-made newsletter, all the law office has to do is add its logo and firm name and address. Newsletters can be purchased from several sources, including the ABA's Client Update, Section on General Practice (www.ABANET.org/genpractice/clientup/clientup.html).

A Word About Our Firm

We are a general practice law firm, established in 1972 with four attorneys. We can handle almost every type of legal work that you, your family or your business may require. We take great pride in our team of lawyers, legal assistants, legal secretaries, and staff members. Each lawyer, legal assistant and legal secretary is an expert in one or more fields. This expertise allows us to provide superior legal services in a number of fields of law (See our "Legal Services" section). We hope you will meet our well-qualified team and allow them to work together for your benefit.

APPOINTMENTS: We prefer to work by appointment. Agreeing on the date and hour to get together allows both of us to make better use of our time. It is more efficient for us and more economical for you if we meet at our office. If due to illness or disability you are unable to come to our office, we can make arrangements to meet in the most convenient place for you. Our office is open from 8:30 to 5:00 Monday through Friday for appointments. If an unusual situation requires, an appointment can be arranged for other days and times. If you are confronted with a legal emergency, you won't need any appointment. Just give us a call!

Selecting a Lawyer

We will help you select the right member of the firm to handle your work. Contact any of our lawyers that you know, or call the office number and speak to the receptionist. When you explain the type of legal matter that concerns you, you will be referred to someone in our firm who is well-qualified for that type of work. We will introduce you, at your convenience, to the lawyer we believe will be able to handle your legal need most effectively (See the bibliographical profiles in the "Our Lawyers" section). If you consider one of our lawyers to be your lawyer, continue to do so and feel free to consult with him at any time. We are here to serve you!

Our Work

When you retain our firm, there should be a clear understanding between us about the extent of the work we are authorized to do. We will discuss the types of legal remedies or legal work required by the situation and the estimated time and legal expense involved. It is a good time to be practical. If, as the work progresses, there are unexpected developments which result in a longer time period or greater expense than anticipated, we will tell you when we recognize this.

DISBURSEMENTS: The work we do for you may require us to make disbursements. Sometimes the estimated disbursements are payable in advance. Sometimes they are b
RETAINERS: In many cases, our office policy requires an advance payment, kn payments are deposited in our trust account and are paid to us periodically as your wor

Our Lawyers

Edward R. Parker (Ned), born Richmond, Virginia, June 19, 1929; admitted to bar, 1952, Virginia. Preparatory education, University of Virginia (B.A., 1951); legal education, University of Virginia (LL.B., 1952). Adjunct Assistant Professor, T.C. Williams School of Law, University of Richmond 1973-1979. Legal Specialities: Estate Planning, Administration of Decedent's Estate, Business Law and Taxation.

Henry R. Pollard, IV (Harry), born Richmond, Virginia, August 5, 1943; admitted to bar 1967, Virginia. Preparatory education, Hampden-Sydney College (B.S., 1964); legal education, University of Richmond (LL.B., 1967). Legal Specialities: Litigation, Business Law, Commercial Real Estate, Securities Law.

William N. Pollard, born Richmond Virginia, April 4, 1945; admitted to bar 1971, Virginia. Preparatory education, Hampden-Sydney College (B.S., 1967); legal education, University of Virginia (J.D., 1971). Legal Specialities: Real Estate, Business Planning and Corporate Law, Litigation, Estate Planning, Administration of Decedent's Estates, Family Law.

Legal Services

BUSINESS AND CORPORATE: Partnerships, incorporation of businesses, advising individuals, partnerships and corporations, business contracts.
PERSONAL INJURY CLAIMS: Investigation and evaluation of claims for injuries resulting from accidents, bringing lawsuits and conduct of trials to enforce claims.
GENERAL TRIAL WORK: Bringing or defending lawsuits in a variety of legal disputes, including bankruptcy.
WORKERS' COMPENSATION: The representation of persons injured on their jobs.
WILLS AND TRUSTS: The preparation of wills, and of revocable and irrevocable trusts.
ESTATE PLANNING: The preparation of a plan for the transfer of your assets prior to or upon your death to carry out your wishes in a cost efficient manner.
ESTATE ADMINISTRATION: Serving as executor or representing the executor or family of the deceased person in settling an estate.
TAX AND FINANCIAL PLANNING: Planning the shape of business and personal transactions for minimum tax impact, representation before Federal and State tax authorities, answering tax questions.
REAL ESTATE TRANSACTIONS: The sale or purchase of real estate, mortgage transactions, leases, contracts, title searches and title insurance.
INVESTMENT MANAGMENT: Offering investment counceling on your investment portfolio through your trust or directly.
FAMILY LAW: Adoptions; appointment of guardians, and conservators; separation agreements, divorces; annulments; and legal separations.

Our Locations

We are easily accessible to you. Richmond: Take the Staples Mill Road West Exit off Interstate 64 and we are at 5511 Staples Mill Road between Southside and Northside Avenues. Tidewater: In Norfolk, travel east on Northampton Boulevard (Route 13) from its intersection with Interstate 64 to the northeast corner of Diamond Springs Road and Northampton Boulevard.

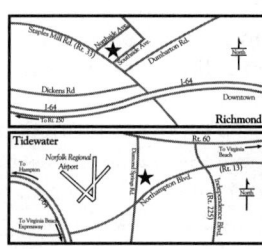

Parker, Pollard & Brown, P.C.
Attorneys at Law

5511 Staples Mill Road
Richmond, Virginia 23228
(804) 262-4042

1300 Diamond Springs Road
Northampton Executive Center
Virginia Beach, Virginia 23455
(804) 460-5050

Parker, Pollard & Brown, P.C.
Attorneys at Law

5511 Staples Mill Road
Richmond, Virginia 23228
(804) 262-4042

1300 Diamond Springs Road
Northampton Executive Center
Virginia Beach, Virginia 23455
(804) 460-5050

Figure 3-8
Small Law Firm Brochure
Printed with permission of Parker, Pollard, and Brown, P.C.

Health Representation – Skills and Experience

Reed Smith's Health Care Group works to solve its clients' problems. Our representation begins by listening to you — the client. Systematically, our lawyers will analyze complex problems, advise you on various courses of action and, when necessary, advocate on your behalf to achieve a prompt and reasonable solution.

Legislative and Regulatory: Legislative representation for health care clients includes drafting and advocacy on proposed and enacted health care legislation. We have successfully challenged major regulatory actions through negotiations with federal agencies, including HCFA, OMB, the FTC, and others, and we regularly advise clients on a host of regulatory compliance issues. The firm assists clients throughout the legislative and regulatory process by drafting comments, testimony and legislative amendments, as well as presenting clients' positions directly to Members of Congress, Administration officials, and key regulatory personnel. A number of our attorneys previously served in high-level positions with both Republican and Democratic administrations, as well as in agency and various congressional positions.

Legal Fees

The particular backgrounds of our health attorneys make it possible for our clients to obtain comprehensive, targeted legal advice at competitive prices. Moreover, we believe that our wide range of specialties saves our clients money, if by using our services they have access to a coordinated team, and can thus avoid the need to consult specialists at a number of firms. Our health group is often retained by other law firms on specific projects requiring a high degree of technical advice, such as reimbursement, fraud and abuse, biotechnology, and the like. We are happy to provide more detailed information on our fee structure and billing procedures.

Future

Reed Smith attorneys welcome the opportunity to talk with you about your company, business, or organization. We would like to hear how the changing health care environment affects you, and discuss how Reed Smith can bring thoughtful, innovative, and responsive solutions to your health care problems. The lawyers in the Reed Smith Health Care Group are listed on the card at the end of this brochure. Please feel free to call any of them to discuss your particular needs.

Source: Reed Smith & McClay. Printed with permission.

Figure 3-9 Large Law Firm—Specific Industry Brochure
Copyright Reed, Smith, Shaw, & McClay. Printed with permission.

- **Informational brochures**—These are brochures that are aimed at informing clients about a specific topic such as "Why You Need a Will," "What to Do in Case of an Auto Accident," "How to Set Up Your Own Business," or "How to Protect Your Ideas through Copyrights, Trademarks, and Patents." They are informational pieces that are used to inform clients about legal problems.
- **Public relations**—Generating goodwill and a positive public image is a long-standing way that firms have marketed themselves. Being members of social groups, churches, committees, nonprofit boards, and associations is a way that legal assistants and attorneys can promote themselves and their firms.

    Speaking at public meetings and association meetings is also a way of attracting interest and goodwill. Handling pro bono cases and issuing press releases when a firm wins a case or achieves other accomplishments that the public would be interested in are other ways of generating and maintaining good public relations.
- **Firm open house**—Some firms hold annual open houses, where clients and visitors can come to the firm and socialize with attorneys and staff members outside the normal pressures of coming to the office with legal problems.
- **Business cards, letterhead, announcement cards**—Announcement cards are used quite frequently by law offices. An announcement card is usually a postcard that is sent to other firms when new attorneys have been added to the firm and it wants to publicize the change or when firms merge.
- **Public advertising—yellow pages, newspaper, television, and radio ads**—Public advertisements also are a popular form of marketing. They come in all sizes and shapes and in all price ranges.
- **Firm seminars**—Some firms put on seminars that are aimed at educating their clients or the general public (prospective clients) on legal issues. They can relate to any legal topic that is of interest. For example, businesses might be interested in the legal issues of hiring, firing, and evaluating employees and employee benefits. Individual clients might be interested in tax planning, trusts and estates, and other issues. Client seminars are usually put on to create client loyalty. Firm seminars should be conducted by an attorney (see *Doe v. Condon*, 2000 WL718448 (S.C.), included at the end of this chapter.
- **Direct mail pieces**—Some firms also send out direct mail pieces aimed at a specific audience. Usually, the pieces are unsolicited; that is, they are sent out to people without being requested. For example, if your firm primarily handles real estate matters, you might send out a letter to all real estate businesses. Note, however, that direct mail is very controversial, especially when the mailing is targeted to a specific group. Ethical rules in some states strictly prohibit targeted mailing under the theory that it is direct solicitation. Attorneys are specifically prohibited from directly soliciting clients.

- **Involvement in legal associations**—Attorneys and legal assistants also can market themselves by being active in local, state, and national bar and legal assistant associations. Many firms that involve themselves in these types of organizations gain the respect and goodwill of others and may gain referrals from another firm that may not have the expertise to handle a particular type of case.
- **Sending information to clients that you know will be of interest to them**—Whenever you come across information that you think will interest clients, bring it to the attention of your supervising attorney and have the attorney send it to them. For example, if you come across a newspaper article that concerns their business or new laws that might affect them, clip it out and have the attorney send it to them. Or, if you come across a case that they might be interested in, get your attorney's approval and send it to them with a note. (And do not bill them for it)! Clients appreciate when the law office takes a personal interest in them.
- **Marketing your services to existing clients**—A firm's current clients are among its biggest assets. Firms not only want to market to new clients but also need to keep the business of their current clients. Thus, firms will typically spend a great deal of time cultivating their existing clients using techniques described earlier, such as newsletters and client seminars. Firms also have other techniques for marketing to existing clients.

    (a) **Cross-selling**—**Cross-selling** refers to selling additional services to existing clients. For instance, suppose a law office represented XYZ business in a tax matter. But XYZ used another firm to handle its personnel disputes. If possible, the law office would like to cross-sell XYZ to use its firm for both the tax matter and the personnel matters.

    (b) **Client questionnaires**—Many firms send out client questionnaires at the end of a legal matter to see how the client felt about the services that were provided. In addition to this being a quality-control device, it also is a marketing technique because it is aimed at correcting problems that the client might have had.

    (c) **Keeping the firm's name in front of the client**—What happens if a client's case is completely finished and the client has no other business at the time? Should the firm forget about the client? No, most firms continue to try to keep in contact with the client with newsletters, seminars, letters, and holiday cards. Firms want clients to feel wanted and be reminded that the firm is there to serve them.

    (d) **Developing client relationships**—Whom would you rather do business with: friends or strangers? Unquestionably friends, because you trust them and feel comfortable with them. It is this kind of relationship that firms want to promote.

    (e) **Thanking clients for referring others to you**—Always send a thank you letter to clients (or other attorneys) for making referrals to the office.

cross-selling
Selling additional services to existing clients.

THE ROLE OF THE RAINMAKER

rainmaking
Bringing in new clients to a law office.

Rainmaking refers to the ability to bring in new clients to a law office. Some law offices bring attorneys into the firm for the sole purpose of being "rainmakers." Some rainmakers are well connected politically or have inroads into certain industries. Rainmakers use their influence and skills to bring new clients into the firm. However, a recent survey of successful rainmakers found, without exception, that helping their clients achieve their business goals and dreams was what made them a good rainmaker. One rainmaker summed it up: "I like to think that I have a special relationship with my clients. My legal antennae are always sensitive to any issues which may affect them. . . . It gives them comfort to know we're here. They can sleep because the 'national guard' is awake." Many private law offices use rainmakers in their marketing scheme.

THE MARKETING PLAN

> *Sadly, although many [firms] would not admit it, they practice a haphazard approach to marketing. They proceed without direction, wasting valuable funds with an unfocused plan. These costly mistakes cause many . . . to question the value of marketing as a component in their firm's budget.*[14]

marketing plan
The goals that a marketing program is to accomplish and a detailed strategy of how the goals will be achieved.

Although there are many options a marketing program can take, it is important that a law practice develop a detailed marketing plan. A **marketing plan** specifies the exact goals that the marketing program is to accomplish and establishes a detailed strategy of how the goals will be achieved. The firm marketing plan should include the following.

- Overall goals of the marketing program
- Strategies and activities that will be necessary to obtain the goals including who, what, when, how, and in what order the activities will be implemented
- Estimated cost of the marketing program
- Estimated profit the successful marketing program would bring in

The marketing plan and the strategic business plan are related documents. To develop an effective marketing plan, consider Figure 3-10. Additional information on law office marketing plans and law office marketing in general can be obtained from the Legal Marketing Association (www.legalmarketing.org).

MARKETING—AN ETHICS PERSPECTIVE

Although ethical limitations on marketing have eased up during the past fifteen years, there are still many pitfalls that can occur from an ethical perspective, including making false or misleading statements in an advertisement, general requirements about any advertisement made, directly soliciting a client, or holding an attorney out as a specialist. Figure 3-11 contains a marketing ethics checklist.

1. **Develop a Strategic Business Plan for the Firm**—The firm needs to know who it is, what business it is in, who its competitors are, what areas are the most profitable, who its clients are, what the client's needs are, and in what direction the firm is headed. All of these things have a direct bearing on the marketing program.
2. **Determine Specifically What Target Market the Marketing Plan Will Be Aimed at and What the Goals of the Marketing Program Will Be**—The firm must decide exactly what the purpose of the marketing plan is. Is it to expand the firm's expertise into additional areas? Is it to expand into different types of clients? Is it into a new geographical area?

Types of Client Markets:
- Government—federal, state, local;
- Business Organizations—publicly owned, privately owned, non profit institutions, small businesses, large businesses;
- Labor organizations;
- Individuals—middle class, wealthy, disadvantaged.

Legal Specialty Markets
- Administrative law
- Admiralty law
- Antitrust law
- Banking law
- Bankruptcy law
- Civil rights law
- Collections law
- Computer law
- Contract law
- Corporate law
- Labor law
- Landlord and tenant law
- Litigation
- Military law
- Municipal finance law
- Oil and Gas law
- Real Estate law
- Criminal law
- Employee benefit law
- Entertainment law
- Environmental law
- Estates, trusts, and probate
- Family law
- Immigration law
- Insurance law
- International law
- Social Security law
- Tax law
- Tort law
- Water law
- Workers' compensation law

3. **Research the Market**—When you have determined what your goals are and what your target group is, you still need to find out about the target group. You need to know its wants and needs, who it is, where it is, and how you can serve it.

Researching the Market:
- Study your own marketing successes/failures;
- Study the marketing efforts of your competitors;
- Survey your target group members (talk to them, know their needs);
- Use in-house surveys to survey your own clients (what do they need/want);
- Talk to consultants;
- If it is a specific group, read its trade journals and find out what issues are important to it.

(continued)

**Figure 3-10
Developing the Marketing Plan**

Adapted from Austin G. Anderson, *Marketing Your Practice* (American Bar Association, 1986), 64. Reprinted by permission of the American Bar Association. Also, from Hollis Weishar and James Durham, *The Complete Guide to Marketing Your Law Practice*, American Bar Association, 1999. Reprinted by permission.

4. **Examine Problems**—Now that you know your goals and you have some market research, what problems will impede the firm from reaching those goals? Anticipate what the problems will be and devise solutions to them.
5. **Develop Specific Strategies and an Action Plan for Meeting the Goals**—In this stage you must set specific strategies for achieving the goal. How are you going to get there? What marketing techniques will convey your message and reach the target group the best? What pricing will you use? A plan or time line should be developed stating exactly when each step of each strategy or marketing technique is to be accomplished, and who is going to accomplish it. All the strategies should be coordinated and complement one another.
6. **Develop a Marketing Budget and Analyze Resources**—In this stage you must determine whether the firm's resources are large enough to carry out the specific marketing plan you laid out in the previous step. It is crucial that enough resources be available to carry out the plan. If the firm does not have the resources to carry out the plan, the plan may need to be scaled back.

Figure 3-11 Marketing the Law Office—Ethics Tips

1. **Do Not Use Examples of Past Performance**
   Do not use examples of past client successes. This may be interpreted as guaranteeing future results, even though every client's case is different and has a different set of factual and legal arguments.
2. **Keep Copies of All Marketing Pieces**
   Ethical rules in most states provide that a copy of the marketing piece or advertisement must be retained by the law office for a certain period of time (sometimes years) after the campaign is completed.
3. **No Direct Solicitation**
   Direct solicitation to unknown, prospective clients is not allowed.
4. **Language Should Be Carefully Drafted**
   The language of all marketing pieces should be carefully drafted to reflect only factual or quantitative information so that it is not subject to interpretation as being false or misleading. Words such as "specializing" and other such words cannot be used in advertisements in some states.
5. **When in Doubt, Have It Approved First**
   If you are uncertain if a marketing piece is ethical, most states will allow the firm to submit it to a disciplinary panel (before publication) where it can be reviewed to see if it complies with the state's ethics rules.

FALSE OR MISLEADING STATEMENTS Attorneys are not allowed to make false or misleading statements in any kind of marketing or advertising piece. Rule 7.1 of the ABA *Model Rules of Professional Conduct* states:

> A lawyer shall not make a false or misleading communication about the lawyer or the lawyer's services. A communication is false or misleading if it:
>
> (a) contains a material misrepresentation of fact or law, or omits a fact necessary to make the statement considered as a whole not materially misleading;
> (b) is likely to create an unjustified expectation about results the lawyer can achieve or states or implies that the lawyer can achieve results by means that violate the Rules of Professional Conduct or other law; or
> (c) compares the lawyer's services with other lawyers' services, unless the comparison can be factually substantiated.

The Ethics 2000 Commission is recommending a substantive change to Rule 7.1 by deleting subsections (a), (b), and (c). Rule 7.1 would simply state: "A lawyer shall not make a false or misleading communication about the lawyer or the lawyer's services." This is a fairly straightforward ethical rule. Attorneys cannot promote themselves using advertisements that are less than truthful. Subpart (b) of the rule prohibits an attorney from running an advertisement about the results in a specific case. Figure 3-12 shows several examples of advertisements that are false or misleading.

ADVERTISING IN GENERAL Rule 7.2 of the *Model Rules* states some general guidelines that apply to all types of advertising.

> Rule 7.2 Advertising
>
> (a) ... [A] lawyer may advertise services through public media, such as telephone directory, legal directory, newspaper or other periodical, outdoor advertising, radio or television, or through written or recorded communication.
> (b) A copy or recording of an advertisement or communication shall be kept for two years after its last dissemination along with a record of when and where it was used.
> (c) A lawyer shall not give anything of value to a person for recommending the lawyer's services, except that a lawyer may (1) pay the reasonable costs of advertisements or communications by this rule. . . .
> (d) Any communication made pursuant to this rule shall include the name of at least one lawyer responsible for its content.

Figure 3-13 shows the recommended changes to Rule 7.2 by the Ethics 2000 Commission. The reason for the two-year rule in subpart (b) is to ensure that if an ethical complaint is made against the law office, a copy of the ad will be available. The Ethics 2000 Commission recommends adding the need to keep an electronic record for Internet sites and related electronic ads. In some instances, ethical complaints are made long after the initial advertisement has run. The rule also prohibits the lawyer from paying someone to refer cases to the attorney. Finally, the rule requires that at least one person's name be on the advertisement somewhere so that, if there is an ethical violation, the authorities will know whom to hold responsible. The Ethics 2000 Commission is recommending an address be in the ad as well.

**Figure 3-12
Examples of False or Misleading Advertisements**

Advertisement	Ethical Analysis
"On personal injury and worker's compensation cases there are no attorney's *fees* unless we win for you."	Most lawyers will charge clients for the *costs* of bringing the claim, whether or not they are successful. Since people do not generally distinguish between *fees* and *costs*, it could be misleading to omit information in an advertisement the clients are responsible for *costs*.[1]
"Our firm recently won a $10,000,000 award—we can do the same for you."	This would create an unjustified expectation and would imply that the next case would have a similar result, even though every case is different.[2]
"We do it well." "Quickly becoming recognized as a premier personal injury law firm." "We are the best and smartest firm in the city."	Generally, the use of unsupportable, absolute terms are prohibited. It is also false or misleading for lawyers to compare their services to those of other lawyers unless that comparison can be factually substantiated.[3]
"We are specialists in personal injury and litigation." "Specializing in medical malpractice."	Violates Rule 7.4 that prohibits attorneys from claiming they are specialists unless it is an area in which some particular certification is required.[4]

[1] *The Legal Assistant's Practical Guide to Professional Responsibility,* American Bar Association, 1998, p. 108. Reprinted by permission.
[2] Ibid.
[3] Ibid.
[4] *Model Rules of Professional Conduct, 4th ed.*, American Bar Association, 1999, p. 534. Reprinted by permission.

**Figure 3-13
Public Discussion Draft to Model Rule 7.2, ABA Ethics 2000 Commission**

Reprinted by permission. Copies of the ABA Model Code of Professional Responsibility, 1999 ed., are available from Service Center, American Bar Association, 750 North Lake Shore Drive, Chicago, IL 60611-4497, 1-800-285-2221.

ADVERTISING
(a) Subject to the requirements of Rules 7.1 and 7.3, a lawyer may advertise services through public media, ~~such as a telephone directory, legal directory, newspaper or other periodical, outdoor advertising, radio or television,~~ or through written ~~or~~, recorded <u>or electronic</u> communication.
(b) A copy ~~or~~, recording <u>or electronic record</u> of an advertisement or communication shall be kept for two years after its last dissemination along with a record of when and where it was used.
(c) A lawyer shall not give anything of value to a person for recommending the lawyer's services except that a lawyer may
  (1) pay the reasonable costs of advertisements or communications permitted by this Rule;
  (2) pay the usual charges of a not-for-profit lawyer referral service or legal service organization; and
  (3) pay for a law practice in accordance with Rule 1.17.
(d) Any communication made pursuant to this rule shall include the name <u>and office address</u> of at least one lawyer <u>or law firm</u> responsible for its content.

NO DIRECT SOLICITATION OR "AMBULANCE CHASING" Rule 7.3 of the ABA *Model Rules* restricts attorneys from directly soliciting persons they do not know.

Rule 7.3 Direct Contact with Prospective Clients

(a) A lawyer shall not by in-person or live telephone contact solicit professional employment from a prospective client with whom the lawyer has no family or prior professional relationship when a significant motive for the lawyer's doing so is the lawyer's pecuniary gain.

(b) A lawyer shall not solicit professional employment from a prospective client by written or recorded communication or by in-person or telephone contact even when not otherwise prohibited by paragraph (a), if: (1) the prospective client has made known to the lawyer a desire not to be solicited by the lawyer; or (2) the solicitation involves coercion, duress, or harassment.

(c) Every written or recorded communication from a lawyer soliciting professional employment from a prospective client known to be in need of legal services in a particular matter, and with whom the lawyer has no family or prior professional relationship, shall include the words "Advertising Material" on the outside envelope and at the beginning and ending of any recorded communication.

DIRECT CONTACT WITH PROSPECTIVE CLIENTS

(a) A lawyer shall not by in-person ~~or~~, live telephone *or real-time electronic* contact solicit professional employment from a prospective client with whom the lawyer has no family, close personal or prior professional relationship when a significant motive for the lawyer's doing so is the lawyer's pecuniary gain.

(b) A lawyer shall not solicit professional employment from a prospective client by written ~~or~~, recorded or electronic communication or by in-person, ~~or~~, telephone or real-time electronic contact even when not otherwise prohibited by paragraph (a), if:
 (1) the prospective client has made known to the lawyer a desire not to be solicited by the lawyer; or
 (2) the solicitation involves coercion, duress or harassment.

(c) Every written ~~or~~, recorded or electronic communication from a lawyer soliciting professional employment from a prospective client known to be in need of legal services in a particular matter, and with whom the lawyer has no family, close personal or prior professional relationship, shall include the words "Advertising Material" on the outside envelope, if any, and at the beginning and ending of any recorded or electronic communication.

(d) Notwithstanding the prohibitions in paragraph (a), a lawyer may participate with a prepaid or group legal service plan operated by an organization not owned or directed by the lawyer which uses in-person or telephone contact to solicit memberships or subscriptions for the plan from persons who are not known to need legal services in a particular matter covered by the plan.

Figure 3-14
Public Discussion Draft to *Model Rule* 7.3, ABA Ethics 2000 Commission

Direct, in-person telephone contact with individuals that the lawyer does not know is prohibited because there may be the possibility of undue influence, intimidation, or overreaching when a skilled attorney contacts a layperson. However, prerecorded communications may be acceptable, as the attorney is not "live." This rule also squarely prohibits attorneys from making harassing communication or bothering persons who do not want to be solicited. Finally, the rule requires that advertisements soliciting business must be labeled as "Advertising Material" to inform persons up front that the communication is an advertisement. The recommended change by the Ethics 2000 Commission adds that real-time electronic solicitation is also prohibited.

A distinction is made in the rule between directly soliciting persons that are known by the attorney, such as family members or past clients, and soliciting unknown individuals. Attorneys and staff may solicit individuals they know. This is quite common, and there is nothing unethical about mentioning to friends and relatives that your law office handles certain types of cases and could help them if the need ever arose. What is prohibited is directly soliciting absolute strangers in person. Written solicitation, such as newsletters, brochures, and in many jurisdictions targeted mail, is allowed.

LAWYER CANNOT STATE HE IS A SPECIALIST Rule 7.4 of the *Model Rules* prohibits attorneys from holding themselves out as specialists.

> Rule 7.4 Communication of Fields of Practice
>
> A lawyer may communicate the fact that the lawyer does or does not practice in particular fields of law. A lawyer shall not state or imply that the lawyer is a specialist in a field of law except . . . the Ethics 2000 Commission is not recommending any changes to this rule.

This rule allows attorneys to list what areas they practice in, but it prohibits them from holding themselves out as specialists or as attorneys who specialize in particular fields. The reason is that the word "specialist" has a secondary meaning, implying formal recognition (this rule would not apply in states that provide procedures for certification in particular areas).

Each state has specific ethical rules about lawyer advertising, so it is important that whoever performs the marketing be familiar with the rules of your state. One option to avoid ethical problems is to show the advertising to the disciplinary administrator for the state before it is run and ask his or her opinion on the matter.

PLANNING

> *The simple fact is that most law offices do not plan for the future. They wait for the future to come get them; then they get pulled into it kicking and screaming. These [firms] are the victims of change; they never truly succeed; they never quite get out of the rut.*[15]

When most people think of law practice management, planning is usually not at the top of the list of things management must do. However, planning is the difference between firms that stay in the past and firms that move ahead. In Chapter 1, **planning** was defined as the process of setting objectives, assessing the future, and developing courses of action to achieve these objectives. Planning is one of the most primary and important things that effective management must do to succeed. Unfortunately in the past, many law practices, including government, corporate, and private firms, have neglected this function. The reason that many firms neglect to plan is because it takes time and energy to do it right. It is easier to deal with the problems of today than to make strategies for the future.

planning
Setting objectives, assessing the future, and developing courses of action to achieve these objectives.

> *Planning skills are very important for a paralegal. One of the keys to good planning is to be organized and proactive. Learn how the attorney does things and stay a step ahead of him or her. If you know a deadline is coming up on the calendar, go to the attorney early to see what you can do to assist him or her. Do not wait for the attorney to come to you because the attorney has many other things to focus on. Poor planning leads to last minute work and rushes. Some things will come up at the last minute that cannot be avoided, but try to limit those occurrences by planning ahead and being prepared.*
>
> Linda Rushton, CLA

WHY LEGAL ASSISTANTS NEED TO LEARN TO DEVELOP PLANS

As a legal assistant's career expands, he or she will be given more complex assignments, job duties, and tasks. As the complexity of assignments increases, the ability to develop and execute plans is crucial. The following are some plans that legal assistants may prepare.

- Budgets for a legal assistant department
- Case budgets for a particular case (i.e. how much the law office will expend to bring a case to trial)
- Case plans (in conjunction with a supervising attorney), including what witnesses need to be deposed, what interrogatories, requests for production, and requests for admissions need to be issued and to whom, what experts need to be hired, what strategies the office should pursue, what further investigation needs to be conducted, etc.
- Large projects, such as developing a litigation-support data base in cases that have thousands of documents (Legal assistants and others must plan how the documents will be entered into the computer, what program, service bureau, or technique will be the most successful, etc.)

- Administrative projects that require planning, including computerizing a law office's time and billing system from a manual system, implementing a computerized docket control system, or setting up a new filing system or law library
- In small law offices, the office's mission statement and some strategic plans
- Their own career plans (where they want to be in two years or five years and how they are going to get there).

THE MISSION STATEMENT AND STRATEGIC PLANS

A mission statement is a particular type of plan. The **mission statement** is a general, enduring statement of what the purpose or intent of the law practice is. The mission statement is a statement about the goals and objectives of the firm. It is a plan or vision stating what the firm is about. It sets out the fundamental and unique purpose that sets it apart from other firms, identifies the firm's scope, and sets out why it exists. For examples, see the mission statements in Figure 3-15.

mission statement
A general, enduring statement of what the purpose or intent of the law practice is.

Figure 3-15
Mission Statements

> **Law Office Mission Statements:**
> #1
> The mission of the Davis, Saunders & Lavely law firm is to deliver high-quality legal services to business clients nationwide through personalized, value-added service and a strict adherence to the highest ethical standards.
> #2
> The KGLPE Law Department seeks to offer the Corporation the best legal services available while containing costs to a minimum. The law department will utilize four divisions—labor, environmental, litigation, and general business. The use of in-house staff will be maximized. Only matters of vital importance to the Corporation will be contracted out. The other departments of the Corporation will be defined as our "clients." Our clients will be given the same high-quality legal services as provided by outside counsel. Our clients will be surveyed on an annual basis, and we will obtain a 90 percent average approval rating.
> #3
> Woodsom and Stetson is a full-service, client-centered law firm. Our goal is to provide outstanding, responsive services to our clients at a reasonable cost. As a full-service law office, we offer many services for our clients. We represent clients as we ourselves would want to be represented. We use a team approach to provide legal services to our clients, including—lawyers, paralegals, and office associates—to ensure a professional level of response to our clients' needs.

All law practices need a vision: they need to know where they have been and where they are going. They need to have a few guiding principles and philosophies that motivate and determine the direction of the firm. The mission statement represents the foundation for priorities and all other plans. If the firm you work for has a mission statement, memorize and use it. Every idea, new client, hiring of an employee, purchase of a piece of equipment,—everything you do should be judged as to whether it advances the mission of the firm. If it does not advance the mission, then it may not be right for the firm.

Mission statements may include when the firm began, who founded the firm, the philosophy of the founder(s), the nature of the practice (areas of experience and expertise), the geographic service area, the departments in the practice, the philosophies toward costs, income, growth, technology, client services, and personnel, and who specifically the firm's clients are. Mission statements are not static; they should be changed and updated as long as everyone in the firm understands the change. A mission statement is a vision that keeps the firm headed in the right direction. Without one, a law practice may spend a considerable amount of time never knowing where it is headed.

> *Strategic planning has always been important, but the present circumstances make it imperative for law offices to consider strengths and weaknesses, evaluate the competition, and devise a game plan that will set the course to the future.*

Strategic planning is the process of determining the major goals of a firm and then adopting the courses of action and allocating resources necessary to achieve those goals. In a strategic plan, a firm decides its long-range goals and prepares a plan of action of how to achieve those goals. For instance, a strategic plan may include expanding a firm's practice in additional areas of the law, such as adding a tax or labor law department. One thing to remember is that before you can sell a legal service to someone, you must have a buyer. That is, you should not focus on what you want to sell but rather on what the buyer or the client wants to buy. Strategic plans usually answer the questions contained in Figure 3-16.

strategic planning
Determining the major goals of a firm and then adopting the courses of action necessary to achieve those goals.

> *[In successful firms there is a] constant action or movement toward objectives. . . . Standing still is viewed as stagnating or losing ground to competitors. There exists a general perception that if the firm is not continually evaluating its position, problems, or opportunities, movement toward the goals might not exist. The old adage, "If it ain't broke, don't fix it," is ignored. [Successful] law offices realize that there are always better ways to accomplish goals more efficiently and effectively.*[16]

**Figure 3-16
Strategic Planning**

Source: Adapted from material supplied by John L. Espy, formerly professor of international business at the Chinese University of Hong Kong.

Key Questions a Strategic Plan Should Answer:
- What legal services will we provide? What services will we add or delete? How profitable are these areas?
- Who are our clients (individuals, businesses, government)? What market segments will we serve? What do our clients need? What do our clients want? What type of clients/cases do we want to pursue (type of clients—insurance companies, doctors, manufacturers; type of cases—personal injury, tax, family law).
- What are the long-term projections for these clients in these areas?
- How will we assure our clients receive quality services?
- How will we attract and hold customers (what will be our basis of competition)?
- Who will own the firm?
- Who will manage the firm? Is our governing structure adequate?
- What sources of finance will we use?
- Will we purchase or rent premises and equipment (new practices typically lease)?
- What kinds of technology and systems will we use to produce our services?
- What marketing channels will we use?
- How will we achieve continuing growth?
- What new area of the country/world will we enter?
- What kinds of insurance will we need to acquire (malpractice, disability, life, health)?
- How many employees will we require to accomplish our goals?
- How will we recruit, train, and retain the right people for our firm?
- Will the firm merge with another firm to obtain a competitive advantage?
- What type of additional staff will we need—attorneys, clerks, administrators?

Additional Factors a Strategic Plan Should Consider:
- Environmental Analysis—Consider demographic, political, and economic factors when considering your strategic plan. How will these things affect who we are going to serve and how we are going to serve them?
- Industry Analysis—Consider the legal environment as a whole, such as surveys of other law firms with average profit margins, growth rate, costs, etc., for your size of firm. How does your particular firm compare with industry averages?
- Competitive Analysis—Identify your major competitors; what are their strengths and weaknesses? What are your competitor's business strategies?
- Internal Analysis—Compre your own strategies with that of your major competitors and consider your strengths and weaknesses as compared with your competitors.
- Determine Threats and Opportunities—Consider what new markets are the most attractive for your firm and then analyze your firm's competitive position in the marketplace, identify any threats that competitors may have, and identify opportunities resulting from market conditions or a competitor's weakness.

1. Gather Facts and Opinions
2. Assess and Organize Information
3. Develop Goals
4. Assess Strengths and Weaknesses of Each Goal
5. Develop Objectives and Strategies for Obtaining the Goal
6. Consider the Resources Necessary to Achieve the Objectives
7. Develop an Action Plan
8. Monitor, Reevaluate, and Make Corrections in the Plan

Figure 3-17
The Planning Process

Source: Henry Ewalt, Practical Planning (American Bar Association, 1985), 23. Reprinted by permission of American Bar Association.

THE PLANNING PROCESS

Going through the planning process step by step is as important as the resulting plan itself (see Figure 3-17). The process of planning makes you wiser, and it forces you to think about and consider factors you might not otherwise.

GATHER FACTS AND OPINIONS The first step in the process is to gather as much relevant and timely information about the subject matter of the plan as possible. You can do this by researching the issue, hiring consultants, researching surveys of other similarly situated law practices, attending seminars, belonging to professional organizations, and reading periodicals. You should also talk to others in the firm about their ideas and opinions regarding the subject matter of the plan and get as many different angles and viewpoints as possible.

ASSESS AND ORGANIZE INFORMATION After you have gathered relevant information, the next step is to organize it and determine which pieces are the most persuasive.

DEVELOP GOALS Take the best information and opinions you have gathered and turn them into goals. These are typically statements of what the firm will accomplish. You should not be bothered with how the goals will be achieved at this stage, but only with what the specific goals of the plan will be (for example, to bring in a minimum of 15 percent more clients). At this stage you will begin to narrow down your ideas and determine exactly what you want to accomplish.

ASSESS STRENGTHS AND WEAKNESSES Assess each goal and determine its strengths and weaknesses. How will attaining these goals help or hurt the firm? Are there negatives? This is one more way to narrow the goals down to make sure you have completely thought through which goals will bring the firm the most benefit.

DEVELOP OBJECTIVES Develop specific objectives of how to accomplish each goal, including what will be achieved, when it will be achieved, how it will be achieved, who will be involved in achieving it, and where it will be achieved.

CONSIDER RESOURCES NECESSARY Look at each strategy or objective and determine whether the firm can allocate the resources (i.e. money, time, people, equipment, etc.) to accomplish each objective. Keep in mind that a plan will fail if it is too large and vast for the amount of resources the firm can devote to it.

DEVELOP AN ACTION PLAN Develop a specific action plan, in writing, as to how the firm will accomplish the goals. For each step, you should designate who is responsible for its achievement and when it will be achieved. You also may want to develop a time line so that you can track the progress of the plan.

MONITOR EVALUATE PLAN Monitor the plan, reevaluate the plan, and make changes as necessary. The planning process is a continuous process of refinement. Remember: for a plan to succeed, many people must be involved to increase support, enthusiasm, and ownership of the plan.

IDEAS ON HOW TO PLAN EFFECTIVELY

The following are some ideas on how to plan effectively.

- **Gather timely, relevant information.** It is axiomatic that, without good information, you cannot possibly make an effective plan. Too many times, people make plans based on faulty information. Gathering timely and relevant information is one of the most important things you can do to make sure your plan will succeed. You can gather information from public libraries, law libraries, the ABA, local, state, and national bar associations, law office surveys, consultants, other firms, and historical records from your own firm. Good information is a key to making good decisions.
- **Write all plans.** Goals and plans should be in writing as constant reminders of where you are supposed to be headed.
- **Involve everyone in the planning process.** Always ask for comments from anyone who would be affected by the plan. You want to build a consensus so that everyone will have input into the plan and will support it when it comes time to implement it. People promote plans that they perceive as being their own, either in part or as a whole. This is the "ownership" concept. Soliciting input from others opens the lines of communication and allows all firm members to feel that they have a stake in the action, that their thoughts are important, and that they are needed. When you are involving others in the process, do not judge their suggestions; listen to them and consider them. Your job is to facilitate communication and to provide a nonthreatening environment so everyone can participate.
- **Stick to the plan.** It takes an amazing amount of patience to stick to a plan and follow through with what you started. It does a firm little good to make a detailed and wonderful plan and then scrap it two months later. It takes commitment from everyone involved to give the plan a chance to succeed.
- **Recognize that planning is a continuous process.** Planning is a continuous process of making improvements; it is not a one-time effort in which you

develop a plan and then never revisit it. If all you do is make a plan and never follow it up or monitor it, all you have done is waste the firm's time.
- **Monitor the plan and communicate the results to others.** Always monitor the progress of the plan. One way to do this is to make a time line or Gantt chart to track the expected progress over time. A **Gantt chart** is a plan or time line of projected begin dates and end dates of a project. A Gantt chart breaks a large project down into specific jobs or items that must be accomplished. As an item is finished, it can be marked completed (see Figure 3-18). Gantt charts also are good at simplifying and communicating complicated projects. Most people find charts more reader-friendly than straight text.

Gantt chart
A plan or time line of projected begin dates and end dates of a project.

Periodically, you should check the progress of the project to determine whether the plan needs to be revised or completely overhauled to accomplish its objectives. One way to do this is to hold monthly planning meetings or to otherwise communicate the progress of the plan to others by keeping them informed about how the project is going. If possible, you want to build into the plan quantifiable means to show others that the plan is working as expected and that resources are not being wasted.

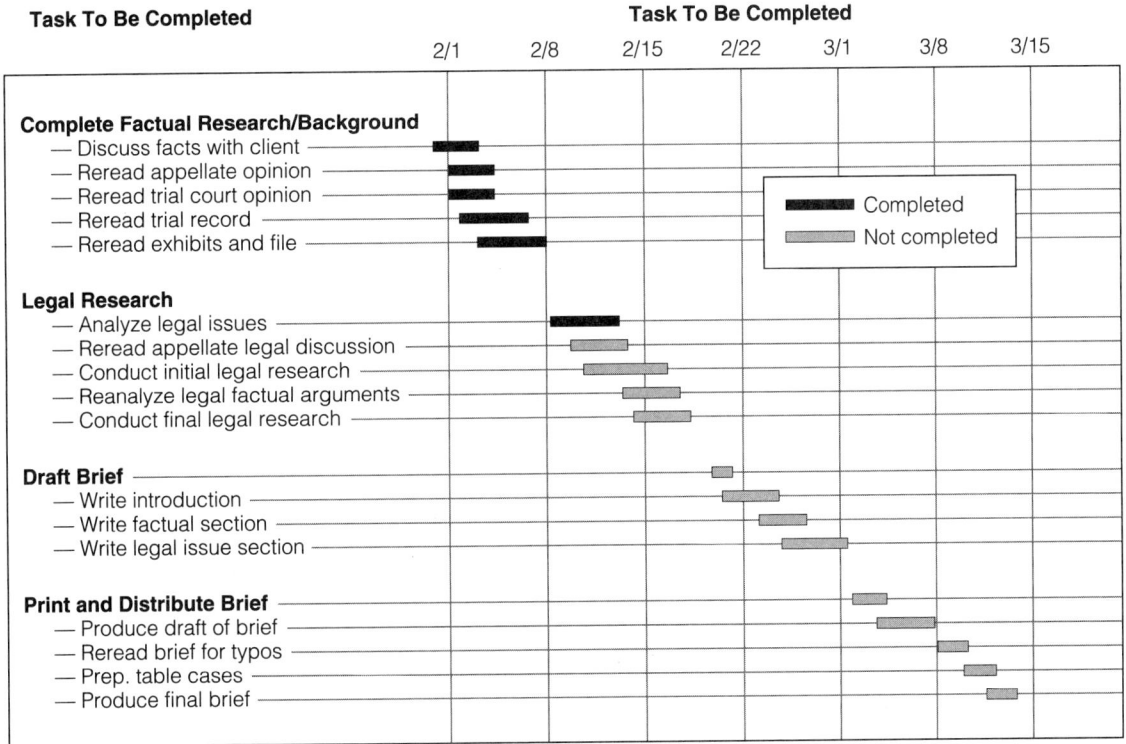

Figure 3-18 A Gantt Chart

Internet Sites

Organization	Description	Internet Address
ABA Law Practice Today	ABA site devoted to law practice management	www.abanet.org/lpm
Association of Legal Administrators	Association of legal administrators, including marketing directors and administrators	www.alanet.org
Legal Marketing Association	Association of legal marketing processionals	www.legalmarketing.org
Red Street, Inc.	Reviews of hundreds of law office Websites; offices Website design tips	www.redstreet.com

Suggested Reading

Complete Guide to Marketing Your Law Practice, Weishar and Durham, American Bar Association, 1999.

Law Firm Marketing: The Move to the Internet, Legal Marketing Association, 1997.

Law Office Policy and Procedures Manual, 4th edition, Wert and Hatoff, American Bar Association, 2000.

Law Office Staff Manual for Solos and Small Law Firms, Demetrious Dimitriou, American Bar Association, 1995.

The Lawyer's Guide to Creating Web Pages, Kenneth Johnson, American Bar Association, 1997.

Legal Marketing, Munneke and Raridon, American Bar Association, 1995.

Legal Resources and Client Development on the Internet, Guy Alvarez, Practicing Law Institute, 1997.

Marketing and Legal Ethics, 3rd edition, William E. Hornsby, Jr., American Bar Association, 2000.

The Quality Pursuit, Robert Michael Greene, American Bar Association, 1989.

Total Quality Management in the Law Office, Alman Weil, Inc., 1993. (*www.altmanweil.com*)

TQM in Action, Walker and Ciaramitaro, American Bar Association, 1993.

Summary

A law office staff manual establishes written policies and procedures regarding the firm's personnel policies, filing procedures, billing procedures, general office procedures, and more. The purpose of a staff manual is to ensure consistent treatment to all clients, to set out minimum standards that the law office expects, to help train new staff members, and to assign responsibility of certain tasks to specific persons.

Total quality management (TQM) is a philosophy that is based on knowing the needs of the client and allowing those needs to drive the organization. It is providing quality legal services to all clients.

Marketing is the process of educating consumers on the quality legal services that a law office provides. Marketing techniques include Websites, firm brochures, newsletters, and client seminars. Marketing works best when the firm establishes a written marketing plan and then sticks to the plan.

Planning is the process of setting objectives, assessing the future, and developing courses of action to achieve these objectives. There are many types of plans, including a mission statement and short- and long-range plans. Planning forces firms to anticipate change and to prepare for ways to handle the change.

Key Terms

Policy
Procedure
Intranet
Total Quality Management (TQM)
Marketing/marketing plan
Cross-selling

Rainmaking
Planning
Mission statement
Strategic planning
Gantt chart

Questions and Exercises

1. You are a legal assistant coordinator in a medium- to large-size law practice. You coordinate approximately fourteen legal assistants. Recently, attorneys in the firm have complained about the coordination of the legal assistants, including complaints of the attorneys needing assistance and no one being available to help them, too many legal assistants working on one particular case, a lack of effective priorities being set, and a lack of communication among the legal assistants. What general measures could you take to help this situation?

2. As a legal assistant in a corporate law department, you are asked to begin working on a department staff manual and later to successfully implement it. You and your superiors are convinced that the department will benefit greatly from such a manual. However, your peers are disturbed that you were chosen to coordinate the effort instead of them. What is your next move and why? Be specific.

3. The attorney you work for asks if you have ever heard of "total quality management." The attorney would specifically like you to discuss what it is and what advantages it might have for the firm. The attorney also would like you to discuss what effect it might have on its marketing plans. Please discuss your understanding of the term and how it differs from the old philosophy the firm had about being well respected in the community and earning a good profit.

4. You and your supervising attorney have just spent three weeks in a complicated products liability trial regarding vaccine immunization shots for children. Your firm's client contracted the disease from the immunization shot. Your firm received the largest verdict in history for this type of case. Given the success of this case, the firm would like to handle more of these. When you get back to the office, you are shown a draft of an advertisement that is going to run in newspapers across the country that reads:

"MILLER AND HASTINGS Law Office SPECIALIZES IN PHARMACEUTICAL CASES!—Recently, our firm won a multi-million-dollar judgment against a drug company for producing an unsafe drug. Please call us if you would like us to represent your interests."

Your supervising attorney asks for your comment. How do you respond? Your client, who is absolutely ecstatic about the verdict, learns of your intentions and volunteers to appear in a television ad to do a testimonial about the verdict and the great services the firm provided.

5. Recently, a senior attorney was reading an article on legal malpractice that stated that every law office should have a person responsible for risk management. That is, someone in every law office should be responsible for thinking of ways to reduce the law office's exposure to legal malpractice. Because you are willing to take on additional responsibilities, you volunteer. Analyze briefly from an ethics and malpractice perspective why every law office should have a staff manual.

6. As a legal assistant for a small but respected firm, you know that the firm wishes to expand and to move into more lucrative legal areas. You think that environmental issues such as toxic

waste are promising. However, before suggesting the idea, you know that you must present solid evidence of feasibility and present a plan for making this happen. Delineate what you would do to research this issue; then develop a draft of how you would sell the partners on it. How will you convince the partners that this can be accomplished?

7. As a legal assistant in a public legal aid clinic, you are asked to draft a policy/procedure regarding incoming and outgoing mail practices. The following should be addressed: who will stamp the incoming mail "received," how it will be stamped, how the mail will be routed, who will process the outgoing mail, when it should be delivered to the post office, and when overnight delivery will be used. Present your draft.

8. Your law office is considering placing a yellow pages ad. You are to research the issue by looking in the yellow pages under "Attorneys." You are to pick out two ads that you think are outstanding. Determine what you like about the ads and their messages. Do the same with television ads. What attorney ads are the best? Why?

9. As you are considering Question 8, look for ads that you think are questionable from an ethics perspective or that exhibit poor taste. Give explanations for your answers.

10. Using a general Internet engine (such as *www.yahoo.com*) or a site specializing in legal Internet sites such as *www.redstreet.com*, find five law firm (or other type of legal organization) Internet sites that you like. Write a brief report explaining what you liked about each of the sites.

11. You work in the small law firm of Skiles and Smith. The partner you work for tells you that she would like you to do research on the Internet and develop a basic design for the firm's new Internet site. The firm handles employment, labor, and benefits law. She tells you that you will be the principal contact with the Website designers. Put together a draft of the site.

12. The partner at Skiles and Smith would also like you to draft a vision statement, marketing plan, and short- and long-range plans. The partner would like to expand the firm into all areas of employment, labor, and benefits law. The purpose of the documents is to set a vision and plan for achieving this growth and expansion. Present your work.

NOTES

1. Robert Greene, *Making Partner,* American Bar Association, 1992, p. 3. Reprinted by permission.
2. *Law Office Policy and Procedures Manual,* 4th ed., Wert and Hatoff, American Bar Association, 2000, p. ix. Reprinted by permission.
3. Robert G. Kurzman and Rita Gilbert, *Paralegals and Successful Law Practice,* Institute for Business Planning, 1984, p. 80.
4. Robert G. Kurzman and Rita Gilbert, *Paralegals and Successful Law Practice,* Institute for Business Planning, 1984.
5. Edward C. Manahan, "Deciding to Train for Quality Service," *Cornerstone,* National Legal Aid and Defender Association 14(2), Fall 1992, p. 11.
6. Thomas Clay and Charles Maddock, "The 12 Deadly Management Sins," *Pennsylvania Lawyer,* January/February, 1999.
7. Ann Massie Nelson, "Work with Support Staff to Promote Quality," *Wisconsin Lawyer,* October, 1999. Reprinted with permission of the October 1999 *Wisconsin Lawyer,* the official publication of the State Bar of Wisconsin.
8. Deborah C. Wahl, "Managing for Quality," *The LAMA Manager,* Spring 1992, p. 21. Reprinted with the permission of the Legal Assistant Management Association.
9. Deborah C. Wahl, "Managing for Quality," *The LAMA Manager,* Spring 1992, p. 7. Reprinted with the permission of the Legal Assistant Management Association.
10. *The Legal Assistant's Practical Guide to Professional Responsibility,* American Bar Association, 1998, p. 105. Reprinted by permission.

11. *The Legal Assistant's Practical Guide to Professional Responsibility,* American Bar Association, 1998, p. 109. Reprinted by permission.
12. Deborah C. Wahl, "Managing for Quality," *The LAMA Manager,* Spring 1992, p. 8. Reprinted with the permission of the Legal Assistant Management Association.
13. Joy M. White, "Trend Setters—Pioneers in the New World of Law Practice," *Law Practice Management,* July/August 1999, p. 55. Reprinted by permission.
14. Leslee M. Stewart and Pamela J. Gonyea, "Marketing for the Small Law Firm," *New Hampshire Bar Journal,* June 1992, p. 389. Reprinted with the permission of the *New Hampshire Bar Journal.*
15. Gary A. Munneka, *Law Practice Management,* West Publishing Group, 1991, p. 570.
16. Thomas S. Clay, "Profile of a Successful Law Firm," *The Law Firm Management Guide* (Pennsylvania: Altman Weil Pensa), 1988, p. A–15. Reprinted with permission from Altman Weil, Inc.

CASE REVIEW

 —*Doe v. Condon, 2000 WL 718448 (S.C.)*

2000 WL 718448
(Cite as: 2000 WL 718448 (S.C.))

Only the Westlaw citation is currently available.

NOTICE: THIS OPINION HAS NOT BEEN RELEASED FOR PUBLICATION IN THE PERMANENT LAW REPORTS. UNTIL RELEASED, IT IS SUBJECT TO REVISION OR WITHDRAWAL.

Supreme Court of South Carolina.

John DOE, Alias, Petitioner,

v.

Charles M. CONDON, Attorney General for the State of South Carolina,

Respondent.

No. 25138.

Submitted May 23, 2000.

Decided June 5, 2000.

Assistant Attorney General Jennifer A. Deitrick, of Columbia, for respondent.

Disciplinary Counsel Henry B. Richardson, Jr., of Columbia, for amicus curiae Office of Disciplinary Counsel.

IN THE ORIGINAL JURISDICTION

PER CURIAM.

*1 Petitioner sought to have the Court accept this matter in its original jurisdiction to determine whether certain tasks performed by a non-attorney employee in a law firm constitute the unauthorized practice of law. Specifically, petitioner asks (1) whether it is the unauthorized practice of law for a paralegal employed by an attorney to conduct informational seminars for the general public on wills and trusts without the attorney being present; (2) whether it is the unauthorized practice of law for a paralegal employed by an attorney to meet with clients privately at the attorney's office, answer general questions about wills and trusts, and gather basic information from clients; and (3) whether a paralegal can receive compensation from the paralegal's law firm/employer through a profit-sharing arrangement based upon the volume and type of cases the paralegal handles. The Office of the Attorney General filed a return opposing the petition for original jurisdiction.

The Court invoked its original jurisdiction to determine whether the paralegal's activities constituted the unauthorized practice of law, and, pursuant to S.C.Code Ann. § 14-3-340 (1976), John W. Kittredge was appointed as referee to make findings of fact and conclusions of law concerning this matter. A hearing was held and the referee issued proposed findings and recommendations.

[1][2] We adopt the referee's findings and recommendations attached to this opinion and hold that a non-lawyer employee conducting unsupervised legal presentations for the public and answering legal questions for the public or for clients of the attorney/employer engages in the unauthorized practice of law. See State v. Despain, 319 S.C. 317, 460 S.E.2d 576 (1995). We further hold that a proposed fee arrangement which compensates non-lawyer employees based upon the number and volume of cases the non-lawyer employee handles for an attorney violates the ethical rules against fee-splitting with non-lawyer employees. Rule 5.4 of the Rules of Professional Conduct, Rule 407, SCACR.

PROPOSED FINDINGS AND RECOMMENDATIONS OF THE REFEREE

This is a declaratory judgment action in the Supreme Court's original jurisdiction. The Court referred this matter to me as Referee. Petitioner, a paralegal, has submitted a generalized list of tasks he wishes to perform and has inquired whether performing them constitutes the unauthorized practice of law. Petitioner also seeks a determination of the propriety of his proposed fee splitting arrangement with his attorney-employer. Despite my repeated offers for an evidentiary hearing, neither party requested a hearing. The record before me is sufficient to address and resolve whether the activities in question constitute the unauthorized practice of law.

I find that a paralegal conducting unsupervised legal presentations for the public and answering legal questions from the audience engages in the unauthorized practice of law. Further, I find that a paralegal meeting individually with clients to answer estate planning questions engages in the unauthorized practice of law. Finally, I find the proposed fee arrangement is improper and violates the ethical prohibition against fee splitting.

BACKGROUND

*2 Petitioner submitted the following questions to the Court:

(1) Is it the unauthorized practice of law for a paralegal employed by an attorney to conduct educational seminars for the general public, to disseminate general information about wills and trusts, including specifically a fair and balanced emphasis on living trusts, including answering general questions, without the attorney being present at the seminar as long as the seminar is sponsored by the attorney's law firm and the attorney has reviewed and approved the format, materials and presentation to be made for content, truthfulness and fairness?

(2) Is it the unauthorized practice of law for a paralegal employed by an attorney to meet with clients privately in the law office for the purpose of answering general questions about wills, trusts, including specifically living trusts, and estate planning in general, and to gather basic information from said clients for such purposes as long as it is done under the attorney's direction, and the clients have a follow-up interview and meeting with the attorney who would have primary responsibility for legal decisions?

(3) Can a paralegal receive compensation from the law firm he is employed by, through a profit-sharing arrangement, which would be based upon the volume and type of cases the paralegal handled?

DISCUSSION

To protect the public from unsound legal advice and incompetent representation, South Carolina, like other jurisdictions, limits the practice of law to licensed attorneys. S.C.Code Ann. § 40-5-310 (1976). While case law provides general guidelines as to what constitutes the practice of law, courts are hesitant to define its exact boundaries. Thus, the analysis in 'practice of law' cases is necessarily fact-driven. The Supreme Court has specifically avoided addressing hypothetical situations, preferring instead to determine what constitutes the unauthorized practice of law on a case by case basis. In Re Unauthorized Practice of Law Rules Proposed by the South Carolina Bar, 309 S.C. 304, 422 S.E.2d 123 (S.C.1992). I find that Petitioner's proposed actions constitute the unauthorized practice of law and that the proposed fee agreement violates the ethical prohibition against fee splitting.

Our Supreme Court has set forth a succinct standard of the proper role of paralegals:

> The activities of a paralegal do not constitute the practice of law as long as they are limited to work of a preparatory nature, such as legal research, investigation, or the composition of legal documents, which enable the licensed attorney-employer to carry a given matter to a conclusion through his own examination, approval or additional effort. Matter of Easler, 275 S.C. 400, 272 S.E.2d 32, 33 (S.C. 1980).

While the important support function of paralegals has increased through the years, the Easler guidelines stand the test of time. As envisioned in Easler, the paralegal plays a supporting role to the supervising attorney. Here, the roles are reversed. The attorney would support the paralegal. Petitioner would play the lead role, with no meaningful attorney supervision and the attorney's presence and involvement only surfaces on the back end. Meaningful attorney supervision must be present throughout the process. The line between what is and what is not permissible conduct by a non-attorney is oftentimes "unclear" and is a potential trap for the unsuspecting client. State v. Buyers Service Co., Inc., 292 S.C. 426, 357 S.E.2d 15, 17 (S.C.1987). The conduct of the paralegal contemplated here clearly crosses the line into the unauthorized practice of law. It is well settled that a paralegal may not give legal advice, consult, offer legal explanations, or make legal recommendations. State v. Despain, 319 S.C. 317, 460 S.E.2d 576 (S.C.1995).

A. Educational Seminars

***3** Petitioner intends to conduct unsupervised "wills and trusts" seminars for the public, "emphasizing" living trusts during the course of his presentation. Petitioner also plans to answer estate planning questions from the audience. I find Petitioner's proposed conduct constitutes the unauthorized practice of law.

I find, as other courts have, that the very structure of such "educational" legal seminars suggests that the presenter will actually be giving legal advice on legal matters. See, In Re Mid-America Living Trust Assoc. Inc., 927 S.W.2d 855 (Mo.banc 1996); People v. Volk, 805 P.2d 1116 (Colo.1991); Oregon State Bar v. John H. Miller & Co. 235 Or. 341, 385 P.2d 181 (Or.1963). At the very least. Petitioner will implicitly advise participants that they require estate planning services. Whether a will or trust is appropriate in any given situation is a function of legal judgment. To be sure, advising a potential client on his or her need for a living trust (or other particular estate planning instrument or device) fits squarely within the practice of law. These matters cry out for the exercise of professional judgment by a licensed attorney. Thus, in conducting these informational seminars, Petitioner would engage in the unauthorized practice of law as a non-attorney offering legal advice.

Petitioner plans to answer "general" questions during his presentation. I have reviewed the Estate Planning Summary submitted by Petitioner and his attorney-employer. This summary sets forth the subject matter to be covered by the paralegal. Petitioner would present information on, among other things, revocable trusts, irrevocable living trusts, credit shelter trusts, qualified terminable interest property trusts, charitable remainder trusts, qualified personal residence trusts, grantor retained annuity trusts, grantor retained unitrusts and charitable lead trusts. It is difficult to imagine such specific estate planning devices eliciting "general" questions or a scenario in which the exercise of legal judgment would not be involved. It is, after all, a legal seminar, apparently for the purpose of soliciting business. [FN1] To suggest that some "plan" would anticipate all possible questions with predetermined nonlegal responses is specious. And so complex is this area of law that many states, including South Carolina, have established stringent standards for an attorney to receive the designation of "specialist" in Estate Planning and Probate Law. SCACR, Part IV, Appendices D and E. This is the practice of law.

I fully recognize the prevailing popularity of 'financial planners' and others "jump[ing] on the estate planning bandwagon." (Estate Planning Summary submitted by Petitioner's attorney-employer, p. 1). This trend in no way affects the decision before the Court. This paralegal would not be presenting the estate planning seminar as a financial planner. This seminar would be conspicuously sponsored by the paralegal's attorney-employer. The attorney's law firm is prominently displayed in the brochure submitted, e.g., name, address, telephone number and "Firm Profile." In promoting the law firm and representing to the public the 'legal' nature of the seminar, neither the paralegal nor his attorney-employer can escape the prohibition against the unauthorized practice of law.

B. Initial Client Interview

***4** Petitioner intends to gather client information and answer general estate planning questions during his proposed "initial client interviews." While Petitioner may properly compile client information, Petitioner may not answer estate planning questions. See Matter of Easler, supra. Petitioner's answering legal questions would constitute the unauthorized practice of law for the reasons stated above. While the law firm in which Petitioner is employed plans to direct clients to an attorney for "follow-up" consultations, a paralegal may not give legal advice in any event. Moreover, permissible preparatory tasks must be performed while under the attorney's supervision. The proposed after the fact attorney review comes too late.

C. Compensation

Petitioner's law firm intends to compensate him based upon the volume and types of cases he "handles." A paralegal, of course, may not "handle" any case. [FN2] This fee arrangement directly violates Rule 5.4 of the Rules of Professional conduct, SCACR 407. [FN3] This limitation serves to "discourage the unauthorized practice of law by lay persons and to prevent a non-lawyer from acquiring a vested pecuniary interest in an attorney's disposition of a case that could possibly take preeminence over a client's best interest." Matter of Anonymous Member of the S.C.Bar, 295 S.C. 25,26, 367 S.E.2d 17, 18 (S.C.1998). This compensation proposal arrangement coupled with Petitioner's desire to market the law firm's services via the educational seminars and meet individually with clients creates a situation ripe for abuse. Indeed, the proposal by Petitioner presents the very evil Rule 5.4 was designed to avoid. Accordingly, I find Petitioner's proposed compensation plan violates both the letter and the spirit of Rule 5.4 prohibiting fee splitting with non-attorneys.

RECOMMENDATIONS

1. Offering legal presentations for the general public constitutes the practice of law.

2. Answering estate planning questions in the context of legal seminars or in private client interviews constitutes the practice of law.

3. Fee sharing arrangements with non-attorneys based on volume and cases "handled" by a paralegal violates Rule 5.4, Rules of Professional Conduct, SCACR 407.

RESPECTFULLY SUBMITTED.

FN1. While this marketing method may raise ethical implications for the attorney involved, the issue before me is whether the activities of the paralegal constitute the unauthorized practice of law. See Rule 7.3, Rules of Professional Conduct, 407 SCACR; Matter of Morris, 270 S.C. 308, 241 S.E.2d 911 (1978) (lawyer improperly solicited employment); Matter of Craven, 267 S.C. 33, 225 S.E.2d 861 (1976) (an attorney's knowledge that his employee is engaged in solicitation of professional employment for attorney constitutes professional misconduct); Matter of Crosby, 256 S.C. 325, 182 S.E.2d 289 (1971) (attorney improperly solicited business). Thus, not only does Petitioner's solicitation of legal clients raise possible ethical concerns for his sponsoring attorney, Petitioner's involvement clearly constitutes the unauthorized practice of law.

FN2. The suggestion that Petitioner and the law firm intend for him to "handle" cases speaks volumes about the anticipated role of Petitioner, far beyond the permissible tasks performed by paralegals.

FN3. Nonlawyer employees may certainly participate "in a compensation or retirement plan, even though the plan is based in whole or in part on a profit sharing arrangement." Rule 5.4(a)(3), Rules of Professional Conduct, SCACR 407.

END OF DOCUMENT

Copr. © West 2000 No Claim to Orig. U.S. Govt. Works

Clients and Communication Skills

CHAPTER OBJECTIVES

After you read this chapter, you will be able to:
- Discuss factors that will promote effective client relationships.
- Discuss ways to communicate effectively.
- Identify communication barriers.
- Explain the importance of good listening skills.
- Identify the pros and cons of using groups to make decisions.
- Discuss the characteristics of a leader.

A client hired an attorney to file a petition. At that time, the client paid the attorney $650. Over the next five months, the client made approximately twenty-five telephone calls to the attorney. The attorney failed to return all of the client's calls. The attorney asked an independent legal assistant to prepare a draft of the petition. The legal assistant prepared a draft of the petition and then made twenty-six attempts to reach the attorney by telephone and by pager, but the attorney failed to respond. The attorney did not pay the legal assistant for the work on the petition, did not review the petition, and did not provide legal services to the client. The attorney was disbarred.[1]

***

Over a two-and-a-half-year period, an attorney failed to perform legal services in thirty-eight client matters. In the thirty-eight matters, the attorney was charged and found culpable in thirty-three cases of failure to competently perform legal services, twenty-seven cases of failure to communicate, thirty cases of failure to refund unearned fees, five cases of aiding others in the unauthorized practice of law, two cases of failure to maintain client funds in trust, two cases of improper withdrawal, and one case of failure to comply with a court order. The attorney's clients were significantly harmed. Some of her clients suffered financial losses, and others suffered stress, loss of sleep, and loss of time because of the attorney's misconduct. The attorney was disbarred.[2]

***

A sole practitioner lost a court case after months of preparation and weeks of trial. The attorney had been representing one of her best corporate clients who had paid her faithfully each month during litigation.

The attorney did not relish the thought of visiting the owner of the company. When she did, she was stunned. The client offered his condolences and expression of support. During the course of the litigation, the attorney and all the members of the attorney's staff had kept the client fully informed of everything that was transpiring in the case. The client knew that the attorney and her staff had worked hard on the case and how intent they had been on winning. He also knew that he had been treated fairly and that the attorney and the staff had acted honestly and ethically in representing his interests. While winning would have been better, the client felt well served.[3]

WHY DO LEGAL ASSISTANTS NEED TO FOSTER GOOD CLIENT RELATIONSHIPS AND COMMUNICATE EFFECTIVELY?

Fostering positive client relationships and communicating effectively with others are absolute necessities for legal assistants to be successful. Customer service and satisfaction are very important to the practice of law, especially considering the number of law offices and the fierce competition that exists. Legal assistants who mishandle client relationships by not putting the client first will cause clients to go elsewhere for legal services. Nearly every task a legal assistant performs requires communication skills such as writing correspondence, drafting briefs, interviewing clients and witnesses, and legal research. The ability to effectively exchange ideas and information with others is an essential part of being a legal assistant.

This section will present an overview of ethical duties to clients and a basic but practical explanation of communication and will give you some ideas on how your communication skills can be improved. Also included in this section are related communication topics such as leadership qualities, the advantages and disadvantages of working with groups, and how to conduct client interviews.

> *Establish a good relationship with a client early by showing him or her respect, listening, and being responsive to his or her needs. If you tell a client that you will get back to him or her, do so, even if you are only telling him or her that you are still working on solving the issue and do not have an answer. If you promise a client that you will send him or her something, stop what you are doing and send it. Offer to help the client while always keeping in mind that you cannot give answers to specific legal questions and the need to avoid the unauthorized practice of law. A paralegal can be accommodating to a client without having to worry about unauthorized practice of law issues.*
>
> Linda Rushton, CLA

ETHICAL DUTY TO COMMUNICATE WITH CLIENTS

While much of this chapter covers how to provide clients with excellent customer service as it relates to providing quality legal services, there is also a strong ethical duty regarding the need to regularly communicate with clients. Keeping a client informed about his or her case, keeping him or her abreast of changes, developing strategy with him or her, and keeping him or her involved in the progress of a case—including communicating settlement offers—is fundamental to the practice of law. Attorneys and legal assistants are bound by this ethical duty. Clients cannot make informed decisions about their case if they do not know what is happening. Rule 1.4 of the *Model Rules* states:

> Rule 1.4 COMMUNICATION
>
> (a) A lawyer shall keep a client reasonably informed about the status of a matter and promptly comply with reasonable requests for information.
>
> (b) A lawyer shall explain a matter to the extent reasonably necessary to permit the client to make informed decisions regarding the representation.

The Ethics 2000 Commission is recommending no changes to this rule.

Rule 1.4 specifically requires the attorney to keep in reasonable contact with the client, to explain general strategy, and to keep the client reasonably informed regarding the status of the client's legal matter. The "reasonableness" of the situation will depend on the facts and circumstances of the particular case. The comment to the rule states that:

> The guiding principle is that the lawyer should fulfill reasonable client expectations for information consistent with the duty to act in the client's best interests, and the client's overall requirements as to the character of representation.

Clients become extremely frustrated when they pay for legal services and the attorney or legal assistant refuses to take their calls, answer their letters, or otherwise communicate with them in any way.

> *Reasonable communication between the lawyer and the client is necessary for the client effectively to participate in the representation. . . . The lawyer must consult with and secure the client's consent prior to taking action unless prior discussions with the client have resolved what action the client wants the lawyer to take. For example, a lawyer who receives from opposing counsel an offer of settlement in a civil controversy or a proffered plea bargain in a criminal case must promptly inform the client of its substance unless the client has previously indicated that the proposal will be acceptable.*
> *Ethics 2000 Commission Comment to Rule 1.4.*

The duty to communicate derives in part from the attorney's fiduciary duty of utmost good faith to the client.[4] Figure 4-1 sets out the specific duties of Rule 1.4 as decided by case law (see *Annotated Model Rules of Professional Conduct,* American Bar Association, 4th ed., 2000, p. 32–39).

DUTY TO INFORM CLIENTS ON THE STATUS OF THEIR CASE There is an affirmative duty by an attorney to generally contact clients and let them know what the status of their case is. The rule does not contemplate how this is done. Arguably, it can be done by personal visits, telephone, voice mail, e-mail, or any other method as long as the client is properly advised of his or her case. While this sounds easy, sometimes it is not. In some instances, cases can drag on for years and years. Nonetheless, the duty continues and clients are entitled to know what is happening in their case.

Model Rule 1.4 on Client Communication Includes a Duty of an Attorney to:
- Inform clients of the status of their case
- Timely respond to a client's request for information
- Inform clients promptly about important information
- Not cover up a matter if the attorney failed to carry out the client's instructions
- Notify clients if he or she is leaving a firm or quitting the practice of law
- Notifying a client if he or she is stopping working on a client's case
- Explain the law and benefits and risks of alternative courses of action
- Notify and communicate settlement offers to clients

Figure 4-1
Requirements of *Model Rule* 1.4

Reprinted by permission. Copies of the ABA Model Code of Professional Responsibility, 1999 edition are available from Service Center, American Bar Association, 750 North Lake Shore Drive, Chicago, IL 60611-4497, 1-800-285-2221.

DUTY TO TIMELY RESPOND TO A CLIENT'S REQUEST FOR INFORMATION
There is an absolute duty for an attorney to respond to reasonable requests for information. While this seems basic, many attorneys still do not return client phone calls, respond to client letters, respond to client e-mails, or show up for client appointments. There are literally thousands of state bar disciplinary opinions where attorneys have been reprimanded, suspended, and disbarred for failing to respond in a timely fashion to their clients.

DUTY TO INFORM CLIENTS PROMPTLY ABOUT IMPORTANT INFORMATION An attorney may not withhold important information that affects a legal matter without telling the client. For example, cases have held that an attorney has a duty to promptly tell a client that the client was named as a defendant in a civil action; an attorney cannot wait six months to tell an incarcerated defendant that the attorney had been appointed to represent the client; and an attorney had to tell a client that a case was set for docket and later dismissed for failure to prosecute.

DUTY TO NOT COVER UP A MATTER IF THE ATTORNEY FAILED TO CARRY OUT THE CLIENT'S INSTRUCTIONS If an attorney fails to carry out the instructions of a client by either neglect or design, the attorney has a duty to be up front and communicate this to the client. There have been many attorney discipline cases where an attorney agreed to file a claim and then did not, either because of negligence or because the attorney later changed his or her mind and then told the client the case was, in fact, filed. This type of behavior is also prohibited by Rule 1.4.

DUTY TO NOTIFY CLIENTS IF AN ATTORNEY IS LEAVING A FIRM OR QUITTING THE PRACTICE OF LAW An attorney has a duty to tell a client that he or she is leaving a firm and, therefore, representation of the client's case will be handled by someone else. The same holds true if the attorney is going to stop practicing law. The client needs to be made aware of this fact so that he or she can get his or her file returned and secure other counsel.

DUTY TO NOTIFY A CLIENT IF HE OR SHE IS STOPPING WORKING ON A CLIENT'S CASE An attorney cannot cease working on a client matter without affirmatively telling the client because doing so without the client's consent or knowledge could injure the client's legal interests. The withdrawal from a client matter should preferably be in writing, in the form of a letter to the client. If formal representation has been made in court, the attorney must file a motion to withdraw.

DUTY TO EXPLAIN THE LAW AND BENEFITS AND RISKS OF ALTERNATIVE COURSES OF ACTION An attorney has a duty to help the client make an informed decision about the client's matter. This may include explaining legal theories to the client, explaining the effects of contracts and other documents, advising a client on the consequences of accepting one alternative over another, and generally giving advice and counseling the client regarding the legal matter.

NOTIFY AND COMMUNICATE SETTLEMENT OFFERS TO CLIENTS An attorney has a duty to notify a client of all settlement offers, including explaining the terms and conditions of the offer and the ramifications to the client. An attorney cannot ordinarily, without the prior direction of the client, unilaterally decline or accept a settlement offer.

THE LEGAL ASSISTANT'S ROLE IN COMMUNICATING WITH CLIENTS Legal assistants can play an active role in communicating with clients. Often, legal assistants are more accessible to clients than attorneys and therefore may have many opportunities to work with clients and to keep them informed. This is admirable and encouraged as long as the attorney is actively involved with the case, is reviewing all documents prepared by the legal assistant, is the only party giving legal advice to the client, and meets with the client as needed.

CLIENT RELATIONSHIPS

A fundamental aspect of law office management is the commitment to provide quality legal service to clients. This is true whether you work in a private law firm or legal aid office with many clients or in a corporation or government practice where you have only one client: service is the key. Providing quality legal services begins with a good working relationship with each client, and this relationship is not just for attorneys. Everyone in the office, including legal assistants, should be committed to this. Remember, the client always comes first; he or she is the one paying your salary in the end. Clients may not have the legal background to know whether or not they are receiving good legal representation. However, clients do know whether their phone calls are being returned, whether documents in their case are poorly written and have typographical errors, whether deadlines are missed, or whether they are being treated respectfully. Merely providing good technical legal skills is not enough to please clients. Most clients are referred to attorneys and law offices by previous clients. If you provide poor service to existing clients, you will be depriving your firm of the best way to expand the practice.

FOSTERING POSITIVE CLIENT RELATIONSHIPS

Figure 4-2 shows a list of things that clients like and dislike about attorneys and law office staff. These likes and dislikes determine whether a client will come back for future business or refer others to the firm. Notice that the issue of winning or losing a case is not included in either list.

It is important to note that many of the items on the list are opinions of how the *client* perceives the legal professional.

- Does the client see you as friendly and willing to help, or inattentive and impersonal?
- Do you come across to the client as prompt and businesslike, or indifferent?
- Do you show common courtesy to the client, or do you come across as rude?

Figure 4-2
What Clients Like and Dislike

Source: *The Lawyer's Handbook*, American Bar Association, 1983. Reprinted by permission.

What Clients Like and Dislike	
Likes	**Dislikes**
Friendliness	Acting impersonal
Prompt and businesslike attitude	Bored or indifferent attitude
Courtesy	A rude and brusque manner
Avoidance of a condescending attitude	A superior attitude
A habit of keeping the client informed	A failure to keep client informed

- Are you respectful of the client and what he or she is going through, or do you have a superior and condescending attitude?
- Do you at every possible opportunity let the client know what is going on with his or her case and establish a feeling of trust and cooperativeness, or is the client ignored?

Each of these areas is critical to the success of the client relationship. Fail in any of these areas, and the relationship is undermined. This section will provide you with some ideas about how to foster excellent client relationships (see Figure 4-3).

KNOW YOUR CLIENT.

> *Leading firms in any endeavor know the key to competitive advantage is to set your sights on being first to market with exceptional ideas and exceptional service offerings. They become obsessed with: "How can we serve clients in a way nobody else can?" "What potential clients are not being served adequately?" "What services can we offer that will make clients go 'wow'? What can we do that will actually lead the market?"*[4]

Knowing your client and your client's individual needs is extremely important. Each client has a unique set of needs, worries, and desires related to his or her legal matter. Firms with outstanding client relations discover what those specific needs are for each client, and then systematically deliver on each need.

Before you can understand a client and his or her needs, it is helpful to understand why a client comes to a legal professional. Like any other relationship, the client relationship is based on trust. Clients come to legal professionals because they need help. They are either in a crisis or trying to avoid a crisis, and this condition of need makes them feel vulnerable.[5] When possible, take the client's emotional, mental, and physical state into consideration and empathize with him or her.

Figure 4-3
Fostering Positive Relationships with Clients

Description	Behavior
Know Your Client	• When dealing with the client, take into account his or her emotional/mental/physical state (consider how you would feel in the same circumstances) and based on this, respond and ask questions appropriately. • Establish basic trust in the relationship at every opportunity by listening to the client's needs, being honest, and being respectful. • Ask your client what his or her concerns are about the matter. • Ask your client what his or her business is about. • Do research on your own about the client's business or industry. • Ask how the client prefers to be communicated with (in-person, e-mail, telephone, voice mail). • Ask the client how often he or she wants to be communicated with. • Ask how you can serve the client better.
Treat Each Client as If He or She Is Your Only Client	• When you meet with a client, only have that client's file on your desk. • Never take another call when meeting with a client and let others know not to disturb you. • Never talk to clients about how busy you are or about other cases.
Send Copies of All Documents to Clients	• Always send copies of documents to the client. This lets the client know what you have been working on and keeps him or her informed. If the document is not particularly sensitive, attach the document as an e-mail to the client.
Do Not Use Legalese	• Talk to clients in lay terms and refrain from using jargon or legalese.
Return All Phone Calls and Reply to E-mails and Voice Mails Immediately	• Always return phone calls, e-mails, and voice mails as soon as possible, but at least by the end of the day.

(continued)

Be Courteous and Professional	▪ Always be courteous, professional, and empathetic with clients. This is extremely important to most clients.
Respond to Clients' Requests and Keep Promises	▪ Always respond to client requests in a timely manner. If you make a promise to get something to a client, do so in a timely manner. Contact the client and let him or her know the status of the matter in question.
Give Periodic Updates	▪ Be proactive. Periodically give updates to a client on the status of thier case.
Never Share Personal Problems with Clients	▪ Avoid sharing personal problems with clients. Clients are there to receive a service.
Preserve Client Confidences	▪ Maintain client confidentiality. This is critical to maintaining the foundation of trust in the relationship.
Survey Clients	▪ Use formal client surveys to find out what clients think about your services.
Management Must Help Promote Good Client Relations	▪ Work with management to let them know how better to support positive client relationships.
Publish a Client Manual	▪ Publish a client manual to help clients understand what to expect from the law office and how the judicial system functions regarding their type of case.

By showing the client that you understand and recognize his or her situation and concerns, you establish trust, which is the foundation of the relationship. Other ways to establish trust is by being respectful and honest with the client at all times.

> *Simply listening is not enough, because clients want more than a legal solution. They want a solution to their unique needs. It's the total experience that counts ... Discover what they think of the way you treat them.*[6]

Once a relationship of trust is established with a client, it is important to know specifics about that individual, such as what his or her business is, what his or her concerns are about the legal matter, and what you can do to serve his or her needs.

Do not assume you know what the client needs or wants. You may or may not be right, but you will know for sure if you ask. Because communication is vitally important, ask the client how he or she wants to receive communication. Are office visits the most convenient? Is e-mail best? Do they prefer telephone or voice mail? Again, the trick is to ask and then deliver services based on the client's needs.

TREAT EACH CLIENT AS IF HE OR SHE IS YOUR ONLY CLIENT. Every client should be treated individually. Behave as if that client's case is the only thing you are working on and as if the case is your most important one. Everyone at the firm needs to put the client at ease. When you meet with a client, have only his or her file on your desk and give the client your undivided attention. Never take a call when meeting with a client and let others know not to disturb you. This is a good idea not only because it shows the client that you are interested in his or her case, but because the confidentiality of your other clients needs to be maintained.

Never tell the client how busy you are or how many other cases you are working on; the client's case is the only one he or she is concerned about and the only one you should be talking to him or her about. If a client calls and asks if you are busy, say something such as "I'm never too busy to take a call from a good client" (even if you are swamped). If a client comes in for an appointment, never make him or her wait in the waiting room. A good law practice makes prompt, *personal* service a high priority. Take a personal interest in the client's affairs and be empathetic. It is always best to be personable with clients because this fosters good working relationships that will continue for years to come.

> *The one thing that I always try to remember is that these clients pay my salary! It is important for them to believe that I am doing my job and that they can talk to me about their case and any questions they have. Throughout a case, I grow to care for my clients very much, and I consider the client relations portion of my job to be THE most important job I do every day.*
> Andrea Blanscet, CLA

> *One law firm's client reported that he was sending additional business—both his own business and referrals—to other law firms in town. When asked why he wasn't sending it to his primary firm, he replied, "Because they're too busy already. The lawyers [and legal assistants] are always telling me how busy they are, and are slow in responding to my requests."[7]*

SEND COPIES OF ALL DOCUMENTS TO CLIENTS. As a matter of practice, it should be the policy of the law office to always send copies of all letters, memos, pleadings, and documents to the client. In nearly all cases, the client will appreciate this, and it will increase his or her confidence, satisfaction, and trust because although this might be just another case to you, this matter is of particular importance to the client. Although many people focus on the results of a case, the documents are a large piece of the product that the client is paying for. Even if the client does not understand everything sent, it still allows him or her to know what is happening in the case and how difficult the theories and complexities of the case are, and it lets the client know that you are actively working on the case. The cost of the copies can be charged to the client's account, so there is no real reason not to do it. Also, if the client has e-mail and the document isn't particularly sensitive, attach it to an e-mail and send it directly to the client. Also, clients are usually more willing to pay their attorney's fees when they have seen the work done on the case. It can be frustrating when a client does not know what is happening and then receives a bill.

DO NOT USE LEGALESE. Do not use legalese or legal jargon when talking with clients. Many clients do not understand legal jargon, and it is confusing and frustrating. Some clients may be too intimidated to ask what the terms mean. Try to explain legal concepts in words that a layperson will understand.

> *"They need to get explanations down to a level people can understand—I recently received an opinion letter from another law firm and was very impressed—it was succinct and easy to read."[8]*

RETURN CLIENT PHONE CALLS IMMEDIATELY. It is essential that you return client phone calls immediately. If that is not possible, at least return the calls on the same day that they are made. It is not uncommon for clients to call legal assistants. Usually, legal assistants are easier to reach than attorneys, and often legal assistants must work with clients quite closely depending on the type of case. Because legal assistants typically are very busy and may be working on many projects at once, you will be inclined to put client calls off, but do not do this. Always return a client's call first and then finish the job at hand. If you do not reach the client on the first try, continue to try to reach the client rather than letting the client call back for you.

> *Believe it or not, one of the key reasons clients feel rejected is the misuse of the telephone. Clients feel that calls are excessively screened. To them, the telephone represents accessibility. [One satisfied client said:]*
> *"He always calls me back the same day. I know I'm not his biggest client, but he makes me feel like my problems are important too."[9]*

BE COURTEOUS, EMPATHETIC, AND PROFESSIONAL AT ALL TIMES. Some clients at times may be abusive. Do not take client comments personally. Never become impatient with a client, "snap" at a client, or act rudely. If you have a problem with a client treating you abusively, mention it to your supervising attorney or legal assistant manager and let him or her handle it. Act professionally in all situations.

Finally, never allow a secretary or receptionist to let a client stay on hold after calling for you. If you are on another call and cannot get to the client immediately, have the receptionist tell the client you will return the call as soon as you get off the phone, then follow it up and call the client.

> *When I talk to new paralegals about dealing with clients, I always tell them to practice common courtesy. Keep "please" and "thank you" active in your vocabulary, and use them frequently. Keep your word: when you tell a client or coworker you will do something, do it. Practice the art of being gracious, even to the most difficult client. Give clients the respect they deserve simply because they are the firm's clients. Treat others as you would like to be treated. This is good service. Good service and good manners never go out of style!*
>
> Vanessa Beam, CLAS

RESPOND TO CLIENT REQUESTS IN A TIMELY FASHION AND KEEP YOUR PROMISES. It is not enough to simply return client phone calls. When clients request answers to questions, send letters, or need things from you, it is absolutely necessary that you respond as quickly as possible. If you tell the client that you will have something to him or her by a particular time or date, keep your promise. If an emergency comes up and you cannot make the deadline, always contact the client and let him or her know and set a new deadline that you can meet.

GIVE CLIENTS PERIODIC STATUS REPORTS. Some cases can be sitting on appeal for months, waiting for a motion to be ruled on, or facing other things that make them lie in a dormant state. This will always frustrate clients, who would like quick remedies to their problems. On a weekly or not less than a monthly basis, review your cases, and, with the approval of your attorney, write or e-mail clients letting them know what is happening in their cases. Word processors can be configured to make this a very quick process by having form letters on file for different situations. If the case is waiting for some kind of action, you should still write the client and let him or her know that you are waiting and have not forgotten the case. If you do not review the case periodically, the case could very well sit for months with no contact with the client. Keeping in touch with the client never hurts; it reiterates that his or her business is important to you.

DO NOT SHARE PERSONAL OR OFFICE PROBLEMS WITH CLIENTS. Always keep your personal problems to yourself and never make comments that are derogatory about your supervising attorney, firm, or other staff members. Clients need to know that their legal matters are in good hands and that everything is under control.

PRESERVE CLIENT CONFIDENCES. Preserving client confidences is very important and cannot be overemphasized. Apart from the ethics question, you should keep in mind that if a release of client information gets back to the client, the relationship is most likely finished.

THE USE OF CLIENT SURVEYS. A client survey is a way to find out exactly what your clients think of your services (see Figure 4-4). Most client questionnaires are given at the conclusion of a case. Anytime you get information directly from a client, you should take it to heart. Most firms allow the client to remain anonymous in completing the questionnaire to ensure truthfulness, and it is usually short, not more than a page long, to make completion as easy as possible.

MANAGEMENT MUST HELP PROMOTE GOOD CLIENT RELATIONSHIPS. Management also has a duty to promote good client relationships. Figure 4-5 contains a list of possible firm policies regarding communication with clients.

**Figure 4-4
A Client Questionnaire**

Adapted from *The Lawyer's Handbook*, American Bar Association, 1983. Reprinted by permission.

In order that we might provide efficient and skillful legal services to our clients at a cost which is not unreasonable, we are asking you to answer the questions listed below in the space provided. After doing so, would you please separate the top portion of this letter from the question section by tearing on the indicated line, and return the question section to us in the enclosed business reply envelope.

We are grateful for your time and effort involved in answering the questionnaire, and sincerely wish that your answers will help us obtain the results that we and our clients are striving for.

Sincerely,

1. Type of case: _____
2. Attorney or legal assistant _____
3. Has any member of our firm represented you before? _____
   If so, how many months/years ago? _____
4. Why did you choose our firm to represent you? _____
5. Were your telephone calls or e-mails to our office returned within a reasonable time? _____
6. Were you treated courteously by the members of our staff? _____
   If not, please explain: _____
7. Did you ever wait in the waiting room for an unreasonable period of time before seeing the attorney or legal assistant you had an appointment with? _____
   If yes, the number of times: _____
8. Were you informed, at the beginning of the case, as to the basis of our charges for legal services? _____
9. Were you sufficiently informed as to the progress of your case by the assigned attorney or legal assistant? _____

10. In your opinion, was the fee charged reasonable? _____
    If no, why not? _____
11. Were you satisfied with the results obtained in your case? _____
    If no, why not? _____
12. Would you recommend our law firm to another? _____
    If yes, why? _____
    If no, why not? _____
13. Please rate the general quality of the services performed by our law firm. _____
    (Excellent, Very Good, Good, Fair, Poor)_____
14. Comments:_____
    _____
    _____
    _____

- Clients should not be kept waiting in the reception area more than _____ minutes . . .
- Copies of documents should be mailed or e-mailed to clients within _____ days . . .
- A new case should be acknowledged in writing to a client within _____ days . . .
- Telephone calls should be answered within _____ rings . . .
- E-mail should be replied to within _____ days.
- Clients should not be left on hold longer than _____ seconds . . .
- All telephone calls should be returned within _____ hours . . .
- A client should receive a status report every _____ days . . .
- When an existing client refers another person to the firm, the client should be thanked for the referral within _____ days . . .

**Figure 4-5
Policies for
Timeliness**

Source: Adapted from "The Power of Communication of the Billing Process," by Milton Zwicker, in *Law Practice Management,* copyright © 1992, American Bar Association. Reprinted by permission.

PUBLISH A CLIENT MANUAL. Some law offices publish a manual for their clients, which explains what to expect from the law office, such as how attorney fees are calculated, how the attorney-client relationship works, what discovery is, how to prepare for a deposition, and what to expect at trial. This type of manual is very beneficial and will save the attorney and legal assistant from answering the same questions over and over for different clients.

RESOLVING CLIENT DISSATISFACTION

Resolving client dissatisfaction is not an easy task and may not be up to the legal assistant to resolve at all. Client dissatisfaction can have many roots, including personality conflicts with the legal staff, disagreement on strategy, misunderstandings, lack of knowledge about the law or facts, or frustration with the legal system. Here are some ideas on resolving client dissatisfaction.

> *I have sincerely tried to respond to every negative person/situation I have encountered in my career with the "kill'em with kindness" philosophy. It may not always soften them up, but it certainly keeps my conscience clear to know that I did not "stoop" to their level.*
>
> Lenette Pinchback, CLA

LISTEN TO THE COMPLAINT; DO NOT INTERRUPT AND DO NOT ARGUE. When a client has a complaint, the first thing to do is to listen carefully and patiently to the client. Listen with empathy and do not react. Avoid interrupting or arguing with the client: this is rude. In some instances, clients just want to vent about something they do not agree with, they see as unfair, or believe was a mistake. The client may be fully satisfied simply by finding someone who will listen patiently and to react in a courteous, professional manner. If the client is satisfied with this, thank him or her for the call, let him or her know you or the firm will try to correct this in the future, and then pass along the information to the appropriate parties who can prevent the problem from recurring.

> *I do not get involved with resolving client dissatisfaction and will leave it for the attorney to handle. In working with a difficult client, be careful about promising something that neither you nor the attorneys are capable of delivering. Be cordial to the difficult client, but do not be afraid to "punt" things to the attorney when necessary.*
>
> Linda Rushton, CLA

> *There are some very simple phrases that clients appreciate: "I will do my best." "I understand." "I know this is difficult for you."*
>
> *One thing to remember is that, no matter what, some clients are not ever going to be happy and you cannot please everyone, but you should at least be able to honestly say you tried.*
>
> Andrea Blanscet, CLA

EMPATHICALLY LISTEN. When speaking with a client regarding a complaint, it is usually good to acknowledge what he or she is saying and that you are listening by saying "Yes," or "Hmmmm," or "I see." Responses like these show that you are actively listening.

DO NOT OVERSTEP YOUR BOUNDS OR PROMISE SOMETHING YOU CANNOT DELIVER. A client may try to extract a promise from you to do something that you do not have the authority to do. Do not let a client force you into doing something you are not comfortable with or that you do not have the authority to do. In those instances, say something like, "I will talk to my supervising attorney and get back to you as soon as possible, hopefully by X." Telling the client an exact time you will get back to him or her should alleviate fears that the complaint will be ignored.

TAKE NOTES. Always take careful notes so that you can recount exactly what the complaint is about, including the fine details. This will allow you to relay it to others for the purpose of resolving the matter.

FORWARD SERIOUS COMPLAINTS TO YOUR SUPERVISING ATTORNEY AND BE HONEST. Serious complaints or complaints from clients who refuse to work with you should be immediately referred to your supervising attorney. If a client is calling to complain about a mistake you made and you know it is a mistake, be honest, admit the mistake to your supervising attorney, generate possible solutions to the problem, and put procedures in place to keep it from happening again.

DO NOT IGNORE THE COMPLAINT. If you receive a client complaint, never ignore or procrastinate on it. If a client believes he or she has been ignored or his or her comments summarily disregarded, he or she will only become more angry. The best thing to do is to resolve the matter as quickly as possible.

RECOGNIZE THAT SOME CLIENTS WILL ALWAYS COMPLAIN. Some clients are seemingly never happy and always have a complaint to make. Hopefully, the number of clients like this is very small, but nonetheless they do exist. The best thing to do is to treat the client as considerately as you can and talk to your supervising attorney. In extreme cases, a firm may decide to simply terminate the relationship and move on.

WORK THROUGH PERSONALITY CONFLICTS. Some client complaints may be the result of personality conflicts. In most instances, you should work through personality conflicts. In severe instances you may be able to request that another staff member handle the matter. This should be asked for as a last resort. In some instances, you may have to handle the matter anyway, either because there is no one else to take over or there is no one else with your experience regarding that client or the legal/factual issues involved.

COMMUNICATION SKILLS

> *Basically, the whole (legal assistant) profession is communication, and many of the problems that arise are going to be in that area.*[10]

**Figure 4-6
How Professionals Spend Their Time**

Source: Deborah Heller and James M. Hunt, *Practicing Law and Managing People* (Butterworth, 1988), 210. Courtesy of Heller, Hunt & Cunningham.

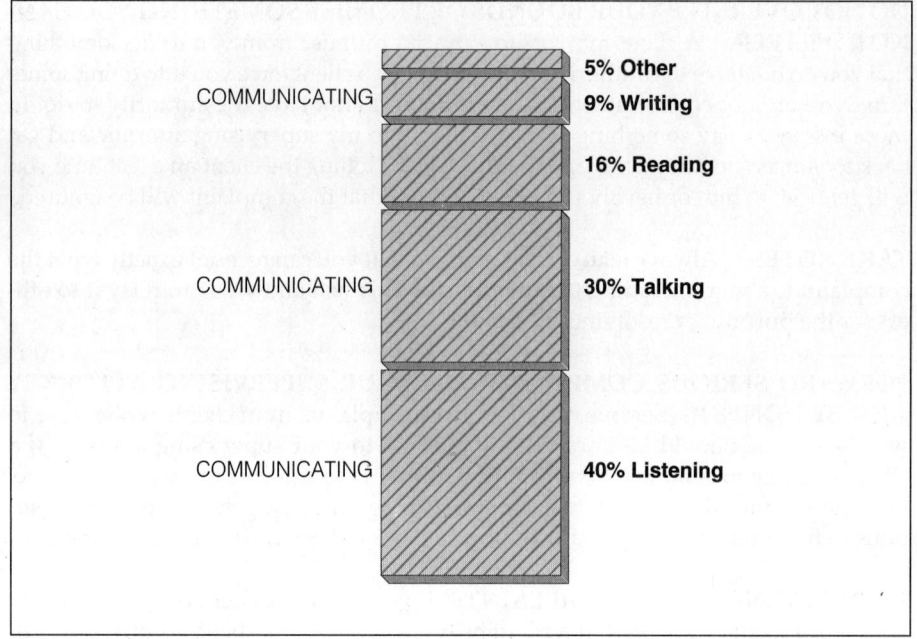

Possessing good communication skills is necessary in most professional jobs, but it is especially important in a law office. Legal assistants must communicate with clients, opposing counsel, supervising attorneys, office staff, court clerks, and witnesses on a daily basis regarding complex and important matters. Having good communication skills also bears directly on the effectiveness of law office management. Communication is an important part of management because, without it, management could not plan, organize, control, or direct the business. Thus, having good communication skills bears directly both on legal services to clients and on law office management.

GENERAL COMMUNICATION

communication
The transfer of a message from a sender to a receiver.

communication barrier
Something that inhibits or prevents the receiver from obtaining the correct message.

noise
Any situation that interferes with or distorts the message being communicated.

Professionals, such as legal assistants and attorneys, typically spend about 79 percent of each day communicating (see Figure 4-6). **Communication** is the transfer of a message from a sender to a receiver. Although communication can be quickly defined, it is more difficult to explain why there is so much poor communication in the world.

Figure 4-7 is a flow chart that shows how information is communicated. The abundance of communication barriers shows why some messages are never properly received. A **communication barrier** inhibits or prevents the receiver from obtaining the correct message from the sender. These barriers include situations where the sender and receiver have different cultural backgrounds, different perceptions, different understandings, and different ages. Noise is also a communication barrier. **Noise** interferes with or distorts the message being communicated. An example of noise is when one person is trying to listen to several senders at one time. The messages are distorted because the receiver cannot understand all the messages at the same time.

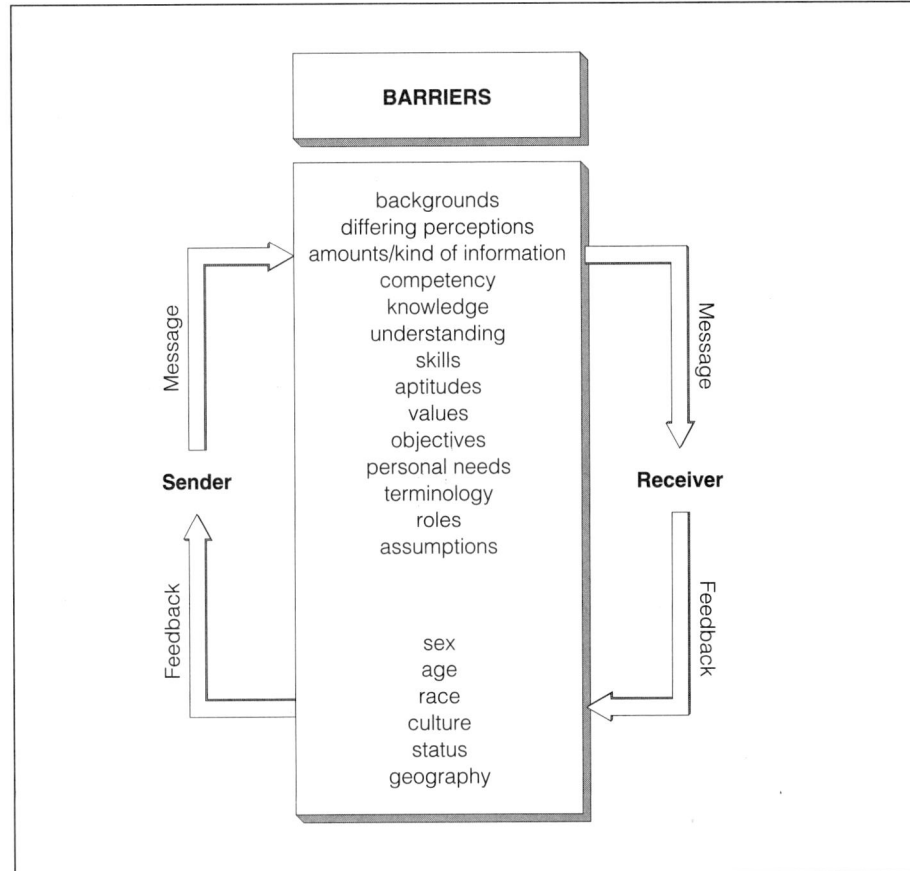

**Figure 4-7
Communication Diagram**

Source: Deborah Heller and James M. Hunt, *Practicing Law and Managing People* (Butterworth, 1988), 212. Courtesy of Heller, Hunt & Cunningham.

There are many other communication barriers as well (see Figure 4-7). Effective communicators are able to overcome these communication barriers and make their point.

Feedback is an important part of effective communication. **Feedback** is information sent in response to the sender's message. There is no way for the sender to know whether his information has been properly received without feedback. Feedback allows the receiver to state his understanding of the message and also allows the sender to evaluate the effectiveness of the message and to clarify misunderstood points. Feedback does not have to be verbal; it can be as simple as a puzzled look on the receiver's face.

feedback
Information sent in response to a message.

NONVERBAL COMMUNICATION

Communication is much more than just speech. There are many nonverbal communicators, such as eye contact, facial expressions, posture, appearance, clothing, tone of voice, and gestures. All these nonverbal means of communication have a hand in determining whether or not a message is properly received.

IMPROVING YOUR COMMUNICATION SKILLS

LISTEN. Listening is one of the most important features of communicating effectively, and although it sounds easy to do, often it is not. The average person forgets 50 percent of what was said to him or her within just a few minutes. We have all caught ourselves in the middle of conversations thinking about something unrelated to the conversation. We become "lazy listeners," only minimally listening. Figure 4-8 contains some excellent rules on listening. A common problem that attorneys and legal assistants are guilty of is that, instead of listening to what another person is saying, they formulate arguments and prepare for when they will speak. This effectively takes the listener out of good listening, and the listener may miss the total message.

> *Too often we listen with the ear of impatience, with the mind of a fixed idea. Sometimes our minds are so firmly fixed on formulating a response that we do not even hear what is being said.*[11]

KEEP IT SIMPLE AND TO THE POINT. Most people understand more of a message when the sender uses short, direct sentences rather than long, complex ones. You can explain complex issues to others: just use words and phrases they will understand. Avoid jargon and legalese when dealing with clients. In the same vein, research has shown that short letters are read sooner than are long ones, and the reader actually remembers the message of the short letter more accurately.

CONSIDER YOUR NONVERBAL SIGNALS. Realize that when you are communicating with people, they look at you and your message as a total package. They are considering how you are dressed, if you are nervous, if you are fidgeting, if you have your hands in your pockets, and if you have confidence in yourself.

DO NOT BECOME EMOTIONAL. Try not to be emotional when communicating. Try to be objective and calm, without being cold and distant.

MAKE EYE CONTACT. Make eye contact with everyone you are talking to, since it conveys honesty and interest. Juries, for instance, often cite the lack of eye contact as a reason that they did not believe a witness.

BE AWARE OF YOUR BODY LANGUAGE. Crossed arms usually mean you are feeling defensive, scared, or cold about something; poor posture is sometimes interpreted as lazy or slothful. One kind of body language that is more important than anything else for setting a positive tone is a simple smile. Smiling relaxes both your audience and you.

BE PRECISE AND CLEAR. Always try to be as precise as possible when communicating with others. How often have you heard someone say, "Well, I thought

> 1. **STOP TALKING!**
>   You cannot listen if you are talking.
> 2. **PUT THE TALKER AT EASE.**
>   Help the person feel that he or she is free to talk.
> 3. **SHOW THE INDIVIDUAL THAT YOU WANT TO LISTEN.**
>   Look and act interested. Do not read your mail while the person talks. Listen to understand, rather than to oppose.
> 4. **REMOVE DISTRACTIONS.**
>   Do not doodle, tap, or shuffle papers. Will it be quieter if you shut the door?
> 5. **EMPATHIZE WITH THE PERSON.**
>   Try to see the other's point of view.
> 6. **BE PATIENT.**
>   Allot plenty of time. Do not interrupt. Don't start for the door or walk away.
> 7. **HOLD YOUR TEMPER.**
>   An angry person gets the wrong meaning from words.
> 8. **GO EASY ON ARGUMENT AND CRITICISM.**
>   This puts the person on the defensive. He or she may "clam up" or get angry. Do not argue: Even if you win, you lose.
> 9. **ASK QUESTIONS.**
>   This encourages the speaker and shows you are listening. It helps to develop points further.
> 10. **STOP TALKING!**
>   This is first and last, because all other commandments depend on it. You cannot do a good listening job while you are talking. Nature gave man two ears but only one tongue, which is a gentle hint that he should listen more than he talks.

**Figure 4-8
The Ten Commandments of Good Listening**

Source: Keith Davis, *Human Behavior at Work*, 7th ed., copyright © 1985, McGraw-Hill. Reprinted with permission of McGraw-Hill.

you meant...." Speak clearly and do not leave anything to the imagination. For example, if you tell a delivery person you need something filed at the courthouse, be sure you are precise and tell him or her whether you need it filed at the federal courthouse, the local courthouse, or the state courthouse. These subtle differences can be very important in a law office, so be absolutely clear when you communicate. Look for feedback. If someone has a puzzled look on his or her face, explain your message again or ask him or her to repeat it to you.

CONSIDER YOUR AUDIENCE. Always tailor your communication to the specific audience with which you are communicating. You can have the best message in the world, but if you are delivering it to someone who does not care about it, you have wasted your effort. If possible, find out what is important to your audience, what concerns it has, and then tailor everything you say to address these concerns.

CONSIDER THE TIMING AND CONTEXT. Timing is everything. A good communicator must know when to communicate his or her message. Be patient and wait until the time is right. Time your message so that noise and barriers are kept to a minimum. You may want to wait until the receiver is in a good mood or has just received good news. Communication is an art; people will react to the same message in different ways depending on the timing. For your message to be effective, you must consider the context in which the communication is being made. Is the receiver having a bad day? Where is the communication taking place: in a crowded hallway or in a private office? What type of relationship have you had with the receiver? Do you respect each other, dislike each other, or distrust each other?

Try to consider the other person's perception of your communication. Consider this: when you find yourself in a disagreement with someone, are you more likely to believe that *your behavior is motivated by context* (i.e. you had a bad day, you're tired, you're stressed out) while you believe that the *other person's behavior is motivated not by context, but by something personal* (such as spite, revenge, meanness, or unreasonableness)? Actually, this is a normal reaction. Consider the context and the environment in which the other person is viewing your communication; look at it from his or her point of view and be aware of your own biases. This will improve your ability to communicate with others.

DO NOT BE JUDGMENTAL/AVOID NEGATIVES. Do not start with negative or judgmental comments such as "That probably will not work." This will only make your audience defensive. Try to be positive and explore the conversation in a positive light. If you do not think an idea will work, ask a question about why you think it might not work, such as "Well, have you considered what would happen if this occurred . . . .? Will your idea still be successful?" This allows the other person to consider your side but in a positive, constructive light.

ASK QUESTIONS. Never assume something based on unsupported evidence. It is very easy for people to misread or assume things about other people. Instead of assuming something incorrectly, ask questions and talk about it. This will allow you to verify whether or not your initial assumptions were accurate.

REPHRASE IDEAS. If you are not sure whether you truly understand what someone has told you, try rephrasing. **Rephrasing** is the technique of telling the sender what your understanding of the conversation is. It allows the sender to clarify information that might not have been understood clearly.

rephrasing
A technique used to improve communication by repeating back to a person what your understanding of the conversation was.

RECOGNIZE THE IMPORTANCE OF GOOD COMMUNICATION WITH THIRD PARTIES. A legal assistant deals with many types of people, including witnesses, court personnel, outside agencies, libraries, businesses, and other law offices. It is very important that you be professional at all times and have good relationships with these third parties, since they may provide information that will help you perform your job. When possible, cultivate these relationships.

TELEPHONE TECHNIQUES

Poor telephone techniques abound in many law offices. Here are some examples of what not to do.

- Office staff: "Law offices."
  Client: "May I speak to Mr. Smith?"
  Office staff: "Sure, just a sec."
- Office staff: "Law offices."
  Client: "May I speak to Mr. Smith?"
  Office staff: "He's yakking on the other line, you want to hold?"
- Office staff: "Law offices."
  Client: "May I speak to Mr. Smith?"
  Office staff: "He's not in. Why don't you call back this afternoon."

Good telephone techniques are important in any legal organization. Most legal professionals spend a great deal of time on the phone and need courteous telephone skills.

ALWAYS COMMUNICATE IN A BUSINESSLIKE, PROFESSIONAL TONE. Because callers cannot see your body language and facial expressions on the phone, what you say and the tone you use are very important. Always be calm and professional when talking on the phone. If you have a million things to do and you are flustered or might get short with the caller, then do not answer the phone. Call back when you are calm.

PUT THE CALLER AT EASE. Whenever possible, listen carefully and make appropriate responses that put the caller at ease. You gain nothing by quick responses that may alienate the caller.

REFER TO THE CALLER BY NAME. When the caller tells you his or her name, call the person by that name: *"Mr. Smith, I'll page her immediately."* This puts the caller at ease and lets him or her know you remember who he or she is. It also communicates personal service.

WHEN TAKING A MESSAGE, ALWAYS OBTAIN THE TELEPHONE NUMBER OF THE CALLER. Many times, callers will say that the person whom they are calling already has their number. Obtain a call-back number from the caller anyway, just in case the number recently changed, number has been lost, the caller has a new number, or just because it is more convenient for the person to return the call.

WHEN TAKING A CALLER'S NAME OR PHONE NUMBER ALWAYS REPEAT BACK THE INFORMATION. By repeating the information back to the caller, you confirm that you received the message correctly and that the name and number are accurate. Think how frustrated you get when someone takes a message and does not record the information accurately.

ALWAYS IDENTIFY YOURSELF AS A LEGAL ASSISTANT. If you are taking a call from a client, attorney, or a third party regarding a case, always identify yourself as a legal assistant early in the conversation.

WHEN TAKING A MESSAGE, GET A GENERAL "FEEL" FOR THE SUBJECT. When taking a message, it is important to get a general "feel" for what the caller needs because you might be able to handle the matter yourself. If you cannot, then do not ask for too much information, from clients in particular. Some clients do not like to give out details about their problems.

BE WARY OF MOBILE PHONES. When speaking on a mobile phone be careful that the conversation is not about sensitive client matters. Although mobile phones are becoming more secure, it is prudent to be careful.

WHEN TAKING A MESSAGE, EXPLAIN BRIEFLY WHY THE INDIVIDUAL CALLED IS NOT IN. Giving a short explanation as to why someone cannot take a call, such as "Susan is in court this morning," lets the caller know that the person is not ducking their call. Avoid saying the person is "unavailable."

TRY TO ANSWER YOUR PHONE WHEN YOU ARE NOT WITH A CLIENT. In the era of e-mail and voice mail, sometimes clients want to talk to a person to discuss a matter. If possible, try to answer your phone instead of letting it roll to voice mail. Clients can become quite frustrated when they cannot reach someone on the phone, particularly when the client has an emergency.

DO NOT KEEP CALLERS ON HOLD EXCEPT FOR A VERY SHORT PERIOD OF TIME. Nothing is more frustrating to a caller than to be indefinitely put on hold. If you must place a caller on hold, do so for only a very short period of time. Continually update the caller as to the status of his or her call.

LEADERSHIP AND COMMUNICATION

Being a leader takes a special type of communication skill. In Chapter 1, leadership was described as the act of motivating or causing others to perform and achieve objectives. Leaders give us direction, vision, and motivation. Leadership is an important part of any organization or department. Legal assistants need to take leadership roles, and there are opportunities for legal assistants who have leadership skills. For instance, legal assistants can be legal assistant managers or law office administrators. Legal assistant "leaders" can take on projects and cases that need innovation and that have never been done before. Legal assistants with leadership characteristics are sought after and are important to growing law offices.

HOW DO I BECOME A LEADER? Having determined that leadership qualities are essential for the legal assistant, the next question is: "How does one become a leader?" This has been a hotly debated issue over the years. Early leadership theories said that only exceptional people were capable of assuming the leadership role (i.e. you either were or were not born with it). But current research overwhelmingly shows that leaders are not born, they are made. The following are some suggestions on how to be a leader.

1. **Be an expert.** Effective leaders are experts in what they do. They know precisely what they are talking about. People around them have confidence in their abilities and rely upon their knowledge and judgment. They are inventive and ingenious and are able to plan, organize, and manage resources to solve problems. Before they give opinions, they do research and master the subject they are talking about. Leaders must be competent, make good decisions, and be able to evaluate situations and act accordingly.
2. **Be honest.** Effective leaders have a reputation for being extremely honest and forthright and possessing a high degree of integrity. These are important qualities; subordinates must respect leaders and must be motivated, inspired, and willing to follow their directives.
3. **Stay calm.** Good leaders stay cool and collected, even when they are "under fire." They have confidence in their own abilities and are not shaken by disagreement or challenge. Instead, they rise to the occasion.
4. **Trust and support those under you.** Good leaders choose effective and competent subordinates and then support them in their efforts. Subordinates know that they are trusted and their abilities and skills are appreciated and thus work even harder for the leader.
5. **Take risks and do not be afraid of failure.** Effective leaders take calculated risks. They focus on the positive and refuse to think about failure. Failures and mistakes are steps in the learning process and are to be expected. Leaders have the ability to make a bold decision and to stand by it when others are backpedaling.
6. **Encourage honest opinions from others.** Effective leaders encourage subordinates to be honest and to articulate their opinions, even if those opinions are in disagreement with the leader's. Debate sharpens the decision-making process so that all alternatives are considered and evaluated based on their merits. This is the only way situations can be properly evaluated. Leaders encourage others around them to cooperate and communicate with each other by listening to everyone's ideas and opinions.
7. **Set goals and visions.** Effective leaders set goals and have specific visions of the future. The goals and visions inspire and empower others to accomplish the goals and to work toward the common dream.
8. **Be respectful.** Good leaders respect others and get along with and care for other people. They foster meaningful, personal, and professional relationships with the people around them.

Communication is at the center of leadership. Leaders emerge when a new crisis arises or when a new challenge surfaces. Leaders are able to put together a solution, empower their subordinates to support it, reshape and retool their resources, and come up with a package that meets the new challenge and solves the problem.

GROUP COMMUNICATION

Communicating in groups involves a whole different set of variables than communicating one-on-one. Legal assistants must routinely work with groups, including groups of attorneys and legal assistants on trials and similar projects, and with clients and attorneys on cases. Additionally, they serve on committees and associations. The following are some commonly known advantages and disadvantages of group work.

- Groups tend to make more accurate decisions than do individuals. As the adage says, "Two heads are better than one." That is, there are more points of view to be heard and considered and a greater number of solutions offered and analyzed in a group.
- Once a group has arrived at a decision, there is an increase in the acceptance of the final choice because group members were involved in the process.
- Group members can communicate and explain the group's decision to others because they were included.
- Once a decision has been made by a group, implementation is easier because the group members were involved in the process and have a "stake in the action."
- Decisions by groups take up to 50 percent longer to make than do decisions by individuals.
- Group decisions are often compromises between different points of view rather than the most appropriate alternative.
- Group decisions can sometimes result in groupthink. **Groupthink** occurs when the desire for group cohesiveness and consensus becomes stronger than the desire for the best possible decision.
- Groups sometimes make more risky decisions than do individuals, especially when there is no one individual responsible for the consequences of the group decision.
- Groups are sometimes dominated by one or more individuals who rank higher in status in the organization.

groupthink
Term for when the desire for group cohesiveness and consensus becomes stronger than the desire for the best possible decision.

COMMUNICATION IN INTERVIEWING CLIENTS, WITNESSES, AND THIRD PARTIES

Interviewing clients, witnesses, and third parties is a specialized communication skill that you will need to possess. In many firms, interviews are conducted by experienced legal assistants or attorneys. However, new legal assistants sit in on interviews with an experienced legal assistant or attorney to learn good interviewing skills.

The initial client interview is very important, because it is usually the first real contact the client may have with the firm. The purpose of the interview is to relax the client, to convince the client that he or she has come to the right firm, and to gather enough information to decide whether your firm and responsible attorney are interested in representing the client or at least finding out more about the case. The following are some suggestions for handling each part of the interview and what to do should you encounter difficulties. Figure 4-9 is an evaluation sheet to evaluate your interviewing skills. While Figure 4-9 is specifically geared toward a client interview, many of the same principles apply to all interviewing.

PREPARE FOR THE INTERVIEW.   One of the simplest things you can do to make sure an interview will go well is to prepare for it. Always try to get as much initial information as possible before the interview. Establish a checklist of questions you want to ask and specific information you want to gather. You must establish what the purpose or goal of the interview is, and then steer the interview toward the direction of the goal. For example, if you routinely interview clients regarding workers' compensation claims, there is certain information that you must have. Establish exactly what information you need and then draft a checklist and an agenda to ensure that you obtain the information.

Many law offices also have an intake form on which the client generally describes why he or she has come to the firm. All this information will help you to prepare for the interview. Also, whoever is setting up the interview should always ask the client to bring in any documentation that may be relevant.

BREAK THE ICE.   The beginning of any interview brings apprehension both for the interviewer and interviewee. Ways to break the ice include meeting the client in

---

Client Interviewing
1. Planning for client interviews
   a. In planning for client interviews generally, do I consider
      (1) the length of the typical first interview?
      (2) the best seating arrangement?
      (3) how to minimize interruptions?
      (4) discouraging the presence of third persons unless absolutely necessary?
      (5) my personal appearance?
      (6) what information I will give to the client?
   b. In planning for specific client interviews, do I
      (1) conduct an initial conflicts check?
      (2) conduct initial legal research or review?
      (3) note appropriate areas of factual inquiry?
      (4) consult checklists of general areas of inquiry?
      (5) identify which documents the client should bring to the interview?
      (6) consider giving the client a written questionnaire to complete and bring to the interview?
   c. Do I have readily available sources to consult in preparation for client interviews, such as
      (1) treatises?
      (2) texts?
      (3) form books?
      (4) sample checklists?
      (5) sample questionnaires?

(continued)

**Figure 4-9
Client Interviewing:
Self-Evaluation**
Copyright 1993 by the American Law Institute. Reprinted with the permission of the American Law Institute—American Bar Association Committee on Continuing Professional Education.

2. Interviewing skills
   a. Do I seek to develop rapport with a client by
      (1) putting the client at ease?
      (2) adopting an attitude of friendliness, courtesy, and patience?
      (3) demonstrating interest without becoming overly emotional or involved?
      (4) maintaining a receptive, nonjudgmental attitude toward the client as a person?
      (5) encouraging and allowing the client to talk openly?
      (6) listening attentively to the client?
      (7) interrupting the client only when necessary?
      (8) using language understandable to the client?
      (9) using active listening responses?
      (10) offering support to the client?
      (11) recognizing communication blocks?
      (12) showing respect for the client and avoiding condescension?
      (13) encouraging client questions?
   b. Do I seek to maximize information gathering by
      (1) encouraging a complete factual narrative?
      (2) avoiding premature diagnosis of the client's problem?
      (3) focusing on topics likely to elicit relevant information?
      (4) identifying additional topics as the interview progresses?
      (5) sequencing questions from general to specific or vice versa?
      (6) avoiding undue influence on client responses?
      (7) using open-ended questions, when appropriate?
      (8) using leading questions, when appropriate?
      (9) making sure that the client understands my questions?
      (10) making sure that I understand the client's answers?
   c. Do I periodically evaluate and attempt to improve my interviewing skills by
      (1) reading current literature on interviewing skills?
      (2) transcribing an interview, with the client's permission?
      (3) reviewing the transcript?
      (4) attending CLE programs designed to enhance interviewing skills?
3. Making a prompt, detailed, and accurate record
   a. Do I have a reliable system for preserving information gained in the interview by
      (1) taking notes during the interview?
      (2) without disrupting communication (e.g., by maintaining eye contact)?
      (3) making a detailed record immediately after the interview?
      (4) including follow-up plans in this record?
      (5) making this record sufficiently clear and detailed so that it could be reviewed or used by another lawyer?

the waiting room, offering your hand for a handshake, accompanying the client back to your office, and talking to the client about the weather or other neutral topics. Always wear a smile and be warm and friendly. Another interesting way to break the ice is to ask the client or witness about his or her family. This allows you to gain some background information. Some people may think this is nosy. You may want to tell the person that the questions are not meant to embarrass him or her, but simply to understand who he or she is and to get the "big picture." You also may want to explain about the confidentiality of everything that he or she tells you.

ALWAYS INFORM THE PERSON YOU ARE INTERVIEWING OF YOUR STATUS AS A LEGAL ASSISTANT. Once the client is relaxed and is ready to talk about why he or she is there, indicate your status as a legal assistant. Do not make a prolonged speech, which may demonstrate your lack of confidence; simply state, "I am a legal assistant, and I work for Ms. Smith, who is an attorney here." You should also tell the person what you will be doing and what the attorney is going to do: "I will initially be talking to you about your case. I will take down the facts of your case and then prepare a memo to the attorney about it. The attorney will then contact you to discuss it more in depth." Once you have done that, you are ready to begin the interview. Many people begin by asking an open-ended statement such as, "Tell me why you are here. Start at the beginning."

LISTEN CAREFULLY. Listening carefully to the client's story is sometimes hard to do. The client may ramble, talk about events out of sequence, and talk about matters that may be irrelevant to the legal problem. However, refrain from leading the conversation, at least during the first part of the interview. Be patient and let the client tell the whole story his or her own way. Then go back and fill in the details by asking questions. Do not take too many notes during the first part of the interview. You should give the client your undivided attention and try to make eye contact. Clients need to be reassured that you are interested in their case. As you listen, determine whether the client's story makes sense and think of what facts the client may be leaving out.

COMMUNICATE SINCERITY. For any interview to be successful, you must communicate that you are sincerely interested in the client's problem. Characteristics such as dominance or defensiveness are counterproductive to establishing sincerity. One of the best ways you can communicate sincerity is to show you are really listening to what the person is saying by asking thoughtful questions. Avoid appearing as if you are "grilling" a client.

BE EMPATHETIC. Be empathetic with the client, letting him or her know that you feel for him or her and for the situation he or she is in. Empathy is distinguished from sympathy, which is feeling sorry for the individual. However, be sure to keep your objectivity. Sometimes the client may have to describe very personal, traumatic, or embarrassing information. In that case, you need to be extra sensitive and inform the client that everything said is confidential and is necessary so that you understand what happened.

ORGANIZE THE INFORMATION. Once you have listened to the client tell his or her story the first time through, you are ready to organize the information. A common way to organize the client's story is to build a chronology of events that starts at the beginning of the problem and works forward. This helps the client relive the facts in a particular order and may cause the client to remember more exact details. However, be aware that clients seldom remember things in exact order, so it usually takes several times through before your chronology is accurate.

ASK APPROPRIATE QUESTIONS. When you want to get detailed information about a particular event, remember to ask who, what, when, and where questions. However, do not ask leading questions that might suggest a particular answer, such as, "You saw the traffic light as you were going through and it was green, right?" Ask your questions carefully. A better approach might be to say, "Describe the intersection before the accident."

Also, avoid compound questions that ask the client to answer two or more questions. For example, "How many cars were in the intersection and when was the first time you saw the blue car?" Ask your questions one at a time.

DO NOT BE JUDGMENTAL. Never be judgmental toward a client. Saying things like "You really need to get a grip on yourself," "You are acting like a child," or "You can't mean that," is the opposite of being empathetic, which is what you ideally want to be. Avoid questions that begin with "Why did you . . .?". This type of question might be viewed as judgmental. These questions put the client on the defensive.

NEVER SAY "YOU HAVE A GREAT CASE." Be very careful about judging the client's case. Do not make any promises to the client and never tell the client what a great case he or she has, since this may be bordering on giving legal advice. At this stage you do not have enough information to make that determination. Lawsuits are usually too complex for this type of statement.

LEAVE FEE DISCUSSIONS TO THE ATTORNEY. Discussions regarding whether the firm is going to take the case and discussions about the amount of the fee should be left to the attorney.

CLOSE THE INTERVIEW APPROPRIATELY. Do not close the interview too quickly. Before you close, be sure to do the following.

- Get copies of all the documentation that the client brought.
- Instruct the client not to discuss the case with anyone else.
- Reassure the client by telling him or her exactly what your office will be doing and when it will be done. For example: "I will draft a memo to the attorney, our office will do some preliminary legal research, and this will be completed by Friday. Our office will call you Friday to set up an appointment for early next week." Never tell the client that "the attorney will get back to you as soon as he can." Clients want to know exactly what is going to happen and when it is going to happen.

- Review your checklist to make sure you have obtained all the information you need.
- Have the client sign any release or authorization you might need to get information, such as a medical release for the client's files from a doctor or hospital.
- List everything the client did *not* bring with him or her. Give a copy of the list to the client with a self-addressed return envelope.
- Thank the client for coming into the office, reassure the client that you will be in contact with him or her shortly, and instruct him or her that, if he or she remembers anything else that is important, to be sure to give you a call. Give the client your business card.

INTERNET SITES

ORGANIZATION	DESCRIPTION	INTERNET ADDRESS
ABA LAW Practice Today	ABA site devoted to law practice management	www.abanet.org/lpm
Association of Legal Administrators	Site for legal administrators	www.alanet.org

SUGGESTED READING

Connecting With Your Client, Noelle Nelson, American Bar Association, 1996.

Easy Self-Audits for the Busy Law Office, Nancy Byerly Jones, American Bar Association, 1999.

How to Get and Keep Good Clients, Jay Foonberg, American Bar Association, 1990.

Through the Client's Eyes, Henry Ewalt, American Bar Association, 1994.

You and Your Clients—A Guide to Client Management Skills for a More Successful Practice, Stanley Clawar, American Bar Association, 1996.

SUMMARY

Attorneys have an ethical duty to communicate with their clients and legal assistants can play an active role in this process. Legal assistants must be able to establish effective client relationships. Clients like attorneys and legal assistants to be friendly, prompt and businesslike, courteous, and informative.

Effective communication is essential in law firms. Communication is the transfer of a message from a sender to a receiver. A communication barrier inhibits or prevents the receiver from obtaining the correct message from the sender. There are many different communication barriers, including the receiver and sender having different cultural backgrounds, using different terminology, and having different values. Interviewing clients is a communication skill that legal assistants use on a consistent basis.

Key Terms

Communication
Communication barrier
Noise

Feedback
Rephrasing
Groupthink

Questions and Exercises

1. You are a legal assistant working for an attorney in a large law firm. A general counsel from one of the corporations you work with calls you and tells you that he had just read the legal arguments regarding a Motion for Summary judgment that the firm prepared and that you worked on. He tells you the legal analysis is extremely weak. You can tell by his voice that he is unhappy. What do you do next?

2. You are a legal assistant for a sole practitioner. The attorney represents a client named Betty Johnson in a probate matter that has dragged on for years. Ms. Johnson calls to inquire about the status of her case. She says that she has not heard from the attorney in over a year, and that she has no idea what is going on in the case. You know that the attorney has long since quit working the case and has closed his file. The file takes up three file drawers in the file room. You tell the attorney about Ms. Johnson's call and he says not to worry about it. What is your analysis of the matter? What would you do next?

3. You are a legal assistant in a legal aid office. The executive director calls you into his office to let you know that he has received complaints from clients regarding legal assistants being less than courteous on the phone and in person. The executive director gives you one week to begin turning this situation around. He mentions on his way out the door that, in addition to a short-term solution, he wants a long-term solution to the problem. How would you proceed?

4. Over the years you have become friends with one of your law office's best clients. The client likes you and believes in your ability as a competent legal assistant. Recently, you have spent many hours, including evenings and weekends, working on the client's case. The client comes in for an appointment to see you about his case. The client notices that you look very tired and ragged. You tell the client how many hours you have been working on the case to let him know about the hard work that the law office is doing. The client responds by saying that he is going to the lead attorney on the case and demand that you be given an increase for all the extra time you have spent on the case. You are flattered that a client would think of your interest and you could certainly use the money. How would you handle this situation?

5. You are a legal assistant manager at a medium-size law office. The Executive Committee thinks that the law office needs to put more emphasis on client services. You are a respected part of the firm and the committee thinks you interact with clients exceptionally well. The committee has approved the development of a client manual that will be given to all its clients. The committee has chosen you to be in charge of developing the manual in the initial stages. Your task is to prepare a client manual that will be presented to the Executive Committee within thirty days. In addition, once the committee approves the manual, you also will be in charge of implementing the manual's use. The committee is giving you control to research and develop the manual.

Assume you have never heard of or developed a client manual before. Assume you can choose to either accept the task or not accept it. Would you accept the assignment? Why or why not? How would you develop the client manual? Would you choose to use a work group or not? What sections or key points would you include in the manual? Give reasons for your answers.

6. From an ethical perspective only, analyze what the benefits are to a law office that routinely sends copies of all documents to its clients.

7. As a legal assistant in a busy office, you try your best to talk to clients when they call and to pass along information from the client to your supervising attorney, but sometimes you forget. On one such occasion, a client called you because she was unable to talk to the attorney. The client called with vital information that the attorney needed regarding an important aspect of the case. Unfortunately, you failed to pass the information along. Discuss from an ethics and malpractice standpoint the importance of communication skills.

8. Think of someone you know that you think is a good leader. Write down why you think this person is a good leader and what outstanding qualities he or she has. How do the qualities listed compare with the information in the chapter? What leadership qualities do you have?

9. Think about a group or committee that you have worked on. Write down the dynamics of how the group interacted. Who emerged as the leader and why? Looking back, do you see any evidence of groupthink? Did the group members communicate with each other effectively? Was the group successful at accomplishing its purpose? Why or why not? Did you feel like an active member of the group? Why or why not? If you could have changed one thing about the group, what would it have been?

NOTES

1. *California Lawyer,* June 2000, p. 71. Reprinted with permission from *California Lawyer.*
2. *California Lawyer,* March 2000, p. 69. Reprinted with permission from *California Lawyer.*
3. Robert Greene, *Making Partner,* American Bar Association, 1992. Reprinted by permission.
4. *Annotated Model Rules of Professional Conduct,* American Bar Association, 4th ed., 2000, p. 32 citing *Sage Realty v. Proskauer Rose Goetz,* 666 N.Y.S.2d 985, 988 (App. Div. 1997). Reprinted by permission. Copies of the ABA Model Code of Professional Responsibility, 1999 edition, are available from Service Center, American Bar Association, 750 North Lake Shore Drive, Chicago, IL 60611-4497, 1-800-285-2221.
5. Patrick J. McKenna, "Develop a 'First Mover' Advantage," *Law Practice Management,* January/February 2000. Reprinted by permission.
6. Stanley Clawar, *You and Your Clients—A Guide to Client Management Skills for a More Successful Practice,* American Bar Association, 1996, p. 3. Reprinted by permission.
7. Milton Zwicker, "What Can You Glean from Client Feedback?" *Law Practice Management,* January/February 2000, p. 51. Reprinted by permission.
8. Sally J. Schmidt, *What Clients Say* (Burnsville, MN: Sally Schmidt Consulting, Inc., 1989) p. 14.
9. Sally J. Schmidt, *What Clients Say* (Burnsville, MN: Sally Schmidt Consulting, Inc., 1989) p. 19.
10. Schmidt, p. 19–20.
11. Cynthia Tokumitsu, "How to Avoid the Top 10 Mistakes Paralegals Make on the Job," *Legal Assistant Today,* November/December 1991, p. 27. Copyright 1991. James Publishing, Inc. Reprinted with permission from *Legal Assistant Today* magazine. For subscription information call 800-394-2626 or visit www.legalassistanttoday.com.
12. Mary H. Mocine, "The Art of Listening," *California Lawyer,* July 2000, p. 23. Reprinted with permission from *California Lawyer.*

Notes

1. Adapted from Robert Michael Greene, *Making Partner* (Chicago: American Bar Association, copyright © 1992). Reprinted with permission.

Case Review

—In re J. Gregory Caver, 97–0823 (La. 5/1/97, 693 So.2d 150.)

(Cite as: 97-0823

(La. 5/1/97), 693 So.2d 150)

Supreme Court of Louisiana.

In re J. Gregory CAVER.

Nos. 97-B-0823, 97-B-0824.

May 1, 1997.

**150 DISCIPLINARY PROCEEDINGS

1 PER CURIAM. [FN]

FN* Kimball, J., not on panel. Supreme Court Rule IV, Part 2, § 3.

On April 5, 1996, respondent, J. Gregory Caver, an attorney licensed to practice in the State of Louisiana, was charged by disciplinary counsel with one count of formal charges, alleging failure to perform work for which he was hired to do, failure to communicate with his clients, failure to return client papers and failure to refund an unearned fee, in violation of Rules 1.1, 1.3, 1.4, 1.5(f), 1.16(d), and 8.4(a)(b) and (c) of the Rules of Professional Conduct.

The underlying facts indicate that on July 30, 1991, respondent was retained by Laura and Larkin Tidwell to expeditiously process a step-parent adoption matter. Although he was paid $500, respondent failed to perform the work, and steadfastly covered up his neglect for almost a year by telling his clients the court docket was "backed up" and that the Office of Family Services had misplaced their file. He advised his clients of an alleged court date and arranged for them to meet at his office, but did not show up for the meeting. Respondent also misrepresented to his clients that the judge would sign the adoption papers on an ex parte basis since they were friends, and that he was waiting on an amended birth certificate, a document usually issued only after a final decree of adoption is rendered.

Subsequently, the Tidwells filed a complaint with the Office of Disciplinary Counsel on April 16, 1992. In addition, they wrote respondent on May 8, 1992 demanding an accounting and that their file be returned. Although they received their file one month later, respondent failed to provide an accounting. As a result, the Tidwells wrote another letter to disciplinary counsel requesting assistance to recover their unearned retainer fee since their file indicated respondent had failed to perform any work.

151 Respondent provided disciplinary counsel with several written responses to the Tidwell's complaints, which included allegations that he prepared (although admittedly did not process) the adoption papers, and that he had issued a reimbursement check to his clients for the unearned ***2 fee on July 9, 1993. However, disciplinary counsel later found that the check was dishonored by the drawee bank as having been drawn against insufficient funds, and the unearned fee was not refunded until December 3, 1996.

On July 13, 1993, respondent appeared for a deposition at the request of disciplinary counsel, but refused to directly answer questions propounded to him. After formal charges were filed, respondent failed to file an answer.

Based on respondent's failure to answer, the matter was submitted to the hearing committee on documentary evidence only. On October 13, 1993, the hearing committee rendered its findings of fact and recommendation. It found that respondent failed to diligently represent his clients, failed to properly communicate with and communicated false information to his clients, failed to return client documents and unearned fees, and engaged in conduct involving dishonesty, fraud, deceit, and misrepresentation in violation of Rules 1.3, 1.4, 1.16(d), and 8.4(a) and (c) of the Rules of Professional Conduct. As such, it determined the appropriate baseline sanction was suspension in light of respondent's other disciplinary transgressions. [FN1] The committee recommended to the disciplinary board that respondent be suspended for one year and a day. As conditions for readmission, it further recommended respondent obtain three (3) hours of law school credit in professional ethics, retake the ethics part of the bar examination, and pay all costs, dues and assessments.

> FN1. Respondent's prior discipline includes:
> 1. Formal private reprimand, conflict of interest, 5/1/85;
> 2. Admonition, 93-ADB-031, 6/24/93, failure to cooperate;
> 3. Public reprimand, 93-2698 (La.1/13/94); 632 So.2d 1157, commingling and conversion of client funds;
> 4. Admonition, 93-ADB-092, 2/2/94, failure to cooperate;
> 5. Admonition, 93-ADB-099, 2/25/94, misrepresentation;
> 6. Admonition, 94-ADB-071, 8/22/94, failure to cooperate;
> 7. Admonition, 93-ADB-078, 9/1/94, failure to cooperate;
> 8. Admonition, 93-ADB-108, 11/16/94, failure to cooperate;
> 9. Admonition, 94-ADB-109, 11/16/94, failure to cooperate;
> 10. Admonition, 94-ADB-111, 11/16/94, failure to cooperate;
> 11. Admonition, 94-ADB-003, 3/30/95, failure to cooperate;
> 12. Admonition, 95-ADB-013, 3/30/95, diligence, communication; and,
> 13. Admonition, 95-ADB-031, failure to cooperate.

The hearing committee's recommendation was considered by a panel of the disciplinary board; however, the board did not issue a written recommendation because the respondent was *3 placed on interim suspension in an unrelated proceeding. In re Caver, 96-0280 (La.3/28/96), 670 So.2d 1217.

Prior to the filing of formal charges arising from this subsequent proceeding, respondent submitted a petition for consent discipline on August 15, 1996 admitting to harming forty-nine (49) clients and proposing his disbarment, with restitution to all victims and payment of costs of the proceedings as conditions to readmission. [FN2] Disciplinary counsel **152 concurred with the consent discipline, noting that respondent had converted $83,092.13 in client funds and had 13 prior disciplinary proceedings dating back to 1985.

> FN2. In the Stipulation of Facts filed with the Petition for Consent Discipline, respondent admitted to the following violations of the Rules of Professional Conduct and other misconduct:
>
> 42 instances of failing to properly withdraw as counsel by failing to return client files, failing to protect a client's interest, failing to return an unearned fee and failing to complete a matter; 41 instances of failing to return unearned fees; 41 instances of failing to communicate with clients and/or misrepresenting cases to clients; 37 instances of failing to use due diligence; 23 instances of engaging in dishonesty, fraud, deceit or misrepresentation (such as lying to clients or falsifying evidence); 19 instances of failing to properly handle client property by failing to render an accounting, failing to inform a client of a settlement, failing to properly remit a settlement, forging a client's signature, converting and commingling a client

and third party funds and failing to use and maintain a trust account; 13 instances of engaging in conduct that is prejudicial to the administration of justice; 7 instances of failing to inform a client he was suspended from the practice of law; 7 instances of knowingly disobeying the rules of a tribunal; 6 instances of being incompetent by allowing a claim to prescribe, failing to appear and failing to complete a matter; 4 instances of failing to cooperate with disciplinary authority; 3 instances of committing a criminal act by forging a client's signature and writing a NSF check; 2 instances of accepting representation which created a conflict of interest between two clients and/or former clients; 2 instances of engaging in the unauthorized practice of law by accepting work while under interim suspension; 2 instances of offering evidence known to be false; 2 instances of converting a nonmeritorious issue; 1 instance of usurping a client's authority; 1 instance of failing to respond to a lawful request for information from a disciplinary authority; and 1 instance of falsifying evidence.

The disciplinary board consolidated both proceedings for purposes of rendering its recommendation. Upon its consideration of the hearing committee's findings in the Tidwell matter and the petition for consent discipline, the board recommended approval of the consent discipline, specifically, that respondent be disbarred from the practice of law and, as conditions for readmission, that he make full restitution to all complainants and pay all costs of these proceedings, including, but not limited to, all investigative costs. Neither disciplinary counsel nor respondent filed objections to the disciplinary board's recommendation in this court.

Upon review of the record of the disciplinary board's findings and recommendations, and the record filed herein, it is the decision of the court that the disciplinary board's recommendations be adopted.

Accordingly, it is ordered that respondent's name be stricken from the roll of attorneys, *4 and that his license to practice law in the State of Louisiana be revoked. It is further ordered that respondent make full restitution in the amount of $83,092.38. Respondent's payment of full restitution or efforts to make restitution will be considered if respondent applies for readmission. All costs of this proceeding including, but not limited to, all investigative costs are assessed to respondent.

END OF DOCUMENT

EXERCISES

1. Given the facts of the case, what *Model Rules* relating only to client communication did the attorney violate? Explain your response.

2. Footnote 2 describes the Stipulation of Facts that the attorney admitted to. Were you surprised by the stipulation?

TIMEKEEPING AND BILLING

CHAPTER OBJECTIVES

After you read this chapter, you will be able to:

- Differentiate between timekeeping and billing.
- Recognize major types of legal fee agreements.
- Know the difference between billable and nonbillable time.
- Explain the concept of value billing.
- Discuss how the billing process works and what it entails.
- Differentiate between an earned and an unearned retainer.

When a Chicago-based law firm submitted its bill, the client company suspected something might have been wrong. Years later, an audit revealed that the invoice included nontechnical deposition summaries by paralegals at four to five pages per hour. The usual rate is twenty to twenty-five pages an hour. The paralegals were apparently working at 20 percent to 25 percent the normal rate, so the client company was being billed four times what it should have been for that service.[1]

***

A federal grand jury indicted two men allegedly conspiring to defraud an insurance company by having tens of thousands of dollars in checks issued for expenses and legal services that were never provided. The defendants are a former litigation supervisor for the insurance company and a former partner in the law firm representing the company. The grand jury indicted them on one felony count of conspiracy, three felony counts of mail fraud, and twenty felony counts of wire fraud as a result of checks written over four years.

THE DIFFERENCE BETWEEN TIMEKEEPING AND BILLING

timekeeping
The process of tracking time for the purpose of billing clients.

billing
The process of issuing invoices for the purpose of collecting monies for legal services performed and being reimbursed for expenses.

In the legal environment, **timekeeping** is the process of tracking time for the purpose of billing clients. The obvious reason private attorneys and legal assistants keep track of their time is to bill clients. However, many corporate, government, and legal aid practices also keep time records for other reasons. Timekeeping can be used to manage and oversee what cases attorneys and legal assistants are working on and whether they are spending too much time or too little time on certain cases. Timekeeping can be used to evaluate the performance of attorneys and legal assistants and can be used in determining promotions and raises. Timekeeping also can be used to evaluate what types of cases are the most beneficial and profitable for the office.

Billing is the process of issuing invoices for the purpose of collecting monies for legal services performed and being reimbursed for expenses. The lifeblood of any organization depends on its ability to raise cash and be paid for the services it renders. In most cases, private law practices must be able to generate billings on at least a monthly basis to generate the cash they need to meet their expenses such as rent, utilities, and salaries. Attorneys and legal assistants in corporate and government practices also need to know about billing to ensure that when they hire outside counsel (private law firms), the corporation or government gets the most for its money.

Why Do Legal Assistants Need to Know Timekeeping and Billing?

There are several reasons why legal assistants need to know about timekeeping and billing. In most private law practices, legal assistants are required to track their time so it can be charged to the case(s) they are working on. Many law practices require legal assistants to bill a minimum number of hours a year. It is important to remember that private law firms are fundamentally businesses, and like any business, their function is to make money, operate at a profit, and earn money for their owners. Therefore, the billing of time to a firm's clients is crucial to its operations and success as a business. A recent survey of legal assistants found that legal assistants were most often expected to bill between 26 and 35 hours a week (1,352 and 1,820 annually). Thus, it is necessary for legal assistants to understand how timekeeping and billing works. **Legal assistants are sometimes discharged from their jobs because they fail to bill the required number of hours.** The issue of tracking time and billing a minimum number of hours is very important in many offices.

In addition, legal assistants are sometimes put in charge of actually running the timekeeping and billing system, including managing the timekeeping process, and generating bills. This usually occurs in smaller law offices. In those cases, it is important for them not only to know the process but also to know how to actually run and operate the system. Timekeeping and billing are important issues because the survival of law offices depends on their ability to track and bill time. However, before exploring the fundamentals of timekeeping and billing in depth, you first need a background in legal fee agreements, legal expenses, and trust accounts.

Kinds of Legal Fee Agreements

Legal fees can be structured in many different ways. The kind of legal fee depends on the type of case or client matter, the specific circumstances of each particular client, and the law practice's preference toward certain types of fee agreements. Fee agreements can be hourly rate fees, contingency fees, flat fees, retainer fees, and others.

HOURLY RATE FEES

An **hourly rate fee** is a fee for legal services that is billed to the client by the hour, at an agreed-upon rate. For example, suppose a client hires an attorney to draft a

hourly rate fee
A fee for legal services that is billed to the client by the hour at an agreed-upon rate.

business contract. The client agrees to pay $200 for every hour the attorney spends drafting the contract and advising the client. If the attorney spent four hours working on the contract, the client would owe the attorney $800 ($200 times 4 hours equals $800).

Hourly rate agreements can be complicated. Law offices have several specific types of hourly rate contracts, including the following.

- Attorney or legal assistant hourly rate
- Client hourly rate
- Blended hourly rate fee
- Activity hourly rate

Some law practices use a combination of these to bill clients.

attorney or **legal assistant hourly rate**
Fee based on the attorney's or legal assistant's level of expertise and experience in a particular area.

ATTORNEY OR LEGAL ASSISTANT HOURLY RATE The **attorney** or **legal assistant hourly rate** is based on the attorney's or legal assistant's level of expertise and experience in a particular area. Figure 5-1 is an example of this type of contract. If a partner or shareholder worked on a case, his or her hourly rate charge might be considerably more than that of an associate or legal assistant's hourly rate charge. Partners typically can earn from $200 to $400 an hour or more compared with associates who might work for $100 to $250 an hour. Legal assistants typically charge from $40 to $85 an hour. The difference in price is based on the expertise and experience of the individual working on the case and on locally acceptable rates. In this type of fee agreement, it is possible for a client to be billed at several different rates in a given period if several attorneys or legal assistants work on a matter because they all may have different rates.

client hourly rate
Fee based on one hourly charge for the client, regardless of which attorney works on the case and what he or she does on the case.

CLIENT HOURLY RATE The **client hourly rate** method is based on one hourly charge for the client, regardless of which attorney works on the case and what he or she does on the case. For example, if an insurance company hired a law practice to represent it, the insurance company and the law practice might negotiate on a client hourly charge of $170 per hour for attorneys and $70 an hour for legal assistants. This means that no matter which attorney or legal assistant works on the case, whether the attorney or legal assistant has one year's or twenty years' experience, and regardless of what the attorney or legal assistant does (e.g., making routine phone calls or appearing in court), the insurance company would be charged $170 an hour for attorney time or $70 an hour for legal assistant time.

blended hourly rate fee
One hourly rate that is set taking into account the blend or mix of attorneys working on the matter.

BLENDED HOURLY RATE FEE A **blended hourly rate fee** is one hourly rate that is set taking into account the blend or mix of law office staff working on the matter. The "mix" includes the mix among associates, partners, and sometimes legal assistants working on the matter. Some states only allow the "blend" to include associates and partners, while other states allow legal assistants to be included. The advantage to this is that billing is simpler because there is one rate for all legal assistant and attorney time spent on the case. The bill is easier for the law office to produce and easier for the client to read. Some states will allow legal assistants to have their

HOURLY RATE CONTRACT FOR LEGAL SERVICES

This contract for legal services is entered into by and between H. Thomas Weber (hereinafter "Client") and Johnson, Beck & Taylor (hereinafter "Attorneys") on this _____ day of December, 200_. The following terms and conditions constitute the entirety of the agreement between Attorneys and Client and said agreement supersedes and is wholly separate and apart from any previous written or oral agreements.

1. Client hereby agrees to employ Attorneys and Attorneys hereby agree to represent Client in connection with a contract dispute in Jefferson County District Court of Client's claim against Westbridge Manufacturing.
2. Client agrees to pay a retainer fee of $2,000.00, which will be held in Attorney's trust account until earned.
3. Client agrees to pay associate attorneys at **$200.00** per hour, partners at **$250** per hour, legal assistants at **$65.00** per hour and senior legal assistants at **$80.00** per hour for legal services rendered regarding the matter in paragraph one. Attorneys are not hereby obligated to take an appeal from any judgment at the trial court level; if an occasion for an appeal arises, Attorneys and Client hereby expressly agree that employment for such an appeal must be arranged by a separate contract between Attorneys and Client.
4. Client agrees to reimburse Attorneys for all expenses incurred in connection with said matter; and, Client agrees to advance all expenses requested by Attorneys during the duration of this contract. Client understands that he is ultimately responsible for the payment of all expenses incurred in connection with this matter.
5. Client understands that Attorneys will bill Client periodically (usually on a monthly or quarterly basis, depending on how quickly the case moves through the system) for copying costs at the rate of $.25 cents per copy, postage and handling costs, long-distance telephone costs, travel costs, and other costs, and that Client is obligated to make payments upon said billing for said fees and expenses described at paragraphs (2), (3) and (4) above, or otherwise satisfy said fees and expenses. Attorneys will also bill Client for all deposition costs incurred and Client is solely responsible for said deposition costs and Client will be required to advance the sum of $1,500.00 (or more as necessary) for trial costs (including subpoenas, travel costs, and preparation costs) once the case is set for trial.
6. Client understands and agrees that this litigation may take two to five years or longer to complete and that he will make himself available for Attorneys to confer with and generally to assist Attorneys in said matter. Client agrees he will not discuss the matter of his litigation with any unauthorized person at any time or in any way. Client understands and agrees that Attorneys may withdraw from representation of Client upon proper notice. Client further understands that he can apply for judicial review and approval of this fee agreement if he so desires.
7. Client agrees that associate counsel may be employed at the discretion of Attorneys and that any attorney so employed may be designated to appear on Client's behalf and undertake Client's representation in this matter and such representation shall be upon the same terms as set out herein. **Client understands that Attorneys cannot and do not guarantee any particular or certain relief and expressly state that they cannot promise or guarantee Client will receive any money damages or money settlement**.

(continued)

Figure 5-1 Attorney/Legal Assistant Hourly Rate Contract

The undersigned hereby voluntarily executes this agreement with a full understanding of same and without coercion or duress. All agreements contained herein are severable and in the event any of them shall be deemed to be invalid by any competent court, this contract shall be interpreted as if such invalid agreements or covenants were not contained herein. Client acknowledges receiving a fully executed copy of this contract.

_____ _____
Date

_____ _____
Date   JOHNSON, BECK & TAYLOR

NOTE: THIS IS ONLY AN EXAMPLE AND IS NOT INTENDED TO BE A FORM, CHECK WITH YOUR STATE BAR FOR A PROPER FORM.

---

own "blend" and have one rate for all legal assistants whether experienced or inexperienced.

activity hourly rate
Fee based on the different hourly rates depending on what type of service or activity is actually performed.

ACTIVITY HOURLY RATE An **activity hourly rate** is based on the different hourly rates depending on what type of service or activity is actually performed. For example, offices using this approach might bill attorney time to clients as follows.

Court appearances	$300 per hour
Legal research by attorneys	$200 per hour
Drafting by attorneys	$150 per hour
Telephone calls by attorneys	$100 per hour
Legal research by legal assistants	$70 per hour
Drafting by legal assistants	$60 per hour

This is sliding-scale hourly fee based on the difficulty of an activity. Hourly rate agreements, no matter what the type, are the most common kind of fee agreement.

CONTINGENCY FEES

contingency fee
Fee collected if the attorney successfully represents the client.

A **contingency fee** is a fee that is collected if the attorney successfully represents the client. The attorney is entitled to a certain percentage of the total amount of money awarded to the client. If the client's case is not won, and no money is recovered, the attorney collects no legal fees but is still entitled to be reimbursed for all expenses incurred (see Figure 5-2). Contingency fees are typically used in representing plaintiffs in personal injury cases, workers' compensation cases, civil rights cases, medical malpractice, and other types of cases in which monetary damages are generated. The individual who would like to bring the lawsuit usually has little or no money to pay legal fees up front. Contingency fees typically range from 20 percent to 50 percent.

For example, suppose a client hires an attorney to file a personal injury claim regarding an automobile accident the client was in. The client has no money, but agrees to pay the attorney 20 percent of any money that is recovered (plus legal expenses) before the case is filed, 25 percent of any money that is recovered after the

CONTINGENCY FEE CONTRACT FOR LEGAL SERVICES

Date:
Name: D.O.B.
Address: Phone:

1. I hereby employ **Johnson, Beck & Taylor** (hereinafter "attorneys") to perform legal services in connection with the following matter as described below:
   Personal injury claims arising out of an automobile accident which occurred January 12, 2003, on Interstate I-70.
2. I agree to pay a nonrefundable retainer fee of $1,000; plus,
3. I agree attorneys will receive ____20%____ of any recovery, if prior to filing suit;
   I agree attorneys will receive ____25%____ of any recovery, if prior to pretrial conference;
   I agree attorneys will receive ____33%____ of any recovery, if after first trial begins;
   I agree attorneys will receive ____33%____ of any recovery, if after appeal or second trial begins.
   Attorneys are not hereby obligated to take an appeal from any judgment at the trial court level; if an occasion for an appeal arises, attorneys and client hereby expressly agree that employment for such an appeal will be arranged by a separate contract between these parties. Further, I agree that attorneys will be entitled to the applicable above-mentioned percentage of recovery minus whatever a court may award, if I am a prevailing party and the court awards fees following my request therefor.
4. As to the expenses of litigation: I agree to reimburse attorneys for all expenses incurred in connection with said matter, and any expenses not fully paid as incurred may be deducted from my portion of any recovery. I agree to advance any and all expenses requested by attorneys during the duration of this contract. I agree to make an advance of expenses upon execution of this contract in the amount of $ 500.00. I understand that these litigation expenses do not pertain to the retainer fee or percentage of any recovery, and I am ultimately responsible for the payment of all litigation expenses.
5. I understand that attorneys will bill client periodically, and that client is obligated to make payments upon said billing for said fees and expenses described at paragraphs (2), and (4), or otherwise satisfy said fees and expenses.
6. I understand and agree that this litigation may take 2 to 5 years, or longer to complete, and that I will make myself available for attorneys to confer with, and generally to assist attorneys in said matter. I will not discuss the matter of my litigation with an unauthorized person at any time in any way. I understand and agree that attorneys may withdraw from representation of client at any time upon proper notice.
7. I agree that associate counsel may be employed at the discretion of JOHNSON, BECK & TAYLOR, and that any attorney so employed may be designated to appear on my behalf and undertake my representation in this matter and such representation shall be upon the same terms as set out herein. Attorneys have **not** guaranteed, nor can they guarantee, any particular or certain relief.

The undersigned herewith executes this agreement with a full understanding of same, without coercion or duress, and understands the same to be the only agreement between the parties with regard to the above matter, and that if any other terms are to be added to this contract, the same will not be binding, unless and until they are reduced to writing and signed by all parties to this contract. I acknowledge receiving

(continued)

Figure 5-2 Contingency Fee Contract

a fully executed copy of this contract. Further, the undersigned Client understands that said Client is entitled to apply for judicial review and approval of this fee agreement, if Client so desires.

_____
Date

_____
Date   JOHNSON, BECK & TAYLOR

NOTE: THIS IS ONLY AN EXAMPLE AND IS NOT INTENDED TO BE A FORM, CHECK YOUR STATE BAR FOR A PROPER FORM.

case is filed but before trial, and 33 percent of any money recovered during trial or after appeal. Suppose the claim is settled after the case is filed but before trial for $10,800. Suppose also that the legal expenses the attorney incurred were $800. Under most state laws, legal expenses are paid first and then the contingency fee is calculated. The attorney would deduct the expenses off the top and the remaining $10,000 would be divided according to the contingency fee agreement. Because the suit was

Figure 5-3 Contingency Fee Example

Written Contingency Fee Agreement Provisions
Attorney receives
- 20% of any money recovered (plus legal expenses) before case is filed;
- 25% of any money recovered (plus legal expenses) after case is filed, but before trial;
- 33% of any money recovered (plus legal expenses) during trial or after appeal.

Settlement
Case is settled for $10,800 after case is filed, but before trial.
Attorney has $800 worth of legal expenses.

Calculation of Contingency Fee
1. Legal expenses are paid first.
    Settlement of $10,800
    Minus legal expenses   −   800
    Balance $10,000
2. Contingency fee is calculated as follows:
    Total recovery minus legal expenses $10,000
    Attorney's 25% Contingency Fee
    ($10,000 x 25% = $2,500)   − 2,500
                       TOTAL TO CLIENT $ 7,500
3. Total fees and expenses to attorney
    Reimbursement of legal expense $ 800
    Contingency fee $ 2,500
                       TOTAL TO ATTORNEY $ 3,300

settled after the case was filed but before the trial, the attorney would be entitled to receive 25 percent of any recovery. The attorney would be entitled to $2,500, and the client would be entitled to 75 percent, or $7,500 (see Figure 5-3).

Contingency fee agreements must be in writing. Figure 5-2 contains a sample contingency fee contract. Some states put a cap or a maximum percentage on what an attorney can collect in areas such as workers' compensation and medical malpractice claims. For example, some states prevent attorneys from receiving more than a 25 percent contingency in a workers' compensation case. Contingency fees by their nature are risky, because if no money is recovered, the attorney receives no fee. However, even if no money is recovered, the client must still pay legal expenses such as filing fees and photocopying. Contingency fees and hourly fees also may be used together. Some offices reduce their hourly fee and charge a contingency fee.

FLAT FEE

A **flat fee** is a fee for legal services that is billed as a flat or fixed amount. Some offices have a set fee for handling certain types of matters, such as preparing a will, or

flat fee
A fee for legal services that is billed as a flat or fixed amount.

⌒ PRICE LIST ⌒

Initial Consultation with Branch Lawyer..........$100.00

REAL ESTATE

Divorce - Uncontested................................1000.00
Domestic contracts and family litigation vary according to time involved.

REAL ESTATE

Purchase or Sale of House..........................1000.00
Each Mortgage—Additional...........................199.00
Each Discharge of Mortgage—Additional........150.00
Refinancing..599.00

WILLS & ESTATES

Basic Will..300.00
Estates, administrations, and estate litigation vary according to time involved

BUSINESS

Consultation...150.00
Incorporation...1000.00
We provide many other business services, including:
- *Commercial Leases*
- *Purchase and Sale of Businesses*
- *Trade Marks & Copyright*

ADDITIONAL SERVICES

Collection—demand letter..........................2000.00
Notarization (per signature)...........................20.00
Power of Attorney / Promissory Note................50.00

⌒ PAYMENT POLICY ⌒

We require a retainer before commencing work on your behalf, which amount is paid into trust. We then draw checks on the retainer to pay out-of-pocket expenses made on your behalf and our fees.

We will advise you of completion of our services to you and ask you to come in and pick up the documentation involved and pay any balance owing at the same time.

In real estate transactions the balance must be paid prior to closing. In litigation and criminal matters, any outstanding account and the estimated fee for the appearance must be paid prior to the court appearance.

ETHICAL NOTE: Even if the firm has a price list, legal assistants should leave the matter of fees to the attorney.

Figure 5-4 Flat Fee Price List.

handling an uncontested divorce, a name change, or a bankruptcy (see Figure 5-4). For example, suppose a client agreed to pay an attorney a flat fee of $300 to prepare a will. No matter how many hours the attorney spends preparing the will, the fee is still $300. Flat fee agreements are usually used when a legal matter is simple, straightforward, and involves few risks.

Figure 5-5 shows a comparison of different methods of billing for drafting a routine or standard will. In routine matters, flat rates will typically be the least expensive for the client. In addition, flat rates and the blended methods are typically the easiest types of bills to both prepare and read.

RETAINER FEES

The word *retainer* has several meanings in the legal environment. Generally retainer fees are monies paid by the client at the beginning of a case or matter. However, there are many types of retainers. When an attorney or legal assistant uses the term *retainer*, it could mean a retainer for general representation, a case retainer, a pure retainer, or a cash advance. In addition, all retainer fees are either earned or unearned.

EARNED V. UNEARNED RETAINERS There is a *very* important difference between an earned retainer and an unearned retainer. An **earned retainer** means that the law office or attorney has earned the money and is entitled to deposit the money in the office's or attorney's own bank account and can use it to pay the attorney's or law office's operating expenses, such as salaries, immediately upon deposit.

For example, suppose an attorney agrees to take a products liability case on a contingency fee basis, but requires that the client pay a nonrefundable (earned) retainer of $2,000. The attorney drafts a contract and both parties sign it. The contract clearly states that the $2,000 is nonrefundable. The earned, nonrefundable retainer is an incentive for the attorney to accept the case on a contingency basis. The attorney may deposit the $2,000 in his or her law office checking account and pay operating expenses out of it. This is an example of a case retainer. Case retainers are discussed in more detail later in this section.

An **unearned retainer** is monies that are paid up front by the client as an advance against the attorney's future fees and expenses as a kind of down payment. Until the monies are actually earned by the attorney or law office, they belong to the client. According to ethical rules, unearned retainers may *not* be deposited in the attorney's or law office's normal operating checking account. Unearned retainers must be deposited into a *separate* trust account and can be transferred into the firm account as it is earned.

For example, suppose a business client wants to sue his or her insurance company for failing to pay a claim submitted by the business. The business signs a contract with the attorney to pay a (unearned) retainer of $10,000. The contract states that the $10,000 will be held in trust and paid to the attorney as the attorney incurs fees and properly bills the client. This is an example of a cash advance retainer. Cash advance retainers are covered in more detail in the next section.

A **trust** or **escrow account** is a separate bank account, apart from a law office's or attorney's operating checking account, where unearned client funds are deposited. As an attorney or law office begins to earn an unearned retainer by pro-

earned retainer
Term for the money the law office or attorney has earned and is entitled to deposit in the office's or attorney's own bank account.

unearned retainer
Monies that are paid up front by the client as an advance against the attorney's future fees and expenses. Until the monies are actually earned by the attorney or law office, they actually belong to the client.

trust or escrow account
A separate bank account, apart from a law office's or attorney's operating checking account, where unearned client funds are deposited.

Kinds of Legal Fee Agreements 205

Services Provided
1. Legal Assistant interviews client (office conf.) regarding the law office drafting a will for client. Legal assistant gets background information including financial holdings, heirs, family tree, etc. .... 1.50 hours
2. Legal Assistant drafts memo to Attorney itemizing the conference with client .... 0.25 hours
3. Attorney reads the legal assistant's memo and talks with client on the telephone .... 0.25 hours
4. Attorney conducts legal research, prepares a draft of the will which meets the expectations of the client .... 1.0 hours
5. Client reviews will, office conf. with attorney, attorney discusses client's changes to the will, makes client's changes to the will and the will is executed, witnessed and notarized .... 1.0 hours
   TOTAL HOURS .... 4.0 hours

- **CLIENT HOURLY RATE**
Assume attorneys agree to charge the client to prepare a will for his/her time as follows:
- $125.00 an hour for the attorney's time (the client is not "rich" and would have to go elsewhere if the firm normal hourly rate were charged)
- $60.00 an hour for his/her legal assistant's time

TOTAL COST $386.25
(Legal Asst. 1.75 hours × $60 = $105; Atty 2.25 × $125 an hour = $281.25; $105 + $281.25 = $386.25)

- **ATTORNEY/LEGAL ASSISTANT HOURLY RATE**
- Assume the attorney is an associate attorney and his/her normal hourly rate is $150.00
- Assume the legal assistant assigned to the case has a normal hourly rate of $55.00

TOTAL COST $433.75
(Legal Asst. 1.75 hours × $55 = $96.25; Atty 2.25 × $150 an hour = $337.50; $96.25 + $337.50 = $433.75)

- **BLENDED (Attorneys and Legal Assistant) HOURLY RATE**
- Assume blended hourly rate for all attorney and legal assistant time is $85 an hour.

TOTAL COST $340 (4 hours × $85 = $340).

ACTIVITY HOURLY RATE
Assume:
- Legal Assistant Office Conference Rate is $40.00 an hour/Atty is $100.00
- Legal Assistant Time for Drafting Memo is $50.00 an hour/Atty is $100.00
- Attorney Time for Phone Conferences $80 an hour
- Attorney Time for Drafting Pleadings, Will, etc. $150 an hour

TOTAL COST $347.50
1.5 × $40 = $60.00; .25 × $50 = $12.50; .25 × $100 = $25; 1.0 × $150; 1.0 × $100 = Total $347.50

FLAT FEE RATE
Assume attorney and client agree on a flat rate of $300.00 to prepare the will.
TOTAL COST $300.00

CONTINGENCY RATE: $0.00 (No Monetary Recovery - not applicable)

Figure 5-5   Comparison Legal Fees to Prepare a Will

viding legal services to the client, the attorney can then bill the client and move the earned portion from the trust account to his or her own law office operating account.

The written contract should set out whether the retainer is earned or unearned. However, in some instances the contract may be vague on this point. Typically, when a contract refers to a "nonrefundable retainer," this means an earned retainer.

Additionally, in many contracts, flat fee rates, as discussed earlier, are said to be "nonrefundable," and thus have been treated as earned. However, some state ethical rules regulate this area heavily, so it depends on the state. Some state ethical rules hold that all flat fees are a retainer, have been unearned, and must be placed in trust until they are earned. Whether a retainer is earned or unearned will depend on your state's ethical rules and on the written contract.

cash advance
Unearned monies that are an advance against the attorney's future fees and expenses.

CASH ADVANCE RETAINER One type of retainer is a cash advance. A **cash advance** is unearned monies and is an advance against the attorney's future fees and expenses. Until the cash advance is earned by the attorney, it actually belongs to the client. The cash advance is a typical type of unearned retainer.

For example, suppose a client wishes to hire an attorney to litigate a contract dispute. The attorney agrees to represent the client only if the client agrees to pay $150 an hour with a $2,500 cash advance against fees and expenses. The attorney must deposit the $2,500 in a trust account. If the attorney deposits the cash advance in his own account (whether it is the firm's account or the attorney's own personal account), the attorney has violated several ethical rules. As the attorney works on the case and bills the client for fees and expenses, the attorney will write himself a check out of the trust account for the amount of the billing. The attorney must tell the client that he is withdrawing the money and keep an accurate balance of how much the client has left in trust. If after a month the attorney billed the client for $500, the attorney would write himself a check for $500 from the trust account, deposit the $500 in the attorney's or the firm's own bank account, and inform the client that there was a remaining balance of $2,000 in trust. Look closely at the payment policy in Figure 5-4. The firm in Figure 5-4 requires a cash advance before it will take any case. Also, recognize that if the case ended at this point, the client would be entitled to a refund of the remaining $2,000 in trust.

retainer for general representation
Retainer typically used when a client such as a corporation or entity requires continuing legal services throughout the year.

RETAINER FOR GENERAL REPRESENTATION Another type of retainer is a **retainer for general representation.** This type of retainer is typically used when a client such as a corporation or entity requires continuing legal services throughout the year. The client pays an amount, typically up front or on a prearranged schedule, to receive these ongoing services. For example, suppose a small school board would like to be able to contact an attorney at any time with general legal questions. The attorney and school board could enter into this type of agreement for a fee of $2,000 every six months, and the school board could contact the attorney at any time and ask general questions and the attorney would never receive more than the $2,000 for the six-month period. Retainers for general representation allow the client to negotiate and anticipate what his or her fee will be for the year. This type of agreement usually only covers general legal advice and would not include matters such as litigation (see Figure 5-6). Depending on the specific arrangements between the client and the attorney, and on the specific

> Ms Gloria Smith, Chairperson
> Unified School District
> No. 453 School Board
>
> Subject: General Representation of the UDS No. 453 School Board
>
> Dear Ms Smith:
>
> Thank you for your letter informing us that the School Board would like to place our law firm on a general retainer of $_____ for the coming year. We will bill on a quarterly basis for the retainer plus any expenses incurred.
>
> The retainer will include general advice concerning business operations, personnel questions, legislative initiative, and attendance at all Board meetings. It will not cover litigated matters requiring appearances at boards or commissions, court or state administrative agencies. Should any of the excluded services appear to be necessary, we shall be happy to discuss the cost of these services with you.
>
> It is our hope that the knowledge that we are ready to serve you under the retainer will provide you with regular advice to avoid any serious problems or litigation. Please sign this letter and return it to us. If you have any questions, please feel free to give me a call.
>
> Kindest Regards,
>
> Sandra W. Johnson
> JOHNSON, BECK & TAYLOR
>
> Accepted for Unified School District No. 453 School Board by:
>
> _____
> Gloria Smith, Chairperson

**Figure 5-6
Retainer for General Representation Agreement**

Source: Adapted from Mary Ann Altman and Robert I. Weil, *How to Manage Your Law Office*. Matthew Bender, 1986, 4–6. Reprinted with the permission of Altman Weil Pensa Publications, Inc., copyright 1991 by Altman Weil Pensa Publications, Inc.

ethical rules in your state, many retainers for general representation are viewed as being earned because the client can call at any time and get legal advice. Retainers for general representation resemble a flat fee agreement. The difference is that, in a flat fee agreement, the attorney or law office is contracting to do a specific thing for a client such as prepare a will or file a bankruptcy. In the case of a retainer for general representation, the attorney is agreeing to make himself or herself available to the client for all nonlitigation needs.

case retainer
A fee that is billed at the beginning of a matter, is not refundable to the client, and is usually paid at the beginning of the case as an incentive for the office to take the case.

CASE RETAINER Another type of retainer is a **case retainer,** which is a fee that is billed at the beginning of a matter, is not refundable to the client, and is usually paid to the office at the beginning of the case as an incentive for the office to take the case. For example, a client comes to an attorney with a criminal matter. The attorney agrees to take on the case only if the client agrees to pay a case retainer of $5,000 up front plus $100 an hour for every hour worked on the case. The $5000 is paid to the attorney as an incentive to take the case and thus is earned. The $100 an hour is a client hourly basis charge. Because the case retainer is earned, the attorney can immediately deposit it in the office's own bank account.

Another example of a case retainer is in a case involving a contingency fee. Suppose a client comes to an attorney to file a civil rights case. The attorney agrees to accept the case only if the client agrees to a 30 percent contingency fee and a nonrefundable or case retainer of $1,000. Again, the earned retainer is an incentive for the attorney to take the case and can be deposited in the attorney's or the office's own bank account.

pure retainer
A fee that obligates the office to be available to represent the client throughout the time period agreed upon.

PURE RETAINER A rather rare type of retainer is a **pure retainer.** A pure retainer obligates the law office to be available to represent the client throughout the time period agreed upon. The part that distinguishes a pure retainer from a retainer for general representation is that the office typically must agree to not represent any of the client's competitors or to undertake any type of adverse representation to the client.

Retainers for general representation, case retainers, and pure retainers are usually earned retainers and a cash advance is an unearned retainer. However, *the language of the contract will determine whether amounts paid to attorneys up front are earned or unearned.* The earned/unearned distinction is extremely important, and is one reason all fee agreements should be in writing.

COURT AWARDED FEES

court awarded fees
Fees given to the prevailing parties pursuant to certain federal and state statutes.

Court awarded fees are another type of fee agreement. In certain federal and state statutes, the prevailing party (i.e., the party that wins the case) is given the right to recover from the opposing side reasonable attorney's fees. The amount of the attorney's fees are decided by the court. This is called **court awarded fees.** Court awarded fees are provided for in civil rights law, antitrust, civil racketeering, and in many other instances and statutes as well. The prevailing party must submit to the court detailed time records showing specifically how much time was spent on the case. If the prevailing law office did not keep such records, the court will not award fees. The purpose of court awarded fees is to encourage potential plaintiffs in public interest issues to pursue legitimate claims while discouraging frivolous claims. For example, if an employee brought a sexual harassment suit against an employer and subsequently won the suit, the employee's attorneys would be entitled to receive reasonable attorney's fees from the defendant.

prepaid legal service
A plan that a person can purchase that entitles the person to receive legal services either free or at a greatly reduced rate.

PREPAID LEGAL SERVICES

A prepaid legal service plan is another type of fee agreement. **Prepaid legal service** is a plan that a person can purchase that entitles the person to receive legal services (as enumerated in the plan) either free or at a greatly reduced rate. In some cases, corporations or labor unions, for example, provide a prepaid legal service plan to their employees as a fringe benefit. For instance, if a person who is a member of a prepaid legal service plan needed a will drafted, that person would go to either an attorney employed by the prepaid plan or a private attorney that the prepaid plan contracted with and get the will drafted free of charge or at a greatly reduced rate.

VALUE BILLING

Recently, much has been written (in the legal press) about why private law practices should stop billing by the hour and use a different billing method. The reasons for the change from hourly billing include the following:

- The client never knows during any stage of the work how much the total legal fee will be.
- Clients sometimes avoid calling legal assistants and attorneys because they know they will be charged for the time, even if it is a simple phone call.
- Clients have trouble seeing the relationship between what is performed by the legal assistant or attorney and the enormous fees that can be generated.
- Hourly billing encourages lawyers and legal assistants to be inefficient. (i.e., the longer it takes to perform a job, the more revenue they earn).
- Many law offices force attorneys and legal assistants to bill a quota number of hours a year, which puts a tremendous amount of pressure on the individual legal assistant and attorney.

So what is value billing? The **value billing** concept represents a type of fee agreement that is based not on the time required to perform the work but on the basis of the perceived value of the services to the client. Value billing typically provides that the attorney and client reach a consensus on the amount of fees to be charged. Because of increased competition in the legal environment and because of the power of the client as a buyer, clients are demanding that they have a say in how much they are going to pay for legal services, what type of service will be provided, and what the quality of the legal services will be for the price.

value billing
A type of fee agreement that is based not on the time to perform the work but on the basis of the perceived value of the services to the client.

THE ETHICS OF TIMEKEEPING AND BILLING

There are more timekeeping- and billing-related ethical complaints filed against attorneys and law offices than all other types of complaints. It is important that legal assistants completely understand the ethics of timekeeping and billing. In years past, timekeeping and billing complaints were viewed as simply "misunderstandings" between the client and the law office. Recently, state bars have viewed timekeeping and billing disputes as having major ethical implications for attorneys. That is, such disputes were simply not misunderstandings, but law offices were sometimes flagrantly violating ethical rules regarding money issues.

Timekeeping and billing complaints by clients are leading not just to ethical complaints against attorneys, but are also turning into criminal fraud charges filed against attorneys and legal assistants.

ETHICAL CONSIDERATIONS REGARDING LEGAL FEE AGREEMENTS

There are several important ethical considerations that need to be stressed about fee agreements. The first is that **all fee agreements should be in writing,** especially when a contingency fee is involved. Second, contingency fees should not be used in criminal or domestic-relation matters.

FEE AGREEMENTS SHOULD BE IN WRITING

It is highly recommended that as a matter of course all fee agreements be in writing. The days of a handshake cementing an agreement between an attorney and the client are long over. There is no substitute for reducing all fee agreements to writing. If the firm and the client have a dispute over fees, the document will clarify the understanding between the parties. The *Model Rules of Professional Conduct* states at 1.5(b):

> (b) When the lawyer has not regularly represented the client, [i.e., the lawyer has never represented the client before], the basis or rate of the fee shall be communicated to the client, preferably in writing, before or within a reasonable time after commencing the representation.

> *A fee agreement allows a lawyer and client to make clear from the inception of the legal representation the scope of that representation and the basis for the lawyer's compensation. A clearly drafted agreement, which is fully explained to the client at the time the representation begins, will minimize disagreement as the representation proceeds and assist in resolving any disputes that may arise when the representation ends.*[2]

Although the *Model Rules* state that the agreement "preferably" be in writing, nearly every authority on this subject, as well as most attorneys who have been in business long, will tell you that the agreement absolutely should be in writing to protect both the attorney and the client. The reasons legal fee agreements should be in writing follow.

1. Clients file more ethical complaints against attorneys and law offices for fee disputes than for any other type of complaint.
2. The client and the attorney may (will) forget what the exact fee agreement was unless it is reduced to writing.
3. In a factual dispute regarding a fee between a client and an attorney, the evidence is typically construed in the light most favorable to the client.

The Ethics 2000 Commission is recommending the following change to Rule 1.5(b):

> (b) When the lawyer has not regularly represented the client, <u>the scope of the representation,</u> the basis or rate of the fee <u>and disbursements for which the client will be responsible</u> shall be communicated to the client, ~~preferably~~ in writing, before or within a reasonable time after commencing the representation. <u>Any changes in these terms of the engagement shall also be communicated in writing.</u>

Notice that the Ethics 2000 Commission is recommending tightening up this rule to require that, in addition to simply stating the basis of the fee and the scope of the representation (exactly what the attorney is to perform), the agreement also include the disbursements or expenses the client is responsible for and that the agreement be in writing. The revision also adds that any changes in the agreement will also be in writing. The Ethics 2000 Commission released the following statement about this revision:

> *Few issues between lawyer and client produce more misunderstandings and disputes than the fee due the lawyer. The present Rule says a written agreement is "preferable," but the Commission believes the time has come to minimize misunderstandings by requiring written fee agreements.*

CONTINGENCY FEE AGREEMENT MUST BE IN WRITING   When a contingency fee is involved, most jurisdictions state that the agreement *must* be in writing for the office to collect the fee. Rule 1.5(c) of the *Model Rules* states:

> (c) ... A contingent fee agreement shall be in writing and shall state the method by which the fee is to be determined, including the percentage or percentages that shall accrue to the lawyer in the event of settlement, trial or appeal. ...

The Ethics 2000 Commission is recommending no changes to this rule. Even the *Model Rules* make a distinction between contingency agreements and other types of fee agreements and require that contingency agreements be in writing. The reason that a contingency fee agreement must be in writing is that in many cases, large sums of money are recovered and the difference between 20 percent and 30 percent may mean tens of thousands of dollars. Contingency agreements are risky for the attorney and they simply must be reduced to writing so that the client and the attorney know what the proper percentage of fees should be. It also is important that the contingency agreement state and the client understand that even if there is no recovery in the case, the client must still pay for expenses.

NO CONTINGENCY FEES IN CRIMINAL AND DOMESTIC-RELATION PROCEEDINGS IN SOME JURISDICTIONS   Many jurisdictions prohibit contingency fees in criminal and domestic-relation proceedings as a matter of public policy. Rule 1.5(d) of the *Model Rules* states:

> (d) A lawyer shall not enter into an arrangement for, charge, or collect:
>
> (1) any fee in a domestic relations matter, the payment or amount of which is contingent upon the securing of a divorce or upon the amount of alimony or support, or property settlement thereof; or
>
> (2) a contingent fee for representing a defendant in a criminal case.

The Ethics 2000 Commission is recommending no change to this rule. For example, an attorney agrees to represent a client in a criminal matter. The client agrees to pay the attorney $10,000 if the client is found innocent, but the attorney will receive nothing if the client is found guilty. This is an unethical contingency fee agreement. The thinking is that contingency fees in these types of cases are against the public policy and should be prohibited.

ONLY A "REASONABLE" FEE CAN BE COLLECTED

> *Billing a senior partner's rate for a lawyer to research discovery documents for several hours is a sure way to drive away clients. The work is essential, requiring someone with knowledge and savvy, but is more suited to a legal assistant who can ensure proficient performance while freeing the senior partner to address those tasks that only a senior partner can do—at a greater billing rate.[3]*

> *Today's clients are discriminating purchasers of legal services. Hourly rates and billing invoices are often challenged by long-standing clients.[4]*

Figure 5-7 shows the recommended changes by the Ethics 2000 Commission. The Commission has changed the wording of the rule to clearly state that an attorney cannot charge or collect an unreasonable fee. The Ethics 2000 Commission stated:

> *The present Rule requires that a lawyer's fee be reasonable, but it does not state a corollary prohibition of a fee that is larger than reasonable. The omission thus makes it harder than necessary to impose discipline for excessive fees.*

The Commission has made it clear that it wants to make it easier to prosecute attorneys for ethical violations related to fee issues.

It is important to keep in mind that no matter what the contract or legal fee agreement is with a client, attorneys and legal assistants can only receive a "reasonable" fee. Unfortunately, there is no absolute standard for determining reasonableness, except that reasonableness will be determined on a case-by-case basis. However, Rule 1.5 of the *Model Rules of Professional Conduct* gives a number of factors to be considered in determining reasonableness.

(a) A lawyer's fee shall be reasonable. The factors to be considered in determining the reasonableness of a fee include the following:

(1) The time and labor required, the novelty and difficulty of the questions involved, and the skill requisite to perform the legal service properly

(2) The likelihood, if apparent to the client, that the acceptance of the particular employment will preclude the other employment by the lawyer

(3) The fee customarily charged in the locality for similar legal services

(4) The amount involved and the results obtained

(5) The time limitations imposed by the client or by the circumstances

(6) The nature and length of the professional relationship with the client

(7) The experience, reputation, and ability of the lawyer or lawyers performing the services

(8) Whether the fee is fixed or contingent

For example, in one case, a court found that a fee of $22,500 pursuant to a written agreement for a real estate matter that involved little time for the attorney and that was not unduly complex was unreasonable. Figure 5-8 shows some additional examples of unreasonable fees.

For many years, it was thought that overbilling and stealing from clients by attorneys was only done by sole practitioners and attorneys in small firms. Figure 5-8 shows that this is probably not true and that these practices happen at all levels.

> ...A lawyer may not bill more than one client for the same hours worked by charging a client for the time it took to produce a document that the lawyer had already created for another client. The lawyer also is prohibited from charging clients for the same hours when the lawyer works on one client's matter while traveling for the benefit of the other client on a different matter.[5]

Proposed Rule 1.5 - Public Discussion Draft
Ethics 2000 Commission

FEES

(a) A ~~lawyer's fee~~ lawyer shall be ~~reasonable~~ not make an agreement for, charge, or collect an unreasonable fee. The factors to be considered in determining the reasonableness of a fee include the following:

(1) the time and labor required, the novelty and difficulty of the questions involved, and the skill requisite to perform the legal service properly;

(2) the likelihood, if apparent to the client, that the acceptance of the particular employment will preclude other employment by the lawyer;

(3) the fee customarily charged in the locality for similar legal services;

(4) the amount involved and the results obtained;

(5) the time limitations imposed by the client or by the circumstances;

(6) the nature and length of the professional relationship with the client;

(7) the experience, reputation, and ability of the lawyer or lawyers performing the services; and

(8) ~~whether~~ the degree of risk assumed by the lawyer when the fee is fixed or contingent on the outcome of the matter.

**Figure 5-7
Proposed Changes to Model Rule 1.5(a)**

Reprinted by permission. Copies of ABA Model Code of Professional Responsibility, 1999 edition, are available from Service Center, American Bar Association, 750 North Lake Shore Drive, Chicago, IL 60611-4497, 1-800-285-2221.

**Figure 5-8
Unethical/Highly
Questionable &
Fraudulent Billing
Practices**

- **Audit Questions Legal Assistant's 12 Hour Work Days**
  An audit of a paralegal's time found that for nearly a two year period the legal assistant worked (i.e., billed) an average of 12.45 hours each day, including Saturdays, Sundays, and holidays without details to support the hours. During the nearly two year period the legal assistant took only one day off (one Christmas day). The audit estimated that the paralegal over billed by 2,220 hours totaling $39,960.

- **Client Charged for Individual Attorneys Billing More than the 24-hour Day**
  A corporation recently received a monthly legal bill in excess of $300,000. The head of the corporate legal department was concerned. After hiring an outside audit firm to audit the billings he discovered that:
  - Individual attorneys were billing in excess of the 24-hour day;
  - Attorneys were assigned to tasks that could have been provided by legal assistants at *greatly* reduced costs;
  - The client was billed by the firm for duplicate items;
  - Conferences were often attended by many attorneys who were not needed and time charged to the client;
  - The client was billed for the same expert witness fees multiple times; and,
  - The firm charged the client for the time the firm spent working with an auditor to show them their overcharges.

- **Overbilling and Fraud by Elite Partners and Firms**
  In the winter of 1999, the *Georgetown Journal of Legal Ethics* published an exhaustive article on overbilling and fraud by 16 elite attorneys and/or law firms. Below are some quotes from the article.
  "In recent years, a disturbing number of well-respected lawyers in large established firms have been caught stealing large amounts of money from their clients and their partners by padding, manipulating and fabricating time sheets and expense vouchers. Some have gone to prison, been disbarred, and/or been fired . . . Billing fraud takes many different forms. Here are some examples:
  - Some lawyers are just sloppy about keeping time records.
  - Some systematically "pad" timesheets, or bill one client for work done for another.
  - Some create entirely fictitious timesheets.
  - Some record hours based on work done by other lawyers, paralegals, or secretaries, representing that they did the work. This may result in non-billable time being billed, or in work being billed at a rate higher than that of the person who actually did the work.

- Some lawyers bill for time that their clients might not regard as legitimately billable—for schmoozing with other lawyers, chatting with clients about sports or families, for doing administrative work that could be done by a non-lawyer, or for thinking about a case while mowing the lawn or watching television.

The methods of expense fraud are equally diverse; the lawyers who engage in expense fraud may be stealing from their clients or their partners or both . . . Billing fraud is far more difficult to detect than expense fraud, unless the lawyer is reckless enough to bill more than twenty-four hours per day. But regulation of this type of conduct is very difficult because no one except the lawyer really knows how much time was spent and how much was billed. . .

I undertook the research for this article because in recent years, I periodically noticed reports of cases of elite lawyers who had gone to jail, been disbarred, or been investigated for stealing by billing and expense fraud. . . . These sixteen cases involve lawyers who came from privileged backgrounds, attended elite schools, and have:

(a) been a managing partner, a member of the executive committee or a rainmaker at a large, respected law firm or a spin-off from such a firm;

(b) been publicly accused of stealing over $100,000 from clients or from his or her law firm by fraudulent representations as to hours worked or expenses incurred;

c) been jailed and/or disbarred for billing or expense fraud.

These lawyers engaged in patterns of fraud that went on for an average of five years. Their collective total proven or admitted theft is about $16 million. These highly educated successful lawyers were at the pinnacle of the profession.

[Here are some specific examples]:

Attorney
$3.1Million Over 5 yr period
- Attorney wrote fake time sheets, engaged in expense fraud, inflated hours, billed for work not done, billed for time of persons who did no work on matters billed on, engaged in "ad hoc value billing." One judge who reviewed the case described the methods as "almost fictional," and offered these examples: $98,700 billed for services never performed by David Levin; almost $500,000 for time attributed to legal assistants, medical experts and law clerks, when the work billed for was in fact done by the firm's receptionist and secretaries, and $66,127.29 for legal and medical research that cost only $394.98.

(continued)

- Attorneys' partners helped cover up the billing fraud after complaints were made. The partners and their wives spent part of a weekend at the firm producing fictitious time sheets to correspond with erroneous bills that had been sent to the client. The wives were enlisted so that time sheets would reflect the handwriting of several people.
- Attorney wrote over 100 checks on firm accounts for personal expenses, claiming they were payments to "expert witnesses" or other law-related work.

Attorney
$1.4M over 5 yr period

- Attorney intentionally overbilled the federal government and destroyed and concealed records to conceal his activities. As managing partner, he reviewed the time records of associates and partners in the firm. He forwarded them to the bookkeeper with written instructions directing the bookkeeper to increase the number of hours billed above the numbers recorded by the lawyers. When audited by FDIC, the attorney gathered the original time records and either concealed them or destroyed them, and directed the firm office manager to provide false information to the government.

Attorney
$1.1M over 5 yr period

- Attorney billed five firm clients (four corporations and one trade union) directly without firm authorization. He claimed to be taking vacation or doing client development during some periods when he was billing these clients. Attorney "had most of the payments mailed directly to his home, so that his secretary would not see them; he also forbade his secretary to open any of his mail. . . . [He] spent many hours typing up facsimile legal bills to present to the clients, himself, rather than having his secretary do them. And, of course, he kept all the records for the bills at his home." He "often shifted fees to expenses and vice-versa, to make the bottom line agree with the billing totals he was submitting to his firm's accounting department." Attorney deceived his firm, sometimes with the knowledge and cooperation of clients. He also deceived clients, sometimes billing over 24 hours per day, or billing one expense to two clients. He billed $16,000 of personal expenses to one client.

Attorney
$500 Thousand over 5 year period

- While at the firm, attorney persuaded a French pharmaceutical client to hire a dummy consulting firm he had set up (which had no clients or employees) to arrange drug testing needed for FDA approval. The client paid nearly $1 million to the consulting firm; Morrell paid about half this amount into his checking account, his profit-sharing plan, or took it in cash.

> **Attorney**
> **$225 Thousand over 4 yrs**
> - Attorney charged personal expenses to the firm and to clients, including $27,000 for flowers for his children's weddings, and the cost of meals, floral displays for the office, plane tickets and hotel accommodations for non-business-related family vacations. (Notice of Charges) Attorney denied most of the charges, but admitted billing clients for airfare and hotel accommodations if he was working on a client's case during a particular vacation. He said his "clients have approved and ratified the specific expenses in question." Attorney also arranged for legal fees to be paid directly to him without firm approval.
>
> **Attorney**
> **over 4 yrs (1991–1995)**
> - Attorney allegedly billed clients for hundreds of hours of work that he did not do; he continued to bill for legal work after he began to spend most of his time on investing that involved a $100 million Ponzi scheme.[6]

MANY STATE BARS' RULES PROVIDE FOR OVERSIGHT/ARBITRATION ON FEE ISSUES

One of the ways that state bar associations and courts have dealt with the abundance of fee disputes is to provide for immediate and informal review/arbitration of fee disputes. Many state ethical rules and court rules provide that clients have the right at any time to request that the judge in the case or an attorney representing the state bar review the reasonableness of the attorney's fees. In many states, the attorney is required to inform the client of this right. In those states, the judge or attorney hearing the matter has the right to set the fee and determine what is reasonable under the particular facts and circumstances of the case.

FRAUD AND CRIMINAL CHARGES

> *Intentionally overbilling clients for work not done is called fraud. You can be criminally prosecuted by government officials and civilly prosecuted by your clients.*

Charging an unreasonable fee is no longer simply a matter of ethics. Recently, attorneys and legal assistants have been criminally charged with fraud for intentionally recording time and sending bills for legal services that were never provided. **Criminal fraud** is a false representation of a present or past fact made by the defendant, upon which the victim relies, resulting in the victim suffering damages.

criminal fraud
A false representation of a present or past fact made by a defendant.

Criminal charges for fraud are not filed against attorneys and legal assistants when there is simply a disagreement over what a reasonable fee is. Criminal charges are filed when an attorney or legal assistant acts intentionally to defraud clients. This usually happens when the attorney or legal assistant bills for time when he or she did not really work on the case, or in instances in which the office intentionally billed a grossly overstated hourly rate far above the market rate.

> *One of the most common temptations that can corrupt a paralegal's ethics is to inflate billable hours, since there is often immense pressure in law offices to bill high hours for job security and upward mobility. Such "creative billing" [or "padding"] is not humorous; it's both morally wrong and illegal.*[7]

Interestingly, many of the most recent criminal cases being brought are against well-respected large and small law offices specializing in insurance defense and corporate work. Some insurance companies and corporations, as a matter of course when a case has been concluded, hire an audit firm or independent attorney to go back and audit the firm's billing and files to be sure they were billed accurately. In some instances, these audits have concluded that intentional criminal fraud has occurred and have been referred to prosecutors where criminal charges have been filed. No matter what type of firm is involved, intentionally overstating bills can lead to very big problems. Most, if not all, of the examples in Figure 5-8 reported in the *Georgetown Journal of Legal Ethics* led to criminal prosecutions of the attorneys.

ETHICAL PROBLEMS

There are several difficult ethical problems with no definite solutions regarding timekeeping and billing that need to be explored. The rule in answering ethical questions such as these is to use your common sense and notions of fairness and honesty.

BILLING MORE THAN ONE CLIENT FOR THE SAME TIME OR "DOUBLE BILLING." A situation happens from time to time in which a legal assistant or attorney has the opportunity to bill more than one client for the same time period. For instance, while you are monitoring the opposing side's inspection of your client's documents in case A, you are drafting discovery for case B. Another example: while traveling to attend an interview with a witness in case A, you work on case B.

If you were the client, would you think it is fair for the attorney to charge full price for travel time related to your case while billing another case? A reasonable approach is to bill only the case you are actively working on, to split the time between the cases, or bill the case you are actively working on at the regular hourly rate and bill the case you are inactively working on at a greatly reduced rate. Be fair and honest; your clients as well as judges and others looking at the time will respect you for it.

WHEN BILLING BY THE HOUR, IS THERE AN ETHICAL OBLIGATION TO BE EFFICIENT? DOES THE FIRM HAVE TO HAVE A FORM FILE IN LIEU OF RESEARCHING EACH DOCUMENT EACH TIME? MUST AN OFFICE USE A COMPUTER TO SAVE TIME? These types of ethical questions are decided on a case-by-case basis. The point is that billing by the hour rewards people to work slowly, since the more slowly they work, the more they are paid.

Common sense tells you that if you were the client, you would want your legal staff to be efficient and not to "milk" you for money. The real issue is whether the attorney or legal assistant acted so inefficiently and charged so much, when compared with what a similar attorney or legal assistant with similar qualifications would charge in the same community, that the fee is clearly unreasonable. When a judge rules on the reasonableness of fees, there is no doubt that he or she will consider what a reasonably efficient attorney or legal assistant in the same circumstances would have charged. Use your common sense and be honest and efficient because someone in your office might have to justify your time and charges someday.

SHOULD YOU BILL FOR CLERICAL OR SECRETARIAL DUTIES? Law offices cannot bill clients for clerical or secretarial tasks. The reason is that these tasks are viewed as overhead costs or are a normal part of doing business. An easy, but unethical way to bill more hours is for a legal assistant to bill time to clients for clerical functions such as copying documents or filing material. Legal assistants clearly should not bill for these types of clerical tasks. Legal assistants bill time for professional services, not for clerical functions. If you are unsure about whether a task is clerical, ask your supervising attorney, or record the time initially and point it out to the supervising attorney and let him or her decide.

SHOULD YOU BILL FOR THE MISTAKES OF THE LAW OFFICE? This is another tough problem. People make mistakes all the time. Clients generally feel that they should not have to pay for mistakes, since the reason they went to an attorney was to get an expert to handle their situation. This is a decision that should be left for every law office to decide, but generally the practice of billing for mistakes should be discouraged.

MUST A TASK BE ASSIGNED TO LESS EXPENSIVE SUPPORT STAFF WHEN POSSIBLE? Common sense and efficiency will tell you that tasks should be delegated as low as possible. Clients should not have to pay for attorney time when the task could be completed by an experienced legal assistant. In addition, this practice is more profitable to the law office because higher-paid persons are free to do tasks for which they can bill clients at their normal rates.

> *Billing is important to the legal assistant because raises and bonuses may be reflected by the amount of time billed. Correctly bill no matter how much pressure there is about maintaining those high billable hours because at the end of the day, you will have to live with your conscience. Fortunately, I have never been placed in a position that I was asked to record time which I did not think was right. If I had that situation, I would obtain clarification for the reasoning because there could be a misunderstanding.*
>
> Linda Rushton, CLA

**Figure 5-9
Expense Slip**

Johnson, Beck & Taylor
Expense Slip

Expense Type & Code
1 Photocopies   4 Filing Fees   7 Facsimile   10 Travel
2 Postage   5 Witness Fees   8 Lodging   11 Overnight Delivery
3 Long Distance 6 WESTLAW/LEXIS   9 Meals   12 Other _____

Date _4-5-03_   Case Name: _Smith v. United_   File No. _118294_
Expense Code: _1_ Quantity _20 pages_ Amount _File rate_ (Billable) Non-Billable
Expense Code: _2_ Quantity _4 packages_ Amount _$4.66_   (Billable) Non-Billable
Expense Code: ____ Quantity _sent_   Amount _____   Billable   Non-Billable
Name of Person Making Expense Slip: _JBP_

Description of Expense(s) Incurred:
Copies and postage re: Motion to compel 4/5/03

LEGAL EXPENSES

In addition to recovering for legal fees, law practices also are entitled to recover from the client reasonable expenses that are incurred by the office in representing the client. For example, in Figure 5-9, the office needed to make copies of a motion to compel and mail them to opposing counsels. The cost of making the copies of the motion and mailing them out is directly related to the case, so the office is entitled to be reimbursed from the client for this expense. In most offices, it is important that you fill out expense slips similar to the one in Figure 5-9 or fill out some type of log regarding expenses that the office can be reimbursed for. Such expenses typically include the costs of photocopying documents, postage, long-distance telephone calls, or travel expenses (see Figure 5-10).

The types of items to be charged back to clients are usually found in the law practice's staff manual. Most law offices charge what appears to be premium prices for legal expenses, such as copying costs of ten cents to twenty-five cents or more, especially when a client sees that print shops charge five to ten cents for a photocopy.

> **Figure 5-10**
> **Expenses Typically Billed to Clients**
>
> Court Reporter Fees (Deposition Transcripts)
> Delivery Charges (Federal Express, etc.)
> Expert Witness Fees
> Facsimile Costs
> Filing Fees
> Long-Distance Phone Calls
> Photocopying
> Postage
> Travel Expenses
> WESTLAW/LEXIS
> Witness Fees

However, at five cents a page you (the customer) provide the labor; if you want the store to do the work it costs more. The same is true for a law office. One way to deal with this situation is to send jobs of fifty or more pages to a copy or printing service. This pleases the client because he or she is not paying as much for copying costs, your copiers do not get as much wear and tear, and the invoice from the copy or printing service can be included on the client's bill for reimbursement.

In cases involving litigation, the expenses alone can run into the tens of thousands of dollars. Therefore, the careful tracking of expenses is no trivial matter. Consider the revenues that would be generated if you billed copies at twenty-five cents and the office made 80,000 copies a year directly related to clients. This would be $20,000. Consider also the additional overhead an office would have if it did not bill clients for the copies.

As a legal assistant, you may be required to pay expenses for a case out of your own pocket from time to time. If this happens, be sure to ask for receipts. It also helps to know in advance what specific expenses the office will reimburse you for before they are incurred.

TIMEKEEPING

Timekeeping is the process of tracking what attorneys and legal assistants do with their time. Although this might seem like an incredibly easy task, it is not. Timekeeping is a necessary evil in most law practices. Keeping careful time records is important both for managerial reasons and for producing income.

From a managerial perspective, time records (a) provide the office with a way to monitor the progress of a case, who is working on the case, and/or who is responsible for the matter; (b) allow the office to determine which cases are the most profitable; and (c) allow office management to monitor the efficiencies of law practice staff.

From an income producing perspective, time records (a) allow offices to bill their time to clients; and (b) allow the office to document its fees in probate matters and in cases where legal fees will be decided by a court.

Notice that managerial reasons could apply to any type of law practice including corporate, government, or legal aid. And, it is not uncommon for corporate, government, and legal aid practices to be given court awarded attorneys fees from time to time.

Figure 5-10 is an example of a typical timesheet. A **timesheet** or **timeslip** is where legal professionals record detailed information about the legal services they provide to each client. Timekeeping entries must contain information such as the name of the case worked on, the date the service was provided, and a description of the service.

timesheet or **timeslip**
A record of detailed information about the legal services professionals provide to each client.

MANUAL TIMEKEEPING

There are many different types of manual timekeeping methods that can be purchased from most legal law office supply catalogs. Figure 5-11 is an example of a multiple-slip timesheet. The timeslips are recorded chronologically. Timeslips will be completed by different billing people within the office for a variety of different cases. At some point, typically once a week, the pages of timeslips will be turned in by everyone in the office to the billing department. Each individual slip can be separated and has adhesive on the back. Each slip is separated and is stuck to each client's timeslip page (see Figure 5-12). This provides a convenient way for tracking time for each client. All client's timeslip pages can be stored in a three-ring notebook in alphabetical order by client name or stored in each individual client's accounting file.

It is important to point out that time records do not automatically get charged to clients. The supervising attorney in the case typically reviews the time records turned in and determines whether they will be charged as is or whether the time should be adjusted upward or downward. It should also be noted that it is common to have clients with more than one matter pending. Separate records need to be kept for each matter, and, typically, separate invoices are generated.

COMPUTERIZED TIMEKEEPING

Some timekeeping and billing computer programs also can provide assistance in keeping track of time. In some programs, the user enters what case is being worked on and whether the time is billable or nonbillable and then turns the "meter" on. The computer keeps track of the time until the user is completed with the project for that client. The computerized timeslip is then stored in the program until a billing is generated. When a bill is generated, the computerized timeslip is automatically calculated and included in the client's bill. There are even some systems that use bar codes. The user simply scans in the client's bar code and the bar code for the type of activity he is delivering. When he or she is finished, the bar code for the activity is scanned back in to show that the work on the matter is completed.

billable time
Actual time that a legal assistant or attorney spends working on a case and that is directly billed to a client's account.

BILLABLE V. NONBILLABLE TIME

One of the basics of timekeeping is the difference between billable and nonbillable time. **Billable time** is actual time that a legal assistant or attorney spends working on a case and that is directly billed to a client's account. Any activity that you perform to further a client's case, other than clerical functions, is usually con-

Timekeeping 223

PC—Phone Conference	R—Review
LR—Legal Research	OC—Office Conference
L—Letter	T—Travel
D—Dictation	CT—Court Hearing

Time Conversion
6 Minutes = .1 Hour   36 Minutes = .6 Hour
12 Minutes = .2 Hour   42 Minutes = .7 Hour
15 Minutes = .25 Hour   45 Minutes = .75 Hour
18 Minutes = .3 Hour   48 Minutes = .8 Hour
24 Minutes = .4 Hour   54 Minutes = .9 Hour
30 Minutes = .5 Hour   60 Minutes = 1.0 Hour

Date	Client/Case	File No.	Services Performed	Attorney	Time Hours & Tenths
5-7-03	Smith v. United Sales	118294	Summarized 6 depositions; Client; Δ (Defendant) Helen; Δ Barney, Δ Rose; Witness Forrest & Johnson	BJP	6.5
5-8-03	Marcel v. True Oil	118003	PC w/Client Re: Settlement offer; Discussions w/Attorney; Memo to file Re: offer	BJP	.3
5-8-03	Johnson v. State	118118	PC w/Client's Mother, PC w/Client; LR Re: Bail; Memo to file; R correspondence	BJP	.75
5-8-03	Potential claim of Watkins v. Leslie Grocery	Not Assigned Yet	OC w/Client; (New client); Reviewed facts; Received medical records Re: accident; Conf. w/atty	BJP	1.50
5-8-03	Smith v. United Sales	118294	Computerized searches on depositions for attorney	BJP	.75
5-8-03	Jay Tiller Bankruptcy	118319	PC w/Creditor, Bank One; Memo to file; Client; LJ to Client	BJP	.3
5-8-03	Potential Claim of Watkins v. Leslie Grocery	—	LR Slip & Fall cases generally; Standard of care	BJP	1.00
5-8-03	Marcel v. True Oil	118003	Conf. w/atty. & Client Re: Settlement; Drafted & prepared LJ to Δ's Re: Settlement offer	BJP	1.10
5-8-03	Jay Tiller Bankruptcy	118319	Drafted Bankruptcy petition; OC w/Client; List of Debts; Fin. Stmt; Conf. w/atty	BJP	1.00
5-8-03	Smith v. United Sales	118294	Drafted and prepared depo notice to Witness Spring	BJP	.25
5-9-03	Seeley Real Estate Matter	118300	Ran amortization schedule to attach to 'Contract for Deed'	BJP	.25

Figure 5-11 Typical Manual Timeslip/Time Record Form

Time Records for Case Name: _Smith v. United Sales_   Case No: _118294_

5-7-03	Smith v. United Sales	118294	Summarized 6 depositions; Client; Δ (Defendant) Allen; Δ Barney, Δ Rose; Witness Forest & Johnson	BJP	6.	5
5-8-03	Smith v. United Sales	118294	Computerized searches on depositions for attorney	BJP		.75
5-8-03	Smith v. United Sales	118294	Drafted and prepared depo notice to Witness Spring	BJP		.25

Figure 5-12   Timesheet Record for a Case

nonbillable time
Time that cannot be directly billed to a paying client.

sidered billable time, including interviewing witnesses, investigating a case, serving subpoenas, performing legal research, drafting, and so forth. **Nonbillable time** is time that cannot be directly billed to a paying client. Nonetheless, it should still be tracked.

There are typically three types of nonbillable time:

(a) general firm activities
(b) personal time
(c) pro bono work

pro bono
Legal services that are provided free of charge to a client who is not able to pay for the services.

General firm activities refer to time spent on personnel materials, planning, marketing, client development, staff/committee meetings, library maintenance, and professional development. Personal time refers to taking breaks, cleaning and organizing, and taking sick/vacation days. **Pro bono** work is legal services that are provided free of charge to a client who is not able to pay for the services. Pro bono may be required by your firm or by some state bars. Typically, pro bono cases are taken to generate goodwill in the community for the office or to provide a community service. Although handling pro bono cases is a morally proper thing to do, nonetheless it is still counted as nonbillable time.

overhead
General administrative costs of doing business, including costs such as rent, utilities, phone, and salary costs for administrators.

Nonbillable time is sometimes referred to as "overhead" or "office hours" because the cost of nonbillable time must be paid for by the office. **Overhead** refers to general administrative costs of doing business. They are incidental costs regarding the management and supervision of the business. Overhead includes costs such as rent, utilities, phones, office supplies, equipment, and salary costs for administrators who manage the business and others. Overhead costs are sometimes defined as any cost not directly associated with the production of goods or services.

> —Then—
> There are only approximately 1,300 fee-earning hours per year unless the lawyer works overtime. Many of the eight hours per day available for office work are consumed in personal, civic, bar, religious, and political activities, general office administration, and other . . . matters. Either five or six hours per day would be realistic, depending upon the habits of the individual lawyer. ABA-1959[8]
> —Now—
> The overwhelming majority of law firms today have a minimum billable hour or target that they like for their legal assistants to achieve. [It's] anywhere from 1,400 to 1,800 billable hours a year depending on the law firm. In the last couple of years, more and more firms have realized they have got to be more strict about billable minimums.[9]

MINIMUM BILLABLE HOURS

Many law offices have a preoccupation with the billable hour concept and set billable hour quotas that legal assistants must meet. Figure 5-13 (top) shows the average number of billable hours for legal assistants, associates, and partners/shareholders according to a recent survey. However, in some offices, legal assistant billable hours can be as high as 1,600 to 1,800 hours annually. Historically, this was not the case. In the early 1960s, 1,300 billable hours was thought to be realistic. The number of minimum billable hours depends greatly on location, the size of the law office, and the types of cases.

> *PARALEGAL TRAPPED*
> A paralegal, on his way to an assignment on another floor, became trapped in an elevator just after getting on. Fellow employees gathered around the elevator door. The time-conscious paralegal called out from inside the elevator, "Is this billable or nonbillable time?"[10]

**Figure 5-13
Average Annual
Billable Hours**

Source: *The 2000 Survey of Law Firm Economics—A Management and Planning Tool,* Altman Weil, Publications, Inc. Reprinted with the permission of Altman Weil Publications, Inc. 2000 by Altman Weil Publications, Inc.

Timekeeper	Average
Legal Assistants	1,408 hours
Sr. Legal Assistants	1,438 hours
Legal Assistant Supervisor	1,503 hours
Associates	1,834 hours
Partners/Shareholders	1,754 hours

RECORDING TIME

There are several different ways to actually record and/or track your time. One method is to bill time in tenths of an hour with .5 being a half-hour and 1.0 being an hour. Every six minutes is a tenth of the hour, so you would be billing on six-minute intervals. Billing in tenths works out as follows.

0–6 minutes	= .1 hour	31–36 minutes =	.6 hour
7–12 minutes	= .2 hour	37–42 minutes =	.7 hour
13–15 minutes	= .25 hour	43–45 minutes =	.75 hour
16–18 minutes	= .3 hour	46–48 minutes =	.8 hour
19–24 minutes	= .4 hour	49–54 minutes =	.9 hour
25–30 minutes	= .5 hour	55–60 minutes	= 1.0 hour

As an alternative, some offices will bill using a quarter of an hour as the basis, as follows.

0–15 minutes	=	.25 hour
16–30 minutes	=	.50 hour
31–45 minutes	=	.75 hour
46–60 minutes	=	1.0 hour

Although the quarterly basis is easier to use, it is not as accurate as the tenth of an hour system. Suppose you took a five-minute phone call from a client and your average billing rate is $40 an hour. Using the tenth of an hour system, the fee for the phone call would be $4 (.1 hour times $40 equals $4). However, using the quarterly system, the fee for the phone call would be $10, since .25 is the smallest interval (.25 times $40 equals $10), or 60 percent more.

Figure 5-14 contains some stock billing phrases. It is important that you include as much detail as possible when completing your time records, that the language is clear and easily understood, and that the time record itself is legibly written. Clients

Figure 5-14
Billing Phrases

E-mail to _____, regarding _____.
Telephone conference with _____, regarding _____.
Office conference with _____, regarding _____.
Interview of _____, regarding _____.
Review of file regarding _____.
Review of incoming correspondence from _____, regarding _____.
Review of incoming legal document entitled _____, from _____.
Review and approval of _____, prepared by _____.
Preparation of _____, regarding _____.
Appearance at _____, regarding _____.
Court appearance at _____, regarding _____.
Drafting of _____, regarding _____.
Revising of _____, regarding _____.
Preparation for _____, regarding _____.
Investigation of _____, regarding _____.
Legal research of _____ issue for the legal document entitled _____.
Travel to _____, regarding _____.
Negotiations with _____, regarding _____.
Status report to _____.
Advice and counsel to _____ concerning _____.
Handling miscellaneous details regarding _____.
Research and analysis of _____, regarding _____.

---

are usually more willing to pay a bill when they know exactly what service was performed for them. For example, compare these general bill statements.

1. "Telephone conference—.50 hr. $20.00"
2. "Telephone conference with client on Plaintiff's Request for Production of Documents regarding whether or not client has copies of the draft contracts at issue—.50 hr. $20.00."

Which of these statements would you rather receive?

Many clients would prefer the latter, since they are able to see, and hopefully remember exactly what specific services they received. The problem with the longer format is that detailed timeslips take longer to complete.

TIMEKEEPING PRACTICES

If the average legal assistant is required to bill between 1,400 and 1,600 hours a year, it is very important that he or she take the timekeeping function extremely seriously. The following are some suggestions to consider regarding keeping track of time.

> *Be very careful with your billing. Billing extra hours just to look good is foolish. Consider how much time it should take you to complete a task and try to work within that time frame. If you are consistently a high biller because you spend an inordinate amount of time on projects, people will assume one of two things: (1) you don't know what you are doing, or (2) you are doing more than needed to accomplish the task. Remember that your client pays the bills. The most important consideration in being competitive is to provide the best service at the best price.*[11]

- *Find out how many hours you must bill annually, monthly, and weekly up front and track where you are in relationship to the quota.* One of the first things you should do when you start a new legal assistant job is to find out how many billable hours you must have. If the office requires that you bill 1,400 to 1,800 hours a year, budget this on a monthly and weekly basis and keep track of where you are so that you will not have to try to "make it all up" at the end of the year.
- *Find out when timesheets are due.* Another thing you should do when starting a new position is to find out exactly what day timesheets are due so that you can submit them on time.
- *Keep copies of your timesheets.* Always keep a copy of your timesheet for your own file in case the original is either lost or misplaced. Having a copy also allows you to go back and calculate your number of billable hours.
- *Record your time contemporaneously on a daily basis.* One of the biggest mistakes you can make is to not record your time as you go along during the day. If you wait until the end of the day to try to remember all the things you did, there is absolutely no way you will be able to accurately reconstruct everything. In the end, you will be the one suffering, doing work you did not get credit for. Be sure to keep a timesheet handy and fill it out as you go along.
- *Record your actual time spent; do not discount your time.* Do not discount your time because you think you should have been able to perform a job faster. If it took you four hours to finish an assignment and you worked the whole four hours, there is no reason to discount the time. **If the supervising attorneys think a discount is warranted, they can decide that, but it is not up to you to do that.** That is not your burden. However, if you made a mistake or had a problem that you do not think the client should be billed for, be up front and tell your supervising attorney and let him or her help you make the decision.
- *Be aware if billable hours are related to bonuses or merit increases.* Be aware as to how billable hours are used. In some law offices, billable hours are used in distributing bonuses and merit increases and can be used in performance evaluations. Some offices discount or "cut" the time actually billed to the client. Always ask whether billable hours means the amount of time submitted or the amount of time actually billed to the client; there is a big difference.

- *Be ethical.* Always be honest and ethical in the way you fill out your timesheets. Padding your timesheet is unethical and simply wrong. Eventually wrongdoing regarding timekeeping, billing, or handling client funds will become apparent.

> *I worked closely with a paralegal who consistently had two or three more [billable] hours a day than I did, although we arrived around the same time and did similar work all day. We usually walked each other out at night (for safety reasons). I'd look at my time for a day: 10.5 hours; and she had 13. She didn't subtract for lunch or breaks. . . . An attorney called me in to ask about the discrepancy between her time and mine. . . . The lawyer talked to her. . . . Her timesheet was accurate after that.*[12]

- *Be aware of things that keep you from billing time.* Be aware of things that keep you from having a productive day such as people who lay their troubles at your feet or who are constantly taking your attention away from your work. An appropriate approach is to say, "I would really like to hear about it at lunch, but right now I am really busy." Also, avoid wasting time trying to track down other people or trying to find information you need. Finally, try to eliminate constant interruptions, including phone calls. If you really need to get something done, go someplace where you can get the work done and tell others to hold your calls. However, check in every once in a while to return client phone calls. Clients should have their phone calls returned as soon as possible.

BILLING

To generate the necessary income to operate the firm, special attention must be paid to billing, the process of issuing bills for the purpose of collecting monies for legal services performed and for being reimbursed for expenses. This section shows how legal assistants are able to bill their time, how billing rates are determined, the difference between manual and computerized billing systems, the billing cycle, how management reports that are generated from many computerized billing systems can help the office make good administrative decisions, and what some successful billing practices are.

BILLING FOR LEGAL ASSISTANT TIME—LEGAL ASSISTANT PROFITABILITY

Many law offices bill for legal assistant time as well as for attorney time. A recent survey found that most of the legal assistants responding to the survey stated that their law office billed clients separately for their work. Many clients prefer this

**Figure 5-15
Average Hourly Billing Rates**

Source: *The 2000 Survey of Law Firm Economics—A Management and Planning Tool,* Altman Weil, Publications, Inc. Reprinted with the permission of Altman Weil Publications, Inc. 2000 by Altman Weil Publications, Inc.

Region	Legal Assistants	Associates	Partners/Shareholders
California	$102	$196	$294
West	$90	$153	$221
South Central	$77	$152	$236
West Central	$74	$130	$185
East Central	$86	$150	$228
South	$69	$134	$204
Northeast	$88	$171	$260

because the legal assistant hourly rates are much lower than attorney hourly rates. Figure 5-15 shows the average hourly rates for legal assistants, associates, and partners/shareholders throughout the country.

For example, assume an associate attorney and a legal assistant can both prepare discovery documents in a case and that the task will take seven hours. Assuming the legal assistant bills at $55 an hour and the associate bills at $100 an hour, the cost to the client if the legal assistant does the job is $385, and the cost if the

---

CLOSE-UP

Successful Billing Practices—Pleasing the Client and Avoiding Accounts Receivable Problems

The following are some successful billing practices.

- Legal fees and expenses should be discussed early in the case.

    Determining legal fees in a case must be performed by an attorney and should be done up front with a client. Clients know that legal matters are expensive, so many are nervous about the cost of the matter from the first moment they walk into the office. The attorney involved should raise the issue first.

    Other matters that should be covered include:
    - What type of billing format the client would like to receive
    - When billings should be sent: biweekly, monthly, bimonthly, annually, etc.
    - Where the billings should be sent. (Some clients do not want the billings going to their office or to their home, so the office needs to know where the billing should be sent.)
    - Introducing the clients to the people, including the legal assistant, assigned to their case
    - An estimate of the length of time it will take to complete the matter (days, months, years)
    - Legal expenses, including exactly what costs they will be billed for, whether clients can pay for outside assistance, such as the costs of investigators and experts, and how much the total expenses might be
- Clients should be asked point-blank whether they will be able to pay the costs as they go along.

    When fee discussions are being held with clients, it is important that clients be directly asked whether they think they will be able to make payments on the case as the costs are incurred. If they do not think they can pay the balance as they go along, it is important that this is known up front to help decide what type of fee agreement is the most appropriate.
- Clients must be screened.

    It is important to realize that some clients simply will not pay their bills. It is important for the law office to learn to screen out and minimize these types of clients. Attorneys and law offices cannot take every case presented to them. Attorneys and law offices must be able to pick out the cases that will be profitable.
- Get the fee agreement in writing.

    There is no substitute for reducing everything related to the billing process to writing. All fee agreements,

associate drafts the discovery is $700. Thus, the client will have saved $315 by simply allowing the legal assistant to do the job. The client would still have to pay for the attorney's time to review the legal assistant's discovery, but the cost would be minimal. This represents substantial savings to clients.

The question of whether law offices can bill for legal assistant time was considered by the United States Court in *Missouri v. Jenkins,* 491 U.S. 274 (1989). In that case, the plaintiff was successful on several counts in a civil rights lawsuit and was attempting to recover attorney's fees from the defendant under a federal statute. The statutory language provided that the prevailing party could recover "reasonable attorney's fees" from the other party. The plaintiff argued for recovery for the time that legal assistants spent working on the case as well as for the time attorneys spent. The defendant argued that legal assistant time was not "attorney's fees." Alternatively, the defendants argued that if they did have to pay something for legal assistant time, they should only have to pay about $15 an hour, which represents the overhead costs to the office for a legal assistant.

The Court found that legal assistants carry out many useful tasks under the direction of attorneys and that "reasonable attorney's fees" referred to the reasonable fee for work produced whether it be by attorneys or legal assistants. The Court also

---

arrangements regarding when billing should be sent, and bill formats should be completed in writing and put into the client's file.
- Accurately track how much a client has paid the firm.

A successful billing system must be able to *accurately* track how much clients have paid the firm. It is important that the firm take great care in what goes in and out of the billing system and that the information be accurate.
- The firm must send regular billings.

Nearly all clients like to receive timely billings. Most clients like to receive billings at least monthly. Imagine the frustration of a client who receives a quarterly billing that is four or five times more expensive than what he planned on. Regular billings will alert the client as to how he or she is being billed and how much he or she needs to budget. In addition, if a client sees timely bills that are more expensive than he or she had planned, he or she can contact the firm to tell it how he or she wants to proceed to limit future bills before they are incurred. This at least gives the client the option of cutting back on legal services instead of getting angry at the firm for not informing him or her of the changes on a timely basis.
- Client billings must be fair and respectful.

Billings that are fair and courteous are essential to a good billing system. If a client thinks that the firm is overcharging him or her for services or that the billings are curt and unprofessional, there is a good chance that he or she will not pay the bill or will hold payment. If you speak to a client regarding a bill, be courteous and respectful and try to understand the situation from his or her point of view. If there is a dispute, take down the client's side of the story, relay the information to the attorney in charge of the matter, and let the attorney resolve it. Also, it is usually not a good practice to bill time for the time spent discussing the bill with a client.
- Client billings must be clear.

Billings should be clear and without legalese. The billings should be easy to read and provide the information that the client wants to see. Payments that are made based on billings that are complicated and hard to read are oftentimes held up while the client tries to decipher the bill.
- Build relationships with clients.

Remember that everything you do to build relationships with your clients, including returning phone calls, listening and being responsive to client needs, keeping your promises, and providing quality services, affects the client when he or she receives a billing. Clients are far less likely to complain or refuse to pay billings when they receive good service from someone they like and trust and who is sincerely interested in their best welfare.

found that, under the federal statute, legal assistant time should not be compensated for at the overhead costs to the office but should be paid at the prevailing market rates in the area for legal assistant time. The Court noted that the prevailing rate for legal assistants in that part of the country at that time was about $40 an hour and held that the office was entitled to receive that amount for legal assistant hours worked on the case. Thus, it is clear that offices can bill for legal assistant time if they choose to do so. The case also reminds us that purely clerical tasks or secretarial tasks should not be billed at the legal assistant rate. This topic was also covered in more detail in Chapter 1.

LEVERAGING AND HOW HOURLY BILLING RATES ARE DETERMINED

leveraging
The process of earning a profit from legal services that are provided by law office personnel (usually partners, associates, and legal assistants).

Leveraging is an important concept in law office billing. **Leveraging** is the process of earning a profit from legal services that are provided by law office personnel (usually partners, associates, and legal assistants). Leveraging allows the office not only to recover the cost of an attorney or legal assistant's salary but also to pay overhead expenses and even make a profit on each such person. Thus, legal assistants are also a profit center for law firms. It is a win-win situation. Clients pay less fees for legal assistants over attorneys and law firms still generate a profit on legal assistant time.

MANUAL BILLING SYSTEMS

Before legal billing software was widely available, billings were generated manually, using typewriters or word processors and timesheets. Law practices typically would store the timesheets in the accounting file of each case and then periodically send a statement. Although a few offices may still produce billings manually, manual systems have certain inherent limitations. Manual billings typically are slow and cumbersome, are prone to mathematical errors, and can take a great deal of overhead time to generate the bill. Thus, manual billings are sent out less frequently than most offices would like, which can cause cash-flow problems. In addition, management reports on manual systems are burdensome to produce. Computerized billing systems automatically produce management reports that tell who is billing the most hours, which clients pay the best, and which types of cases generate the most money.

COMPUTERIZED BILLING SYSTEMS

Computerized billing systems solve many of the problems associated with manual systems. Generally, timekeepers still must record what they do with their time on a timeslip or timesheet or record the entry directly into the program. If the timeslips are completed manually, then they must be entered into the legal billing software, usually on a daily or weekly basis. It is common for offices using computerized billing systems to produce monthly or even biweekly bills according to the wishes of the client. In addition to solving cash-flow problems, most legal billing software programs produce reports that can help the office make good management decisions. (This is covered in more detail later in the chapter.) Computerized timekeeping and billing also produces billings that are more accurate than manual

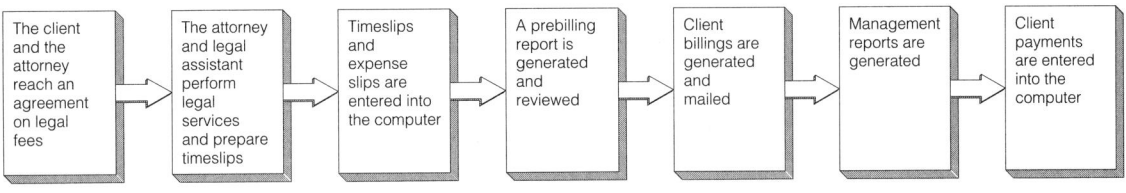

Figure 5-16 Computerized Timekeeping and Billing Cycle

methods because all mathematical computations are performed automatically by the computer. Because legal timekeeping and billing software prices have plunged to below even $100, nearly any office can afford these types of programs.

THE TIMEKEEPING AND BILLING CYCLE

Although all law offices have their own timekeeping and billing practices, most computerized systems follow a cycle or process (see Figure 5-16).

1. *Client and attorney reach an agreement on legal fees.* At the outset of most cases, the client and attorney reach an agreement regarding how much the attorney will charge for services.
2. *Attorneys and legal assistants perform legal services and prepare manual timeslips.* After the client and attorney reach an agreement on how legal fees will be figured, the attorneys and legal assistants begin work on the matter. When an attorney/legal assistant performs work, he or she fills out a timeslip to track the exact services performed for the client. As noted earlier, although some computer programs can keep track of time automatically and make computerized timeslips, many people still use the old manual method.
3. *Timeslips and out-of-pocket expense slips are entered into the computer.* Once the work has been performed on a case, and manual timeslips filled out, the timeslips must be entered into the computer. In addition, expense slips are entered into the computer to track the expenses an office incurs on behalf of a client.
4. *Prebilling report is generated and reviewed by managing attorney (and discounted if necessary.)* After legal services have been performed and recorded in the time and billing software, the next step is for a prebilling report to be generated. This is done before the final client bills are generated. A prebilling report is a rough draft of billings that eventually will be sent to clients (see Figure 5-17). The prebilling report is given to the attorney in charge of the case for review or to a billing committee to make sure the billing is accurate.

Attorneys may choose to discount bills for a variety of reasons, including thinking the task should have taken less time than it actually did. Discounts also are used for good customers because of the client's hardship, for professional courtesy or for friends, or because the billing looks unreasonable. This can, however, be very frustrating to a legal assistant who has his or her time cut back. Typically, only the amount that is actually billed gets counted against the target or minimum billable set number of hours.

Figure 5-17
Prebilling Report

```
                    JOHNSON, BECK & TAYLOR
    8/12/01              Prebilling Report                    Page 1
```

Refrigeration, Inc.   Corporate Matters
Miscellaneous Corporate Matters   Monthly
Case Number: Refrig-002   Trust Balance: $2,825
P.O. Box 10083   Case Rate: $125
500 East Fifth Street   Case Attorney: MJB
Los Angeles, CA 90014
Phone: (213) 553-9342

Previous Bill Owed $470.20

—Legal Fees—

7/6/01	MJB	Telephone conference with Stevenson re: June 2001 minutes	.50 hr	$62.50
7/7/01	MJB	Preparation of June 2001 minutes; prepared for review at next meeting of the board of directors	1.00 ~~1.50~~ hr	$125.00 MJB ~~$187.50~~
7/9/01	MJB	Conference with Stevenson at home	.25 hr	none
		Total Legal Fees	1.75 ~~2.25~~ hr	$187.50 MJB ~~$250.00~~

—Costs Advanced—

| 7/7/01 | MJB | Photocopy documents; June 2001 minutes (for board meeting) | $.25 ea 100 items | $25.00 |
| | | **Total Costs Advanced** .... | | $25.00 |

Continued on Page Two

Changes can be made directly on the prebilling report and then entered into the computer.
5. *Client billings are generated and mailed.* Once the prebilling report has been reviewed and any changes made, formal client billings are generated by the computer (see Figure 5-18). There are many billing formats that most timekeeping and billing software can produce. The computer automatically prints the bills, and they are subsequently mailed to the clients.
6. *Management reports are generated.* Most computerized timekeeping and billing programs have a wide variety of management reports available. Management reports are not used for billing clients; they are used to evaluate the effectiveness of the office. For example, most programs generate a report that shows how much time is nonbillable. If an office has a great deal of nonbillable time, it might indicate the office is not productive and is losing valuable time from its timekeepers.
7. *Client payments entered in computer.* Finally, once the legal services have been performed and billings made to clients, payments made as a result of the billings must be recorded or entered into the computer, giving the client proper credit for the payment.

The timekeeping and billing process is a recurring cycle. Once billings are produced and payments made for a period, the process starts over if more work is performed on the case. The timeslips for the new period must be entered, billings generated, and so forth. Once a year or so, old timeslips should be purged or deleted from the computer. This allows the computer to operate faster.

BILL FORMATS

Generating bills is the most important aspect of any timekeeping and billing program. There is no uniform way that all law offices bill clients. The look and format of billings depend on the law office, its clients, the type of law it practices, etc. Thus, it is important that any timekeeping and billing system used, whether it is manual or computerized, be flexible in the number of client billing formats that are available. For example, some bill formats contain only general information about the services provided, while others show greater detail about what services were provided. In many computerized systems, the format of the bill is set up when the client's case is first entered into the system.

Historically, many offices did not itemize their billing, simply stating "For Services Rendered $XXX" on the bill. Although each client is different, most clients like to receive detailed billings of exactly what services are being provided. This allows the client to see what he is paying for. This also is beneficial to the office, since clients are more willing to pay the bill when they know what it is for. Producing detailed bills takes work. It requires timekeepers to make accurate, current timeslips of what work they have provided. Although this seems enough, it is not. It is very hard to persuade timekeepers to write down each service they perform (i.e., 12/22/01, Telephone call to Larry Jones, witness, regarding statement given 10/10/00........15 minutes). Yet, the whole point of billing is to be paid. So, if an office produces a bill that is not itemized and therefore the client does not pay it, nothing has been gained. Although itemized billings are sometimes inconvenient for the timekeeper and take longer to produce, if the bill is paid in the end, the extra work has paid off.

**Figure 5-18
Final Client Billing**

JOHNSON, BECK & TAYLOR
555 Flowers Street, Suite 200
Los Angeles, California 90038
(212) 585-2342

Mary Smith
Refrigeration, Inc.
P.O. Box 10083
500 East Fifth Street
Los Angeles, CA 90014

Billing Date: 08/15/01

Acct. Number: 4345AS3234
Previous Bal. in Trust
$2,825.00

RE: Refrigeration Miscellaneous Corporate Matters

DATE	PROFESSIONAL SERVICES	INDIV.	TIME	
7/6/01	Telephone conference with Stevenson re June 2001 minutes	MJB	.50	$62.50
7/7/01	Preparation of June 2001 minutes: prepared for review at next meeting of the board of directors	MJB	1.00	$125.00
7/9/01	Conference with Stevenson at home	MJB	.25	$-0-
TOTAL FOR THE ABOVE SERVICES			1.75	**$187.50**

DATE	EXPENSES	
7/7/01	Photocopy documents; June 2001 minutes (for board meeting)	$25.00
TOTAL FOR ABOVE EXPENSES		**$25.00**
TOTAL BILLING		**$212.50**
CURRENT BALANCE IN TRUST		**$2,612.50**

MANAGEMENT REPORTS

Almost all timekeeping and billing software packages produce a wide variety of management reports. **Management reports** are used to help management analyze whether the timekeeper is operating in an efficient and effective manner. Management reports can be used to track problems an office may be experiencing and to help devise ways to correct the problems. The following are explanations of some common management reports and how they are used by offices.

management reports
Reports used to help management analyze whether the office is operating in an efficient and effective manner.

CASE/CLIENT LIST   Most billing packages allow the user to produce a case or client list. A list of all active cases an office has is very important in trying to effectively manage a large caseload. Most reports not only will list the client names but also will list the appropriate account number (also called "client identification number" by some programs). This is useful when trying to locate a client's identification number.

AGED ACCOUNTS RECEIVABLE REPORT   The **aged accounts receivable report** shows all cases that have outstanding balances due to the office and how long these balances are past due (see Figure 5-19). The report breaks down the current balances due and the balances thirty, sixty, and more than ninety days past due. Using this report, management can clearly see which clients are not paying and how old the balances are. This report also is helpful for following up on clients who are slow in paying their bills. Most programs allow the report to be run according to the type of case. Thus, management can see what types of cases (i.e. criminal, divorce, tax, etc.) have the most aged accounts. If one particular type of case has more than its share of aged accounts, it might be more profitable to stop taking that type. So, from a management perspective, this can be a very important report. It should be noted that aged account information should not appear on bills sent to clients. Bills that are more than thirty days old should simply say "past due."

aged accounts receivable report
Report showing all cases that have outstanding balances due and how long these balances are past due.

TIMEKEEPER PRODUCTIVITY REPORT   The **timekeeper productivity report** shows how much billable and nonbillable time is being spent by each timekeeper (see Figure 5-19). This report can be used to identify which timekeepers are the most diligent in their work. For example, notice in Figure 5-19 that "Arthur A. Alexander" billed a total of only 77.75 hours for the month, while the other attorneys billed more than 100 hours. Also, notice that "Byron B. Brown" produced the most billable hours and payments received by the office.

Finally, note the totals section, which shows that although the office billed 280.25 hours for a total of $31,130.25, the office received to date $27,778.00. Although the report in Figure 5-19 shows the results for only one month, most packages allow the productivity report to be run for a quarter or even for a year.

timekeeper productivity report
Report showing how much billable and nonbillable time is being spent by each timekeeper.

CASE TYPE PRODUCTIVITY REPORT   The **case type productivity report** shows which type of cases (i.e., criminal, personal injury, bankruptcy, etc.) are the most profitable (see Figure 5-20). For example, in Figure 5-20 note that the bankruptcy and litigation areas of the law office brought in $17,500.50 and $44,550.75 respectively for the month of July, or 11.73 percent and 29.87 percent of the income earned. This report obviously shows which types of cases are the most profitable and which cases are the least profitable. Management will again use this type of report to decide which areas to concentrate more on to become more profitable.

case type productivity report
Report showing which types of cases (i.e., criminal, personal injury, bankruptcy, etc.) are the most profitable.

A. Aged Accounts Receivable Report

```
                    LAW OFFICES OF SMITH, SMITH AND JONES
5/ 1/02                  Aged Accounts Receivable                    PAGE 1
Entire Alphabet                                                 All Bill Types
All Attorneys                                                   All Case Types
Cycle: All Cycles (All Months)                           Ignore Cycle Due Date
```

Client/Matter	Balance	Current	30 Days	60 Days	Over 90
All Right Manufacturing C					
General Corporate Matt	127.50	None	127.50	None	None
Hinge Division - Paten	975.00	975.00	None	None	None
	1,102.50	975.00	127.50	None	None
Alta Loma Bookkeeping					
Purchase of Johnson Ch	800.00	175.00	175.00	450.00	None
Burton, Sarah					
Divorce	147.50	None	147.50	None	None
Protective order	440.00	None	None	440.00	None
	587.50	None	147.50	440.00	None
Carla's Hard to Fit					
Incorporation	1,500.00	1,500.00	None	None	None
Chuck's Artist Supplies					
Liquidation	607.50	None	505.00	102.50	None
Drummond, Lester B.					
I.R.S. Matter	427.75	427.75	None	None	None
Long Beach Property	1,775.00	None	None	1,775.00	None
Possession	500.00	None	None	500.00	None
	2,702.75	427.75	None	2,275.00	None
Servi...	175.00	175.00	None	None	None
iness...	725.00	None	None	None	725.00
	112.50	None	None	None	112.50
	75.00	None	None	75.00	None
	912.50	None	None	75.00	837.50
Abe...	632.75	None	632.75	None	None
napt Inc.	7,500.00	7,500.00	None	None	None
	4,410.00	None	1,410.00	3,000.00	None
ncy aud	475.00	475.00	None	None	None
ive	12,559.99	550.00	9,405.00	2,425.00	170.00
	330.00	330.00	None	None	None
	485.00	None	None	485.00	None
ted)	34,770.50	12,107.75	12,402.75	9,252.50	1,007.50

B. Timekeeper Productivity Report

```
                  LAW OFFICES OF SMITH, SMITH AND JONES
5/ 1/02              Attorney Time/Productivity Analysis        PAGE 1

                                              Fees            Hours

                      April 2002

Arthur A. Alexander           Billed:         $8,852.50       77.75
                              On Hold:        $100.00         1.00
   Payments Rec'd   $7,277.50 Non Chargeable: $100.00          .75
   Standard Rate:      $75.00 Written Off:    $125.00         2.00
   Realized Rate:     $112.00 Administrative: $125.00         1.00

                              . . . .

Byron B. Brown                Billed:         $10,527.75      101.50
                              On Hold:        None            None
   Payments Rec'd  $10,950.50 Non Chargeable: None            None
   Standard Rate:      $95.00 Written Off:    None            None
   Realized Rate:      $93.00 Administrative: None            None

                              . . . .

Andrew B. Cabellero           Billed:         $12,750.00      101.00
                              On Hold:        $1,250.00       10.00
   Payments Rec'd   $9,550.50 Non Chargeable: $100.00         1.00
   Standard Rate:     $125.00 Written Off:    $250.00         2.20
   Realized Rate:     $125.00 Administrative: $125.00         1.00

                              . . . .

Monthly Summary - All Attorneys Listed
=======================================
                              Billed:         $31,130.25      280.25
   Payments Rec'd              On Hold:        $1,350.00       11.00
   This Month:      $27,778.00 Non Chargeable: $200.00         1.75
                              Written Off:    $375.00         4.20
   Realized Rate:     $110.00 Administrative: $250.00         2.00
```

Figure 5-19 Aged Accounts Receivable Report and Timekeeper Productivity Report
Source: Courtesy CompuLaw, Inc.

Figure 5-20
Case Type Productivity Report
Source: Courtesy CompuLaw, Inc.

```
                    FENWICK, QUINT GERSON AND PECK
7/31/02                Case Type Productivity                         PAGE 1
                    Hours         Fees          Fees       % Total    % Total
Case Type          Billable      Billed        Income      Fee Inc    Hours

                                 July 2002

Bankruptcies        252.75     $26,450.00    $17,500.50    11.73      17.48
Civil Matters        32.50      $4,142.75     $3,655.75     2.45       2.24
Corporate Matters   125.75     $19,855.50    $12,500.25     8.38       8.70
Criminal Matters     22.00      $1,875.00     $2,250.00     1.51       1.52
Estate Planning      87.75      $9,475.00     $8,875.00     5.95       6.07
Family Law           52.25      $6,175.75     $5,495.75     3.68       3.61
General Business    108.70      $9,775.50     $8,975.50     5.95       7.52
General Practice     61.00      $6,552.75     $7,275.50     4.88       4.22
Litigation          225.00     $37,750.00    $44,550.75    29.87      15.56
Personal Injury      35.00      $4,500.00     $4,125.25     2.76       2.42
Probate Matters       0.00          0.00          0.00      0.00       0.00
Real Estate Matters  18.00      $2,150.00     $2,100.00     1.40       1.24
Taxation Matters     24.75      $2,650.00     $2,655.00     1.78       1.71
Other                 9.00      $1,253.00     $1,253.50      .84        .62
Patents & Trademarks 36.50      $4,141.75     $4,155.50     2.78       2.52
International Law    44.00      $8,645.25     $3,440.00     2.31       3.04
Immigration Law      27.00      $3,150.00       $750.00      .50       1.86
Insurance Defense   111.50     $10,950.75     $7,555.25     5.06       7.71
Insurance Plaintiff  88.00      $8,125.00     $6,550.75     4.39       6.08
Consumer Law          6.75        $595.00       $500.00      .33        .46
Labor Unions         77.00      $5,845.00     $4,995.50     3.35       5.32

July Totals       1,445.20    $174,058.00   $149,161.00
```

TIMEKEEPING AND BILLING SERVICE BUREAUS

Some law offices use third-party timekeeping and billing service bureaus to generate their billings. A **timekeeping and billing service bureau** is a company that for a fee processes attorney and legal assistant timesheets (usually on a monthly basis), generates billings, and records client payments for a law practice. Service bureaus are in the business of producing billings and tracking the financial management of other offices, including law offices. Whether it is cheaper to use a service bureau to produce billings or to do it in-house depends on the size of the office, type of clients, etc.

timekeeping and billing service bureau A company that for a fee produces attorney and legal assistant timesheets (usually on a monthly basis), generates billings, and records client payments for a law practice.

BILLING FROM THE CORPORATE AND GOVERNMENT PERSPECTIVE

Corporate and government law practices sometimes hire outside counsel (i.e., private law offices). **Outside counsel** refers to when corporate and government law practices contract with private law offices (i.e., outside of the corporation or government practice) to help them with legal matters, such as litigation, specialized contracts, stock/bond offerings, etc. Thus, corporate and government law practices are purchasers of legal services and tend to look at billing from a different perspective.

outside counsel Term referring to when corporate and government law practices contract with private law offices (i.e., outside of the corporation or government practice) to help them with legal matters, such as litigation, specialized contracts, stock/bond offerings, etc.

Corporate and government law practices are concerned with limiting the costs of legal fees. Many corporate clients will state that they will not pay more than a certain amount, perhaps $200 an hour, for any attorney regardless of experience. If the office wants to maintain the particular client, it will agree to the terms. Because corporations and governments have access to large sums of money and typically are good-paying clients, many offices will reduce the price to get and keep the business.

Corporate and government clients usually require very detailed bills to control what is being done on the case and to control costs. In some cases, corporations and governments use a competitive bidding process to select outside counsel. Thus, summary billings are usually not accepted. They also typically will limit the type and cost of expenses that are billed to them. For instance, some corporations require that computerized legal research (WESTLAW, LEXIS, etc.), postage, fax costs, and similar expenses be borne by the office.

It is not uncommon for a corporate law practice to publish policies and guidelines covering exactly what outside counsel will charge, when it will charge, how payments will be made, how much and what type of legal expenses will be reimbursed, and so on. Figure 5-21 shows the top ten reasons corporate law departments fail to pay private law offices.

Figure 5-21 Reasons Corporate Law Departments Sometimes Refuse or Negotiate on Legal Bills

Reason	Explanation
Legal services are below standard	The legal services provided were below standard or didn't meet the needs of the corporate client. Corporate law departments will typically attempt to negotiate down the fees. In these instances, the corporate law department staff must take the time to correct the problems even though they paid to have it done correctly.
Too many attorneys and legal assistants working the case	When multiple timekeepers attend the same deposition, or bill for the same work provided the costs rise quickly. Many corporate law departments will try to set limits on the number of timekeepers working a case at one time. Also, if the attorneys or legal assistants that are working the case change, then the client must pay for the new attorneys or legal assistants to get up to speed.
Billing lacks detail	Most law departments want to see detailed reports of how timekeepers spent their time and not "for legal services provided."
Billing is incomplete	A bill doesn't include previous payments made or is otherwise incomplete.
Billing has numerical errors	The bill doesn't add up or wrong billing rates are used.

Sticker-Shock	The corporate law department expects a bill for $5,000 and receives a bill for $25,000.	
Attorneys and Legal Assistants Conferencing with Each Other Frequently	It is frustrating for a client to receive a bill where attorneys and legal assistants are frequently meeting to discuss strategy or otherwise because this greatly increases the client's bill. This is particularly frustrating for the client when the bill does not say why the staff working the case were meeting.	
Billing Sent to the Wrong Person	Sending the bill to the wrong person can be frustrating in a large corporation. The bill can literally get lost inside the corporation unless the bill is sent to the correct person.	
Billing Every Little Thing	Clients strongly dislike being billed for every five-minute phone call, being billed for the time it takes to prepare the bill itself, or other items that in the big picture do not amount to much.	
Being Billed for Another Case	Occasionally, a client will be billed for time spent on another case. This undermines the whole billing process.	
Billing is received late	Corporate clients become frustrated when they receive a bill for services that were delivered five months ago. Not only is the billing late, but it is difficult to remember that far back as to the details of the service.	

INTERNET SITES

GENERAL

ORGANIZATION	DESCRIPTION	INTERNET ADDRESS
ABA Law Practice Today	ABA site devoted to law practice management	www.abanet.org/lpm
Association of Legal Administrators	Site for legal administrators	www.alanet.org
Altman Weil Pensa	National legal consultants with excellent books and publications on fees and billing	www.altmanweil.com
Legal Technology News	Information on legal technology issues including timekeeping and billing	www.lawtechnews.com
Legal Technology Online	Resources regarding legal technology issues including timekeeping and billing	www.digital-lawyer.com
Law Research	Sites with links to many legal software vendors	www.lawresearch.com

TIMEKEEPING AND BILLING

Organization	Description	World Wide Web Address
Software Technology	TABS legal timekeeping	www.stilegal.com
Alumni Computer Group	PC LAW legal timekeeping	www.pclaw.com
BytePro	Time and Profit legal timekeeping	www.bytepro.com
Sage U.S.	Timeslips legal timekeeping	www.timeslips.com
Prolaw	Prolaw legal timekeeping	www.prolaw.com
Juris	Juris legal timekeeping	www.juris.com

Suggested Reading

Beyond the Billable Hour, Richard C. Reed, American Bar Association, 1989.

Billing Innovations, Richard C. Reed, American Bar Association, 1996.

How to Draft Bills Clients Rush to Pay, J. Harris Morgan and Julie Tamminen, American Bar Association, 1995.

Leveraging With Legal Assistants, Arthur G. Greene, American Bar Association, p. 1993.

Small Law Firm Economics, Altman Weil, Inc. (produced annually).

Survey of Law Firm Economics, Altman Weil, Inc. (produced annually).

Win-Win Billing Strategies: Alternatives That Satisfy Your Clients and You, Richard C. Reed, American Bar Association, 1992.

Summary

Although timekeeping, billing, and managing client funds are not glamorous tasks, they are essential to the survival of most law practices. Timekeeping is the process of tracking attorneys' and legal assistants' time for the purpose of billing clients. Billing is the process of issuing invoices and collecting monies for legal service performed and being reimbursed for expenses. Typical kinds of legal fee agreements include hourly rate, contingency, flat, retainer, court awarded fees, and prepaid legal service plans.

A trust account is a separate bank account, apart from an office's general accounts, where unearned client funds are deposited. The use of trust accounts is mandated by ethical rules for all unearned monies that an office receives.

Leveraging is the process of earning a profit from legal services that are provided by the law office staff.

Computerized billing programs allow offices to quickly and easily send out regular billings, produce management reports that administrators can use to help direct the office, and can typically produce many different types of bill formats.

Key Terms

Timekeeping
Billing
Hourly rate fee
Attorney or legal assistant hourly rate

Client hourly rate
Blended hourly rate fee
Activity hourly rate
Contingency fee
Flat fee
Earned retainer
Unearned retainer
Trust or escrow account
Cash advance
Retainer for general representation
Case retainer
Pure retainer
Court awarded fees
Prepaid legal service

Value billing
Criminal fraud
Timesheet or timeslip
Billable time
Nonbillable time
Pro Bono
Overhead
Leveraging
Management reports
Aged accounts receivable report
Timekeeper productivity report
Case type productivity report
Timekeeping and billing service bureau
Outside counsel

QUESTIONS AND EXERCISES

1. You are a new legal assistant and have worked for a medium-sized law office for three months. It has been a tremendous learning experience for you. It has taken time to learn how the office does business, its policies and procedures, what type of service you are expected to give to clients, where resources are and how to use them, such as the office's computer systems, law library, copy machines, and form files. Although it has taken time for you to learn these things, you also have been productive and have received several compliments on the quality of your work.

One day, you read in the office's staff manual that all legal assistants are required to bill 1,500 hours annually or face possible discipline. You immediately contact your supervisor and ask whether, as a new legal assistant, you will be expected to bill this amount. Your supervisor responds, "Of course. You were told that when you were hired." You immediately begin gathering copies of your timesheets to compile your total. You also request that the billing department send you the total numbers of hours you have billed to date. When you get the report from billing, you panic; you have billed only 300 hours. You are 75 hours behind where you should be (1,500 divided by four [i.e., one-fourth the way through the year] equals 375). What do you do now, and how could you have avoided this unfortunate situation?

2. On April 1, a billing goes out to John Myers, one of the clients whose cases you have been working on. Mr. Myers calls you a few days later and complains about the amount of time shown on the bill. He is extremely rude and discourteous. Mr. Myers flatly states that he thinks he is being overbilled. How do you handle the phone call?

3. Your office is on the same side of the city as a major manufacturing plant. You notice that many of the plant's employees come to your office for routine legal services, such as wills, adoptions, and name changes. Although the office has been charging these clients on an hourly basis, you think that there might be alternatives. You talk to one of the partners, and she suggests that you look into the alternatives. Prepare a memorandum to the partner discussing billing options for this situation.

4. You are interviewing a new client. The client wants to hire your office to help negotiate the purchase of a small business. The seller has offered $20,000. The new client would be willing to pay this amount, although she thinks it is a bit high, but does not feel comfortable negotiating with the seller and would rather have an attorney involved in the deal for her protection. The new client is suspicious of legal assistants and attorneys and is especially concerned about how much her case will cost. You inform the client that the attorney will be the one who

actually talks to her about the fee issue, but that typically this type of case is taken on an hourly basis and that the attorney will only be able to give her a very broad estimate of what the total matter will cost. The client states that this would be unacceptable to her because she does not have a lot of money to pay overpriced attorneys. The client also states that she would like this matter settled as soon as possible. You must prepare a memorandum to the attorney outlining the facts of the case. What type of fee arrangement would you suggest to the attorney? Please keep in mind the client's anxieties and her particular needs.

5. Recently, your office has found a niche in representing spouses collecting on past-due child support. In most cases, your clients have little money to pay you with and are financially strapped as they no longer have the income of their former spouses to support their children and do not have the child support. In some cases, large amounts of money are owed, but finding the former spouses has proved difficult. Your supervising attorney decides that the best way to handle these types of cases is on a one-third contingency basis. Your supervising attorney asks for your comments. How do you respond?

6. You work for a firm with seventeen attorneys. The firm has always done well financially, but recently it is struggling. There is a great deal of pressure for you to meet your billing requirements of 1,550 hours, even if no one has work for you to do. The firm will not accept the answer, "No one is giving me any work." You are being encouraged to go to each attorney's office and drum something up. Discuss the ethical situation you are being placed in and how you would handle it.

7. Approximately three months ago you and another legal assistant, Jonathan, were hired in a medium-sized law office. You work very hard at your job, record your hours honestly, and always receive compliments on the quality of your work. However, your supervising attorney constantly compares you with Jonathan, who consistently bills more hours than you do. You suspect that Jonathan is padding his time. How would you handle the matter?

8. A client contacts your law office for representation regarding the routine sale of a piece of property. The client appears to be fairly wealthy. Your supervising attorney charges the client what amounts to be about double what the firm regularly charges. You know this because the office uses an internal fee schedule to help the attorneys set a proper fee. Discuss the ethical considerations. How would you handle the situation?

9. You work in a relatively small law office. The office is having a cash-flow problem and has requested that staff members bill as much as they can and really work on cases in which the firm may be able to solve some of its cash-flow problem. The office manager comes to you and tells you that a client whose case you are working on has several thousands of dollars in the trust account. Although not telling you directly, the office manager lets you know that she wants you to bill some hours to this client so the firm can get some of the money in the trust account. Discuss the ethical problems associated with this. Assume you bill the client when in fact no hours were worked on the case. What problems arise?

10. You just finished a hectic morning. Before you go to lunch, you fill out your timekeeping report for the day. Although you wanted to record your time earlier, you just could not get to it. Please record your time on a blank piece of paper; have columns set up for the date, client/case name, timekeeper, services rendered, billable or nonbillable, and the amount of time spent on the matter (see Figure 5-11). For each activity listed, decide whether it is billable or not billable. Record your time, first using tenths of hours. Also, you should fill out expense slips for items that should be charged back to clients. Record the expenses on a blank piece of paper and include date, client/case name, your name, type of expense, and cost. Please total the cost of each expense slip. The firm charges 25 cents each for copies and 50 cents per page to send a fax. Assume long-distance phone calls cost 25 cents a minute.

As best you can recall, this is how your day went:

8:00 A.M.—8:12 A.M.	Got a cup of coffee, talked to other law office staff members, reviewed your schedule/things to do sheet for the day, and reviewed your e-mail inbox.
8:13 A.M.—8:25 A.M.	Talked to your supervising attorney (Jan Mitchell) about some research she needs done on the standards necessary to file a motion to dismiss in *Johnson v. Cuttingham Steel.* Ms. Mitchell also asks you to find a bankruptcy statute she needs for *Halvert v. Shawnee Saving & Loan.*
8:26 A.M.—8:37 A.M.	A legal assistant from another office calls to remind you that the legal assistant association you belong to is having a meeting at noon and that you are running the meeting.
8:38 A.M.—8:40 A.M.	One of your least favorite clients, John Hamilton, calls to ask you when he is supposed to be at your office to prepare for his deposition tomorrow. You access the weekly schedule electronically and read him the information he needs.
8:40 A.M.—8:50 A.M.	You find the information you need re: the motion to dismiss in *Johnson v. Cuttingham Steel* in a motion in another case you helped prepare last month. The research is still current so Ms. Mitchell will be pleased you found it so fast. You note that it took you two hours to research this issue when you did it the first time. You copy the material Ms. Mitchell needed (five pages) and put it in her box and send it to her electronically.
8:55 A.M.—9:30 A.M.	You get hold of a witness you have been trying to contact in *Menly v. Menly.* The call was long-distance. The call lasted fifteen minutes and the memo to the file documenting the call took twenty minutes.
9:30 A.M.—9:54 A.M.	Ms. Mitchell asks you to contact the attorney in *Glass v. Huron* regarding a discovery question. You spend ten minutes on hold. The call is long-distance but you get an answer to Ms. Mitchell's question.
10:00 A.M.—10:45 A.M.	One of the secretaries informs you that you must interview a new client, Richard Sherman. The person that was supposed to see Mr. Sherman got delayed. Mr. Sherman comes to your office regarding a simple adoption. However, in talking to Mr. Sherman you find out that he also needs someone to incorporate a small business that he is getting ready to open. You gladly note that your office has a department that handles this type of matter. You take the basic information down regarding both matters. You tell the client that you will prepare a memo regarding these matters to the appropriate attorney and one of the office's attorneys will contact him within two days to further discuss the matter. You also copy ten pages of information that Mr. Sherman brought.
10:45 A.M.—10:54 A.M.	One of the secretaries asks

	you to cover her phone for her while she takes a quick break. Because the secretary always helps you when you ask for it, you gladly cover the phone for a few minutes. Ms. Mitchell asks you to send a fax in *Stewart v. Layhorn Glass*, so you use this time to send the six-page fax.
10:55 A.M.—12:00 NOON	You were given the job of organizing some exhibits in *Ranking v. Siefkin* yesterday by Ms. Mitchell. You finally have some free time to organize the exhibits.
12:00 NOON—1:00 P.M.	You attend the legal assistant association lunch.
1:00 P.M.—2:00 P.M.	You work on a pro bono criminal case that Ms. Mitchell is representing on appeal. In an effort to become familiar with the case, you read some of the transcripts from the trial.
2:00 P.M.—5:30 P.M.	Ms. Mitchell hands you a new case. Ms. Mitchell says that we will be representing the defendant. She asks you to read the petition and our client file, analyze the case, and draft interrogatories to send the plaintiff. You spend the rest of the day working on this case.

11. You have just been hired by a private law practice. You begin to get a little worried because your employers say you should "hold on" to your paycheck for an extra day to make sure it will clear the bank. You notice that many times staff members "forget" to fill out slips for charging expenses back to the clients, that bills are usually done on a quarterly basis, and that many expenses (such as copying expense) are included in the overhead of the office and not billed to the clients at all. Please identify what the problems are with the office and give a detailed answer on how you would go about addressing the problems.

12. You work for an insurance company. The head of the legal department asks you to begin drafting some billing guidelines for private law practices that represent your interests. Currently the department reviews bills at varying hourly rates from firm to firm and law offices are passing on to your office all types of expenses that they should not be including. Please draft a set of guidelines as requested.

13. Assume for this exercise that you can bill for all activities that relate to learning. Keep a detailed record for all your activities for one day, from when you wake up until you go to sleep. Record your time in tenths (i.e., on six-minute intervals). At the end of the day, calculate the amount due based on your timesheet.

14. Your law office recently began representing a client who had been defrauded in a security scam at a national brokerage firm. The client signed a 40 percent contingency contract. You know that the only thing your office has done on the case is to meet with the client several times, do some general research regarding the case, and prepare a demand letter to the brokerage firm setting out the facts of the case. The brokerage firm does not want bad publicity and has agreed to settle the claim for $1.2 million dollars. The client is going to accept the offer. Discuss the ethical implications. What should the law firm do?

NOTES

1. *Legal Assistant Today,* November/December 1992, p. 25. Copyright 1992. James Publishing, Inc. Reprinted with permission from *Legal Assistant Today* magazine. For subscription information call 800-394-2626, or visit www.legalassistanttoday.com.

2. *The Legal Assistant's Practical Guide to Professional Responsibility,* American Bar Association, 1998, p. 118. Reprinted by permission.
3. Kenny C. Bailey, "All I Really Need to Know I Learned from a Paralegal," *Facts and Findings,* August 2000, p. 29. Reprinted with the permission of the National Association of Legal Assistants, 1516 S. Boston, #200, Tulsa. www.nala.org.
4. Terry Conner, "The Challenges Facing Law Firms," *Texas Bar Journal,* January 2000, p. 22.
5. *The Legal Assistant's Practical Guide to Professional Responsibility,* American Bar Association, 1998, p. 121. Reprinted by permission.
6. "Blue Chip Biling: Regulation of Billing and Expense Fraud by Lawyers," Lisa Lerman, *Georgetown Journal of Legal Ethics* 12 (2), 1999, p. 205. Reprinted with permission of the publisher, Georgetown University and *Georgetown Journal of Legal Ethics,* copyright 1999.l
7. Smith, "AAFPE National Conference Highlights," *Legal Assistant Today,* January/February 1991, p. 103. Copyright 1991. James Publishing, Inc. Reprinted with permission from *Legal Assistant Today* magazine. For subscription information call 800-394-2626, or visit www.legalassistanttoday.com.
8. Special Committee on Economics of Law Practice of the American Bar Association, 1959. Reprinted by permission.
9. John P. Mello, Jr., "Paralegal Billing Trends," *Legal Assistant Today,* September/October 1993, p. 127. Copyright 1993. James Publishing, Inc. Reprinted with permission from *Legal Assistant Today* magazine. For subscription information call 800-394-2626, or visit www.legalassistanttoday.com.
10. William Statsky, *Introduction to Paralegalism,* 4th ed. (St. Paul, MN: West Publishing Co., 1992) p. 826, citing *A Lighter Note,* NALA Advance 15, Summer 1989.
11. Terrie I. Murray, "The Unwritten Rules: Survival in a Law Firm," *Legal Assistant Today,* May/June 1998, p. 13. Copyright 1998. James Publishing, Inc. Reprinted with permission from *Legal Assistant Today* magazine. For subscription information call 800-394-2626, or visit www.legalassistanttoday.com.
12. Carol Milano, "Hard Choices: Dealing with Ethical Dilemmas on the Job," *Legal Assistant Today,* March/April 1992, p. 79. Copyright 1992. James Publishing, Inc. Reprinted with permission from *Legal Assistant Today* magazine. For subscription information call 800-394-2626, or visit www.legalassistanttoday.com.

CASE REVIEW

Committee for Public Counsel Services v. Lookner, 47 Mass.App.Ct. 833, 716 N.E. 2d 690 (1999).

(Cite as: 47 Mass.App.Ct. 833, 716 N.E.2d 690)

Appeals Court of Massachusetts, Suffolk.

COMMITTEE FOR PUBIC COUNSEL SERVICES

v.

Norman S. LOOKNER.

No, 97-P-2138.

Argued April 8, 1999.

Decided Sept. 29, 1999.

Mary Murphy-Hensley, Boston, Assistant Attorney General, for the plaintiff.

Present: LAURENCE, SMITH, & SPINA, JJ.

LAURENCE, J.

Norman S. Lookner is an attorney licensed to practice in the Commonwealth. As part of his practice, he was certified to, and did, accept paid assignments from the Committee for Public Counsel Services (committee) (see G.L. c. 211D) to represent indigent clients in cases involving custody of children, delinquency charges, and termination of parental rights. In early

1995, he was the subject of an audit by the committee which investigated his billing practices (see G.L. c. 211D, § 12).

A committee auditor found that Lookner had overbilled the committee $18,445 in fiscal year 1994 by billing at least .25 hours for each task, such as a short telephone call, as opposed to billing the actual time worked in a given day rounded off to the nearest quarter of an hour. In addition, Lookner's time sheets did not record the actual amount of time spent on billable *834 tasks or explain the nature of the work performed. Lookner had billed the committee 2,327 hours over 364 days of the fiscal year and was paid $79,022.63 for fiscal year 1994 services. The auditor recommended to the committee's executive committee that Lookner repay $18,445 in overbillings within twenty-four months.

Lookner appealed the auditor's recommendation and requested a hearing. On November 1, 1995, pursuant to the procedures set forth in Section E of the committee's Manual for Counsel Assigned Through the Committee for Public Counsel Services—Policies and Procedures (June 1995) (manual), a hearing officer conducted a hearing at which Lookner was represented by an attorney. The manual, which is binding upon all "[a]ttorneys who accept **692 assignments of cases through the Committee," expressly provides that "[t]he action of the Executive Committee Hearing Officer shall be final." On February 28, 1996, the hearing officer issued his findings and final decision, concurring with the auditor's findings but reducing the overbilled amount to $11,130, payable within twelve months on terms to be mutually agreed upon by Lookner's attorney and the committee's audit staff.

After a hearing on the committee's motion to dismiss the complaint on August 16, 1996, a judge of the Superior Court ruled that the time for seeking relief under G.L. c. 249, § 4, had expired but that Lookner's count for declaratory relief had been timely asserted. After a further hearing, on December 19, 1996, a second Superior Court judge allowed the committee's motion to dismiss, not only on the ground that it was untimely, [FN1] but also because Lookner's claim for declaratory relief could not be maintained against the judiciary department (see G.L. c. 231A, § 2), of which the committee is a part. We conclude that the dismissal of Lookner's certiorari count was correct on this record. [FN2]

EXERCISES

1. Do you think Mr. Lookner expected the Committee for Public Counsel Services to conduct an audit of his billings?

2. Do you think a court would take into account the types of clients Lookner would be representing and the fact that the Committee is a nonprofit/governmental entity?

3. What do you think of the auditor's conclusion that the Committee had been overbilled by Lookner's rounding tasks to .25 hours instead of billing for the actual time incurred?

4. What if Lookner had argued that in some instances he billed .25 when the service was actually .30 or .35, that he actually rounded down, and that therefore it "all came out in the wash" and was, in fact, reasonably fair. Is this argument compelling to you?

5. Lookner failed to keep detailed records of exactly what he did on cases, but did record the amount of time he spent. Why was this not enough to please the auditors? What other fact concerned the auditors and led them to question even the amount of time that he recorded?

6. Did Lookner's billing practices violate the *Model Rules?* Why?

Case Review

In the Matter of Lloyd Clareman, 219 A.D.2d 195 (640 N.Y.S.2d 84 (1996).

640 N.Y.S.2d 84
(Cite as: 219 A.D.2d 195, 640 N.Y.S.2d 84)

Supreme Court, Appellate Division, First Department, New York.

In the Matter of Lloyd CLAREMAN, Esq. (admitted as Lloyd Samuel Clareman), an

attorney and counselor-at-law:

Departmental Disciplinary Committee for the First Judicial Department,

Petitioner,

Lloyd Clareman, Esq., Respondent.

April 4, 1996.

Raymond Vallejo, of counsel (Hal R. Lieberman, attorney), for petitioner.

Frank H. Wright, of counsel (Wright & Manning, attorneys), for respondent.

Before SULLIVAN, J.P., and MILONAS, ROSENBERGER, KUPFERMAN and NARDELLI, JJ.

PER CURIAM.

Respondent was admitted to the practice of law in the State *196 of New York by the First Judicial Department, as Lloyd Samuel Clareman, on April 11, 1977. At all times relevant to these proceedings, he has maintained an office within the First Department.

After his second year of law school, the respondent was a summer associate at the now defunct law firm of Webster & Sheffield, where he met one of the firm's star litigation partners, Harvey Myerson. After completing the bar exam, he returned to the firm as an associate, working almost exclusively on litigation matters for Myerson. The Hearing Panel classified the relationship between Myerson and the associates of the firm as one of domineering manipulation. It found that Myerson virtually controlled the lives of the respondent and the other young associates at the firm by convincing them that their careers depended upon how he felt and what he said about them.

In 1983, while at Webster & Sheffield, the respondent became concerned about the legitimacy of a disbursement requested by Myerson on a matter over which the respondent had primary day-to-day responsibility. The request was for $70,000 in outside counsel fees for an attorney with whom the respondent was not familiar. Despite the risks to his career, the respondent brought the suspicious request to the attention of the managing partner of the firm. Although it later came to light that the requested disbursement was a fraud which the firm had agreed to ignore, the respondent incurred the wrath of Myerson for his actions, his mentor accusing the respondent of a rash act of betrayal.

Shortly after this incident, Myerson left Webster & Sheffield to become a partner at Finley, Kumble, Wagner, Heine, Underberg, Manley, Myerson & Casey. The respondent joined him in the move, and also became a partner at this firm. When this firm collapsed in 1987 and filed for bankruptcy, the respondent lost over $150,000.

In early 1988, Myerson formed Myerson & Kuhn, where the respondent became a litigation partner, while also serving on the executive committee which was dominated and controlled by Myerson. The respondent was also the attorney in charge of most of the litigation conducted on behalf of one of Myerson's major clients, Shearson Lehman Hutton. In April 1988, Myerson confided to respondent that Shearson had agreed to pay the firm a flat fee of up to $800,000 per month to handle its litigation. Under

Myerson's direction and assurance of propriety, the respondent and another attorney, Mark Segall, were to *197 prepare monthly statements for Shearson, reflecting charges of at least $800,000, even when the actual monthly fees were considerably less. During the period from April 1988 through January 1989, respondent assisted in preparing statements reflecting about $1.2 million worth of excess time, a major portion of the $2 million Shearson was defrauded under this overbilling scheme. When the respondent expressed misgivings to Myerson about the billing practices, Myerson screamed at him: "You are just to do it. I am instructing you to do it." The respondent was subjected to numerous tirades from Myerson each time he was resistant to Myerson's orders. Ultimately, the firm went under, and again respondent paid all his debts. His full cooperation with government investigators, including testimony before the grand jury and in court, led to successful prosecution of Myerson (see, Matter of Myerson, 182 A.D.2d 242, 588 N.Y.S.2d 142; In re Myerson, 206 A.D.2d 299, 615 N.Y.S.2d 271) and others. The assistant United States attorney assigned to the Myerson investigation noted that the respondent **86 was the government's best cooperating witness. Meanwhile, adverse publicity surrounding the investigation made it difficult for the respondent to find work.

There are substantial mitigating factors in this case, including respondent's subordinate level of participation in the overbilling scheme, from which he received no personal financial benefit; his early, truthful, and complete cooperation; his immediate acknowledgement of wrongdoing and sincere expression of remorse; the significant adverse personal and professional consequences he has suffered as a result of his affiliation with Myerson; his hard-fought attempt to obtain restitution for Shearson; and his otherwise clean record and good moral character. Viewing the misconduct in light of these mitigating factors, the Hearing Panel recommended a public censure.

Respondent is guilty of engaging in misconduct involving dishonesty, fraud, deceit or misrepresentation (Code of Professional Responsibility DR 1-102[A] [4] [22 NYCRR 1200.3]), which adversely reflects on his fitness to practice law (DR 1-102[A][8]). In Matter of Segall, 218 A.D.2d 331, 638 N.Y.S.2d 444, this court sanctioned another attorney to a public censure for violation of the same disciplinary rules based upon the identical acts of misconduct at issue here. The same considerations which guided our decision in Segall lead us to conclude that a public censure is also appropriate here. In fact, we find the mitigating factors in the respondent's case to be even more compelling than those present in Segall. Accordingly, the motion to *198 confirm the Hearing Panel's report and recommendation is granted, and respondent is publicly censured for his misconduct.

Respondent is publicly censured.

All concur.

END OF DOCUMENT

EXERCISES

1. Clareman admitted to helping Myerson defraud their clients of more than a million dollars of the client's money. Why was Clareman not disbarred?

2. What did Clareman do correctly concerning this matter and at what cost?

3. What *Model Rules* regarding fees did Clareman violate?

Hands-On Exercises

ABACUS LAW DOCKET CONTROL IN ONE-HOUR TRAINING MANUAL

TRAINING MANUAL OUTLINE

Lesson 1: Entering a Docket Slip
Lesson 2: Viewing the Docket Slip You Just Entered
Lesson 3: Entering Many Docket Slips
Lesson 4: Printing Reports

WELCOME TO JOHNSON AND SULLIVAN

Welcome to Johnson and Sullivan! We are an active and growing law office with five attorneys and two legal assistants. As you know, you have been hired as a legal assistant intern. We are very happy to have you on board; we can certainly use your help.

At Johnson and Sullivan, we put an emphasis on providing quality legal services to our clients. All of our staff make docket entries into our docket control computer program, Abacus Law Plus. We have developed this training manual to help you learn Abacus Law Plus.

GETTING STARTED
OVERVIEW

Abacus Law Plus is a docket control program made specifically for law offices. It allows law offices to track appointments, deadlines, and court appearances and to manage cases. Abacus Law Plus is very easy to use.

Some data may have already been entered into Abacus Law Plus for you. So do not be surprised to see docket entries that you did not enter on reports you print out.

INTRODUCTION TO THIS TRAINING MANUAL

Throughout this training manual, information you need to enter into the program will be designated in several different ways. Keys to be pressed on the keyboard will be designated in brackets, in all caps, and in bold type (i.e., press the **[ENTER]** key). Movements with the mouse will be designated in bold and italics (i.e., *point to File on the Menu Bar and click the mouse*). Words or letters that should be typed will be designated in bold (i.e., type **Training Program**). Information that is or should be displayed on your computer screen is shown in the following style: **Press ENTER** to continue.

LESSON 1: ENTERING A DOCKET SLIP

In this lesson, you will load Abacus Law Plus and enter your first docket slip in the computer.

1. *Load Abacus.*
2. You should be at the **User Log On** window.
3. *At the* **User ID** *prompt, type* **AAA**
4. *At* **Today**, *type* **12/02/02**
5. *Click on* **OK**.
6. *Point and click on* **OK** *again if you are asked to confirm that AAA is the only valid operator.*
7. *Point and click on* **OK** *on the* **Tip of the Day**.
8. You are now ready to begin entering a docket slip. *Point and click on Events from the Tool Bar and then click on Add a New Event.*
9. *Point and click on the* **Down Arrow** *icon next to* **Who**, *then on* **NPB**, *and then* **OK**.
10. *Point and click on the* **Down Arrow** *icon next to* **What** *and use the scroll bar to point and click on* **C-Client** *(Client conference). Point and click on* **OK**. (*Note:* you can move forward in the fields using the **[TAB]** key or backward using **[SHIFT]-[TAB]**.)
11. *Press [TAB] to go to the* **When** *field. Type 12/06/02.*
12. *Point and click on the field next to* **Time**. *Enter* **10:00a**.
13. *Press the [TAB] key on the keyboard to go to the* **Hours:** *field. Type* **1**.
14. *Press the [TAB] key on the keyboard to go to the* **Reminders** *field. Type* **1** *and then press* **[TAB][TAB]**.
15. *Point and click on the* **Down Arrow** *icon next to* **Where** *and then use the scroll bar to point and click on* **Here** *(Office) and on* **OK**.
16. *Press the [TAB] key on the keyboard to go to the* **Name** *field.*
17. *Point and click on the* **Down Arrow** *icon next to* **Name** *and use the scroll bar to point and click on* **Abacus Data Systems** *and on* **OK**.

18. *Press* **[TAB][TAB]** *to go to the* **Type** *field.*

19. *Point and click on the* **Down Arrow** *icon next to* **Type** *and then use the scroll bar to point and click on* **Appointment** *and* **OK**.

20. *Press* **[TAB][TAB]** *to go to the* **Notes** *field and type* **Discuss IGS**.

21. *Point and click on* **Save** *in the upper right of the window.*

22. *Point and click on* **Close** *in the upper right of the window.*

This concludes Lesson 1.

To exit Abacus Law, *point and click on Files from the Menu Bar and then click on Exit.*

To go to Lesson 2, stay at the current screen.

LESSON 2: VIEWING THE DOCKET SLIP YOU JUST ENTERED

In this short lesson, you will make sure that the docket slip you entered in Lesson 1 was entered into the computer. You will do this by displaying a daily calendar on the screen. If you did not exit Abacus after Lesson 1, skip numbers 1 through 7 and go directly to number 8.

1. *Load Abacus.*

2. *You should be at the* **User Log On** *window.*

3. *At the* **User ID** *prompt, type* AAA.

4. *AT* **Today,** *type:* **12/02/02**.

5. *Click on* **OK**.

6. *Point and click on* **OK** *again if you are asked to confirm that* **AAA** *is the only valid operator.*

7. *Point and click on* **OK** *on the* **Tip of the Day.**

8. *Point and click with the mouse on the Monthly Calendar icon on the Tool Bar (the sixth icon from the left that looks like a calendar with most of the days highlighted).*

9. *You should now see a calendar for December 2002.*

10. *Point and double click on the square of the calendar for Friday the 6th.*

11. *You should now see the appointment you just entered.*

12. *Point and click on* **Close.**

13. *Point and click with the mouse on the Weekly Calendar icon on the Tool Bar (the fifth icon from the left that looks like a calendar with a horizontal bar across it).*

14. You should now see a calendar for the week of December 2, 2002 and you should see the appointment you just entered on Friday, December 6, 2002.

15. *Point and click on* **Close.**

16. *Point and click on the* **Close** *button in the upper right-hand portion of the* **December 2002** *window. (It looks like an X.)*

17. *Point and click with the mouse on the Daily Organizer icon on the Tool Bar (the fourth icon from the left that looks like a calendar with one square highlighted).*

18. *Type* **12/06/02** *in the* **date** *field at the top of the window and then press* **[TAB].** You should now see the entry that you made in Lesson 1.

19. *Type* **12/05/02** *in the* **date** *field at the top of window and then press* **[TAB].** Notice in the **Reminders** section of the screen that a reminder for the appointment on the 6th is displayed.

20. *Point and click on the* **Close** *button in the upper right-hand portion of the* **Daily Organizer—Thursday, December 5, 2002** *window (it looks like an X).*

This concludes Lesson 2.

To exit Abacus Law, point and click on Files from the Menu Bar and then click on Exit.

To go to Lesson 3, stay at the current screen.

LESSON 3: ENTERING MANY DOCKET SLIPS

You now know the basics of entering docket slips and displaying information on the screen. In this lesson, you will enter several different docket slips into Abacus. If you did not exit Abacus after Lesson 1, skip numbers 1 through 7 and go directly to number 8.

1. *Load Abacus.*

2. You should be at the **User Log On** window.

3. *At the* **User ID** *prompt, type* **AAA.**

4. *At* **Today,** *type* 12/02/02

5. *Click on* **OK.**

6. *Point and click on* **OK** *again if you are asked to confirm that AAA is the only valid operator.*

7. *Point and click on* **OK** *on the* **Tip of the Day.**

8. Enter the following docket slips into Abacus. Remember that you enter docket slips by clicking on Events Add Events from the Menu Bar.

1. Who: **NPB**
    What: **INTERROG**
    When: **12/13/02**
    Time: (Nothing goes here; press **[TAB]** to skip)
    Hours: (Nothing goes here; press **[TAB]** to skip)
    Reminders: **1** (press **[TAB]** to skip the second reminder date; it is not needed)
    Where: (Nothing goes here; press **[TAB]** to skip)
    Name: **Abacus Data Systems, Inc.**
    Matter: (Nothing goes here; press **[TAB]** to skip)
    Priority: **1**
    Type: **D**
    Status: **N**
    Notes: **IGs of client are due**
    Point and click on **Save** *at the top right of the window.*
    Point and click on **Add** *at the bottom of the window.*

2. Who: **NPB**
    What: **DEPO**
    When: **12/16/02**
    Time: **10:00a**
    Hours: **2**
    Reminders: **2, 5**
    Where: **Here**
    Name: **Abacus Data Systems, Inc.**
    Matter: (Nothing goes here; press **[TAB]** to skip)
    Priority: **1**
    Type: **A**
    Status: **N**
    Notes: **Deposition of Client**
    Point and click on **Save** *at the top right of the window.*
    Point and click on **Add** *at the bottom of the window.*

3. Who: **NPB**
    What: **DEPO**
    When: **12/19/02**
    Time: **9:00a**
    Hours: **2**
    Reminders: **2, 7**
    Where: **Here**
    Name: **Abacus Data Systems, Inc.**
    Matter: (Nothing goes here; press **[TAB]** to skip)
    Priority: **1**
    Type: **A**
    Status: **N**

Notes: **Deposition of Defendant**
Point and click on **Save** *at the top right of the window.*
Point and click on **Add** *at the bottom of the window.*

4. Who: **NPB**
   What: **C-SETTLE**
   When: **12/20/02**
   Time: **9:00a**
   Hours: **1**
   Reminders: **1, 2**
   Where: (Nothing goes here; press [ENTER] to skip)
   Name: **Abacus Data Systems, Inc.**
   Matter: (Nothing goes here; press [TAB] to skip)
   Priority: **1**
   Type: **A**
   Status: **N**
   Notes: **Settlement Conference**
   Point and click on **Save** *at the top right of the window.*
   Point and click on **Add** *at the bottom of the window.*

5. Who: **NPB**
   What: **H-STATUS**
   When: **12/23/02**
   Time: **9:00a**
   Hours: **1**
   Reminders: **1, 0**
   Where: (Nothing goes here; press [ENTER] to skip)
   Name: **Abacus Data Systems, Inc.**
   Matter: (Nothing goes here; press [TAB] to skip)
   Priority: **1**
   Type: **A**
   Status: **N**
   Notes: **Pre-Trial Status Hearing**
   Point and click on **Save** *at the top right of the window.*
   Point and click on **Close**.

This concludes Lesson 3.

To exit Abacus Law, point and click on Files from the Menu Bar and then click on Exit.

To go to Lesson 4, stay at the current screen.

LESSON 4: PRINTING REPORTS

You now know the basics of entering docket slips and displaying information on the screen. In this lesson, you will print some reports. Abacus has a powerful report writer program, but the easiest way to print out reports is to use the Daily Organizer, Weekly Calendar, or Monthly Calendar icons on the Tool Bar (see Lesson 2) and then click on the Printer icon from the Tool Bar (the third icon from the right on the toolbar). If you did not exit from Lesson 3, then skip number 1 through 7 and go directly to 8.

1. *Load Abacus.*

2. *You should be at the* **User Log On** *window.*

3. *At the* **User ID** *prompt, type* **AAA**.

4. *At* **Today,** *type* **12/02/02**

5. *Click on* **OK**.

6. *Point and click on* **OK** *again if you are asked to confirm that AAA is the only valid operator.*

7. *Point and click on* **OK** *on the* **Tip of the Day.**

8. *Point and click with the mouse on the Monthly Calendar icon on the Tool Bar (the sixth icon from the left that looks like a calendar with most of the days highlighted).*

9. *You should now see a calendar for December 2002.*

10. *Point and click with the mouse on the Printer icon on the Tool Bar (the third icon from the right).*

11. *Point and click with the mouse on* **OK**.

12. *Point and click with the mouse on* **Output to** *and on* **Printer,** *to print, or* **Screen,** *for the monthly report to be displayed on your screen.*

13. *Point and click with the mouse on* **OK**.

14. *Point and click with the mouse on* **Print**. *(Note: If you printed the report to the screen, point and click on the icon of a door after you have viewed the report on the screen.)*

15. *Point and click on* **OK,** *if you printed the report to a printer.*

16. *Point and click on* **Close**.

17. *Point and click on* **Close**.

18. *Close the* **December 2002** *window by clicking on the* **Close** *icon (an X in the upper right-hand corner of the window).*

19. *To exit Abacus Law, point and click on Files from the Menu Bar and then click on Exit.*

This concludes the Abacus lessons.

Hands-on Exercises

TIMESLIPS FOR WINDOWS IN ONE-HOUR TRAINING MANUAL

TRAINING MANUAL OUTLINE

Lesson 1: Configuring Timeslips and Entering Law Firm Information
Lesson 2: Entering Activity Codes
Lesson 3: Entering a New Client
Lesson 4: Entering Timeslips and Expense Slips
Lesson 5: Printing a Prebilling Report and a Final Bill

WELCOME TO JOHNSON AND SULLIVAN

Welcome to Johnson and Sullivan! We are an active and growing firm with five attorneys and two legal assistants. As you know, you have been hired as a legal assistant intern. We are very happy to have you on board; we can certainly use your help.

At Johnson and Sullivan, we put an emphasis on providing quality legal services to our clients. We bill our clients on a regular basis for these quality services, typically either biweekly or monthly, depending on the needs of the client. We strive to make sure our billings are timely and without errors. Because billings and fee disputes are some of the most common types of ethical complaints filed against lawyers, we require that all staff members understand the billing process. In addition, we want our staff members to have many job skills and to be flexible enough to enter their own timeslips into the computer. All staff members are required to have at least minimal training in our billing system. We have developed this training manual to help you learn our system.

We currently use the Timeslips for Windows timekeeping and billing program. One of the reasons we chose Timeslips is because it is easy to learn and to use. Please note that during this training you will be entering information for one attorney, Roger S. Sullivan (RSS).

We know you want to begin using Timeslips immediately, so you only need to read a short Getting Started section before you get on the computer.

Getting Started
Overview of Timeslips

Timeslips allows law offices to track attorney and legal assistant timeslips, track expense slips, issue client billings, track client payments, and generally manage client accounts.

Introduction to This Training Manual

Throughout this training manual, information you need to enter into the program will be designated in several different ways. Keys to be pressed on the keyboard will be designated in brackets, in all caps, and in bold type (i.e., press the **[ENTER]** key). Movements with the mouse will be designated in bold and italics (i.e., ***point to File on the Menu Bar and click the mouse***). Words or letters that should be typed will be designated in bold and enlarged (i.e., type **Training Program**). Information that is or should be displayed on your computer screen is shown in the following style: **Press ENTER to continue.**

Moving Around in Timeslips Entry Fields

When you are entering information in Timeslips, you can go between entry fields by pressing the [TAB] key on the keyboard to go forward and the [SHIFT]-[TAB] key on the keyboard to go backwards.

Overview of the Lessons

In Lesson 1, you will set up Timeslips for our firm by entering our firm name, address, attorneys, and other information. In Lesson 2, you will enter timekeeper activity codes for work that will be completed such as legal research, phone calls, and drafting. You will also enter some expense activity codes such as copying, postage, and long distance. In Lesson 3, you will add a new client to Timeslips. In Lesson 4, you will enter timekeeping timeslips in the program and in Lesson 5, you will enter expense slips into the program. In Lesson 6, you will print a prebilling report and a final client bill. You are now ready to get on the computer and use Timeslips.

Lesson 1: Configuring Timeslips and Entering Law Firm Information

In this lesson, you will load Timeslips, configure the system, and enter information about our law firm.

1. Load Timeslips following the directions given to you by your instructor.

Hands-On Exercises

2. You will be at the **Timeslips Trial Version** screen. In the middle of the screen, it will say **Please select a level.** *The program should be on* **Level One.** *If* **Level One** *is not selected, point and click with the mouse on the drop down arrow and select* **Level One.**

3. *Point and click with the mouse on the* **Proceed** *button at the bottom right of the screen.*

4. You will now be at the **No Database Selected** screen. *Point and click with the mouse on* **Make a New Database.**

5. You will be at the **Create a New Database** screen. The **Empty database** option should be selected, but if it is not, *point and click with the mouse on* **Empty database** *and then point and click with the mouse on* **Next.**

6. You will be asked to **Please choose the location where you would like the new database. . . .** *Point and click with the mouse on* **Next** *(unless your instructor advises you otherwise).*

7. You will be told **Timeslips v9 Trial Version can track money in one currency format per database. . . . Please confirm the number of decimal places in the currency you will track.** Because there are two decimal places in the format we use, *point and click with the mouse on* **Next.**

8. The message **Options are now established. Click Next to create the database, or Back to review and change settings** will be displayed. *Point and click with the mouse on* **Next.** This will create your database.

9. The message **The database has been created successfully** should be displayed. *Point and click with the mouse on Finish.*

10. You should now be at the **General Settings** screen at the **Firm Info** tab. *Enter the following information in the indicated fields (note: you can move to the next field by pressing the* [TAB] *key on the keyboard or move backward to the previous field by pressing the* [SHIFT]-[TAB] *keys on the keyboard):*

Name	JOHNSON & SULLIVAN
Address	10232 23rd ST NW
City	Washington
State	D.C.
ZIP Code	20211
Other	
Phone 1	202/674-2343
Phone 2	
Fax 1	202/675-4534
Fax 2	

11. We do not need to change any of the other settings, so *point and click with the mouse on* **OK.**

12. You will then be at the **Use Timeslips Accounting Link** screen. Since we do not need this feature, *point and click on* **No.**

13. You should now see the **Getting Started** screen. *Point and click on* **Next.**

14. *Enter your name and initials (to go from one field to another press the [TAB] key on the keyboard). When you are done entering your name and initials, point and click with the mouse on* **Next.**

15. You will then be told **Enter up to two shorthand names . . .** *Enter your first name as Nickname 1 and then point and click on the* **Finish** *button.*

16. You are now through with the general set-up of the program. You should be at the **Bill and Aging Date** screen. For this training exercise, we will use a date of May 1, 2002.

17. *Point and click with the mouse on the month that is displayed and then select* **May** *from the list.*

18. *Point and click with the mouse on the year that is displayed and then select* **2002** *from the list.*

19. *Point and click with the mouse on the* **1** *on the calendar and then point and click with the mouse on the* **OK** *button.* (*Note:* if you are asked whether or not you would like to take a tour of Timeslips—select No.).

20. You should now be at the **Basic Navigator** screen. This screen is a flowchart for how to perform different activities in the program. Notice that there are large icons to the left in the **Basic Navigator** screen and that **Prepare and Print Bills** is currently selected. The flowchart now in the **Basic Navigator** screen explains the process for preparing and printing bills. If you select other icons/items on the left side of the **Basic Navigator** screen, the flowchart will change to show the process for that function.

21. The next thing we need to do is add a timekeeper, Roger S. Sullivan, to Timeslips. You will set up his default billing rate so Timeslips will know how much to charge (assuming this particular client is billed at the timekeeper's default hourly rate).

22. *Point and click with the mouse on* **Names** *from the Menu Bar at the top of the screen. Then point and click with the mouse on* **Timekeeper Info.** *Your name should be shown as a timekeeper in the* **Timekeeper List** *window.*

23. *Point and click with the mouse on the* **New** *command in the* **Timekeeper List Window** *(note: it looks like a yellow plus (+) sign—also, if you point at an icon and leave it there for a second it will display the name of the icon).*

24. The **Timekeeper Information** window should now be displayed. In the field just to the right of the number **1,** type **Roger** and then *point and click with the mouse on the* **Apply Defaults** *button, which is in the Timekeeper Information Window (in the middle at the bottom of the window).*

25. *In the* **Name** *field type* **Roger S. Sullivan** *and then press the* **[TAB]** *key on the keyboard.*

26. *In the* **Initials** *field type* **RSS** *and then press* **[TAB][TAB]** *on the keyboard.*

27. You should now be at the **Rate Table 1** field. *In the* **Rate Table 1** *field type* **200.** This indicates that Roger Sullivan's default hourly billing rate is $200 an hour.

28. *Now point and click with the mouse on the* **Save** *command icon in the* **Timekeeper Information** *window; it is on the right, the fourth icon from the bottom and it looks like a floppy disk.*

29. *Now point and click with the mouse on the* **Close** *command icon in the* **Timekeeper Information** *window; it is in the upper right-hand corner of the screen and it looks like an* **X.**

30. The **Timekeeper List** window should be on your screen, and Roger S. Sullivan should now be listed as a timekeeper. *Now point and click with the mouse on the* **Close** *command icon in the* **Timekeeper List** *window; it is in the upper right-hand corner of the screen and it looks like an* **X.**

31. You should now be back at the **Basic Navigator** screen.

This concludes Lesson 1.

To exit Timeslips, *click with your mouse on* **File** *from the Menu Bar and then point and click with your mouse on* **Exit.** *Point and click with the mouse on* **No** *when you are asked whether you want to back up your data.*

To go to Lesson 2, stay at the current screen.

LESSON 2: ENTERING ACTIVITY CODES

In this lesson, you will enter timekeeper and expense activity codes. If you did not exit Timeslips from Lesson 1, then skip numbers 1 through 7 below and go directly to number 8.

1. Load Timeslips following the directions given to you by your instructor.

2. You will be at the **Timeslips Trial Version** screen. In the middle of the screen, it will say **Please select a level.** *The program should be on* **Level One.** *If* **Level One** *is not selected, point and click with the mouse on the drop down arrow and select* **Level One.**

3. *Point and click with the mouse on the* **Proceed** *button at the bottom right of the screen.*

4. You should be at the **Bill and Aging Date** screen. For this training exercise, we will use the date May 1, 2002.

5. *Point and click with the mouse on the month that is displayed and then select* May *from the list.*

6. *Point and click with the mouse on the year that is displayed and then select* 2002 *from the list.*

7. *Point and click with the mouse on the 1 on the calendar and then point and click with the mouse on the* **OK** *button.* (*Note:* if you are asked whether or not you would like to take a tour of Timeslips—select **No**.)

8. You should be at the **Basic Navigator** screen. We are now ready to enter timekeeper activity codes.

9. *Point and click with the mouse on* **Names** *from the Menu Bar at the top of the screen and then point and click on* **Task Info.**

10. You should now be at the **Task List** window. *Point and click with the mouse on the* **New** *icon in the* **Task List** *window (i.e., it looks like a yellow plus (+) sign).*

11. The **Task Information** window should now be displayed. In the field just to the right of the number 1, type **Drafting** and then *point and click with the mouse on the* **Apply Defaults** *button, which is at the bottom middle of the* **Task Information** *window.*

12. *In the* **Name** *field, type* **Drafting** *and then press the [TAB] key on the keyboard.*

13. You should now be at the **Rate Table 1** field. *In the* **Rate Table 1** *field type* **200**. This is the default hourly rate (i.e., $200 an hour) for drafting.

14. *Press the [TAB] key nine times until you are at the* **Bill Status** *field.*

15. *Point and click with the mouse on* **Ignore** *in the* **Bill Status** *field and then point and click with the mouse on* **Billable.**

16. *Point and click with the mouse on the* **Save** *command icon in the* **Task Information** *window; it is on the right, the fourth icon from the bottom and it looks like a floppy disk.*

17. You are now ready to enter several more timekeeping/tasks.

18. *Point and click with the mouse on the* **New** *icon in the* **Task Information** *window. It is on the right, the fifth icon from the bottom and it looks like a yellow plus (+) sign.*

19. Enter the following four timekeeper/task activities using the same process as above. (You only need to change/enter the following information—you can leave all other fields as they are). Remember to enter the information in the **1** field and then select **Apply Defaults**. When you have entered all the information for each activity, remember to save each task (the icon

that looks like a floppy disk) and then click on the **New** *icon (the yellow plus (+) sign) to go to the next item.*

1	2	Name	Rate Table 1	Billing Status
Phone Call	Phone Call		$200	Billable
Investigation	Investigation		$200	Billable
Depo	Deposition		$200	Billable
Office Conf.	Office Conference		$200	Billable

20. After you have entered all the timekeeper tasks/activities, *point and click on the* **List** *command icon in the* **Task Information** *screen; it is the icon that is at the top right in the* **Task Information** *window that looks like a piece of paper with information written on it.*

21. You should now see the **Task List** screen, which shows all five timekeeper tasks/activities.

22. *Point and click with the mouse on the* **Close** *command icon in the* **Task List** *window. It is in the upper right-hand corner of the* **Task List** *window and it looks like an* **X**.

23. *Point and click with the mouse on the* **Close** *command icon in the* **Task Information** *window. It is in the upper right-hand corner of the* **Task Information** *window and it looks like an* **X**.

24. You should now be at the **Basic Navigator** screen.

25. You will use the same basic process to enter expense activities (such as photocopying, postage, etc.).

26. *Point and click with the mouse on* **Names** *from the Menu Bar at the top of the screen and then point and click on* **Expense Info**.

27. You should now be at the **Expense List** window. *Point and click with the mouse on the* **New** *icon in the* **Expense List** *window (i.e., it looks like a yellow plus (+) sign and it is all the way to the left).*

28. The **Expense Information** window should now be displayed. In the field just to the right of the number 1, type **Copies** and then *point and click with the mouse on the* **Apply Defaults** *button, which is at the bottom middle of the* **Expense Information** *window.*

29. *In the* **Name** *field, type* **Photocopying** *and then press the [TAB] key on the keyboard.*

30. You should now be at the **Price** field. *In the* **Price** *field type .25.* This is the default rate for photocopying expenses (i.e., 25 cents per copy).

31. *Press the* **[TAB]** *key twice until you are at the* **Bill Status** *field.*

32. *Point and click with the mouse on* **Ignore** *in the* **Bill Status** *field and then point and click with the mouse on* **Billable.**

33. *Point and click with the mouse on the* **Save** *command icon in the* **Task Information** *window; it is on the right, the fourth icon from the bottom and it looks like a floppy disk.*

34. You are now ready to enter several more expense activities. *Point and click with the mouse on the* **New** *icon in the* **Expense Information** *window. It is on the right, the fifth icon from the bottom and it looks like a yellow plus (+) sign.*

35. Enter the following two expense activities using the same process as above. You only need to change/enter the following information—you can leave all other fields as they are. Remember to enter the information in the **1** field and then select **Apply Defaults.** When you have entered all the information for each activity, remember to save each task (the icon that looks like a floppy disk) and then press the **New** icon (the yellow plus (+) sign) to go to the next item.

1	2 Name	Price	Billing Status
Long Distance	Long Distance	$2.50	Billable
Filing Fee	Filing Fee	$150	Billable

36. After you have entered all the expense activities, *point and click on the* **List** *command icon in the* **Expense Information** *screen; it is the icon that is at the top right in the* **Expense Information** *window that looks like a piece of paper with information written on it.*

37. You should now see the **Expense List** screen, which shows all three expense activities.

38. *Point and click with the mouse on the* **Close** *command icon in the* **Expense List** *window. It is in the upper right-hand corner of the* **Expense List** *window and looks like an* **X.**

39. *Point and click with the mouse on the* **Close** *command icon in the* **Expense Information** *window. It is in the upper right-hand corner of the* **Expense Information** *window and looks like an* **X.**

40. You should now be at the **Basic Navigator** screen.

This concludes Lesson 2.

To exit Timeslips, *click with your mouse on* **File** *from the Menu Bar and then point and click with your mouse on* **Exit.** *Point and click with the mouse on* **No** *when you are asked whether you want to back up your data.*

To go to Lesson 3, stay at the current screen.

LESSON 3: ENTERING A NEW CLIENT

In this lesson, you will enter a new client, Bill Jones, into Timeslips. If you did not exit Timeslips from Lesson 2, then skip numbers 1 through 7 below and go directly to number 8.

1. Load Timeslips following the directions given to you by your instructor.

2. You will be at the **Timeslips Trial Version** screen. In the middle of the screen, it will say **Please select a level.** *The program should be on* **Level One.** *If* **Level One** *is not selected, point and click with the mouse on the drop down arrow and select* **Level One.**

3. *Point and click with the mouse on the* **Proceed** *button at the bottom right of the screen.*

4. You should be at the **Bill and Aging Date** screen. For this training exercise, we will use the date May 1, 2002.

5. *Point and click with the mouse on the month that is displayed and then select* **May** *from the list.*

6. *Point and click with the mouse on the year that is displayed and then select* **2002** *from the list.*

7. *Point and click with the mouse on the* **1** *on the calendar and then point and click with the mouse on the* **OK** *button.* (*Note:* if you are asked whether or not you would like to take a tour of Timeslips—select No.)

8. You should now be at the **Basic Navigator** screen. We are now ready to enter timekeeper activity codes.

9. *Point and click with the mouse on* **Names** *from the Menu Bar at the top of the screen and then point and click on* **Client Info.**

10. You should now be at the **Client List** window. *Point and click with the mouse on the* **New** *icon in the* **Client List** *window (i.e., it looks like a yellow plus (+) sign and it is all the way to the left).*

11. The **Client Information** window should now be displayed. In the field just to the right of the number **1**, type **Bill Jones** and then *point and click with the mouse on the* **Apply Defaults** *button, which is at the bottom middle of the* **Client Information** *window.*

12. Notice that the **Client Information** window has several fields including name, address, city, state, zip, and others. Also, notice at the very bottom of the Client Information window (*note:* you might have to use the vertical scroll bar to scroll down) that there are several tabs including **General, Rate, Arrangement 1,** etc. where you will need to enter information about the client's case. You will start by entering information into the **General** tab.

13. *Enter the following information into the* **Client Information General** *tab screen for Bill Jones:*

Name	**Bill Jones**
Address	**P.O. Box 46285**
City	**Washington**
State	**D.C.**
ZIP Code	**20204**
Attn	
Phone	**202/483-9989**
Fax	**202/483-9990**
Home	**202/843-1231**
Other	
In reference to	**Jones v. Power Automotive Industries**

14. Once you have entered the above information into the **General** tab, *point and click with the mouse on the* **Rates** *tab.* This is where you will enter billing information.

15. *At the* **Rate Table 1** *field, type* **200.** This shows that the default billing rate for this client is $200 an hour. This is all the information we need to enter into this tab.

16. *Now you should point and click with the mouse on each of the other tabs (i.e.,* **Arrangement 1, Arrangement 2, Accounts Receivable,** *etc.) and review the options that are available.* Timeslips is very flexible and can accommodate the needs of most clients.

17. We do not need to change any information in the other tabs.

18. *Point and click with the mouse on the* **Save** *command icon in the* **Client Information** *window. It is on the right, the fourth icon from the bottom and looks like a floppy disk.*

19. *Point and click on the* **List** *command icon on the* **Client Information** *screen. It is the icon that is at the top right in the* **Client Information** *window that looks like a piece of paper with information written on it.*

20. You should now see the **Client List** window, which shows Bill Jones as our only client.

21 *Point and click with the mouse on the* **Close** *command icon in the* **Client List** *window. It is in the upper right-hand corner of the* **Client List** *window and it looks like an* **X.**

22. *Point and click with the mouse on the* **Close** *command icon in the* **Client Information** *window. It is in the upper right-hand corner of the* **Client Information** *window and it looks like an* **X.**

23. You should now be at the **Basic Navigator** screen.

This concludes Lesson 3.

To exit Timeslips, *click with your mouse on* **File** *from the Menu Bar and then point and click with your mouse on* **Exit**. *Point and click with the mouse on* **No** *when you are asked whether you want to back up your data.*

To go to Lesson 4, stay at the current screen.

LESSON 4: ENTERING TIMESLIPS AND EXPENSE SLIPS

In this lesson, you will enter timeslips and expense slips into the Timeslips program. If you did not exit Timeslips from Lesson 2, then skip numbers 1 through 7 below and go directly to number 8.

1. Load Timeslips following the directions given to you by your instructor.

2. You will be at the **Timeslips Trial Version** screen. In the middle of the screen, it will say **Please select a level.** *The program should be on* **Level One**. *If* **Level One** *is not selected, point and click with the mouse on the drop down arrow and select* **Level One**.

3. *Point and click with the mouse on the* **Proceed** *button at the bottom right of the screen.*

4. You should be at the **Bill and Aging Date** screen. For this training exercise, we will use the date May 1, 2002.

5. *Point and click with the mouse on the month that is displayed and then select* **May** *from the list.*

6. *Point and click with the mouse on the year that is displayed and then select* **2002** *from the list.*

7. *Point and click with the mouse on the* **1** *on the calendar and then point and click with the mouse on the* **OK** *button.* (*Note:* If you are asked whether or not you would like to take a tour of Timeslips, select No.)

8. You should now be at the **Basic Navigator** screen. We are now ready to enter timekeeper activity codes.

9. *Point and click with the mouse on the down arrow icon just to the right of the* **New** *icon on the Tool Bar.* (*Note: the* **New** *icon looks like a yellow plus (+) sign; the down arrow icon is between the yellow plus (+) sign and the icon that looks like a telephone.*)

10. *Point and click with the mouse on* **Slip**.

11. You should now be at the **Slip Entry** window. Notice that the **Type** field shows **Time**. Since you are going to enter a timeslip, *press the [TAB] key on the keyboard.*

12. *Point and click with the mouse on the down arrow key just to the right of the* **Timekeeper** *field and then point and click with the mouse on* **Roger**.

13. *Press the [TAB] key on the keyboard to go to the* **Task** *field.*
14. *Point and click with the mouse on the down arrow key just to the right of the* **Task** *field and then point and click with the mouse on* **Phone Call.**
15. *Press the [TAB] key on the keyboard to go to the* **Client** *field.*
16. *Point and click with the mouse on the down arrow key just to the right of the* **Client** *field and then point and click with the mouse on* **Bill Jones.**
17. *Press the [TAB][TAB] key to go to the* **Reference** *field.*
18. *In the* **reference** *field (the large blank open field under the word reference), type* **Phone Call to Witness.**
19. *Press the [TAB] key on the keyboard to go to the* **Start date** *field.*
20. *In the* **Start date** *field, type* **05/01/2002** or click on the calendar icon next to the field to enter the date.
21. *Press the [TAB] key on the keyboard to go to the* **End date** *field.*
22. *Press [TAB][TAB] on the keyboard to go to the* **Time Spent** *field.*
23. *In the* **Time spent** *field, type* **0:30:00.**
24. Because the rest of the information on the timeslip is accurate, *point and click with the mouse on the* **Save** *command icon in the* **Slip Entry** *window. It is on the right, the fourth icon from the bottom and it looks like a floppy disk.*
25. You are now ready to enter several more timeslips. *Point and click with the mouse on the* **New** *icon in the* **Slip Entry** *window. It is all the way to the right, the sixth icon from the bottom and it looks like a yellow plus (+) sign.*
26. Enter the following timeslips using the same process as above. (You only need to change/enter the following information—you can leave all other fields as they are). When you have entered all the information for each timeslip, remember to save each slip (the icon that looks like a floppy disk) and then click on the **New** *icon (the yellow plus (+) sign) to go to the next item.*

Type	Timekeeper	Task	Client	Reference	Start Date/ End Date	Time Spent
Time	Roger	Office Conf.	Bill Jones	Conf. With Client	05/06/02	0:30:00
Time	Roger	Investigation	Bill Jones	Investigation of Key Witness	05/12/02	4:00:00
Time	Roger	Depo	Bill Jones	Deposition of Client	05/15/02	6:30:00
Time	Roger	Drafting	Bill Jones	Drafting of Summary Judgment Response	05/23/02	5:00:00

27. Now you are ready to enter some expense slips into the program. *Enter the following timeslips using the same process as above. (You only need to change/enter the following information—you can leave all other fields as they are.) When you have entered all the information for each expense slip, remember to save each slip (the icon that looks like a floppy disk) and then press the* **New** *icon (the yellow plus (+) sign) to go to the next item.*

Type	Timekeeper	Task	Client	Reference	Start Date/ End Date	Quantity	Price
Expense	Roger	Copying	Bill Jones	Copies of IGs	05/13/02	100	.25
Expense	Roger	Long Distance	Bill Jones	Call with Expert	05/14/02	1	5.00 (*Note:* type over the $2.50 default.)
Expense	Roger	Copying	Bill Jones	Copies of MSJ Resp.	05/24/02	125	.25

28. After you have entered all the timeslips and expense slips and have saved them, *point and click on the* **List** *command icon in the* **Slip Entry** *window. It is the icon that is at the top right in the* **Slip Entry** *window that looks like a piece of paper with information written on it.*

29. You should now see the **Time and Expense Slip List** screen, which shows all the time and expense slips you entered.

30. *Point and click with the mouse on the* **Close** *commmand icon in the* **Time and Expense Slip List** *window; it is in the upper right-hand corner of the* **Time and Expense Slip List** *window and it looks like an* **X**.

31. *Point and click with the mouse on the* **Close** *command icon in the* **Slip Entry** *window; it is in the upper right-hand corner of the* **Slip Entry** *window and it looks like an* **X**.

32. You should now be at the **Basic Navigator** screen.

This concludes Lesson 4.

To exit Timeslips, *click with your mouse on* **File** *from the Menu Bar and then point and click with your mouse on* **Exit**. *Point and click with the mouse on* **No** *when you are asked whether you want to back up your data.*

To go to Lesson 5, stay at the current screen.

LESSON 5: PRINTING A PREBILLING REPORT AND A FINAL BILL

In this lesson, you will print a prebilling report and a final bill. If you did not exit Timeslips from Lesson 4, then skip numbers 1 through 7 and go directly to number 8.

1. Load Timeslips following the directions given to you by your instructor.

2. You will be at the **Timeslips Trial Version** screen. In the middle of the screen, it will say **Please select a level.** *The program should be on* **Level One.** *If* **Level One** *is not selected, point and click with the mouse on the drop down arrow and select* **Level One.**

3. *Point and click with the mouse on the* **Proceed** *button at the bottom right of the screen.*

4. You should be at the **Bill and Aging Date** screen. For this training exercise, we will use the date May 1, 2002.

5. *Point and click with the mouse on the month that is displayed and then select* **May** *from the list.*

6. *Point and click with the mouse on the year that is displayed and then select* **2002** *from the list.*

7. *Point and click with the mouse on the* **1** *on the calendar and then point and click with the mouse on the* **OK** *button.* (*Note:* If you are asked whether or not you would like to take a tour of Timeslips, select No.)

8. You should now be at the **Basic Navigator** screen.

9. *Point and click with the mouse on* **Bills** *from the Menu Bar at the top of the screen and then point and click with the mouse on* **Pre-bill Worksheet.**

10. The **Reports** window is then displayed with the **Pre-Bill worksheet** report highlighted. Notice that the **Print to** field shows **Display.** This means that the report will print to your screen. You could also change this to print to a printer. *Point and click with the mouse on the* **Print** *button at the bottom of the page.*

11. Scroll through the report to make sure it looks accurate. The total timekeeping charges for Bill Jones should be $3,300 and the total expenses should be $61.25. If your pre-billing worksheet is accurate, then continue to number 34. If it is not, you can go back and correct the individual time-slips or expense slips by closing out of the windows you have open. You can do this by pointing and clicking with the mouse on the **Close** command icon in the **Print Preview** and **Reports** window in the upper right-hand corner of the windows; it looks like an **X.** Then point and click with the mouse on **Transactions** and then on **Time and Expense Slips.**

This will display a list of all the slips you have entered. If you made a mistake, just double click with the mouse on the slip that is incorrect and edit it as needed.

12. *Point and click with the mouse on the* **Close** *command icon in the* **Print Preview** *and* **Reports** *window. It is in the upper right-hand corner of the windows and it looks like an* **X.** You should now be at the **Basic Navigator** screen.

13. *Point and click with the mouse on* **Bills** *from the Menu Bar at the top of the screen and then point and click with the mouse on* **Generate Bills.**

14. *Point and click with the mouse on* **Display next to the Print to** *field. Then point and click with the mouse on* **Printer** *and then on* **Print.**

15. From the **Generation of Bills Completed** window, *point and click with the mouse on* **Approve all bills just printed** *and point and click with the mouse on* **OK.**

16. *Point and click with the mouse on the* **Close** *command icon in the* **Reports** *window. It is in the upper right-hand corner of the* **Reports** *window and it looks like an* **X.**

17. You should now be at the **Basic Navigator** screen.

This concludes the Timeslips tutorial.

To exit Timeslips, *click with your mouse on File from the Menu Bar and then point and click with your mouse on Exit. Point and click with the mouse on* **No** *when you are asked whether you want to back up your data.*

Client Trust Funds and Law Office Accounting

CHAPTER OBJECTIVES

After you read this chapter, you will be able to:

- Understand the purpose and importance of trust/escrow accounts.
- Discuss the ethics rules regarding safeguarding client funds.
- Explain the budgeting process.

An attorney represented a married couple in mediation and settled the case for $107,500. The money was to be held in trust for the clients. The attorney was to disburse $16,651 to the wife, $18,920 to an insurance company, and $71,928 to a second insurance company. The $107,500 was deposited into the attorney's trust account. After one month, the attorney wrote $42,789 in checks against the client trust account. One check was used to obtain a cashier's check for $17,439, paid to a Jaguar dealer. After five months, the balance in the client trust account was $494. The attorney failed to pay the second insurance company the funds it was supposed to receive. The second insurance company sent repeated letters to the attorney for payment. The attorney told the insurance company that he was waiting to disburse the funds until the clients had signed releases. The insurance company later sued the attorney. The attorney wrote the insurance company and told them that he had sent the funds to settle the case, but that the settlement check had been returned by the post office marked "refused." The insurance company denied refusing the check. A court issued a judgment in favor of the insurance company for $88,466, which included $10,000 in punitive damages and costs. The attorney was also disbarred for failing to maintain client funds in trust, misappropriation, failure to competently perform legal services, and engaging in acts of moral turpitude.[1]

Why Legal Assistants Need a Basic Understanding of Law Office Accounting

Legal assistants need to have a basic understanding of law office accounting for several reasons. One reason is that legal assistants either directly or indirectly work with trust/escrow accounts on a regular basis and thus need to have an understanding of what they are and how they work. Another reason is that financial decisions drive the law office. It is important to understand how and why a law office operates and to know some basic accounting concepts. In smaller law offices, legal assistants may actually have some bookkeeping or accounting responsibilities. Finally, in some firms legal assistants will help prepare office or department budgets. Thus, it is important to have at least a basic knowledge of how to prepare a budget.

CLIENT FUNDS—TRUST/ESCROW ACCOUNTS

A trust account, sometimes called an "escrow account" or "client account," is an important part of how law practices manage money. A *trust* or *escrow account* is a bank account, separate from a law office's or attorney's business or operating checking account, where unearned client funds are deposited. Nearly all private law practices have at least two checking accounts, one checking account from which normal business deposits and expenses are paid and a separate trust account, typically a checking account as opposed to a savings account, where only client funds are kept (see Figure 6-1). Checks used with the trust/escrow account will carry the title of "Trust Account," "Client Trust Account," or "Escrow Account." Deposit slips also will have this designation. A separate bank statement also will be received for the trust account.

> *It is important to manage a client's trust account accurately. This goes back to gaining and keeping the trust and respect of the client. The monies in the trust account belong to the client, so there must be a high level of responsibility owed to the client to manage those funds correctly.*
>
> Linda Rushton, CLA

NO COMMINGLING OF CLIENT AND LAW OFFICE FUNDS

Ethical rules prohibit the commingling of client funds and law office funds in the same account. This rule cannot be overemphasized, and there is virtually no flexibility regarding this rule.

EXAMPLES OF HOW A TRUST ACCOUNT IS USED

There are times when clients will pay a cash advance or an unearned retainer to an office to apply against future fees and expenses. Until the office has actually earned these monies, it must keep these funds in the trust account. The reason is simple: if client funds are commingled in the same bank account with general law practice funds, creditors could seize these funds to repay debts of the law practice.

The cash advance is just one way that the trust account is used. Trust accounts also are used in other ways, such as for distributing settlement checks. A **settlement** occurs when both parties in a dispute mutually agree to resolve the dispute on specified terms, such as for one party to pay to the other party a certain sum of money.

settlement
A mutual agreement to resolve a dispute on specified terms.

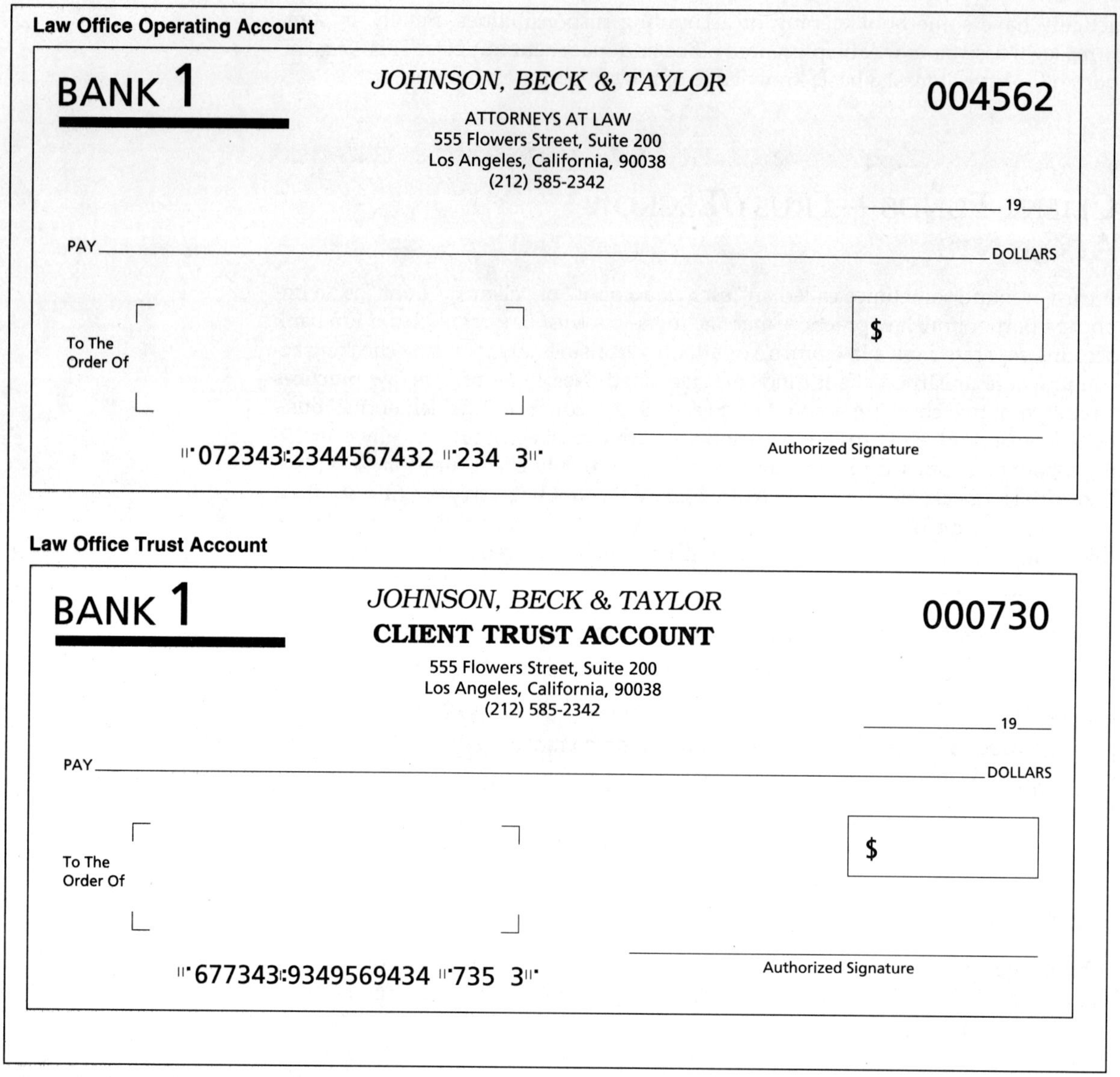

Law Office Operating Account

BANK 1

JOHNSON, BECK & TAYLOR
ATTORNEYS AT LAW
555 Flowers Street, Suite 200
Los Angeles, California, 90038
(212) 585-2342

004562

_____ 19___

PAY _____ DOLLARS

To The Order Of

$ _____

⑈072343⑆2344567432 ⑈234 3⑈

Authorized Signature

Law Office Trust Account

BANK 1

JOHNSON, BECK & TAYLOR
CLIENT TRUST ACCOUNT
555 Flowers Street, Suite 200
Los Angeles, California, 90038
(212) 585-2342

000730

_____ 19___

PAY _____ DOLLARS

To The Order Of

$ _____

⑈677343⑆9349569434 ⑈735 3⑈

Authorized Signature

Figure 6–1 Operating and Trust Checks

For example, suppose that an attorney represented a client in a personal injury case and the matter was settled out of court for $10,000. Suppose that the defendant issued a $10,000 check made payable to both the attorney and the client and that the attorney was entitled to $2,000 and the client to $8,000. The proper way to dispose of the monies would be for both the attorney and the client to endorse the settlement check. Then, the attorney would deposit the $10,000 settlement check in the trust account and subsequently write an $8,000 check from the trust account to the client and a $2,000 check from the trust account to the law office.

ETHICS AND TRUST ACCOUNTS

> *Most courts treat misappropriation of client funds as an ethical violation warranting [attorney] disbarment. Even inadvertent breaches frequently result in discipline by regulatory authorities. The Rules offer protection for clients by imposing three obligations: the lawyer must segregate funds and property of clients, keep careful and correct financial records, and make timely notification to clients of the receipt of funds on their behalf.[2]*

TRUST FUNDS AND OFFICE OPERATING FUNDS CANNOT BE COMMINGLED

Every state bar's ethical rules prohibit the commingling of client and law office funds. Rule 1.15 of the *Model Rules of Professional Conduct* states:

> (a) A lawyer shall hold property of client or third persons that is in a lawyer's possession in connection with a representation separate from the lawyer's own property. Funds shall be kept in a separate account. . . . Complete records of such account funds and other property shall be kept by the lawyer and shall be preserved for a period of five years after termination of the representation.

The Ethics 2000 Commission is not recommending any revisions to Rule 1.15(a).

Notice in Rule 1.15 (a) that not only must the lawyer keep the client's and the lawyer's property separate from each other, but that complete records regarding these accounts must be maintained for at least five years after termination of the representation. There is an affirmative duty not only to have the trust account but also to keep complete and proper records. It is permissible to use one trust account for all client funds as long as there is sufficient record keeping to know how much each client has in the trust account. Law practices do not have to have separate trust accounts for every client. In fact, many law offices have only one trust account for all client monies. Larger offices may choose to have several trust accounts to help organize and control the large numbers of cases they have.

For example, suppose Attorney A has twenty-five clients who have monies deposited in one trust account, and each client has differing amounts in the account. This is perfectly acceptable, as long as Attorney A knows and has records to prove exactly how much each client has in the trust account and maintains a running ledger to show what money was taken out check by check and what amounts were deposited for each client (see Figure 6–2). This is why good record keeping regarding trust accounts is crucial. Law offices must know to the penny how much each client has in the trust account so that when it comes time to give the money back to the client, the money will be there. Most state bars require that

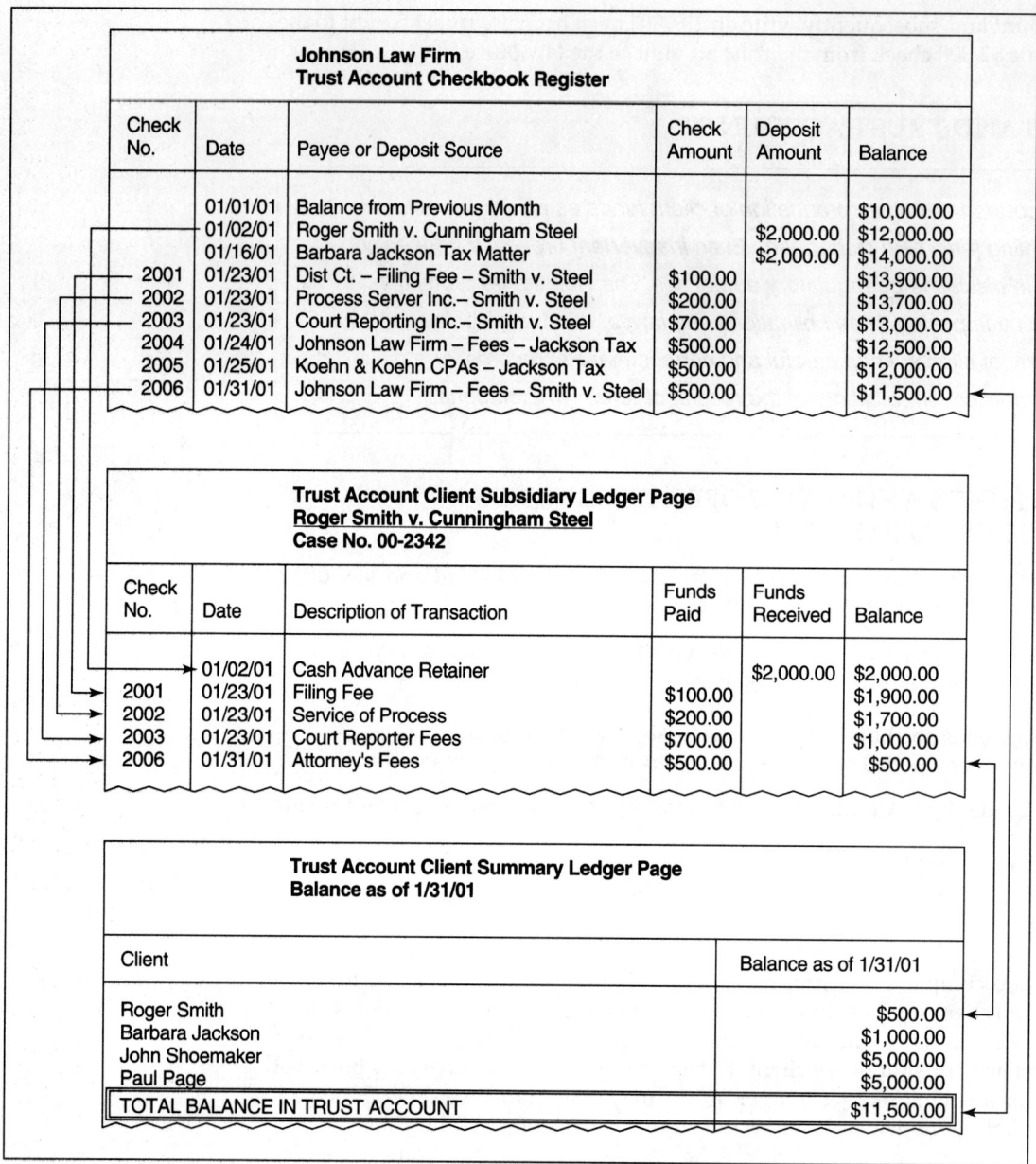

Figure 6–2 Trust Account Ledgers

the bank statement for the trust account be reconciled every month, showing exactly which clients have what amounts in the trust account. A failure of the law office to keep detailed records could result in a finding by the state bar that the attorney is subject to disciplinary action.

TRUST ACCOUNT CANNOT BE USED TO PAY LAW OFFICE OR PERSONAL EXPENSES Ethical rules also prohibit attorneys from using trust funds to pay for general office expenses. For example, if an attorney had client money in the trust account but did not have enough money in the law office checking account to cover his rent, the attorney would be absolutely prohibited from writing the rent check on the trust account.

Sometimes attorneys will say that they are simply "borrowing" money from the trust fund and will pay it back. This, too, is a violation of the ethical rules, even if the money is in fact repaid to the trust account within the same day. Client funds simply cannot be used in any way for the personal use of the law office or attorney.

Rule 1.15(b) of the *Model Rules of Professional Conduct* states:

> (b) . . . [A] lawyer shall promptly deliver to the client or third person any funds or other property the client or third person is entitled to receive . . . and, shall promptly render a full accounting regarding such property.

The Ethics 2000 Commission is not recommending any revisions to Rule 1.15(b). Under Rule 1.15(b), once the client is entitled to receive monies held in trust, the attorney must deliver the monies promptly. For example, if a client's case is concluded and the client still has money left in trust from a cash advance, the attorney has a duty to promptly return the funds.

COMMINGLING OF CLIENT FUNDS A COMMON PROBLEM

The commingling of client funds with attorneys' or law office funds is not a trivial or uncommon matter (see Figure 6–3). Hundreds of attorneys are disbarred or suspended from practice every year for commingling client funds. In nearly every issue of every state's bar association journal, one can read about an attorney being disciplined for commingling client monies. Funds that *must* be held in a client trust account include:

- client funds
- third party funds
- funds that belong partly to a client and partly to an attorney (such as settlement funds)
- retainers for legal services that are unearned and that are the client's property until they are earned

Funds that *cannot* be held in a client trust account include:

- personal funds of the attorney or staff
- business funds of the law firm
- investment funds of the law firm
- earned fee payments that have become the property of the attorney or law firm

State disciplinary authorities have taken notice of the problem of attorneys commingling client and business funds and attorneys stealing from their clients. Many jurisdictions now have rules in place that require a bank or financial institution to contact the state disciplinary authorities when any attorney trust account has checks that return as insufficient. When this happens, state disciplinary authorities conduct

Christina M. Arnall, (*California Lawyer,* July 2000, p. 79) An attorney represented a three-generation extended family regarding an elevator incident at a hotel. The case was settled for $20,000. A total of $11,221 was placed in trust for the benefit of the attorney's clients. The attorney failed to disburse any of the funds to the clients. The balance in the trust account eventually fell to a negative $333. The clients hired new counsel and the attorney stipulated in a judgment of $30,000. The attorney agreed to pay the money to the clients at a rate of $500 per month. The attorney made four payments and then quit. The attorney was suspended for two years and placed on probation for three years and until she makes restitution.

Melanie Lorraine Jones, (*California Lawyer,* May 2000, p. 79) Attorney commingled personal funds with client funds by failing to timely remove the attorney's fees from the trust account. The attorney wrote 52 checks against the trust account for personal and nonclient purposes. At a later time, the attorney wrote 16 checks against the trust account when there were insufficient funds in the account to cover them. The attorney was suspended for six months and placed on probation.

In Re Rivlin, (*Legal Times,* October 26, 1998) Attorney asked his client to invest in a venture the attorney had formed to purchase and resell diamonds and gold from the Central African Republic. The client agree to invest $48,000, but only if the new company was a partnership, not a corporation. The attorney agreed to prepare the necessary documents to make the company a limited partnership. The client in fact paid the $48,000 and the attorney deposited it in his trust account. The attorney withdrew monies from the trust account and paid them to people associated with the company, his wife, his dentist, and to others. Within a couple of months, the balance in the trust account fell to $666.65. The client later demanded his money back and the attorney agreed to pay it back, but never did. The disciplinary authorities charged the attorney with representing a client in a matter when the attorney's own professional judgment was reasonably adversely affected by a third party or financial interest, entered into a business transaction with a client in which the terms were not fair to the client or fully disclosed; failed to deliver funds that the client was entitled to, and committed fraud or theft.

In re Cavuto, New Jersey Supreme Court, D-122, July 30, 1999 Attorney had practiced law for 33 years. In 1986, attorney settled a personal injury claim for a client for $36,000. The settlement proceeds were deposited in the attorney's trust account. The attorney was to pay himself a fee of $12,000, to pay the client's health care providers of $12,727 and the rest to the client. Within a month of depositing the funds in this trust account in 1986, the attorney paid himself 22 checks from the trust account for a total of $26,259. The attorney never paid the medical expenses. The client did not discover that the medical expenses had not been paid until more than five years later when the doctor refused to treat the client because the client's bill had not been paid. The client complained to the disciplinary authorities and an audit was done. The audit showed that the attorney had very few trust account matters and that the attorney did not keep a trust account receipts journal, a disbursement journal, or client record cards. The attorney did not reconcile his trust account. The

Figure 6–3 Commingling and Misappropriation of Client Trust Funds

Reprinted by permission from *California Lawyer;* © 2000 NLPLP Company. All rights reserved. Reprinted with permission of *Legal Times,* 1730 M Street NW, Suite 802, Washington, DC 20036. (202)457-0686.

attorney tracked his trust account through the running balance on the checks stubs. The attorney said that he kept fees in his trust account to keep them from the attorney's spouse since the spouse had authority to sign checks on the attorney's business account. The attorney said that he had tried to review the file after the client complained, but that the file had been mistakenly purged his spouse. The attorney then asked the client to bring in the client's records. Still, the attorney could not remember whether the medical providers had been paid. The attorney told the client that he did not have the money to pay the bills at that time, but that he would pay them from another settlement that he was handling for the client. The attorney never paid the medical providers. The attorney suffered from diabetes, depress, fatigue, forgetfulness, and memory loss. The New Jersey Supreme Court found that the attorney knowingly misappropriated client funds and disbarred the attorney. At the time of the disbarment, the actions of the attorney were 13 years old.

Committee on Professional Ethics and Conduct of the Iowa State Bar Association v. Minette, 499 N.W. 2d 303 (Ia. 1993) Attorney was client's financial advisor. Client was the recipient of a $40,000,000 trust funded through 842,120 shares of stock. Attorney was authorized to write checks on client's bank account and to approve the sale of stock from the trust when greater funds were needed to pay client's expenses. Attorney paid himself $9,000 from client's account to settle a professional negligence claim against him and paid himself a $2,500 a month retainer. When the complaint was received, attorney had misappropriated about $88,000 in client funds. Attorney had no written fee agreement to establish any of these payments. Attorney was disbarred.

Non-Published California Case (*California Lawyer,* September 1993, p. 76) Attorney entered into an arrangement with a non-lawyer in which the non-lawyer offered to provide the overhead to operate a law office (including legal work) and to provide the expenses of start-up costs. The non-lawyer also agreed to pay the attorney a monthly draw of $500 plus expenses. The attorney agreed to do legal work in the office for one day a week. After one year, the attorney's salary increased to $3,000 a month and his hours increased to three days a week. The non-lawyer and the attorney both had signature authority on the office checking account. The attorney gave the non-lawyer a power of attorney authorizing him to sign for the attorney. For the first two years, the office did not have a client trust account. Client settlement funds were all deposited in an operating account under the non-lawyer's control. After the State Bar requested copy of the law office's trust account records, the attorney opened a trust account and made the non-lawyer a signatory to it. Non-client funds were commingled in the trust account on three occasions. The non-lawyer embezzled $120,000 from client settlements. The attorney received a six-month suspension, and was placed on three years of probation.

In re petition for Disciplinary Action Against Erickson, 1993 WL 408187 (Minn.) In February 1992, Norwest Bank notified the state bar that the attorney's trust account was overdrawn. The state bar found that the attorney's trust account records were incomplete; that client subsidiary ledgers for several clients had not been timely established; and that on occasion the trust account had contained both client and personal funds, because attorney had not promptly withdrawn earned fees. In three instances, where there were no client funds in the trust account, only earned fees, respondent wrote checks on the account for filing fees, thus using the trust account as a personal business account. Attorney was suspended for 60 days.

(continued)

> *In the matter of Discipline of Tidball* 503 N.W.2d 850 (SD. 1993) Attorney practiced law for more than 20 years. Attorney fell on hard times and was being pressed by creditors. To avoid their garnishment attempts, he placed his personal funds in his trust account. Deposits and withdrawals were made with such randomness that it was impossible to tell with exactness which transactions were of a personal nature and which involved a specific client. He failed to keep contemporaneous ledgers or other records regarding the trust account. In one case, attorney received some $62,000 for settlement of case. Of that, $40,000 never went into this trust account at all. Attorney received a three-year suspension.
>
> *Stegal v. Mississippi Bar*, 618 So.2d 1291 (MS. 1993) Attorney received a $2,500 payment from client. Attorney maintained he was waiting for a second payment of $2,500 before he completed any work for client. Client stated that he did not know that attorney never refunded the money or performed the work. Client was not told the payment was non-refundable and no written fee agreement was signed. Attorney did not respond to the letters and phone calls of clients. Attorney had four prior complaint proceedings brought against him. Attorney was disbarred.

an audit of the law firm's trust account. In addition, many state disciplinary authorities conduct random audits of attorney trust accounts in an effort to prevent these problems from occurring. Commingling of client funds is a common problem that nearly always results in harsh discipline being levied against the attorney.

BONDING FOR PEOPLE HANDLING FUNDS Law offices should routinely buy a dishonesty bond from an insurance company to cover all employees handling client or law office funds. If an employee covered by an employee dishonesty bond were to steal client or law office funds, the insurance company would cover the loss up to the amount of the bond. Bonding is a prudent way to protect funds.

BUDGETING

Budgeting in any kind of law office is a good tool to control expenses and make a profit. Firms that develop and use budgets recognize that the budgeting process allows them to project and manipulate the profitability they want.

A **budget** is a projected plan of income and expenses for a set period of time, usually a year. Budgets allow firms to plan for the future, to anticipate problems, needs, and goals for the firm, and to allocate and manage resources. A budget also is a management tool used to keep revenues and expenses moving toward the profit goal. Figure 6–4 shows an example of a typical law office budget. Notice that the budgeting process involves careful development of planned operating expenses, professional and administrative staff sizes, professional and administrative salaries, desired income, and planned capital expenditures for items such as computers, copiers, and furniture.

It is not uncommon for legal assistants to prepare budgets for their department, their office, or, in small firms, for the whole practice.

budget
A projected plan of income and expenses for a set period of time, usually a year.

Figure 6–4
Law Firm Budget—Master Budget

Step 1—Income Budget	Hours	Rate	Total
R. Johnson, Partner	1700	$175	$297,500
C. Beck, Partner	1700	$175	$297,500
J. Taylor, Partner	1700	$175	$297,500
J. B. Ring, Associate	1800	$125	$225,000
H. S. Hendershot, Associate	1800	$125	$225,000
B. D. Smith, Legal Assistant	1750	$50	$87,500
C. A. Sullivan, Legal Assistant	1750	$50	$87,500
Other Income			$35,000
SUBTOTAL (Total Billings)			1,552,500
Time to Billing Percentage			95%
TOTAL TO BE BILLED			$1,474,875
Realization Rate			90%
TOTAL GROSS INCOME			$1,327,388

Step 2—Staffing Plan

EXPENSE BUDGET
Salary Expenses:

J. B. Ring, Associate	$70,000
H. S. Hendershot, Associate	$70,000
B. D. Smith, Legal Assistant	$35,000
C. A. Sullivan, Legal Assistant	$35,000
M. J. Johnson, Administrator	$40,000
J. T. Thomas, Secretary	$25,000
J. J. Statzman, Secretary	$21,000
H. V. Billingsley, Secretary	$20,250
B. J. Wickert, Librarian	$24,000
C. M. Hunt, Receptionist	$17,000

Step 3—Estimated Expenses

All Other Expenses:

Accounting/professional services	$3,500
Amortization of leasehold improvements	$1,000
Association/Membership Dues	$2,500
Client billings written off	$10,000
Continuing legal education	$13,000
Copying expenses (not billed to clients)	$18,000
Depreciation	$10,000
Employee benefits & taxes	$72,000
Entertainment	$2,500
Equipment purchase/computers	$50,000
Equipment rental	$8,500
Forms & stationery	$6,000
General liability & property ins.	$3,000
Housekeeping/cleaning services	
Malpractice/errors & omissions ins.	$70,000
Marketing	$10,000
Miscellaneous	$2,000

(continued)

Office supplies	$12,500
Other taxes	$2,500
Postage	$10,000
Reference materials/subscriptions/library	$8,000
Rent expense	$94,000
Repairs and maintenance	$8,600
Telephone & fax exp. (not billed to clients)	$20,000
Travel (not billed to clients)	$3,000
Utilities	$34,000
TOTAL EXPENSES	$835,850

Step 4—Determine Acceptable Profit Goal

NET INCOME TO BE DISTRIBUTED	$491,538

BUDGETING AND PLANNING

Planning and budgeting go hand in hand. A budget is just a specific type of plan. For example, if a firm's long-term strategic plan and marketing plan call for $10,000 of marketing expenditures, the budget also needs to reflect the $10,000 planned marketing expenditure.

STEPS IN THE BUDGET PROCESS

income budget
Estimate of how many partners, associates, legal assistants, and others will bill for their time, what the appropriate rates of hourly charge should be, and the number of billable hours each timekeeper will be responsible for billing.

time to billing percentage
System of adjusting downward the actual amount that will be billed to clients during the budget process, taking into account the fact that timekeepers are not always able to bill at their optimum levels.

Step 1. Income budget One of the first steps in developing a firmwide budget is to draft an income budget (see Figure 6–4). An **income budget** estimates how many partners, associates, legal assistants, and others will bill for their time, what the appropriate rates or hourly charge should be, and the number of billable hours each timekeeper will be responsible for billing.

When preparing an income budget, it is recommended that you estimate as close to possible what the actual amount will be. However, if you are unsure of something, it is usually recommended that you be *conservative* in estimating the income budget. The reason for being conservative is that if you overestimate income and then rely on the overestimate in the expense budget and spend it, and income is actually lower than expected, you have a net loss. However, if you underestimate income and then the actual income is above the level (and expenses stay the same as budgeted), it simply means that the firm makes a larger profit than was estimated and there is no harm done. One way to minimize this problem is to use a "time to billing" percentage. The **time to billing percentage** adjusts downward the actual amount that will be billed to clients, taking into account the fact that timekeepers are not always able to bill at their optimum levels due to vacations, sickness, and other unforeseeable events. Notice in Figure 6–4 that the firm used a time to billing of 95 percent, thus reducing its billing estimate by 5 percent. The time to billing percentage for most firms ranges from 85 percent to 100 percent. The purpose of the time to billing percentage is to build into the budget the fact that the firm may not bill all the hours it would like to.

Reasons that timekeepers may not bill their required number of hours include the following.

- Extended medical leave of timekeepers
- Too few clients
- Procrastination or other bad work habits
- Disorganization or inefficiencies in case management
- Failure to consistently report all billable hours
- Extensive use of the timekeeper on pro bono or other nonbillable tasks

In some instances, legal assistants' and attorneys' actual hours end up being greater than the budgeted hours. When this happens, the firm makes an even larger profit than expected, as long as expenses remain as budgeted.

Realization also is an important concept in budgeting income. **Realization** is what a firm actually receives in income as opposed to the amount it bills. In Figure 6–4, the firm anticipates that it will actually receive or collect 90 percent of what it bills for. Some firms strive for a 95 percent rate, while others are comfortable with a rate as low as 80 percent.

realization
Amount a firm actually receives in income as opposed to the amount it bills.

Notice in Figure 6–4 that the firm usually sets the hourly rates for the year at this point. Setting rates in the income budget can be difficult. If a firm sets the rate too high, clients may take their business to a competing firm, but if rates are too low, it could mean a loss of revenue. It also is quite difficult to try to project income if the firm has many contingency fee arrangements. One way to do it is to look at gross income figures for contingency fees for the past several years to help in estimating future contingencies.

Step 2. Staffing plan A staffing plan also should be established early in the budgeting process. A **staffing plan** estimates how many employees will be hired or funded by the firm, what positions or capacities they will serve, what positions will need to be added, what positions will be deleted, and how much compensation each employee will receive. One of the largest expenses of any professional service business is salary costs, usually about 80 percent. Thus, it is important that the firm determine whether positions will be added or cut or whether existing staff members will receive cost-of-living adjustments or merit increases. A staffing plan also goes hand in hand with preparing the income budget.

staffing plan
Estimate of how many employees will be hired or funded by the firm, what positions or capacities they will serve in, what positions will need to be added, what old positions will be deleted, and how much compensation each employee will receive.

Step 3. Estimating overhead expenses Firms also must accurately estimate their general operating or overhead expenses. This can be fairly tricky because, in many cases, the estimates are covering a period that ends at a minimum of a year in advance. For example, if a person is preparing a budget in November 2002, and the budget covers the period of January 2003 to December 2003, the person will not know until fourteen months later whether the estimates were accurate. The time problem makes budgeting difficult. For example, if insurance rates go up unexpectedly, if postage costs go up, or if large equipment breaks down unexpectedly, then your budget will be greatly affected. When discussing the income budget, it was noted that the preparer should be conservative in estimating income. However, when you get to the expense budget, the opposite is true. As always, you should try to be as accurate as possible in estimating expenses. However, if you question the validity of an item, you should be liberal in estimating the expense. This allows the firm to forecast unforeseeable events that might otherwise leave the budget short.

Step 4. Profit margin The last step is to calculate income and expenses so that the firm budgets the targeted profit margin it needs. That is, if after the draft budget the firm is not happy with the profit margin, the preparer can manipulate and make changes in the budget such as adding additional profit-making positions or cutting expenses further to reach the desired goal.

Here are some additional suggestions about budgets.

- **Communicate the budget to everyone involved.** For a budget to be effective, everyone in the firm should be aware of it, and there should be a consensus reached by the firm's management on major issues such as desired profits and equipment purchases. For instance, if even one timekeeper fails to charge the number of estimated hours, it could completely throw the budget off. Thus, it is very important that management stress the importance of the budget and communicate it effectively.
- **Track budgets year-round and consult them regularly.** For budgets to be useful, they must be taken out of the desk drawer. That is, if a firm wants to purchase a piece of equipment, it is important that the budget be consulted to see if the purchase was planned or if there is room in the budget for it.
- **Track the progress of the budget on a monthly basis.** As suggested before, budgets are of little value if they are not updated and used throughout the year. One way to use the budget year-round is to compare "budget" v. "actual." This allows the firm to know whether it is staying in line with its budget and/or if it needs to make midyear adjustments.
- **Always document your budget.** Always document budgets well, making notes and narrative statements in the budget itself. It is common to make assumptions when formulating a budget, and unless the preparer notes why the assumption was made he or she may forget its purpose. It also helps in preparing the budget for next year.
- **Use zero-based budgets.** Although it is common for organizations to start the budgeting process of a new year by using the actual figures from the previous year and adding 4 percent or 5 percent, this is not an effective way of controlling costs and managing the firm. By using a **zero-based budgeting system,** everyone in the organization must justify and explain his or her budget figures in depth without using last year's figures as justification. In short, each year's budget is taken on its own merit.

zero-based budgeting system
Procedure that forces everyone in the organization to justify and explain his budget figures in depth without using prior year's figures as justification.

INTERNAL CONTROLS

Law offices of every type—private, corporate, government, and legal aid—must establish good internal control procedures. **Internal control** refers to procedures that an organization establishes to set up checks and balances so that no one individual in the organization has exclusive control over any part of the accounting system. Internal controls discussions are usually saved for accounting professionals. However, embezzlement by law practice personnel has become a major issue (see Figure 6–5) and is quite prevalent. If embezzlement occurs in an organization, it signals that its internal controls are weak and ineffective.

internal control
Procedures that an organization establishes to set up checks and balances so that no individual in the organization has exclusive control over any part of the accounting system.

LEGAL ASSISTANT ALLEGEDLY LAUNDERS INSURANCE REBATE CHECKS

A legal assistant allegedly stole approximately $724,000 from an insurance company over a two-month period. The legal assistant allegedly conspired with another person to issue thirty-four fraudulent rebate checks to policyholders. The legal assistant allegedly laundered the checks through a number of different accounts. The insurance company realized that something was wrong and started an investigation, but not before nearly three-quarters of a million dollars was gone. The legal assistant was charged with five counts of money laundering, fourteen counts of embezzlement, and conspiracy and forgery charges.[1]

[1] *Legal Assistant Today,* "A 'Clean' Get-Away . . . Almost," May/June, 1999, p. 19.

FORMER PARALEGAL SENTENCED IN EMBEZZLEMENT CASE

A former paralegal was sentenced to two months of home detention and one year of probation for having embezzled $8,000 in funds belonging to a bankruptcy debtor while employed as a paralegal at a East Coast law firm. The paralegal faced a maximum penalty of five years' imprisonment and a $250,000 fine. The paralegal was custodian of the bankruptcy debtor's account and was responsible for preparing checks for the bankruptcy trustee. The embezzlement was discovered a few months after the paralegal left the firm while he was working at another firm. "We discovered certain irregularities during a routine inventory of accounts and turned the information over to the proper authorities" said one of the firm's directors. The case was investigated by the FBI. At the time of sentencing the paralegal informed the U.S. attorney's office that he was no longer working at the new firm and that he voluntarily withdrew from law school entirely.

Legal Assistant Today, July/August 1992, p. 27.

BOOKKEEPER ALLEGEDLY EMBEZZLES $2 MILLION OVER 15-YEAR PERIOD

A Boston personal injury attorney alleges that his bookkeeper of 15 years stole $2 million from him. The bookkeeper had complete authority over the office's finances. She was able to write and sign checks for unlimited amounts of money without the attorney's approval. The attorney felt confident about the bookkeeper. Then one day, he discovered that some checks were missing and that there were inaccuracies in the case settlement and disbursement records. One of the bookkeeper's schemes was to write partial settlement checks between $3,000 and $6,000. She would then endorse these in clients' names, take them to the bank and cash them as a "favor" to the clients. But she kept the money. Among other things, the bookkeeper converted $30,000 which she used to make a down payment on a condominium in the Caribbean.

"Stealing Your Practice Blind Embezzlement in the Law Office," *ABA Journal* 73, August 1987, p. 78.

$400,000 EMBEZZLED FROM LEGAL AID ORGANIZATION

A neighborhood legal service's history of 25 years of service was overshadowed by the shocking revelation that the program executive director confessed that he was a compulsive gambler and had diverted nearly $400,000 in program funds to feed his addiction. Apparently the executive director forged Board member signatures to documents that enabled him to open a false corporate account, giving a post office box as the program address. He was able to intercept and deposit program checks into the phony account and later withdraw such funds by using his own signature. The embezzlement took place during a two and a half year time span before the embezzlement was discovered.

Lew Hollman, "Overcoming the Shock of Embezzlement," *Los Angeles Lawyer,* October 1992, p. 18.

Figure 6–5   Embezzlement Is Common In Law Practices

Internal controls must be established in both large and small firms. Interestingly enough, small law offices need internal controls more than large firms do. Why? Because fewer people handle the finances in a small office, and there are typically fewer written and strict procedures. Thus the opportunity to embezzle tends to be greater in a smaller office. Therefore, it is absolutely critical in a small law office to have exceptionally good internal controls. The downside of internal controls is that it takes time to do them right and they can slow down the financial process (i.e., such as requiring a partner to sign all checks instead of having a bookkeeper sign checks). This is particularly true in small firms. But it is the only way to ensure that embezzlement and fraud do not take place.

What type of internal control procedures could limit the possibility of embezzlement? There are several.

- **Never allow a bookkeeper or person preparing checks to sign checks or to sign on the account.**

Never let the individual who writes the checks sign on the account. A bookkeeper should never be allowed to sign on the account. In addition, never let any one person record the check in the checkbook (or equivalent), prepare the check, obtain signature(s) on the check, and mail the check. Embezzlement is more likely to happen in that case. A partner or ranking member of the firm should sign all checks, if possible. An alternative is to require two signatures on all checks.

- **Have careful, unannounced, routine examination of the books.**

A partner or other ranking member of the law office with no direct accounting responsibilities should carefully look over the books on a weekly basis. A partner also should account for all monies on a regular basis (once a week or once every two weeks) by reviewing bank statements and canceled checks for the authenticity of the signatures, reviewing the reconciliation register, ensuring that check numbers out of sequence are not being cashed, and looking through cash disbursement records carefully. These procedures must be done for both the office business account and the trust account.

- **All documents must routinely be read and examined—no exceptions.**

Never sign or let someone else sign checks, correspondence, or other important documents without carefully reading the material. It is very easy to hand documents to people and ask for their signature immediately. Do not do this and do not let someone else do it. It is very important that everyone involved always check all the supporting documentation of a check.

- **All checks should be stored in a locked cabinet.**

All checks should be kept under lock and key at all times when not in use, and access for writing checks should be given to as few people as possible.

- **Never let the person signing the checks reconcile the account.**

The person writing checks or the person signing the checks should not be allowed to reconcile the bank account. If the person who is preparing and signing the checks is allowed to reconcile the account, that person will be able to write herself a check, sign it, and destroy the check when it comes in the bank statement. This might even tempt a basically honest person. Oversight is the key. Never let anyone have the opportunity to embezzle; set up good procedures and follow them.

- **Use check request forms.**

Check request forms also are used to bolster internal control procedures. If, for instance, an employee or attorney needed a check for a client expense or for an expense charged to the firm, the person would be required to complete a form similar to the one shown in Figure 6–6. Small law offices also should use check requests whenever possible.

- **Establish guidelines for how the mail should be opened.**

The mail should be opened by someone with no accounting duties, such as a receptionist, secretary, or mailing clerk. When a check is received, the person opening the mail should be instructed to immediately endorse the check on the back "FOR DEPOSIT ONLY" in ink or with a stamp. If the bookkeeper or someone in accounting opens the mail, there is absolutely nothing to stop that person from taking the check and cashing it. This would be easy to do because the firm would have no record of it.

- **Use nonaccounting personnel to help with internal controls.**

An additional internal control would be for the receptionist, secretary, or another person to prepare the bank deposits because he or she would be separated from the accounting department and would not have recorded the cash receipts in the accounts receivable system. In this way, all cash receipts and bank deposits are independently verified by someone completely outside the accounting department who has no access to accounting records.

A very common way embezzlement occurs is on refund checks. For example, it is not uncommon for firms to receive large refund checks from insurance companies and other vendors. If a person in the accounting department opens the mail, he could endorse the check and deposit it in his own account with little possibility of someone finding out about it. Why? Because the original invoice would be shown as paid on the firm's books, and no one else would know that he had received the refund.

- **Require two signatures on checks over $10,000.**

Checks over a certain dollar amount might also be required to be signed by a second individual (i.e., two signatures on the check). This is another example of an internal control. This would limit large checks from going out of the firm with the authority of only one individual.

- **Stamp invoices "Canceled."**

Once a check has been paid, the invoice should be stamped "CANCELED" so that no one could intentionally resubmit the same invoice for payment.

- **Have an audit done once a year or hire a CPA to help you set up internal controls.**

A yearly audit by an accounting firm can help find embezzlement and strengthen and monitor internal control procedures. If your firm cannot justify the cost of an audit, hire a CPA to help you set up good internal controls and have him or her come in once a year to review them.

JOHNSON, BECK & TAYLOR
ATTORNEYS AT LAW
555 Flowers Street, Suite 200
Los Angeles, California, 90038
(212) 585-2342

CHECK REQUEST FORM

Client Name and File Number: _____

Date of Request: _____

Request Made By: _____

Bank Account: General Business Account   Trust Account   (Circle One)

Amount of Check: $ _____

Check Should Be Made Payable To: _____

Address of Payee: _____

Detailed Description: _____
_____
_____
_____

Accounting Use Only

Account No./Code: _____

Approved by: _____   Date: _____

Figure 6–6   Check Request Form

Lawyers and Nonlawyers Cannot Share Fees

Attorneys are generally barred from directly sharing their legal fees with a non-lawyer, such as a legal assistant. The ABA *Model Rules of Professional Conduct* state:

Rule 5.4 (a) A lawyer or law firm shall not share legal fees with a nonlawyer . . . .

(d) A lawyer shall not practice with or in the form of a professional corporate or association authorized to practice law for a profit, if:

(1) A nonlawyer owns any interest therein . . . .

The reasoning for the rule is that the sharing of a fee between a lawyer and a non-lawyer could interfere with the lawyer's professional judgment and lead to the nonlawyer being concerned only with profits and not the best interests of his or her clients. Regarding legal assistants, this typically arises when a legal assistant refers a person to an attorney for representation. The attorney is prohibited from sharing the representation fee with the legal assistant or paying the legal assistant specifically for the referral. Figure 6–7 shows an example of lawyers sharing fees with nonlawyers.

Figure 6–7
Lawyers Cannot Share Fees with Nonlawyers
Source: *California Lawyer*, June 2000, p. 73. Reprinted by permission of *California Lawyer*.

Charles Harold Kavalaris, State Bar # 46853, San Jose (December 15). Kavalaris, 56, was suspended for one year and placed on four years of probation for splitting fees with nonattorneys, commingling, writing checks against a client trust account when there were insufficient funds in the account, engaging in acts of moral turpitude, and practicing law while suspended.

Beginning in 1985 Kavalaris and his law partner had an agreement with a nonlawyer, an officer of the local Teamsters Union, to refer personal injury cases to the law firm. During the time of the agreement, 1985 to 1991, Kavalaris and his partner paid the Teamsters' officer approximately $130,000 in referral fees. The money represented 10 percent of the attorneys fees the law firm realized from the cases. Also, beginning in 1987 and continuing into 1991, Kavalaris and his partner paid $150,000 to other nonlawyers in exchange for case referrals.

In November 1991 a federal investigator was appointed by a federal judge to look into Teamsters Union activities. The investigator conducted the deposition of the Teamsters' officer that Kavalaris had paid for case referrals. In 1995 the Teamsters' officer was indicted for perjury for giving false testimony during his deposition. The Teamsters' officer pleaded guilty and was sentenced in 1996. The State Bar learned about Kavalaris in November 1995, when a State Bar attorney read a newspaper article about the Teamsters' officer's guilty plea and that Kavalaris had been named as a participant in a kickback scheme.

(continued)

> In a second matter, in August 1996 Kavalaris wrote two checks against his client trust account totaling $4,770. There were insufficient funds in the account to cover the amount of the checks. In November 1996 he commingled funds by depositing $1,000 in personal funds into the client trust account.
>
> In a third matter, in March 1998 Kavalaris was suspended for failure to pass the professional responsibility exam. During the time of his suspension, he represented clients at two arbitrations, made a court appearance, and settled a case.
>
> In aggravation, Kavalaris had a prior record of discipline. In February 1997 he was placed on two years of probation for failure to communicate, improper withdrawal, failure to pay court-imposed sanctions, failure to report court-ordered sanctions to the State Bar, and failure to comply with the laws of California. In 1998 he was suspended for 60 days for failure to comply in a timely fashion with conditions to the previous probation. In mitigation, Kavalaris admitted to being an alcoholic. He has remained sober since March 1997 and attends meetings several times a week of Alcoholics Anonymous and the Other Bar. Kavalaris cooperated with the State Bar during its investigation of the kickback scheme, and he and his partner admitted their role in the kickbacks.
>
> The suspension order took effect January 14.

SUMMARY

Financial management is an important part of any successful law office, whether it be private, corporate, legal aid, or government.

Ethical rules require that client funds not be commingled with law office operating funds. This usually means that a law office must have a trust or escrow account. A trust account is a bank account, separate from a law office's or attorney's operating checking account, where unearned client funds are deposited.

A key aspect of financial management relates to budgeting. A budget is a projected plan of income and expenses for a set period of time, usually a year. Most budgets consist of an income budget, staffing plan, general overhead expenses, and an estimated profit. A firm must safeguard its assets by having internal control procedures that establish checks and balances so that no individual in the firm has exclusive control over any accounting system. Finally, there is an ethical prohibition against lawyers and nonlawyers sharing fees.

Internet Sites

Organization	Description	Internet Address
ABA Law Practice Today	ABA site devoted to law practice management	www.abanet.org/lpm
Association of Legal Administrators	Site for legal administrators	www.alanet.org
ABA Model Rule for Financial Recordkeeping	Rules for maintaining and tracking client funds	www.abanet.org/cpr/clientpro/fpreface.html
ABA Model Rule for Trust Account Overdraft Notification	Rules for trust account overdraft notification	www.abanet.org/cpr/clientpro/opreface.html
ABA Model Rule for Auditing Lawyer Trust Accounts	Rules of auditing lawyer trust accounts	www.abanet.org/cpr/clientpro/apreface.html

Suggested Reading

Lawyer Trust Accounts, Jag G. Foonberg, American Bar Association, 1996.

ABA Model Rules for Client Protection: Model Rule on Financial Recordkeeping Preface, American Bar Association; 1995.

ABA Model Rules for Client Protection: Model Rules for Trust Account Overdraft Notification, American Bar Association; 1995.

ABA Model Rules for Client Protection: Model Rule for Random Audit of Lawyer Trust Accounts, American Bar Association; 1995.

Key Terms

Settlement
Budget
Income budget
Time to billing percentage

Realization
Staffing plan
Zero-based budgeting system
Internal control

Questions and Exercises

1. You are a legal assistant in a five-attorney legal aid practice. The office manager who writes all the checks for the organization will not be back for several hours. Your supervising attorney asks you to get the checkbook out of the office manager's desk and issue a check that she needs right now. You fill in the manual check stub and type the check. Because the office manager is not there to sign the check, you hand the check to your supervising attorney to sign with several other papers. The attorney quickly signs her name while looking at the other documents. On your way to your office, the receptionist asks you to drop off the office manager's mail in his office. You notice that one of the envelopes appears to be a check from the local bar association that makes contributions to the practice as a community service. You also notice that another of the envelopes appears to be a bank statement and returned checks for the previous month. The office manager uses the returned checks and bank statement to reconcile the bank account. You place all the items on the office manager's desk as requested. Do you see any potential problems? Would it matter if the office manager had been there for twenty years, was extremely trustworthy, and refused to even take a vacation in that it might take him away from work? What recommendations would you make?

2. Your office represented a business client in litigation. During the litigation, the client made several cash advances. The matter has been concluded for approximately two months and the client has a balance in the trust account of about $20,000. The client has requested that the money be returned, but the supervising attorney has not gotten around to it yet. How do you analyze the situation and what would you do?

3. You have just been given the assignment to begin work on incorporating a new business. At the first meeting with the client, the client hands you a check for $1,000 and states that although no work has been performed on the case, this was the agreement that the client and your supervising attorney worked out last week on the telephone. Later, you hand the check to the supervising attorney. The attorney says to just deposit it in the office's account. What problems do you see, and what would you do and why?

4. As a legal assistant in a sole practitioner's office, you sometimes become "burned out" and tired. The attorney you work for is very appreciative of your hard work and would like to give you incentives when possible to keep you motivated. The attorney mentions that she will pay you a bonus equal to 10 percent of any new client retainers you are responsible for bringing in. How does this sound to you? Analyze this arrangement from an ethics perspective.

5. You are a legal assistant in a relatively small office. One day, one of the partners in the office instructs you to transfer $5,000 from the trust account into the office's general account. You ask him what case is involved. The partner says "There is no case name, but it doesn't concern you." What would you do? Explain your answer.

6. Using your state's bar association magazine, turn to the section that reports what disciplinary action has been taken against attorneys in your state and find one case wherein an attorney mishandled client funds. (There is usually at least one in every issue.) Answer the following questions.

- Why was the attorney disciplined?
- How were client funds mishandled?
- What kind of discipline did the attorney receive?
- Do you agree with the discipline? Why or why not?
- How could the situation have been avoided?

7. At 8:00 on a Monday morning, your supervising attorney rushes into your office. She states that at 10:00 A.M. she has a meeting with one of the firm's administrators to go over her draft version of the proposed budget for her satellite office. Although the office is relatively small, she must submit a budget that will produce a reasonable profit for the firm. Unfortunately, she has a meeting with a client and a court appearance to go to before the 10:00 A.M. meeting. She hands you a list of her notes and asks you to please come through for her on this one. You reluctantly agree, but then remember that your bonus at the end of the year will depend on how profitable your office is. Suddenly, you feel better about the assignment.

Here are the attorney's notes.

- Rent is $5,000 a month, but halfway through the year the lease calls for a 5 percent increase.
- The legal assistants will bill at $70.00 an hour and must work a minimum of 1,750 hours. You think that they will do this, since they will not be eligible to receive a bonus unless they work this amount.
- Utilities are included in the lease agreement, so do not worry about these.
- Associates will bill at $150 an hour. You

figure that they will bill no less than 1,900 hours because if they do not, they will not look good for a partnership position.
- From past history, the firm has determined that its time to billing percentage is 98 percent and the realization rate is 92 percent.
- Telephone cost is expected to be $4,000 a month.
- Staffing is as follows:
  Two legal assistants
  Four secretaries
  Three associates

Last year, legal assistants were paid on average $40,000, secretaries, $30,000 and associates, $70,000. Budget a 3.5 percent cost-of-living adjustment and a 2.5 percent merit increase.

- Fringe benefits and taxes are figured at 25 percent of the total of the salaries.
- Office supplies and stationery expenses will be about $20,000.
- The office must purchase four computers. Your best estimate is that they will cost about $5,000 each when all costs are included (installation, cabling, software, printers, training, maintenance contract, etc.).
- All other items such as malpractice and general liability insurance and professional services will be prorated to your office by the accounting office. You do not need to worry about this now.

What profit or loss is the office budgeted for?

8. You are a legal assistant manager in a small- to medium-sized firm. The firm administrator asks you to prepare a proposed income budget for your department of six legal assistants. You are not required to do an expense budget, as this is handled by the administrators and the accounting department. From years past, you know that you must sit down with each of the legal assistants and discuss billable hours, hourly rates, etc. You don't relish this much because the firm has consistently pressed for more and more billable hours. Thus, this topic can be somewhat touchy for you as a manager. Below is the information you obtained to help you. Also, note that time to billing percentage is figured at 95 percent and the realization rate also is 95 percent.

Legal assistant #1 typically works for one of the firm's general litigators. Because of her extensive background in this area, her hourly charge is about $60 an hour. However, during trial and trial preparation, her hourly charge is usually about $70 an hour. She figures that about 40 percent of her time will be either in trial or in preparing for trial. About 10 percent of her time is spent traveling to and from trials, finding witnesses, etc. Her travel time is billed at $35 an hour. She is a very hard worker, and although she billed 1,900 last year, she is requesting that her billable hours be lowered to 1,800. You tentatively agree.

Legal assistant #2 has recently been given a new assignment: to work almost exclusively on insurance defense cases. His typical hourly billing rate was $65 an hour. However, you know that the insurance company he will be primarily working for will only pay a maximum of $52 an hour for legal assistant time. In addition, the insurance company is extremely picky about its invoices and absolutely refuses to pay for anything even remotely close to secretarial functions. The legal assistant states he thinks that 1,750 is a reasonable number of billable hours when considering his present salary. You note that, based on your experience, you figure the insurance company will either reasonably or unreasonably question about 40 hours that he bills. You reduce your estimate by this amount just to be safe.

Legal assistant #3 handles workers' compensation cases. Unfortunately, these cases are almost all taken on a contingency basis. The firm typically recovers 25 percent of these types of cases. You estimate that the firm will receive about $300,000 in revenues from this small part of its practice. You also note that about one-third of this is usually allocated to the work of the legal assistant.

Legal assistant #4 works mainly in the probate area. She typically receives about $50 per hour for her work. You note that although she billed more than 2,000 hours last year, she did not take any vacation and took very little time off. Your conversation reveals that she is going to take three weeks off for an extensive vacation and that she may need to take an additional week off for medical reasons.

Legal assistant #5 is new to the firm. From your past experience, you do not want to burn him out by putting too many billable hours on him at first. You also recognize that he will have many nonbillable hours during the first several months due to staff training and general unfamiliarity with the firm. You budget him for 1,600 hours. He will be a rover, working for many different people, and thus his hourly billing rate is hard to estimate, but you budget $45.00 an hour.

Finally legal assistant #6, yourself. You have many administrative responsibilities. You would like to set a good example, so you budget yourself at 1,400 hours. You bill at $75 per hour. You are responsible for coordinating the efforts of the legal assistants under you, for handling personnel-related issues, and many other duties. You also remember that you are to take a greater role in marketing this year and that approximately 160 hours of your time will be nonbillable handling this function.

Finally, you note that the economy may be turning down. So, you propose to lower your billable hour estimates by 10 percent. You will talk to the administrators about this.

NOTES

1. *California Lawyer,* April 2000, p. 77.
2. *The Legal Assistant's Practical Guide to Professional Responsibility,* American Bar Association, 1998, p. 92. Reprinted by permission.

CASE REVIEW

Iowa Supreme Court Board of Professional Ethics and Conduct v. Sunleaf, 588 N.W.2d 126 (1999).

588 N.W.2d 126
(Cite as: 588 N.W.2d 126)

Supreme Court of Iowa.

IOWA SUPREME COURT BOARD OF PROFESSIONAL ETHICS AND CONDUCT,

Complainant,

v.

Roger W. SUNLEAF, Respondent.

No. 98-1644.

Jan. 21, 1999.

Mark McCormick of Belin Lamson McCormick Zumbach Flynn, a P.C., Des Moines, and Roger W. Sunleaf, Montezuma, pro se, for respondent.

Considered by HARRIS, P.J., and CARTER, NEUMAN, SNELL, and TERNUS, JJ.

HARRIS, Justice.

In myriad lawyer disciplinary cases we have noted the axiom that we give respectful consideration to the sanction recommended by the grievance commission, but must reserve to ourselves the ultimate responsibility in the matter. A corollary to the axiom is that the commission's recommendation weighs most heavily in cases where the appropriate discipline is most difficult to assess. The misconduct in the present case lies at the precise boundary between suspension and public reprimand. Under the circumstances we impose the public reprimand recommended by the commission.

[1] Roger W. Sunleaf, the respondent attorney, was admitted to practice in 1963 and has concentrated on probate and personal injury cases. Our ethics board was alerted to this matter by a letter from Sunleaf's former secretary, accusing him of commingling his own funds with his clients' trust accounts. Although Sunleaf vigorously denied the charge in a letter he sent in response to an inquiry by the board, the commingling was established as true by an audit directed by our client security and disciplinary commission. Sunleaf used his trust account for the deposit of earned fees and for the payment of both personal and business expenses. He did so in order to hide funds from the federal internal revenue service which had levied on his business account for two unpaid payroll tax obligations. The commingling violated DR 9-102(A) of the Iowa *127 code of professional responsibility for lawyers.

[2] Sunleaf compounded the commingling by his letter to the board denying it, and also by certifying there was no commingling of funds on his 1997 combined statement and questionnaire to our client security and attorney disciplinary commission, a clear violation of DR 1-102(A)(4) of the Iowa code of professional responsibility for lawyers.

[3] The commission was on track in discounting the factors Sunleaf suggested in palliation for his misconduct: a personal health crisis, pressing financial problems, and a bout with alcoholism. We regularly see this trio lurking in the background of lawyer disciplinary cases, and routinely explain that, although our sympathy is frequently aroused, protection of the public interest prevents us from being swayed by them. In Committee on Professional Ethics & Conduct v. Cook, 409 N.W.2d 469, 470 (Iowa 1987), we put it this way:

> Nearly every lawyer involved in these cases could cite personal problems as the cause of the professional downfall. But life in general is a series of problems and it is the fundamental purpose of our profession to face and solve them. Our profession certainly cannot excuse misconduct on the basis of personal problems.

[4] The commission was also correct in refusing to give consideration to the motive of Sunleaf's former secretary in alerting the board to Sunleaf's misconduct. In In re Boyer, 231 Iowa 597, 600, 1 N.W.2d 707, 709 (1942), we said a complainant's motives were not a bar to disbarment. We now prefer to say that a complainant's motives are irrelevant in lawyer disciplinary cases.

The commission was prompted to its recommendation after becoming convinced this episode is an aberration, wholly out of plumb with Sunleaf's many years of practice which appear to have been honorable. His reputation for honesty was established by lawyers of unquestioned ability and discernment. Sunleaf has come to terms with his alcoholism. The audit uncovered no evidence of misappropriation of client funds. We accordingly accede to the commission's recommendation.

Roger W. Sunleaf is hereby publicly reprimanded for the misconduct hereinbefore described.

ATTORNEY REPRIMANDED.

END OF DOCUMENT

EXERCISES

1. How did substance abuse and the attorney's reputation play a part in the case?

2. Why was the court not concerned about the ill motives of the attorney's former secretary? Why did the court not dismiss these allegations of the former secretary as simply "sour grapes"?

3. The attorney's clients did not seem to be harmed by any of the attorney's activity. That is, the attorney was never even accused of misappropriating client funds. So what harm was done?

Case Review

In the Matter of Hawk, 269 Ga. 165, 496 S.E.2d 261 (1998).

496 S.E.2d 261
98 FCDR 707
(Cite as: 269 Ga. 165, 496 S.E.2d 261)

Supreme Court of Georgia.

In the Matter of Charles N. HAWK, III.

No. S98Y0774.

March 2, 1998.

Charles N. Hawk, III, Atlanta, for Charles N. Hawk, III.

George R. Reinhardt, Jr., Chairperson, Review Panel, Joel E. Dodson, Douglasville, for other interested parties.

***165** PER CURIAM

This disciplinary matter is before the Court on the special master's recommendation that Respondent Charles N. Hawk, III be disbarred for violations of disciplinary standards 4 (lawyer shall not ***166** engage in professional conduct involving dishonesty, fraud, deceit, or wilful misrepresentation); 45(b) (lawyer shall not knowingly make a false statement of law or fact); 45(e) (lawyer shall not knowingly engage in other illegal conduct or conduct contrary to a disciplinary rule); 45(f) (lawyer shall not institute, cause to be instituted or settle a legal proceeding or claim without proper authorization); 61 (lawyer shall promptly notify client of the receipt of client's funds, securities or other properties and shall promptly deliver such funds, securities or other properties to the client); 63 (lawyer shall maintain complete records of a client's properties and render appropriate accounts to the client); 65(A) (lawyer shall not commingle client's funds with his own nor fail to account for trust property); 65(D) (no personal funds shall be deposited into trust account, no funds shall be withdrawn from trust account for lawyer's personal use); and 68 (failure to respond to disciplinary ****262** authorities) of Bar Rule 4-102(d). The State Bar filed Formal Complaints against Hawk in three separate matters, which were consolidated for hearing purposes. Because Hawk failed to respond to discovery (failed to appear at depositions and failed to produce documents, despite agreeing to do so), the special master found that he intentionally or consciously failed to act as required under the discovery rules and granted the State Bar's motion for sanctions, striking Hawk's answers. Therefore, the facts alleged and violations charged in the Formal Complaints are deemed admitted. Based on those admissions, we agree with the special master that Hawk should be disbarred.

In one of the cases before the Court, Hawk represented to an insurance company representative that he still represented a client who had fired him, and he negotiated a settlement without the client's knowledge or authorization. When he received the settlement funds, Hawk deposited them into his firm's operating account based on a forged endorsement. He did not notify the client, deliver the funds to her, or account to her for the funds, despite her requests for same. In another case, Hawk failed to respond to a Notice of Investigation within the time prescribed under Bar Rule 4-204.3 and, in the last case, Hawk prepared and presented numerous checks written on his trust account that were returned for insufficient funds. He commingled trust funds with his personal funds and made personal use of the trust funds.

We agree with the special master that disbarment is warranted as a result of Hawk's violations of Standards 4, 45(b); 45(e); 45(f); 61; 63; 65(A); 65(D); and 68. We also agree that the following aggravating circumstances are present in this case: dishonest or selfish motive; multiple offenses; a pattern of misconduct; obstruction of the disciplinary process by intentionally failing to comply with the rules of the disciplinary agency; refusal to acknowledge the wrongful

*167 nature of his conduct; and substantial experience in the practice of law. See ABA Standards for Imposing Lawyer Sanctions (1991), Standard 9.22(b); (c); (d); (e); (g); and (l).

Accordingly, Hawk is disbarred from the practice of law in the state of Georgia. He is reminded of his duties under Bar Rule 4-219(c).

Disbarred.

All the Justices concur.

END OF DOCUMENT

Exercises

1. Distinguish this case from the *Sunleaf* case. What is different about the two cases?

2. List each act that the attorney did that was unethical and state why it was unethical.

Case Review

In the Matter of James A. Cleland, 2p.3d 700 (2000).

2 p.3D 700
2000 CJ C.A.R. 2672
(Cite as: 2 P.3d 700)

Supreme Court of Colorado,

En Banc.

In the Matter of James A. CLELAND, Attorney-Respondent.

No. 99SA89.

May 22, 2000.

*700 John S. Gleason, Attorney Regulation Counsel, James C. Coyle, Assistant Regulation Counsel, Denver, Colorado, Attorneys for Complainant.

No Appearance By or on Behalf of Attorney-Respondent.

PER CURIAM.

The respondent in this attorney regulation case, James A. Cleland, admitted that he knowingly misappropriated funds belonging to his clients. We have consistently held that disbarment is the appropriate sanction for this type of misconduct, unless significant extenuating circumstances are present. No such circumstances exist in this case. Nevertheless, a hearing panel of our former grievance committee [FN1] accepted the findings and recommendation of a hearing board that Cleland should be suspended for three years, rather than disbarred. The complainant filed exceptions to the findings and recommendation, contending that Cleland should be disbarred. On review, we determine that certain of the board's findings are clearly erroneous, and we disagree with some of its legal conclusions. On the other hand, we agree with the complainant that disbarment is the only appropriate sanction in this case. Accordingly, we reject the panel's and board's recommendations and we order that Cleland be disbarred, effective immediately.

FN1. By order of the supreme court dated June 30, 1998, effective January 1, 1999, the grievance committee was superseded by the reorganization of the attorney regulation system. The same order provided: "All attorney discipline cases in which trial has occurred prior to January 1, 1999 before a Hearing Board . . . shall be reviewed by the applicable Hearing Panel at a final meeting to be held in 1999. . . ." Order re Reorganization of the Attorney Regulation System (Colo. June 30, 1998), reprinted in 12 C.R.S. at 605 (1999). This case was tried on April 29, 1998, and was reviewed by the hearing panel on February 20, 1999.

I.

James A. Cleland was first licensed to practice law in Colorado in 1989.

2 P.3d 700

(Cite as: 2 P.3d 700, *700)

[FN2] The amended complaint contained six counts. Count I charged Cleland with commingling his personal funds with a client's funds, knowingly mishandling contested funds, and knowingly misappropriating funds belonging to the client. Count II alleged that Cleland ***701** knowingly misappropriated $5000 of his client's funds to reimburse a third party for an earnest money deposit that Cleland was supposed to have held in trust. Count III of the complaint charged that Cleland consistently mismanaged his trust account from September 1995 to February 1996. Count IV alleged that Cleland unilaterally charged his client interest on past-due attorney's fees, without the client's authorization. In Count V, the complainant asserted that Cleland had failed to file a collection matter for a client; that he failed to keep the client reasonably informed about the status of the matter; and that he misrepresented that he had settled the case when in fact he had not. Finally, Count VI charged Cleland with making misrepresentations to one of the complainant's investigators and a paralegal during the investigation of Count V. [FN3]

> FN2. In an unrelated attorney regulation matter heard after the hearing panel acted in this case, the presiding disciplinary judge and hearing board suspended Cleland for two years, effective October 18, 1999. See In re Cleland, No. GC98B118, slip op. at 14 (Colo. PDJ Sept. 17, 1999).

FN3. The hearing board found that the charges in Count VI had not been proven by clear and convincing evidence. The complainant did not except to this finding; we therefore dismiss Count VI and do not discuss it further.

The evidence before the hearing board consisted of the testimony of the complainant's and respondent's witnesses (including Cleland himself), documents, and a stipulation of facts contained in the trial management order the parties submitted. As the facts are sometimes complex, we address each count of the complaint separately, together with the hearing board's findings and conclusions pertaining to that count.

A. Count I—The Kasnoff Funds

Cleland represented George M. Kasnoff Jr. and his various business entities. In 1994, however, Cleland and Kasnoff had a disagreement over the attorney's fees Kasnoff owed Cleland. One of the business entities involved was Kas-Don Enterprises, Inc., which was owned by Kasnoff and Don Shank. Kasnoff and Shank decided to dissolve Kas-Don in the summer of 1995, Shank agreed to buy out Kasnoff's interest in the real estate the corporation owned. Cleland was to prepare the documents that were necessary to transfer the property and to terminate Kas-Don. This was completed in August 1995 and the corporation was dissolved.

Because he was on his honeymoon in Europe on the closing date, Kasnoff made arrangements for Cleland to deposit the net proceeds from the closing into Cleland's trust account. The parties agreed that once the funds were in the trust account, they would be disbursed for certain business expenses. In addition, Kasnoff authorized Cleland to pay himself $5000 for past attorney's fees. Cleland was to deposit the balance of the funds in Kasnoff's bride's bank account.

On August 16, 1995, Cleland deposited proceeds from the closing in the amount of $16,576.56 into his trust account. With his client's permission, Cleland paid certain business expenses that Kasnoff owed with funds from the trust account. On August 17, 1995, Cleland asked Kasnoff to pay attorney's fees over and above the $5000 that Kasnoff had agreed to pay. Kasnoff did not authorize any additional sums to be taken out. Nevertheless, Cleland paid himself an additional $4581.94 for legal services, including $600 for fees that had not yet been earned. Cleland deposited these unauthorized funds into his operating account and used them for his own purposes. When Kasnoff called from Europe on August 16, Cleland told him that he had deposited the balance of the funds (including the $4581.94 he had paid himself without permission) into Kasnoff's wife's bank account. This was untrue.

The hearing board found that Kasnoff frequently paid the attorney's fees he owed Cleland slowly. Cleland also reasonably believed that Kasnoff was in financial difficulties. The exact amount of attorney's fees that Kasnoff owed was in dispute even at the hearing (although after these disciplinary proceedings were underway, Cleland returned the clearly unearned $600 in fees through his lawyer). The hearing board also found that at the time he paid himself the unauthorized funds, Cleland was under considerable financial and personal pressure, and that he was clinically depressed.

The board concluded that Cleland's conduct violated Colo. RPC 1.15(a) (failing to keep the client's property—in this case, the $4581.94—separate from the lawyer's own *702 property), and 1.15(c) (failing to hold separate any property that the lawyer and another—in this case, the client—both claim an interest in). The board found, however, that the complainant did not prove by clear and convincing evidence that Cleland violated Colo. RPC 8.4(c) (engaging in conduct involving dishonesty, fraud, deceit, or misrepresentation). The complainant did not specifically complain about this finding in his opening brief, and we find it unnecessary to address it.

B. Count II—The Clearly Colorado Matter

On June 19, 1995, about two months before Kas-Don was dissolved, Clearly Colorado, L.L.C. entered into a contract with Kasnoff to purchase the latter's one-half interest in Kas-Don real estate. The contract provided that Clearly Colorado would pay a $5000 earnest money deposit, and that this would be held in Cleland's trust account. After receiving the $5000, Cleland used the trust funds for his own use. This was not authorized. [FN4] The real estate transaction fell through and Clearly Colorado demanded the return of its $5000 deposit. Because he had already diverted the trust funds, however, the balance in Cleland's trust account on August 3, 1995, was only $66.40. Nevertheless, on August 15, 1995, Cleland wrote a $5000 check drawn on his trust account as a refund to Clearly Colorado. This $5000 was paid from the proceeds of the Kas-Don transaction referred to in Count I above.

> FN4. It is unclear why Cleland was not charged with initially misappropriating this $5000 from his trust account.

The board concluded that Cleland knowingly misappropriated client funds to reimburse Clearly Colorado in violation of Colo. RPC 8.4(c) (engaging in conduct involving dishonesty, fraud, deceit, or misrepresentation).

C. Count III—Commingling and Misappropriation

Count II details numerous transactions that Cleland engaged in with respect to client funds and his trust account. For our purposes here, it is sufficient to note that Cleland admitted to commingling his own funds with those belonging to his clients in his trust account and that he knowingly misappropriated client funds without the authorization or knowledge of the clients affected. [FN5]

> FN5. The board did find that client funds belonging to Donna Nazario were transferred to Cleland's operating account by mistake, and thus did not constitute commingling or misappropriation.

In particular, the hearing board found that Cleland: (1) knowingly misappropriated $1376.95 of client funds from his trust account to repay another client; (2) commingled personal funds with client funds in his trust account on numerous occasions between November 1995 and August 1996; and (3) disbursed trust account funds belonging to various clients to other clients, without the authorization or knowledge of the clients affected. The board thus concluded that Cleland's conduct violated Colo. RPC 8.4(c).

D. Count IV—Kasnoff Interest

Without his client's consent or agreement, Cleland charged interest on Kasnoff's past-due accounts. The board found that this practice violated Colo. RPC 1.5(a) (charging an unreasonable fee), and 8.4(c) (conduct involving dishonesty).

E. Count V—Robin Caspari

Robin Caspari hired Cleland to prosecute a landlord-tenant dispute, and gave him $91 to file suit against two tenants for past-due rent. The hearing board concluded that Cleland failed to keep Caspari reasonably informed about the status of the matter, in violation of Colo. RPC 1.4(a). In addition, Cleland told the client, falsely, that he had filed an action against one of the tenants, when he had not; that hearings had been set and orders had been entered in the case, when in fact there was no case; and that he had settled the matter with one of the clients for $600 which he then paid to the client. The $600 was actually from Cleland's personal funds. This conduct violated Colo. RPC 1.3 (neglecting a legal matter), and 8.4(c) (engaging in dishonest conduct).

*703 II.

[1] The hearing panel approved the hearing board's recommendation that Cleland be suspended for three years, with conditions. The complainant filed exceptions, claiming that certain of the board's factual and legal conclusions were erroneous, and that the appropriate disciplinary sanction was disbarment. The key to the appropriate discipline is also the most serious misconduct here - the knowing misappropriation of client funds in Counts II and III.

[2] As we have said numerous times before, disbarment is the presumed sanction when a lawyer knowingly misappropriates funds belonging to a client or a third person. "When a lawyer knowingly converts client funds, disbarment is 'virtually automatic,' at least in the absence of significant factors in mitigation." People v. Young, 864 P.2d 563, 564 (Colo.1993) (knowing misappropriation of clients' funds warrants disbarment even absent prior disciplinary history and despite cooperation and making restitution); see also In re Thompson, 991 P.2d 820, 823 (Colo.1999) (disbarring lawyer who knowingly misappropriated law firm funds); People v. Varallo, 913 P.2d 1, 12 (Colo. 1996) (disbarring lawyer who knowingly misappropriated client funds); People v. Ogborn, 887 P.2d 21, 23 (Colo.1994) (misappropriating client funds warrants disbarment even in absence of prior discipline and presence of personal and emotional problems); People v. Robbins, 869 P.2d 517, 518 (Colo.1994) (converting client trust funds warrants disbarment even if funds are restored before clients learn they are missing but not before the conversion is discovered by the lawyer's law firm).

[3] Consistent with our approach, the ABA Standards for Imposing Lawyer Sanctions (1991 & Supp.1992) provides that, in the absence of mitigating circumstances, "[d]isbarment is generally appropriate when a lawyer knowingly converts client property and causes injury or potential injury to a client." Id. at 4.11. Neither this standard nor our cases require serious injury before disbarment is appropriate. On the other hand, "[s]uspension is generally appropriate when a lawyer knows or should know that he is dealing improperly with client property and causes injury or potential injury to a client." Id. at 4.12.

The hearing board found that the following aggravating and mitigating factors were present. In aggravation, Cleland has prior discipline in the form of a letter of admonition for neglecting a legal matter, see id. at 9.22(a); and multiple offenses are present, see id. at 9.22(d). The board also determined that there was a pattern of misconduct, see id. at 9.22(c), but only with respect to Cleland's "continuing recklessness and gross negligence in management of his trust account from approximately mid-1995 to mid-August 1996."

According to the board, mitigating factors included the absence of a dishonest motive or intention on Cleland's part, see id. at 9.32(b); Cleland admitted that he committed some of the misconduct and otherwise cooperated in the proceedings, see id. at 9.32(e), Cleland was relatively inexperienced in the practice of law, see id. at 9.32(f); and he has expressed remorse, see id. at 9.32(1). Additional mitigating factors found were the presence of personal financial and emotional problems, see id. at 9.32(c); and a timely good faith effort to rectify the consequences of at least part of his misconduct, see id. at 9.32(d). The board noted that Cleland was diagnosed with a depressive disorder that impaired his judgment, concentration, and thinking. The conclusion that Cleland tried to rectify some of the consequences of his misconduct stems from the board's belief that he offered to arbitrate the fee dispute with Kasnoff before he was aware that he was under investigation.

While acknowledging our statement in Varallo, 913 P.2d at 12, that disbarment is the presumed sanction when knowing misappropriation is shown, the board declined to apply what it deemed such a "bright-line" rule to the facts in this case. In particular, the hearing board cited three cases that we decided after Varallo that it believed contradicted a literal reading of the case: People v. Zimmermann, 922 P.2d 325 (Colo.1996); People v. Reynolds, 933 P.2d 1295 (Colo.1997); and People v. Schaefer, 938 P.2d 147 *704 (Colo.1997). However, these cases did not modify Varallo's "bright-line" rule. [FN6]

> FN6. The virtue of a bright-line rule like this one is not that it is easy to apply, although it is. Rather, such a rule strives to eliminate the disparate treatment of lawyers who have committed serious misconduct, when the unequal treatment may otherwise be based on invidious and irrelevant factors.

We decided Zimmermann three months after Varallo. The respondent in Zimmermann, John Delos Zimmermann, seriously mismanaged the funds in his trust account. He commingled funds that should have been placed in his trust account with funds that should have been deposited in his operating account; he improperly used clients' funds to pay his personal or business expenses; and refunded unearned attorney's fees to clients from funds advanced by different clients. See 922 P.2d at 326-29. We suspended Zimmermann for one year and one day. See id. at 330. Zimmermann's misconduct is similar to that charged in Count III of the complaint in this case, with one important exception. That exception serves to distinguish Zimmermann from this case, however, in the same way that we distinguished Zimmermann from Varallo. We stated that:

> The single most important factor in determining the appropriate level of discipline in this case is whether [Zimmermann's] misappropriation of client funds was knowing, in which case disbarment is the presumed sanction, People v. Varallo, 913 P.2d 1, 12 (Colo.1996), or whether it was reckless, or merely negligent, suggesting that a period of suspension is adequate. People v. Dickinson, 903 P.2d 1132, 1138 (Colo.1995).

Zimmermann, 922 P.2d at 329 (emphasis added). However, the hearing board specifically found that Zimmermann's mental state when he was mismanaging his trust account was one of recklessness. See id. We noted that although the evidence before the board would have supported a finding that Zimmermann's conduct was knowing, rather than reckless, the board's conclusion found support in the record and we would not overturn it. See id. at 329 n. 1. Zimmermann therefore stands for the same proposition as Varallo—the lawyer's actual mental state is the most significant factor for determining the proper discipline. Because the board found that Zimmermann's mental state when he mismanaged his trust and operating accounts was reckless, not knowing, Dickinson (suspension) governed the result, not Varallo (disbarment).

We suspended the respondent in People v. Reynolds, 933 P.2d 1295 (Colo.1997), for three years. John Kerz Reynolds engaged in an extensive pattern of "neglect of client matters, misrepresentations to clients, dishonesty, misuse of client funds, and assisting a nonlawyer in the unauthorized practice of law." Id. at 1305. He also failed to account for, or return, unearned advance fees he received from various clients. See id. at 1296-1301. The case did not involve the knowing misappropriation of client funds, however. Reynolds was not charged with misappropriation, nor did the hearing board in that case make any findings on the issue. Reynolds is therefore distinguishable.

Finally, in People v. Schaefer, 938 P.2d 147 (Colo.1997), we suspended Richard A. Schaefer for two years. Citing Zimmermann and Varallo, we concluded that "[t]he hearing board's determination that [Schaefer's] mishandling of his client's funds was negligent rather than intentional is not clearly erroneous and we will not overturn it." Id. at 150. Schaefer is thus completely consistent with Varallo.

The present case cannot be distinguished from Varallo. In two separate counts, Cleland admitted, and the hearing board found, that he knowingly misappropriated client funds. The board erred when it did not just accept Cleland's admissions and its own initial findings, and then go on to determine whether the factors in mitigation were weighty enough to justify a sanction less than disbarment. Because there is no evidence in the record that supports the conclusion that Cleland's mental state was merely reckless or negligent, that finding is clearly erroneous, and we reject it.

Having determined that disbarment is the presumed sanction in this case, we must now independently review the record with an eye *705 towards the factors in mitigation. The hearing board first found that Cleland did not have a dishonest motive or intention when he committed the misconduct. As the complainant points out, this is directly contrary to the stipulation and a large part of the evidence. The hearing board specifically concluded that Cleland engaged in conduct involving dishonesty, fraud, deceit, or misrepresentation in Counts II (knowing misappropriation of client funds), III (knowing misappropriation of client funds), IV (unilaterally charging unauthorized interest), and V (misrepresenting the status of a case and that it had settled), in violation of Colo. RPC 8.4(c). The fact that Cleland may not have had a dishonest motive in every single instance of misconduct does not demonstrate that the mitigating factor exists. We reject this as a mitigating factor.

Next, the board found that Cleland's admissions of misconduct and his cooperative attitude in the proceedings were mitigating factors. See ABA Standards, supra, at 9.32(e). We agree that these constitute bona fide mitigating circumstances, but we accord them little ultimate weight, given Cleland's failure to appear and participate in this court, and his noncooperation and default in the proceedings before the PDJ for the misconduct (similar to that in this case because it involved mismanagement of trust funds) that earned him a two-year suspension. The reason we consider mitigating factors at all is so we may gauge the level of danger that an attorney poses to the public and, ideally, to arrive at a disciplinary sanction that adequately balances the seriousness of the danger against the gravity of the misconduct.

Although Cleland's cooperation before the hearing board warrants some consideration, we are troubled by his later noncooperation, and feel that this does not bode well for Cleland's future as a lawyer.

The board also considered Cleland's relative inexperience in the practice of law as a mitigating factor. It is such a factor; but inexperience does not go far in our view to excuse or to mitigate dishonesty, misrepresentation, or misappropriation. Little experience in the practice of law is necessary to appreciate such actual wrongdoing. On the other hand, Cleland's expressions of remorse are mitigating, as the board found. See id. at 9.32(l).

The hearing board also considered that the personal, financial, and emotional problems that Cleland was experiencing were mitigating. See id. at 9.32(c). Specifically, the board noted that Cleland had been diagnosed with a depressive disorder that impaired his judgment, concentration, and thinking. However, we deem it worthy of note that, despite the advice of the psychiatrist who testified for him, Cleland had not sought treatment for the disorder. Moreover, we reject the proposition that Cleland's financial difficulties mitigate his misappropriation of client funds in any way. Finally, the board found that by offering to arbitrate the fee dispute with Kasnoff, Cleland made some effort to rectify the consequences of at least part of his misconduct. See id. at 9.32(d). Despite the fact that Cleland's clients may not have suffered significant actual damages, as the hearing board found (a point that is debatable given the record in this case), the potential for injury was nevertheless substantial.

Taking all of the above factors into consideration, we conclude that they are not significant enough to call for any result other than disbarment. However, two members of the court disagree and would approve the recommendation to suspend Cleland for three years. Accordingly, we reject the board's and panel's recommendation, and we order that Cleland be disbarred.

III.

We hereby order that James A. Cleland be disbarred, effective immediately. Should Cleland ever seek readmission to practice law pursuant to C.R.C.P. 251.29, he must first demonstrate that he has complied with the following conditions:

(1) Cleland must pay George M. Kasnoff Jr. any amount awarded in Kasnoff's favor in the fee arbitration proceedings between Cleland and Kasnoff;

(2) Cleland must pay the costs incurred in this proceeding in the amount of $2,188.73, to the Attorney Regulation *706 Committee, 600 Seventeenth Street, Suite 200 South, Denver, Colorado 80202.

END OF DOCUMENT

EXERCISES

1. Why did the Court disagree with the board's findings that the attorney should only be suspended for three years and instead find that the attorney should be disbarred?

2. Why do you think the attorney requested disbarment?

3. How did the attorney "consistently mismanage" his trust account?

4. In the Kasnoff matter (Count I), why could the attorney not place the $600 of unearned fees in his operating account?

5. How did the attorney complicate matters by writing a check in *The Clearly Colorado Matter* (Count II) for $5,000 when there was only $66.40 in the account at the time? Apparently, the check cashed because another deposit was made. Where did this money come from?

6. In the Robin Caspari matter (Count V), what was wrong with the attorney's taking the $600 from his own personal account, as a client actually received a benefit and no client was harmed?

7. When considering mitigation, was the court persuaded by the fact that the attorney had been diagnosed with a depressive disorder that impaired his judgment, concentration, and thinking? Why or why not?

Calendaring, Docket Control, and Case Management

CHAPTER OBJECTIVES

After you read this chapter, you will be able to:

- Explain how to make docketing entries.
- Discuss how to calculate court deadlines.
- Explain why a poor docket system is harmful to a law office.
- Differentiate between manual and computerized docket systems.
- Explain how a poor docket control system leads to ethical and malpractice claims.

A client sued his former attorney (and the attorney's partners) for legal malpractice for failing to timely file a medical malpractice claim. In October the client met with a Michigan attorney regarding a claim against a hospital for medical malpractice. After the initial meetings, the client made repeated telephone calls and sent letters to the attorney. However, the attorney never responded to the client's communications. Eighteen months later, the attorney finally responded. The client received a letter from the attorney.

My sincere apologies for the delay in responding to your earlier communications; however, we have been making a thorough inquiry into the facts of your alleged complaints. We have not been able to find an expert to make the appropriate causal relationship to support our theories of possible malpractice. Accordingly, we are not going to be proceeding on your claim and will close our file.

Within two weeks, the client sought the advice of another attorney and filed a legal malpractice claim against the first attorney. A jury awarded the client $150,000 in damages against the attorney for allowing the statute of limitations on the medical malpractice claim to lapse.[1]

CALENDARING, DOCKET CONTROL, AND CASE MANAGEMENT DEFINITIONS

The practice of law is filled with appointments, deadlines, hearings, and other commitments for every case that is handled. It is extremely important that these dates be carefully tracked for legal ethical reasons, customer service reasons and general business reasons. Most, but not all legal organizations track these deadlines by computer. This chapter introduces calendaring, docket control, and case management. These terms are somewhat confusing and are often used interchangeably.

Calendaring is typically a generic term used to describe the recording of appointments for any type of business. For example, an accounting or engineering firm might use a generic calendaring or scheduling form that comes with an office suite of software programs to track their appointments.

calendaring
Typically a generic term that is used to describe the function of recording appointments for any type of business.

Docket control is typically a law office specific term that refers to entering, organizing, and controlling all the appointments, deadlines, and due dates for a legal organization. There are many legal specific software programs and manual systems that perform docket control functions for law offices, corporate law departments, and government law departments.

Case management is also a law office specific term, but it always means more than just tracking dates. Case management usually refers to docket control (e.g., controlling and tracking appointments and deadlines) and other related functions, such as tracking the names and addresses of clients, attorneys, and court contacts by case; tracking other case information (e.g., the causes of action alleged by the claim or the amount sued for); and merging names, addresses, and case information into word processing documents. A final term that is sometimes used to describe docket control is *tickler* because it "tickles" the memory for upcoming events.

> As a paralegal, how can you accommodate each client individually, while still effectively handling the many demands competing for your time? How can you better organize your work to prevent rush jobs? How can you promptly take care of the little things to keep a case or file moving forward—and still keep the client and yourself content? One of the best ways to achieve your goals is to invest your time and energy in a tickler [docket control] system.[2]

In many law offices, legal assistants operate the docket control system for the whole office, while in others, legal assistants only use the system to manage and track cases. Although the calendaring and docketing subject may seem trivial at first, the examples of dire consequences resulting from docketing system failures at the beginning of this chapter should indicate the grave nature and importance of this subject. Thus, it is critical for the legal assistant to know how to use docket control so that important deadlines are tracked and kept.

APPOINTMENTS

During the course of a case or legal matter, a legal professional will have many appointments: meetings with clients and co-counsel, witness interviews, interoffice meetings, and so forth. Keeping appointments is very important. Law offices that must constantly reschedule appointments with clients may find their clients going to other attorneys who provide better service. The concept of rescheduling appointments or legal deadlines is often called getting a **continuance** (e.g., the deposition was continued because the witness was sick).

docket control
A law office specific term that refers to entering, organizing, and controlling all the appointments, deadlines, and due dates for a legal organization.

case management
Usually refers to docket control (e.g., controlling and tracking appointments and deadlines) and also other related functions such as tracking the names and addresses of clients, attorneys, and court contacts by case; tracking other case information; merging names, addresses, and case information into word processing documents.

continuance
Rescheduling an appointment or court date.

DEADLINES AND REMINDERS

The practice of law is filled with deadlines at practically every stage of a legal matter. One of the most important types of deadlines is a statute of limitations. A **statute of limitations** is a statute or law that sets a limit on the length of time a party has to file a suit. For instance, some states impose a five-year statute of limitations on lawsuits alleging a breach of a written contract. That is, if a lawsuit is brought or filed more than five years after a contract is breached or broken, the lawsuit is barred by the statute, and a court will dismiss the action. The purpose of a statute of limitations is to force parties to bring lawsuits in a timely fashion so that evidence is not destroyed, or before witnesses leave the area, and so forth. If an attorney allows a statute of limitations to run, or expire, without filing a case he or she may be liable for legal malpractice.

There also are many deadlines that are set after a case has been filed. In some courts, the judge and the attorneys on both sides sit down and schedule a list of deadlines that the case must follow. The schedule may look something like the one shown in Figure 7-1. These deadlines must be tracked and adhered to. An attorney who does not adhere to the deadlines may cause the case to be dismissed or may be penalized. Some courts are very reluctant to continue deadlines once they have been set.

Because attorneys and legal assistants are busy, usually working on many cases, the law office must have a system of tracking upcoming deadlines. This is done not only by calendaring the deadline itself but also by creating reminder notices in the calendar so that a deadline does not catch a person by surprise. These reminders also are called warnings. For example, in Figure 7-1, regarding the January 30 motion to dismiss, the attorney or legal assistant may want to be reminded thirty, fifteen, and five days before the deadline. Therefore, reminder notices would be made on January 1, January 15, and January 25, in addition to the deadline itself being

statute of limitations
A statute or law that sets a limit on the length of time a party has to file a suit. If a case is filed after the statute of limitations, the claim is barred and is dismissed as a matter of law.

Figure 7-1
A Typical Case Schedule

Deadline Item	Deadline Date
All Motions to Dismiss must be filed by:	Jan. 30
Responses to Motions to Dismiss must be filed by:	Mar. 1
Discovery (depositions, interrogatories, request for production) to be completed by:	Dec. 20
Summary Judgment Motions to be filed by:	Feb. 1
Responses to Summary Judgment Motions to be filed by:	Mar. 1
Pretrial order to be filed by:	June 1
Settlement Conferences to be completed by:	June 30
Pretrial Motions to be completed and decided by:	July 15
Trial to start no later than:	Sept. 1

recorded on January 30. It is common for an attorney or legal assistant to request from one to four reminders for each deadline. If reminders are not entered in the docket system, it may make it hard to meet the deadline. Thus, logging reminder notices of upcoming events is crucial to the effective practice of law.

Some deadlines are automatically set by the rules of procedure that are in effect in any given court. Rules of procedure are court rules that govern and tell parties what procedures they must follow when bringing and litigating cases. For instance, in some courts, the rules of procedure hold that after a final decision in a case has been rendered, all parties have thirty days after that to file an appeal.

For a law office that practices in the tax area, April 15, the date that federal income tax returns are due, is an example of an automatic or procedural deadline that must be tracked. Thus, this automatic or procedural deadline must be tracked by the office's docket system and appropriate reminders must be made so that returns are not filed late and penalties assessed.

> *Docket control is not just a "secretarial" function. The importance of working closely with the secretarial staff in calendaring and docketing matters cannot be stressed enough. In litigation firms, one of the legal assistant's primary responsibilities is tracking deadlines relating to timeliness of pleadings, discovery requests, interrogatories and answers, mediation statements, pretrial requirements, timely notification and service regarding discovery and trial subpoenas. All deadlines, dates, and appointments should be maintained on one central calendar (preferably computerized) for each attorney. This calendar should be accessible by the attorney, the secretary, and the legal assistant. All three should be cognizant of all deadlines, depositions, appointments, meetings, and hearings. All three should review upcoming deadlines and docket (tickler) notes on a daily basis.*
>
> Lenette Pinchback, CLA

HEARINGS AND COURT DATES

Hearings and court dates are formal proceedings before a court. It is extremely important that these dates be carefully tracked. Most courts have little tolerance for attorneys who fail to show up for court. In some instances, the attorney can be fined or disciplined for missing court dates.

In larger cases, especially when the case is being litigated in court, there may be hundreds of entries into the docket system. Figure 7-2 includes a list of common docket entries, including both substantive and law office management-related entries.

**Figure 7-2
Common Docket
Control Entries**

- Expiration dates for statutes of limitations
- Judgment renewal dates
- Employee-benefit annual filings
- Renewal dates for copyrights, trademarks, and patents
- Renewal dates for leases and licenses
- Renewal dates for insurance coverage
- Trial court appearance dates
- Due dates for trial court briefs
- Due dates on various pleadings: answers; depositions; replies to interrogatories and requests for admissions; various motions and notices, etc.
- Due dates in probate proceedings such as inventory and appraisal dates
- Appearances in bankruptcy proceedings
- Action dates in commercial law matters
- Due dates in corporate or security matters
- Closing dates for real estate transactions
- Due dates for appellate briefs and arguments
- Tax return due dates
- Due dates in estate matters such as tax return dates, valuation dates, and hearing dates
- Dates of stockholder meetings
- Dates of board of directors meetings
- Review dates for wills
- Review dates for buy and sell valuations of business interests
- Review dates for trusts
- Renewal dates for lease on offices
- Renewal dates for attorney licenses
- Expiration dates on notary certificates
- Renewal dates for malpractice and other insurance
- Personal property tax return dates
- Dates for partners (and other recurring and nonrecurring) meetings
- Review dates for billings and accounts receivable
- Review dates for work-in-process
- Review dates for evaluation of associates and staff
- Review dates for raises and bonuses
- Quarterly payroll withholding reports due

Receiving Documents, Following Court Rules, and Calculating Deadlines

Receiving documents that need to be calendared, calculating deadlines, and following the local court rules are important aspects of docket control.

RECEIVING DOCUMENTS

It is important when documents come in the mail, e-mail, or otherwise that response dates and other deadlines be immediately and systematically entered in the law office's docket system. For example, pleadings, motions, discovery documents, and other documents that need to be responded to within a certain time period should be immediately entered in the office's system.

Suppose your office received interrogatories (i.e., written questions that your client must complete and send back) for one of your clients in the mail. Also, suppose in the particular court where the suit is filed, interrogatory responses must be answered within thirty calendar days from the date they are received. It is important when the interrogatories are received by the mail department or whoever opens the mail that the documents with calendar entries be routed immediately to someone who has the responsibility to record the deadlines in the docket control system. If there is confusion as to whose responsibility it is to enter the calendar item or confusion as to when the documents should be calendared (i.e. no systematic system), there is an excellent chance the calendar dates will not be entered in the docket system. If that happens, it is virtually guaranteed that deadlines, response dates, etc., will be missed and ethical problems will follow.

KNOW THE LOCAL COURT RULES

It is imperative to know the local court rules for each court your office has cases in. Even courts in the same state can have vastly different rules depending on the internal operating procedure of each court.

CALCULATING DEADLINES

Calculating deadlines depends on the local rules. However, the following are some of the different ways that deadlines can be calculated and some problems that may arise in making calculations.

CALENDAR DAYS V. WORKDAYS Some courts make a distinction between calendar days and workdays. For example, if a court rule says that a party responding to a motion has fifteen days from the file date to file a response, you need to know if the fifteen days refers to all days (i.e., calendar days) or only to workdays.

calendar days
System for calculating deadlines that counts all days including weekends and holidays.

When calculating deadlines, **calendar days** typically mean literal days, counting all days including weekends and holidays. For example, if a motion is filed on the 1st and you have fifteen calendar days to respond, the response must be filed by Tuesday the 16th. When you count days, you count from one day to the next. For example, the 1st to the 2d is one day, the 2d to the 3d is two days, and so on. So, you actually start your count on the next day after you receive it. When using the calendar-day method, a deadline may fall on a Saturday or Sunday. In many courts, the due date would simply be the Monday after the Saturday or Sunday. If the deadline falls on a holiday, the deadline is typically the next day the court is open for business.

workdays
System for calculating deadlines that refers to only days when the court is open.

When calculating deadlines, **workdays** typically refer to only days when the court is open. Because courts usually are not open on holidays and weekends, these days are omitted from the calculation. For example, if a motion is filed on the 1st and you have fifteen workdays to respond, and assuming the 1st is a Monday (with no holidays in between), the response would be due on Monday the 22d (see Figure 7-3).

Monday	Tuesday	Wednesday	Thursday	Friday	Saturday	Sunday
1 Motion filed	**2**	**3**	**4**	**5**	**6**	**7**
8	**9**	**10**	**11**	**12**	**13**	**14**
15	**16** Response Due if 15 Calendar Days	**17**	**18**	**19**	**20**	**21**
22 Response Due if 15 Work Days						

Sample Event:
Motion filed on 1st
Motion filed on 1st

Number of days:
15 Calendar Days
15 Work Days

Due Date:
Tuesday, 16th
Monday, 22nd

Figure 7-3 Calendar for Calculating Calendar Days and Workdays Example

As you can see, it is important that you know whether the court rules are figured on calendar days or workdays because there is a big difference between the two.

FILE DATE V. DOCUMENT RECEIPT DATE

Typically court rules will state when deadlines are. Deadlines can be calculated either on the date the person actually receives the document or on the date when the document is actually stamped "FILED" at the clerk's office.

FILE DATE   A typical court rule may state for a civil action that a party has thirty days from when the judgment is "FILED" to file an appeal. Assume the court files a judgment on the 1st and that the party receives the judgment on the 3d. The deadline is calculated from the file date, and if there were thirty days in the month, the appeal would have to be filed by the 1st of the next month.

DOCUMENT RECEIPT DATE   Discovery document deadlines typically are calculated by receipt date. For example, a typical court rule may state that a party has thirty days to answer interrogatories. This is usually calculated when the document is actually received by the law office needing to respond to them. So, if the document was mailed on the 1st and actually received on the 3d, then the party has until the 4th of the next month to send his responses to the opposing side. Thus, it can be very important for the law office to establish when a document was received. All law offices should routinely stamp all documents that come into the office with a received stamp that shows the date the document was received (e.g., "RECEIVED 10/1/2003").

In addition, typically when a party prepares a court document in a case there is a **"Certificate of Service"** at the very end of the document. The purpose of the "Certificate of Service" is to certify and establish when the document was placed in the mail. The "Certificate of Service" must also be signed. This way, the clerk of the court and the parties know when a document was placed in the mails.

Also, a **"Bates stamp"** is sometimes used to number every page of a document. A "Bates stamp" stamps a document with a sequential number and then automatically advances to the next number. In this way, it is possible to establish the order of every page in a document, particularly large documents such as those that have been produced for evidence.

DUE DATE——FILE DATE V. MAIL DATE

It is important when reading court rules to know whether documents can be mailed in or if they must be actually "FILED" within the specified deadline. For example, assume you receive a document on the 1st and the court rule says you have twenty days to respond. Thus, the response would be due on the 21st. In some courts it is acceptable to put the response in the mail on the 21st. That is, you do not actually have to get the document stamped "FILED" on the 21st. Some courts automatically give you three days' mail time before they say the document is late. Different courts have different rules; again, be sure you know if due dates are calculated on file dates or mail dates. This distinction becomes more important in rural areas.

Certificate of Service
A statement at the end of a court document that certifies or establishes when a document was placed in the mail.

Bates stamp
Stamps a document with a sequential number and then automatically advances to the next number.

ETHICAL AND MALPRACTICE CONSIDERATIONS

The ramifications of missing deadlines and otherwise failing to track the progress of cases can be severe. In fact, there are two types of negative outcomes that can result from case neglect: an ethical proceeding against the attorney and a legal malpractice claim filed against the attorney or firm. An attorney who neglects a case can be disciplined by a state ethics board. Such discipline in an ethics case may include reprimand, suspension, or even disbarment. In a legal malpractice case, the attorney involved is sued for damages for providing substandard legal work. These types of cases are not remote or obscure. There are thousands of legal ethics and malpractice proceedings filed throughout the country every year alleging case neglect.

ETHICAL CONSIDERATIONS

A recent nationwide statistical study of attorney disciplinary opinions by *West's Legal News* found that the number one and two reasons that clients file disciplinary proceedings against attorneys and that courts discipline attorneys are (1) attorneys failing to communicate with their clients and (2) attorneys neglecting or not pursuing client cases diligently. This confirms what studies have shown since the early 1980s. Both of these problems are easily preventable when attorneys and legal assistants use good docket control systems and effective time management.

The *ABA Model Rules of Professional Conduct* give direct guidance on these issues. The *Model Rules* state that attorneys should be competent in the area they are practicing in and that they be reasonably prepared to represent the client. The *Model Rules* state that the attorney must act with reasonable diligence and promptness when representing a client, and, finally, the *Model Rules* state that an attorney must keep the client reasonably informed with what is going on in the representation of the client. While these ethical rules have been discussed in previous chapters, it is important to include them again in the context of docket control because it is through docket control and organization that a legal professional complies with these rules. It is important to note that the Ethics 2000 Commission is not recommending any changes to these rules. Each of these areas is explored in detail.

COMPETENCE AND ADEQUATE PREPARATION The *Model Rules* hold that an attorney must be competent to represent the client. That is, that he or she reasonably know the area of law that the client needs representation in and, assuming the attorney does know the area of law, that he or she take the preparation time to become familiar with the case to represent the client adequately. *Model Rule* 1.1 states:

> Rule 1.1 Competence
> A lawyer shall provide competent representation to a client. Competent representation requires the legal knowledge, skill, thoroughness, <u>and preparation</u> reasonably necessary for the representation.[3]

The purpose of this rule is to ensure that an attorney does not undertake a matter that he or she is not competent in and to ensure that the attorney has had adequate preparation. The amount of "adequate preparation" depends on what type of legal matter the client has. Major litigation, for example, will require far more preparation time than the amount of time it takes to prepare a will. The point is that attorneys should not undertake to represent a client if for some reason they cannot do it with the skill and preparation time necessary. Legal professionals use docket control systems to plan adequate preparation time for cases.

> *At one point in time, because we were so busy—we were in the process of bringing on another person for clerical support—we missed a deadline for filing [a] response to requests for admissions. . . . We did file a motion to approve an extension of time in order to file [a response], and we were granted that . . . but had that not been the case, the admission would have been deemed admissible or admitted and that could have really hindered the defense of the case. That was a horror story I about had a nervous break down over. . . . You never want that. Your heart drops to the floor.[6]*

DILIGENCE *Model Rule* 1.3 requires that an attorney act with a reasonable degree of diligence in pursuing the client's case:

Rule 1.3 Diligence
A lawyer shall act with reasonable diligence and promptness in representing a client.

Rule 1.3 specifically requires an attorney to act with commitment and dedication when representing a client and to avoid procrastination. Further insight into the rule is contained in the comment to the rule:

A client's interests can be adversely affected by the passage of time or the change of conditions; in extreme instances, as when a lawyer overlooks a statute of limitations, the client's legal position may be destroyed. Even when the client's interests are not affected in substance, however, unreasonable delay can cause a client needless anxiety and undermine confidence in the lawyer's trustworthiness.[4]

The comment to this rule also notes that the attorney should carry through to conclusion all legal matters undertaken for a client unless the relationship is properly and clearly terminated. If doubt exists about whether an attorney-client relationship exists, the attorney should clarify the situation "in writing so that the client will not mistakenly suppose the attorney is looking after the client's affairs when the lawyer has ceased to do so." The purpose of this rule is to ensure that attorneys put forth reasonable effort and diligence to represent a client. Attorneys cannot adequately represent the interests of clients if they ignore the case, if they are lazy and do not work the case, or if they do not have the systems in place to manage deadlines, appointments, and things to be done.

COMMUNICATION WITH CLIENTS An attorney also must communicate regularly with a client. Rule 1.4 of the *Model Rules* states:

> Rule 1.4 Communication
> (a) A lawyer shall keep a client reasonably informed about the status of a matter and promptly comply with reasonable requests for information.
> (b) A lawyer shall explain a matter to the extent reasonably necessary to permit the client to make informed decisions regarding the representation.

This rule specifically requires the attorney to keep in reasonable contact with the client, to explain general strategy, and to keep the client reasonably informed regarding the status of the client's legal matter. The "reasonableness" of the situation will depend on the facts and circumstances of the particular case. The comment to the rule states:

> The guiding principle is that the lawyer should fulfill reasonable client expectations for information consistent with the duty to act in the client's best interests, and the client's overall requirements as to the character of representation.[5]

Figure 7-4 shows only a few examples of attorneys and law firms failing to follow up on client cases. A basic element of due diligence to a client requires an attorney to meet deadlines and limitation periods and appear at requisite legal proceedings. Many of these failures could have been avoided by a good docket control system and attorneys' and legal professionals' willingness to plan, organize, and simply get the work done. There is little excuse for poor organization and poor docket control in the modern law office. Firms today have access to an unlimited supply of excellent manual docket control systems, outstanding computerized docket control systems, and case management programs made specifically for law firms, and an even greater supply of generic calendaring software that comes with most computers. With all these systems and technology, however, failure to properly perform work on time is a major reason that attorneys are disciplined in this country.

LEGAL MALPRACTICE CONSIDERATIONS

> *[A] client sued his former attorney(s) alleging that they neglected his case by among other things: not taking the depositions of the defendants, not taking depositions of related witnesses, and failing to secure expert witness testimony which all led to the dismissal of the client's case. The client also testified that when he questioned the attorney about when the depositions would be taken, the attorney responded "all in due time."*
> *The client was awarded a judgment of $700,000.00 against his former attorneys.[10]*

Figure 7-4
Ethical Cases Regarding Lack of Diligence

Attorney Receives One-Year Suspension for Neglecting Legal Matters
A New York attorney of 25 years received a one-year suspension for misconduct in neglecting legal matters which caused harm to his clients. This came after the attorney previously received a letter of caution and letter of admonition as a result of his neglect of other legal matters from the court. *Matter of Aiello,* 246 A.D.2d 55, 676 N.Y.S.2d 385 (1998).

Attorney of 37 Years Receives a Public Censure for Neglecting a Client's Case and Lying About Not Neglecting It
An attorney of 37 years was publicly censured after he neglected a personal injury action he had commenced on behalf of a client. The client's case was eventually dismissed with prejudice due to the attorney's neglect of the case. In addition, after the case was dismissed the attorney repeatedly and falsely advised his client that the matter was still pending and after the client discharged him the attorney failed to forward the file to the new attorney. *Matter of Welt,* 1999 WL 130600 (N.Y.A.D. 3 Dept.).

Oregon Attorney Suspended for One Year for Failing to File Documents His Client Executed and for Failing to Respond to a Show Cause Order
An Oregon attorney failed to file a Uniform Support Affidavit that his client had executed in a divorce action and he failed to respond to a show cause order. The attorney also failed to respond to numerous telephone calls from his client and several letters from counsel. The Court suspended the attorney for one year. *Conduct of Meyer,* 970 P.2d 647 (1999).

Minnesota Attorney Appeals a Client's Case but Neglects to File a Brief to the Court and Writes a Hot Check to the Appellate Court Clerk as Well
A Minnesota attorney filed a lawsuit for a client. The lawsuit was dismissed and the client paid $250 to file an appeal. The attorney wrote a $250 check out of his law office account to pay the filing fee for the appeal. The attorney failed to file a brief to the court and the attorney's check returned insufficient funds. After numerous requests for repayment of the fee and submission of the brief the court of appeals dismissed the appeal and issued an order directing entry of a $250 judgment against the attorney personally. The attorney did not satisfy the judgment. The attorney also neglected other cases as well. The attorney was disbarred. *Disciplinary Action Against Grzybek,* 567 N.W.2d 259 (1997).

Attorney Failed to Tell Convicted Client He Needed Five Extensions of Time to File an Appeal and Failed to Communicate with Client About the Appeal at All—Attorney Disbarred
Attorney filed an appeal of a criminal conviction for first degree theft for a client. The attorney filed the brief but only after the court granted him five extensions of time. The attorney never communicated with the client, never advised the client of the five extensions, never discussed or reviewed the brief

(continued)

with the client, never told the client that the brief was filed or gave him a copy, never told the client about the oral arguments, never told the client about the court's decision to affirm the conviction and never gave the client a copy of the decision. The attorney was disbarred. *Conduct of Bourcier*, 325 Or. 429, 939 P.2d 604 (1997).

Attorney of 30 Years Fails to File Action Within Statute of Limitations and Lies to Client for Seven Years—Suspended for 60 Days and On Probation for Two Years—An attorney with 30 years experience was paid $1,000 to file a breach of contract case. The attorney failed to file the breach of contract lawsuit within the statute of limitations. For seven years the attorney allowed the client to believe the breach of contract complaint had been filed. The attorney also advised the client's bankruptcy attorney that a civil complaint was filed in the breach of contract case, and even provided the other attorney with a fake case number. The attorney finally admitted his misconduct to the client and refunded the money.[7]

Attorney Fails to Record Deed—Costs Client $1.3 million dollars—An attorney was hired by a client to provide legal representation regarding the sale of the client's lease. The attorney did not timely execute the deed of trust in the lease matter and did not secure or record the deed, resulting in the loss of $1.3 million. The attorney accepted a six-month suspension.[8]

Attorney Forgets to Defend the Corporate Client—An attorney was hired by a counsel for a corporation to defend them in a federal civil lawsuit. The attorney filed the "Answer" to the complaint and filed a statement of claim with the National Association of Securities Dealers to submit the matter to arbitration. After that, the attorney failed to take any further action on the client's behalf and stopped communicating with the corporation's counsel. The attorney was served with a notice to appear for a hearing but did not notify the corporate counsel of the hearing or otherwise notify the client. Later, a conference call was scheduled with the arbitrator, but the attorney failed to participate. The corporate counsel requested status reports several times but the attorney never responded. After the initial work, the attorney failed to respond to the client entirely. The attorney was suspended for 90 days.[9]

legal malpractice
A claim that an attorney breached an ordinary standard of care that a reasonable attorney would have adhered to in that same circumstance.

In addition to the ethical considerations of neglecting a client's legal matter, the client may also have a legal malpractice claim against the attorney for negligence. The general theory in a **legal malpractice** claim is that the attorney breached an ordinary standard of care applicable to a reasonable attorney under those circumstances. In a legal malpractice case, both the plaintiff and defendant must rely on attorneys who are expert witnesses to testify that the defendant either did or did not act like a reasonable attorney would in the same situation.

Figure 7-5
Common Reasons for Malpractice Claims

1. Expiration of the statute of limitations.
2. Failure to appear or plead resulting in a default judgment.
3. Dismissal of a lawsuit for lack of prosecution.
4. Failure to file tax returns or other documents within the time required.
5. Failure to file pleadings or to comply with an order within the time required.
6. Failure to answer interrogatories within the time required.
7. Failure to give timely notice when such notice is a precondition to a recovery of damages.
8. Failure to communicate with clients.
9. Not knowing what to do next (i.e., the attorney not being competent in an area).

Figure 7-5 shows some common deadlines that, when missed, may lead to malpractice claims. In fact, many malpractice insurers will refuse to write malpractice insurance for a law office that does not have an effective docket control system.

In the hurry-up world of law and order, how you use your time and resources can be the difference between success or malpractice.[11]

In recent years, the number of legal malpractice claims that have been filed has gone up dramatically. In some cases, the amount of damages can be substantial. Some insurance companies that offer legal malpractice coverage actually meet with staff members who are in charge of docket control to ensure that a docket control system is being used. Thus, attorneys and law offices have two powerful reasons to maintain a quality docket system.

MANUAL DOCKET CONTROL SYSTEMS

There are many types of manual docketing systems, including a simple calendar, a card system, and others. Manual docketing systems work best for fairly small law offices. As a law office grows, manual systems become more difficult to manage.

CALENDAR Small law offices may use simple computer calendar programs or a page-a-day calendaring system. Many calendars provide a section to record "things to do" or reminders, in addition to providing a place to schedule appointments.

As cases or legal matters are opened, deadlines and reminders (i.e. ticklers) are entered into the calendar. Notices from courts, attorneys, and so forth also are entered. In addition to the due dates or appointment date being entered, reminders also must be manually entered into the calendar. This process of manually entering due dates and reminders can be very time-consuming. For instance, if a deadline was entered that had two reminders, the whole entry would have to be manually entered a total of three times in three places.

In some offices, each attorney and legal assistant maintains his or her own separate calendar. The problem with this approach is that often the attorneys and legal assistants fail to coordinate their schedules and calendars. This can be a serious problem.

Finally, if attorneys wanted a short list of things to be done, appointments, or critical deadlines for a day, week, or month, it would have to be compiled and entered into a word processor by a staff member.

CARD SYSTEM A card system (sometimes called a "tickler card system") uses index cards or their equivalent to track deadlines and things to be done. A manual card or form is used for each deadline or task to be completed and includes client name, action to be performed, client number, reminder date, and due date. Cards can be color-coded to indicate different types of deadlines. In most cases, the card or slip of paper is kept in duplicate or triplicate. Copies are used as reminders and filed before the actual due date. An index card holder or expanding file folder with dividers for each month and for each day must be maintained to file each card under. When the date on which a card tickler is reached, the card is pulled and given to the appropriate person to perform the task or a list of the deadlines and things to do is made.

To work properly, the individual must check the system every day. However, if a slip is lost or is misfiled, the system breaks down. Although computerized systems also may occasionally break down, manual systems are far more likely to be error prone than their computerized counterparts. In addition, like the manual calendar, any daily, weekly, or monthly report must be typed by hand.

Manual calendaring systems also lack the ability to track information by case. For example, if a client asked to see all the upcoming events for his or her case, a staff person would have to go through the calendar and manually put together a list. Depending on the case, there could be many entries. Again, this is a time-consuming process.

Another problem with a manual calendaring system is that successive calendars must be purchased every year (e.g., one for 2002, one for 2003, one for 2004, etc.). It is also difficult to schedule dates far in the future—five years down the road for a statute of limitations entry, for instance—because you will need the appropriate calendar.

Manual calendaring systems are prone to error and are tedious and time-consuming to administer. Because the process is slow and tedious, it encourages users to make as few docket entries as possible. Further, manual systems simply do not have the flexibility and reporting capabilities that computerized versions can deliver.

> *An effective [docket control/tickler] system weaves the fabric of a case together, propelling each element of a case toward its conclusion. . . .*
> *Maintaining a tickler [docket control] system, keeping it updated, and making total use of it would be very beneficial to your performance as a paralegal.*[12]

Types of Computerized Docket Control Systems

There are a variety of computer programs that can be used to schedule and track events for a legal organization. These include generic calendaring and personal information manager programs, legal specific docket control, legal personal information manager, and full case management programs. Most of these programs can be purchased for stand-alone computers or for local area networks. Networked docket control systems, whether they are generic or legal, specific have the principal advantage of allowing individual users throughout an organization to see and have access to the calendars of other users in the office.

GENERIC CALENDARING AND PERSONAL INFORMATION MANAGER PROGRAMS

Generic calendaring programs computerize the functions of a paper desk calendar. Since they are generic and can be used by any type of business, they lack many features that are helpful to a legal organization. These types of programs are usually very inexpensive, come free with many computers, and typically manage only the calendar function.

A generic **personal information manager (PIM)** program consolidates a number of different tasks into one computer program. Most PIMs include calendaring, things to do, a contact database that tracks names and addresses of people, note taking, e-mail, and other tasks as well. Figure 7-6 shows Microsoft Outlook, which is a type of PIM that can come bundled with Microsoft's Office Suite of programs. Outlook is an extremely powerful program. As the generic calendaring and scheduling software market has matured, most new programs are PIMs. PIMs are very popular and convenient to use because they allow a user to organize a number of related tasks into one easy-to-use interface. Generic PIMs, such as Outlook, are not specifically suited to the needs of legal professionals but they still have many useful features and some legal organizations use these programs. For example, for consistency purposes a corporate law department might use a product like Microsoft Outlook, which can be implemented throughout the corporation, instead of a legal-specific program that only their department could use.

personal information manager (PIM)
Consolidates a number of different tasks into one computer program. Most PIMs include calendaring, things to do, a contact database that tracks names and addresses of people, note taking, and other tasks as well.

LEGAL-SPECIFIC CALENDARING, PERSONAL INFORMATION MANAGER, AND FULL CASE MANAGEMENT PROGRAMS

There are many legal-specific calendaring, personal information managers, and full case management programs that are designed to meet the specific needs of legal organizations. Legal calendaring programs computerize only the calendaring and scheduling function.

Legal-specific PIMs usually consolidate calendaring and planning, and have note taking and a contact database that tracks names and addresses of people, and other features (see Figure 7-7). Unlike generic PIMs, legal-specific PIMs are written

324 CHAPTER 7 Calendaring, Docket Control, and Case Management

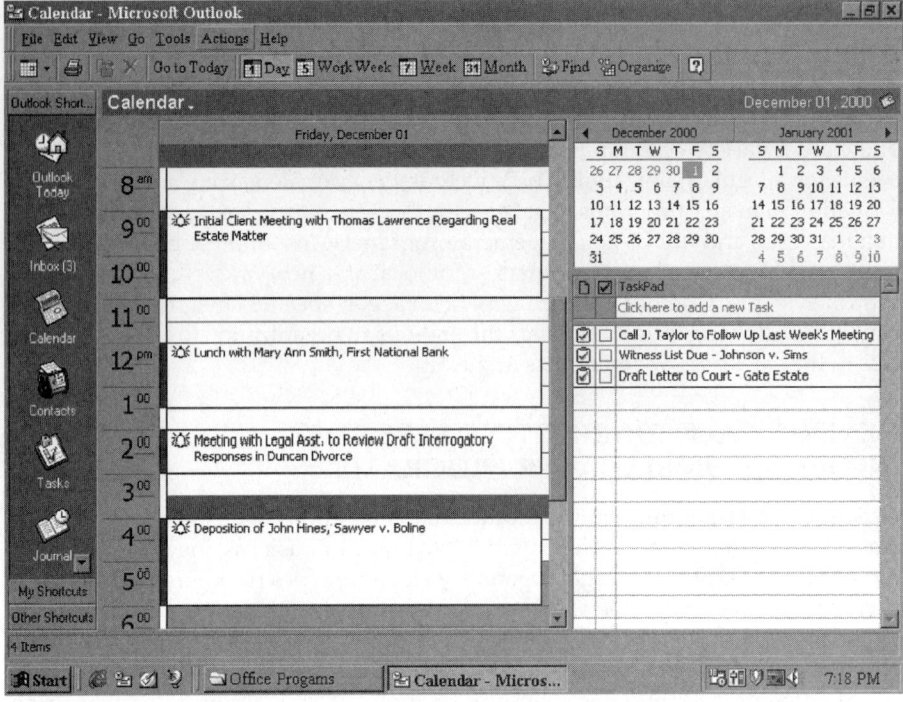

**Figure 7-6
Microsoft Outlook—
Generic Personal
Information Manager**

Screen shot reprinted by permission from Microsoft Corporation

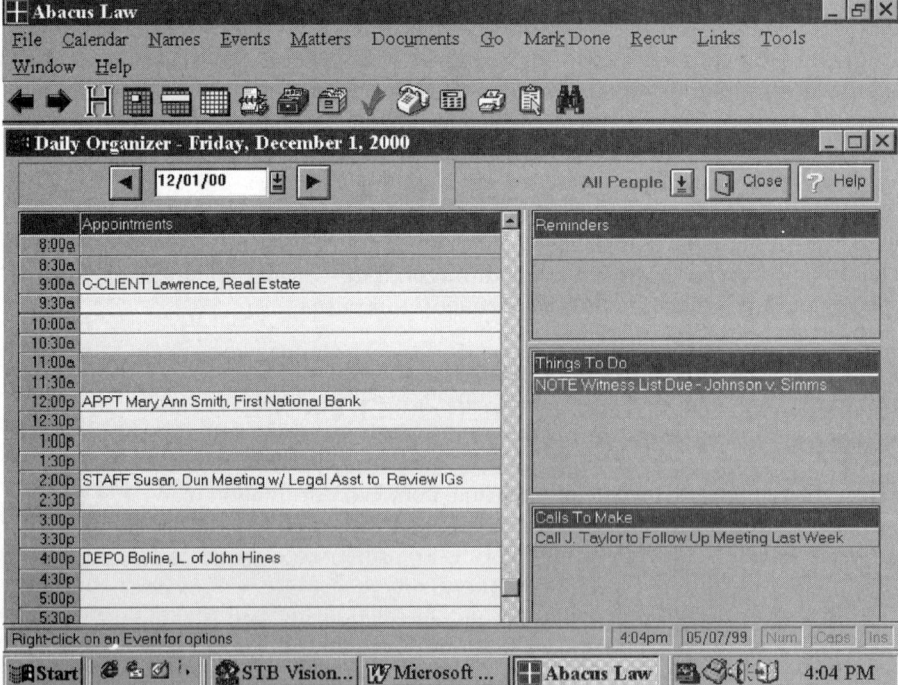

**Figure 7-7
Legal-Specific PIM**

Copyright 1999 Abacus Data Systems, Inc.

for legal professionals and include many features that are very helpful to users in the legal profession. The distinction between docket control programs that manage only the calendaring function and legal-specific PIMs that also manage other functions is usually easy to spot.

Legal-specific case management programs nearly always include docket control and calendaring, but they also offer features such as the ability to manage cases and to track case-related information like the subject matter of cases, causes of actions pleaded, and more. Some case management programs are written for specific types of law such as collection law, criminal law, or real estate, while others can be used for generic cases. Distinguishing between legal-specific PIMs and case management programs can be difficult. Many legal-specific PIMs market themselves as case management programs because they can track some information by case. Legal-specific docket control/PIMs and case management programs will be discussed in more detail later in this chapter.

OVERVIEW OF COMPUTERIZED LEGAL DOCKET CONTROL FEATURES

Most legal-specific programs that handle docket control, whether they are called calendaring, PIMs, or case management, include the following features.

MONTHLY, DAILY, AND WEEKLY CALENDAR VIEWS

Figure 7-8 shows a monthly display screen for a computerized docket control program. Almost all docket control programs have some type of monthly display, which allows the user to get an overview of his or her schedule. Notice in Figure 7-8 that small numbers appear below the date for December 3–7. In this program, the numbers on the bottom left of each box represent the number of events the user has in the morning for that day, and the numbers on the bottom right represent the number of events in the afternoon. The user can go to a daily view (see Figure 7-7) from the monthly view by simply clicking on one day. In addition to monthly and daily views, most docket control programs allow users to see a weekly view of their schedules as well (see Figure 7-9).

EVENT ENTRY SCREEN

A typical event entry screen is shown in Figure 7-10. This is where new entries are entered into the docket control program. The data entry process for most programs is easy and straightforward.

Who The "Who" in Figure 7-10 refers to the user the event is scheduled for. In Figure 7-10, the user is "BDR." In most docket control programs, you can schedule events to a variety of users.

What "What" refers to the type of event that is being scheduled. In Figure 7-10, the event is a deposition. Most docket control programs allow users to enter many types of events such as appointments, trials, hearings, settlement conferences, pretrial conferences, and hearings.

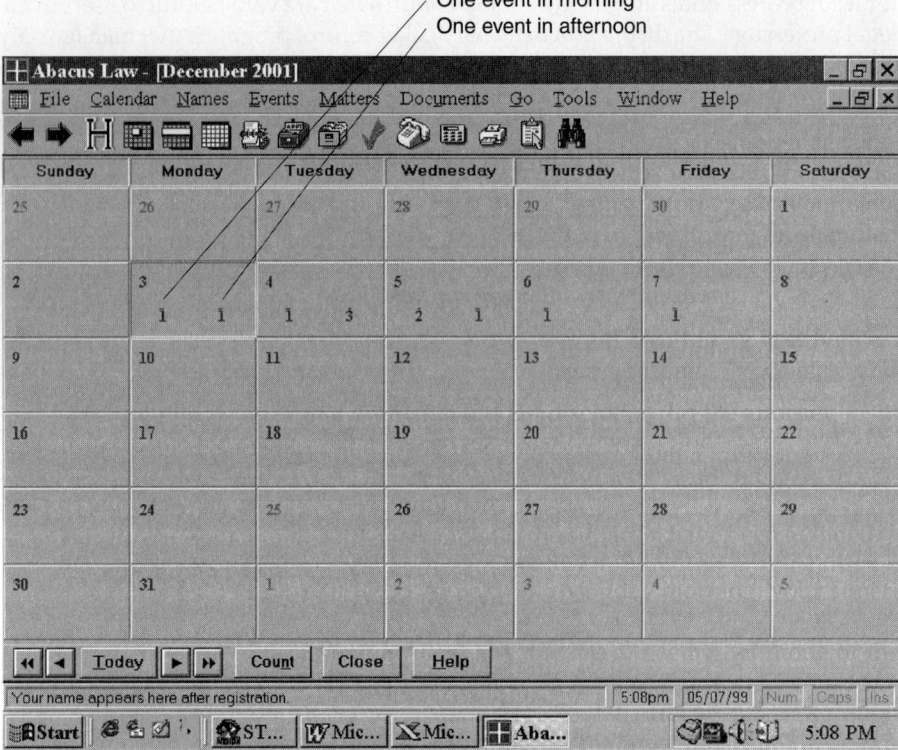

**Figure 7-8
Monthly Calendar
Screen**

Courtesy Abacus Data Systems

**Figure 7-9
Weekly Calendar
Screen**

Courtesy Abacus Data Systems

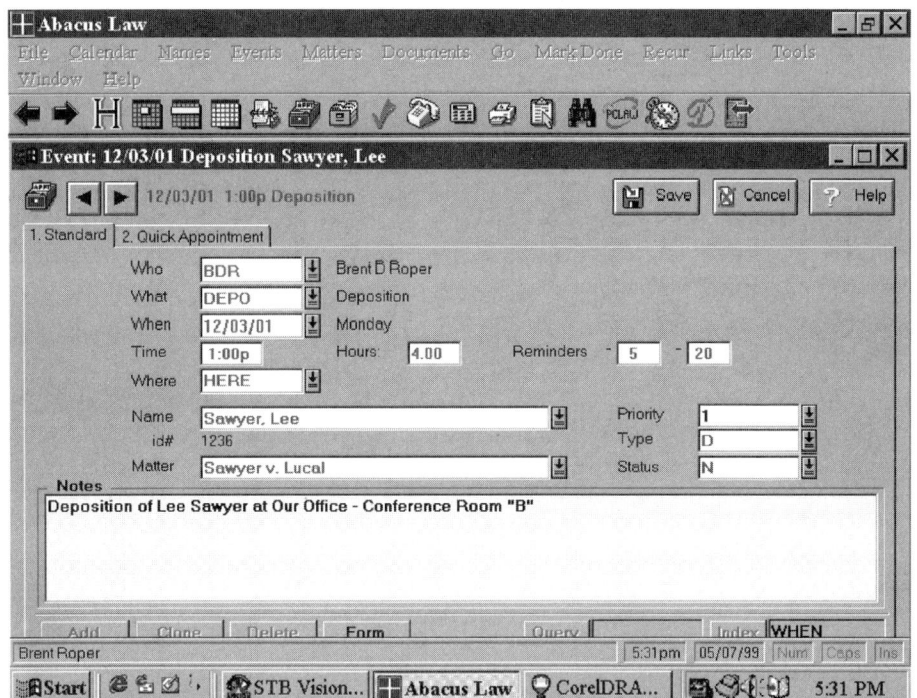

**Figure 7-10
Docket Program
Event Entry Screen**

Courtesy Abacus Data Systems

When "When" refers to the day the event is to be scheduled. Most programs allow users either to enter a day in numerical format or to pop-up a calendar where the user can graphically choose the day.

Time This refers to the time of the event.

Hours "Hours" refers to the duration of the event. In Figure 7-10, the deposition is scheduled to last four hours.

Reminders This allows the user to enter a reminder of an upcoming event and its due date in his or her schedule. For example, in Figure 7-10 a reminder is set for five days before the event. Thus, the upcoming deposition will appear on the user's schedule on November 28, 2001 (e.g. five days before the event is to take place on December 3, 2001). The reminder on November 28 would prompt the user to begin to prepare for the deposition. The second reminder of "20" in Figure 7-10 is a post-event reminder. A reminder on December 23 will appear on the user's schedule regarding the December 3 deposition. A user might use this reminder to follow up on an event, such as to see if the deposition transcript has been completed by the court reporter yet.

Where This refers to the place of the event, such as the user's office, a courthouse, or some other location.

Name This is the name of the client the event belongs to. In Figure 7-10, the client is Lee Sawyer.

Matter "Matter" refers to the client matter that the event involves. In Figure 7-10, the matter is *Sawyer v. Lucal.* There are separate data entry fields for Name and Matter because the firm may be handling multiple matters for a client.

Priority, Type, Status, and Notes In Figure 7-10, "Priority" allows a user to assign different priorities to events, such as high or low priority. "Type" lets a user define the event as a phone call, reminder, deadline, or other type of event. In "Status," the user marks whether the event was completed or not. In Figure 7-10, the *N* in Status stands for "Not Done." Finally, the user can enter additional information about the event in the "Notes" section.

PERPETUAL CALENDARS

Most computerized docketing systems have built-in perpetual calendars that allow a person to see and enter data that will be used many years into the future. Unlike manual calendars, a computerized system does not have to be updated annually (although purchasing updated versions of the software may be desirable). The perpetual calendar is an important feature of a computerized system because it allows the user to make entries concerning dates that are far in the future, such as a statute of limitations.

RECURRING ENTRIES

recurring entry
A calendar entry that typically recurs daily, weekly, monthly, or annually.

One advantage of using computerized docket systems is that the user can automatically make recurring entries. A **recurring entry** is a calendar entry that typically recurs daily, weekly, monthly, or annually. For instance, if an office has a staff meeting every Wednesday morning, the entry could be entered once as a weekly recurring appointment because most computerized docket systems can make recurring docket entries daily, weekly, monthly, quarterly, and annually. Thus, an entry that would have had to be entered fifty-two times in a year would only have to be entered once in a computerized docket control program.

DATE CALCULATOR

Some docket systems have a date calculator that automatically calculates the number of days between dates. For instance, suppose you have forty-five calendar days from a specific date to file a motion. The date calculator feature will automatically calculate the deadline. This is useful when you have deadlines that take into account only workdays (i.e., do not count Saturdays, Sundays, and holidays).

CONFLICT ALERT

Some docket systems automatically alert the user to possible conflicts. For instance, if a user mistakenly tries to schedule two appointments for the same date and time, nearly all computerized docket systems will automatically alert the user to the possible conflict. If the user knows of the conflict, most systems can be overridden and both appointments entered anyway. Some systems have a "lockout" feature that prevents users from scheduling more than one appointment for a given time period.

Some systems even allow the user to enter such information as the individual's regular office hours and days of the week that are usually taken off. If, for instance, an individual's office hours are from 7:00 A.M. to 4:00 P.M. and an entry is made for 4:30 P.M., some systems will automatically recognize the problem and alert the user.

SCHEDULING MULTIPLE PARTIES

Scheduling free time for an interoffice meeting can sometimes be difficult because all parties must have an open block of time. Many docketing systems that operate on a local area network (i.e., where individual workstations are all linked together) can automatically bring up dates and times that a group of people have free, thus making scheduling meetings easy.

A computerized docketing system also allows other individuals working on a case to see what docketing entries have been made and to find out what is going on in the case. This eases the process of multiple people working on the same case.

CENTRALIZED AND DECENTRALIZED SYSTEMS

Most docketing systems work well in either a centralized or decentralized system. That is, in a centralized system one person (for example, a secretary), can make time entries for many individuals. A centralized system is beneficial because one individual is responsible for making the docketing entries. A decentralized system where the attorney or legal assistant enters her or his own deadlines into the docket program also works well for some offices.

AUTOMATIC REMINDERS

Most computerized docketing systems allow the user to make one entry into the system that also contains the reminder dates. For instance, when an appointment or deadline is entered into the computer, the system automatically asks the user when he or she wants to be reminded of it. If a reminder date is entered, the computerized method automatically makes reminder entries (see Figure 7-10). This is a great timesaving feature over manual systems where every reminder must be entered individually.

CALENDARING A SERIES OF EVENTS FROM A RULE

Some docketing programs allow a user to enter one event that, in turn, automatically triggers a list of subsequent calendaring events based on court rules. For instance, in Figure 7-11, a complaint is filed. Sixty days after the complaint is filed, according to court rules the complaint must have been served. Therefore, the docketing program automatically enters a deadline to serve the complaint sixty days after the complaint is filed. Figure 7-11 lists seven events that the filing of a complaint will automatically trigger. This kind of feature is very powerful and can be a real time-saver. Many docketing programs allow the user to program his or her own court rules into the docketing program or to add on purchased court rule setups.

**Figure 7-11
Calendaring a Series of Events from a Rule**
Courtesy Abacus Data Systems

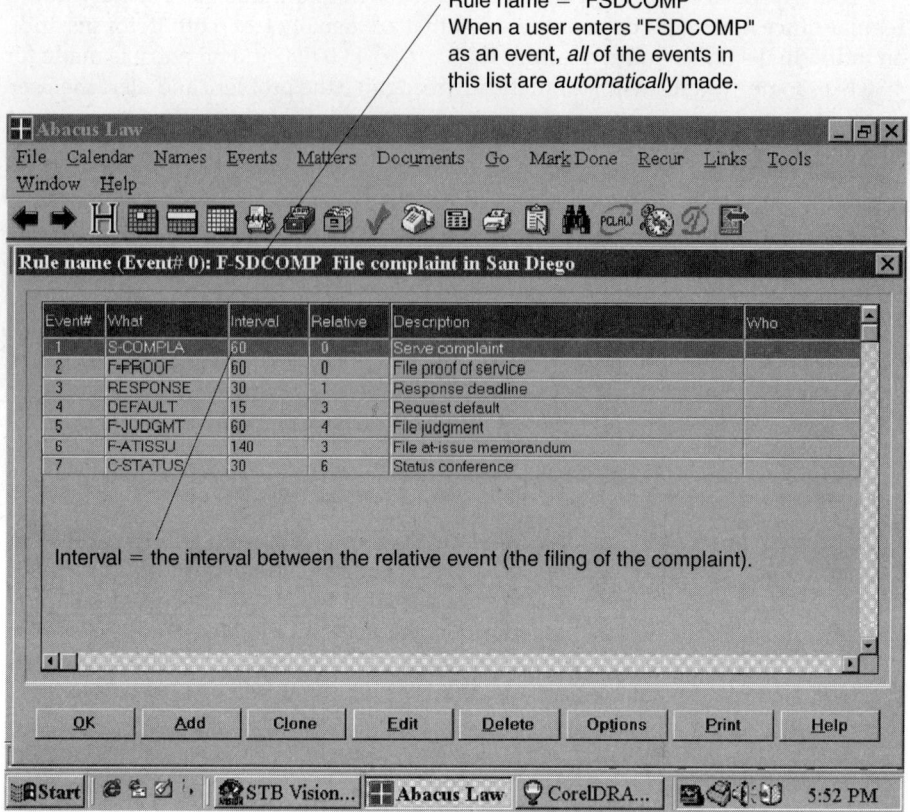

REPORTING

Most computerized systems allow the user to generate a variety of reports that manual systems cannot produce including daily, weekly, or monthly schedules and things-to-do entries for one person or a group of people. Most systems also can search and sort the entries in a variety of different formats.

DAILY CALENDAR REPORTS This is an in-depth listing of a timekeeper's or office's daily schedule. The daily report, which is similar to the daily screen view in Figure 7-7, is sometimes called a "daysheet." Daysheets for an entire office also can be produced. Many attorneys and legal assistants will use this report every day for an accurate listing of the day's events.

DAILY CALENDAR REPORT FOR A WEEK This is similar to the daily calendar report except that the report shows docket entries for the entire week. Again, legal assistants and attorneys may want this report at the beginning of the week to get a "snapshot" of what their schedule looks like, so they can plan accordingly. The weekly report is similar to the weekly screen view in Figure 7-9.

			Brent Roper			
			Schedule for Boline v. McPherson			
			Case Number: 1237			
Day	When	Time	Last, First	What	Who	Note
Fri	09/28/01	8:30a	Boline, L.	DISCOVER	AMS	Discovery Deadline
Tue	10/02/01	9:00a	Boline, L.	HEARING	AMS	Hearing on Pending Motions
Thu	11/01/01	9:00a	Boline, L.	C-STATUS	AMS	Status Conference
Thu	11/15/01	1:00p	Boline, L.	PRETRIAL	AMS	Pretrial Conference
Thu	11/29/01	10:00a	Boline, L.	C-SETTLE	AMS	Settlement Conference
Thu	12/06/01	8:00a	Boline, L.	TR PR	AMS	Trial Preparation
Fri	12/07/01	8:00a	Boline, L.	TRIAL	AMS	TRIAL

Number of Events: 7

Figure 7-12 Docket Report for a Case

PER CASE DOCKET REPORT Most computerized docket systems allow the user to generate a docket report by case—that is, a report showing all the docketing dates for any one case (see Figure 7-12). This report can be very helpful in trying to determine how to proceed with certain cases. Figure 7-12 shows a listing of all entries for the case *Boline v. McPherson.* This is particularly helpful when scheduling other events for the same case and also to give to clients. Keeping clients informed about their cases is very important when it comes to client satisfaction and when it is time for the client to pay the legal bill. A client who is consulted often and kept aware of the progress of the case is more likely to pay the bill and generally will be more satisfied than a client who is not notified about a case's progress. Again, this report is very beneficial to clients who want to know what is going on in a case and to attorneys or legal assistants who have just been assigned to the case to see what has happened and where the case is headed.

PAST DUE REPORT The past due report prints a listing of all docket entries that are past due (i.e., the deadline or due date has passed), and the entry has not been marked "Done." The past due report is a safeguard against forgetting or not completing items.

SEARCHING

Most computerized docketing systems allow the user to search for entries. For instance, if a client calls and wants to know when his or her deposition is, the user could enter the client's name into the computer, and the system would retrieve the entry showing the date of the deposition.

```
┌─────────────────────────────────────────────────────────────────────────────┐
│  JOHNSON, BECK & TAYLOR        DOCKET SLIP                                  │
│                                                                             │
│  Client/Case Matter: _Smith v. United Sales_____    File No.: _118294__     │
│                                                                             │
│  Event: _Pre-Trial Hearing_____   │
│                                                                             │
│  Date of Event: __10/1/2001_____   Time of Event: _10:00 AM – 1:00 PM__   │
│                                                                             │
│  Place of Event: _U.S. Ct. House, Div. 8_____    │
│                                                                             │
│  To Be Handled By: __MJB_____  Reminder Dates: ____9/15/2001_____    │
│                                                                             │
│  Priority: ①  2  3  4  5  (Circle one, Top Priority is 1).                  │
│                                                           ┌───────────────────────────────┐
│  Slip Completed By: _BRR_ Date Slip Completed: 8/15/2001  │ Docket Clerk Use Only         │
│                                                           │ Date Entered in Docket: 8/17/2001 │
│  Notes: _Meet client at 9:45 at Ct. House_____   │ Entered By: __JCC__           │
│                                                           └───────────────────────────────┘
└─────────────────────────────────────────────────────────────────────────────┘
```

Figure 7-13 Sample Docket Slip

THE DOCKET CYCLE

The docket cycle refers to how information is entered into a docket control program. There are three primary ways that information can flow into and out of a docket control program. These include a centralized method, decentralized method, and a combined method.

CENTRALIZED DOCKET CONTROL CYCLE

In a centralized docket control cycle, one person typically is responsible for entering all docket entries into the docket program. This is usually a secretary or in some cases a legal assistant. In this type of system, step one would be for a user to manually complete a docket slip (see Figure 7-13). The second step would be for the secretary to enter the event into the docket control program. The third step would be for reports to be generated, and the last step would be for entries to be marked "Done."

DECENTRALIZED DOCKET CONTROL CYCLE

In a decentralized docket control cycle, the user enters docket information directly into the computer, controlling his or her own docket. In this type of system, the first step would be for the user to enter a docket entry into the docket control program. The second step would be for the user to view or print reports as necessary and the third step would be for the user to mark entries "Done." The advantage of this system is that the user has ultimate control over his or her own docket. The disadvantage is that the user instead of a clerk or secretary is doing the data entry.

COMBINED DOCKET CONTROL CYCLE

In a combined docket control cycle, a user can decide whether to enter information into the program or have a clerk or secretary do it. Some docket control programs allow multiple people to enter data into a user's schedule. For example, some networked docket programs allow both an attorney and his or her secretary to enter information into the attorney's schedule. Both have full access to the attorney's calendar.

In this type of system, the first step would be for either the user or a third party to enter a docket entry into the docket control program. The second step would be for either the user or the third party to view or print reports as necessary, and the third step would be for either the user or third party to mark entries "Done." In some ways, this is the best of both worlds because the user still has control over his or her calendar, but can delegate the data entry to someone else.

USING A WORD PROCESSOR FOR DOCKET CONTROL

Some law offices use a word processor to do docket controls. That is, docketing entries are written down and given to the docketing clerk. The docketing clerk then records the docketing in a word processing document. This typically only works well for relatively small law offices. The docketing entries typically are arranged in the word processing document chronologically. Because the document can quickly become extremely long, reminder dates are sometimes not entered at all, and only deadlines and appointments are entered. Word processors simply do not have the reporting capability or flexibility of a computerized docket system, but they typically are easier to use than a strictly manual system.

CASE MANAGEMENT

As mentioned earlier, case management programs usually include docket control, but they also include functions such as maintaining a database of information about each client's case. They typically include the ability to merge that database of information into word processing documents to produce letters, pleadings, and other legal work by case. Another feature of some case management programs is the ability to enter notes about client phone conferences, conversations with attorneys, and other information about the case as it progresses.

HOW CASE MANAGEMENT WORKS

In addition to docket control, there are two basic functions that most case management systems address. First, case management systems create a database of case and client information. Figure 7-14 shows an example of a case management system developed for representing lenders on collection cases. The case database in Figure 7-14 tracks eighteen pieces of information about the case. This information would be readily available in the case management program if, for instance, a debtor called and wanted to know the amount he owed on the debt. While having access to this information electronically is important, the power of case management is its ability

CASE DATABASE

Client Name:	First National Bank
Contact Person–First Name	Sam
Contact Person–Last Name	Johnson
Client Address:	P.O. Box 1000
Client City:	Philadelphia
Client State:	Pennsylvania
Client Zip:	98934
Client Phone:	943/233-9983
Case Number:	2001-9353
Court:	Philadelphia Superior Court—District 13, Philadelphia, Pennsylvania
Debtor Name:	Philip Jones
Debtor Address:	3242 Wilson Ave. SW
Debtor City:	Philadelphia
Debtor State:	Pennsylvania
Debtor Zip:	98984
Amount Owed to Client:	$25,234
Type of Debt:	Mortgage
Type of Asset:	House at 3242 Wilson Ave SW, Philadelphia, Pennsylvania

DOCUMENT TEMPLATE 1—"Complaint"

In the {Court}
{Client name}
Plaintiff
Case No. {Case Number}
{Debtor Name}
{Debtor Address}
{Debtor City}{Debtor State}{Debtor Zip}

Defendant.

COMPLAINT

Comes now the plaintiff, {Client Name}, and states that the defendant, {Debtor Name}, is indebted to the plaintiff in the amount of {Amount Owed to Client} on a {Type of Debt} regarding a {Type of Asset}. Attached to this complaint as Appendix "A" is a fully executed copy of the mortgage above referenced.

Merge function

MERGED DOCUMENT—"Complaint"

In the Philadelphia Superior Court – District 13, Philadelphia, Pennsylvania

First National Bank
Plaintiff
Case No. 2001-9353
Philip Jones
3242 Wilson Ave. SW
Philadelphia, Pennsylvania 98984

Defendant.

COMPLAINT

Comes now the plaintiff, First National Bank, and states that the Debtor, Philip Jones, is indebted to the plaintiff in the amount of $25,234 on a mortgage regarding a house at 3242 Wilson Ave. SW, Philadelphia, Pennsylvania. Attached to this complaint as Appendix "A" is a fully executed copy of the mortgage above referenced.

Figure 7-14
Case Management for Collection Cases

to combine the information into a document template (see Figure 7-14). Many case management programs allow users to build document templates either in a stand-alone word processor or in a word processor supplied with the case management program. Users are then able to merge the case database with the document template to create a merged document (see Figure 7-14).

It would be very beneficial to an attorney or legal assistant working fifty collection cases to have nearly all of the forty documents necessary to litigate a collection case in document templates. If the case management software could also maintain docket control/calendaring and case note information by case, it would give the attorney or legal assistant nearly complete control over a case in one program. This is the power of case management software. It combines the benefits of word processing, document generation, docket control, and personal information managers into one program.

INTERNET SITES

GENERAL

ORGANIZATION	DESCRIPTION	WORLD WIDE WEB ADDRESS
ABA Law Practice Today	ABA site devoted to law practice management	www.abanet.org/lpm
Association of Legal Administrators	Site for legal administrators	www.alanet.org

DOCKET CONTROL/CALENDARING/CASE MANAGEMENT

ORGANIZATION	PRODUCT/SERVICE	WORLD WIDE WEB ADDRESS
Abacus Data Systems	Abacus Law (legal PIM/case management)	www.abacuslaw.com
Bridgeway Software	Law Quest (case management for corporate law departments)	www.bridge-way.com
Chesapeake Interlink Ltd.	Needles (legal PIM/case management)	www.needpins.com
Compulaw	Compulaw (legal calendar)	www.compulaw.com
Computer Law Systems	CLS/Summit (legal PIM/case management)	www.clswin.com
Corel	Corel Central/GroupWise (PIM/groupware)	www.corel.com
Data.txt Corp.	Time Matters (legal PIM/case management)	www.timematters.com
De Novo Systems Inc.	Trial De Novo (legal PIM/case management)	www.denovosys.com
Gavel & Gown Software	Amicus Attorney (legal PIM/case management)	www.amicus.ca
Gryphon Law, Inc.	Gryphon (legal PIM/case management)	www.gryphonlaw.com
KeyPoint	Case management for criminal defense attorneys	www.key-point.com
Legal Files Software	Legal Files (legal PIM/case management)	www.legalfiles.com
LegalEdge Software	Case management for criminal defense attorneys, prosecutors, and general law offices	www.legaledge.com
Lotus	Organizer/Lotus Notes/Domino (PIM/groupware)	www.lotus.com
Microsoft	Outlook (PIM/groupware)	www.microsoft.com
Software Technology	Case Master III (legal PIM/case management)	www.stilegal.com/loc.html

Suggested Reading

Computerized Case Management Systems, American Bar Association, 1998.

Practical Systems: Tips for Organizing Your Law Office, American Bar Association, 1991.

You and Your Clients: A Guide to Client Management Skills for a More Successful Practice, Second Edition, American Bar Association, 1996.

Summary

The practice of law is filled with appointments, deadlines, hearings, and other commitments that must be carefully tracked. A docket is a calendaring or scheduling system that tracks and organizes these events.

Attorneys and law offices that fail to operate an accurate docket may be subject to ethical sanctions and malpractice lawsuits. In some offices, a legal assistant is responsible for maintaining a law office's docketing system.

The two types of manual docket control systems include calendaring and card systems. A card system uses duplicate or triplicate docket control slips that are filed according to the event's date. Manual docketing systems typically are only used for very small offices.

Computerized docketing systems have perpetual calendars that can make recurring entries with one entry, can alert the user to possible scheduling conflicts, and can generate past due reports to name just a few of their features.

Key Terms

continuance
statute of limitations
calendaring
docket control
case management
calendar days

Certificate of Service
Bates stamp
legal malpractice
personal information manager
recurring entry
workdays

Questions and Exercises

1. Your law office currently uses a manual docket system. It works fairly well because the office is small. However, several clients have requested a detailed listing of what is going on in their case and what is coming up in the future. To do this, it takes a staff member quite a while to compile the information. Even though the office's manual system is working, should the office consider a change? What benefits would be realized? Please note that the office is driven by quality and productivity.

2. As a legal assistant in a legal aid practice, you notice that one of the attorneys in the office filed a case on behalf of an indigent client. The defendant's attorney has attempted on three separate occasions to take the client's deposition. However, the attorney asked for and received continuances on

each occasion. The client's health is deteriorating and the client has anxiety over the deposition. The client's deposition is set for tomorrow and the attorney tells you that something has "come up" and to please call the defendant's counsel, the court reporter, and the client and get it continued. Although you have covered for the attorney on multiple occasions, you know that the client really wants to talk to the attorney and not to you and that the client would like to finish the deposition as soon as possible. Please respond to the attorney's request.

3. From time to time, you see new clients who come into the office. On this occasion, you interview a client who has a potential workers' compensation claim. After the client has left, you note that in a month the statute of limitations on the claim will expire. After discussing the case with your supervising attorney, the attorney says that he does not believe that the client has a viable case. The attorney tells you to not waste any more time on the matter and that you should simply call the client and tell her that the office will not be representing her. As you pick up the phone, you hesitate and then put the phone down. You go back into the attorney's office. What would you tell your supervising attorney?

4. You and your supervising attorney are overworked. You have two days to prepare for a trial that you really need eight to ten days to adequately prepare for. Your supervising attorney says "It's okay, we'll just do the best we can." Discuss this situation from an ethical perspective.

5. One of the five attorneys you work for is taking on a new case. Unfortunately, the attorney has never handled a case like this before. This is particularly troubling to you because you doubt if the attorney or you have the time or inclination to do the necessary research to handle the case properly. Address any concerns you might have to the attorney. Try to be diplomatic. Give the attorney options that will address your concerns, but will still allow the attorney to work on the case in some capacity.

6. Calculate the following due dates.
   a. Motion for Summary Judgment filed 8/1/03; response due seventeen days from file date. Court rules in this case use calendar days.
   b. Motion to Compel filed 3/5/03; response due ten days from file date. Court rules in this case use workdays only. Assume there is one weekend.
   c. Request for Admissions is received 6/1/04; response is due twenty-five days from receipt. Court rules in this case use calendar days. Response must be mailed by what date?
   d. Request for Production of Documents is received 12/10/04; response is due within ten days. Court rules in this case use workdays only. Assume there is one weekend and two holidays.

7. Set up and maintain a docket of class assignments for a semester. Use index cards to represent each assignment and file them in chronological order, or use a computerized calendaring program. For quizzes and assignments, give yourself one three-day reminder before the assignment or quiz is due in addition to recording the quiz or assignment itself. For exams or lengthy papers, give yourself three reminders: a ten-day reminder before it is due, a five-day reminder, and a three-day reminder in addition to docketing the deadline itself.

8. Read the disciplinary report section of your State Bar Association journal or magazine and prepare a short memorandum on several cases related to diligence and/or docket control.

9. Using the Internet, go to *www.findlaw.com* and click on *Ethics and Professional Responsibility.* Use the resources in this section to find an article on case management, how to work with clients, docket control, or a related subject. Prepare a report summarizing the article.

10. Using the Internet Sites section of this text or a general search engine such as *www.yahoo.com*, review two to three docket control, legal personal information managers, or legal case management programs. Prepare a short report on the product that you believe is the best. Defend your choice.

NOTES

1. Gore v. Rains & Block, 189 Mich. App. 729, 473 N.W.2d 813 (1991).
2. Kathy Ruff, "Time Out—Incorporation of a Tickler System Will Help You Best Utilize Your Time, Energy, and Resources," *Legal Assistant Today,* September/October, 1999, p. 70.
3. Reprinted by permission. Copies of the *ABA Model Code of Professional Responsibility*, 1999 edition, are available from Service Center, American Bar Association, 750 North Lake Shore Drive, Chicago, IL 60611-4497, 1-800-285-2221.
4. Reprinted by permission. Copies of the *ABA Model Code of Professional Responsibility*, 1999 edition, are available from Service Center, American Bar Association, 750 North Lake Shore Drive, Chicago, IL 60611-4497, 1-800-285-2221.
5. Reprinted by permission. Copies of the *ABA Model Code of Professional Responsibility*, 1999 edition, are available from Service Center, American Bar Association, 750 North Lake Shore Drive, Chicago, IL 60611-4497, 1-800-285-2221.
6. Kathy Ruff, "Time Out—Incorporation of a Tickler System Will Help You Best Utilize Your Time, Energy, and Resources," *Legal Assistant Today,* September/October, 1999, p. 70.
7. *California Lawyer,* June 2000, p. 73. Reprinted by permission.
8. *Texas Bar Journal,* March 2000, p. 298.
9. *California Lawyer,* May 2000, p. 78. Reprinted by permission.
10. Mayol v. Summers, 223 Ill. App. 3d 794, 585 N.E.2d 1176 (1992).
11. Kathy Ruff, "Time Out—Incorporation of a Tickler System Will Help You Best Utilize Your Time, Energy, and Resources," *Legal Assistant Today,* September/October, 1999, p. 70.
12. Kathy Ruff, "Time Out—Incorporation of a Tickler System Will Help You Best Utilize Your Time, Energy, and Resources," *Legal Assistant Today,* September/October, 1999, p. 72.

CASE REVIEW

In the Matter of Riva, 157 N.J. 34, 722 A.2d 933 (N.J. 1999).

722 A.2d 933
(Cite as: 157 N.J. 34, 722 A.2d 933)

Supreme Court of New Jersey.

In the Matter of Robert E. RIVA, an Attorney at Law.

Argued Sept. 28, 1998.

Decided Feb. 5, 1999.

**934 *35 Lee A. Gronikowski, Deputy Ethics Counsel, argued the cause on behalf of the Office of Attorney Ethics.

Robert E. Riva, argued the cause pro se.

PER CURIAM.

This attorney discipline matter arises from a Report and Recommendation of the Disciplinary Review Board (DRB) that respondent be publicly reprimanded. Three members of the DRB concluded that a public reprimand would be insufficient discipline and recommended a three-month suspension. The majority recommendation is based on findings of the District VB Ethics ***36** Committee (DEC), concurred in by the DRB, that respondent had been guilty of gross neglect, a violation of RPC 1.1(a), and a lack of diligence, a violation of RPC 1.3. The misconduct involved the failure to file a timely answer to a complaint against his clients and his subsequent failure to act with necessary diligence to vacate a default entered on the complaint. Respondent also failed to communicate with his clients in a timely manner and misrepresented the status of the matter.

Respondent does not deny the essential facts but asserts that the conduct resulted from a misunderstanding that his adversary had withdrawn the complaint and his failure to have received notice of the proposed default judgment. Respondent contends that the Court should not follow the DRB's recommendation that he be publicly reprimanded.

Based on our independent review of the record, we find clear and convincing evidence that respondent engaged in conduct proscribed by RPC 1.1(a) and RPC 1.3, and that a public reprimand is warranted.

**935I

The matter involves respondent's representation of Robert Palceski and his wife Janet, who owned a company against which a former employee threatened to file an employment-practices claim. The disgruntled employee had hired an attorney in 1992. Respondent told that attorney that if the employee sued, the employer would file a counterclaim based on alleged financial improprieties engaged in by the employee. That attorney did not file an action. The employee hired a new attorney.

In January 1993, the new attorney served a summons and complaint on the employer. The employer retained respondent again. After some modification of the documents, respondent obtained a stipulation to extend the time for filing an answer to the complaint.

*37 Respondent never filed the stipulation or the answer and counterclaim. Although he testified that his conversation with the employee's attorney led him to believe that she would voluntarily dismiss the matter, the adversary testified that she had never made such a statement because her client was "adamant" about pursuing the claim. Meanwhile, respondent had told the Palceskis that he had filed the answering papers and that, because he had heard nothing further from opposing counsel, the case would just "go away."

The employee's attorney said that she called respondent several times and left a number of messages on his answering machine between March and May 1993 to determine whether respondent intended to file an answer to the complaint. She eventually learned by calling the court that respondent had never filed an answer on behalf of his client.

In May 1993, the employee's attorney obtained an order entering default. Her transmittal letter to the court and an affidavit of service prepared by her secretary indicated that the request for entry of default and a copy of the proposed default order had been sent to respondent by regular mail. Respondent denied receiving them.

The court entered a default judgment against the employer for $1.7 million in September 1993. A court officer seized the trucks, tools and bank accounts of the employer. A constable sought to seize the personal cars and other assets of the Palceskis.

Robert Palceski telephoned respondent while the constable was at his home. Respondent assured him that he would go to court the next day to have their assets returned to them. He went to the Palceskis' home that evening to obtain copies of the papers served on them to prepare an emergent motion to vacate the default and assured them that he was working on the motion. The Palceskis asked for a copy of the motion, but respondent "put them off." It was only when Robert Palceski threatened to drive to respondent's office to pick up a copy of the motion that respondent agreed to fax him a copy. The faxed copy consisted of ***38** fourteen blank pages. When later asked about the blank pages, respondent stated that he might have put the pages in the machine backwards or improperly transmitted the document.

When respondent went to court two days later, he was only able to obtain the release of the Palceskis' trucks and tools. (Respondent contends that the default judgment improperly included a business entity not named in the original complaint.) Although respondent filed a later motion to vacate the default in full, the trial court held that respondent's papers were deficient and that additional information was needed to set forth a meritorious defense to the claim.

From September through December 1993, respondent told the Palceskis on a number of occasions that he was consulting with other attorneys and conducting research on their defense. By the time that the court considered the motion again in December, the Palceskis had retained a new attorney. It was several weeks before respondent turned over the file. The only papers in the file were the motion to vacate the default with its accompanying inadequate certification, a cover letter to the employee's attorney with the draft stipulation extending the time to answer, and the draft answer and counterclaim. Only the motion to vacate had been filed with the **936 court. The Palceskis later settled the lawsuit of the employee by a payment of $11,500.

In his testimony before the DEC, respondent acknowledged that although he knew that a stipulation of dismissal was necessary to have resolved the litigation once the complaint had been filed, he never obtained one. He believed that he had resolved the problem with the employee's attorneys.

The DRB agreed with the DEC that respondent's conduct displayed gross neglect and a lack of diligence from the time that he failed to file a timely answer to the complaint through his failure to act with necessary haste to vacate the default.

The dissenting members stressed respondent's continuous misrepresentations to his clients about the status of the matter both *39 before and after the entry of the default, and the great financial and emotional injury suffered by the clients, who had relied on respondent's false assurances that their interests were being protected. The experience was a "nightmare" for respondent's clients, who were threatened with bankruptcy and the loss of their personal assets. In the dissenters' view

> this is precisely the sort of attorney who contributes to the lamentable state of disrepute in which the attorney population has fallen, and who is responsible for the public's loss of trust in the legal profession. In order to assure the public that such conduct will never be tolerated, we believe that a period of suspension must be imposed. We would suspend this respondent for three months.

II

We have attempted to establish over a long period of years predictable standards for the imposition of discipline in cases of attorney misconduct. On one end of the spectrum are the cases in which disbarment of an attorney will be "almost invariable." In re Wilson, 81 N.J. 451, 453, 409 A.2d 1153 (1979) (misappropriating client funds).

Crimes of dishonesty touch upon a central trait of character that members of the bar must possess. In re Di Biasi, 102 N.J. 152, 506 A.2d 719 (1986). Such crimes are defined as a "serious crime" pursuant to Rule 1:20-13b(2). We have repeatedly held that "when a crime of dishonesty touches upon the administration of justice," id. at 155, 506 A.2d 719, the offense "is deserving of severe sanctions and would ordinarily require disbarment." In re Verdiramo, 96 N.J. 183, 186, 475 A.2d 45 (1984); In re Edson, 108 N.J. 464, 530 A.2d 1246 (1987) (counseling client to commit perjury and lying to prosecutor). Such conduct "poisons the well of justice." In re Pajerowski, 156 N.J. 509, 721 A.2d 992 (1998) (quoting In re Verdiramo, supra, 96 N.J. at 185, 475 A.2d 45). Serious crimes not touching on the administration of justice often warrant the same penalty of disbarment. In re Lunetta, 118 N.J. 443, 572 A.2d 586 (1989) (conspiring to receive and sell stolen securities); In re Mallon, 118 N.J. 663, 573 A.2d 921 (1990) (conspiring to commit tax fraud).

*40 Nevertheless, "even in proceedings involving 'serious crimes,' mitigating factors may justify imposition of sanctions less severe than disbarment or extended suspension." Compare In re Imbriani, 149 N.J. 521, 533, 694 A.2d 1030 (1997) (disbarment for engaging in numerous acts of misconduct that involved substantial amounts of money) with In re Litwin, 104 N.J. 362, 517 A.2d 378 (1986) (five-year suspension for arson); In re Kushner, 101 N.J. 397, 502 A.2d 32 (1986) (three-year suspension for false certification); In re Labendz, 95 N.J. 273, 471 A.2d 21 (1984) (one-year suspension for instigating fraudulent representations to federally-insured lender for purposes of obtaining a mortgage, despite excellent reputation, unblemished record and lack of personal gain); and In re Silverman, 80 N.J. 489, 404 A.2d 301 (1979) (eighteen-month suspension for filing false answer with the bankruptcy court to retain custody of certain assets).

Other crimes of dishonesty not touching upon the administration of justice nonetheless demonstrate an absence of character that ordinarily warrants extended periods of suspension.

[1] Crimes that subvert the public policy and good order of the State will ordinarily warrant a period of suspension. In re Kinnear, **937 105 N.J. 391, 522 A.2d 414 (1987) (one-year suspension for criminal drug use); In re Herman, 108 N.J. 66, 527 A.2d 868 (1987) (three-year suspension for criminal sexual contact).

[2] Material misrepresentations of fact in sworn affidavits will warrant a long period of suspension. In re Lunn, 118 N.J. 163, 570 A.2d 940 (1990) (three years). Even misrepresenting a reason for an overlooked court appearance may result in a suspension. In re Johnson, 102 N.J. 504, 509 A.2d 171 (1986) (three months).

[3] Charges of client neglect "are serious and can have a detrimental impact on the confidence the public should have in the [b]ar of this state." In re O'Gorman, 99 N.J. 482, 492, 493 A.2d 1233 (1985) (citation omitted). When such ethical infractions demonstrate a pattern of neglect and of misrepresentation to clients, a period of suspension is warranted. In re Cullen, 112 *41 N.J. 13, 20, 547 A.2d 697 (1988); In re O'Gorman, supra, 99 N.J. at 492, 493 A.2d 1233; In re Getchius, 88 N.J. 269, 276, 440 A.2d 1341 (1982).

We have noted, however, in such cases that "the picture presented is not that of an isolated instance of aberrant behavior unlikely to be repeated. [The attorney's] conduct over a period of years has exhibited a 'pattern of negligence or neglect in the handling of matters.' " In re Getchius, supra, 88 N.J. at 276, 440 A.2d 1341 (quoting In re Fusciello, 81 N.J. 307, 310, 406 A.2d 1316 (1979)). The Cullen case involved two instances of neglect; O'Gorman involved four instances of neglect after being suspended for five prior similar complaints; and Getchius involved six instances of neglect. Other cases of suspension for client neglect and misrepresentation include In re Terner, 120 N.J. 706, 577 A.2d 511 (1990) (three-year suspension for pattern of neglect for failure to communicate with thirteen clients despite potential mitigating factor of drug addiction, which respondent denied); In re Stein, 97 N.J. 550, 483 A.2d 109 (1984) (six-month suspension for "pattern of neglect" in handling three matters coupled with self-dealing in another matter); In re Goldstaub, 90 N.J. 1, 446 A.2d 1192 (1982) (one-year suspension for pattern of neglect involving three civil cases and one criminal case combined with long history of ethical complaints). In light of respondent's unblemished record for almost two decades, he does not fall within the end of the spectrum that warrants suspension.

III

[4][5][6][7] "[T]he principal reason for discipline is to preserve the confidence of the public in the integrity and trustworthiness of lawyers in general." In re Kushner, supra, 101 N.J. at 400, 502 A.2d 32 (quoting In re Wilson, supra, 81 N.J. at 456, 409 A.2d 1153). In making disciplinary decisions, we must consider the interests of the public as well as of the bar and the individual involved. Ibid. "The severity of discipline to be imposed must comport with the seriousness of the ethical infractions in light of *42 all the relevant circumstances." In re Nigohosian, 88 N.J. 308, 315, 442 A.2d 1007 (1982). For that reason, we consider factors in mitigation of the seriousness of the offense. In re Hughes, 90 N.J. 32, 36, 446 A.2d 1208 (1982).

Although respondent's conduct was inexcusable in that he had compounded his initial neglect in not filing an answer with his later neglect and misrepresentation concerning his efforts to vacate the default judgment, the ethical misconduct is related to one client transaction. The closest analogous case, In re Kantor, 118 N.J. 434, 435, 572 A.2d 196 (1990), also involved a single failure to file an appellate brief and to represent truthfully the status of the appeal, but the one-year suspension reflected that it was conduct "viewed in combination with a prior ethics infraction and lack of mitigating factors." Generally, in the absence of conduct evidencing a disregard for the ethics system, cases involving a similar mixture of ethics infractions have resulted in a reprimand. See, e.g., In re Onorevole, 144 N.J. 477, 677 A.2d 210 (1996) (reprimand for gross neglect, lack of diligence, failure to communicate, failure to cooperate with disciplinary authorities and misrepresentation; attorney misrepresented to client that he had filed a complaint and that court was backlogged in filing complaints, when in fact attorney had not filed the complaint at all); In re **938 Horton, 132 N.J.266, 624 A.2d 1367 (1993) (reprimand for lack of diligence, failure to communicate, failure to provide sufficient information to allow client to make informed decisions and misrepresentation; attorney allowed an appeal to be procedurally dismissed, based on his belief that he could not win appeal, first allowing his client to believe that appeal was pending and then attempting to mislead client into believing that appeal was dismissed on merits).

[8][9] "We ordinarily place great weight on the recommendation of the Disciplinary Review Board." In re Kushner, supra, 101 N.J. at 403, 502 A.2d 32; see also In re Vaughn, 123 N.J. 576, 589 A.2d 610 (1991) (adopting DRB's recommendation to reprimand publicly attorney who had failed to keep client informed, *43 displayed pattern of neglect and had failed to reply to DEC investigation). We greatly respect, as well, the views of the dissenting members of the DRB but believe that predictability and uniformity in the imposition of ethical decisions call for a public reprimand in these circumstances. We do not find that respondent's misconduct demonstrates dishonesty, deceit, or contempt for law, but rather an aberrational neglect of his responsibilities as an attorney. Respondent will suffer the reproach of his peers for the suffering inflicted on his client. Finally, we cannot overlook the fact that the default judgment of $1,700,000 was entered (perhaps against the wrong parties) in a case that settled for $11,500.

For all of these reasons, we conclude that the appropriate discipline is a public reprimand.

Respondent shall reimburse the Disciplinary Oversight Committee for appropriate administrative costs, including the costs of transcripts.

For reprimand—Chief Justice PORITZ and Justices HANDLER, POLLOCK, O'HERN, GARIBALDI, STEIN, and COLEMAN—7.

Opposed—None

ORDER

It is ORDERED that ROBERT E. RIVA of SHORT HILLS, who was admitted to the bar of this State in 1979, is reprimanded; and it is further

ORDERED that the entire record of this matter be made a permanent part of respondent's file as an attorney at law of this State; and it is further

ORDERED that respondent reimburse the Disciplinary Oversight Committee for appropriate administrative costs incurred in the prosecution of this matter.

END OF DOCUMENT

EXERCISES

1. List each of the attorney's actions in this case that amounted to a lack of diligence, incompetence, or failure to communicate with his client.

2. Discuss how you might have felt if you had been the attorney's client in this matter.

3. Why did the New Jersey Supreme Court only reprimand the attorney?

4. After reading the case, did you tend to agree with the New Jersey Supreme Court that ordered the attorney be reprimanded or with the Disciplinary Review Board that recommended a three-month suspension of the attorney? Explain your answer.

HUMAN RESOURCE MANAGEMENT

8

CHAPTER OBJECTIVES

After you read this chapter, you will be able to:
- Define and discuss the term *employment-at-will*.
- Discuss the Americans with Disabilities Act.
- Define what sexually harassing conduct is.
- List questions that cannot lawfully be asked in an employment interview.
- List questions that should be covered when performing reference checks.
- Explain the coaching technique.
- Discuss when terminating an employee is appropriate.
- Explain what positive discipline is.

The field of employment law has developed only during the past twenty years and is changing rapidly. Hiring, firing, reference checks, evaluations—everything has to be done just right or you can find yourself in trouble with low morale, high turnover rates, and even lawsuits. Then there are all the federal regulations: ADA (Americans with Disabilities Act), FMLA (Family and Medical Leave Act), FLSA (Fair Labor Standards Act), the Civil Rights Act, the Age Discrimination in Employment Act, and many more. Law offices have to be very careful to manage their human resources carefully and lawfully.

INTRODUCTION TO HUMAN RESOURCE MANAGEMENT

A law office has many types of resources, including computers, books, financial resources, and information, yet none is more important than its human resources—its people. Because law offices are in a service industry, they must rely on the expertise and performance of their employees to provide quality legal services to clients. Like any resource, a law office's human resources must be carefully managed. Human resource management is particularly important because in nearly every type of business, including law offices, roughly 75-80 percent of all expenses are for salaries and personnel-related matters.

In Chapter 1, **human resource management** was defined as the process of recruiting, hiring, training, evaluating, maintaining, and directing the human resources (i.e. the personnel) that will provide quality legal services to the clients. Some firms may refer to these duties as "personnel management" or "employee relations." In larger law firms and in corporate and many government practices, there is a human resources department. In smaller law offices and in many legal aid practices, an office manager or partner will handle these responsibilities. It is important to note that this chapter contains general information about human resource, personnel, and labor-related subjects. Because every state has its own statutes and rules that cover these areas, it is important to research the specific statutes in your state.

human resource management
The process of recruiting, hiring, training, evaluating, maintaining, and directing the human resources (i.e. the personnel) that will provide quality legal services to the clients.

WHY HUMAN RESOURCE MANAGEMENT FOR LEGAL ASSISTANTS?

The whole issue of human resources is profoundly important to most legal assistants. The obvious reason is that they personally are affected by human resource decisions, including being hired, receiving performance evaluations, and avoiding discipline problems. It is in a legal assistant's best interest to have an understanding of these issues. In addition, many legal assistants participate in hiring secretaries, clerks, and other legal assistants. Some law offices also have managing legal assistants who administer and run a legal assistant department. They typically are responsible for writing job descriptions for their department, interviewing and hiring personnel, and evaluating and disciplining people.

THE HIRING PROCESS

At some point in your career, you may be required to hire someone, such as a legal secretary, another legal assistant, or a clerk. It is important that you hire the right individual for the job the first time. A poor hiring decision can cost a law office literally thousands of dollars in wasted salary, wasted training expenses, wasted time, and potential malpractice problems. In addition, if the right person is not hired the first time, the firm must hire another individual and incur the cost of readvertising and retraining.

The hiring process is fairly detailed. Typically, a detailed job description is drafted, ads are placed in newspapers (or recruitment is started), resumes and employment applications are analyzed, candidates are interviewed, references are checked, and a final selection is made.

WRITING JOB DESCRIPTIONS

The first step in the hiring process is to write a detailed job description that explains what the duties of the position will be. If an employer does not know what the new hire is going to do, there is no way the employer can recognize the best person for the position. A detailed job description lets the employer match the strengths of candidates to the particular position that is being filled. Job descriptions also help the employee to understand his or her role in the firm and what will be expected. Most job descriptions include a job title, a summary of the position, a list of duties, and minimum qualifications that the new employee must have. (A salary range is optional; see Figure 8-1.)

All organizations should have job titles, even if there are only a few people in the law office. This gives each position an identity and a way to refer to the position itself. The "Summary" provides a brief overview of the position and describes who supervises the position. Essential "Duties and Responsibilities" is a list of the essential job functions. **Essential job functions** are job duties or tasks that are necessary for the completion of the job and that will take up a significant part of the employee's time. Care should be taken in drafting these essential job functions, especially when considering the Americans with Disabilities (ADA), which bans discrimination against persons with disabilities. If a job duty is included in the job description that is not essential and that might screen out otherwise qualified applicants who are disabled, the employer might be inviting an ADA complaint.

Suppose in the job description it is said that the legal assistant must be able to lift fifty-pound storage boxes, but in fact the legal assistant may only have to do this once

essential job functions
Job duties or tasks that are necessary to the completion of the job and that will take up a significant part of the employee's time.

**Figure 8-1
Sample Litigation
Legal Assistant Job
Description**

Job Description
JOB TITLE: **LEGAL ASSISTANT** (Litigation)

EXEMPT:		**GRADE LEVEL:**	10
DIVISION:	Legal	**LOCATION:**	Headquarters
DEPARTMENT:	Litigation		
INCUMBENT:			
REPORTS TO:	Attorney		
PREPARED BY:	Antonio Brown	**DATE:**	January 2003
APPROVED BY:	Susan Smith	**DATE:**	January 2003

SUMMARY:
Under supervision of an attorney, provides a broad range of professional and technical duties related to litigation. Performs factual investigations including gathering documents, researching records, and interviewing witnesses/clients. Works with the supervising attorney and client to prepare and answer discovery documents in draft form. Prepares deposition summaries, witness summaries and case chronologies or timelines. Manages and organizes litigation files and exhibits. Prepares drafts of pleadings and correspondence. Conducts legal research as needed. Manages the computerized litigation support for each case as needed.

ESSENTIAL DUTIES AND RESPONSIBILITIES (and other duties as assigned):
1. Performs factual investigations including gathering, analyzing and organizing documents such as medical records, police records, birth and death records, motor vehicle records, incorporation records and other documents using a variety of sources including the Internet, government agencies and other contacts. Compiles and summarizes data as necessary. Conducts interviews with clients and witnesses as needed. Works with expert witnesses as needed.
2. Performs a variety of tasks related to discovery under the supervision of an attorney including preparing drafts of interrogatories, requests for admissions, and requests for production of documents. Works with the attorney and client to prepare and coordinate drafts of discovery responses. May prepare drafts of deposition questions, coordinate deposition scheduling, and prepare case chronologies and timelines as necessary. Prepares deposition and witness summaries.
3. Organizes and maintains litigation files, prepares trial notebooks and assists in organizing, maintaining and indexing trial exhibits. Performs case management, docketing, scheduling and planning as needed.
4. Conducts drafts of legal research memorandums using the Internet, WESTLAW, LEXIS, CD-ROM databases and the law library as needed.

5. Prepares drafts of a variety of litigation-related legal documents under the supervision of an attorney including pleadings, motions, discovery documents and general correspondence.
6. Reviews, analyzes, organizes, indexes discovery documents and all case-related documents including managing the computerized litigation support for each case.

QUALIFICATION REQUIREMENTS:
To perform this job successfully, an individual must be able to perform each essential duty satisfactorily. The requirements listed below are representative of the knowledge, skill, and/or ability required. Reasonable accommodations may be made to enable individuals with disabilities to perform the essential functions.

MINIMUM EDUCATION AND EXPERIENCE:
Bachelor's degree (B.A.) from four-year college or university (major: legal assistance); or one to two years related experience; and/or training or equivalent work experience.

LICENSES/CERTIFICATIONS REQUIRED:
Paralegal certificate

KNOWLEDGE, SKILLS, AND ABILITIES REQUIRED:
Knowledge of the principles and procedures of legal research. Strong interpersonal and communication skills and the ability to work effectively with a wide range of constituencies in a diverse community. Skill in the use of personal computers and related software applications. Ability to draft legal documents, such as pleadings, legal responses, affidavits, position statements and briefs. Ability to develop and maintain recordkeeping systems and procedures. Database management skills. Ability to gather and organize legal evidence. Knowledge of litigation and civil procedure helpful. Knowledge of planning and scheduling techniques. Skill in organizing resources and establishing priorities. Ability to maintain confidentiality of records and information.

REASONING ABILITY:
Ability to define problems, collect data, establish facts and draw valid conclusions. Ability to interpret an extensive variety of legal instructions in different areas of the law and deal with several abstract and concrete variables.

LANGUAGE ABILITY:
Ability to read, analyze and interpret legal documents. Ability to write legal documents, and legal and business correspondence. Ability to effectively present information and respond to clients, attorneys, witnesses, opposing counsel and the general public.

(continued)

> **MATHEMATICAL SKILLS:**
> Ability to calculate figures and amounts such as percentages, discounts, interest, and general business and financial data.
>
> **PHYSICAL DEMANDS/WORK ENVIRONMENT:**
> The physical demands described here are representative of those that must be met by an employee to successfully perform the essential functions of this job. Reasonable accommodations may be made to enable individuals with disabilities to perform the essential functions.
>
> While performing the duties of this job, the employee is regularly required to sit; use hands to finger, handle, or feel objects, tools, or controls; and talk or hear. The employee frequently is required to reach with hands and arms. The employee is occasionally required to stand and walk.
>
> The employee must regularly lift and/or move up to 10 pounds, and frequently lift and/or move up to 25 pounds. Specific vision abilities required by this job include close vision.
>
> **WORK ENVIRONMENT:**
> The work environment characteristics described here are representative of those an employee encounters while performing the essential functions of this job. Reasonable accommodations may be made to enable individuals with disabilities to perform the essential functions. The noise level in the work environment is usually quiet.

or twice a year. This probably would not be an "essential job function" or a "significant" task. If a qualified applicant could show that he or she could perform all the truly essential job functions, the employer might be subject to an ADA complaint if the person is not hired because he or she cannot lift fifty pounds due to a disability.

When writing job descriptions, use simple, clear, concise, and easy-to-read language. When possible, use action verbs such as *prepares, maintains, performs, conducts, oversees, assists,* and *manages.* Refrain from using technical language because new employees and others will not be able to easily understand the job description. There is no way to anticipate every job duty. A technique for drafting good job descriptions is to talk to people who already are in the position being covered or who are in similar positions. They will have the most accurate information about the position.

Always include as a job duty a catch-all phrase stating that the applicant will be required to perform other functions not specifically listed as assigned by the supervisor, or words to the effect that the employee will act in the best interest of the firm, even if doing so requires actions or responsibilities not listed in the job description. This prevents individuals from saying, "It's not in my job description."

It is a good idea to periodically review existing job descriptions to monitor work load. It is important to note that job descriptions for existing positions should be made based on the *position* itself, not based on the individual holding the position. Think *positions,* not people. Do not draft or redraft job descriptions for specific individuals. At this stage, you cannot think about who will fill the position, only what duties and qualifications will best meet the needs of the organization.

ADVERTISING AND RECRUITING

After a detailed and accurate job description is drafted, organizations begin the actual hiring process. This includes either promoting from within the organization or recruiting candidates outside the organization. Recruiting candidates can include using newspaper advertisements, interviewing candidates at specific schools or institutions, using employment agencies and search firms, contacting professional associations, using the Internet, or receiving referrals from the organization's own employees on possible candidates.

Advertising in the Sunday issue of the newspaper gets more response than advertising on weekdays. A common question is whether employers *must* advertise positions in the newspaper, on the Internet, and other places. In many cases, employers hire from within their organizations, and it is not necessary to advertise positions to the public. In fact, there is no requirement that employers advertise at all, and they generally are free to hire individuals any way they like. However, if an organization wants to demonstrate that it is truly an equal opportunity employer, public advertisements provide an excellent way of doing this.

EMPLOYMENT APPLICATIONS AND RESUMES

Once an employer has drafted a detailed job description and advertised the position, the next step is to review the employment applications or resumes received.

In many cases, an organization will receive a resume first and then subsequently have the individual fill out a formal application for employment. An application for employment is a good idea because resumes are inconsistent and may not provide all the information needed to make a good decision.

Employment applications must comply with legal requirements and not ask for information that the employer is not entitled to have, such as information regarding race, religion, or age. Some organizations may use a resume evaluation form similar to Figure 8-2 to rank resumes and to make the hiring process as objective as possible.

INTERVIEWING

Once resumes and employment applications have been analyzed and the field of candidates narrowed, the next step is the interview process. The interview is typically the most dynamic part of the hiring process. This is the point where the interviewer decides which applicant is the most qualified and which one will "fit" with the organization. Below are some general insights regarding interviews.

RESUME EVALUATION FORM

Date: _____ Scoring: 70 points possible

Position: _____

Name of Candidate: _____

- SATISFIES MINIMUM QUALIFICATIONS OF THE POSITION:

    YES   NO
    If the candidate does not meet the minimum qualifications, do not continue.

1. RESUME (0–10 points)

    (Circle the description that best describes the category and award points accordingly; numbers in parentheses show the points available for that selection)

_____	(5–10)	neat, current, good format, professional looking
_____	(3–7)	typos, unclear, long, grammatical problems, not current
_____	(0–5)	unreadable, sloppy, careless
_____	(0)	resume not included
_____	(0–10)	other_____

2. EDUCATION (0–20 points)

_____	(15–20)	applicant's education — highly appropriate for the position
_____	(10–15)	applicant's education — average qualifications for the position
_____	(10–15)	applicant's education — overqualified for the position
_____	(0–10)	applicant's education — underqualified for the position
_____	(0)	no related education

3. WORK EXPERIENCE (0–20 points)

_____	(15–20)	applicant's experience shows he/she is highly qualified
_____	(10–15)	applicant's experience shows he/she has average qualifications
_____	(10–15)	applicant's work experience shows he/she is overqualified
_____	(0–10)	applicant's experience shows he/she is underqualified
_____	(0)	no related work experience

4. OTHER QUALIFICATIONS OR EXPERIENCES (0–10)

_____	(0–10)	active in community, serves on social boards, has contacts or experiences valuable to our organization
_____	(0–5)	other_____

5. OVERALL IMPRESSION (10)

_____	(0–10)	this score shows my overall impression of the candidate

TOTAL SCORE_____   Reviewer's Name: _____

NOTES:

This is only a sample and is not intended to be all-inclusive. Always consult your attorney before using any personnel-related form.

Figure 8-2   Resume Evaluation Form

SCREEN APPLICANTS TO BE INTERVIEWED A common problem that occurs during the interview is finding out that, while an applicant may look qualified on paper, it becomes clear that the organization is not interested in the applicant. In that case, the whole interview is a waste of both the employer's and applicant's time. One way to avoid this is to conduct a casual, phone screen of all applicants. By asking some salient questions on the phone, an interviewer can determine whether it is appropriate to have the applicant come in for a formal interview.

INSURE THAT ALL INTERVIEWS ARE CONSISTENT It is extremely important that all interviews conducted for a position are consistently done. The interviewer must make sure that all candidates are asked the same questions and that all candidates are treated fairly. It is easy during the interview process for an interviewer to think of additional questions and to ask different questions of candidates who come at the end of the process than those at the beginning. If interviews are not performed consistently, an interviewer may be giving preference or special treatment to one candidate over another. One way to maintain consistency is to have a written list of all questions to be asked and to follow a "script" of the interview. This will insure that everything done in each interview is the same. The more consistent the interview is, the less likely an organization will be susceptible to a discrimination complaint.

THE INTERVIEWER SHOULD TALK LESS AND LISTEN MORE The interviewer should talk as little as possible. Any time the interviewer is talking, he or she is giving up the opportunity to hear from the candidate, which is the whole purpose of the interview. Interviewers should avoid filling in pauses or completing sentences for candidates. Interviewers should also refrain from giving occupational or career advice to candidates. The purpose of the interview is to select the candidate who is the best for the job, not to counsel and give advice to the applicant.

ASK OPEN-ENDED AND BEHAVIORAL-BASED QUESTIONS Most questions in interviews today are open-ended in that no specific answer is hinted at or suggested by how the interview question is asked. The applicant must decide how to answer the question. For example, a typical open-ended question might be "Review your work experience for me and tell me how it prepares you for the position you have applied for." Another type of question that is typically asked in interviews is a behavioral-based question. A behavioral-based question asks the candidate to give a specific example from his or her past. For example, a typical behavioral-based question is "Tell me about a time you had a particularly difficult legal ethics problem and how you handled it." Many organizations use behavioral-based questions because it is believed that it is more difficult for an applicant to rehearse answers to behavioral-based questions. Good interviewers will ask candidates a variety of open-ended and behavioral-based questions that call for concrete examples relating to the candidate's personality, job history, education, and experience related to the job that they are hiring for (see Figure 8-3). A good interviewer will also make the candidate feel relaxed and comfortable during the interview so that he or she can obtain as much information as possible from the candidate.

**Figure 8-3
Open-Ended and
Behavioral-Based
Interview Questions**

Common Open-Ended Questions
- What experience do you have related to being a litigation legal assistant?
- What did you do to prepare for this interview and what do you know about our law firm?
- What are your strengths and weaknesses?
- What interests you in this position?
- What is your philosophy about serving clients?
- What kind of personal/professional characteristics do you work best with regarding your supervising attorney?

Common Behavioral-Based Questions
- Tell me about a time you used initiative and hard work to complete a project.
- What is your worst work-related failure?
- Give me an example of when you had to work with a difficult client.
- Tell me about a time you had a disagreement with your supervising attorney.
- What is the hardest case you ever worked on and what was your role?

**Figure 8-4
Interview Questions
that Should *Not* Be
Asked**

Race/Color/Religion/Sex:
Any question that is related to a candidate's race, color, religion, sex, national origin, age, disability, sexual orientation or veteran status.

Name/Marital Status:
- What was your maiden name?
- Have you ever used another name?
- Are you married? (permissible after hiring)
- What is your spouse's occupation?

Ancestry:
- Where were you born?
- Where does your family come from?
- That is an interesting last name. Where does it come from?

Residence:
- How long have you lived at this address?
- Do you own your house?
- Do you live with your parents?

Family/Personal:
- How many children do you have?
- How will you provide child care?
- Are you pregnant?
- Do you have a car?

> Credit/Financial:
> - Have you ever taken bankruptcy?
> - Have you been garnisheed?
>
> Age:
> - What is your date of birth? (permissible after hiring)
> - How old are you?
> - When did you graduate from elementary or high school?
>
> Organizations:
> - What organizations do you belong to? (You can ask this if you instruct them to delete organizations related to race, religion, color, disability, age, etc.).
> - Questions regarding union activity.
>
> Religion:
> - What church do you belong to?
> - What holidays do you celebrate?
> - Does your religion prevent you from working weekends?
>
> Medical:
> - Are you disabled or taking medication regularly? (You can ask whether they have the ability to perform the essential functions of job.)
> - Have you had any recent illnesses?
>
> Arrest Record:
> - Have you ever been arrested? (You can ask about convictions.)
>
> Military:
> - What type of discharge did you receive from the military?

USE DIVERSE INTERVIEW TEAMS Many organizations routinely use diverse interview teams to ensure that the selection process is fair. Diverse interview teams include team members that are culturally diverse and are also made up of males and females. Using a diverse team approach allows multiple people with different views and backgrounds to select candidates based on objective rather than discriminatory reasons. Using diverse interview teams helps to protect the organization from discrimination claims as well as to select the best candidate.

AVOID DISCRIMINATORY QUESTIONS Particular caution should be used when deciding what interview questions to ask. There are many questions that should be avoided because they might be considered discriminatory (see Figure 8-4). Figure 8-4 is not an all inclusive list, as many states and local governments have additional anti-discrimination laws. As a rule, if a question is not directly relevant to the position or to job performance, an interviewer should not ask it. There is no reason to take unnecessary risks. Questions that are personal or family-related should be avoided. The problem with most personal questions is that they relate to the applicant's race, color, religion, sex, national origin, age, or disability. Many city statutes and ordinances prevent discrimination on the basis of sexual orientation, so questions related to this should be avoided as well.

REFERENCE CHECKS

Once the employer has narrowed the list to two or three final candidates, the only thing left to do is to check references. Checking references is an important part of the hiring process and should never be left out (see Figure 8-5). Researchers have found that nearly 30 percent of all resumes contain exaggerated statements or misstatements

---

Applicant Name: _____ Date: _____
Employer/reference name: _____
Organization: _____
Dates known: From_____ To _____
Job Title/Duties: _____

Quality/quantity of applicant's work: _____

What kind of communications skills did the applicant have: _____

How did the applicant get along with clients, peers, attorneys, and other team members? _____

Was the applicant dependable? _____

Did the applicant have any outstanding skills or abilities? _____

Did the applicant have any problems or shortcomings? _____

Describe applicant's work style or potential: _____

Supervisory/managerial skills or potential: _____

Why did the applicant leave? _____

Eligible for rehire: Yes   No
Recommendation for this job: _____

Comments: _____

By: _____ Date: _____

Figure 8-5 Reference Check Questionnaire

about education or employment history. In addition, employers have been held liable for negligent hiring. **Negligent hiring** is when an employer hires an employee without sufficiently and reasonably checking the employee's background. In one case, an apartment complex was found liable after a new manager used a pass key to enter an apartment and rape a tenant. The apartment complex failed to check the new manager's references and reasonably investigate the person's background for felony convictions, fighting, and other criminal activity. Thus, references should always be checked and gaps in employment and other indicators of such behavior should be investigated.

> **negligent hiring**
> Hiring an employee without sufficiently and reasonably checking the employee's background.

The following are some hints on how to get good information when performing reference checks.

CALL PAST EMPLOYERS/SUPERVISORS Typically, the most relevant information an employer can gather is from the candidate's last employer or supervisor. Call these people first. Although some of these people will refuse to give out any information for fear of being sued for defamation if they say something negative, many will still answer your questions. A way around this problem is to ask potential candidates to sign a release or waiver that allows the past employer to talk to you openly and freely without fear of being sued for defamation.

BE PREPARED AND KNOW WHAT YOU WANT TO ASK Before you call, have a list of questions you want to ask. Ask specific questions about the candidate's dates of employment, job duties and responsibilities, quality and quantity of work, disciplinary problems, work attitude, communication skills, dependability, ability to be a team player, and reason for leaving. Also ask whether the former employer would rehire the person. You also might want to confirm the information in the candidate's resume. Always avoid questions related to race, religion, national origin, age, etc.

CALL INSTITUTIONS/SCHOOLS If a candidate lists graduation from a school or institution, call the school and confirm it. This usually does not take a great deal of time. This is seldom done and many candidates claim that they have finished degrees when, in fact, they have not. Also, if a candidate claims he or she was in the top 5 percent of the class or received an honor, check on it.

BE FRIENDLY When calling references, always be friendly and tell them that you are calling because a candidate has applied for a job with your organization. It is not necessary that you give them any other information. Your goal is to encourage the reference to give you information about the candidate's previous work.

CALL CHARACTER REFERENCES LAST Candidates only give potential employers character references who will give them a glowing recommendation. Expect this, but ask specific questions as well.

AFTER THE SELECTION

Once the employer has checked references and selected an individual, and the individual has agreed to work for the employer, it is a good idea on the employee's first day of work to give him or her a thorough orientation to your office. Figure 8-6 shows an example of a orientation checklist. Special attention should be made to the

**Figure 8-6
New Employee
Checklist**

Name: _____ Hire Date: _____
Title: _____ Phone Number: _____
Address: _____
Employee Number: _____

WELCOME
- Welcome the employee to the organization
- Introduce the employee to fellow staff members
- Show the employee his or her work area
- Give employee key to office/building
- Explain how to request supplies
- Issue computer access

FORMS, BENEFITS, POLICIES
- Give the employee a copy of the personnel handbook
- Give the employee a copy of the staff manual
- Complete Form I–9
- Complete Application for Employment
- Complete W–4
- Explain Insurance Plans/Complete Forms
    - Group Life
    - Group Health
    - Group Disability
    - Retirement Plan
- Explain Pay Procedures
- Explain billing requirement/practices

GENERAL INFORMATION
- Assign parking
- Explain timesheets
- Explain telephone procedures
- Explain office hours
- Explain vacation and sick-leave policy
- Explain overtime policy
- Explain ethics and confidentiality policy
- Show employee location of restrooms
- Show employee break rooms and explain break policy
- Explain lunch policy
- Explain smoking policy
- Explain dress policy
- Explain evaluation procedures
- Explain bonus policy

INS (Immigration and Naturalization Service) I-9 Form. This form establishes that the individual can legally work in this country. An I-9 Form *must* be completed according to federal law and must be retained by the employer. In addition, a W-4 Form showing withholding deductions *must* be completed and retained for the employee file.

FAIR CREDIT REPORTING ACT   **The Fair Credit Reporting Act** governs the use of "consumer reports" in all employment decisons. **The Fair Credit Reporting Act** is federal legislation that limits how "consumer reports" are used. "Consumer reports" is defined very broadly and includes reference checks, education checks, credit history reports, and criminal background checks when an employer hires a third party to conduct these checks. If an employer conducts these checks himself or herself, compliance with the Fair Credit Reporting Act is not required. However, if a third party is used, the organization must comply. The employer must give prior written notice to the applicant before procuring the consumer report, and obtain prior written authorization by the applicant before obtaining the consumer report. Before "adverse action" is taking against the applicant (such as not hiring the applicant based on the consumer report), the applicant must be provided with a copy of his or her report and notified of his or her legal rights regarding the consumer report.

> **Fair Credit Reporting Act**
> Federal legislation that governs the use of consumer reports in all employment decisions.

PERFORMANCE EVALUATIONS

Timely performance evaluations are a strong human resource development technique. Employees need to know on a regular basis what they are doing right and where they need to improve. Performance evaluations allow employees to know where they stand and to help them to grow and progress. It is important to see a performance evaluation not as a heavy object to beat or threaten employees with, but as a part of the communication process of working with employees toward a common goal.

If done correctly, evaluations can strengthen ties with employees by allowing them to participate in the evaluation process. In the end, a well-defined evaluation process can make the organization more efficient. Employee evaluations should be conducted privately, and, when possible, the evaluation itself should be given to the employee before the meeting so that he or she is prepared to talk about the evaluation and its findings. The evaluation should always be performed in writing and should be kept in the employee's personnel file.

EVALUATIONS SHOULD BE DONE REGULARLY   To be effective, evaluations should be done on a regular basis. Some offices evaluate employees quarterly, biannually, or annually. Quarterly or biannually is recommended because criticism or praise usually has more effect soon after an incident has happened.

EVALUATIONS SHOULD BE OBJECTIVE AND MATCH RATINGS WITH PERFORMANCE   Evaluations should be based on objective performance by an employee and not on any personal likes or dislikes the employer has for an employee. It is particularly important to match ratings with performance and to be fair about it. Do not set quotas, such as mandating that 70 percent of employee evaluations be "average," 20 percent "above average," and 10 percent "outstanding." Employees often complain about evaluations being unfair in that, although they might have worked particularly hard, they were still given an "average" rating. This is very discouraging for most employees. It is important that employers communicate with employees on a regular basis and take a "hands-on" approach to knowing whether or not employees really deserve a certain rating. Using objective criteria and actual examples of the employee's performance will help in this process. Examples of how the employee earned the "excellent" or "average" performance rating will help identify what he or she is doing correctly or incorrectly.

EVALUATION METHODS SHOULD BE CONSISTENT It is a good idea to use the same evaluation method so that evaluations done at different times can be compared. This will allow you to track the process of an individual consistently.

ELICIT OPEN COMMUNICATION AND SET MUTUAL GOALS FOR IMPROVEMENT Any evaluation method must allow the employee to participate in the process by communicating how he or she feels about the evaluation, including what he or she likes or dislikes and what both parties can do to help solve problems. There must be a give-and-take relationship in the evaluation process to make it work. One technique is to ask the employee how he or she feels the year went; what went right or wrong. Let him or her do the talking. This will put him or her at ease and will let the person feel that he or she has taken part in the process. Setting realistic goals to solve the problems also helps to communicate what is expected of the employee in the future. One way of doing this is for the employer to set certain goals and then have the employee set certain goals as well.

COACHING TECHNIQUE—ONGOING EVALUATION

coaching technique
Counseling that focuses on the positive aspects of the employee's performance and explores alternative ways to improve his or her performance.

One way to help an employee succeed in his or her job is to coach and counsel the employee on a daily ongoing basis. The **coaching technique** focuses on the positive aspects of the employee's performance and explores alternative ways to improve his or her performance. Most people are more willing to listen to advice from a "friend" who is interested in their well being than from a disinterested and heavy-handed "boss." The coaching technique is borrowed from sports, where a coach works with an individual to overcome deficiencies by counseling and by explaining problems to the person.

The coaching technique works best when the supervisor has had direct experience in the employee's position. This allows the supervisor to give good, concrete tips, examples, information, and opinions that the employee can use. Employees typically are more willing to accept the advice if the supervisor has been in the same position. When discussing areas that need improvement, try not to be judgmental, but instead give advice on exactly how to correct a deficiency. This technique is especially useful when an employee lacks knowledge about a situation. One of the

> 1. Event—Describe exactly what happened; do not be negative, just state the fact.
> 2. Effect—Describe the impact of the event, who or what was adversely affected and why; be specific. Let the employee know why the behavior should be changed.
> 3. Advice—Describe exactly how the employee can improve performance in the future.
> 4. Remind—Emphasize that you believe the employee is competent and that this was just a lapse.
> 5. Reinforce—Monitor the employee's performance. If the employee corrects the mistake, let him or her know that he or she is doing it right. Reinforce the positive change he or she made.

Figure 8-7
The Coaching Technique

Source: Adapted from *Complete Personnel Administration Handbook for Law Firms,* Altman Weil Pensa. 1991, 8.4.2. Reprinted with the permission of Altman Weil Pensa Publications, Inc., copyright 1991 by Altman Weil Pensa Publications, Inc., Newtown Square, Inc.

most positive aspects of the coaching technique is that it does not place blame on the employee; the employee is able to retain his or her self-esteem, which can be lost when an employee is simply reprimanded. Figure 8-7 explains how the coaching technique works. The coaching technique is not a substitute for a regular evaluation, but it is a technique for helping an employee be successful in his or her job.

EVALUATION FORMS AND TECHNIQUES

There are many techniques and forms that can be used when completing a formal evaluation, including general performance evaluations, job-based/job-description, and goal setting methods such as management by objectives (MBO), which is discussed later in this section. The evaluation technique used depends on the needs of the employer.

GENERAL PERFORMANCE EVALUATION FORM Figure 8-8 contains a general performance evaluation form that could be used for many law office support jobs. This type of evaluation is quick to prepare and straightforward. However, this type of checklist is not job-specific and does not allow a great deal of interaction on the part of the employee. If possible, it is beneficial to allow the employee to make comments and to be an active participant in the evaluation process.

JOB-SPECIFIC FORM BASED ON THE JOB DESCRIPTION One technique of analyzing performance is to use the job description as a guide for evaluating performance. Since the job description sets out the essential functions of the position, an employer should be able to go down the list of duties and responsibilities and talk about the employee's performance regarding each duty. This allows the employer to accurately break down the employee's performance so that he or she knows exactly what areas need improvement.

GOAL SETTING AND MANAGEMENT BY OBJECTIVES (MBO) Another type of performance system is based on goal setting, also commonly referred to as

LEGAL ASSISTANT PERFORMANCE EVALUATION

Name: _____ Title: _____

Evaluation Type: Introductory Period   Six Month   Annual   Special: _____

Date: _____ Score: _____

Evaluate the staff member's performance using the following rating criteria and make comments as necessary.

Rating: Description:
  5 — **Outstanding**—Employee's performance is exceptional and far exceeds normal expectations.
  4 — **Above Average**—Employee's performance is very good and exceeds expectations.
  3 — **Average**—Employee performs to normal expectations of the position.
  2 — **Below Average**—Employee's performance falls below acceptable levels from time to time.
  1 — **Unacceptable**—Employee's performance is completely unacceptable.

1. **Competence in the Law Office**
   _____ a. Is technically competent in all areas of work.
   _____ b. Other staff members have confidence in and trust the employee's work.
   _____ c. Continuously strives to learn and expand his/her competence level.
   Comments: _____
   _____
   _____

2. **Quality of Work**
   _____ a. Is accurate in all work.
   _____ b. Is thorough and complete in all work.
   _____ c. Takes pride in work.
   _____ d. Work is consistently of high quality.
   Comments: _____
   _____
   _____

3. **Dependability**
   _____ a. Highly dependable.
   _____ b. Good attendance.
   _____ c. Work is always turned in timely.
   _____ d. Can be counted on in a crisis.
   _____ e. Works independently without need of supervision.
   Comments: _____
   _____
   _____

Figure 8-8 Legal Assistant Performance Evaluation

4. **Work Habits/Attitude**
   _____ a. Has excellent work habits.
   _____ b. Is neat in appearance and in work habits.
   _____ c. Works hard and efficiently.
   _____ d. Is conscientious and contributes new ideas.
   _____ e. Accepts criticism professionally.
   _____ f. Has a positive and enthusiastic attitude.
   _____ g. Acts as a team player.
   _____ h. Gets along with other staff members and supervisors.
   Comments: _____

5. **Communication/Relationships**
   _____ a. Treats clients professionally.
   _____ b. Treats other staff members professionally.
   _____ c. Can write effectively.
   _____ d. Has good grammar skills.
   _____ e. Listens effectively.
   _____ f. Can make self understood orally.
   _____ g. Develops and maintains efficient relationships.
   Comments: _____

6. **Judgment**
   _____ a. Makes sound judgment calls.
   _____ b. Exercises appropriate discretion.
   _____ c. Intelligently arrives at decisions.
   _____ d. Thinks through decisions.
   Comments: _____

7. **Initiative**
   _____ a. Accepts new assignments willingly.
   _____ b. Takes on new responsibilities without being asked.
   Comments: _____

OVERALL RATING: **Outstanding   Above Average   Average   Below Average   Unacceptable**

(continued)

General Comments:
_____
_____
_____
_____

Employee's Strengths:
_____
_____
_____
_____
_____
_____

Areas Which Need Improving/Recommendations:
_____
_____
_____
_____
_____

Supervisor Signature:_____ Employee Signature: _____
Date: _____ Date: _____

Employee signature only verifies that this evaluation has been discussed and does not indicate agreement with the evaluation.

EMPLOYEE SELF-APPRAISAL

A. What were your achievements this year?

B. List any goals you would like to achieve next year.

C. What strengths do you have in performing this position?

D. What areas do you think you can improve upon?

E. What can your supervisor do to help you reach your goals?

F. Overall, how would you rate your own performance level?

**Figure 8-9
Management by
Objectives Process**

1. Employee and supervisor agree on the employee's major performance objectives for the coming period, including target dates for accomplishing each part of them.
2. Employee and supervisor agree on how the objectives will be measured and how it will be decided if the objectives have been met.
3. Employee and supervisor meet periodically to discuss the employee's progress toward meeting the goals.
4. At the end of the period, an accomplishment report is prepared stating which objectives were met or not met.
5. Awards or incentives are given depending on whether the objectives were met.

"management by objectives" (see Figure 8-9). In a **management by objectives** performance program, the employee and employer agree at the beginning of the evaluation period what the goals for the employee will be. Also included will be target dates for reviewing the employee's progress toward the goals and a determination for how it will be decided whether the goal was achieved or not. An accomplishment report is prepared detailing which goals were accomplished, and rewards or incentives are given for meeting the goals. For example, a goal might be to reduce nonbillable hours by 5 percent or increase billable hours by fifty hours during the fourth quarter. MBO programs generally require quite a bit of time, planning, and paperwork, but they can be very successful programs if managed correctly.

management by objectives
A performance program in which the individual employee and the employer agree on goals for the employee.

EMPLOYEE ATTITUDE SURVEYS

If an employer is willing to evaluate the performance of its staff, it also should be prepared to allow the staff to evaluate it. An **employee attitude survey** is a survey that is given to the employees of an organization asking them to rate the effectiveness of the organization in many specific areas. Management can gain a great deal of information from its employees on how the organization can be run more effectively. Figure 8-10 shows an example of an employee attitude survey. These surveys allow employees to be critical of management and to suggest ways that management can improve the way in which it meets the needs of the staff. They allow the staff members to suggest and share ideas that they otherwise might not. They also are a very good way to test employee morale and discover how morale might be increased. Employee attitude surveys are another means of increasing communication between employers and employees.

In addition, employee attitude surveys help law offices keep the staff turnover rate down. Staff turnover is very costly. Every time a law office hires an employee, the office must invest a large amount of resources, including the time and energy of existing staff, to train the employee. Other factors are the time and cost of the mistakes of new employees as they learn about the employer's business, Social Security

employee attitude survey
A survey that is given to an organization's employees asking them to rate the effectiveness of the organization in many specific areas.

Employee Attitude Survey

Introduction

The purpose of this survey is to give you a chance to express your feelings about various aspects of your work. These aspects include such things as working conditions, pay, benefits, etc. The survey consists of two sections:

In Section I, we ask several questions to determine what you like and don't like about your present job, and how satisfied you are with different aspects of your present job.

In Section II, we ask for your written comments in areas of general interest.

Your answers to the survey questions will be *confidential.* We want to encourage you to be completely frank in telling us how you feel about the different aspects of your job. Only then will your survey have any real meaning.

Thank you for taking part in this survey.

Section I

Following you will find statements about certain aspects of your present job. Read each statement carefully and decide how satisfied you are with the aspect to which it refers.

- Circle "1" if you are *not satisfied* with that aspect of your job
- Circle "2" if you are *only slightly satisfied* with that aspect of your job
- Circle "3" if you are *satisfied* with that aspect of your job
- Circle "4" if you are *very satisfied* with that aspect of your job
- Circle "5" if you are *extremely satisfied* with that aspect of your job

ON MY PRESENT JOB, THIS IS HOW I FEEL ABOUT

For Each Statement Circle a Number

1. My job in general, considering all things. 1 2 3 4 5
2. The chance to do something that makes use of my abilities. 1 2 3 4 5
3. My present salary or pay rate. 1 2 3 4 5
4. My pay when compared to the amount of work I do. 1 2 3 4 5
5. How well my pay compares with that of others outside the office. 1 2 3 4 5
6. How substantial my pay raises are. 1 2 3 4 5
7. My overall benefit program. 1 2 3 4 5
8. The way my vacation, sick leave and holiday schedules compare with those of other offices. 1 2 3 4 5
9. The way my medical, dental and life insurance plans compare with those of other offices. 1 2 3 4 5
10. My working conditions (heating, lighting, office equipment/supplies, work space). 1 2 3 4 5
11. The opportunities for promotion for me. 1 2 3 4 5
12. The degree to which my performance appraisal is based on what I do. 1 2 3 4 5
13. The way my supervisor(s) treats me. 1 2 3 4 5
14. The way my attorney(s) treat me. 1 2 3 4 5
15. How the office values my opinions and suggestions. 1 2 3 4 5
16. The personnel policies and practices of the office. 1 2 3 4 5
17. The recognition I get for the work I do. 1 2 3 4 5
18. How clearly I understand everything I am required to do. 1 2 3 4 5
19. How clearly the offices aims and plans are stated. 1 2 3 4 5
20. The orientation and training I receive. 1 2 3 4 5
21. The way the office hires qualified people. 1 2 3 4 5
22. My knowledge of what my supervisor(s) expects from me. 1 2 3 4 5
23. My knowledge of what my attorney(s) expects from me. 1 2 3 4 5
24. My job security. 1 2 3 4 5
25. The ease of approaching personnel and management with work-related problems. 1 2 3 4 5

(continued)

Figure 8-10 Employee Attitude Survey

Section II

On this and the following pages, you will be asked to comment on several general topics. This section gives you opportunity to express your opinions regarding both satisfaction and dissatisfaction in your working environment.

Your frank and thoughtful comments will be appreciated.

1. The suggestion I would make to improve the office's physical environment or technology is: _____
_____
_____
_____

2. My thoughts regarding the pay and benefit package are: _____
_____
_____
_____

3. What I like most about the supervisor for whom I work is (answer if applicable): _____
_____
_____
_____

4. What I like most about the attorney(s) for whom I work is (answer if applicable): _____
_____
_____
_____

5. What bothers me most about the supervisor(s) for whom I work is (answer if applicable): _____
_____
_____
_____

6. What bothers me most about the attorney(s) for whom I work is (answer if applicable): _____
_____
_____
_____

7. What I need to get my current job done that I don't already have is: _____
_____
_____
_____

(continued)

8. My thoughts about the overall office management are: _____
_____
_____
_____

9. This law office could do the following to make my job more satisfying: _____
_____
_____
_____

10. Any other comments and/or suggestions concerning your work relationship with this law office? _____
_____
_____
_____

11. Any comments and/or suggestions concerning this survey? _____
_____
_____
_____

tax that every employer must pay on the employee, and additional seminars or other training the employee may need. Also, when a well-trained employee leaves, he or she takes all the knowledge he or she gained from the employer (this hurts the employer, since his or her expertise is now gone and that employee must be replaced), and, in some cases, the employee actually may leave to go to work for one of the office's competitors. Another way of trying to reduce staff turnover is to hold an exit conference with employees who choose to leave the law office. This allows the law office to find out why the employee was unhappy so the employer can take positive steps to prevent others from leaving.

TERMINATION

In all organizations, it is necessary to terminate employees at some time or another. For many people, terminating employees is hard to do. However, it can be the only reasonable recourse in circumstances in which an employee is acting in a counterproductive manner to the goals of the organization. It can be a positive experience for the remaining employees of the organization, in cases in which the employee's conduct has brought down employee morale or when others have had to work harder to make up for the employee's poor performance. There are many nuances to terminating people correctly so that costly lawsuits and other unpleasant situations are avoided.

WHEN CAN AN EMPLOYEE BE TERMINATED?

In many states, an employer is allowed to terminate an employee for any reason as long as it is nondiscriminatory and does not violate a public policy. This is called "employment-at-will." In these instances, an employee serves at the leisure of the employer. Some states do not recognize the employment-at-will doctrine, but instead require that an employer terminate employees only when "just cause" exists. Employment-at-will does not apply if an employment contract exists between the employer and employee or in a collective-bargaining agreement. Instead, the contract or bargaining agreement determines when termination is allowed.

However, even in an employment-at-will situation, an employer should always avoid terminating an employee for arbitrary reasons. Terminating an employee for unjustified or arbitrary reasons can be as harmful to employee morale as the failure to terminate a nonproductive worker. Whenever possible, employees should only be terminated as a last resort and for "just cause." That is, employers should have a good reason for taking the action, should follow their own rules, and give the employee notice and opportunity to be heard regarding the charges.

There are three general and justifiable reasons for terminating an employee.

1. Disciplinary causes—This includes violating the organization's policies or known rules, such as acting dishonestly or unethically, falsifying records, fighting, being intoxicated, or using illegal substances.
2. Poor job performance—This includes failure to perform work, poor attitude, uncooperative behavior, excessive absenteeism, insubordination, and others.
3. Economic conditions—This includes layoffs and cutbacks because of poor economic conditions for the organization.

It is important that a list of unacceptable behaviors be included in an organization's employee handbook. Employees also can be terminated for serious misconduct off the job, but the employee handbook should define what type of misconduct would lead to dismissal.

WHAT IS NOT CAUSE FOR EMPLOYEE TERMINATION

An employer cannot terminate employees based on any kind of discriminatory reason related to race, color, religion, sex, or disability (and sexual orientation by ordinance in some cities/states). The organization should always avoid even the appearance of discrimination. An employer should never terminate employees for petty or personal reasons because it may appear that the termination was done for an unlawful purpose such as discrimination, and can lead to a wrongful termination lawsuit. In a **wrongful termination lawsuit,** the former employee alleges that an employer unlawfully terminated the employee. Depending on the former employee's allegations, he or she can recover back pay and punitive damages and be reinstated.

wrongful termination lawsuit
A lawsuit in which a former employee alleges that an employer unlawfully terminated the employee.

Personnel Policies

One of the most useful things a law office of any type can do to effectively manage its human resources is to create a comprehensive and up-to-date personnel handbook. A **personnel handbook** (sometimes called an employee handbook or it also can be a part of the law office staff manual) lists the formal personnel policies of an organization. Personnel handbooks (1) establish formal policies on personnel matters so staff members will know what to expect of management and what management expects of them regarding personnel issues; (2) establish a standard so that all employees are treated fairly and uniformly; and (3) help to protect the law office if it is involved in litigation regarding personnel matters and to avoid government-compliance problems. In some law offices, the staff manual covers both substantive law office policies and personnel policies.

personnel handbook
A manual that lists the formal personnel policies of an organization.

WRITING PERSONNEL POLICIES

Personnel policies are best when written in clear, specific language that is easy to read and understand. The drafter should explain personnel-related procedures leaving little room for interpretation. Figure 8-11 contains an anti-harassment policy. Notice in Figure 8-11 that the policy is quite specific in that it defines what harassment is, states how such complaints will be investigated, and gives the possible punishment.

Generally, personnel policies should cover any matter that concerns the employee and employer relationship. This is particularly true of frequently asked questions regarding employee benefits (compensation and fringe benefits), vacation and sick-leave time, termination, and so on. It is axiomatic that if an employer develops and publishes a personnel handbook, the office must be willing to be bound by these policies and to follow its own rules and regulations.

Some courts have interpreted personnel handbooks as an enforceable contract between the employer and employee. Thus, careful thought must go into any personnel policy. It is imperative that personnel policies be kept up-to-date to reflect the rules and regulations of the company. It also is recommended that each personnel policy include the date it was put into effect. In this way, a reader can tell how old each policy is. This can be helpful when updating policies.

Personnel handbooks should be easy to use and include a table of contents and possibly an index as well to encourage employees to use it.

Current Personnel Law Issues

Personnel-related issues are highly regulated and often litigated. The following is a sampling of some of the more important areas related to federal personnel/labor law.

> **ANTI-HARASSMENT**
>
> We are strongly committed to the principle of fair employment, and it is our policy to provide employees a work environment free from all forms of discrimination. In recognition of each person's individual dignity, harassment of employees will not be tolerated.
>
> Unwelcome harassment is verbal or physical conduct by an employee or any individual (including customers, vendors, or suppliers) which denigrates or shows hostility or aversion toward an employee and/or his or her relatives, friends or associates because of his or her race, color, sex, religion, age, national origin, handicap or disability, veteran status, sexual orientation or other status protected by law, and which:
>
> 1. has the purpose or effect of creating an intimidating, hostile, abusive or offensive working environment; or
> 2. has the purpose or effect of unreasonably interfering with an individual's work performance; or
> 3. otherwise adversely affects an individual's work performance.
>
> This includes acts which, are intended to be "jokes" or "pranks" but which are hostile or demeaning with regard to race, color, religion, gender, national origin, age, handicap or disability, veteran status, sexual orientation or other status protected by law.
>
> As part of this anti-harassment policy, no employee or any other individual (including customers, vendors, or suppliers) may sexually harass any employee. Sexual harassment includes unwelcome sexual advances, sexual jokes or comments, requests for sexual favors or other unwelcome verbal or physical conduct of a sexual nature. This policy is violated when:
>
> 1. submission to such conduct is made, either explicitly or implicitly, a condition of employment,
> 2. submission to or rejection of such conduct is used as a basis for employment-related decisions such as promotion, discharge, performance evaluation, pay adjustment, discipline, work assignment, or any other condition of employment or career development; or
> 3. such conduct otherwise unreasonably interferes with work performance or creates an intimidating, abusive or offensive working environment, even if it leads to no adverse job consequences.
>
> Any employee who has a question, concern, or complaint of discrimination, including harassment, based on race, color, sex, religion, age, national origin, handicap or disability, veteran status, sexual orientation or other protected
>
> *(continued)*

Figure 8-11
Anti-Harassment Policy

> status is encouraged to bring the matter to the immediate attention of his or her supervisor or manager. If for any reason the employee would feel uncomfortable discussing the situation with his or her supervisor or manager, or if he or she feels further discussion is needed, the employee should contact the Human Resources Manager.
>
> All reports of inappropriate conduct will be promptly and thoroughly investigated, and we ensure that any improper conduct will cease immediately and corrective action is taken to prevent a recurrence. Any employee who violates this policy will be subject to the full range of disciplinary action, up to and including termination of employment. We will inform the complaining employee of the resolution of the complaint as appropriate.
>
> All complaints will be treated confidential to the extent practical for an effective resolution. No employee will suffer adverse employment consequences as a result of making a good faith complaint or taking part in the investigation of a complaint. An employee who knowingly alleges a false claim against a manager, supervisor, or other employee or individual will be subject to the full range of disciplinary action, up to and including termination of employment. (1/2003)

EMPLOYMENT-AT-WILL DOCTRINE

employment-at-will doctrine
Doctrine that states that an employer and employee freely enter into an employment relationship and that either party has the right to sever the relationship at any time without reason.

The **employment-at-will doctrine** states that an employer and employee freely enter into an employment relationship and that either party has the right to sever the relationship at any time without reason. If an employee is covered by a union collective-bargaining agreement, employment contract, or civil service regulations, the employment-at-will doctrine does not apply, and the employer must comply with the terms of the contract or regulations. Employment-at-will typically happens when an employee works for an employer without any type of written agreement or reference to how long the employee will work. For example, suppose a law office hired a legal secretary in an employment-at-will state. The legal secretary did good work, but the firm subsequently changed its mind and decided that it did not need the extra position and terminated the secretary. This would be perfectly acceptable, and the secretary would have no basis for a lawsuit against the law office. For another example, suppose that the legal secretary gets a better-paying job at another law office and quits without giving notice. This also would be acceptable under employment-at-will status.

Organizations should be careful when drafting their personnel handbook to state that the policies in the handbook are not a contract or that employees will be retained for a certain amount of time. For example, an employer should not include language such as "If you do your work satisfactorily, you will always have a job here." The reason is that if a court finds that the employer gave an expectation to an employee that he would have a job forever (as long as the work was satisfactory) or that the policies in the personnel handbook were a type of contract, this would upset the normal expectation of employment-at-will. Personnel handbooks should contain a simple employment-at-will statement, typically near the front, that states:

> Employment-At-Will
> It is understood that these personnel policies and any other firm document do not constitute a contract for employment, and that any person who is hired may voluntarily leave employment upon proper notice, and may be terminated by the firm any time and for any reasons.

In addition, some employers require employees to sign a statement such as the one above as of employment or place the statement on the employment application form.

The employment-at-will doctrine does, of course, have limitations. Courts have found that at-will employees may have legal rights against employers, even though the employer is supposed to be able to terminate the employee without any reason. Instances include when the employer violates public policies, such as firing an employee for filing a workers' compensation claim, firing an employee for refusing to commit perjury, or terminating an employee to avoid paying retirement benefits or sales commissions. Other instances include terminating an employee based on discrimination (see below) or terminating an employee when the employer promised to retain the employee as long as the employee did a good job. Thus, although employment-at-will is a doctrine that runs in favor of employers, it is by no means absolute. In addition, some states by statute limit the employment-at-will doctrine, so any organization should know its own state laws as well.

When employment-at-will is not in effect or if there is an employment contract in place, the typical standard is "just cause." An employment contract is a contract between the employer and an employee setting out the terms and conditions of the employment relationship. "Just cause" means that before an employer can terminate an employee, the employer must have just cause or reasonable cause to do so. Just cause can include many things such as violating the company's rules and regulations, insubordination, and dishonesty.

THE FAMILY AND MEDICAL LEAVE ACT OF 1993

The **Family and Medical Leave Act of 1993 (FMLA)** applies to employers with fifty or more employees (and any public agency and any private elementary or secondary school) and provides that eligible employees be allowed up to twelve workweeks of unpaid leave within any twelve month period for (a) the birth or adoption of a child or placement of a child for foster care; (b) the care of a child, spouse, or parent with a serious health condition; and (c) the employee's own serious health condition. To be eligible for FMLA, an employee must have one year of service with the organization and worked at least 1,250 hours in the last year. The FMLA requires that an employee granted leave under the act be returned to the same position held before the leave or be given one that is equivalent in pay, benefits, privileges, and other terms and conditions of employment. The employee also is entitled to health care benefits during the leave. The purpose of the FMLA is to assist workers to better balance the demands of the workplace with the needs of their families.

Family and Medical Leave Act of 1993 (FMLA)
Legislation that allows employees in certain circumstances to have up to twelve workweeks of unpaid leave from their jobs for family or health-related reasons.

FAIR LABOR STANDARDS ACT

The Fair Labor Standards Act sets minimum wage and maximum hours of work for employees. It also requires that overtime pay (one-and-one-half times their normal rate) be paid to employees who work in excess of forty hours a week. Employees do not need to be paid overtime if they fall into one of the four "white-collar" exemptions: executive, administrative, professional, or outside sales (see Figure 8-12).

If an employee is exempt, it means that he or she is not required to be paid overtime wages. If an employee is nonexempt, it means he or she is required to be paid overtime wages. Whether legal assistants are exempt or nonexempt is a hotly debated issue. (See chapter 1 for a detailed discussion.)

EQUAL EMPLOYMENT OPPORTUNITY

Equal employment opportunity means that employers make employment-related decisions without arbitrarily discriminating against an individual. This is a statement that is often seen in want ads, employment applications, and other employment-related documents. Federal laws, including the **Civil Rights Act of 1964,** prohibit employers from discriminating against employees or applicants on the basis of race, color, national origin, religion, or gender. The **Americans with Disabilities Act of 1990 (ADA)** prohibits employers from discriminating against employees or applicants with disabilities (see the following section on the ADA). The **Age Discrimination in Employment Act of 1967** prohibits employers from discriminating against employees and applicants on the basis of age where the individual is forty or older. The **Equal Pay Act of 1963** prohibits employers from paying workers of one sex less than the rate paid an employee of the opposite sex for work on jobs that require equal skill, effort, and responsibility and that are performed under the same working conditions (see Figure 8-13). There are several other federal laws that legislate in this area. Most of the laws cited here make it unlawful for an employer to arbitrarily discriminate against employees or applicants.

Every personnel handbook should have a policy stating the law office's position on equal employment opportunity, such as:

Equal Employment Opportunity Statement
It is the policy of the firm to apply recruiting, hiring, promotion, compensation and professional development practices without regard to race, religion, color, national origin, sex, age, creed, handicap, veteran status or any other characteristic protected by law.

An exception to equal employment opportunity is when age, sex, or religion is a **bona fide occupational qualification** (BFOQ). A BFOQ means that to perform a specific job adequately, an employee must be of a certain age or sex or religion. A BFOQ does not apply to race or color. An example of a BFOQ would be for a position as a Catholic priest. The employer could reasonably discriminate against non-Catholics because the candidate must believe in and have knowledge of the Catholic religion to qualify. BFOQs generally have been narrowly construed by most courts, and there are few if any positions in a law office that would qualify.

---

equal employment opportunity
Concept that means that employers make employment-related decisions without arbitrarily discriminating against an individual.

Civil Rights Act of 1964
Legislation that prohibits employers from discriminating against employees or applicants on the basis of race, color, national origin, religion, or gender.

Americans with Disabilities Act of 1990 (ADA)
Legislation that prohibits employers from discriminating against employees or applicants with disabilities.

Age Discrimination in Employment Act of 1967
Legislation that prohibits employers from discriminating against employees and applicants on the basis of age when the individual is forty or older.

Equal Pay Act of 1963
Legislation that prohibits employers from paying workers of one sex less than the rate paid an employee of the opposite sex for work on jobs that require equal skill, effort, and responsibility and that are performed under the same working conditions.

bona fide occupational qualification
An allowable exception to equal employment opportunity. For example, for an employee to perform a specific job, the employee must be of a certain age or sex or of a certain religion.

Summary of White-Collar Exemptions Under the FLSA Short Test

- Exemptions are construed narrowly and against the employer.
- Exemptions must be plain and unmistakable.
- Each element of an exemption must be proven by substantial evidence by the employer.
- **MUST COMPLY WITH ALL REQUIREMENTS IN EACH COLUMN**

Description	EXECUTIVE EXEMPTION 29 C.F.R. Sect. 541.101	ADMINISTRATIVE EXEMPTION 29 C.F.R. Sect. 541.201	PROFESSIONAL EXEMPTION 29 C.F.R. Sect. 541.301	PROFESSIONAL (COMPUTER PROGRAMMING) EXEMPTION 29 C.F.R. Sect. 541.303	OUTSIDE SALES EXEMPTION 29 C.F.R. Sect. 541.500
Primary Duties:	– Primarily manages the agency, department or subdivision. (Usually over 50% of the employee's time must be in *managing and (supervising people)*. This includes interviewing, selecting, and training employees; setting and adjusting employees rates of pay and hours of work; directing employee work; appraising employees of their productivity and efficiency; handling employee complaints; planning employee work; controlling the flow and distribution of work; determining employee techniques to use; and providing for employee safety. – Customarily and regularly directs two or more "full-time" employees (80 hours a week of direct reports).	– Primarily performance of office work related to *management policies or business operations* (usually 50% or more of time). – Management policies/business operations = advising mgmt, planning, negotiating, representing the org, purchasing, research, etc. – Requires *actual discretion and independent judgment* in significant matters = independent choice free from immediate direction; – Not prescribed procedures or prescribed processes in manuals, etc. Person can have skills but not be truly independent. – Cannot be in "*production*" of a product, must be in management policy or business operations.	– Primarily consist of performing work requiring *advanced learning or that is original and creative* in a recognized artistic field or work as a teacher. – Requires the consistent exercise of discretion and judgment or consists of work requiring invention, imagination or talent in a recognized field of artistic endeavor. – Learned professions = law, medicine, nursing, teaching, accounting, actuarial, engineering, biology, data processing (computers) – Does NOT including any of the above in entry level positions. – Artistic Professions—music, theatre, creative writing, painters, etc.	– Highly skilled in computer systems analysis or programming. – "Application of systems analysis techniques and procedures including consulting with users to determine hardware, software, or system functions" – "Design development, documentation, analysis, creation, testing, or modification of computer systems or programs. – Does not include "trainees, entry level positions, employees engaged in operation of computers, manufacture, repair or maintenance of computer hardware."	– Employed for the purpose of *making sales or obtaining orders or contracts for services*. – Customarily and regularly engaged away from his or her employer's place or places of business typically devoted to retail or service establishment – Telephone sales are not outside.
Time Requirement	Usually 50% or more of time spent managing employees.	Usually 50% or more of time spent with management policy/business operations.	Usually 50% or more of time spent in above areas.	Usually 50% or more of time spent in above areas.	Cannot spend more than 20% of the normal workweek of the employer's nonexempt employees doing nonexempt wk.
Salary Requirement	Paid not less than $250 a week $13,000 yr.	Paid not less than $250 a week $13,000 yr.	Paid not less than $250 a week $13,000 yr.	Salary - Paid not less than $250 a week $13,000 yr. Hourly - Or $27.63 an hr.	None
Typical Examples:	Directors, Managers, Project Managers and Assistant Managers that have two or more people reporting to them.	Exec. Asst. to President; Asst. Manager, Insurance Expert, Tax Expert, Research Expert, Senior systems analysts (computer prof. re: business operations).	Doctors, lawyers, dentists, accountants, teachers, professors, registered nurses, engineers, scientists, composers, painters, soloists.	– Highly skilled, computer systems analysts, software engineers, and computer programmers".	– Commissioned outside sales people.

Figure 8-12 Who Are Exempt Employees?

Family and Medical Leave Act of 1993	Provides that eligible employees be allowed up to twelve workweeks of unpaid leave within any twelve-month period for: a) the birth or adoption of a child or placement of a child for foster care; b) the care of a child, spouse, or parent with a serious health condition; and c) the employee's own serious health condition.
Civil Rights Act of 1964	Prohibits discrimination against employees on the basis of race, color, religion, sex, or national origin. The Equal Employment Opportunity Commission (EEOC) was established to enforce this law.
Equal Pay Act of 1963	Prohibits employers from basing arbitrary wage differences on gender.
Age Discrimination in Employment Act of 1967 (ADEA) (Amended 1978)	Prohibits employers from discriminating against persons age forty or more on the basis of their age unless age is a bona fide occupational qualification.
Pregnancy Discrimination Act of 1978	Prohibits discriminating against women because of pregnancy.
Americans with Disabilities Act of 1990 (ADA)	Prohibits employers from discriminating against persons with disabilities in several different areas.
Civil Rights Act of 1991	Relaxed the burden of proof in discrimination claims and allows for greater recovery of damages.
Fair Labor Standards Act	Sets minimum wage and maximum basic hours of work for employees, and requires overtime pay for nonexempt employees.
Fair Credit Reporting Act	Limits and restrains the use of consumer reports (including reference and other employment checks on job applicants).

Figure 8-13 Partial List of Federal Employment Related Laws

AMERICANS WITH DISABILITIES ACT

The Americans with Disabilities Act of 1990 (ADA), among other things, makes it unlawful to discriminate in employment against qualified applicants and employees with disabilities. Under the ADA, a person has a "disability" if he or she has a physical or mental impairment that substantially limits a major life activity, such as seeing, hearing, breathing, speaking, walking, performing manual tasks, working, or learning. This does not include a minor impairment that is of short duration such as a broken limb, infection, or sprain. An individual with a disability also must be qualified to perform the essential functions of the job, with or without reasonable accommodation. That is, the applicant or employee must be able to satisfy the job requirements, including education, experience, skills, and licenses, and be able to perform the job. The ADA does not interfere with an employer's right to hire the best-qualified applicant but simply prohibits employers from discriminating against a qualified applicant or employee because of his disability.

The ADA also requires that employers "reasonably accommodate" persons with disabilities. An employer must make **"reasonable accommodation"** for a person with a disability, which may include existing facilities readily accessible, restructuring the job, or modifying work schedules. The ADA provides that individuals with disabilities have the same rights and privileges in employment as employees without disabilities. For example, if an employee lounge is in a place inaccessible to a person using a wheelchair, the lounge might be modified or relocated, or comparable facilities might be provided in a location that would enable the individual to take a break with co-workers. This is an example of "reasonable accommodations." Persons who have been discriminated against because of a disability can receive back-pay damages, reinstatement, punitive damages, and other remedies.

"reasonable accommodation"
Accommodating a person with a disability, which may include making existing facilities readily accessible, restructuring the job, or modifying work schedules.

SEXUAL HARASSMENT

Sexual harassment means unwelcome sexual advances, requests for sexual favors, and other verbal or physical conduct of a sexual nature that creates an intimidating, hostile, or offensive working environment.

Many people typically think of sexual harassment as a male supervisor sexually coercing a female subordinate in order for her to keep her position or to be promoted. Sexual harassment is much broader than this, however. Sexual harassment can include unwelcome sexual jokes, inappropriate sexual remarks, innuendos, insults, leering, subtle forms of pressure for sexual activity, vulgar or indecent language, sexual propositions, displaying sexually oriented photographs, and unwelcome and inappropriate touching, patting, and pinching.

Sexual harassment does not have to involve a subordinate and a supervisor; it also can take place with persons at the same job level. In addition, sexual harassment can involve clients as well. It has been reported that clients sometimes sexually harass law office staff. The law office also has as a duty to investigate a client harassing a staff member. The law office may be liable if it does not take appropriate action to protect its employees. Finally, although the majority of sexual harassment cases involve male employees harassing female employees, women also have been accused of sexually harassing male subordinates. In any case, the employer is responsible for taking corrective action.

sexual harassment
Unwelcome sexual advances, requests for sexual favors, and other verbal or physical conduct of a sexual nature that create an intimidating, hostile, or offensive working environment.

> Paralegal managers play a key role in preventing harassment by communicating policies and by keeping the door open to complaints . . . [W]e need to convey to legal assistants that we are sensitive to the situation and to assure them that they do not need to tolerate harassment. . . . The way to preempt problems down the road is to develop policies which prohibit sexual harassment, then communicate the policies to employees. Firms with a policy in place are less likely to face litigation because people have a place to go and feel as though they will be treated fairly.[1]

Managing Stress

A law office is an inherently stressful place with a constantly changing array of clients, activities, deadlines, appointments, problems, trials, and conflicts. All legal professionals must learn to manage stress. If you do not manage stress, the stress will manage you. Work-related stress, particularly in a law office, can come from an unlimited number of sources.

- A lack of ability to control one's surroundings
- Lack of recognition or feedback
- Uncertainty about the future
- Inability to guarantee a particular outcome
- Poor interpersonal relationships with other staff or clients
- Feeling threatened
- Inability to balance career and family obligations
- Not enough time to get everything done

People deal with stress in many different ways including feeling burned out, tense, anxious, and frustrated; becoming depressed; lashing out at others; experiencing health problems (high blood pressure/heart attacks, ulcers, headaches); having insomnia/sleep disorders; engaging in drug/alcohol abuse; or abusing children/spouses.

One way to prevent or deal positively with stress is to analyze what stressors are present in your life. You can then identify ways to reduce stress.

- **Identify areas of conflict, possible solutions, and take appropriate action.** Identify areas of conflict that are causing you stress, identify possible solutions, and then take action to eliminate or reduce whatever is causing you stress. Ignoring the problem or procrastinating only makes the matter worse and increases the stress to unbearable proportions.
- **Take counsel with others and identify a support system.** After identifying the underlying issues that cause you stress, talk with trusted friends and coworkers. Ask them to help analyze and identify alternative ways (you may not have thought of alone) to deal with the situation. Use the support system of family and friends to help you deal with stressful issues.
- **Get regular exercise.** Regular exercise is an excellent way to reduce stress. Walk, run, row, swim, or bike.
- **Maintain a healthy diet.** Maintaining a well-balanced and healthy diet is another way to reduce stress.
- **Know what you like.** Identify things at work and in your life that you like and reduce exposure to the things that you do not like.
- **Organize and delegate tasks.** When dealing with work-related stressors, organize your work, develop plans and timelines, minimize interruptions, get the most important things done first, and appropriately delegate tasks as much as possible. These strategies will help you feel in control and off-load work that is not yours to begin with.

- **Take vacations.** Take a vacation at least once a year, if not more often. People need to rest and get away from the office from time to time. People who take regular vacations instead of constantly building vacation time are often less stressed.
- **Remember your family.** Do not let your work rule your life. To be a complete person, you must work hard, but you also have responsibilities to your family. Try not to go too far in either direction. All people need balance in their lives.
- **Participate in relaxing activities.** Learn to relax and participate in activities you enjoy. Other forms of relaxation (besides personal hobbies) include deep breathing, gentle muscle stretching, walking, visualizing peaceful settings you enjoy, and music therapy.
- **Consider your environment.** Consider where your stress comes from and how you can change your work environment to reduce the cause of your stress.
- **Decide what's important.** Decide on the things in your life that are important and then focus on those things and avoid spreading yourself too thin. You must learn to set limits and to say "no" to projects.
- **Live within your means.** Financial matters cause many people stress. Living within your means reduces the stress caused by spreading your finances too thin.
- **Accept the things you cannot change.** Some things you cannot change. You must either learn to accept those things or change the environment.

INTERNET SITES

ORGANIZATION	DESCRIPTION	INTERNET ADDRESS
ABA Law Practice Today	ABA site devoted to law practice management	www.abanet.org/lpm
Society for Human Resources Management	Site devoted to human resource issues	www.shrm.org
Workforce	Site devoted to human resource issues	www.workforce.com
World At Work	Site devoted to human resources issues	www.acaonline.org

SUGGESTED READING

Compensation Plans for Law Firms, James Cotterman, American Bar Association, 1995.

Law Office Policy and Procedures Manual, 4th ed., Robert Wert and Howard Hatoff, American Bar Association, 2000.

Julie Tamminen, *Living with the Law: Strategies to Avoid Burnout and Create Balance*, American Bar Association, 1996.

SUMMARY

Because a poor hiring decision can cost an organization literally thousands of dollars, it should take great care in hiring individuals, including writing detailed job descriptions, advertising positions, analyzing resumes, interviewing candidates correctly, and checking references to select the best candidate available.

Performance evaluations are an important human resource technique that is designed to communicate with employees what they are doing right and where they need to improve on a timely basis. In some situations, termination actually can be positive for an organization, eliminating employees who are "dead-wood" or who do not contribute.

Human resources are regulated by many rules, regulations, and statutes. The employment-at-will doctrine states that an employer and employee freely enter into an employment relationship and that either party has the right to sever the relationship at any time without reason. However, there are many exceptions to employment-at-will, including laws aimed at equal employment opportunity. The Americans with Disabilities Act is one such law that makes it unlawful to discriminate in employment against a qualified individual with a disability. Sexual harassment is another type of conduct that is prohibited by law. This includes unwelcome sexual advances, requests for sexual favors, and other verbal or physical conduct of a sexual nature that creates an intimidating, hostile, or offensive working environment.

KEY TERMS

Human resource management
Essential job functions
Negligent hiring
Fair Credit Reporting Act
Coaching technique
Management by objectives
Employee attitude survey
Wrongful termination lawsuit
Personnel handbook
Employment-at-will doctrine
Family and Medical Leave Act of 1993 (FMLA)

Fair Labor Standards Act
Equal employment opportunity
Civil Rights Act of 1964
Americans with Disabilities Act of 1990 (ADA)
Age Discrimination in Employment Act of 1967
Equal Pay Act of 1963
Bona fide occupational qualification
"Reasonable accommodation"
Sexual harassment

QUESTIONS AND EXERCISES

1. As a legal assistant manager in a large law firm, you have the opportunity to see pay scales, budgets, and other financial data. During your long career with the firm, you have held many positions. From your experience, you know that the file clerks in the probate department perform substantially the same functions as the file clerks in the tax department. The only difference is that the file clerks in the probate department are nearly all female, while most of the file clerks in the tax department are male. In looking through the firm's budget for next year, you notice that the file clerks in the tax department are paid nearly $3.00 more an hour than are their counterparts in probate. You know that the firm is only motivated by good intentions. However, does this pose any potential problems for the firm? Is there any other information you would like to know?

2. You are a new legal assistant at a medium-sized law firm. You are currently making just enough for you, your spouse, and your children to get by, but hope that in a year or two the firm will recognize your hard work and promote you. Your supervising attorney is well respected at the firm. Recently, you have had to work many long hours on a particular case with the attorney. One evening when you are alone, the attorney unexpectedly propositions you. You politely refuse. However, the propositions continue. They are quite annoying and unsettling and are affecting your performance. You worry about whether anyone will believe your story because you are new and the matter concerns a well-liked and respected attorney in the firm. What are your options? What would you do?

3. You are a legal assistant manager, and one of your top assistants just quit to take another job at a competing firm. You must fill the position in at least three weeks with a qualified candidate. You would like the candidate to be "young and aggressive." You know of an acquaintance who is a legal assistant and who is looking for a job. Explain how you would fill the position.

4. As a legal assistant, you need to hire a temporary document clerk to help you with a particularly large case. You expect the position to last about six months. After carefully drafting a detailed job description, advertising, and interviewing, you determine that the best candidate happens to be an individual who uses a wheelchair. This presents some problems because your firm is somewhat wheelchair accessible, but not entirely so. You figure that the improvements would cost about two thousand dollars. You doubt that your office will want to put in the necessary improvements. Briefly, what are your obligations?

5. You are a new legal assistant manager at a medium-sized law firm. The individual who managed the department before you did an incredibly poor job. Morale is low, and people under you are threatening to quit. The situation looks bleak. You must take quick action to ensure that people do not quit and that they understand you are here to make changes and to listen. Can you think of anything you can do relatively quickly that might help in this situation? Explain your answer.

6. Your office has put you in charge of hiring a clerk. You advertise for the position, conduct interviews, and make a selection. Because you have all your regular job duties to perform in addition to hiring the clerk, you only casually call his references and do not call his past employers at all. You do, however, feel very confident that you have hired the best individual for the position. After three weeks, one of the other staff members quits, stating that the new clerk has been harassing her and threatening her into going out with him. You feel particularly bad about the situation because you were responsible for hiring him and she has always been a good employee. You feel even worse when the law office is served with a negligent hiring lawsuit. The lawsuit alleges that the clerk spent the last two years in prison for a sexual-related crime and before that had been fired from a job for sexual harassment. What could you have done to prevent this?

7. The law office you work for failed to perform routine evaluations on a certain legal assistant. The firm subsequently received a complaint from a client regarding the legal assistant's work. The office investigated the matter and found that the legal assistant had been performing work far below an acceptable level and in some cases had even compromised a client's case. Discuss the law office's ethical duties to adequately supervise a legal assistant.

8. Recently, your firm terminated an employee. Unfortunately, the employee's keys were not taken and the locks were not changed. Later, the employee returned and stole vital information from the office's files regarding a client. The information, if released, would be very detrimental to the client. Did the office act in a prudent way to safeguard client confidences?

9. You are a legal assistant manager and a subordinate, legal assistant one, comes to you and

reports that legal assistant two propositioned her. He became belligerent when she refused and threatened to get her fired if she told anyone. You have never had any trouble with either one of them. They currently are working on the same case together. It is your job to investigate the complaint. You initially call in legal assistant two and tell him about the complaint. Legal assistant two appears shocked and states that it is completely unfounded, that he would never do such a thing, and that he is completely innocent. He further states that legal assistant one has a vendetta against him and wants him fired and that no one else in the firm has ever complained about his conduct in any regard. Both individuals appear completely honest and their stories are believable. Indicate what steps you would take to further investigate this matter; be specific. What steps would you take if there were no other credible evidence available and nothing else to corroborate either story? What steps would you take to prevent this from happening in the future?

10. You work closely with a secretary in your office. During the past three weeks, the secretary's quality of work has deteriorated. Three assignments you have given to her were late and not completed correctly. The secretary also has been moody, belligerent to other staff members and clients, and generally hard to get along with. You have avoided her on several occasions and have seen others doing so, too. You have been asked by the firm to handle the situation. You have looked for the right opportunity to talk to the secretary, but have not done it yet. Today, a client complained about the secretary's poor quality of work. You know that the situation must be dealt with now. On your way to the secretary's office, you meet her in the hall. State step-by-step how you would handle the situation. Explain your answer.

11. You have worked for a law office for several years and your hard work finally has paid off. The office is going to create a legal assistant manager position to manage the firm's other legal assistants. The law office has selected you to fill that position. The office has asked you to write the job description. Keep in mind that you must supervise other legal assistants, do performance evaluations, manage and coordinate their caseloads, prepare a budget for your department, and handle your own cases. Draft the job description.

12. You are a legal assistant manager and must prepare interview questions for a new legal assistant position you are filling. You want to find out the following information about the candidates, but do not want to ask a question that is illegal. Draft legal questions to find out the following information.

- You have had trouble with employee's cars breaking down, making them late for work; you want to make sure this is not a problem.
- You want to make sure the person is stable, committed, and will not leave town after you have trained him or her.
- You want to make sure that the person will not be continually receiving phone calls from children, relatives, and others, taking him or her away from his or her work.
- You want to hire persons who are interested in community projects and organizations because it looks good for your firm to have employees who are involved in community affairs.
- You want to make sure that the person will be able to work on Saturdays, even if the person has religious observances on that day.
- You want to make sure that if you invest your time and train this individual, he or she will not have to take a medical leave of absence after you have trained him or her.
- You want to make sure that you hire a reputable person who does not pose a threat to co-workers.

13. After looking at your firm's performance evaluation procedures, you realize that they desperately need to be updated. Draft an evaluation policy stating who will conduct performance evaluations, what the evaluations will involve, and when, where, and how they will be conducted. You want to make sure the employee not only knows how he or she is performing, but also takes an active part in the process and knows exactly what he or she should be accomplishing or working on for his or her next evaluation.

14. It has recently come to your attention that your secretary has stolen money out of the petty cash

fund that your office keeps. In addition, the secretary has recently on at least two occasions violated the firm's confidentiality policy by telling people outside the office about cases that your office handles. Your supervisor thinks the secretary should be fired, but will defer to your judgment for now. After investigating the petty cash allegation, you find out that the secretary claims he borrowed the money to pay for an emergency and that he then put the money back. You do confirm, however, that the confidentiality policies were in fact violated and could have serious implications to your clients. Explain how you would handle the matter.

NOTES

1. Phillip M. Perry, "Sexual Harassment," *Legal Assistant Today,* July/August 1992, p. 66. Copyright 1992. James Publishing, Inc. Reprinted with permission from *Legal Assistant Today* magazine. For subscription information call (800) 394-2626, or visit www.legalassistanttoday.com.

CASE REVIEW

Smith v. Chrysler Financial Corporation, 101 F.Supp.2d 534 (E.D. Mich. 2000).

101 F.Supp.2d 534
(Cite as: 101 F.Supp.2d 534)

United States District Court,

E.D. Michigan,

Southern Division.

Karen SMITH, Plaintiff,

v.

CHRYSLER FINANCIAL CORPORATION, Chrysler Corporation,

James Kozik and Allan

Ronquillo, jointly and severally, Defendants.

No. 97-CV-60309-AA.

May 30, 2000.

I.

Background

Plaintiff Karen Smith filed a First Amended Complaint on November 12, 1999 alleging she and Jessica Framer were employed by defendant CFC as paralegal, *537 and were supervised by CFC's then Assistant General Counsel James Kozik. Plaintiff alleges Kozik made repeated sexual advances and comments to Farmer. Plaintiff alleges that, once others reported Kozik's misconduct to CFC, Kozik retaliated against her by recommending that she receive only marginal pay raises, and by denying her certain performance reviews. Plaintiff alleges she thereafter filed a confidential sexual harassment complaint with CFC's Sexual Harassment Committee on August 12, 1996, which determined after an internal investigation that there was "reason to believe" Kozik had committed sexual harassment. Plaintiff initially filed a sex discrimination lawsuit in state court on October 15, 1996. Six days later, on October 21, 1996, she was removed from her CFC paralegal position by CFC's then General Counsel Allan Ronquillo and was transferred to a non-paralegal position away from CFC Headquarters. Plaintiff alleges she has since been denied opportunities to apply for any CFC paralegal positions by current CFC General Counsel Christopher Taravella. Smith alleges hostile work environment sexual harassment (Count I) and retaliation and reprisal (Count II), each in violation of Title VII of the Civil Rights Act of 1964, 42 U.S.C. §2000e et seq.

III.

Motions for Summary Judgment

A.

Standard of Review

Federal Rule of Civil Procedure 56(c) empowers the court to render summary judgment "forthwith if the pleadings, depositions, answers to interrogatories and admissions on file, together with the affidavits, *540 if any, show that there is no genuine issue as to any material fact at that the moving party is entitled to judgment as a matter of law." See FDIC v. Alexander, 78 F.3d 1103, 1106 (6th Cir.1996). The standard for determining whether summary judgment is appropriate is " 'whether the evidence presents a sufficient disagreement to require submission to a jury or whether it is so one-sided that one party must prevail as a matter of law.' " Winningham v. North Am. Resources Corp., 42 F.3d 981, 984 (6th Cir.1994) (citing Booker v. Brown & Williamson Tobacco Co., 879 F.2d 1304, 1310 (6th Cir.1989)). The evidence and all inferences therefrom must be construed in the light most favorable to the non-moving party. Matsushita Elec. Indus. Co., Ltd. v. Zenith Radio Corp., 475 U.S. 574, 587, 106 S.Ct. 1348, 89 L.Ed.2d 538 (1986); Enertech Elec., Inc. v. Mahoning County Comm'r, 85 F.3d 257, 259 (6th Cir.1996); Wilson v. Stroh Cos., Inc., 952 F.2d 942, 945 (6th Cir.1992).

If the movant establishes by use of the material specified in Rule 56(c) that there is no genuine issue of material fact and that it is entitled to judgment as a matter of law, the opposing party must come forward with "specific facts showing that there is a genuine issue for trial." First Nat'l Bank v. Cities Serv. Co., 391 U.S. 253, 270, 88 S.Ct. 1575, 20 L.Ed.2d 569 (1968); see also Adams v. Philip Morris, Inc., 67 F.3d 580, 583 (6th Cir.1995). The nonmoving party cannot rest on its pleadings to avoid summary judgment, but must support its claims with probative evidence. Kraft v. United States, 991 F.2d 292, 296 (6th Cir.), cert. denied, 510 U.S. 976, 114 S.Ct. 467, 126 L.Ed.2d 419 (1993); Anderson v. Liberty Lobby, Inc., 477 U.S. 242, 248, 106 S.Ct. 2505, 91 L.Ed.2d 202 (1986).

B.

Plaintiff's Motion for Summary Judgment as to Liability Only

Plaintiff moves for summary judgment as to liability only, as to the Title VII retaliation claims only, proffering: (1) Ronquillo's and CFC Human Resource Manager Linda Rumshlag's testimony that Smith was transferred out of her CFC paralegal position on October 21, 1996 because she filed a discrimination lawsuit and; (2) CFC Associate General Counsel Tracy Hackman's testimony that Smith has not since been considered for a paralegal position because of plaintiff's state and federal lawsuits.

Defendants counter that plaintiff has misconstrued the testimony, and assert that the reason plaintiff was reassigned and is not now eligible to occupy a paralegal position is for the protection of corporate security, to wit, defendants fear that a disgruntled plaintiff Smith will leak confidential and sensitive legal information. Defendants also assert plaintiff was transferred out of her paralegal position, and is currently ineligible for a paralegal position, consistent with her professional and ethical duty to eliminate conflicts of interest; defendants maintain plaintiff cannot properly represent her former client and employer CFC while, at the same time, she is suing them.

[7] To demonstrate a prima facie case of unlawful retaliation under Title VII, the plaintiff must prove: (1) she engaged in protected activity; (2) the exercise of protected rights was known to the defendant; (3) the defendant thereafter took adverse employment action against the plaintiff, or subjected the plaintiff to severe or pervasive retaliatory harassment by a supervisor, and; (4) a causal connection between the protected activity and the adverse employment action or harassment. Morris v. Oldham County Fiscal Court, 201 F.3d 784, 792 (6th Cir.2000). If the plaintiff establishes a prima facie case, the burden of production shifts to the defendant employer to articulate a legitimate, nondiscriminatory reason for its actions. Id. at 793. The plaintiff

then bears the burden *541 of demonstrating that the proffered reason was not the true reason for the employment decision. Id.

[8] Construing the pleadings and evidence in a light most favorable to defendants CFC and Chrysler, the evidence in the record presents a sufficient disagreement as to CFC's true motivations for transferring plaintiff out of her paralegal position on October 21, 1996, and for continuing to refuse to consider her for other CFC paralegal positions that the issue of CFC's true motivation for these employment decisions must be submitted to a jury. Winningham, 42 F.3d at 984. The proffered testimony of Ronquillo, Rumshlag, Hackman and Travella demonstrates, as plaintiff argues, that plaintiff was transferred out of her CFC paralegal position, and is not currently considered eligible for a CFC paralegal position, as a direct result of the sex discrimination lawsuits she filed and continues to pursue. Defendant does not dispute that filing a sex discrimination lawsuit against an employer constitutes an exercise of activity protected by Title VII. What remains to be decided by a jury, however, is whether defendant CFC retaliated against plaintiff for filing and maintaining the lawsuits, or whether CFC legitimately reasoned that plaintiff posed a potential threat to corporate security if she occupied a paralegal position while her lawsuits remained pending. The "only effect of the employer's nondiscriminatory explanation is to convert the inference of discrimination based upon the plaintiff's prima facie case from a mandatory one which the jury must draw, to a permissive one the jury may draw, provided that the jury finds the employer's explanation 'unworthy of belief.'" Manzer v. Diamond Shamrock Chemicals Co., 29 F.3d 1078, 1083 (6th Cir.1994). Plaintiff now bears the burden of proving that the defendants' proffered reasons are simply unworthy of belief given plaintiff has never before leaked confidential client information, and has not threatened to leak such information. Oldham County, 201 F.3d at 793. Evidence in the record construed in a light most favorable to the defendants nonetheless indicates that CFC attempted, albeit briefly, to build a "firewall" between plaintiff and her access to confidential CFC information before plaintiff was transferred, lending support to the proffered legitimate reason of protecting corporate security. Construing this and other evidence in light most favorable to the defendants, the issue of CFC's true motivation remains for the jury to decide.

The court notes that the defendants' more recent argument that plaintiff was transferred due to ethical considerations is not supported by the proffered testimony; the court is not cited to any deposition testimony by Ronquillo, Rumshlag, Hackman or Taravella, or any other agent of CFC or Chrysler, who has testified to date that plaintiff was removed from her paralegal position, and is no currently eligible for a paralegal position, because plaintiff cannot ethically occupy the position as a legal professional. The issue is not whether a legitimate reason exists, but whether CFC and Chrysler relied upon a legitimate reason for their challenged employment decisions. Nonetheless, the true causal connection between plaintiff's transfer from her paralegal position and her filing of sex discrimination lawsuits, as well as the nondiscriminatory justification proffered by defendants, should be submitted to a jury. Plaintiff's motion for partial summary judgment as to liability only, as to her retaliation claims only, must therefore be denied. Winningham, 42 F.3d at 984.

C.

Defendants' Motions for Summary Judgment

i.

Defendants move for summary judgment of plaintiff's retaliation claims predating August 12, 1996—the alleged hostile work environment created by Kozik, an alleged retaliatory January 1996 performance *542 appraisal, and an alleged retaliatory April 4, 1996 low salary increase—arguing the court lacks subject matter jurisdiction over these claims because they are broader than the claims plaintiff made in her May 14, 1997 Charge of Discrimination submitted to the EEOC. Defendants also argue references made in plaintiff's complaint regarding comments about "African-Americans" and "physically disabled employees" are likewise outside the scope of the Charge of Discrimination.

Plaintiff's EEOC Charge of Discrimination, set forth in an EEOC form, reads:

> I began employment for CFC's Legal Department in May, 1989.
>
> I performed my job duties in an exemplary manner and regularly received merit raises based upon my performance. My supervisor was CFC's Assistant General Counsel and was responsible for my merit raises, performance reviews, job assignments and positions with CFC's Legal Department.
>
> At various times while the Assistant General Counsel supervised me, he subjected me to demeaning and harassing remarks and behavior intended to denigrate myself and/or women in general. After I reported his conduct to CFC's General Counsel, his illegal misconduct continued and he vowed to "get rid of" and retaliate against those CFC employees he suspected reported his conduct to General Counsel.
>
> On or about August 12, 1996, I filed a confidential sexual harassment complaint with CFC's Sexual Harassment Committee pursuant to CFC's sexual harassment policy. In response to my complaint, CFC and Chrysler purportedly conducted a thorough investigation into my sexual harassment claim.
>
> On September 16, 1996, CFC and Chrysler provided the harasser [sic] with a promotion from CFC to Chrysler's Legal Department. On October 15, 1996, I filed a lawsuit against the Defendants alleging, inter, violations of the Elliott-Larsen Civil Rights Act (ELCRA). On or about October 21, 1996, in response to filing a lawsuit alleging violations of the ELCRA, CFC demoted and/or involuntarily transferred me to a different, non-paralegal position at a location away from CFC's headquarters.
>
> I believe that I have been wrongfully sexually harassed, based on my sex, female, and demoted, in retaliation for reporting sexual harassment and for filing a lawsuit, in violation of Title VII of the Civil Rights Act of 1964, as amended.

As to the alleged cause of discrimination, plaintiff checked the boxes in the form titled "sex" and "retaliation". Describing the dates of discrimination, plaintiff wrote "unknown" for the "earliest" date, "ongoing" for the "latest" date, and checked the box "continuing action."

[9][10] This court enjoys jurisdiction over claims explicitly filed in the EEOC charge as well as claims that were reasonably expected to grow out of the charge. See Abeita v. TransAmerica Mailings, Inc., 159 F.3d 246, 254 (6th Cir. 1998) (Citing Ang v. Procter & Gamble Co., 932 F.2d 540, 544-45 (6th Cir. 1991)). Construing the pleadings and evidence in a light most favorable to plaintiff Smith, plaintiff's pre-August 12, 1996 sexual harassment and retaliation claims can reasonable and fairly be read as growing out of the broad allegations set forth in her Charge of Discrimination, which begin with the date May 1989, allege subsequent misconduct and threats of retaliation, continue through to August 12, 1996 and the filing of the internal confidential sexual harassment complaint, and continue further through plaintiff's October 21, 1996 transfer from her paralegal position, all allegations consistent with an alleged "continuing action". The court need not apply a "liberal construction" applicable to pro se claimant's in reaching this conclusion. See Ang, 932 F.2d at 546. As to plaintiff's allegations in this lawsuit regarding comments made about "African-Americans" and "physically disabled employees", plaintiff is not alleging *543 race or disability discrimination claims, and thus, the court has not improperly exercised jurisdiction over such claims. Defendants are not entitled to summary judgment based on lack of subject matter jurisdiction. Winningham, 42 F.3d at 984.

ii.

Defendants move for summary judgment of plaintiff's claims pre-dating August 16, 1996 arguing any such claims are untimely because they arose more than 300 days prior to June 12, 1997, or August 16, 1996, the date the EEOC first filed plaintiff's charge with Michigan's "deferral agency" the Michigan Department of Civil Rights or, in the alternative, 300 days prior to April 23, 1997, or July 2, 1996, the date the EEOC first received plaintiff's April 22, 1997 letter.

[11] Generally under 42 U.S.C. § 2000e-5(e)(1) and 42 U.S.C. § 2000e-5(c) of Title VII, no charge may be filed with the EEOC until 60 days have elapsed from the time a charge is filed with a local state agency having the authority to administer state civil rights laws that prohibit unlawful employment practices. The purpose of this 60 day deferral period is "to give States and localities an opportunity to combat discrimination free from premature federal intervention." Equal Employment Opportunity Commission v. Commercial Office Products Co., 486 U.S. 107, 110-11, 108 S.Ct. 1666, 100 L.Ed.2d 96 (1988). Mohasco Corp. v. Silver, 447 U.S. 807, 100 S.Ct. 2486, 65 L.Ed.2d 532 (1980) held that, consistent with this deferral period, a complainant must either file a charge with the state agency, or have the EEOC refer the charge to the state agency, within 240 days of the alleged discriminatory event. See Commercial Office Products, 486 U.S. at 111, 108 S.Ct. 1666 (citing Mohasco, 447 U.S. at 814 n. 16, 100 S.Ct. 2486 (1980)). However, if the EEOC enters into work sharing agreements with a state agency authorized to enforce state employment discrimination laws, and the state waives the Title VII statutory 60 day deferral period, the state's investigation is considered "terminated", and a claimant may file a discrimination charge directly with the EEOC within 300 days after the alleged discriminatory conduct—even if the claimant has not filed a timely state charge. Commercial Office Products, 486 U.S. at 124-25, 108 S.Ct. 1666. See also Janikowski v. Bendix Corp., 823 F.2d 945, 947 (1987) ("In states such as Michigan, which have their own laws forbidding age discrimination, a plaintiff must file a claim of ADEA violation 'within 300 days after the alleged unlawful practice occurred.'"). Consequently, plaintiff's claims based on discriminatory conduct that occurred 300 days before the EEOC received plaintiff's April 23, 1997 Charge of Discrimination, being claims based on conduct that occurred on or after July 2, 1996, are timely as a matter of law.

[12] Further, plaintiff may also pursue pre-July 2, 1996 hostile work environment and retaliation claims pursuant to the "continuing violation" doctrine. Plaintiff has produced evidence indicating Kozik made sexually hostile remarks to former co-employee Jessica Farmer within plaintiff's working environment after July 2, 1996, specifically, on July 25, 1996, August 13, 1996, and August 16, 1996. A confidential memo regarding harassment/fear of retaliation was allegedly submitted to CFC on August 12, 1996, and Kozik was not removed from the work environment until August 16, 1996. Otherwise time-barred unlawful discriminatory acts may be actionable if, as here, the plaintiff can establish a continuous pattern discrimination throughout her term of employment that continued into the EEOC charge-filing period. See Held v. Gulf Oil Co., 684 F.2d 427, 430 (6th Cir.1982) ("[s]ince [the evidence] supports a finding that discriminatory acts continued throughout her period of employment, the plaintiff's action is not time barred"). See also Hull v. Cuyahoga Valley Joint Vocational School District Board of Education, 926 F.2d 505, 510-11 (6th Cir.1991) (stating "there are important *544 policy reasons not to require a discrimination suit be filed at the first instance of discrimination or not at all."). Defendants are not entitled to summary judgment based on the asserted untimeliness of plaintiff's claims. Winningham, 42 F.3d at 984.

iii.

Defendants move for summary judgment of plaintiff's claims post-dating August 16, 1996 arguing: (1) plaintiff cannot prove that she suffered an objective, material adverse employment action as a result of other transfers from the CFC paralegal position to Discount Supervisor, to Receptionist, and on to her current position as a Bankruptcy Specialist/Supervisor because plaintiff cannot prove she has lost any pay or benefits; (2) plaintiff cannot prove she suffered emotional damages after October 12, 1997 when she was promoted to the position of Bankruptcy Specialist/Supervisor, and; (3) plaintiff has not rebutted defendants' legitimate reasons for her transfer out of the paralegal position.

[13][14][15] On October 28, 1996, plaintiff was transferred to the position of Discount Supervisor in CFC's Troy, Michigan office, where she worked until March 1997 when she took a medical leave of absence. Upon her return to work on July 5, 1997, she was assigned a position as a Receptionist. In October 1997,

plaintiff was transferred to her current position as a Bankruptcy Specialist/Supervisor. A tangible employment action includes reassignment to a position with "significantly different responsibilities." Burlington Industries, Inc. v. Ellerth, 524 U.S. 742, 761, 118 S.Ct. 2257, 141 L.Ed.2d 633 (1998). In determining whether an employment action was materially adverse, and thus actionable, a court should consider such factors as a demotion evidenced by a decrease in wages or salary, a less distinguished title, a material loss of benefits, significantly diminished responsibilities, or other indices unique to the situation. See Kocsis v. Multi-Care Mgt., Inc., 97 F.3d 876, 886 (6th Cir.1996) (cited in Burlington Industries, 524 U.S. at 761, 118 S.Ct. 2257). A plaintiff's subjective personal preferences are insufficient to prove an actionable adverse employment action. See Brown v. Brody, 199 F.3d 446, 455 (D.C.Cir.1999).

[16] Plaintiff Smith has produced evidence that her transfer from her position as a CFC paralegal to Discount Supervisor, and then to the position of Receptionist, resulted in changes a professional to clerical positions, resulted in a less distinguished title, significantly diminished her job responsibilities, and resulted in the loss of a private office. Although plaintiff may have been required to work as a Receptionist on her return from medical leave because the Discount Supervisor position had been filled, it must be remembered that plaintiff was initially transferred to the Discount Supervisor position by CFC. The court also concludes that, in construing the evidence in a light most favorable to plaintiff, a jury could further conclude that the transfer from the CFC paralegal position to the current Bankruptcy Specialist/Supervisor position likewise represents a tangible adverse employment action accompanied by objective loss. The increase in actual and potential pay and benefits is not dispositive, especially in this unique situation involving several job transfers. See Kocsis, 97 F.3d at 886. The court is not prepared to find that plaintiff cannot recover post-October 1997 emotional damages solely because she now occupies a position that pays better than the paralegal position she occupied on October 27, 1996. The issue of plaintiff's damages, and the defendants mitigation of same, should be submitted to the jury.

As pointed out in Section III, B, supra, plaintiff Smith may rebut the proffered legitimate reasons of corporate security and potential ethical breaches by showing: (1) the reasons have no basis in fact; (2) these reasons did not actually motivate he challenged decisions, or; (3) the reasons are insufficient to motivate the transfer decision. See Manzer, 29 F.3d at 1084. *545 Defendants are not entitled to summary judgment based on the absence of an actionable adverse employment action, an inability to prove post-October 12, 1997 emotional damages, or an inability to rebut defendants' proffered reasons for the employment decisions made. Winningham, 42 F.3d at 984.

iv.

[17][18][19] Defendants move for summary judgment of plaintiff's hostile work environment claims arguing plaintiff has not plead requisite severe and pervasive conduct, nor does plaintiff allege she was the target of Kozik's sexual advances. A hostile work environment claim requires proof that the discrimination is so severe or pervasive as to alter the conditions of the plaintiff's employment. See Oldham County, 201 F.3d at 790; Hafford v. Seidner, 183 F.3d 506, 512 (6th Cir.1999) (quoting Meritor Sav. Bank, FSB v. Vinson, 477 U.S. 57, 67, 106 S.Ct. 2399, 91 L.Ed.2d 49 (1986)) (deciding issue of race discrimination). In order to prove a prima facie hostile environment claim, the plaintiff must establish five elements: (1) she is a member of the protected class; (2) she was subjected to unwelcome harassment; (3) the harassment was based on sex; (4) the harassment had the effect of unreasonably interfering with her work performance by creating an intimidating hostile or offensive work environment and (5) the existence of employer liability. Seidner, 183 F.3d at 512.

> In determining whether an environment is one that a reasonable person would find hostile or abusive and that the plaintiff in fact did perceive to be so, courts look at all of the circumstances, including: [T]he frequency of the discriminatory conduct; its severity; whether it is physically threatening or humiliating, or a mere offensive utterance; and whether it unreasonably interferes with an employee's work performance.

Harris [v. Forklift Sys. Inc.], 510 U.S. [17,] 23, 114 S.Ct. 367, 126 L.Ed.2d 295; Abeita v. TransAmerica Mailings, Inc., 159 F.3d 246, 251 (6th Cir.1998). "A recurring point" in the Supreme Court's opinions is that " 'simple teasing,' offhand comments, and isolated incidents (unless extremely serious) will not amount to discriminatory changes in the 'terms and conditions of employment'" and that "conduct must be extreme to amount to a change in the terms and conditions of employment." Faragher v. City of Boca Raton, 524 U.S. 775, 785-86, 118 S.CT. 2275, 2283-84, 141 L.Ed.2d 662 (1998) (citations omitted).

Seidner, 183 F.3d at 512-13. See also Oldham County, 201 F.3d at 790. Isolated incidents and remarks do not give rise to Title VII liability unless they are extremely serious because Title VII is not a "general civility code." Faragher, 524 U.S. at 781, 118 S.Ct. 2275.

[20] To determine if an abusive work environment existed, the court must apply a two part totality of the circumstances test, requiring an analysis under both an objective reasonable person standard and a subjective standard. Seidner, 183 F.3d at 512.

> Conduct that is not severe or pervasive enough to create an objectively hostile or abusive work environment—an environment that a reasonable person would find hostile or abusive—is beyond Title VII's purview. Likewise, if the victim does not subjectively perceive the environment to be abusive, the conduct has not actually altered the conditions of the victim's employment, and there is no Title VII violation.

Harris, 510 U.S. at 21-22, 114 S.Ct. 367. A court must review the work environment as a whole because, under certain circumstances, a hostile work environment may be proven by establishing the cumulative effect of related acts of abuse. See Williams v. General Motors Corp., 187 F.3d 553, 563 (6th Cir.1999).

[21] Construing the pleadings and available evidence in a light most favorable *546 to plaintiff Smith, the issue of whether plaintiff was subjected to an actionable sexually hostile work environment must be submitted to the jury. The fact the Kozik's alleged sexual comments were not directed at plaintiff is relevant to the determination of whether an objectively hostile work environment existed, but is not dispositive. See Oldham County, 201 F.3d at 790. See also Jackson v. Quanex Corp., 191 F.3d 647, 660 (6th Cir.1999) (rejecting view that harassment, to be actionable, must be aimed at the plaintiff); Equal Opportunity Commission v. Ohio Edison, 7 F.3d 541 (6th cir.1993) (Title VII prohibits discrimination against an employee who "opposes any practice" unlawful under Title VII). As determined in Section III, C, ii, supra, the "continuing violation" doctrine permits plaintiff to pursue her hostile work environment claims based on all of Kozik's alleged harassment, including any pre-July 2, 1996 conduct. Consistent with this determination, and reviewing plaintiff's work environment as a whole, including pre-July 2, 1996 conduct, this record does not preclude Smith's claims that Kozik's conduct in the CFC work environment went beyond simple teasing, offhand comments, or isolated incidents directed at paralegal Farmer. The court awaits full development of the work environment at trial. Defendants are not entitled to summary judgment based on plaintiff's asserted inability to prove she was subjected to a sufficiently severe or pervasive sexually hostile conduct. Winningham, 42 F.3d at 984.

IV.

Conclusion

For the reasons set forth above, defendants CFC's and Chrysler's motion to compel arbitration is hereby DENIED. Plaintiff Smith's motion for partial summary judgment as to liability only is hereby DENIED. Defendants CFC's and Chrysler's motions for summary judgment are hereby DENIED.

IT IS ORDERED.

END OF DOCUMENT

EXERCISES

1. If the Assistant General Counsel, in fact, made repeated sexual advances and comments about others to the paralegal, do you believe this constitutes sexual harassment?

2. Based on the facts of the case, do you believe the defendants transferred the paralegal based on their belief that she would leak confidential and sensitive information or because the paralegal filed a sexual harassment lawsuit?

3. Did you agree with the court that the paralegal's transfer to clerical positions could indeed be construed as "adverse employment action"?

4. Did you generally agree or disagree with the decision?

FILE AND LAW LIBRARY MANAGEMENT

CHAPTER OBJECTIVES

After you read this chapter you will be able to:

- Discuss why file management is important.
- Explain centralized and decentralized filing systems.
- Discuss the importance of closing and purging files.
- Explain why library ordering should be centralized.
- Give examples of how law library costs can be reduced.

- For 2½ hours I searched for our file on tax issues in the State of Maine. I found it under "S."
- We finally located the agreement with Boeing under "N." It was labeled 1979 Aircraft Contracts by the lawyer and filed under "N" for "Nineteen" by the secretary.
- I waited two weeks for Alice to return to ask her about her previous work on a particular issue. She told me that Alan was the one who worked on it. He [Alan] said that his work would probably help me but that it wasn't the main issue in his case and he couldn't remember the file name.[1]
- The library is, without a doubt, the heart of the law office. Lawyers [and legal assistants] are in the business of doing legal research and reporting the results of that research to the courts, to their clients, and to each other.[2]

Why Legal Assistants Need an Understanding of File and Law Library Management

Legal assistants work with files every single day. It is crucial that they know how to organize, track, and store client files. If a file or parts of a file are lost, misplaced, or misfiled, the effects can be devastating both to the office and to the client's case. Information must be stored so that it can be quickly found and retrieved. In many instances, legal assistants are responsible for organizing case files. In addition, many legal organizations are using automated file management systems. Legal assistants must have a good understanding of automated systems as law firms progress toward a paperless office.

Legal assistants also must have a basic understanding of law library management. Legal assistants use the law library to conduct legal research, so it is important that they know how libraries work and be familiar with electronic research resources. In addition, many legal assistants, especially in smaller offices, actually may be in charge of maintaining the library.

> *I worked at a firm where the Records Department constantly struggled with proper maintenance of the files. Loose filing that was sometimes a year old stacked up in the file area. When an attorney needed something, hours if not days were spent looking for it. The alternative was to call co-counsel to request another copy, but we could only call so many times before the other attorney's office got frustrated. I ended up making working copies of important documents and stashing them in my office, but there was only so much room in my office. The Records Department was using bar coding technology, but when the documents themselves do not make it into the files, using a bar code to "find" material is moot.*
> Linda Rushton, CLA

INTRODUCTION TO FILE MANAGEMENT

Law offices of all types need a file system that allows them to store, track, and retrieve information about cases in a logical, efficient, and expeditious manner. The outcome of many legal matters depends on the case information gathered, including evidence, depositions, pleadings, discovery requests, and witness interviews. File information generally is worthless unless it is organized and available to the legal assistants and attorneys who will use it. File management is a large task no matter the size of the law practice.

Figure 9-1 contains characteristics that a good file system has whether the system uses paper or is paperless. Each of these areas is vital to a law office, and none can be compromised. A poor file system has some or all of the following problems.

1. Files are lost and cannot be found.
2. Files are messy and disorganized.
3. Office staff is unclear about how the filing system works.
4. Attorneys and legal assistants do not trust the file system and keep their own files or keep the office's files in their possession.
5. Staff is constantly aggravated and frustrated over the file system.
6. Large amounts of time and money are wasted trying to find the file and information.
7. Poor-quality legal services are given to clients because of the poor filing system.
8. Electronic file systems are unreliable, do not work.

**Figure 9-1
An Effective File Management System**

Source: Adapted from Deborah Heller and James M. Hunt. *Practing Law and Managing People: How to Be Successful* (Butterworth, 1988), 62. Courtesy of Heller, Hunt & Cunningham, Stoneham, MA.

1. **Completeness**—The files (hardcopy and/or electronic) are complete and contain all of the information relevant to the case or matter.
2. **Retention**—Filing procedures ensure that all items are retained for the appropriate length of time.
3. **Integrity**—Files are maintained so that they are accurate, sound, and reliable.
4. **Ease of Use**—The file structure and file access provide for quick and easy location of files. Electronic file systems are readily available to all staff.
5. **Security**—Files (hardcopy and electronic) are maintained in a safe environment which prevents unauthorized access to the system as a whole or to individual files.
6. **Ease of Learning**—The file system is candid, straightforward, and easy for others to learn.
7. **Adaptability**—The file system is flexible and easy to modify if structural or functional changes in the organization are necessary.

File management is an important topic because law office management is responsible for providing an effective system that adequately supports its attorneys and legal assistants. Files and file systems represent a tool that the attorney and legal assistant use to provide their services.

FILING METHODS AND TECHNIQUES

There are different variations or filing methods that accomplish the objectives in Figure 9-1. Which filing method is used depends on the particular needs of each law office. These needs may be based on such factors as the number of attorneys in the firm, the number of cases that will be tracked and stored, the type and power of computer hardware and software in use, the size and length of time typical cases are kept open or active, how much paper typical cases generate, the amount of space available for storage, whether the files will be kept in a central location, or whether departments or attorneys will keep their own files.

EACH LEGAL MATTER IS MAINTAINED SEPARATELY

No matter which filing method is used in a law office, it is essential that each case or legal matter be maintained separately. Even if one client has several legal matters pending, each case/legal matter should have its own separate file and should be given its own file number. There is the danger that documents will be misplaced or lost if all documents are commingled.

When matters are commingled, it affects other law office systems, such as conflict-of-interest checking (which determines whether the law office has a conflict of interest), docket control, and billing. Each case should be checked for conflict-of-interest problems, should have its own distinct and separate deadlines entered into the docket control system, and should be billed to the client separately.

ALPHABETIC SYSTEMS

In an **alphabetic filing system,** cases are stored based on the last name of the client or name of the organization. There is a natural tendency to alphabetize because it is a system that most people understand. In addition, staff members do not need to memorize case numbers or use numerical lists: a user knows exactly where the file should be in the drawer.

The larger the number of cases the law office is handling, the more problems it will experience with an alphabetical system. This is because names are not all that unique; many clients may have the same last name. It is not efficient to search through four or five file drawers or cabinets of "Smith" files looking for the right case. It also is not uncommon for clients to have the same first and last names. Other systems, such as a numerical system or an electronic system, can track an almost infinite number of cases with a unique number and also can protect the confidentiality of the client better because the client's name is not the identifier for the file and is not on all the files. In offices with a large number of cases, an alphabetic system may not be the best kind of filing system. Alphabetic systems also are difficult to expand and can mean constantly shifting files to make room for more.

alphabetic filing system
Filing method in which cases are stored based on the last name of the client or organization.

NUMERICAL SYSTEMS

In a numerical filing system, each case or legal matter is given a separate file number. This is similar to when a case is filed with a court; a clerk assigns each action or lawsuit a separate case number. Case identifiers can be, but do not necessarily have to be, all numbers (i.e., 234552). Variations can be used, such as alphanumeric in which letters and numbers are used. For instance, a letter might be used in the case number to reflect which branch office is handling the case and two of the numbers might reflect the year the case was filed, such as LA04-990004. The "LA" might stand for the office's Los Angeles office, and "04" stand for 2004, the year the case was initiated.

Letters also may stand for types of cases: "PB" for probate, "TX" for tax, for a particular attorney—"Patricia Burns," and so forth. Even in a numerical system, however, legal matters for the same client can be kept together. For instance, in the example "LA04-990004," "99" could represent the client's personal number and "4" could mean that this is the fourth case that the office is handling for the client.

Another numerical filing method is to assign a range of numbers to a particular type of case, such as 000–999 for trusts, 1,000–1,999 for tax matters, and 2,000–2,999 for criminal matters.

A filing rule that sometimes bears out is that the longer the case number, the more misfiling and other types of errors occur. Also, shorter numbers can be remembered more easily. Numerical filing also solves the shifting problems with alphabetical systems. When a new case is taken, the next sequential number is given to the file, and it is stored accordingly. This is opposed to an alphabetic system, where a new file is stored by the client's name. When the new file is added to the existing drawer, the drawer already may be filled and then someone must shift or move files to make room for the new file.

BAR CODING

Bar coding is a file management technique in which each file is tracked according to the file's bar code. Each time a user takes a file, the file's bar code and user's bar code are scanned into a computer. The computerized system then tracks which user checked out which file. When the file is returned, the file's bar code is scanned back into the computer. A report can be generated any time listing what files are checked out and by whom. Using this system, it is possible to find the location of files quite easily. Bar codes are used in many libraries to track the library's collection. Bar coding of law office files works much the same way.

bar coding
A file management technique in which each file is tracked according to the file's bar code.

AUTOMATED AND ELECTRONIC FILE/RECORDS MANAGEMENT

An automated file/record management system tracks information about a file in a computerized database. Records management software tracks files from when they are opened until they are closed. Records management software allows many reports to be generated regarding the records that are being kept. Records can be printed regarding files assigned to specific attorneys, types of cases being handled, files by legal departments, different types of administrative files, and much more.

In addition to tracking and reporting information about files, some records management systems also allow for imaging. **Imaging** refers to the capture, retrieval, and storage of document images electronically. Images are captured and stored electronically and are available to a number of staff members at virtually the same time. In addition, misfiling of information is greatly reduced. Imaging allows a legal organization to store potentially thousands and thousands of documents electronically, saving space and making it more convenient to track, search for, and retrieve the information.

imaging
The capture, retrieval, and storage of document images electronically.

Nearly all legal organizations must also track electronic mail, client-related word processing, spreadsheets, databases, and other types of documents generated by law office staff. Many legal organizations do this using sophisticated computerized networks. As technology continues to expand and evolve, legal organizations must develop sophisticated computerized systems that organize all of this information into a user-friendly system. The procedures used for each legal organization will be different, but tracking client-related information electronically in an organized fashion so the information can be retrieved at a later time is crucial.

Computerized record management systems also allow staff to create back-up copies of data. Having current back-up copies of electronic data is crucial as more and more legal organizations depend on electronic data. If a legal organization's computers malfunctioned and vital client information were deleted without a backup, it could have disastrous implications for the client. Also, as client files are closed, information can be stored using a variety of electronic means.

CORPORATE, GOVERNMENT, AND LEGAL AID FILING METHODS

Corporate law departments and government departments may arrange their matters differently. They may file matters by subject, by department, or by other means that suit their particular industry or need. Legal aid offices typically file cases alphabetically or even geographically, by city or county.

CENTRALIZED V. DECENTRALIZED

A fundamental law office filing consideration is whether the filing system will be centralized or decentralized. A **centralized file system** is where a file department or file clerk stores and manages all active law office files in one or more file rooms. In a **decentralized file system,** files are kept in various locations throughout the law office, such as each department storing its own files or each attorney keeping his own files.

A centralized system is typically used when the office has a complex filing procedure best handled by one department or file clerk staff; when the office wants a highly controlled system; or when several attorneys or legal assistants work on the same cases. Even though a law office may want a centralized system, the office must have the physical space to accommodate it. Law offices in which a single attorney or legal assistant works on each case, such as real estate matters, or needs the case files for long periods of time may use a decentralized file system where the files are located in an individual's office or in a secretarial area. Some offices use a "pod," or team filing system, where several people—perhaps two or three attorneys, a secretary, and a legal assistant or two—have offices located close to one another and have their files stored next to them. Some offices may use a combination. Whether an office uses a centralized or decentralized system depends on the size of the office, type of cases handled, and the needs of the personnel involved. Closed files are almost always kept in a centralized location.

centralized file system
Method in which a file department or file clerk stores and manages all active law office files in one or more file rooms.

decentralized file system
System in which files are kept in various locations throughout the law office.

OPENING FILES

When a new or existing client comes into the office with a new legal matter, a new file should be immediately opened. The opening of a file should be standardized and should require certain information about the legal matter. A file opening form or an electronic version (sometimes called a new client/matter form or casesheet) is customarily completed when opening a new file (see Figure 9-2).

The **file opening form** is used for a variety of purposes, including to check potential conflicts of interest, to assign a new case number and attorney to the matter, to track the area or specialty of the case, to set forth the type of fee agreement and billing frequency in the case, to enter the case in the timekeeping and billing system, to make docketing entries such as when the statute of limitations in the matter might run, and to find out how the client was referred to the law office. Although file opening forms are commercially available, most law offices choose to customize the form to reflect their own needs.

Copies of the file opening form may be sent to the managing partner, other attorneys, accounting department, docket-control department, and the responsible attorney.

file opening form
A standardized form that is filled out when a new case is started. The form contains important information about the client and the case.

New File

Client (Check one)
_____ INDIVIDUAL
_____
                      Last   First   Middle Initial
_____ ENTITY
        (Use complete name & common abbreviations; place articles [e.g., The] at end.)
_____ CLASS ACTION _____
                      (File Name, ex.: Popcorn Antitrust Litigation)

Matter (Check One)
_____ NON-LITIGATION
_____ LITIGATION
     _____ Approved for litigation by—MUST BE INITIALED by submitting attorney!!

Nature of the Case
    Area of law code _____   Summary of work or dispute: _____
_____

Client Contact (N/A for Class Actions)
Name:
Company:
Street:
City, State, Zip:
Telephone:

*New Adverse Parties:
_____
_____

*New Related Parties (for Class Actions, Named Plaintiffs Only):
_____
_____

*Will be entered into computer system by Bus. Dept. *AFTER* approval by Managing Partner.

Closed File

Date Closed: _____   **Atty. Or Sec. Initials:** _____
_____ Attach Pleadings and/or File Indexes. If indexes are not available, attach brief description of what is contained in the file(s). SEND FILES, THIS FORM, AND INDEX TO FILE ROOM.

Routing Lists

	(Initial)			
	New File:	Date:	Closed File:	Date:
Submitted by	_____	_____	_____	_____
Sec. of Submitting Person	_____	_____	_____	_____
Managing Partner	_____	_____	_____	_____
Business Department	_____	_____	_____	_____
File Department	_____	_____	_____	_____
Firm Newsletter	_____	_____	_____	_____
Docket for Litigation	_____	_____	_____	_____
EnviroLaw (Computer Center) Add?	_____			
IdeaLaw (Computer Center) Add?	_____			
JobLaw (Computer Center) Add?	_____			

Figure 9-2 File Opening Form

Billing Address (N/A for Class Actions)
   Name: _____
   Company: _____
   Street: _____
   City, State, Zip: _____
   Telephone: _____

Team Information (Use initials)
_____ _____ _____ Managing Attorney(s) (for non-litigation cases only)
_____ _____ _____ Bill Review Attorney(s)
_____ _____ _____ Originating Attorney(s)
_____ Calendar Attorney (for litigation cases only)
_____ Legal Assistant (for litigation cases only)
_____ Secretary to Calendar Attorney (for litigation cases only)

Referral Source (Check one)
_____ Existing Client _____
                  (Name)
_____ Non-Firm Attorney _____
                  (Name)
_____ Firm Attorney or Employee _____
_____ Martindale-Hubbell _____
_____ Other _____

Fee Agreement (Check those that apply)
_____ Hourly
_____ Contingent _____ %
_____ Fee Petition
_____ Fixed Fee $_____ or Fixed Range from $_____ to $_____
_____ Retainer $_____
_____ Letter of Retainer sent by _____ on _____
                          (Initials)   (Date)

Statement Format (Check those that apply)
Do you want identical disbursements grouped? _____ Yes _____ No
Do you want attorney hours reflected on *each* time entry? _____ Yes _____ No
Do you want fees extended on *each* time entry? _____ Yes _____ No

Conflict Check

Conflict Check Completed By: _____   Date: _____
                         (Initials)

Conflict Check Not Needed: _____
              (Initials of Submitting Person)

Check One:
_____ No conflicts
_____ Potential conflict with the following existing parties (from computer system):
_____
_____

(Or attach computer printout from Conflict Check System.)

**Figure 9-3
Typical Subcategories of Files**

Accounting
Correspondence with Client
Correspondence with Attorneys
Deposition Summaries
Discovery
Evidence
General Correspondence
Investigation
Legal Research
Memorandums
Notes & Miscellaneous
Witnesses

FILE FORMAT/INTERNAL FILE RULES

The format or how case files are set up and organized depends on the needs of the office and how the office thinks the organization will best be served. The type of file format will depend on the filing system that is used. As an example, vertical file drawers require tabs at different places while an open-shelf filing system requires tabs on the side.

Many offices use separate manila files as subdivisions in the same case to differentiate information in the same file, such as having files for "Accounting," "Discovery," "Pleadings," "Client Correspondence," and others (see Figure 9-3). The individual manila files are stored in one or more expanding files, so that all the files for one case are kept together. Also, many offices use metal fasteners in the manila files to hold the papers securely in place. The exception to this is that original documents should not be punched. Instead, they should be maintained separately and a copy put in the regular file. Finally, information typically is placed in each manila file in chronological order, with the oldest on the bottom and newest on the top of the file. This gives the user a systematic way of finding information. It is routine to find duplicate and draft copies of documents in a file. However, duplicates and drafts only make the organization process more difficult. If duplicates must be kept, they should be in a separate file folder labeled "Duplicates."

COLOR CODING

Color coding files is a simple but effective way to reduce the number of misfiled documents. Files can be color coded in a variety of ways; for example, red-labeled files for probate and green files for criminal matters. Color coding also can be done according to the year the case was opened or according to the attorney handling the matter.

Color coding also can be used for cases that are especially sensitive or that need to be especially secure. For example, if the law office is trying to create a "Chinese wall" to keep a staff member from participating in a case, it can alert others to the need for security by assigning a certain color of file label to the case. Finally, color coding can be used in an alphabetic filing system. For example, A to E equals blue; F to J equals green, and so forth.

CHECKING FILES OUT

In some law offices where many people have access to files, users are required to check out files electronically, in a process similar to one used in a public library. It can be quite frustrating to search and search for a client file and discover that someone else took the file home to work on it, or that the file is lost. Tracking the location of files is crucial to an effective file/record management system.

CLOSING, STORING, AND PURGING FILES

After a legal matter has come to a conclusion, and after the final bill has been paid, the file is closed and taken out of the storage area of active files. It is boxed up and kept in the office's basement or an off-site storage facility for a certain number of years until it is destroyed, or put on microfilm, microfiche, or other electronic storage system.

A closed file is sometimes called a "dead file" or a "retired file." When a case is closed, some offices give the case a new number to differentiate it from active cases. The closing of cases represents a problem for many law offices. Attorneys like to have access to closed files in case they need the information in them someday. Storage space can be quite expensive. Most law offices are continually opening and closing cases, which means that the flow of files never stops and that the required storage area gets larger and larger. To reduce file storage requirements, duplicate copies of documents should be removed.

Before a client file is closed, it is important for the client to be completely aware that the file is being closed. It is strongly recommended that the law firm send a disengagement letter to the client, letting him or her know in writing that the file is being closed, that the client can have documents, evidence, or other information returned to him or her, or the whole file returned if he or she would like. Electronic records also need to be purged or backed-up at the same time the hard copy of the file is closed.

> *Most attorneys cannot rest comfortably knowing that closed client files have been destroyed, yet the actual frequency of need for a file which has been closed for more than one year is very low. Because of unwillingness to authorize file destruction, most law offices build up huge quantities of old paper which often end up in lofts, basements, barns, abandoned buildings, or worst of all, on the office's premises in increasingly expensive space.*

One solution to storage problems is to purge or destroy files after a certain period of time (see Figure 9-4). Some state ethical rules also govern file retention. Some law offices purge all files after a certain number of years, such as seven or eight, while others purge only selected files. Destroying files usually means shredding,

**Figure 9-4
Sample Record
Retention Periods**

Source: Adapted from Association of Legal Administrators. Reprinted with permission.

Law Office Administration	Retention Period
Accounts Payable and Receivable Ledgers	7 yrs.
Audit Reports	Permanently
Bank Statement and Reconciliations	3 yrs.
Cash Receipt Books	Permanently
Canceled Checks (except for payments of taxes, real estate, and other important payments—permanently)	7 yrs.
Contracts, mortgages, notes, and leases (still in effect)	Permanently
Contracts, mortgages, notes, and leases (expired)	7 yrs.
Correspondence, general (except important matters—permanently)	7 yrs.
Deeds, Mortgages, etc.	Permanently
Employment Applications	3 yrs.
Financial Statements (Year End)	Permanently
Insurance policies (expired)	3 yrs.
Invoices	7 yrs.
Minutes of directors and stockholders meetings	Permanently
Payroll records	7 yrs.
Retirement and Pension Records	Permanently
Tax Returns	Permanently
Timecards	7 yrs.

Client Files and Documents

- Retention of client files and client-related documents depends on the ethical rules in your state.
- Before destroying a client file, contact the client to make sure she does not want the file or want something out of the file.
- When destroying client files, burn, shred, or recycle them to ensure client confidentiality.

burning, or recycling them. Simply throwing them away does not protect the client's confidentiality and should not be done. Another alternative is to microfilm closed files. Drawbacks are that microfilming can be fairly expensive and the information is not as usable as the original document. However, when considering the cost of long-term storage, microfilming actually may be less expensive in the long run.

ORGANIZATION OF FILES—
A MAJOR LEGAL ASSISTANT DUTY

File organization is a large part of what many legal assistants do. They must use files on a daily basis. Therefore, for most legal assistants to become efficient at what they do, they must be able to organize and in some cases index case files in a logical and systematic fashion so they can quickly find information. Case material also must be organized in such a way that others, such as attorneys, can find the information quickly. A file that is a disorganized mess is useless in a law office. For instance, if the legal assistant is assisting an attorney at a deposition and the attorney asks him or her to find a specific answer in the discovery request, she must be able to quickly locate it. If the legal assistant is not familiar with the case, does not have the file organized, or misfiled the document, he or she will not have the ability to find the information quickly, and the client's case may suffer.

FILE MANAGEMENT AND ETHICS

There are several ethical questions that should be addressed when considering filing and filing systems. These issues include performing conflict-of-interest checks before a new case is taken, maintaining client-related property that is turned over to the law office during representation, maintaining trust and client-related accounting records, returning a client's file to him if he decides to change attorneys, and ensuring that the office's filing system and/or file destruction procedures maintain client confidentiality.

CLIENT PROPERTY

Offices should be careful when closing files and especially in destroying files where documents or other information were given to the attorney by a client. Rule 1.15 of the *Model Rules of Professional Conduct* states:

> Rule 1.15 Safekeeping Property
> (a) A lawyer shall hold property of clients or third persons that is in a lawyer's possession in connection with a representation separate from the lawyer's own property.... Other property shall be identified as such and appropriately safeguarded....[3]

The Ethics 2000 Commission is not recommending any changes to this rule. A law office has a duty at the end of a case to give the client the option to pick up information that was delivered to the attorney for representation in the matter. Generally, unless the client consents, a lawyer should not destroy or discard items that clearly or probably belong to the client. In addition, an attorney should be especially careful not to destroy client information where the applicable statutory limitations period has not expired.

DUTY TO TURN OVER FILE WHEN CLIENT FIRES ATTORNEY

An attorney also has a duty to turn over to a client his or her file when the client decides to fire an attorney and hire another one. What must be turned over to the client depends on the ethical rules and case law in each state. For example, Rule 3-700(D) of the *California Revised Rules of Professional Conduct* states:

> (a) [An attorney] whose employment has terminated shall ... promptly release to the client, all the client papers and property. Client papers and property include correspondence, pleadings, deposition transcripts, exhibits, physical evidence, expert's reports, and other items reasonably necessary to the client's representation, whether the client has paid for them or not.

In most states, the attorney must turn over the documents the new counsel will need to reasonably handle the matter. In some states, such as California, a law office cannot refuse to release a client's file just because the client still owes fees and expenses.

DESTRUCTION OF RECORDS OF ACCOUNT

Rule 1.15(a) of the *Model Rules of Professional Conduct* states the minimum rules for how long attorneys should keep client account/fund information:

> . . . Complete records of . . . account funds and other property shall be kept by the lawyer and shall be preserved for a period of [five years] after termination of the representation.[4]

The Ethics 2000 Commission is not recommending any changes to this rule. Law offices should carefully maintain accurate and complete records of the lawyer's receipt and disbursement of trust funds in every case.

CONFIDENTIALITY

An attorney's duty to maintain the confidentiality of client-related matters should be a factor when considering a law office file management system. Files must be maintained so that sensitive information about a case or client is maintained. Also, the confidentiality rule does not stop once the case is closed. Law offices should be careful to destroy or dispose of files in a manner consistent with the confidentiality requirements.

FORM FILES

form file
A file that contains examples of documents used in a law office, including pleadings, contracts, letters, discovery documents, wills, and incorporation papers.

A **form file** contains examples of documents that are commonly used in the law office, including pleadings, contracts, letters, discovery documents, wills, and incorporation papers. As a practical matter, any time a new type of document is prepared, a copy of the document should be placed in the form file. Depending on the size of the law office, the office itself may keep a form file, or attorneys, legal assistants, and legal secretaries may keep their own form files. Form files are critical to practicing law efficiently: if a firm does not keep a form file, staff members are forced to recreate documents over and over. Sometimes hours of research go into producing a new document. Thus, the law office does not want to duplicate this research time over and over.

Form files are kept electronically, in three-ring notebooks, expanding file folders, or manila files. Form files can be arranged alphabetically or can be grouped according to type, such as bankruptcy. Any form file should have some type of alphabetical index so that users can quickly find the document for which they are looking. In addition to keeping hard copies of documents, many offices also keep copies of the documents on a word processor or a firm intranet so that they can be quickly pulled up and edited as needed. This, too, can save hours. Although form files are great time-savers, users must be sure to update the forms and/or research on a regular basis to keep forms current.

Finally, in addition to each office keeping a form file, many state bar associations or legal secretary associations publish forms for their particular state. The cost of such forms is usually several hundred dollars, although in many states the set contains literally hundreds of different forms and checklists for many areas of law. This type of form file can pay for itself in legal research savings very quickly. Most law libraries have form books, but in many cases the books are not specifically made for a particular state.

INTRODUCTION TO LAW LIBRARY MANAGEMENT

> *Even though the library remains the single most valuable tangible asset of a law office or corporate legal department, it must justify the continuing investment that it requires.*[5]

Nearly every law office has some type of law library. From an administrative standpoint, the library must be managed correctly to ensure that the law office gets its money's worth from it, especially when considering the high cost of maintaining a law library. In medium-sized to large law offices, professional librarians may coordinate and manage the law library. In smaller law offices, legal assistants or associate attorneys may perform these duties. Figure 9-5 contains a list of librarian-related duties.

Depending on the structure of the law office, the library may be supervised by a library committee, a managing partner, or an office administrator, or all functions may be controlled by the librarian.

- Trains and supervises staff.
- Explains research techniques to lawyers and legal assistants and answers questions.
- Compiles legislative histories and bibliographies.
- Selects and orders books, CD-ROM libraries, and other library resources.
- Reviews and approves bills for payment.
- Plans library growth.
- Catalogs and tracks library resources using computerized methods.
- Routes library-related materials to appropriate staff.
- Files loose-leaf services and other library-related documents.
- Manages check out of books and reshelves material.
- Performs or assists legal professionals in legal research particularly regarding computed-assisted legal research and legal and factual research on the Internet.

**Figure 9-5
Librarian-Related Duties**

Law libraries generally are thought of as an overhead expense and, regardless of size, are costly to maintain. Proper library management can, however, reduce overhead expenses and increase the quality of services to clients at the same time.

Some legal assistants may be put in charge of the law library. Managing a law library may not seem at first like a difficult job, but in many instances it is. Books, periodicals, CD-ROM libraries, and other materials must be ordered on a regular basis to ensure the library is kept current, supplements to books (sometimes called "pocket parts") must be ordered and replaced regularly, the collection must be tracked using some type of computer or card catalog system (this requires quite a bit of time), books must be shelved and maintained, a library budget must be kept and tracked, and, from time to time, books must be tracked down and found. Many librarians themselves perform legal research as well. Proper law library management can be a time-consuming task.

DEVELOPING A LIBRARY COLLECTION

What distinguishes an excellent library from a mediocre one . . . is not its size but its usefulness to the practitioners who rely on it. Its worth depends not merely on the amount of information they can find there but on the quality of that information and the ease of gathering it.[6]

There are many different types of materials that can be found in a law office library. The office's collection should mirror the type of practice and specialties it practices in. As a law office's practice changes, the library also will need to change to keep information that is current with the needs of the law office. Figure 9-6 shows typical types of publications that are found in many law office library collections.

The extent of an office's collection will depend on many factors. Larger offices that have been in existence for many years will have much larger collections than will newer or smaller law offices. Some offices think that most, if not all, research should be performed in their own library, while other law offices that have large collections nearby, such as a law school or state or county law library, may want to keep their costs low and use these resources to the fullest extent possible.

**Figure 9-6
Possible Holdings in a Law Library**

- Case Law
- Citators
- Digests
- Encyclopedias
- Index to Periodicals
- Periodicals
- Reference Works
- Statutes
- Treatises
- CD-ROM Libraries
- LEXIS
- WESTLAW
- Internet Access

One popular option to keep overhead costs low in the library is to purchase CD-ROM libraries, include internet access, maintain LEXIS or WESTLAW, and maintain hard copy books and periodicals only as needed. This strategy limits the space requirements needed for most libraries and maximizes the use of computers already on the desks of most staff.

CD-ROM LEGAL DATABASES

A **CD-ROM legal database** is a database like one found on WESTLAW or LEXIS, but packaged on one or more CD-ROMs. For example, the complete set of Federal Reporters, which contains federal appellate court decisions from 1880 to the present, takes up more than 150 linear feet of shelf space in a law library, and this does not count the indexes necessary to use the reporters. The same Federal Reporters come on twelve CD-ROM disks, take up a few inches of shelf space, and come with a search engine that allows the user to search for needed material. Many CD-ROM publishers also offer connections to the Internet or online service so that research can be updated.

CD-ROM legal database
A database like one found on WESTLAW or LEXIS, but packaged on CD-ROMs.

CD-ROM LEGAL LIBRARIES There are hundreds and hundreds of CD-ROM legal libraries currently available. Many books and periodicals published for the legal industry are available on CD-ROM. This includes everything from criminal law and family law to European tax laws, and everything in between. One of the best places to find a listing of law related CD-ROMs is in a book from Infosources Publishing (www.infosourcespub.com) called the *Directory of Law-Related CD-ROMs*. The directory lists more than 1,200 law-related CD-ROM products and is cross-referenced by title, subject, publisher, and computer type. Most of the major legal book publishers, including West, BNA, Matthew Bender, and many others offer a wide variety of CD-ROM products.

CD-ROM SEARCH ENGINES Searching CD-ROM legal databases is similar to searching on WESTLAW and LEXIS. Every CD-ROM legal database uses a search engine, typically either Premise or Folio Views, to perform the search. Users are able to use terms and connectors including proximity searches, wild card searches, and other searches similar to WESTLAW and LEXIS. Most search engines also have hypertext, which allows a user to go directly to another referenced document immediately (similar to the Internet). For example, if a user is reading a case and another case is referenced, the user can click the mouse on the reference to the second citation, and the computer will immediately take the user to the second case.

ADVANTAGES AND DISADVANTAGES OF CD-ROM LEGAL LIBRARIES
There are many advantages to using CD-ROM legal libraries.

- *Reduced Space and Reduced Expense Considerations* CD-ROM legal libraries take up a fraction of the space that similar information in book form would. While most law libraries will want some information in book form, there is much information that can be stored on CD-ROM. This has a tremendous impact on the annual operating cost of a law library for any legal organization. If a law firm or corporate law department can cut the size of its law library in half, it can save a tremendous amount on lease space, shelving, and other items. Because many legal organizations are in the business of making money, this is a very important consideration.

- *Portability* Unlike rows and rows of books, CD-ROM legal libraries are inherently portable. Users can take the entire body of a state's case law into a courtroom on a laptop computer and have the information at their fingertips. This can prove extremely beneficial to the attorney or legal assistant.
- *Convenience* Users can access information on their own computers without going to a library or even leaving their office. In addition, information on CD-ROM can be copied into a user's word processor just like WESTLAW and LEXIS.
- *Cost* The total cost of a CD-ROM legal library is often less than for hardcopy books or for performing the research on-line using WESTLAW or LEXIS. It is also more cost effective for anyone who does a significant amount of legal research because it can usually be done at the person's desk and, in many circumstances, electronic research is substantially faster than using books and indexes to do the same research.
- *Maintenance* The cost of maintaining books and adding and deleting supplements and loose-leaf pages should not be underestimated, particularly in a large law library. It takes library personnel numerous hours to do this, as compared to installing a new CD-ROM to replace an old one. There are, however, some maintenance disadvantages to CD-ROM that will be discussed later in this section. As library personnel maintenance time lessens, productivity should increase in other areas, such as the amount of time library staff can spend to assist customers with research projects.

Disadvantages to CD-ROM legal libraries include the following.

- *Maintenance* Maintenance of the computer software can be an issue: most CD-ROM databases have a monthly or quarterly subscription service that must be purchased to keep it up to date. New CD-ROMs and updates must be installed. In addition, search engines must be upgraded to new versions from time to time. Depending on the environment, such as whether the computers are networked or are stand-alone, this can be quite time-consuming. Keeping hardware requirements, including RAM and hard disk space, and networking requirements current can also be time-consuming. In addition, sometimes the technology involved (including interfacing with a network) is a problem. The systems may not work or may be incompatible. Technical experts must be called in to make modifications, which can be both expensive and time-consuming.
- *CD-ROM versus the Internet* There is some question regarding the long-term validity of CD-ROMs, particularly when compared to the Internet. CD-ROMs must be continually updated whereas Internet products never need to be updated because the user connects to the Internet where the product is always current.

- *Switching CD-ROMs* While there are CD-ROM towers that can handle multiple CD-ROMs, many systems still require users or information system professionals to change CD-ROM disks. This can be inconvenient and time-consuming. Some legal organizations copy all their CD-ROMs to large network servers so that CD-ROM towers are not necessary. This also makes accessing the information faster, as server access is much faster than CD-ROM access.
- *Training* Training users to use CD-ROMs legal databases can be a problem when different publishers or search engines are used.

CATALOGING AND CLASSIFYING THE COLLECTION

Proper classification and organization of a collection are imperative for the office to know what material it has and where it is. If information is not arranged or organized in such a manner so that attorneys and legal assistants can easily find it without wasting time, the whole purpose of an in-house library is thwarted.

Cataloging is the process of listing and organizing the inventory of a library. This usually includes giving each book a separate call number and listing the book's author, title, publisher, subject, publication date, and so forth. Some offices classify and catalog their collections according to the Library of Congress classification system or the Dewey decimal system. The Library of Congress system uses the alphabet for its general divisions. For instance, "K" is the letter that represents American Law. Figure 9-7 contains a list of selected Library of Congress legal classifications. Other offices may simply group materials together, such as a tax section, labor section, or real property section. This is sometimes called a "neighborhood" classification system.

Administrative Law	Constitutional Law
KF5401	KF4501
Agency	Consumer Law
KF1341	KF1601
Appellate Advocacy	Contracts
KF9050	KF801
Civil Procedure	Corporations
KF8810	KF1384
Commercial Transactions	Criminal Law
KF871	KF9201
Conflict of laws	Criminal Procedure
KF8810	KF9601
Conservation of Natural Resources	Decedents' Estates & Trusts
KF5505	KF746

Figure 9-7
Modified Library of Congress Classification Numbers

Computerized catalog systems can be created using almost any data-base management program. They are very easy to set up and are very flexible. There also are some commercially available library cataloging systems for many types of microcomputers.

Technology and the Law Library

COMPUTER-ASSISTED LEGAL RESEARCH (CALR)

Computer-assisted legal research uses computers to search the words of cases, statutes, and documents themselves. Two familiar legal-information services include WESTLAW and LEXIS.

Because CALR systems use the full text of the document, there is no need for indexes or digests. Instead, the user simply enters common words that describe the issue that might appear in the full text of the case or document and the system retrieves all cases and documents that meet the request. Since the information is stored on large mainframes, the data base can be searched and the documents quickly retrieved. The documents that are retrieved can be read on-line, can be sent off-line to your printer, or the full text can be downloaded to the user's computer. **On-line** means that the user is connected to an information system and is running up charges. **Off-line** means that a user is no longer connected to an information service and that no charges are accruing except possibly a printing or downloading charge. Alternatively, a list of the appropriate cases or documents also can be printed or downloaded so that if the user likes, he or she can go to a library and examine the full text of the cases or documents.

CALR can be significantly quicker than manual researching techniques. Further, when CALR is used correctly, it also can find or retrieve cases that might not otherwise have been found using manual methods because of poor indexing or other errors. CALR is also faster than manual methods because it is possible to search many data bases (such as searching the case law of all fifty states on a specific subject). Using manual methods, the user would have to search through several sets of digests, supplements, and indexes.

CALR, in addition to being quicker and sometimes being more accurate than manual researching, also can be more convenient. Nearly all legal-information services are available twenty-four hours a day, unlike many law libraries. Also, the research can be done from the legal professional's office. As mentioned before, when using a law library, it is possible that an important book might already be checked out or unavailable. Sources are always available on-line with CALR. Another important factor to consider is that new cases are entered into legal-information services usually within a few days of being handed down or decided. Therefore, the information that is available on-line is almost always more up-to-date than information available in books.

Although CALR is both fast and convenient, it is not free. Most legal-information services charge a yearly subscription fee and a fee based on the amount of time connected to their system. Some services also charge a fee for every search that is done

on-line
The user is connected to an information system and is running up charges.

off-line
The user is not connected to an information service and no charges are accruing except possibly a printing or downloading charge.

on their system. Some services have connect-time charges of more than two hundred dollars an hour. In addition, some services have a minimum monthly charge even if the service is not used. Because CALR is so expensive, new users can run up large bills quickly. Therefore, it is particularly important that new users have a thorough understanding of the CALR system they will be using. This is usually not a problem because most CALR systems have off-line training tutorials. On the average though, most legal issues take approximately fifteen minutes to research. Most offices bill this expense back to their clients; some even do so at a higher rate than charged to help cover related expenses such as long-distance charges. The office must be careful, however, to not bill the client for general overhead costs. General overhead costs should already be figured in the office's attorney and legal assistant billing rate, so it would be inappropriate for the client to be billed for general overhead costs again.

WESTLAW

WESTLAW is a full-text legal information service provided by West Group. According to West, it is one of the largest law libraries in the world, with more than 10,000 separate databases available for its users. It contains cases from all West reporters as well as slip opinions, unreported cases, interactive databases from Dow Jones DIALOG databases, and much more. This site gives WESTLAW users access to an enormous body of legal and nonlegal resources. Many of WESTLAW's features are covered here, including its databases, types of search queries, and special WESTLAW features.

WESTLAW can be accessed by using a microcomputer and WESTLAW-specific proprietary software called Westmate, or by using a microcomputer and a standard Web browser to connect to WESTLAW via the Internet.

LEXIS-NEXIS

LEXIS-NEXIS is a full-text legal information service. It was the first on-line full-text legal information service and is one of the world's largest. LEXIS and WESTLAW are similar in many respects, with a few differences. LEXIS can be accessed by using a microcomputer and specific proprietary software or by using a microcomputer and a standard Web browser and connecting to LEXIS via the Internet.

THE INTERNET

Many, if not most, legal professionals are connected to the Internet and are using it in a variety of ways (see Figure 9-8). Some of the most common include performing legal research, performing factual or business research, using e-mail to communicate with clients and colleagues, accessing court records, and performing marketing functions.

A recent survey by *Legal Assistant Today* indicated that nearly 80 percent of the legal assistants surveyed were connected to the Internet at work. Nearly 75 percent had a work e-mail address, while 22 percent used the Internet primarily to conduct legal research.

**Figure 9-8
How Legal
Organizations Are
Using the Internet**

Small Law Firm Technology Survey, Large Law Firm Technology Survey, Corporate Law Department Technology Survey, © 1998, American Bar Association. Reprinted by Permission.

Internet Activities	Small Firms	Large Firms	Corp. Law Dept.
Legal Research	86.4%	95.4%	89.0%
Non-Legal Research (Factual or Business Research)	66.1%	82.5%	70.1%
E-Mail Communication with Clients	53.6%	93.5%	—
E-Mail Communication with Colleagues	52.7%	83.7%	63.6%
Accessing Court Records	34.1%	83.0%	33.8%
Marketing	18.8%	73.2%	—
Participating in Discussion Groups	17.2%	40.5%	11.0%
Locating an Expert Witness	15.9%	46.4%	8.4%
Continuing Legal Education	11.7%	28.1%	15.6%
Electronically Filing SEC Documents	1.7%	54.9%	32.5%
Filing Court Document Electronically	2.5%	40.5%	4.5%

Sources: ABA 1998 Small Firm Technology Survey
ABA 1998 Large Firm Technology Survey
ABA 1998 Corporate Law Department Technology Survey

PERFORMING LEGAL RESEARCH ON THE INTERNET Performing legal research on the Internet can be done, but it is not at all like researching on WESTLAW or LEXIS. In WESTLAW and LEXIS, a user can look up, choose, and go to thousands of databases instantly; there is a uniform search engine and uniform Boolean language; and information is formatted neatly, succinctly, and uniformly. Even with all that, it still takes time, training, and experience to be proficient on WESTLAW and LEXIS.

In performing legal research on the Internet, little is uniform. You must search for and find information where you can, and you must learn the nuances of many different searching techniques and search languages. There is no one central depository of information. As with any kind of legal research, the more experience you have the better, but it takes time, training, and experience to be good at it.

Following are some strategies, adapted from *The Legal List—Research on the Internet,* to consider when beginning an Internet legal research project.

1. Is the Internet an appropriate place to find the legal information? If the user is looking for historic documents, including articles and statutes, or a solid case law background that dates before 1990, the Internet is probably not the place to search. It is better suited for current law, or recent cases or information. In short, the Internet is not a replacement for a traditional law library. With that said, depending on the subject matter, the Internet can have rich treasures of information, but you have to look for them.

A cost conscience legal researcher should start by researching any CD-ROM databases and hard copy books that he or she has, since they are cheap and convenient. The user could then explore the Internet to see what is available on-line. Again, this is cheap (actually free) and handy. Finally, the user could go to WESTLAW or LEXIS to double check and confirm the research, fill in any holes, and check citations (Shepardize).

2. **Understand your legal project and have a strategy.** It is important when doing legal research on the Internet to understand exactly what you are looking for and to have a strategy for finding it. The problem with looking for something on the Internet with no plan in mind is that you can easily spend three to four hours "surfing" from site to site without finding what you are looking for because the amount of information available on the Web is so vast.

3. **Choose a finding tool.** Choose a finding tool or search engine that is suited to the type of information for which you are looking. Some tools are better than others for finding specific kinds of information. FindLaw and LawCrawler are usually good legal finding tools.

4. **To find precise legal information, use a guidebook.** If you are looking for precise information on the Internet, it is highly recommended that you purchase a legal guidebook. A guidebook will help you get an on-line starting point (lists of specific legal Internet sites by topic) which will greatly improve your ability to find the information you need. There are many Internet guidebooks published by most major legal publishers.

5. **Get help.** Not only is the Internet a good source for legal and non-legal information, it is also a good resource for getting help. It is advantageous to belong to listservs and discussion groups regarding the type of law in which you work. When you get stuck or need help on a research project, ask for help. It is possible, if not probable, that others have experienced the same problem you have. You must, of course, be discreet in how you ask for help.

6. **Use an on-line starting point.** It is important to have a starting point when performing legal research on the Internet. However, a good starting point for one type of legal research might be poor for others. Guidebooks will help you find the right starting point. Also, Figure 9-9 shows some of the best legal research sites on the Web; they provide a wide variety of legal information.

PROBLEMS WITH RESEARCHING ON THE INTERNET There are inherent problems with researching on the Internet that legal professionals should consider before beginning.

- *Research on the Internet can take longer to perform.* This is especially true when looking for cases, statutes, and other primary information because it is spread over so many different sites. It takes experience to know where certain kinds of information reside on the Internet and which sites are better than others, especially for looking for historical cases or data.
- *Research on the Internet must be checked for accuracy and given a citation.* Unlike WESTLAW, LEXIS, and other fee-based information services, it is necessary to make sure that the data you have collected on the Internet is genuine. You must be able to cite the source of the information.
- *There are no added features to information.* The legal researcher needs to remember that cases and other material on the Internet are raw in nature. There are usually no additional features like the case synopsis and keynotes at the beginning of the case that WESTLAW adds. For the most part, the information has not been managed, at least not to the extent that a fee-based service would.

Legal Search Engines

Subject	Additional Information	Web URL (Address)
FindLaw	Legal search engine	www.findlaw.com
LawCrawler	Legal search engine	www.lawcrawler.com
Counsel Quest	Legal search engine	www.counselquest.com
The Law Engine	Legal search engine	www.fastsearch.com/law
GSU College of Law	Meta search engine—runs several legal search engines at once	www.gsulaw.gsu/metaindex/
Lawguru	Legal search engine	www.lawguru.com/search/lawsearch.html
All Law	Legal search engine	www.alllaw.com

General Starting Points (Including Federal and State Case Law and Statutes)

Subject	Additional Information	Web URL (Address)
Legal Information Institute at Cornell	One of the best sources of legal information on the Web	www.law.cornell.edu
CataLaw	General law-related information	www.CataLaw.com
WashLaw Web at Washburn University	Well-organized and comprehensive legal information	www.washlaw.edu
World Wide Web Virtual Library: Law at Indiana University	General law-related information	www.law.indiana.edu/law/v-lib/lawindex.html
CLR Internet Law Library (formerly hosted by the U.S. House of Representatives)	General law-related information	www.currentlegal.com/lawlibrary/
Hieros Gamos	Large collection of links to legal resources	www.hg.org

Federal Government Information, Regulations, and Laws

Subject	Additional Information	Web URL (Address)
Federal Web Locator—Villanova Center for Information Law and Policy	Federal regulations and information	www.law.vill.edu/Fed-Agency/fedwebloc.html
FedWorld	Federal information	www.fedworld.gov
GOVBOT	Search engine for government sites	www.ciir.cs.umass.edu/ciirdemo/govbot
Thomas	Searchable database of historical document including the Constitution and much more	www.thomas.loc.gov

International Law

Subject	Additional Information	Web URL (Address)
Library of Congress Guide to Law Online	Includes law-related information from around the world	www.lcweb2.loc.gov/glin/worldaw.html
N.Y. University School of Law—Foreign and International Materials	International law	www.nyu.edu/law/library/forint.html
Washburn's International Page	International law	www.lawlib.wuacc.edu/forint/forintmain.html

Figure 9-9   Law-Related Starting Points

INTERNET SITES

ORGANIZATION	DESCRIPTION	INTERNET ADDRESS
ABA Law Practice Today	ABA site devoted to law practice management	www.abanet.org/lpm
American Association of Law Libraries	Site devoted to topics related to law libraries	www.aallnet.org
ARMA—The Association for Information Management Professionals	International association devoted to record, file, information, and library management	www.arma.org
Association of Legal Administrators	Site devoted to administration of law office	www.alanet.org

SUGGESTED READING

Alphabetic Filing Rules, ARMA, 1995

Computer-Assisted Legal Research, Susan Cochard and Samantha Whitney-Ulane, American Bar Association, 1997

Converting from a Manual System to an Automated System: A Guidelines, ARMA, 1992

Electronic Records Retention, David Stephens, ARMA, 1997

Introduction to Electronic Imaging, 3rd ed., Don Avedon, ARMA, 1996

Law, Law, Law on the Internet, Erik Heels and Richard Klau, American Bar Association, 1998

Managing Electronic Records, 2nd ed., William Saffady, ARMA, 1998

Records Retention Law and Practice, Ronald Anson-Cartwright, ARMA, 1999

Report on Issues Surrounding Retention of Client Files in Law Firms, Helen Andrews, ARMA, 1993

The Legal List: Research on the Internet, Diana Botluk, West Group, 1998

SUMMARY

Law offices of all types need a file system that allows them to store, track, and retrieve information about cases in a logical, efficient, and expeditious manner. When considering filing management techniques, each legal matter should be maintained separately and have its own case number. How a law office sets up its case numbering system is up to the office and its own needs. Alphabetical and numerical systems are common. In addition, the law office must decide whether files should be kept in a central location in the office or whether they should be kept throughout the office using a decentralized approach.

Color coding is a file management technique that is used to reduce the number of misfiled documents and lost files. Because most offices cannot keep all files indefinitely, an office should close inactive files and destroy the closed files from time to time to reduce file-storage requirements.

Nearly every law office has some type of law library. The law office library must be managed correctly to ensure that the law office gets its money's worth from it, especially when considering the high cost of maintaining a law library.

The use of computerized legal research has grown substantially in recent years. Most law libraries today include CD-ROM libraries, WESTLAW or LEXIS or both, and the Internet.

Key Terms

Alphabetic filing system
Bar coding
Imaging
Centralized file system
Decentralized file system

File opening form
Form file
CD-ROM legal database
On-line
Off-line

Questions and Exercises

1. Law libraries represent a large overhead cost to nearly every type of law office. List ways to reduce overhead costs of the library.

2. Your supervising attorney hands you a case file that she would like you to do some work on. It appears from the file that the client saw the attorney on two different cases: the purchase of a piece of property and a medical malpractice matter. When you ask the attorney, she states that the client has recently raised the medical malpractice matter, but that the client's primary focus is on the purchase of a piece of real estate. The attorney also states that she does not think the medical malpractice matter is significant and that is why a separate file is not being opened. The attorney tells you not to worry about it. To your knowledge, the attorney is not doing any research on the malpractice matter. How would you handle the situation?

3. The solo practitioner you worked for is moving across the country and wishes to close his law practice. The attorney is going to destroy all files related to the law practice because he does not want to have to rent storage space in a city he will no longer live in. The attorney is getting ready to dispose of the records by hauling them out to the dumpster. What is your advice to the attorney?

4. Your office represents a client who is suing his former partner in a business venture that went sour. Your office has represented the client for two years and has put about three hundred hours into the case. In addition, your office has taken five depositions and paid for the transcripts. Your office also has hired an expert witness. The expert witness prepared a report that supports your client's case. The office has about $30,000 worth of fees and expenses in the case. One afternoon, the client comes into the office and gives the receptionist a letter stating that he is terminating the relationship with the law office and that he wants his files returned to him within one week. The attorney in the case states that there is no way he is going to hand over anything until the client pays the office's expenses. The attorney states that because the client has not paid for any work, the files are not legally his, and because the law office fronted the expenses, the law office at least owns the deposition transcripts and expert witness report. How would you handle the matter?

5. You have known for several months that your office's filing system is terrible. Documents are routinely lost, files are misplaced, and information is never filed in a timely manner. From an ethics and malpractice perspective, discuss the problems that may arise if a client's file or a piece of evidence regarding a client file is lost and cannot be found.

6. The office you work for has recently added six attorneys and three legal assistants. The file system is no longer efficient. Finding files is time-consuming. You have been asked to come up with a new filing system. The following are some of the details you should keep in mind when determining the new system.

- The three tax attorneys want to start their own department. The tax attorneys will shortly move their offices to the basement, and they want to keep their own files so they

do not have to run up and down the stairs to get to them. None of the other attorneys use or need access to the tax files.
- Staff employees can be very reckless about the condition in which they leave files.
- When a case is opened, all the documents are kept in a large expanding file folder.
- Documents tend to fall out of the files, and there is little organization to the case files.
- Many of the attorneys work on cases together and need access to the cases.
- People constantly are looking through the office trying to find a file.
- Last week, the accounting department found out for the first time that the office has been handling a case for about four months. The client has never received a bill.
- The office wants a file system in which it can immediately tell when the case is filed, what type of case it is (the office mainly handles tax, probate, corporate, and general litigation matters), and which partner is responsible for the case (there are five partners).

Develop a strategy that will help eliminate these problems.

7. The partners in your office are displeased with the way the office's library is being maintained. They say that the library is hemorrhaging money with increased costs, which is crippling the office's profits. Your job is to draw up a plan to bring this situation under control. You have noticed the following.

- Several copies of books are purchased by different partners and placed on their bookshelves.
- The library is a mess most of the time. Books are kept in attorneys' and legal assistants' offices (they rarely check out the books and then fail to get them back to the library), there is not enough room for the materials the library does have, and books are stacked up on the floor.
- Many of the materials the library does have are outdated and no longer of use.
- You asked for several books, and, while you know they were ordered, you have not seen them yet.
- The library has no budget as such; purchases are made when the office thinks it needs them. In addition, when an attorney orders a book, the book is sometimes kept on the attorney's own bookshelf.
- All library costs, including WESTLAW and LEXIS, are absorbed by the office.
- The library has no Internet access, although it has been talked about.
- The library has one old desktop computer that has WESTLAW and LEXIS only.

NOTES

1. Deborah Heller and James M. Hunt, *Practicing Law and Managing People: How to Be Successful* (Butterworth, 1988), p. 60.
2. Gary A. Munneke, *Law Practice Management* (St. Paul, MN: West Publishing Co., 1991), p. 199.
3. Reprinted by permission. Copies of the ABA Model Code of Professional Responsibility, 1999 ed., are available from Service Center, American Bar Association, 750 North Lake Shore Drive, Chicago, IL 60611-4497, 1-800-285-2221.
4. Reprinted by permission. Copies of the ABA Model Code of Professional Responsibility, 1999 ed., are available from Service Center, American Bar Association, 750 North Lake Shore Drive, Chicago, IL 60611-4497, 1-800-285-2221.
5. Richard Sloane, "The Law Office Library," *The Lawyer's Handbook,* American Bar Association, 1983, B3-1. Reprinted by permission.
6. Richard Sloane, "The Law Office Library," *The Lawyer's Handbook,* American Bar Association, 1983, B3-2. Reprinted by permission.

CASE REVIEW

In re Cameron, 270 Ga. 512, 511 S.E.2d 514 (Ga. 1999).

Supreme Court of Georgia.

In the Matter of Johnnie CAMERON (Two Cases).

Nos. S99Y0257, S99Y0258.

Feb. 8, 1999.

*512 PER CURIAM.

The State Bar filed two Notices of Discipline against Respondent Johnnie Cameron alleging violations of Standards 4 (professional conduct involving dishonesty, fraud, deceit, or wilful misrepresentation); 22 (withdrawal from employment without taking reasonable steps to avoid foreseeable prejudice to the rights of the client, including giving due notice to the client, allowing time for employment of other counsel, delivering to the client all papers and property to which the client is entitled and complying with applicable laws and rules); and 44 (wilful abandonment or disregard of a legal matter to the client's detriment) of Bar Rule 4-102(d). Upon Cameron's failure to respond to either of the Notices of Discipline within the time set by Bar Rule 4-208.3(a), Cameron was in default pursuant to Bar *513 Rule 4-208.1(b) and subject to discipline by this Court. The State Bar has recommended disbarment as an appropriate sanction for Cameron's violations of Standards 4, 22,and 44 of Bar Rule 4-102(d). We agree.

In one disciplinary matter, Cameron was hired by a client to represent him in a social security disability claim. The client gave Cameron documents pertaining to the claim and tried to reach Cameron by telephone numerous times. Cameron did not return the client's calls even when the client tried to reach Cameron regarding an appointment scheduled with a physician regarding the client's disability claim. On July 28, 1997, the client spoke with Cameron by telephone and Cameron promised to return the call on July 30, 1997 but failed to do so. After the Social Security Administration scheduled a disability hearing, the client again tried unsuccessfully to reach Cameron. Subsequently, the hearing was postponed when the hearing officer also could not reach Cameron. The client, in making additional attempts to reach Cameron, learned that Cameron's office had been vacated and his home telephone number disconnected. On September 5, 1997, the client wrote a letter to Cameron terminating Cameron's services and demanding the return of all documents. Cameron again failed to respond. Due to Cameron's failure to represent the client, the client was not able to present his disability case to the administrative law judge.

In a second matter, a client hired Cameron on or about November 14, 1997 to advise her on a will and property deeds and gave the original documents plus $50 to Cameron. Although Cameron stated that he would copy the documents and return the originals to the client, he failed to return the documents or to contact the client. The client made numerous attempts to call Cameron at his home and his office but was not able to reach him; she also learned that Cameron's fax number was disconnected. The client and the client's daughter contacted Cameron at his part-time job and requested the return of the original documents. Although in both instances Cameron promised to return the documents on the day of the telephone conversations, he did not keep the appointments or return the documents. In sum, Cameron did not do any work on the client's behalf, did not return any portion of the $50 fee, and failed to return the client's documents.

Although Cameron has no disciplinary history, the State Bar noted the pattern of dishonesty and abandonment evidenced by the two grievances filed and Cameron's failure to respond to the Notices of Investigation as aggravating factors in its recommendation for disbarment. Cameron has failed to respond to disciplinary authorities during the investigation of these matters and the Court finds no evidence of mitigating circumstances.

*514 We agree with the State Bar that disbarment is warranted as a result of Cameron's violation of Standards 4, 22, and 44 of Bar Rule 4-102(d). Accordingly, Cameron is disbarred from the practice of law in Georgia. He is reminded of his duties under Bar Rule 4-219(c).

Disbarred.

All the Justices concur.

END OF DOCUMENT

Exercises

1. List each act committed by the attorney that violated Standard 22 of the state Bar Rules regarding the "withdrawal from employment without taking reasonable steps to avoid foreseeable prejudice to the rights of the client . . . "

2. If the attorney had argued that he should not be disciplined because the client had not paid him for the time spent on the case(s) (assuming it was true), would this have changed the outcome of the case?

3. What duty did the attorney have to his client(s) when he moved his office and had his home telephone number and office fax number disconnected?

4. Once the attorney took a part-time job, and assuming he quit the practice of law, what should the attorney have done?

5. Given the fact that the attorney had no prior discipline, do you think disbarment was appropriate?

10

Law Office Equipment, Technology, Space Management, Security, and Leases

CHAPTER OBJECTIVES

After you read this chapter, you will be able to:

- Discuss ethical considerations regarding faxes and e-mail.
- Explain which equipment should be rented instead of purchased.
- Discuss why just-in-time inventory allows businesses to maximize cash flow.
- Distinguish between usable and rentable office space.

> More than ever, it is critical that legal organizations maintain a competitive advantage by using technology to its fullest. While technology represents a tremendous investment, it allows legal organizations to be more responsive, to better communicate with their clients, and to provide higher quality services to clients.

LAW OFFICE EQUIPMENT AND TECHNOLOGY

Law offices of all types have discovered the benefits of technology. Nearly all law offices have a variety of sophisticated equipment such as copy machines, voice mail, computers, e-mail and facsimile (fax) machines. Using technology, staff members can increase productivity; that is, do more work with the same amount of effort. Thus, for legal assistants to be as productive as possible, they need to have a basic understanding of the technologies used in law offices.

In addition, in many instances technology allows a law office to improve the quality of the legal services that are provided. In large offices, it is not uncommon for millions of dollars to be spent on technology every year. Many managers think that by purchasing technology, they are investing in the future of the law office.

> *Keeping abreast of the latest changes in technology and online information resources will continue to be extremely important for our [legal assistant] profession. "Cyberparalegals" with the ability to find information quickly and then analyze, sort, and pare it down into a more manageable, useful format will be in high demand.[1]*

As law offices become increasingly technologically sophisticated, they must carefully choose the types of technologies that are purchased. There are hundreds of options for nearly every piece of equipment. Offices also must manage the system implementation, staff training, how the equipment can be used most effectively, how it will be maintained, and how it will be paid for. Managing equipment and technology has become a major responsibility of managing law offices of all types. In some instances, legal assistants are the persons managing these resources. Different types of equipment are presented in this section.

COPY MACHINES

Copy machines are a staple of every law office regardless of size or type. Law offices must routinely copy documents for internal files, clients, courts, opposing counsel, and others. It is not uncommon, even in a solo practitioner's office, to make tens of thousands of copies a year. Some larger offices have a centralized copy center or department that has its own staff. Other law offices have one or more copy machines located throughout the office that are self-serve. Some offices have both a centralized department, which handles large documents, and self-serve copy machines for smaller jobs.

As an alternative to the high cost of purchasing and maintaining copy machines, some law offices have chosen to have their copiers supplied by facility management operations such as Xerox and others. Facility management operations provide the copy machine, maintenance, supplies, and personnel in an office.

BILLING FOR CLIENT COPIES Making sure that clients are properly billed for copies made for their case can be problematic given the larger number of cases and copies. Some offices have staff members complete expense slips detailing which client the copies were made for, how many copies were made, and why the copies were made. Some copy machines allow the user to enter a client identification number, which then tracks the number of copies to be billed to each client. Some copy machines use client copy cards to calculate the number of copies. The issue of tracking and billing clients for copies should be considered when purchasing a copier.

POSTAGE MACHINES

Law offices use the U.S. Postal Service quite heavily. Given this large usage, most offices use a postage machine in lieu of stamps. Once postage has been placed on the machine, users simply run an envelope or label through the machine and the postage seal and amount are stamped onto the envelope or label.

There are many styles and types of postage machines based on the features and the volume of mail. Not only are postage machines more convenient to use than stamps, but one source indicates that metered mail skips many steps in the automated postal system and can be delivered up to twenty-four hours sooner than mail with a postage stamp. Postage costs, like long-distance and photocopying expenses, also are tracked and charged back to the client for reimbursement purposes by many law offices. Expense slips typically are used to charge this cost back to the client.

TELECOMMUNICATIONS

Telecommunications is a rapidly evolving area that has many aspects important to law offices. Among these are telephone systems, voice mail, facsimile equipment, and electronic mail.

TELEPHONE EQUIPMENT Telephones are vital to any law office because they are the means by which staff members communicate with clients, opposing counsel, courts, witnesses, and one another.

Telephone systems for law offices can cost from one thousand to one hundred thousand dollars or more depending on the number of phone stations needed and the number of outgoing lines needed. As with any equipment purchase, reliability is a key feature that must be researched carefully. Office managers obtain independent reviews of the equipment.

VOICE MAIL Voice mail is a computerized telecommunications system that stores and delivers voice messages. Callers are able to leave a detailed message directly without going through a secretary or other individual where messages can be distorted or miscommunication can take place. The individual can then retrieve either on or off site his or her messages by dialing his or her "mailbox." Voice mail also is available twenty-four hours a day so clients can leave messages for people even when the office is not open. Voice mail is an integral part of many law offices.

FACSIMILE (FAX) MACHINES Fax machines are used extensively by nearly every type and size of law office. Fax machines allow a user to electronically transmit a document's image to a receiving fax machine at another location, which prints the document that was sent. Fax machines are easy to operate and come in hundreds of styles with many features. Prices range from one hundred to two thousand dollars or more. Some fax machines work in conjunction with a computer system and are installed inside the computer system. This allows a user to fax a document, such as a word processing file, without even having to leave his or her desk.

Faxes have become so accepted in the legal community that many courts allow documents to be faxed if the documents are not more than ten to fifteen pages long.

FAXES AND CONFIDENTIALITY Faxes should be sent very carefully because an improper or misdirected fax transmission can lead to breach of client confidentiality, loss of attorney-client privilege, and legal malpractice. All fax cover pages for law offices should have some kind of confidentiality disclaimer on them such as the following.

> CONFIDENTIALITY NOTICE—This fax message contains legally confidential and privileged information intended for the sole use of the individual(s) or organizations named above. If you are not the intended recipient of this fax message, you are hereby notified that any dissemination, distribution, or copy of this message is strictly prohibited. If you have received this fax in error, please notify us immediately by telephone and return this fax to us by mail.

Other precautions that can be taken to ensure fax information stays confidential include assuring that everyone using the fax machine knows how to use it correctly; making sure that everyone operating the fax machine understands that a misdirected fax can destroy client confidentiality and the attorney-client privilege and can result in charges of malpractice; and requiring the sender to check to make sure the material has been received.

TELECOMMUNICATIONS AND CLIENT CONFIDENTIALITY Client confidentiality should always be considered when dealing with phone systems. This is especially true considering the amount of time that legal assistants spend on the phone. Users should never broadcast client names over the law office's intercom/paging system. Users should be very careful about who is in the room when a client's case is being discussed on the phone. Conversations on mobile phones, particularly those that include confidential or sensitive information, should be limited, if possible. Some radios/scanners have the ability to pick up these frequencies.

ELECTRONIC MAIL

Electronic mail (e-mail) allows users to send and receive messages using a computer. When an Internet account is opened, the user is given an e-mail address and can then send and receive messages. Tens of millions of people use e-mail every day to communicate.

There are many advantages to using e-mail. Messages can be sent almost instantaneously nearly anywhere in the world; e-mail is very inexpensive (the cost of an Internet account); word processing, sound, and graphic files can be attached to e-mail messages; messages can be sent, read, and replied to at the user's convenience; e-mail prevents telephone tag; messages can be sent to groups of people at the same time; users can get their messages from anywhere; and messages can be saved, tracked, and managed electronically. A common client complaint is that legal professionals are often very busy and hard to reach. E-mail allows legal professionals and clients to communicate with one another quickly and conveniently. E-mail is a mainstay in most legal organizations.

E-MAIL SOFTWARE To send and receive e-mail requires e-mail software. Two of the most popular e-mail programs are Microsoft Outlook (see Figure 10-1) and Netscape Messenger. E-mail software performs a variety of functions, including storing names and e-mail addresses in an address book, retrieving messages, forwarding messages, storing sent messages, and attaching files to messages.

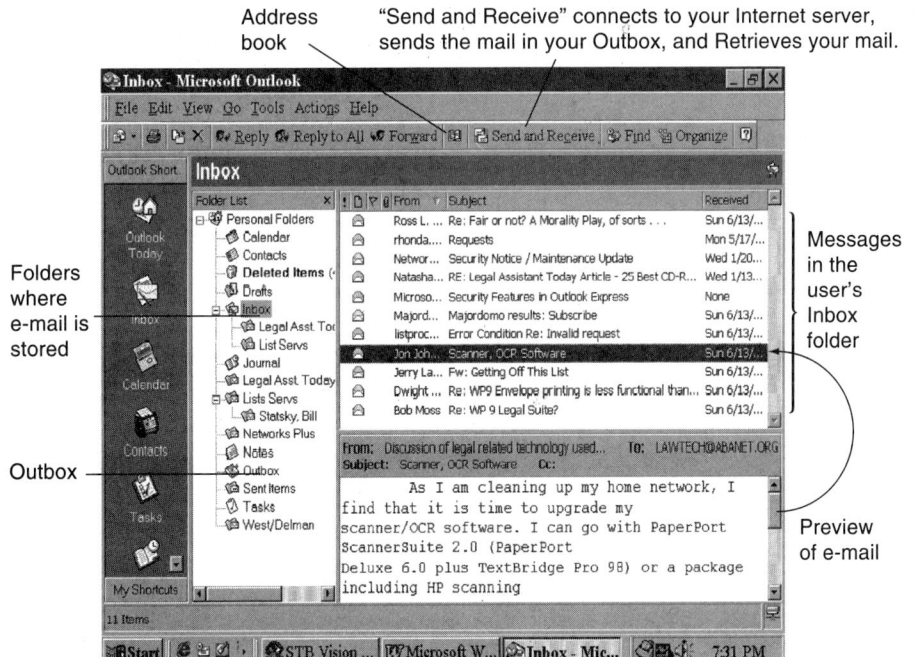

**Figure 10-1
Microsoft Outlook
E-mail Software**

Screen shot reprinted by permission from Microsoft Corporation.

E-MAIL ETIQUETTE Following e-mail etiquette will help you communicate your messages effectively to the reader.

- *Be succinct and clear, and use short paragraphs.* Whenever possible, keep your e-mails short and to the point. You should be as clear as possible in your messages so the reader does not have to ask for clarification regarding something you wrote. Use paragraphs liberally. Long paragraphs are hard to read on a computer screen, and it is easy to lose your place, particularly if you have to scroll up and down the message.
- *Spell check and reread your e-mails.* Most e-mail programs have a spell-check function. Use it whenever possible. Many users send e-mails that are full of spelling and grammar errors that can sometimes change the meaning of the message. Before sending your e-mails, reread them to make sure they make sense.
- *Be careful to treat e-mail as business correspondence.* E-mails cannot be retrieved once they are sent. They are written records that are kept by the recipients, so be extremely careful about what you send and make sure that you can live with the message. When in doubt, do not send it. Also, remember that the recipient cannot see your body language or interpret your tone, so word your e-mails carefully.
- *Do not use ALL CAPS.* Using all caps is equivalent to SHOUTING! Use all caps only when absolutely necessary.
- *If a message is unclear, ask for clarification.* If you are unsure about a message someone has sent you, ask for clarification. Do not assume you know the answer.
- *Be careful of Reply All.* Sometimes users get e-mail with twenty other people copied on it. If the user selects Reply, only the sender of the original e-mail will get a response, but selecting Reply All will send a reply to all twenty of the recipients. Far too often, a user intends to send a personal message to the sender of the e-mail and mistakenly selects Reply All. Before you select Reply All, make sure you really want to send it to everyone on the original message.
- *Check e-mail daily.* If possible, check e-mails daily and do not allow them to stack up, particularly if clients e-mail you regularly.
- *Do not use e-mail to communicate with clients regarding sensitive information.* For communicating with clients about sensitive information, it is probably better not to use e-mail at all, but if in doubt, always ask the client first. Because Internet e-mail can pass through many network servers where the e-mail can be read, it is better not to use e-mail for sensitive information.
- *Double check the recipient of your e-mail.* Often users intend to send e-mail to one person and accidentally select the wrong person. Always double check the e-mail address to make sure you entered the correct one.
- *Limit each e-mail message to one topic.* It is difficult to decide where to file multiple-topic e-mails and it is sometimes difficult to follow-up on them. There could be multiple follow-up actions buried in the e-mail.

PROBLEMS WITH E-MAIL While e-mail is inexpensive and convenient, it is not perfect. Keep the following considerations in mind when using e-mail.

- *Do not assume that an e-mail was read just because you sent it.* Like any other form of written communication, e-mail can be lost, the message not opened, or the message accidentally deleted.
- *E-mail relies on computer technology that fails from time to time.* E-mail only works if the computer networks are functioning correctly, if the telephone lines or other technology is working, and if a recipient's computer hardware and software are working correctly. If any of these fail, your message will not reach the recipient.
- *Be careful what you say in e-mails, as they can be forwarded to others.* The nature of an e-mail is that it can be easily forwarded to another person. For example, you send an e-mail to X about Y and X receives the e-mail and immediately forwards it to Y.

E-MAIL CONFIDENTIALITY Confidentiality while using e-mail to communicate with clients is an important issue. From the client's perspective, there are many advantages to using e-mail to communicate with legal professionals. The problem with e-mail is the level of confidentiality and security that it affords. Internet e-mail passes through many network servers and could be intercepted or read by others at any level. Therefore, many legal professionals are worried about violating client confidentiality and the possibility that attorney-client privilege has been waived if third parties have access to such information. While there is encryption software available that scrambles e-mail so that others cannot read it during transmission and then unscrambles it at the other end, the software has not matured to an acceptable standard yet. In addition, some encryption programs are very easy to break.

The *ABA Model Rules of Professional Conduct* state:

> Rule 1.6 Confidentiality of Information
> (a) A lawyer shall not reveal information relating to representation of a client unless the client consents after consultation, except for disclosures that are impliedly authorized in order to carry out the representation. . . .[2]

The Ethics 2000 Commission is considering the following revision to Model Rule 1.6.

"A lawyer shall not reveal information relating to the representation of a client or a former client unless the client ~~consents after consultation, except for disclosures that are~~ gives informed consent, the disclosure is impliedly authorized in order to carry out the representation. . . ."

The ABA recently issued a formal opinion on this issue (see ABA Standing Committee on Ethics and Professional Responsibility, Formal Opinion No. 99-413, March 10, 1999—Protecting the Confidentiality of Unencrypted E-mail). The committee stated

> A lawyer may transmit information relating to the representation of a client by unencrypted e-mail sent over the Internet without violating the *Model Rules of*

Professional Conduct because the mode of transmission affords a reasonable expectation of privacy from a technological and legal standpoint. The same privacy accorded U.S. and commercial mail, land-line telephonic transmissions, and facsimiles applies to Internet e-mail. A lawyer should consult with the client and follow her instructions, however, as to the mode of transmitting highly sensitive information relating to the client's representation.

The ABA found that e-mail affords users with a reasonable standard of expectation of privacy and therefore concluded that unencrypted e-mail could be used to communicate with a client. However, the ABA also found that an attorney had a duty to consider the sensitivity of the issue being communicated, what it would mean to the client's representation if the communication were disclosed, and the relative security of the contemplated means of communication. Arguably, the ABA wants legal professionals to exercise a common-sense standard when using e-mail or other forms of communicating with clients. If communication with a client is highly sensitive, then the attorney or legal assistant should consult with the client about whether a more secure form of communication is warranted.

Practical considerations for using e-mail ethically include the following.

- Have a policy for the legal organization regarding the use of e-mail and how it will be used to communicate with clients.
- Consult with clients about what type of information they want to communicate via e-mail, how often the client receives or responds to e-mail, and other information about the particulars of the client's specific e-mail system or habits.
- Make sure e-mail addresses are accurately entered so that client communication is not sent to others by mistake.
- Send a test e-mail to a client to ensure the right e-mail address is being used.
- Add a confidentiality statement to all client e-mails. This is similar to statements that accompany many fax cover pages that state that the information is intended solely for the recipient and any third party who receives it should immediately forward it or destroy it.
- Do not use e-mail at all for particularly sensitive information.

E-MAIL ERRORS It is important to be careful when using e-mail. Errors can happen several different ways and could result in malpractice claims against the legal organization. Some common errors include the following.

- *Sending an ill-conceived e-mail to a client or others before it is carefully considered.* Unlike a letter placed in the outgoing mailbox that can be retrieved a few hours later, once the user presses the send button, e-mail is gone.
- *Sending e-mail to unintended parties.* It is easy to use the Reply All command to send a private message to a group of people unintentionally, or to click on the wrong e-mail address. Depending on the content of the message, errors like these can damage a client's case, particularly when e-mail is sent to the opposition.
- *Sending the wrong attachments.* Because files can be sent with e-mails as an attachment, it is particularly important to ensure that the correct file is

attached. It is easy to attach the wrong file to an e-mail and that might be devastating to a client's case. This can be avoided by opening the file after it is attached to the e-mail to make sure it is the correct one.
- *Typing errors.* Typing errors, such as leaving words out, can substantially change the meaning of a sentence. For example, in a client e-mail you might intend to type "We don't recommend that you do this," but instead you type "We recommend that you do this." While you have only left one word out, that word could be crucial to how the client proceeds.

PAPER SHREDDERS

Paper shredders are a necessity in most law offices to ensure that client confidences are maintained. Paper shredders cost from one hundred to several thousand dollars. They are easy to use and safe (if they are used correctly). The size and volume of the shredder will dictate how many pieces of paper can be shredded at a time. Many shredders can "shred" staples, paper clips, diskettes, and cardboard as well.

PURCHASING EQUIPMENT AND SUPPLIES

It is not entirely uncommon for legal assistants to be involved in the purchase of equipment. Purchasing equipment is, of course, an important part of law office management, especially considering the mass use of technology. Making good purchasing decisions also is important considering the amount of resources and the dollar commitment that go into such purchases.

For example, if an office spends $10,000 on a computer system that never gets used or does not work properly, not only has the office lost the money that it invested, but also it has lost other opportunities as well. The office passed up an opportunity to purchase a computer that would have worked. This is called *opportunity costs*. The term **opportunity costs** refers to the costs of forgoing or passing up other alternatives. The law office's costs include the time and energy spent on the unsuccessful system but most importantly include the computer systems that were passed up that might have been successful and that could have raised the quality of the office's legal services.

opportunity costs
The costs of forgoing or passing up other alternatives.

MAKING THE PURCHASE DECISION

Careful thought and consideration should be given to making a purchase decision. Figure 10-2 shows a list of purchase factors that should be given consideration. Never rush into a decision. Whenever possible, try to project what your needs will be in three to four years. Obsolescence, especially when considering computers, can be a significant factor.

When considering purchase decisions, make sure that the product is currently available. Generally, consider the product you see before you, not something a salesperson or an advertisement may offer you in the future.

Does the equipment you are considering meet your needs?

- Ensure that the equipment truly meets your needs.
- Does the equipment have the ability to do the job now? What about your future needs? In two years? In five years?
- Is the equipment state-of-the-art?
- Will the equipment be obsolete in the near future?
- Is the equipment upgradable?

How long will the equipment last?

- What is the useful life of this piece of equipment?
- Is the product currently available?
- Is the equipment available now (not "soon" or "we are working on that")?

Financial considerations

- Is the equipment a good value?
- Can the firm afford the equipment? Is it within your means?
- Does new equipment or used equipment represent the best value?

Is the equipment/vendor reliable?

- Has sufficient evidence been *produced* to show that the equipment is reliable?
- Does the equipment have a maintenance contract? Is the maintenance contract affordable?
- Is the vendor who is selling the equipment reputable? How long in business?
- Were you given the opportunity to test the equipment?
- How much downtime is estimated with this machine?

Implementing considerations

- Will the equipment work in your law office? Is there proper electricity, enough space, etc.?
- Will the firm's staff need training on the equipment? If so, who will provide it? How much will it cost? How long will it take? How many staff members can attend? (It is best to have at least three or more people to know how to operate each machine in case of staff turnover.)
- Is the equipment safe to operate?
- When will the equipment be delivered? How will it be installed? How will it be implemented or introduced into the office effectively?
- Is the product truly compatible with other items or equipment you already have?

Figure 10-2   Factors to Consider When Purchasing Equipment

One of the most compelling factors to consider is, of course, the price of the product and whether or not it is a good value for the money. Remember that although price is important, so is common sense. If another product is a bit more expensive but is more reliable, is state-of-the-art, and is not subject to rapid obsolescence, it is usually wiser to spend the extra dollars to get exactly what you need.

FINANCING DECISIONS

Once a law office has established what equipment to purchase, the office must then decide how to pay for it. The major alternatives for acquiring equipment include outright purchase, lease, and rental.

PURCHASE When equipment is purchased, the buyer makes payment in full for the equipment (or obtains a separate loan) and subsequently takes title to the equipment. Outright purchase is the typical method for some types of law office equipment, such as dictation equipment or typewriters. The advantage to purchasing equipment is that the total cost is less than renting or leasing because no finance or interest charges are incurred. The major disadvantage is that a purchase immediately reduces cash flow in the month that it is incurred.

RENTAL In a rental agreement, the user typically pays a monthly rental fee, which usually includes maintenance and use of the equipment, but the vendor retains title to the equipment at all times. Rental agreements can be made for varying time periods but typically are six months to a year or more and usually include the right to terminate the agreement with thirty to ninety days' notice. Advantages include the flexibility to cancel or terminate the contract when the equipment becomes dated in order to replace it with new equipment or, in cases where the office grossly underestimates its own needs, upgrade to a system that will meet its needs. Rental agreements also reduce the strain on cash flow because payments are made over a period of time and without a large outlay of cash at any one time. Disadvantages of rental agreements include that rental payments typically are higher than purchase or lease, that rental prices may rise with little notice, and that after years of paying rent, the office never acquires title or interest in the equipment even though the payments may have paid for the equipment two or three times over.

LEASE There are two main types of leasing arrangements. If equipment is purchased under an **operating lease,** the lessee (user) agrees to make payments for a specific period of time, typically one to five years or more. An operating lease is similar to a rental agreement except that the period is quite a bit longer. In a **lease-to-purchase** agreement, the lessee agrees to lease the equipment and make payments to the lessor for a specific period of time, but at the end of the lease term the lessee is given the option to purchase the equipment for its fair market value at the time or a prearranged figure, such as five percent of the purchase price.

Equipment leases may be written with either the manufacturer or an independent leasing company. This distinction can be important. If the leasing company is an independent, it may have little or no responsibility to complete agreements or promises of the vendor. The advantages of a lease include that leases provide for lower payments than do rental agreements and that certain tax advantages apply to some types of leases. The disadvantages of leases are that the period is usually longer than a rental agreement, there may be no ability to upgrade the equipment, and the lessee may or may not have any title to the equipment at the end of the lease period.

operating lease
A lease for equipment that typically runs for one to five years.

lease-to-purchase
A lease agreement for a period of time, but after the period is up the lessee is given the option of purchasing the equipment for a prearranged amount.

The type of financing used in any one situation will depend on the needs of the law office and the type of equipment being acquired. Generally, in situations where technology is changing rapidly, leasing or renting, if available, may be better than purchasing.

INVENTORY RECORDS AND INSURANCE

Once equipment is purchased and paid for, the equipment management process is not over. It is important to maintain inventory records of all equipment purchases, including information about the vendor, records of purchase/lease, serial number of the equipment, maintenance and service agreements, warranty information, installation instructions, and manuals. If regular maintenance is required, the law office should take care to calendar the appointments. It is in the office's best interest to maintain the equipment so as to get as many useful years out of it as possible. Inventory records also are important to establish and back up depreciation schedules for tax purposes and for establishing insurance losses in the case of theft, fire, or other catastrophe.

Part of the maintenance effort is to ensure that all law office equipment is covered by adequate property loss insurance in case of theft, fire, or other catastrophe. Be sure that the property loss insurance allows for replacement costs if possible and adequately covers the property insured. The office does not want to be in the undesirable position of being underinsured. Also, be aware that electronic equipment is usually covered under separate insurance riders that require the office to list individually each piece of equipment with appropriate serial numbers.

OFFICE SUPPLIES

Law offices must maintain an adequate level of office supplies. Supplies include everything from paper clips and pencils to legal pads, copy paper, staples, and envelopes. Management of office supplies is important because offices rely quite heavily on them and in many cases cannot perform needed tasks without them. For example, if an office had a large document to be copied on a weekend and subsequently discovered it did not have enough paper to finish the job, this could cause significant problems. Law offices must regularly manage and keep track of office supplies so that shortages do not occur.

just-in-time inventory
An inventory concept that maximizes an office's cash flow by keeping low amounts of inventory on hand but having access to needed supplies by contracting with vendors that fill orders in one or two days.

JUST-IN-TIME INVENTORY There are many ways to manage office supplies, but they all usually require an individual to monitor the supply situation on a regular basis, such as every week or two, and make necessary orders as needed. Although law offices do not want to run out of supplies, they also do not want to tie up money or office storage space in supplies that sit month after month on the supply shelf. Just-in-time inventory is an inventory concept made popular by Japanese manufacturing companies. **Just-in-time inventory** promotes the idea that offices should maintain minimum inventory levels. This allows the office to maximize its cash flow (i.e., it is not tied up in large inventories leading to higher financing charges, etc.), but just-in-time also promotes the idea that offices should build relationships with suppliers so that inventories can be ordered and received within a day or two of when they are needed. Thus, just-in-time allows offices to have the supplies they need, when they are needed, and without shortages, while still maximizing their cash flow.

Just-in-time also points out the advantages of dealing with reputable suppliers who can be counted on and who give good service. It is important to find office suppliers who give reliable service without a large price markup. There are many office suppliers, both at the local level and at the national level, from which to choose.

PILFERAGE Nearly every law office manager or administrator will concede that many supplies are taken home by office employees and that copy machines, fax machines, and postage machines are used for personal use by employees. This practice is commonly known as pilferage. Although pilferage probably will always exist, one way to limit it is to restrict access to the item, such as by locking supply rooms or having careful control over copy machines and other equipment. Establishing strict policy guidelines can also help in this matter.

LAW OFFICE LAYOUT, SPACE MANAGEMENT, SECURITY, AND LEASES

In this section, a variety of office layout, space management, and law office leasing topics are discussed. These topics are sometimes referred to as facility management. **Facility management** refers to law office management's responsibility to plan, design, and control a law office's building or office space effectively.

facility management
Law office management's responsibility to manage, plan, design, and control an office's building or office space effectively.

CONSIDERATIONS IN SELECTING NEW FACILITIES OR REMODELING OLD FACILITIES

Effectively controlling a law office's facilities is one area that law office management is responsible for, and legal assistants may be asked to play a role in choosing new office space, laying out their own office or a secretary's office, or moving a law office. In smaller law offices, legal assistants may play a larger role in this process. This section describes some factors to consider in selecting new facilities or remodeling existing facilities. From time to time, law offices must consider a move. Reasons include generally being unhappy with the office's current location, a need to expand beyond the capabilities of existing facilities, opening a new office, or merging with another law office.

REMODELING V. MOVING Consideration should be given to remodeling the office or expanding existing facilities v. moving the office entirely. The cost of moving and thereby losing some clients (if the office is moved, the new location may not be as convenient for everyone) should be taken into account when making such a decision.

BUILDING LOCATION Consideration should be given to the physical location of the law office, including whether the new building is on public transportation routes, is accessible from major highways, is convenient for existing clients access, is reasonably close or accessible to the courthouse(s) and law libraries, and whether the new location and surrounding area maintain and support the office's image. The type of law practice also should be considered. For example, corporate practices may need to be downtown, domestic-relation offices may want to be in suburbs, and some smaller client-based firms may want to be in a mall. The type of client the firm is trying to attract may be a factor in building location.

PARKING Adequate parking for both employees and clients should be taken into consideration when choosing office space. Poor parking is a common complaint of law offices in downtown business districts.

SPACE PLANNING

Office space is important for many reasons. Office space and office decor help define the image of the law office. It is important that the facility be functional, practical, and work for the particular law office's structure and needs.

One of the first aspects of space planning that must be considered is the organization of the law office. Law office management must decide what the needs of the office are. For example, management must decide whether practice groups will be grouped together or apart; whether computers, files, and other equipment will be centralized or decentralized; what types of offices are needed (e.g., number and size of conference rooms, kitchen area, and separate postage and copy areas); and whether the office will need to expand in the near future. An effective way of determining needs is to survey the staff members and ask them what they think they need and then use that information in the planning process. Some offices, especially medium- to larger-sized offices, hire consultants to help with these as well as other issues.

USABLE V. RENTABLE SPACE **Usable space,** as the name implies, refers to space that is actually available for offices, equipment, furniture, or occupiable area but does not include hallways, stairwells, and like areas. Usable space is what is important to law offices.

Rental space, on the other hand, is what rent is based on and includes usable space plus the tenant's pro-rata share of all common space on the floor, such as hallways, stairwells, restrooms, etc., whether or not the space is occupiable. The tenant's pro-rata share of common space is called a **loss factor** (also called a load factor). Rentable space is what is important to a landlord, since the tenant pays rent on the total rentable space. For example, if a tenant had 2,000 square feet of rentable space but only 1,750 square feet of usable space, the tenant would pay rent (usually so much per square foot) on the 2,000 square feet.

In buildings or floors where hallways, bathrooms, and elevators are shared by many tenants, each tenant is required to pay his or her loss factor. For example, if a tenant had 2,000 feet of usable space and the tenant's share of the loss factor were five percent, the tenant's rentable space (i.e., what he or she would pay rent on) would be 2,100 feet (2,000 times 1.05 equals 2,100). Load factors will, of course, vary from building to building.

usable space
Space that is actually available for offices, equipment, furniture, or occupiable area. Usable space is what is important to law offices.

rentable space
Usable space plus common areas also known as a loss factor. Rentable space is what is important to landlords because this is what rental payments are based on.

loss factor
A tenant's pro-rata share of common spaces, including hallways, restrooms, etc., in a multitenant floor or building.

FURNITURE Furniture must not only project an office's image but also provide sufficient work surfaces, be comfortable and usable, and efficiently use the space the law office has. There are thousands of different styles of furniture, including traditional (wood and plastic laminate); contemporary (wood, metal, and laminate); high-tech (glass, wood, and metal); and ergonomic (laminate, wood, and metal).

Some offices use interior landscaping, also called *system furniture* or *module design*. **Interior landscaping** uses movable partitions, or panels, and work surfaces, file cabinets, and drawers that attach to the partitions instead of interior walls. The panels typically have electric cabling that runs through the bottom of each for electrical outlets. In this way, law offices can be completely flexible and use their space more wisely than ever before. The major disadvantages of interior landscaping are increased noise and decreased privacy. The reason interior landscaping has gained in popularity is because of the increased cost of office space, and minimizing the amount of space a law office uses reduces rent and maintenance costs.

Some studies have shown that the most negative feature of interior landscaping is not the increased noise problem but the lack of personal privacy, especially when short partitions are used that allow people to see over the top and where the entryways face out allowing others to see into the work space.

interior landscaping
Movable partitions, or panels, and work surfaces, file cabinets, and drawers that attach to the partitions.

CORRELATION BETWEEN SPACE AND COST Any law office administrator will tell you that there is a direct correlation between the amount of office space needed and cost. Office space has become increasingly more expensive, especially in metropolitan areas. Lease payments represent a large overhead expense, which can put pressure on cash flow because it is a fixed cost, meaning that it is incurred every month without relation to whether the office is having a good month, financially speaking. Thus, offices have struggled to become physically smaller and more compact and to use the space they have wisely.

PROFESSIONAL HELP Many offices hire space planners, architects, designers, electricians, and consultants to help them lay out and design effective and functional law offices. This helps a law office avoid problems that other law offices have encountered.

OTHER CONSIDERATIONS When planning space, remember that there are considerations other than just taking measurements. Physical location of offices, lounges, and libraries and the effects on social relationships should all be taken into account. Consider the following.

> A large law office was moving to new offices. It seemed natural and cost-effective to put all administrative services, including the office's administrator, on a specially designed administration floor of its own. The administrator had been a powerful force in the office—one who participated in major decisions and policymaking. Within a year of having been physically separated from the office owners, he began to notice that he was not being consulted as frequently as he had been. His credibility had begun to disintegrate. By the second year he was regarded by the partners as part of the accounting department. By the third year he was felt to be expendable and was asked to leave the office.

And another example.

> A mid-size office . . . made a decision to eliminate a central lunch/lounge facility in its new offices. Each floor would have its own lunchroom and coffee area. The staff of the sixth, seventh, and eighth floors used to meet in the one large lunchroom. After the move they hardly saw one another. Gradually the camaraderie which used to exist among all personnel began to erode.

Human factors and tendencies must be taken into account when planning space, or there may be unwanted side effects.

ENVIRONMENTAL CONSIDERATIONS

In addition to simply planning how space in a law office will be used, management must also consider environmental factors such as lighting, noise, climate control, color, image/appearance, elevators, electrical requirements, accessibility for persons with disabilities, and accessibility of the building to its clients, employees, and others. Figure 10-3 shows the results of a law office survey that was given to a variety of employees regarding environmental factors and shows that these factors do have an impact.

LIGHTING Lighting is an environmental factor that is important when considering productivity. Studies have shown that lighting that projects downward, including bright fluorescent lights or large window lighting, creates glare and causes the eye to constantly adapt, resulting in eye fatigue. In addition, bright surfaces such as walls, floors, and equipment also can be a source of glare. High-quality light is free from glare and is dispersed throughout the room.

Many individuals prefer **task lighting,** wherein lights are attached to work surfaces or furniture or are freestanding. In many cases, task lighting also is adjustable so that light can be positioned when and where it is needed and projects to the ceiling and other directions instead of straight down, a measure that reduces glare. Also, soft lighting, especially in close quarters, is preferable to hard or bright lights.

task lighting
Lights that are attached to work surfaces or furniture or that are freestanding.

Figure 10-3
Law Office Study Regarding the Importance of Environmental Factors

Source: Marjorie Miller, *Designing Your Law Office* (American Bar Association, copyright 1988). Reprinted with permission.

Question	Response Yes	No
1. Do you feel that a change in your working environment would have a positive effect on your productivity or efficiency?	92%	8%
2. Are you aware of the temperature in your office?	84%	16%
3. Are you aware of the lighting in your office?	52%	48%
4. Are you aware of the color in your office?	92%	8%
5. Do you feel these colors have any effect on you?	68%	32%
6. Would you like background music while you work?	68%	32%
7. Do you feel a change in your office environment would have a positive effect on your productivity or efficiency?	80%	20%

A typical office will be outfitted with standard fluorescent lights. However, fluorescent lights can be fitted with diffusers that deflect light at a forty-five degree angle. This is particularly helpful when employees use computer screens. Fluorescent lights, which typically have cool white fluorescent bulbs, can be replaced with warm white bulbs that generate a softer light. The effect of harsh lighting can also be reduced by additional sources of light, such as natural light and task lighting.

NOISE Noise also can measurably affect an employee's productivity. Studies have shown that unwanted noise produces tension, fatigue, higher error rates, decreased concentration, and low morale. In addition to productivity issues, confidentiality also should be a reason to control noise and to ensure that private conversations are kept private. Sound leakage is particularly a problem in offices with thin walls, walls that are not continuous, offices with hollow-core doors, and in offices that use interior landscaping. Ceiling panels, carpet, wall coverings, acoustical panels, and insulation can reduce and absorb unwanted noise.

Also, typewriters, printers, and other equipment that produce noise can be fitted with sound-absorbing hoods, and equipment such as copiers can be placed in soundproof rooms. However, most of the noise generated in a law office is by people. Soft background music also can be used to increase the pleasantness of office surroundings and to reduce unwanted and disrupting noise.

COLOR Of the environmental conditions addressed in this section, color would seem to be one of the least important factors. This may or may not be the case. Many people are quite adamant about the colors that they find appealing and are the most comfortable with day in and day out. Some studies have found that surrounding colors can influence the effectiveness and productivity of workers. Figure 10-4 shows the effects of different colors on worker productivity. Color also can make an office more comfortable and pleasing to the eye.

ELECTRICAL REQUIREMENTS Electrical requirements are another environmental factor that should be researched before leasing or purchasing property. This is particularly true when an office has large computer equipment, copy machines, fax machines, printers, scanners, telephone systems, and other equipment. This type of equipment can strain electrical systems, especially in older buildings. It is extremely important that a law office have a steady and reliable source of electricity that is sufficient to meet and exceed its needs.

CLIMATE CONTROL Climate control, commonly referred to as heating, ventilation, and air-conditioning (HVAC), also is an environmental factor that should be considered carefully. The average office worker requires approximately two thousand cubic feet of fresh air per hour. An HVAC system should economically

**Figure 10-4
Effects of Color on Worker Well-Being and Productivity**

Source: Marjorie Miller, *Designing Your Law Office* (American Bar Association, copyright 1988). Reprinted with permission.

Color	Effects
Red	Overstimulates.
	Increases blood pressure.
	Creates feelings of physical warmth.
	Effective in areas where people spend short periods of time and stimulation is desired.
Black and brown	Create feelings of fatigue, often to the point of workers feeling ill.
	Decrease perception of light.
White	No strong reactions.
	Increases perception of light and space.
Blue	Very relaxing.
	Reduces blood pressure and the effects of stress.
	Perceived, physically, as being cold.
	Sedative effect, occasionally to the point of depression.
	Overuse can cause sluggish behavior.
Yellow	No blood-pressure change.
	If tone is too bright or overused, can cause eyestrain.
	Is perceived as warm.
	Can stimulate a cheerful mood and often raises spirits.
Green	Considered the most normal color.
	No abnormal reactions.
	Can have a light sedative effect.
	May be perceived, physically, as cool or cold.
	In a test of rooms, each painted with a different color, a green room was selected as the favorite of the participants.

control an office's climate and provide clean and safe working conditions free of odors, dust, dirt, and smoke. Changes in air temperature also have been known to decrease worker productivity. Thus, the HVAC system must be stable and produce a constant temperature.

ACCESSIBILITY TO PERSONS WITH DISABILITIES Whenever possible, law offices also should be accessible to persons with disabilities. Making law offices truly accessible to persons with disabilities is more complicated than might first be realized.

ELEVATORS Elevators should be quick and responsive and large enough to handle the number of people who are using them, especially during peak times. Long elevator waits can be quite frustrating, especially if they happen on a regular basis.

MAINTENANCE AND CLEANING SERVICES When considering a move, check on whose responsibility it is to take care of routine maintenance and other related issues, such as whether the cleaning service is included with the lease or is contracted for separately with a third party. It is important to make sure that the cleaning service is bonded. This means that if the cleaning service steals from you, an insurance company will pay for the loss.

SPACE MANAGEMENT FOR THE LEGAL ASSISTANT

When setting up an office, resist the urge to act quickly or without forethought. Take the time to set up your office right; do it in the evening after work or early in the morning before work if you have to. Think about your particular work habits and how the office can be laid out to be functional and efficient for your particular needs. Remember that you will be spending about one-fourth of your life in this office, day in and day out, so take the time to make it comfortable and practical. Every person and every office is different. Some employers may be willing to purchase items to make your office more efficient.

In the long run, it probably makes more sense to spend a little extra money to make the office practical and easy to work in. The long-term productivity gains save far more time and money in the end than not purchasing such items. Figure 10-5 will give you some ideas about setting up and managing your own office.

Many legal assistants work in cubicles. Working in cubicles is somewhat different than working in private offices. In a cubicle, it is extremely important to be considerate of others, particularly regarding sound. It is important to keep your voice down when having conversations in hallways where there are people in cubicles nearby. In addition, sit down to talk when you are in a cubicle; most cubicles have acoustic dividers that will absorb some of the sound. In addition, if you need to have extended conversations, it is best to use a conference room. It also helps to keep computer sound levels low so as not to disturb others.

SECURITY AND SAFETY

Security is a topic that has previously not been taken very seriously by law offices. Tragically, violence to attorneys, legal assistants, legal secretaries, and court personnel has jumped at a dramatic and alarming rate in recent years. It is crucial that security be taken seriously. Disgruntled litigants assault all kinds of law offices all over the country from the rural solo practitioner to large firms in downtown skyscrapers.

There are many ways to provide security, including installing security systems, limiting access into private areas of the office using locked doors, installing locking doors with "buzzers" at reception areas, using security guards, installing security cameras, issuing identification and/or building passes, and limiting elevator service after certain hours. Law offices simply cannot afford to ignore the security issues that face them. Figure 10-6 lists suggestions for tightening security. The type of security you use depends on the size of the firm, type of building, and many other factors.

- **Work Space**—Legal assistants typically need as much usable work space as they can get to lay out documents they are working with, to organize files, and to do legal research. (When drafting, it is typical to have many books on your desk, including statutes and reporter.) Maximize your usable work space whenever possible.
- **Mount Telephone on Wall**—Telephones typically sit on desks. However, nearly all telephones can be mounted on the wall. This gives you more usable work space on your desk and often puts the phone closer to you.
- **Replace Handset of Phone with Earpiece/Microphone**—Legal assistants can spend many hours on the phone. Most telephone headsets can be replaced with an earpiece/microphone unit that allows the user to talk on the phone hands free. They also are very comfortable to use and do not have the confidentiality problems that a speaker phone has.
- **Put Client Chairs Next to the Desk, Not Across the Desk**—Be sure to have an extra chair in the office for clients and other people. Place the chair so that you do not have to talk across the desk to the client. This helps prevent you from being in a superior position to the client and creates a more amicable setting.
- **Keep Reference Books Next to You**—Keep reference books (*Black's Law Dictionary,*, phone book, dictionary, form files, state statutes, and so forth) nearby so you do not have to get out of your chair to get them.
- **Background Music**—Many offices will allow you to play soft background music. This can set a relaxed mood or environment for your office and also can reduce stress.
- **Comfortable Chair**—Do what you have to do to get a chair that is comfortable to you, even if it means bringing one from home or buying your own. Many times, people spend day in and day out in lumpy, worn out, uncomfortable, broken chairs and then wonder why they have backaches and do not want to come in for work. Never let someone buy you a chair or get one for you without trying it out. Ergonomic chairs that move up and down and that have adjustable arm rests are recommended.
- **File Cabinet and Bookshelf**—Obtain a file cabinet and bookshelf and place them as close to your desk as possible. Legal assistants typically acquire important books, articles, and research material that should be saved. In addition, a file cabinet for the temporary storage of files while you are working with them will help keep you organized.
- **Glare Screen for Monitor**—If you use a computer, never put the monitor directly across from a window or directly under a fluorescent light. Either of these will create a large amount of glare. When possible, use a glare guard or some type of glare-reducing filter to place over the monitor. This can be purchased at most computer stores for a few dollars. Eyestrain can be a problem for legal assistants who frequently work on a computer.
- **Put Computer on Floor or on a Separate Desk**—If you are using a computer, do not put it on the desk itself unless you absolutely have to because this will take up a great deal of space. Place the computer on the floor, if possible, and keep only the monitor and keyboard on the desk. If your computer cables are too short, cable extenders of all types can be purchased at most computer stores. In addition, separate keyboard drawers can be purchased from most office suppliers. Keyboard drawers allow you to mount the keyboard under the top of the desk, to pull it out when you need it, and push it back under the top of the desk when you do not. (These only work if your desk does not have a "middle" drawer that goes over legs.)

  If possible, separate and compact computer tables can be purchased at most office supply stores. These have a place for the keyboard, monitor, computer, and printer.

Figure 10-5 Considerations When Setting Up a Legal Assistant's Area

- **Never Allow Free Access Throughout Your Office**—The golden rule of security is to **never** allow people free access throughout your office. Access to your office can be limited by restricting points of entry. If you are in a small building, lock the back door and do not allow the public to use it. Require the public to use the front door and have a receptionist there at all times monitoring the entrance.

    If your office is in a high rise, security stations can be posted at the entrance to the building and/or a receptionist at the entrance to your suite.
- **Limit the Public to a Waiting Room with a Locked Door to Inner Offices**—A good way to limit access to your office is to secure your waiting room. Simply put, the door from your waiting room to your inner offices should be locked and have a "buzzer" installed. By having a locked door to your inner offices, you restrict access and require the visitor to check in with the receptionist. This is similar to many doctor's offices, where a receptionist sits behind a sliding window and sounds a buzzer for a visitor to come into the internal part of the office.
- **Issue Security Badges**—Another way to limit access in larger offices is to issue security cards or badges to personnel and to require visitors to check in and to issue them a visitor badge.
- **Use Security Cards**—Many offices use electronic locked doors that use a keyless entry system. If a person does not have a security card, he or she cannot open the locked door.
- **Monitor Entrances**—Entrances to the building or suites should be monitored, when possible, by using security cameras, buzzers that go off when a person crosses the beam of light, posting security guards, keyless entry systems, or other such methods.
- **Remind Staff About Security Issues and Issue Policies**—Always remind staff about the importance of security issues and draft policies regarding security issues. Always be prepared.
- **Train Staff Members on Security Issues**—Whenever possible, staff members should be trained regarding safety awareness and security issues.
- **Large Buildings May Install Metal Detectors**—Metal detectors may be installed in large offices.

Figure 10-6   Strengthening Law Office Security

SAFETY   Safety also should be considered when looking for office space. Find out whether the building has a sprinkler system, fire alarms, emergency power/lighting, fire escapes, and other features that enhance safety.

LAW OFFICE LEASE

Negotiating an office lease is a typical law office management duty. The state of the economy is a major factor when discussing bargaining position in a lease arrangement. When demand for office space is high, it is a seller's market, and the landlord can take a hard-line approach to the lease. However, when demand for space is down or if there is a glut of commercial property, it is a buyer's market, and buyers have a wide latitude in negotiating a lease. This section briefly covers the work letter and different types of leases.

work letter
The part of every lease that states what construction the landlord must perform before the tenant occupies the space.

THE WORK LETTER The **work letter** is the part of the lease that states what construction the landlord must perform before the tenant occupies the space. An adequate work letter will set out the specifications of the office space the landlord will be required to supply to the tenant before the tenant takes possession. In effect, the work letter determines what the tenant is going to get for his or her money. A typical work letter will cover the following areas.

HEATING, VENTILATION, AND AIR-CONDITIONING (HVAC) The work letter should include information regarding acceptable temperature and humidity conditions to be maintained in each season, the quantity and quality of air to be delivered, how control of the temperature will be maintained and by whom, and a description of the HVAC system. Poor HVAC systems can pose a problem in older buildings. HVAC also is important for law offices that have computer equipment that requires stable temperatures within a specified level. In addition, make sure the lease provides the days of the week and hours the HVAC system will run. This can be a problem if people may need to work late and no air is being circulated.

floor-load capacity
The weight per square foot the floor can hold without collapsing.

FLOORING/WALL COVERING Floor covering, floor-load capacities, and wall coverings also are covered in a work letter. Some computers require raised platforms for the computer room so that computer cables can be run under the floor and carpet. Other rooms, such as a law library or file room, require floor-load capacities of up to 125 pounds per square foot. **Floor-load capacity** refers to the weight per square foot the floor can hold without collapsing. Normal floor-load capacity is 75 to 100 pounds per square foot. If the floor-load capacity is not adequate, additional supports may be added. Carpet/floor tile allowances (if any) also are included. Wall covering such as paint and wallpaper also may be included.

CEILING Information regarding the type of ceiling tile may be included, especially if the tenants want acoustical ceiling tiles. Acoustical ceiling tiles are preferable because they improve privacy and help to preserve confidential information. Ceiling heights also may be included here.

WINDOW COVERING The type of window covering (horizontal/vertical blinds or drapes) is covered in a work letter.

ELECTRICAL The amount of electrical power to be supplied also should be included. This is especially important if the law office has a great deal of computer equipment. Also, lighting requirements such as so many watts of fluorescent lighting per square foot, number of telephone and wall outlets, and like information are included in this section of the work letter.

DOORS/HARDWARE Doors and door hardware such as the type and size of doors (e.g., steel doors, hollow-core wood doors, solid wood doors, etc.), types of locks and door hinges, door closers, and door stops should be addressed in the work letter.

WALLS A work letter also refers to the types of walls ("partitions" in work letters). This may include ordinary Sheetrock walls but also may include special requirements, such as additional layers of Sheetrock for copy rooms, computer rooms, or kitchens/lounges with significant amounts of noise or other types of material for noise reduction.

LEASING When negotiating the lease and work letter, always know what concessions you want in advance and bargain for those items that are the most important. You should ask to see the plans and specifications of the building. Be prepared to negotiate not only on the items in the work letter, but also on such matters as the term of the lease, the amount of rentable space and cost per square foot, parking spaces, whether signs are allowed and who pays for them, and how improvements are handled.

TYPES OF LEASES There are many types of leases. Among these are net leases and gross leases. In a **net lease,** the tenant pays a base rent plus real estate taxes (either in whole or in part). In some types of net leases, the tenant may also pay for insurance on the building and repair and maintenance charges. In a **gross lease,** the tenant pays only for base rent, and the landlord covers all other building-related expenses. (This may or may not include cleaning services, utilities, etc.)

In both net and gross leases, the lease agreement typically will include annual increases. It is common for base rents to increase by a fixed amount, such as two percent to seven percent annually, or be tied to an increase in the Consumer Price Index or other such indexes that track inflation. Some leases also will include increases regarding building repair and maintenance charges. Beware of complicated formulas for calculating increases that can be manipulated by the landlord. Some law offices hire leasing services to audit leases to determine whether the office was charged for services that exceeded the terms of the lease. One way to avoid these problems is to hire a leasing consultant or real estate broker to negotiate the terms of the lease for you. In many instances, the landlord pays the broker's commission without cost to the tenant.

net lease
A lease in which the tenant pays a base rent plus real estate taxes (either in whole or in part).

gross lease
A lease in which the tenant pays only for base rent, and the landlord covers all other building-related expenses.

MOVING CONSIDERATIONS

Moving a law office from one physical location to another may seem simple, but that is rarely the case. It takes a great deal of planning and organization to pull a move off successfully without offending clients who still expect their matters to be tended to, losing or misplacing important information or files, breaking or damaging expensive equipment, and paying an enormous amount for moving costs, employee downtime, and restoring office productivity.

The keys to a successful move are to plan thoroughly well in advance and to organize the moving process by leaving little to chance. Most law offices begin the planning process three to twenty-four months in advance of a move, depending on their size.

Figure 10-7 contains a sample moving checklist of things to accomplish. When setting a moving date, be aware that weekend and holiday moves many times are

- Secure new office space.
- Give notice to employees of the decision to move and solicit their input.
- Assign office space, parking spaces, etc.
- Order new or upgrade current telephone system.
- Order new telephone number for new office, if necessary.
- Order new letterhead, envelopes, business cards, billing statements, checks, rubber stamp(s), mailing labels, etc.
- Order new sign for the office.
- Order furniture for the new office, if necessary.
- Establish who will coordinate and be responsible for the move.
- Determine what dates and times the move will occur (e.g., weekends, holidays, evenings, etc.).
- Confirm moving dates with landlord.
- Determine how long the move will take and place schedules accordingly.
- Select a moving company.
- Assemble a list of equipment and furniture to be moved.
- Establish a list of equipment/furniture that will be sold, stored, or otherwise disposed of.
- Establish packing requirements.
- Prepare a basic move plan for the mover.
- Confirm delivery dates of new furniture, vending machines, utilities.
- Send out new address cards to clients, bar associations, other firms, judiciary, Martindale Hubbell, telephone directory, library subscription services, bank, vendors, post office, insurance carriers, utilities.
- Order office keys.
- Establish when staff will stop working on client matters and begin moving.
- Secure needed packing materials, cartons, etc., if not provided by movers. (Always have a large supply of extras.)
- Consider whether additional insurance will be needed if additional furniture or equipment is purchased.
- Determine the order of the move (what gets moved first, moved last, set up first, etc.).
- Make necessary arrangements for moving of electronic equipment such as computers, copy machines, and/or rental equipment. This equipment should usually not be moved by the moving company.
- Test new phone equipment.
- Distribute office keys to employees.
- Clean out and throw away items not to be removed (housecleaning).
- Have employees remove personal property.
- Request employees to close or put away as many files as possible.
- Pack contents of offices.
- Assign code numbers and tag equipment.
- Cut over telephone system.
- Move!
- Reduce access of employees to the new location until after everything is moved. (This will cut down on confusion.)

Figure 10-7 Moving Details

done to reduce interference that might occur when trying to move during a normal workday. Selecting a mover is an important consideration and usually can be done by calling references. Always meet with the mover and communicate exactly what your moving plans are. Additional suggestions follow.

- Prepare an inventory of what the mover is going to move.
- Calculate overall costs of the move, will including hourly rates.
- Decide whether the mover must provide boxes and cartons.
- Determine who will be responsible for coordinating the move with the new landlord.
- Give detailed instructions to the mover, including the layout of each new office.
- Provide information regarding particularly heavy equipment, loose material, etc.

All boxes, equipment, and furniture should be tagged with a code number indicating where they go on a detailed map of the new location. The numbering system should take into account floor and room numbers. Copy machines and computer equipment can be very sensitive and should be moved by the vendor that services the equipment.

Figure 10-8 gives a graphic account of a move for one office and shows how a move can be completed successfully.

INTERNET SITES

ORGANIZATION	DESCRIPTION	INTERNET ADDRESS
ABA Law Practice Today	ABA site devoted to law practice management	www.abanet.org/lpm
Association of Legal Administrators	Site devoted to administration of law office	www.alanet.org

20 years of Collecting "Stuff"
Moving a law firm is a daunting and traumatic event. We moved 350 people from an office overstuffed from 20 years of doing business. Not only were we physically moving, we were simultaneously implementing a new computer system network, new software, and new telephone system and voice mail.

Teamwork is Needed at All Levels
You will need the cooperation and effort of every person in the law firm to conduct a successful move. We held periodic staff meetings, assigned activity coordinators, and generally tried to get all the employees on the team. This. . .allowed the administration to regularly communicate with the staff about tasks that needed to be completed on a timely basis. . . [and] helped us stay on schedule.

Planning
You simply can't overplan a move. . . . Think through as many of the details as you can and develop a schedule. We began planning a year in advance, but most of the real work was done in the five months prior to the move.

Clean Out "Stuff"—Be Ruthless!—11 Bottles of Whiteout in One Desk
Make decisions about what documents will be retained, what will be discarded, and what will be sent to storage. We gave each timekeeper a list of items he or she could keep and which types of material he or she could discard. Go through everything!! Be ruthless! Electronic documents can be cleaned out, too. 100,000 documents were cleared off the existing computer system. The savings in electronic and hard-copy storage space was dramatic. Clean out those desks. Make the supplies hoarders return surplus supplies. One desk alone produced eleven bottles of Whiteout! You will be absolutely amazed at the amount of material that is squirreled away in lawyer's offices.

Have Letterhead Delivered to the New Location
Monitor levels of letterhead and other customized supplies so that there is not a large excess at move time. Plan to have the new letterhead delivered to the new location. . . .Don't pay to move it twice.

Personal Belongings Go Home
Insist that all personal belongings go home well in advance of the move. Moving personal belongings presents several problems, including insurance liability and unnecessary moving charges. Personal effects should not be returned until well after the move.

Communicate with Office Staff—Moving Is Traumatic—Solicit Staff Input at All Phases
Keep all firm personnel fully informed of the moving plans. Don't underestimate how traumatic a move can be. Our move updates were distributed on bright green paper. We also staged frequent staff meetings during which we provided status reports on our preparation progress. These meetings kept everyone informed and motivated. Solicit staff input at all phases of the planning process. Let them test equipment and furniture being considered.

Appoint an "Answer Person"
Several weeks prior to the move, appoint an experienced staff member to be the "Answer Person"—someone who can be trained to provide the answers on any question concerning the upcoming move. Since many middle management will be unavailable during this point, having a stationary "Answer Person" to provide a triage of sorts to field the inevitable questions about parking, security cards, voice mail, supplies, etc., can really help to alleviate staff confusion and anxieties.

Communicate with Vendors
Meet with all your vendors and let them know your move timetable. It's a good idea to take equipment and service vendors on a tour of the new facility, in case. . . any changes in equipment are necessary. Some vendors insist on moving their own equipment. This is good to know and plan for in advance.

(continued)

Figure 10-8 Blueprint for Relocating the Law Firm Office

Source: *Arizona Attorney*, April 1993, 17. Reprinted with permission from *Arizona Attorney*. Copyright State Bar of Arizona, 1993. Reprinted with permission of the authors: Victoria Trotta, Jo Ann Harrington, Susan Price, and Janie Conrad.

Provide Training on New Equipment to Staff

If you are changing a major system (changing voice mail, changing software, etc.), plan your training and documentation for several weeks prior to the move. This gives people a chance to become familiar with the new systems. . . . This is important even if the new equipment is not yet available to them.

Provide "Care Packages" to Staff

Provide detailed instructions about the move and information about the new location. We had a "care package" on everyone's chair that contained labeled floor plans, new telephone directories, a list of who to call for what, how to work the phones, and other helpful information to ease the anxiety of new surroundings and to minimize postmove work inefficiency.

Provide Documentation to the Movers

Provide adequate documentation for the movers. This includes portable maps of office/department layouts with preassigned room labels to help movers know where to go. Every room that is a destination for any box, equipment, furniture, or supplies should have a number assigned to it. There should be detailed library layouts specifying precisely where particular book sets should be shelved.

Take Care of the Telephone System Early

Telephone lines must be installed and operational before the phone company will assign phone numbers. If you want to maintain the same phone prefix for all your employees, you will have to be sure to reserve it well in advance of the move. The phone company won't guarantee the exact phone numbers you have reserved, but its your only chance to do so. Besides, you can't order the stationary, business cards, and other personalized supplies until those phone numbers are finalized. During the move, be sure to have the phone and computer vendors on hand to troubleshoot the inevitable malfunctioning cable, unprogrammed telephones, and the like. Don't let the vendor leave until the equipment works to your satisfaction. Hang on to them by their ankles if need be.

Install Technology in New Offices First

Arrange to install the computers, phones, copiers, and fax machines before the furniture and boxes are moved. This is critical for a number of reasons. The installers can work faster if they don't have to contend with the clutter of furniture or boxes. The movers can work faster if the "tekkies" are out of the way. Lastly, having the technology up and running allows a lawyer [and legal assistant] to begin work immediately upon moving. Of course, back up all computer and telephone systems before anything is moved.

The Move

Secure access to elevators in both the new and the old office locations. Don't let them assign you just the service elevator. Many a firm relocation has become a disaster due to inadequate elevator access. Allow only those persons directly involved in the physical move to be on the old or new premises. This means no partners, no associates, no children. Moreover, no one should be admitted to the new office location until the all-clear sign has been given. An office move is no time for spectators. Retain one fully functional office/secretarial station until after the move is completed. Include fax, word processor, a copy machine, and WESTLAW/LEXIS access. This will allow client business to continue during the most chaotic time.

After the Move

Institute a six-month "No Complaints" period. This separates the anxiety-driven complaints from the rest and gives everyone a chance to get used to the new surroundings and troubleshoot the problems. Realize that the job is not over once moving day is finished. The key to any successful move is planning and working with all of your peers and your vendors so that everyone has the information they need to move in an efficient and effective way. Such an effort takes planning, teamwork, communication, and documentation.

Suggested Reading

Complete Book of Equipment Leasing Agreements, Forms, Worksheets, and Checklists, Association of Legal Administrators, 1999

Legal Technology Survey, American Bar Association, 1999

Managing Emergency Situations in Law Firms: Minimizing the Damage, Nina Wendt and L. pJ. Sklenar, American Bar Association, 1993

Summary

Law offices of all types have discovered the increased productivity and quality of legal services that can be provided to clients by using technology that includes copy machines, facsimile machines, and telecommunication equipment. Technology, however, must be carefully managed, given its high cost. Every time a law office purchases equipment, an opportunity cost is involved. Opportunity cost refers to the cost of forgoing or passing up other alternatives. By carefully determining an office's current and future needs, researching the purchase, generating competition, and making purchase decisions wisely, a law office can go a long way toward making sure it is making intelligent purchases for equipment that will serve the office for many years to come.

Facility management refers to management's responsibility to manage, plan, design, and control a law office's building or office space effectively. When choosing an office, careful consideration should be given to the building's location, effective space planning, space utilization, and environmental matters such as lighting, noise, color, climate, security, and safety. An office's usable space is actual occupiable area that the firm can use for office and equipment. A loss factor is the tenant's pro-rata share of common space in a multitenant floor or building. Rentable space is what a tenant pays rent on and includes usable space plus a loss factor. A work letter is that part of the lease that sets out the specifications of the office space the landlord will be required to provide. There are several types of leases, including net leases, where tenants pay a base rent plus other expenses such as real estate taxes, and gross leases, where the tenant pays only for base rent. When a law office must go through a move, it must be carefully planned well in advance with attention paid to all the necessary details.

Key Terms

Opportunity costs
Operating lease
Lease-to-purchase
Just-in-time inventory
Facility management
Usable space
Rentable space

Loss factor
Interior landscaping
Task lighting
Work letter
Floor-load capacity
Net lease
Gross lease

QUESTIONS AND EXERCISES

1. Your law office recently purchased a piece of equipment. The equipment never worked properly, and after three months the vendor picked it up. The vendor agreed to refund the office its money. Comment on this situation. Did the office lose anything? Would your answer change if the vendor did not refund the money and the office were forced to sue the vendor to recover the purchase price?

2. Your office needs to rent 5,000 square feet of usable office space. You have been given a great bid on an office with 5,000 square feet that suits your new and expanding image. The lease term can be a minimum of two years. However, within the next three years, the office is expecting to double its growth. The current space is a little cramped but could get you by for a year longer. Discuss the office's situation. What do you recommend? What additional information would you like to have? Give reasons for your responses.

3. As the law office manager for a legal aid practice, you must consider how the office is going to finance a new copier it must have. The purchase price of a mid-size copier you are looking at is $7,500. The rental price on the machine is $250 per month. A lease-to-purchase agreement is $200 per month for four years; the office would have an option to buy the equipment under the agreement at ten percent of the purchase price. The useful life of the copier is not more than five years. If the office purchased the machine, it would hurt its cash flow, but, on the other hand, the office doesn't want to pay a great deal extra if it uses the rent or lease option. List the factors that will influence your decision and present the approximate cost of the machine under each option. Discuss the pros and cons of each option.

4. You must purchase office supplies for your office. Nothing makes the partners more upset than to go into the supply room for supplies and be out of the item they are looking for. In fact, they like to see stacks of supplies. You are considering starting a just-in-time inventory system. Explain to the partners the benefits of this system. Also, explain how you will implement the system. They will specifically be curious to know how you will ensure that there are no supply shortages.

5. Recently, you notice that your office's secretarial pool is taking more and more sick days, that morale is dropping, that productivity is off, and that several secretaries are discussing filing workers' compensation claims. You have heard the secretaries complain about glare from their computer screens, the institutional-type atmosphere, and the uncomfortable, old secretarial chairs. You hear one of the administrators mentioning that the secretaries are just lazy and that their equipment is fine. However, to your recollection no one has checked the validity of their complaints. Recommend to the administrator ways to handle the situation. The administrator will surely discredit your ideas unless you are prepared to answer questions about how the cost of any new equipment could be justified to the partners.

6. As a legal assistant at a legal aid organization, you see all types of people. Although you are compassionate about their needs, you realize that some of the people coming into the office have extensive criminal records. Recently, you were working in your office when you heard one of the attorneys over the intercom call for help. A client was apparently threatening the attorney. In addition, several weeks ago one of the new clients was making the receptionist feel uncomfortable by asking her for a date and not taking "no" for an answer. The legal aid organization does not have a great deal of money, but is concerned about the safety of its staff. People are free to come and go as they like. The office is in a small building and has three doors leading in and out of the building. The front door opens into a small waiting room. The receptionist sits at a desk in the waiting room. The parking lot is very small and unlighted. Staff members must occasionally work late

and typically leave the doors unlocked. Prepare a short memorandum to the director of the legal aid organization discussing your analysis of the security situation at the office. Prioritize a list of three things that could be done to increase the security at the building. Include the cost of any measure taken. In addition to "gadgets," discuss policies that could be changed.

7. Many of the attorneys in your office have mobile phones and use e-mail extensively. Discuss from an ethical perspective the problems related to these technologies.

8. Staff members in your office routinely use the office intercom system's all-call/paging feature that goes officewide to announce who is in the waiting room or who is on the phone needing to talk to a specific attorney. Is there any problem with this?

9. Discuss the problems with fax machines from an ethical perspective.

10. You are working on a particularly sensitive case for a good client. You are handling many confidential documents, some of which need to be trashed. The office is small and thus does not shred all documents, just the ones that each employee thinks need to be shredded. The office shredder is several offices away. It is inconvenient for you to get up and shred a document every time you throw away a sensitive paper, so you have just been putting it in the regular trash can. Discuss the ethical considerations.

11. You have been charged with doing the research necessary to purchase a copier for your law office. You will research the purchase, get bids, and then present your recommendations to a committee. Your first step was to talk to law office staff members, and get their comments on what features they wanted in a machine and to generally research what size machine the office needed. Your research revealed the following.

- The law office appears to be making about 15,000 copies a month in high-volume months, and about 10,000 in lower-volume months.
- The office handles cases in which employees must make as many as twenty separate copies of briefs and other large documents. Many of the briefs and documents eventually are mailed out.
- Everyone in the office agrees that having cost-saving features in the machine is important (both in time and in other costs), and that the machine purchased should be extremely reliable and large enough to handle the firm's needs. Reliability is a feature that everyone agrees cannot be compromised on.
- The office wants to get a competitive maintenance contract that includes all supplies (other than paper).
- The office occasionally uses legal-size paper, but the predominance of its paper need is letter size. This is especially true when copying large briefs.

What additional piece of information is critical before you can make this determination? (Think in terms of time.) Prepare a brief specification sheet on the type of copier and/or features you might be looking for. The committee will be interested in your justification and support of the specifications you choose.

12. You have the task of researching the decision to purchase a phone system for your office. The office is looking for a system for ten staff members. You will report to an office administrator, but the administrator expects you to do the legwork and to present her with good information that she can use to make the final decision and plan/budget for how to pay for the purchase. The administrator expects the system to cost not less than $10,000. Given the amount of money involved, you are a little nervous about the assignment. However, you are determined to get every scrap of relevant information so that the administrator will have the information necessary to make a good decision. Plan how you would complete the assignment, step-by-step.

13. Your office has narrowed a search to two new office location alternatives, both of which are in multitenant office buildings. The first alternative has

2,000 square feet of usable space with a loss factor of twelve percent and a cost of $17 per square foot. The second alternative has 2,000 square feet of usable space with a loss factor of seven percent and a cost of $22 per square foot. If everything else is equal, what do you recommend?

14. You have been appointed as the point person to arrange a solo practitioner's move to a new location. He put the decision off to decide to move or not until the last minute. It is now June 1. You must be out of your current building by June 30 and you can take possession of the new building on June 25. Time is of the essence, and you must quickly lay out a game plan to get the impossible done. The solo practitioner is changing his image and ordering three new desks and credenzas, which must be arranged with the office equipment company, and a new phone system. You must contact all necessary vendors and clients about the move. Construct a detailed plan for your employer's move.

15. Contact a law office in your area and discuss what it is doing to ensure the safety and security of its staff. Ask what its future plans are and what its philosophy on the topic is. Ask for examples of security or safety problems the office has had.

NOTES

1. Casey Anderson, "Technology Trends," *Legal Assistant Today,* January/February 1999, p. 52.
2. The *Model Rules of Professional Conduct,* 1999. Reprinted by permission of the American Bar Association. Copies of the ABA *Model Rules of Professional Conduct* (1999) and ABA Ethics Opinions are available from Service Center, American Bar Association, 750 North Lake Shore Drive, Chicago, IL 60611-4497, 1-800-285-2221.

APPENDIX A

SUCCEEDING AS A LEGAL ASSISTANT

> *The biggest reason we let legal assistants go is because they do not have the management skills necessary to perform adequately. They come out of school with a theoretical knowledge of law, but with few practical skills to manage themselves so as to succeed at our firm.[1]*

In order to succeed, legal assistants must develop good management skills. They need to be accurate and thorough in everything they do. They must be routinely organized, prompt, and prepared. They must be team players and communicate effectively. These things do not come naturally; most are learned the hard, old-fashioned way, by trial and error, over years. Read this section with the idea that you can pick up some good ideas now that will save you many headaches once on the job. Some of the suggestions may sound simplistic. They really are not. The suggestions in this chapter come from many legal assistants and from many experiences. These suggestions really work, and while some are fundamental, all of them are still important.

ACCURACY, THOROUGHNESS, AND QUALITY

"Accuracy" and "thoroughness" are easy to say but hard to accomplish. However, high quality work is vital to the performance of a professional. A law office is a team, and everyone must be able to rely on the others; each client is paying for and deserves the absolute best work product the team can provide.

One element of quality work is careful documentation. It is important that, when you talk to witnesses, clients, opposing counsel, or others, you keep written notes of your conversation and send a confirming letter that documents your conversation. Some cases can drag on for years; if proper notes are not kept in the file, vital information can be lost. Keeping proper documentation about the work you have done on a case is very important.

Mistakes happen. If something does slip by, do not try to cover it up. Admit and/or report the mistake, correct the mistake to the best of your ability as quickly as possible, take precautions to make sure it does not happen again, apologize, and go on. Because mistakes are natural and almost inevitable, being accurate and putting out quality work is a daily battle.

Ideas on how to improve the quality of your work are given here.

- **Create forms and systems.** If you do a job more than once, create a system using forms and instructions for yourself. This will evoke your memories from the last time you performed the job and speed up the work.
- **Create checklists.** Make a checklist for the jobs you regularly perform. Checklists will keep you from failing to perform specific details of a job that otherwise might be forgotten. In this way, the high quality of your work is maintained.
- **Be careful and complete.** Be prudent and careful in your work. Do not hurry your work to the degree that accuracy and thoroughness are compromised. Your work should always be neat and complete.
- **Keep written documentation and notes.** Keeping proper documentation about work you have done on a case is very important.
- **Take pride in your work.** Do not let work go out with your name on it that you are not proud to call your own.
- **Work hard.** Accuracy and thoroughness are seldom reached by slothfulness. Work hard in what you do and your quality will always be better.
- **Ask for peer review.** If you have a particularly important project due and you have a question about the accuracy of your work, have another legal assistant or other staff member look it over before it is turned in. While you do not want to become dependent on others or disrupt their productivity, sometimes a second opinion can really help, especially if you are new to the organization.
- **Never assume.** Do not assume anything. If you have the slightest doubt, check it out, research it, make sure that you pay attention to details, and double check the accuracy of your work.
- **Use firm resources.** Use firm resources like intranets, brief banks, and tools to their fullest. By using the collective knowledge of other experienced staff, you will learn from others and your work will be of higher quality.

THE ASSIGNMENT

A senior partner thinks he has told a legal assistant to take care of an important filing. In actuality, all he told the legal assistant to do was to draft the necessary documents to make the filing. The legal assistant drafts the documents and puts them in the senior partner's box for review. The filing deadline is missed. The senior partner blames the legal assistant for the job not being done properly.[2]

When a task is being assigned, make sure you understand exactly what the assignment is and what the supervising attorney wants. Be absolutely certain that you understand the whole assignment; do not guess or extrapolate. One of the most common mistakes a new legal assistant makes is to not ask questions. It takes a certain amount of maturity to say, "I do not understand," but it is absolutely critical. Your supervising attorney will not think any worse of you for it, and your chance of success on the task will be greatly enhanced. Also, it is a good idea to repeat the assignment back to the supervisor to make sure you understand all of the details of the assignment. If a task is extremely complicated, ask the supervisor to help you break it down into smaller parts. You might say: "This appears to be a fairly good sized job. Where do you recommend I start and how should I proceed; what steps should I take?"

It is also a good idea to write down your assignment. Have a pencil and a notebook or steno pad with you any time you talk to your supervisor about an assignment. A steno pad can serve as a journal, allowing you to keep all of your assignments in one place. If you record assignments, you will be able to refer back to them later if someone has a question or problem about an assignment they gave you. Be sure to write down what the assignment is, who gave it to you, any comments the person made about the assignment, and when it is due. It is always a good idea to ask the exact date an assignment is due, not "sometime next week" or "whenever you get to it." Also be sure to write down when it was completed.

If an assignment gets a little fuzzy to you after you start it, ask the supervisor questions about it while you are still in the middle of it. Do not wait until the end of the assignment to realize you did something wrong; check in periodically and have the supervisor quickly review it. This is particularly important with large and complex tasks.

> *You start with real basic things like you bring a pad and pencil with you. You don't get grabbed in the hallway and get an oral assignment of some significance and not write it down.*[3]

To communicate effectively when receiving assignments, do the following.

- **Ask questions when the assignment is given.** Ask questions about the assignment until you fully understand what you are being asked to perform. Be aware that miscommunication problems occur more frequently regarding assignments you have never done before.
- **Repeat the assignment to your supervisor.** Repeat the assignment back to the supervisor to make sure you understand all details.
- **Break down complex assignments into small tasks.** On complex assignments, ask the supervisor to help you break the assignment down into smaller tasks and help you organize the priority of those tasks.
- **Have a pen and paper ready.** Always have a pen and paper (a steno pad works best) with you when you are being given as assignment. It allows you to remember when the assignment was given, by whom, any comments from the supervisor about it, and when it is due.

- **Always ask for a due date.** Always ask for a specific due date. This prevents miscommunication regarding when an assignment should be completed.
- **Continue to ask questions and check in periodically.** As you work on the assignment, continue to ask clarifying questions and periodically check in with your supervisor to keep him or her updated on your progress.

PREPARATION AND ORGANIZATION

Successful legal assistants are organized and prepared for everything they do. Being organized is not hard; it just takes planning and time. Always have an appointment calendar with you so that you can record important appointments and deadlines. In addition, use a "things-to-do" list each day and try to plan and prioritize tasks so that assignments and projects are never late. Begin with the most important assignment you have to do or with the task that has the most pressing deadline. When you are working on projects for two or more attorneys, ask someone to prioritize the tasks for you. If you have a computer program that has these features, use it.

These ideas will improve your preparation and organization.

- **Have an appointment calendar.** Carry an appointment calendar with you at all times or be sure to constantly update your computerized versions and print out hard copies regularly. This way, if you are caught in the hallway and given an assignment or meeting date, you will know if you have a conflict.
- **Make a things-to-do list.** Plan your day in advance, every day. Make a "things-to-do" list and try to complete your list every day, marking off items that are completed.
- **Prioritize tasks.** When you are preparing your "things-to-do" list, always prioritize the tasks so that you turn in assignments on time. Give priority to assignments that have the most pressing deadlines. If you have a question about what assignment needs to be done first, ask your managing attorney for direction.
- **Be on time.** Always be on time when completing assignments, and attending meetings, and always take good notes when attending meetings so that you will remember important facts or information from the meeting.

MANAGE YOUR TIME

Are you using your time effectively, or wasting it? Time management and organization go hand in hand.

The following ideas can help you manage your time effectively.

- **Set daily objectives.** Always plan your day by setting daily objectives and prioritizing them accordingly. Try to stick to your plan and achieve your objectives every day. Do the most important things first.
- **Do not waste your time on irrelevant tasks.** Do not waste your time on unnecessary tasks. When someone walks into your office to talk about an

irrelevant subject and you have a job due, tell him or her politely to come back another time when you are free.
- **Avoid procrastination.** Do not put off what you can do today. Procrastination is unprofessional and leads to dissatisfied clients. Stick to your daily schedule and do not put things off unless you have a good reason.
- **Avoid socializing in hallways.** Socializing is not only a waste of your time, but also a distraction to others around you. It also looks very unprofessional to clients.
- **Make a timeline or Gantt chart.** When you have a large project, take the time to make a Gantt chart. A Gantt chart is a plan or timeline of projected begin dates and end dates for the various parts of a project. A Gantt chart will help you plan how you will complete the project and also allow you to track the progress of the work.
- **Have reference material close by.** Lay out your desk and office so that important reference materials are located within arm's reach to minimize time spent looking for things.

EFFECTIVE COMMUNICATION WITH ATTORNEYS

One of your most important tasks will be to establish mutual confidence between yourself and your supervisor. Because legal assistants and attorneys must work together very closely, good communication is an absolute necessity.

> *If you want respect in this profession, you must command it. To command this respect, you must be an intelligent professional willing to take on responsibility without having to be asked. Find ways to make yourself even more valuable than you already appear to be. Don't sit and complain about the way things are. Take charge and change them.*[4]

These practices will help maintain effective communication with your supervisor.

- **Always ask questions.** If you do not understand something, ask questions.
- **Listen.** Do not forget to listen carefully when communicating with your supervising attorney. Listen and make notes so that you remember the details you will need to complete assignments.
- **Be confident.** Do not be so intimidated by attorneys that you act timidly and fail to communicate. Carry yourself with confidence and authority. When you talk, always make eye contact.
- **Check in.** Check in with your supervising attorney on a daily basis so that he or she is informed of your progress on your assignments.
- **Do not make important decisions unilaterally.** Include the supervising attorney in the decision-making process.

- **Establish mutual confidence.** Establishing mutual confidence with your supervising attorney is crucial. Your supervising attorney needs to have confidence in your work and you need to have confidence in his or her work.
- **Establish your limit of authority.** Ask your supervising attorney what your limit of authority is when making decisions. You need to know as clearly as possible when he or she should be involved in decisions and what types of decisions they are.

THE CLIENT COMES FIRST

When you are with a client, he or she should be given your undivided attention. Do not take phone calls, be interrupted, play with your nails, or do anything else that would take your attention away from the client. Treat each client courteously and respectfully, and as if he or she is the only client you have.

These measures will help ensure that "the client comes first."

- **Give clients your undivided attention.** When you are with a client, be sure that you give the client your undivided attention. Do not take phone calls, open mail, or do anything else that would take your attention away from the client.
- **Give clients fast, courteous, respectful treatment.** Treat the client courteously and respectfully at *all* times. Always return client phone calls and e-mails as quickly as possible, but never later than the same day, and always try to answer their questions as quickly as possible.
- **Treat each client as if he or she were your only client.** A client's case is very important to him or her and should be important to you. Let your clients know that their welfare genuinely concerns you.
- **Serve clients, but do not overstep your bounds.** Do not let your zeal to serve clients cause you to overstep your bounds. Let the attorney answer complex client questions and give legal advice.
- **Maintain client confidence.** Always maintain the strictest standards regarding client confidentiality.

KEEP ACCURATE, CONTEMPORANEOUS TIMESHEETS

Attorneys and legal assistants keep time records for the amount of time spent on each case so that management will know how much to bill each client. Many firms require legal assistants to bill a certain number of hours of billable time to clients each year or each month, so when you start with a firm always be sure to ask how many hours of billable time you are expected to have per month and annually. Also, ask when time sheets are due and when they are monitored for compliance (i.e., weekly, monthly, quarterly). It is a good idea to budget your time so that you know how many billable hours each month, week, or even day you will need to meet your goal, and then monitor yourself on your progress. Do not let yourself get behind, as you will not be able to make it up. If you are given a non-billable task, delegate the task as much as possible to secretaries and clerks. There are a few simple techniques to keeping accurate timesheets. Always record the necessary information on your timesheet *as the day progresses*. Do not try and go back at the end of the day or week and try to remember what you did; write it down as you perform the work.

Timekeepers, especially new timekeepers, have a tendency to subjectively discount their hours because they feel guilty for billing their time to clients. Record the time you *actually* spent working on a client's case: if it took six hours to research a legal issue, record the whole six hours. If your supervisor does not believe the finished product is worth that much, he or she can adjust the time billed. Simply put, it is not your call to reduce your hours. Record your actual time and go on.

To keep accurate time records, implement the following measures.

- **Keep track of budgeted and actual billable hours.** Your supervisor may tell you that you are responsible for billing 100 hours a month (i.e., 25 hours a week). You want to be sure every week that the timesheets you turn in to management show as close to the amount budgeted as possible. You need to track this.
- **Keep a timesheet near your phone and computer.** Always keep a timesheet next to your phone or computer so when you pick up the phone or prepare work on the computer, you can record the time for it.
- **Fill out the timesheet throughout the day.** Fill out your timesheet as you go throughout the day instead of trying to play the "memory game" to remember all the things you accomplished that day.
- **Record the actual time you spent on a case.** Always record the actual time it took you to perform the legal service. Let your supervisor make any decision to adjust or reduce time to be billed to the client.
- **Be absolutely honest and ethical.** Never bill a client for administrative tasks or for time you did not actually spend working on his or her case.

WORK HARD AND EFFICIENTLY

Everyone knows the difference between working hard and coasting. If you work hard, people will respect you and recognize you for it; if you do not, people will recognize this also and typically will resent you for it.

Do not be surprised if you must work overtime. The question as to whether legal assistants should be paid for overtime is a hot topic. Some firms pay overtime compensation and some do not. In any event, if you have to work overtime, do it with a positive attitude. Be honest and sincere. Also, try to work as efficiently as possible.

- **Pull your weight.** Do what is asked of you and produce quality work.
- **Put in overtime when required.** Be ready to put in overtime when it is required. Try to be pleasant and professional about it.
- **Work efficiently.** Work as efficiently as possible. If you have access to a computer, it makes sense to use it instead of doing something by hand.

POSITIVE ATTITUDE AND TEAM SPIRIT

> *The greatest key to success is something no one can give you—a good attitude! Enthusiasm has nothing to do with noise; it has more to do with motivation. It deals with our attitude. An attitude is something you can do something about. I can choose to be enthusiastic or I can choose not to be. Excitement is infectious; it's sort of like a case of the measles. You can't infect someone unless you have the real thing.[5]*

Essentially, a law office is a team that, to be successful, must rely on many different people to work together harmoniously. Approach your job with the goal of being a good team player and helping your team. Put the good of the firm above your own personal interest, and help the firm whenever you can, whether or not it is in your job description.

Good team players help other members of the team by passing along information and by cooperating on tasks. They are able to give and receive help when it is needed. Another aspect of being a team player is how to constructively criticize other players. First of all, be cordial and professional. Never criticize another staff member in front of a client, an attorney, or other staff members. Do not become emotional. Politely explain what the problem is and then suggest a reasonable solution for solving the problem. Treat the other person as an equal. When you are the one being criticized, do not take the criticism personally; look beyond the finding of fault and try to make the adjustments suggested by the firm. Listen carefully and ask questions so that you know exactly what the problem is.

Your own effectiveness as a legal assistant may depend on how well you work with others at your own level on the team. There may be some people whom you strongly dislike. You will need patience and interpersonal skills to learn to work with them and develop mutual trust and confidence.

- **Put the team first.** Always put the needs of the team before your own personal interests. In the long run, what is good for the team is good for you.
- **Delegate.** When possible delegate tasks to other team members. Use the team.
- **Help other team members.** Always remember to take time to help other team members. Otherwise, they will not be willing to help you when you need it.
- **Share information.** Never horde information. Pass information along to other staff members, remembering to put the team first.
- **Constructively and professionally criticize other team members.** Just because you are a team player does not mean you cannot constructively criticize others. Try to be respectful, professional, and non-emotional. Explain the criticism, then suggest ways to fix the problem. Treat others as equals.
- **Take criticism professionally.** Try to avoid becoming defensive and listen to what is being said. As soon as possible, try to implement the suggestions of the other party.

- **Get along with those you do not like.** It is probable that you will not like everyone you work with. But, for the good of the team, work at relationships and treat all co-workers with courtesy and respect.

> *My secretary always backs me up, and she knows I'll back her up. One night she had a critical mailing to get out, and I stayed late with her so she could leave a little sooner. It's important to have a social relationship with her—you're concerned about her kids and she's concerned about how your weekend went.*[6]

- **Know the employees of your firm.** Get to know the employees of your firm and treat all employees as you would like to be treated.

BE A SELF-STARTER

> *In order to advance as a paralegal, you must prove that you are capable of taking on greater responsibility by performing your present duties exceptionally well. Show your initiative by anticipating the next stage of any assignment and completing it before you are asked to do it.*[7]

Self-starters are valuable employees. Self-starters are people who do not need to be told what to do; they see a job that should be done or a need that should be fulfilled and they do the job or meet the need without having to be told. They seek out and volunteer for new work, assume responsibility willingly, and anticipate future needs.

> *If you're in a meeting and everyone's talking about something, volunteer for it. Don't wait for them to point out, "That's something a paralegal could do."*[8]

Be flexible, open-minded, and creative; be a problem solver. Do not hesitate to courteously suggest new ways of doing things as long as the idea is well thought out (not off-the-cuff) and would provide the firm with a real benefit over the present way. However, before you try to implement a new idea or approach, be sure that you have researched, organized, and planned the project well in advance and have assessed the chances or risk of failure and the consequences of such a failure. Get others involved in the project, ask for their help and input; this will help them accept the system later on.

Ideas on being a self-starter follow.

- **Anticipate.** Anticipate what jobs need to be done or what need is unfilled, and then do the job or fulfill the need without being asked to do it.

- **Seek out and volunteer for assignments.** If a new assignment comes up (especially one with a lot of responsibility), volunteer for it.
- **Be flexible and open-minded.** Always be flexible and open-minded; have a positive attitude. All businesses must change with the times; be adaptable.
- **Be aware of risk.** Before taking on a new assignment, research, organize, and plan. Assess your chances of success.
- **Get others involved.** Always include others in your development of new ideas. Get their thoughts and their feedback. Not only is the information helpful, but people are far more willing to implement an idea to which they have contributed.

STRESS MANAGEMENT

A law office is a very stressful place with lots of activities, deadlines, appointments, and problems. You must learn to manage your own stress or it will manage you. Do not be so consumed with your work as to put it above your family or your own happiness. Learn to relax and participate in activities that allow you to relax. A healthy lifestyle and exercise can reduce your stress. You should also consider what causes your stress and how you can change your work environment to reduce your stress. Being a workaholic will only lead to burnout and frustration. Also, it is important that you take a vacation every year; everyone needs an extended rest at least once a year.

To manage stress, follow these guidelines.

- **Remember your family.** Do not let your work rule your life. To be a complete person, you must work hard but you also have responsibilities to your family. Try not to go too far in either direction. You need a balance.
- **Participate in relaxing activities.** Learn to relax and participate in activities you enjoy.
- **Exercise.** A healthy lifestyle and regular exercise is another good way to reduce stress.
- **Consider your environment.** Consider where your stress comes from and how you can change your work environment to reduce the cause of your stress.
- **Take a vacation.** Take a vacation at least once a year. You need to rest and get away from the office from time to time.

CONCLUSION There are many attributes that a successful legal assistant must have in addition to good technical skills. Being a team player, having a positive attitude, working hard, and keeping accurate records are just a few of the skills that legal assistants must have.

Everything in this appendix must be considered in light of the corporate culture of the particular law practice in which you are working. **Corporate culture** refers to generally accepted behavior patterns within an organization. This will include the firm's values, personality, heroes, and mores. Most firms have written procedures or a staff manual that contains some of this information. However, many policies are never reduced to writing. Make it your business to understand your firm's position and how the firm views its clients, staff, and so on. Understanding how your particular firm looks at the world is very important.

NOTES

1. A legal administrator at a large Kansas City, Missouri firm.
2. William Statsky, *Introduction to Paralegalism*, West Publishing, 1992, p. 180, citing Sgarlat, *The Scape Goat Phenomenon*, 6 The Journal 10 (Sacramento Ass'n of Legal Assistants, June 1986).
3. Cynthia Tokumitsu, "How to Avoid the Top 10 Mistakes Paralegals Make on the Job," *Legal Assistant Today*, Nov/Dec. 1991, p. 31.
4. William Statsky, *Introduction to Paralegalism*, West Publishing, 1992, p. 192, citing Roselle, *I Don't Get No Respect!*, 9 Nat'l Paralegal Reporter 2 (NFPA, November, 1984).
5. William Statsky, *Introduction to Paralegalism*, West Publishing, 1992, p. 192, citing Johnson, President's Message, *Newsletter* 1 (Arizona Paralegal Ass'n, July 1988).
6. Cynthia Tokumitsu, "How to Avoid the Top 10 Mistakes Paralegals Make on the Job," *Legal Assistant Today*, Nov/Dec. 1991, p. 30.
7. Cynthia Tokumitsu, "How to Avoid the Top 10 Mistakes Paralegals Make on the Job," *Legal Assistant Today*, Nov/Dec. 1991, p. 30.
8. William Statsky, *Introduction to Paralegalism*, West Publishing, 1992, p. 192, citing Coyne, *Strategies for Paralegal Career Development*, Nat'l Paralegal Reporter 20 (NFPA, Winter 1990).
9. Cynthia Tokumitsu "How to Avoid the Top 10 Mistakes Paralegals Make on the Job," *Legal Assistant Today*, Nov/Dec, 1991, p. 29.

APPENDIX B

National Law Office Management, Legal Assistant, and Related Associations

Legal Administrators:
Association of Legal Administrators (ALA), 175 Hawthorn Parkway, Suite 325, Vernon Hills, IL 60061-1428 (847) 816-1212, www.ALANET.org

Legal Assistant Managers:
Legal Assistant Management Association (LAMA), 2965 Flowers Road South, Suite 105, Atlanta, GA 30341 (770) 457-7746, www.LAMANET.org

General Legal Assistant Associations:
National Federation of Paralegal Associations, Inc., P.O. Box 33108, Kansas City, MO 64114 (816) 941-4000, www.paralegals.org
National Association of Legal Assistants, Inc., 1516 S. Boston, #200, Tulsa, OK 74119 (918) 587-6828, www.NALA.org
American Association for Paralegal Education, 2965 Flowers Road South, Suite 105, Atlanta, GA 30341 (770) 452-9877, www.AAFPE.org

Independent Legal Assistants:
The National Association for Independent Paralegals, 2020 Pennsylvania Ave, NW Washington, D.C. 20006-PMB 690, www.thelawclub.com

Legal Marketing Managers:
Legal Marketing Association, 401 North Michigan, Chicago, IL 60611-4267 (312) 245-1592, www.legalmarketing.org

Filing and Records Management:
Association of Records Managers and Administrators, 4200 Somerset, Suite 215, Prairie Village, KS 66208, (913) 341-3808, (800) 422-2762, www.arma.org

Law Libraries:
American Association of Law Libraries, 53 West Jackson Boulevard, Suite 940, Chicago, IL 60604 (312) 939-4764, www.aallnet.org

GLOSSARY

accounting software Program that uses a computer to track and maintain the financial data and records of a business.

activity hourly rate Fee based on the different hourly rates depending on what type of service or activity is actually performed.

administrative management Management decisions relating to operating or managing a law office, including financial and personnel matters.

administrative task A task relating to the internal practices and duties involved with operating or managing a law office.

administrator Person responsible for some type of law office administrative system such as general management, finance and accounting, human resources, marketing, or computer systems.

aged accounts receivable report A report showing all cases that have outstanding balances due and how long these balances are past due.

Age Discrimination in Employment Act of 1967 Federal legislation that prohibits employers from discriminating against employees and applicants on the basis of age when the individual is forty or older.

Alphabetic filing system Filing method in which cases are stored based on the last name of the client or organization.

Americans with Disabilities Act of 1990 (ADA) Federal legislation that prohibits employers from discriminating against employees or applicants with disabilities.

application software Instructs the computer to perform a specific application or task, such as word processing.

associate attorney An attorney who is a salaried employee of the law firm, does not have an ownership interest in the firm, does not share in the profits, and has no vote regarding management decisions.

attorneys Attorneys counsel clients regarding their legal rights, represent clients in litigation, and negotiate agreements for clients.

attorney-client privilege A standard that precludes the disclosure of confidential communications between a lawyer and a client by the lawyer.

attorney/legal assistant hourly rate A fee based on the attorney's or legal assistant's expertise and experience in a particular area.

bar coding A file management technique in which each file is tracked according to the file's bar code.

billable time Actual time that a legal assistant or attorney spends working on a case and that is directly billed to a client's account.

billing The process of issuing invoices for the purpose of collecting monies for legal services performed and being reimbursed for expenses.

blended hourly rate fee One hourly rate that is set taking into account the blend or mix of attorneys working on the matter.

bona fide occupation qualification An allowable exception to equal employment opportunity. For example, for an employee to perform a specific job, the employee must be of a certain age or sex or of a certain religion.

boutique firm A small law office that specializes in only one or two areas of the law.

budget A projected plan of income and expenses for a set period of time, usually a year.

CD-ROM Peripheral device that uses optical technology, or laser beams, to store large quantities of data on a small laser disk.

calendar days System for calculating deadlines that refers to only days when the court is open.

case advance Unearned monies that are an advance against the attorney's future fees and expenses.

case retainer A fee that is billed at the beginning of a matter, is not refundable to the client, and is usually paid at the beginning of the case as an incentive for the office to take the case.

case type productivity report Report showing which types of cases (i.e., criminal, personal injury, bankruptcy, etc.) are the most profitable.

centralized file system Method in which a file department or file clerk stores and manages all active law office files in one or more file rooms.

certificate of service Establishes when a legal document was placed in the mail.

Chinese Wall Term for a technique used to isolate the legal assistant or attorney with a conflict of interest from having anything to do with a case.

Civil Rights Act of 1964 Federal legislation that prohibits employers from discriminating against employees or applicants on the basis of race, color, national origin, religion, or gender.

clerks Clerks provide support to other staff positions in a variety of miscellaneous functions.

client confidentiality Keeping information exchanged between a client and law office staff confidential.

client hourly rate Fee based on one hourly charge for the client, regardless of which attorney works on the case and what he or she does on the case.

coaching technique Counseling that focuses on the positive aspects of the employee's performance and explores alternative ways to improve his or her performance.

communication The transfer of a message from a sender to a receiver.

communication barrier Something that inhibits or prevents the receiver from obtaining the correct message.

communication device Device that allows computers to exchange information with one another. It is technically both an input and an output device.

computer An electronic device that accepts, processes, outputs, and stores information.

computer programs The step-by-step instructions that direct the computer to do certain tasks.

computer virus A computer program that is destructive in nature and can bury itself within other programs.

conflict of interest A competing personal or professional interest that would preclude an attorney or legal assistant from acting impartially toward the client.

contract attorney An attorney temporarily hired by the law office for a specific job or period. When the job or period is finished, the relationship with the firm is over.

contingency fee A fee that is collected if the attorney successfully represents the client. The attorney is entitled to a percentage of the monies awarded to the client.

continuance Rescheduling an appointment or court date.

controlling The process of determining whether the law practice is achieving its objectives.

court awarded fees Attorneys fees given to the prevailing party in a lawsuit pursuant to certain federal and state statutes.

criminal fraud   A false representation of a present or past fact made by a defendant.

cross-selling   Refers to selling additional services to existing clients.

data base   A computer program that organizes, searches, and sorts data.

decentralized file system   System in which files are kept in various locations throughout the law office.

docket   A calendaring or scheduling system that tracks and organizes appointments, deadlines, and commitments.

earned retainer   An earned retainer is monies that the law office or attorney has earned and is entitled to deposit in the office's or attorney's own bank account.

employee attitude survey   A survey that is given to an organization's employees and asks the employees to rate the effectiveness of the organization in many specific areas.

equal employment opportunity   Concept that means that employers make employment-related decisions without arbitrarily discriminating against an individual.

Equal Pay Act of 1963   Federal legislation that prohibits employers from paying workers of one sex less than the rate paid to employee of the opposite sex for work on jobs that require equal skill, effort, and responsibility and that are performed under the same working conditions.

escrow account   A separate bank account (also called a trust account), apart from a law office's or attorney's operating checking account, where unearned client funds are deposited.

essential job functions   Job duties or tasks that are necessary to the completion of the job and that will take up a significant part of the employee's time.

ethical rule   A minimal standard of conduct.

expense   A cost that the firm has incurred for the purpose of earning income.

expert witness   A person who has technical expertise in a specific field and agrees to give testimony for a client at trial.

facility management   Refers to law office management's responsibility to plan, design, and control a law office's own building or office space effectively.

Fair Credit Reporting Act   A Federal Law that limits the use of consumer reports (including reference check) in all employment decisions.

Fair Labor Standard Act (FLSA)   A Federal Law that sets minimum wage and overtime pay requirements for employees.

Family and Medical Leave Act of 1993   Federal legislation that allows employees in certain circumstances to have up to twelve worksheets of unpaid leave from their jobs for family or health-related reasons.

feedback   Information sent in response to a message.

financial management   The oversight of a firm's financial assets and profitability to ensure overall financial health.

file opening form   A standardized form that is filled out when a new case is opened.

flat fee   A fee for legal services that is billed as a flat or fixed amount.

floor load capacity   Refers to the weight per square foot the floor can hold without collapsing.

form file   A file that contains examples of documents used in a law office, including pleadings, contracts, wills, and discovery documents.

freelance legal assistants   Self-employed legal assistants that market and sell their services to law offices on a per job basis.

Gantt chart   A plan or time line of projected begin dates and end dates of a project.

general counsel   The chief for a corporate legal department.

gross income   Monies that are received before expenses are deducted.

gross lease The tenant pays only for base rent, and the landlord covers all other building-related expenses.

groupthink The desire for group cohesiveness and consensus becomes stronger than the desire for the best possible decision.

hardware The actual physical components of a computer system.

hourly rate fee A fee for legal services that is billed to the client by the hour at an agreed-upon rate.

human resource management Recruiting, hiring, training, evaluating, maintaining, and directing the personnel that will provide quality legal services to the clients.

imaging The capture, retrieval, and storage of document images electronically.

income Something of value that a law office receives from a client in exchange for the law office providing professional legal services.

income budget Estimate of how many partners, associates, legal assistants, and others will bill for their time, what the appropriate rates of hourly charge should be, and the number of billable hours each timekeeper will be responsible for billing.

integrated software Software that combines several application functions into one.

interior landscaping Uses movable partitions, or panels, and work surfaces, file cabinets, and drawers that attach to the partitions instead of interior walls.

internal control Procedures that an organization establishes to set up checks and balances so that no individual in the organization has exclusive control over any part of the accounting system.

Intranet An internal information distribution system based on Internet technology.

just-in-time inventory An inventory method that maintains minimum inventory levels to maximize cash flow.

law clerk A law student working for a law firm on a part-time basis while he or she is finishing a law degree. Law clerk duties revolve almost exclusively around legal research and writing.

law office information system A combination of human involvement, computer hardware and software, and raw information that work together to solve problems in a law office.

law librarian A librarian responsible for maintaining a law library. Maintenance includes purchasing new books and periodicals, classifying, storing, indexing, and updating the holdings, and coordinating computer-assisted legal research (i.e., WESTLAW, LEXIS, and other services).

leadership The act of motivating or causing others to perform and achieve objectives.

lease-to-purchase A lease where the lessee agrees to make payments for a specific period of time, but at the end of the lease term the lessee is given the option to purchase the equipment.

legal aid office A not-for-profit law office that receives grants from the government and private donations to pay for representation of disadvantaged persons who otherwise could not afford legal services.

legal assistants A distinguishing group of persons who assist attorneys in the delivery of legal services. They have knowledge and expertise regarding the legal system and substantive and procedural law that qualifies them to do work of a legal nature under the supervision of an attorney.

legal assistant manager One who supervises, recruits, trains, distributes, sets priorities, and directs the overall management of a group of legal assistants.

legal malpractice Possible consequences when an attorney's or law office's conduct falls below the standard skill, prudence, and diligence that an ordinary lawyer would possess or that is commonly available in the legal community.

legal team A group made up of attorneys, administrators, law clerks, librarians, legal assistants, secretaries, clerks, and other third parties. Each provides a distinct range of services to clients and each has a place on the legal team.

legal technicians People who market their legal services directly to the public.

leveraging The process of earning a profit from legal services that are provided by law office personnel (usually partners, associates, and legal assistants).

local area network A multiuser system that links independent microcomputers together that are close in proximity for the purpose of sharing information, printers, and storage devices.

loss factor The tenant's pro-rata share of common space.

management The administration of people and other resources to accomplish objectives.

management by objectives A performance program in which the individual employee and the employer agree on goals for the employee.

management reports Reports used to help management analyze whether the office is operating in an efficient and effective manner.

managing partner An attorney in a law firm chosen by the partnership or the shareholders to run the firm on a day-to-day basis, make administrative decisions, and set policies.

marketing The process of educating consumers on the quality legal services that a law office can provide.

marketing plan The goals that a marketing program is to accomplish and a detailed strategy of how the goals will be achieved.

mission statement A general, enduring statement of what the purpose or intent of the law practice is.

Model Code of Professional Responsibility American Bar Association (ABA) code of ethics published in 1983 which are self-imposed ethical standards for ABA members, but it can also serve as a prototype of legal ethic standards for state court systems.

Model Rules of Professional Conduct American Bar Association (ABA) code of ethics published in 1969 which are self-imposed ethical standards for ABA members, but it can also serve as a prototype of legal ethical standards for state court systems.

multitask operating system System that allows the execution of several application programs at the same time.

negligent hiring Hiring an employee without sufficiently and reasonably checking the employee's background.

net income Monies that are left after expenses are deducted from gross income.

net lease The tenant pays a base rent plus real estate taxes.

noise Any situation that interferes with or distorts the message being communicated from the sender to the receiver.

nonbillable time Time that cannot be directly billed to a paying client.

nonequity partner A partner who does not share in the profits or losses of the firm but may be entitled to certain benefits not given to associates.

of counsel An attorney affiliated with the firm in some way such as a retired or semiretired partner.

office manager Manager who handles day-to-day operations of the law office, such as accounting, supervision of the clerical support staff, and assisting the managing partner.

off-line The user is not connected to an information service and no charges are accruing except possibly a printing or downloading charge.

on-line The user is connected to an information system and is running up charges.

operating system software Instructs the computer how to operate its circuitry and how to communicate with input, output, and storage devices.

operating lease A lease where the lessee agrees to make payments for a specific period of time.

opportunity costs Refers to the costs of forgoing or passing up other alternatives.

organizing The process of arranging people and physical resources to carry out plans and accomplish objectives.

outside counsel Refers to when a corporate or governmental law practice hires a private law office to help them with legal matters.

overhead General administrative costs of doing business, including costs such as rent, utilities, phone, and salary costs for administrators.

partner An owner in a private law practice that has the partnership form of business structure that shares in the practice's profits and losses.

personnel handbook A manual that lists the formal personnel policies of an organization.

personal information manager (PIM) Consolidates a number of different tasks into one computer program. Most PIMs include calendaring, things to do, a contact database that tracks names and addresses of people, note taking, and other tasks as well.

planning The process of setting objectives, assessing the future, and developing courses of action to achieve those objectives.

policy A specific statement that sets out what is or is not acceptable.

powerful managing partner A management structure in which a single partner is responsible for managing the firm.

practice management Management decisions about how a law office will practice law and handle its cases.

prepaid legal service A plan that a person can purchase that entitles the person to receive legal services either free or at a greatly reduced rate.

pro bono Legal services that are provided free of charge to a client who is not able to pay for the services.

procedure A series of steps that must be followed to accomplish a task.

pure retainer A fee that obligates the office to be available to represent the client throughout the time period agreed upon.

rainmaking The ability to bring in new clients to a law office.

reasonable accommodation Accommodating a person with a disability, which may include making existing facilities readily accessible, restructuring the job, or modifying work schedules.

realization Amount a firm actually receives in income as opposed to the amount it bills.

recurring entry A calendar entry that recurs typically either daily, weekly, monthly, or annually.

rephrasing A technique used to improve communication by repeating back to a person what your understanding of the conversation was.

rental space What rent is based on and includes usable space plus the tenant's prorata share of all common space on the floor such as hallways, stairwells, and bathrooms.

retainer for general representation Retainer typically used when a client such as a corporation or school board requires continuing legal services throughout the year.

rule by all partners/shareholders A management structure in which all partners/shareholders are included in decisions that affect the firm.

rule by management committee/board Management structure that uses a committee structure to make management decisions for the firm.

secretaries Employees who provide assistance and support to the law office staff by taking dictation, performing typing and filing functions, and aiding in scheduling of appointments.

settlement A mutual agreement to resolve a dispute on specified terms.

sexual harassment Unwelcome sexual advances, requests for sexual favors, and other verbal or physical conduct of a sexual nature that creates an intimidating, hostile, or offensive working environment.

shareholder An owner in a private law practice that is a corporation that shares in the practice's profits and losses.

staff attorney An attorney hired by a firm with the knowledge and understanding that he or she will never be considered for partnership.

staffing plan Estimate of how many employees will be hired or funded by the firm, what positions or capacities they will serve in, what positions will need to be added, what old positions will be deleted, and how much compensation each employee will receive.

statute of limitations A statute or law that sets a limit on the length of time a party has to file a suit. If a case is filed after the statute of limitations, the claim is barred and is dismissed as a matter of law.

storage capacity The maximum amount of data that can be stored on a device.

storage device Stores data that can be retrieved later.

strategic planning The process of determining the major goals of a firm and then adopting the courses of action necessary to achieve those goals.

substantive task A task that relates to the process of actually performing legal work for clients.

system A consistent or organized way of doing something.

task lighting Where lights are attached to work surfaces or furniture or are free standing.

terminal A keyboard and monitor that are used to communicate with computers.

time to billing percentage System of adjusting downward the actual amount that will be billed to clients during the budget process, taking into account the fact that timekeepers are not always able to bill at their optimum levels.

timekeeper productivity report Report showing how much billable and nonbillable time is being spent by each timekeeper.

timekeeping The process of tracking how attorneys and legal assistants use their time.

timekeeping and billing service bureau A company that for a fee processes attorney and legal assistant timesheets (usually a monthly basis), generates billings, and records client payments for a law practice.

timesheet/timesheet A record of information about the legal services professionals provide to each client.

total quality management A management philosophy based upon knowing the needs of each client and allowing those needs to drive the legal organization at all levels of activity, from the receptionist to the senior partner.

trust account A separate bank account (also called an escrow account), apart from a law office's or attorney's operating checking account, where unearned client funds are deposited.

unearned retainer Monies that are paid up front by the client as an advance against the attorney's future fees and expenses. Until the monies are actually earned by the attorney or law office, they actually belong to the client.

usable space Space that is actually available for offices, equipment, furniture, or occupiable area but does not include hallways, stairwells, and like areas.

value billing A type of fee agreement that is based not on the time to perform the legal work but on the basis of the perceived value of services to the client.

word processing program Program used to edit, manipulate, and revise text to create documents.

work days System of calculating deadlines that refers to only days when the court is open.

work letter The part of the lease that states what construction the landlord must perform before the tenant occupies the space.

wrongful termination A lawsuit in which a former employee alleges that an employer unlawfully terminated the employee.

zero-based budgeting A type of budget that forces everyone in the organization to justify and explain his or her budget figures in depth without using prior year's figures as justification.

INDEX

Advertising, and hiring process, 349
AAfPe; *see* American Association for Paralegal Education
ABA; *see* American Bar Association
ABA Center for Professional Responsibility, 89
ABA Law Practice Today, 35, 189, 241, 271
ABA Model Rule for Auditing Lawyer Trust Accounts, 271
ABA Model Rule for Financial Recordkeeping, 271
ABA Model Rule for Trust Account Overdraft Notification, 271
ABA Standing Committee on Legal Assistants, 35
  Internet site, 89
Abacus Data Systems, 335
Accounting
  budget and planning, 262–264
  budgeting, 260–264
  cannot be held in client trust, 257
  check request form, 268
  client trust account, 253
  commingling funds example cases, 258–260
  commingling of funds, 257–260
  embezzlement examples, 265
  embezzlement, 266–267
  escrow account, 253
  estimating overhead, 263
  internal controls, 264–268
  Internet sites, 271
  master budget, 261–262
  must be held in client trust, 257
  profit margins, 264
  time to billing percentage, 262–263
  trust account, 253
  trust account checks, 254
  trust account examples, 253–254
  trust account ledger, 256
  trust and operating funds separation, 255–257

Accounts payable, 30
Accounts receivable, 30
Activity hourly rates; *see* Hourly rate fee
ADA; *see* Americans with Disabilities Act of 1990
Administrative management, 29
Administrative task, 34
Administrators, 5
Advertising, 127, 134; *see also* Marketing
  false and misleading statements, 140
Age Discrimination in Employment Act of 1967, 372
Aged accounts receivable report, 237, 238
ALA; *see* Association of Legal Administrators
Alphabetic systems, 393
Altman Weil Pensa, 241
Alumni Computer Group, 242
American Association for Paralegal Education (AAfPe), 6–7
American Bar Association (ABA), 6–7, 35; *see also* Canons of professional ethics; Ethics 2000;Model rules of professional conduct
  Canons of Professional Ethics, 48
  Ethics 2000, 48
Americans with Disabilities Act of 1990 (ADA), 374
American Legal Ethics Library, 89
Application, and hiring process; *see* Hiring process
Appointments, 309
Arizona Republic, 126
Assets, 30
Association of Legal Administrators (ALA), 5, 35, 189, 241, 271
Attorney, 4
  associate, 4–5
  and ethical standards, 48–49
  and management, 28
  of counsel, 5
  partner/shareholder, 4–5, 24

Attorney-client privilege, 64–65
  avoiding confidentiality problems, 66–70
Attorney hourly rates; *see* Hourly rate fee
Automatic reminders, 329; *see also* computers

Bar coding, 394
Bates stamp, 315
Bates v. State Bar of Arizona, 433 U.S. 350 (1977), 126
Billable time, 222; *see also* Timekeeping
  average, 226
  minimum hours, 225
Billing, 196–197; *see also* Timekeeping and billing
  average billing rates, 230
  computerized, 232–233
  copy machines, 420–421
  corporate and government perspective, 239–241, 240–241
  determination of rates, 232
  legal assistant time, 229–232
  manual systems, 232
  successful practices, 230–231
Blended hourly rate fees; *see* Hourly rate fee
Bona fide occupational qualification, 372
Boutique firm, 21
Bridgeway Software, 335
Brochure; *see also* Marketing
  informational, 134
  and marketing, 131
  sample of, 132
  specific industry sample, 133
Budget, 260; *see also* Accounting
Business stationary, and marketing, 134; *see also* Marketing
BytePro, 242

Calendar days, 314; *see also* Deadlines
Calendaring, 308; *see also* Deadlines; Docket control systems; Scheduling

473

California Revised Rules of Professional Conduct, 401
CALR; *see* Computers, computer-assisted legal research
Canons of Professional Ethics, 48
Card system; *see* Docket control systems
Case management, 309, 333–335; *see also* Practice management
 and word processor, 333–335
 example of, 334
 Internet sites, 335
Case retainer, 204; *see also* Retainer fees
Case schedule, 310; *see also* scheduling
Case type productivity report, 237, 239
Case/Client list, 237
Cash advance retainer, 204; *see also* Retainer fees
CD-ROM legal database, 405–407
CD-ROM legal libraries, 405–407
 advantages of, 405–406
 cataloging and classifying, 407–408
 disadvantages of, 406–407
Centralized file system, 395
Centralized systems, 329; *see also* Computers
Certificate of service, 315
Chinese wall, 76–78
Chinese wall, Rivera v. Chicago Pneumatic, 1991 WL 151892 (Conn. Super.), 77–78
Cincinnati Bar Association v. Bertsche, 58
Civil Rights Act, 13–14, 372
Clerks, 16
Client communication, 64–70; *see also* Clients and communication skills
 and e-mail, 70
Client confidentiality, 64–65; *see also* Attorney-client privilege; Ethics 2000; Legal assistant;Model rules of professional conduct; Client communication
 avoiding confidentiality problems, 66–70
 and e-mail, 425–426
 and fax machines, 422
 and telecommunications, 422
Client dissatisfaction; *see* Clients and communication skills
Client hourly rates; *see* Hourly rate fee
Client manual; *see* Clients and communication skills
Client questionnaire; *see* Clients and communication skills
Client surveys; *see* Clients and communication skills
Client trust account; *see* Accounting; Escrow account; Trust account
Clients and communication skills; *see also* Interviewing
 audience, 179
 client confidences, 172

client dissatisfaction, 173–174
client manual, 173
client questionnaire, 172–173
client relationship, 165–175
client surveys, 172
clients likes and dislikes, 166
communication diagram, 177
communication with clients, 318
complaints, 175
copies of documents, 169–170
courteous behavior, 170
explain the law and risks, 164
fostering positive relationship, 165–166, 167–168
general communication, 176
group communication, 184
improvement of, 178–184
attorney leaving office, 164
important information, 164, 171
status of case, 163
interviewing clients, witnesses, and third parties, 185–189
know your client, 166, 168–169
leadership and communication, 183–184
and legal assistants, 161
legal assistant's role, 165
and legalese, 170
listening, 174, 178, 179
nonverbal communication, 177, 178
not to cover up information, 164
notify of settlement offers, 165
personal and office problems, 171
personality conflicts, 175
phone calls, 170
and promises, 175
status reports, 171
stopping work on a case, 164
taking notes, 175
telephone techniques, 181–182
timely response to client's request, 164
treatment of clients, 169
Coaching technique; *see* Performance evaluations
Color coding, 398-399
Communication, 176; *see also* Clients and communication skills
Communication barrier, 176; *see also* Clients and communication skills
Communication skills; *see* Clients and communication skills
Competence and Adequate preparation, 316–317
Competence and Diligence, 61–63
Compulaw, 335
Computer Law Systems, 3135
Computers; *see also* Equipment and technology
 and bar coding, 394
 computer-assisted legal research (CALR)

and Docket control system, 323–332
and file management, 394
and imaging, 394
and law libraries, 405–412
and legal specific management programs, 323–325
calendaring events from a rule, 330
docket report, 331
event entry screen, 327
legal specific PIM, 324
legal specific PIMs features, 325–331
monthly calendar screen, 326
weekly calendar screen, 326
word processor, 333–335
Confidentiality; *see* Client confidentiality
Conflict of interest, 71–75
 avoiding conflict of interest, 79–80
 conflict checks, 75–76
Contingency fee, 200–203
 contract for, 201–202
 example of, 202
Continuance, 309
Contract attorney, 5
Controlling, 34
Copy machines, 420–421
 and billing, 421
Corel, 335
Corporate law management structure, 26–27
Corporation, 24
Court awarded fee, 208
Court rules; *see* Scheduling
Criminal fraud, 217–218
Cross-selling, 135; *see also* Marketing

Dabney v. Investment Corp. of America, 82 F.R.D. 464, 465 (E.D. Pa. 1979), 64
Data.txt Corp., 335
De Novo Systems Inc., 335
Deadlines, 310–311; *see also* Scheduling
 calculation example, 314
 calculation of, 313–315
 calendar days v. workdays, 313–315
 communication with clients, 318
 diligence, 317
 due date, 315
 ethical and malpractice considerations, 316–321
 file date v. document receipt date, 315
 file date v. mail date, 315
 judge and attorney, 310
 workday example, 314
Decentralized file system, 395
Decentralized systems; *see also* Computers
Diligence, 317
Diligence, lack of, 319–320
Discovery document, 315
Disengagement letter, 86–88
Docket control, 309, 317

Index

Docket control systems; *see also* Computers
   calendar, 321–322
   card system, 322
   case management, 333
   centralized cycle, 332
   combined cycle, 333
   computerized, 323–325
   decentralized cycle, 332
   Internet sites, 335
   manual, 321–322
   and word processor, 333–335
Docket cycle, 332–333
Docket slip, 332
Documents; *see also* Deadlines; Scheduling
   receipt date, 315
   receiving of, 313
Double billing; *see* Timekeeping and billing
Due date, 315; *see also* Deadlines
Due diligence, 317

E-mail
   confidentiality, 70, 425–426
   errors, 426–427
   etiquette, 424
   and ethical use, 426
   problems with, 425
   software, 423–427
Earned retainer; *see* Retainer fees
Electronic mail; *see* E-mail
Employee attitude survey; *see* Performance evaluations
Employment-at-will doctrine, 370–371
Embezzlement, 265; *see also* Accounting
   limitation of, 266–267
Engagement letter, 86–87
Equal Pay Act of 1963, 372
Equipment and supplies purchases, 427–431
   decision, 427–428
   factors to consider, 428
   financing decisions, 429–430
   inventory and insurance records, 430–431
Equipment and technology, 420–427
Essential job function; *see* Job descriptions
Equity partner; *see* Partner
Escrow account, 253 *see also* Accounting; Trust account
Escrow, 204; *see also* Escrow account
Ethical rule, 48
Ethical wall; *see* Chinese wall
Ethics 2000, 48
   False and misleading statements, 139
   Internet site, 89
   revision of rule 1.5(b) fees in writing, 211
   revision of rule 1.6 confidentiality of information, 65

   revision of rule 1.7 conflict of interest, 72
   revision of rule 1.8 conflict of interest, 72–75
   Rule 7.3 direct contact with prospective clients, 141
Ethics
   and deadlines, 316–321
   and e-mail, 426
   and file management, 401–402
   fraudulent billing practices, 214–217
   Internet sites, 89
   legal assistant questions, 84
   and marketing, 136–142
   marketing tips, 138
   and policy and procedure manual, 118–119
   professional responsibility, 47–48
   resolving problems of, 80–83
   timekeeping and billing, 209–219
Exempt, 12
Exempt employees, 373
Expense slip, 220–221
Expert witness, 16

Facility management, 431; *see also* Law offices
Fair Credit Reporting Act, The, 337
Fair Labor Standard Act (FLSA), 12–13, 372
Family and Medical Leave Act of 1993 (FMLA), 371
Federal employment related laws, 374
Feedback, 177; *see also* Clients and communication skills
Fees, 197–209; *see also* Specific type of fee; Timekeeping and billing
   comparison example, 205
   fraudulent billing practices, 214–217
   in writing, 210–211
   sharing of example, 269–270
   sharing of, 269–270
File date, 315; *see also* Deadlines
File format, 398
File management, 391–403; *see also* File system
   and ethics, 401–402
   form files, 402–43
   methods and techniques, 392–401
File opening form, 395, 396–397
File system
   alphabetic, 393
   bar coding, 394
   checking out, 399
   closing, storing, and purging, 399–400
   color coding, 398–399
   format of, 398
   numerical, 393–394
   organization of, 400–401
   retention periods, 400

Financial management, 30
   and systems, 34–35
Financing decisions, 429–430
Firm, 20–23; *see also* law practices
   defense, 23
   large, 22
   medium, 21
   plaintiff, 23
   small, 20–21
Flat fee, 203–204
   example of, 203
FLSA; *see* Fair Labor Standard Act
FMLA; *see* Family and Medical Leave Act of 1993
Form file, 402–403

Gantt chart, 149
   appellate brief, 149
General counsel, 17
General representation; *see* Retainer fee
Georgetown Journal of Legal Ethics, 218
Government law office management, 26–27
Gravel & Gown Software, 335
Gross lease; *see* Lease
Gryphon Law, Inc., 335

Hearing and court dates; *see* Scheduling
Hiring process, 345–357; *see also* Job descriptions
   advertising, 349
   after selection of, 355–357
   applications, 349
   discriminatory questions, 353–354
   interview questions, 352–353
   interview teams, 353
   interviewing, 349–354
   recruiting, 349
   reference checks, 354–357
   resumes, 349, 350
Hourly rate fee, 197–200
   activity, 200
   attorney or legal assistant, 198
   blended, 198
   client, 198
   contract for, 199–200
   stop use of, 209
Human resource management, 31, 344; *see also* Hiring process
   systems for, 34–35

Imaging, 394
In re Canter, Tenn. Sup. Ct., Nos. 95–831-O-H, etc (6/5/97)
In re Houston, 57
Income budget, 262; *see also* Accounting
Independent legal assistant, 8
Internal computer network (LAN), 115
Internal control, 264–268; *see also* Accounting

Internet, 409–411
  law related sites, 413
  and legal organizations, 410
  and legal research, 410–412
  and marketing, 128–129
  marketing example, 130; *see also* Marketing
  problems with, 411
Interviewing
  client, 185–186
  closing of, 189
  and hiring process, 349
  inform of status, 187
  listen, 187
  preparation for, 187
  process of, 187–189
Intranet, 119

Job descriptions, 345–349, 346–348
  essential job functions, 345, 348–349
  writing of, 345
Juris, 242
Just-in-time inventory, 430–431

KeyPoint, 335

LAN; *see* Internal computer network
Lateral hire, 4
Law clerk, 15
Law library management; *see also* CD-ROM law library
  CD-ROM, 405–408
  developing a library, 404–405
  duties, 403
  introduction of, 403–408
  law library holdings, 404
Law librarian, 15
Law Office Handbook, 35
Law offices, 2
  environmental considerations, 434–437
  interior landscaping, 433
  lease, 439–441
  and legal assistant profitability, 14
  legal assistants area, 438–439
  legal structure, 23–24
  loss factor, 432
  and moving, 441–443
  moving details, 442
  new and old facilities, 431–434
  rentable space, 432
  security and safety, 437
  space management, 437
  usable space, 432
Law practices; *see also* Legal aid office
  corporate, 16–17
  firm, 20–22
  government, 17–18
  legal aid, 18
  private, 18–19
  sole practitioner, 19–20
Law Research, 241

Leadership, 34, 183–184; *see also* Clients and communication skills
  how to become, 183–184
Lease, 429–430, 441
  gross, 441
  net, 441
Legal advice, 56–57
Legal aid office, 18
  management structure, 26–27
Legal assistant hourly rates; *see* Hourly rate fee
Legal Assistant Management Association, 35
  Internet site, 89
Legal assistant, 6–7 *see also* Clients and communication skills
  accounting, 252–253
  compensation, 11–12
  contract, 6–8
  daily functions and duties, 9
  and ethical importance, 47
  ethical questions, 84
  exempt vs. non-exempt, 12–13
  failing to act competently and diligently, 63
  and file and law library management, 390–391
  freelance, 6–8
  and human resource management, 344–345
  independent, 8
  and judicial system's recognition, 13–14
  and law office area, 438–439
  legal technicians, 6
  managers, 8
  Model Code of Professional Responsibility, 49–51
  Model Rules of Professional Conduct, 49–51
  non-traditional, 6
  roles and responsibility, 8–11
  specialty areas, 10
  and systems, 34–35
  ten commandments of a conservative, 83
  timekeeping and billing, 197
  timekeeping practices, 227–228
  traditional, 6
Legal Assistant Today, 36
Legal associations, and marketing, 135; *see also* Marketing; Specific association
Legal expenses, 220–221
Legal fee agreements; *see* Fees
Legal Files Software, 335
Legal malpractice; *see* Malpractice
Legal team, 2–16
  administrators, 5
  attorney, 4–5
  clerks, 16

law clerk, 15
law librarian, 15
legal assistants, 6–8
office manager, 14
secretaries, 15
Legal technicians, 6–8, 59
Legal Technology News, 241
Legal Technology Online, 241
LegalEdge Software, 335
Legalethics.com, 89
Leveraging, 232; *see also* Billing
LEXIS-NEXIS, 405, 409
Limited liability company (LLC), 24
Listening; *see* Clients and communication skills
LLC; *see* limited liability company
Lotus, 335
Lease-to-purchase, 429

Mail date, 315
Mail, direct mail pieces, 134; *see also* Marketing
Malpractice; *see also* Ethics
  claims by area of law, 85
  claims by type of alleged error, 86
  claims of, 321
  legal, 85, 320
  prevention of, 87
Management, 29; *see also* Total quality management
  functions of law office, 29–34
  Internet sites, 35–36
  law firm responsibilities, 32–33
  law office principles, 27
  practice vs. administrative, 28–29
  timekeeping and billing, 237–239
Managing partners; *see* Partner
Management by objective, 363; *see also* Performance evaluations
Marketing, 33, 126–142; *see also* Model Rules of Professional Conduct
  and ethics, 136–142
  and legal assistants, 126
  and rainmaker, 136
  Bates v. State Bar of Arizona, 433 U.S. 350 (1977), 126, 231
  false and misleading statements, 140
  goals for, 127
  options, 129
  plan, 136, 137–138
  restrictions of, 127
  typical options, 128–135
Microsoft Outlook, 323–324
Microsoft, 335
Misrepresentation of status, 57–59
  and case work, 58–59
  and fees, 59
  legal analysis and legal documents, 58
  representing clients in court proceeding, 58

Mission statement, 144–145; *see also* Planning
Missouri v. Jenkins, 491 U.S. 274, 109 S. Ct. 2463, 105 L.Ed. 2d 229 (1989), 13–14
Model Code of Professional Responsibility, 48
Model Rules of Professional Conduct, 48; *see also* Ethics 2000
   Advertising, 139
   Rule 1.1 Competence, 316
   Rule 1.3 Diligence, 317
   Rule 1.4 Communication, 318
   Rule 1.15 Client and Operating funds, 255–256
   Rule 5.4 Fee Sharing, 269
   Rule 1.1 Competence, 61
   Rule 1.3 Diligence, 62
   Rule 1.4 Communication, 162, 163
   Rule 1.5(b) Fees in writing, 210–211
   Rule 1.5(c) Contingency fee in writing, 211
   Rule 1.5(d) Criminal and Domestic-Relation Fees, 211–212
   Rule 1.5(e) Determining reasonableness, 212–213
   Rule 1.15 Safekeeping Property, 401–402
   Rule 1.6 Confidentiality of Information, 65–66
   Rule 1.7 Conflict of Interest, 71
   Rule 1.8 Conflict of Interest, 73
   Rule 7.1 false or misleading statements, 139
   Rule 7.3 No Direct Solicitation, 141
   Rule 7.4 Specialist
   unauthorized practice of law, 54–55

NALA; *see* National Association of Legal Assistants
National Association of Legal Assistants (NALA), 6–7, 36
   ethical codes, 51–52
   Internet site, 89
   misrepresentation of status, 57
National Federation of Paralegal Associations (NFPA), 6–7, 35
   ethical codes, 51, 53
   Internet site, 89
Negligent hiring, 355
Net lease; *see* Lease
Newsletter; *see also* Marketing and marketing, 131
NFPA; *see* National Federation of Paralegal Associations
Noise, 176; *see also* Clients and communication skills
Non-exempt, 12
Nonbillable time, 224; *see also* Timekeeping
Nonequity partner, 5; *see also* Associate attorney

Nonverbal communication; *see* Clients and communication skills
Numerical system, 393–394

of counsel, 5; *see also* Attorney
office manager, 14
Open house; *see also* Marketing and marketing, 134
Operating funds; *see* Accounting
Organizational charts, 25
Organizing, 31
Ortiz v. Gavenda, 590 N.W.2d 119 (Minn. 1999), 63
Outside counsel, 17, 239
Overhead cost, 20, 225
Overhead expense, estimating, 263

Paper shredders, 427
Paralegal; *see* Legal assistant
Partner, 4; *see also* Attorney
   equity, 4
   managing, 4, 24–26
Partnership track, 4–5; *see also* Associate attorney
Partnership, 24
Performance evaluations
   coaching technique, 358–363
   employee attitude survey, 363–366
   employee attitude survey sample, 364–366
   forms and techniques, 359–363
   guidelines for, 357–358
   management by objective, 363
   sample form, 360–362
Personal policies, 368
Personal information manager (PIM), 323
Personnel law issues, 368–374
Pilferage, 431
PIM; *see* Personal information manager
Planning, 31, 143–152
   and legal assistants, 143–144
   efficiency for, 148–149
   Gantt chart, 149
   mission statement, 144–145
   process for, 147–151
   strategic, 145–146
Plant management; *see* Administrative management
Policy, 115; *see also* Policy and procedure manual; Personnel policies
   conflict of interest, 76
   anti-harassment, 369–370
   for timeliness, 173
Policy and procedure manual, 111–115
   and Intranet, 119–120
   assembling or revising, 115, 118
   ethical considerations, 118–119
   process for, 116–117
   table of contents sample, 112–114
Practice management, 28–29, 30–31
Prepaid legal services, 208–209

Private law firm management, 18–19
   management structure, 24–26
   organizational charts, 25
   powerful managing structure, 24
   rule by all partners/shareholders, 26
   rule by management committee/board, 26
Pro bono, 224–225
Procedure, 115; *see also* Policy and procedure manual
Profit margins, 264; *see also* Accounting
Prolaw, 242
Public relations; *see also* Marketing and marketing, 134
Pure retainer; *see* Retainer fees
Postage machines, 421

Questionnaire; *see* Clients and communication skills

Rainmaking, 136; *see also* Marketing
Realization, 263; *see also* Accounting
Reasonable accommodation, 375
Recruiting, and hiring process; *see* Hiring process
Recurring event, 328
Reference checks, 354–355
   questionnaire, 354
Reminders, 310–311; *see also* Scheduling and warnings, 310
Rephrasing, 181
Resume; *see also* Hiring process; Marketing
   and marketing, 131
   case, 204, 207–208
   cash advance, 204, 206
   earned, 204
   general representation example, 207
   general representation, 206
   pure, 208
   unearned, 204
Riech v. Page & Addison, P.C., 12–13
Rivera v. Chicago Pneumatic, 1991 WL 151892 (Conn. Super.), 77–78
Rules of procedure, 311; *see also* Scheduling

Sage U.S., 242
Scheduling; *see also* Computers; Deadlines; Docket control systems
   appointments, 309
   case schedule, 310
   deadlines and reminders, 310–311
   docket control systems, 321–333
   documents, court rules, and calculating deadlines, 313–315
   hearings and court dates, 311
   Internet sites, 335
   judge and attorney setting of, 310
   rules of procedure, 311
   system of tracking, 310–311

Secretaries, 15
Seminars; *see also* Marketing and marketing, 134
Settlement, 253
Sexual harassment, 375
Shareholder, 4; *see also* Attorney
Society for Human Resources Management, 377
Software Technology, 242, 335
Sole practitioner, 19–20; *see also* Law practices
Sole proprietorship, 23
Solicitation, 141–142
Specialty, 142
Staff attorney, 5; *see also* Associate attorney
Staff manual; *see* Policy and procedure manual
Staffing plan, 263
Statute of limitations, 310
Strategic planning, 145; *see also* planning questions for, 146
Stress, management of, 376–377
Substantive management; *see* Practice management
Substantive task, 34
Surveys; *see* Clients and communication skills
System, 31
System, and management, 34–35

Telecommunications, 421–422
and voice mail, 422
Telephone technique; *see* Clients and communication skills
Termination, 366–367
what is not, 367
when, 367
wrongful termination lawsuit, 367
Tickler card system; *see* Card system
Time to billing percentage, 262; *see also* Accounting
Timekeeper productivity report, 237, 238
Timekeeping and billing; *see also* Accounting; Billing; Timekeeping
bill formats, 235
clerical and secretarial duties, 219
computerized cycle, 233
cycle of, 233, 235
double billing, 218
ethics, 209–219
expense slip, 220
fees, 197–209
final client billing, 236
hourly rate, 197–200
Internet sites, 241–242
itemized, 235
law office mistakes, 219
management reports, 237–239
prebilling report, 234
retainers, 204–208
service bureaus, 239
Timekeeping, 196–197 ; *see also* Timekeeping and billing
billing phrases, 227
computerized, 222
manual, 222
practices for, 227–229
recording of, 226
timesheet record, 224
timeslip/time record form, 223
types of nonbillable, 224–225
Timesheet, 222
Timeslip, 222
Total quality management (TQM), 121–126
and legal assistants, 125–126
client-centered, 122
implementation of, 125
philosophical benefits, 124–125
philosophies of, 122–124
product-centered, 122
TQM; *see* Total quality management
Trust account, 253; *see also* Accounting; Escrow account
Trust, 204; *see also* Trust account

Unauthorized practice of law, 54–61
avoidance of, 60–61
and legal advice, 56–57
misrepresentation of status, 57–59
and other work, 55
Unearned retainer; *see* retainer
United States Department of Labor, 12

Value billing, 209

WESTLAW, 405, 409
West's Legal News, 316
white-collar exemptions, 12
Will, fee example, 205
Workdays, 314; *see also* Deadlines
Workforce, 377
World At Work, 377
World Wide Web; *see also* Internet, law-related sites
www.abacuslaw.com, 335
www.abanet.org/cpr, 89
www.abanet.org/cpr/clientpro/aprefac e.html, 271
www.abanet.org/cpr/clientpro/fpreface .html, 271
www.abanet.org/cpr/ethics2k.html, 89
www.abanet.org/legalassts, 35, 89
www.abanet.org/lpm, 35, 189, 241, 271, 335
www.abnet.org, 35
www.acaonline.org, 377
www.alanet.org, 35, 189, 239, 271, 335
www.altmanweil.com, 241
www.amicus.ca, 335
www.bridge-way.com, 335
www.bytepro.com, 241
www.clswin.com, 335
www.compulaw.com, 335
www.corel.com, 335
www.denovosys.com, 335
www.digital-lawyer.com, 241
www.gryphonlaw.com, 335
www.hornbook.com, 35
www.juris.com, 241
www.key-point.com, 335
www.lamanet.org, 35
www.lamanet.org/Resources/ethics.ht ml, 89
www.law.cornell.edu/ethics, 89
www.lawresearch.com, 241
www.legalassistanttoday.com, 36
www.legaledge.com, 335
www.legalethics.com, 89
www.legalfiles.com, 335
www.lotus.com, 335
www.microsoft.com, 335
www.nala.org, 36
www.nala.org/stand.htm, 89
www.needpins.com, 335
www.paralegals.org, 36
www.paralegals.org/Development/hom e.html, 89
www.pclaw.com, 241
www.prolaw.com, 241
www.shrm.org, 377
www.stilegal.com, 241, 335
www.timematters.com, 335
www.workforce.com, 377

We're adding an office.

Timeslips BackOffice – the fully integrated accounting solution for Timeslips users.

Sure, we've streamlined time tracking and billing for hundreds of thousands of firms worldwide, and we've been doing it for over 16 years, but we always felt that we could do more - and now we can!

For us to offer an accounting solution especially for Timeslips we knew that it had to be seamlessly integrated with the Timeslips billing engine, and it absolutely had to surpass our customer's expectations for functionality and ease of use. To accomplish these two goals we enlisted the help of Peachtree Software, sister company to Timeslips, and accounting software veteran of more than 20 years.

The result of this effort is the ultimate accounting solution for Timeslips, offering its users general ledger and accounts payable modules that share data with perfect synchronization. What this means for you is bill payments that move directly from Timeslips to your bank accounts, and expenses that effortlessly flow from your checkbook onto your client's bill.

So, if you're a Timeslips user looking to eliminate the redundancies of separate billing and accounting packages, call us and ask for your $50 Timeslips customer discount. If you don't have Timeslips yet, but are in need of a complete billing and accounting solution, get the best of both worlds with Timeslips and Timeslips BackOffice.

888-651-3144
www.timeslips.com

©2001 Sage U.S. Holdings, Inc. All rights reserved.
All other trademarks are the property of their respective owners.

Special Student Offer

For only $29, you can own your very own copy of **AbacusLaw,** the best-selling case management and calendaring software for law offices. Use it as your personal information manger. Increase your skills and value to employers. Discover why over 95,000 lawyers already rely on **AbacusLaw** to manage their law office calendars and cases.

Why are we offering you **AbacusLaw** at a fraction of it's regular price? We are betting that when you discover the real power and benefits of **AbacusLaw** by using it for your own everyday use, you'll enthusiastically support it's use in law offices you work at, and we will expand our growing number of satisfied users.

You will receive the complete **AbacusLaw** stand-alone version, including all the program options, for only $29, plus $15 shipping and handling. The regular price is $299. The software will be registered to you, so your name will appear on all reports and calendars. You will be able to install the software on any computer you choose. You can even take **AbacusLaw** with you to your employer's law office, demonstrate it's uses, and show your proficiency with the software. And if you place an order for your employer's purchase of **AbacusLaw,** you will earn a referral fee of 10% of the purchase price.

To order, call 800-726-3339 and ask for the special student offer.

Windows System Requirements

- Microsoft® Windows® 95 OSR 2.0, Windows 98 SE, Windows Millennium, Windows NT® 4.0, or Windows 2000 Intel® Pentium® processor
- 24 MB of RAM (32 MB recommended)
- 40 MB of available hard-disk space